HEALTH PSYCHOLOGY AND PUBLIC HEALTH

(PGPS-156)

Pergamon Titles of Related Interest

Belar/Deardorff/Kelly THE PRACTICE OF CLINICAL
HEALTH PSYCHOLOGY
Blechman/Brownell HANDBOOK OF BEHAVIORAL MEDICINE
FOR WOMEN

Related Interest
(Free sample copies available upon request.)

CLINICAL PSYCHOLOGY REVIEW

PERGAMON GENERAL PSYCHOLOGY SERIES

EDITORS

Arnold P. Goldstein, Syracuse University
Leonard Krasner, Stanford University & SUNY at Stony Brook

HEALTH PSYCHOLOGY AND PUBLIC HEALTH

An Integrative Approach

RICHARD A. WINETT

Virginia Polytechnic Institute and State University

ABBY C. KING

DAVID G. ALTMAN

Stanford University

PERGAMON PRESS

New York   Oxford   Beijing   Frankfurt
São Paulo   Sydney   Tokyo   Toronto

Pergamon Press Offices:

U.S.A.   Pergamon Press, Inc., Maxwell House, Fairview Park,
              Elmsford, New York 10523, U.S.A.

U.K.   Pergamon Press plc, Headington Hill Hall,
              Oxford OX3 0BW, England

PEOPLE'S REPUBLIC   Pergamon Press, Qianmen Hotel, Beijing,
OF CHINA   People's Republic of China

FEDERAL REPUBLIC   Pergamon Press GmbH, Hammerweg 6,
OF GERMANY   D-6242 Kronberg, Federal Republic of Germany

BRAZIL   Pergamon Editora Ltda, Rua Eça de Queiros, 346,
              CEP 04011, São Paulo, Brazil

AUSTRALIA   Pergamon Press (Aust.) Pty. Ltd., P.O. Box 544,
              Potts Point, NSW 2011, Australia

JAPAN   Pergamon Press, 8th Floor, Matsuoka Central Building,
              1-7-1 Nishishinjuku, Shinjuku-ku, Tokyo 160, Japan

CANADA   Pergamon Press Canada Ltd., Suite 271, 253 College Street,
              Toronto, Ontario M5T 1R5, Canada

Copyright © 1989 Pergamon Press, Inc.

Library of Congress Cataloging in Publication Data

Winett, Richard A. (Richard Allen), 1945-
    Health psychology and public health.

    (Pergamon general psychology series ; 156)
    Includes index.
    1. Medicine and psychology. 2. Health promotion.
3. Health behavior. 4. Public health. I. King,
Abby C. II. Altman, David C. III. Title. IV. Series.
R726.5.W55   1988   613   88-15171
ISBN 0-08-033641-8
ISBN 0-08-033640-X (pbk.)

Printed in the United States of America

Dedication

FOR RW: to my wife Sheila and daughter Emily for their love and support, and to my late friend Robin C. Winkler for his faith and inspiration.

FOR AK: to my parents Lenore and Sheldon King for their love and guidance throughout the years and to my husband Steven for his enduring support.

FOR DA: to my parents Gloria and Irwin and brother Bill who were always there when needed, to my in-laws, Phyllis, Joe, Debbi, and Mark, who understood the demands of the project and encouraged me constantly, to my wife Judith, who was a pillar of support and positive reinforcement, and to Rebecca Sarah, who waited patiently for me to make sufficient progress on this book before initiating the process of entering this world.

Acknowledgments

We wish to express appreciation to Leonard Krasner for helping us from start to finish with this project and to Jerry Frank and Mary Grace Luke and the staff at Pergamon Press for bearing with us through delays and deadlines. We want to acknowledge the support of faculty and staff in the Department of Psychology at Virginia Polytechnic Institute and State University, and the support from the National Science Foundation and the National Cancer Institute. Special acknowledgment is made to John Moore of Educational Technologies (LRC) at Virginia Tech for his help and guidance in many projects and to a number of excellent students who have worked on these projects, especially Kathryn Kramer, Anne Riley, Jana Wagner, and Bruce Walker. Colleagues at the Stanford Center for Research in Disease Prevention provided the models and support that challenged us to do our best. Most of all we want to acknowledge the love and support of family members — without their understanding this project would not have been completed.

Blacksburg, Virginia
Stanford, California
September 1988

Contents

Preface

The major purpose of this book is to draw together the strengths of health psychology and public health into an integrative conceptual and strategic framework. At the time this book was written, there was surprisingly little integration between these fields. Health psychology research is perhaps best characterized as the application of clinical psychology principles and methods to physical health. There are few examples of health psychologists working on macro-level public health issues. At the same time, the field of public health tends not to draw extensively on the theories and techniques of health psychology. We believe that working closely together, the fields of health psychology and public health can achieve more than each field could achieve independently. We hope that this book will help the reader to remove any disciplinary "blinders" that can inhibit innovative solutions to complex health problems society faces.

The framework presented here provides a basis for bridging health psychology and public health by linking theoretical, empirical, and applied multilevel analyses with a systematic approach to large-scale intervention programs aimed at disease prevention and health enhancement. The intervention methods proposed in this book primarily involve incentives, media, and community health promotion. Interventions are discussed within the context of six exemplar areas including mental health, maternal and child health and the reduction of teenage pregnancy, changes in nutritional practices, worksite health and safety, environmental problems, and enhancement of old age. Besides their common derivation from the framework, the proposed interventions are largely multilevel and preventive in focus.

Each of these six content chapters provides an overview of the particular health problem, presenting background epidemiological and behavioral data, as well as relevant theories and interventions that have been used to address the problem. Throughout the text, tensions which exist between individual and societal analyses are also discussed.

The foregoing description of this book, its length, and the size of the reference list may suggest that the reader is embarking on a comprehensive study of contemporary health problems. This is not the case. First, we have limited our discussion to six out of many possible content areas. Second, each chapter is written from a particular perspective. While, as noted, background information is provided, the chapters do not provide exhaustive reviews.

Rather, this book is best seen as an initial attempt to formalize the union of health psychology and public health. The reader should consider our framework as dynamic and evolving rather than finalized. The health problems discussed and intervention strategies proposed in this book are merely one set of analyses and applications.

Writing this book has been both a humbling and uplifting experience. It is humbling to recognize that our framework is in an early stage of development, with much room left for reformulation and expansion. It is also humbling to believe that one has a promising set of ideas for ameliorating a problem, and then to quickly see a myriad of influences alter the scope and texture of the problem. Such was our experience in trying to provide analyses and programs for the AIDS epidemic.

However, such feelings have been offset by our growing conviction in writing this book of the exciting potential of effective integrations of health psychology and public health. And, even more so, excitement has been generated in watching, via our own work and the work of our colleagues, the concepts and strategies in this book come alive, and most importantly begin to have some discernible impacts.

It is our hope that readers of this book will formulate extensions of the framework and applications to new domains to further the development of the integration of health psychology and public health. We do not promise smooth sailing, but we do promise an exciting journey.

SECTION I

INTRODUCTION

INTRODUCTION

Last March, I was diagnosed as having AIDS. This altered my life so profoundly that seven months later I am still struggling to adjust to the change . . . The doctor was very compassionate, saying that this was probably the worst news I had ever received in my life, and he was right. All of my mental preparation was insufficient to thwart the tidal wave of emotion that swept over me as I received what, at the time, I regarded as a death sentence. I went home that evening in the company of my lover Michael, feeling the weight of two worlds — mine and his — on my shoulders . . . I have always considered myself an independent person, tough enough to brave everything life had to throw at me. In fact, I took pride in my ability to 'tough things out' — alone, if necessary . . . It is OK, from my perspective, for other people to cry, but not for me. It has not been easy allowing myself the relief — the freedom — such crying brings . . . It is also extremely difficult for me to make others understand that I do not want sympathy. It is demeaning and humiliating to me when I perceive that someone feels sorry for me . . . Probably the most heartbreaking thing for me has been the realization that physical fitness and other abilities I have always taken for granted are becoming more difficult to maintain, and my daily regimen has become more and more of an effort . . . I finally realized what was going to happen to me — I was going to die. From the very first moment of that realization to this very day, it is not the act of passing from life to death that frightens me but the events that lead up to that point. The body and physical abilities of which I have been so proud and for which I have worked so hard are deteriorating with cancer and weakness . . . To those of you not afflicted goes the task of ensuring that our cause is not forgotten by the politicians and civic leaders responsible for allocating funds to carry on the research that feeds our hopes. To you is assigned the work of keeping our plight in the public eye so that those who would ignore the problem in the hope

1

that it will go away, or those who would declare it to be a problem afflicting only a single segment of our society, cannot accomplish what people of good conscience know is patently wrong. It is up to you to correct the public's misperception, fostered by often insensitive media representation, that all AIDS patients are ignoble, drug-abusing people who are undeserving of attention, let alone the benefits of a worldwide quest to save them from a devastating disease. We are not bad people. We are merely gay, and that is no reason to regard us with disdain. Those of us physically unable to carry on this message look to you for champions (the late Anthony J. Ferrara, 1984).

Anthony J. Ferrara's account of his battle with acquired immune deficiency syndrome (AIDS) serves to highlight poignantly a goal of this book: to bring together psychological and public health approaches to the study of mental and physical health problems. We argue in this book that to fully understand the complex nature of our current health problems, a multifaceted approach such as this is necessary, if not essential. In the case of AIDS, for example, the public health implications are immense. As of February 1988, over 52,000 Americans had been diagnosed with AIDS and over 29,000 had died (Centers for Disease Control, personal communication, February 4, 1988). By 1991, the U.S. Public Health Service estimates that there will be a cumulative total of 270,000 AIDS cases and 179,000 deaths. During that year alone, 54,000 people will die from AIDS, thereby making it one of the leading causes of death in this country. The Centers for Disease Control (1987a) estimated that between 1 and 1.5 million Americans are currently infected with HIV virus (the mean interval between infection and the onset of AIDS is seven years). Thus, within a relatively short period of time, AIDS has become a public health problem of epidemic proportions.

Research on the etiology of AIDS suggests that the cause is a viral pathogen that negatively affects immunologic functioning and results in secondary illness (e.g., cancer, pneumonia) and eventually death (Martin & Vance, 1984). Since the disease is spread through bodily fluids, particularly blood and semen, a variety of public health measures have been taken (e.g., ordering the closure of gay bathhouses, testing blood bank samples for the HIV virus, making sterile syringes available for drug addicts, and educating the public about "safe" sex).

Psychologists are also devoting considerable time to the AIDS epidemic. From a psychoneuroimmunologic perspective, there is evidence that environmental and mental events affect immune response and disease outcome (Levy, 1985). That is, vulnerability to the HIV virus is in part dependent upon psychological factors. The psychological implications of AIDS are also immense. As Anthony Ferrara discussed, the disease alters dramatically the lives of the afflicted individual, his or her family and friends, and acquaintances in work and other settings.

At the community level of analysis, the effects are also apparent. For example, in some cities gays are subject to overt and covert discrimination.

In other cities, people in low-risk groups are highly fearful of any type of contact (e.g., being in the same restaurant) with those at high risk. While the disease tends to be concentrated predominantly in subsegments of the population (gays, intravenous drug abusers), the ramifications of the disease are most certainly not limited only to these groups of people.

The message contained in this brief examination of AIDS is clear and serves as the major focus of this book. The prevention and treatment of our nation's killers at the individual as well as community levels of analysis requires sensitivity to both public health and psychological issues. As with most health issues in this day and age, reliance on any one disciplinary perspective limits effective analysis and intervention.

In the next section of this chapter, other examples of the need for linking these two disciplines are discussed within the context of cardiovascular disease, cancer, substance abuse, accidents and injuries, and adolescent pregnancy. A review of the epidemiologic data associated with these health problems is presented to provide a context within which to place further discussion. This is followed by a summary of the history of the fields of public health and health psychology and a further rationale for bringing these fields together.

1
Overview of Health Psychology and Public Health

OVERVIEW: HEALTH AND ILLNESS IN THE UNITED STATES

In 1985, over 2 million people died in the United States. Of these deaths, 44 percent were due to cardiovascular disease (CVD), 22 percent to cancer, 5 percent to accidents, 4 percent to chronic obstructive pulmonary disease, 3 percent to pneumonia and influenza, and 22 percent to all other causes (National Center for Health Statistics, 1987).

Disadvantaged segments of the population experience significant health problems, and the gap between the rich and poor with respect to health status and health care is actually widening. In the United States today, more than 35 million people do not have medical insurance, Medicaid only covers half of poor people in need, one child in four under the age of six lives in poverty, and the bottom 40 percent of the population receives under 16 percent of the national income (Sidel, 1987).

While our nation struggles to control rising health care costs with various advanced treatment-based technologies, a report from The Carter Center indicated that in this country, roughly two thirds of all deaths (65%) and of the 8.4 million years lost before the age of 65 (63%) are preventable (Foege, Amler, & White, 1985). As discussed in detail later, the specific risk factors and behaviors associated with this premature morbidity and mortality include tobacco and substance abuse, high blood pressure, improper nutrition, and lack of preventive screening and prevention services.

Given the dramatic findings of the Carter Center and other similar data, it is unfortunate that less than one percent of the U.S. "health" care budget is earmarked for health promotion and disease prevention (Califano, 1986). Joseph A. Califano, Jr., former secretary of Health, Education, and Welfare, an architect of Medicare and Medicaid, chairman of Chrysler Corporation's committee on health care, and an attorney in Washington, D.C., crystallizes the problems of the present U.S. health care system in his 1986 book, *America's Health Care Revolution: Who Lives? Who Dies? Who Pays?*

The "health industry colossus," as he refers to it, has become one of the nation's biggest businesses — it is the country's third largest industry in consumer spending and also its second largest employer, providing jobs to 1 of every 14 Americans. There are now almost 7000 hospitals, 1.3 million hospital beds, and 7.9 million people employed by the health care industry in the United States (U.S. Department of Health and Human Services, 1986). Health care costs are the fastest rising expense for the business community, more so than even labor or raw materials. In 1985, the nation spent $425 billion dollars (or an average of $1,721 per person) on health care. About 40 percent of this went to hospitals, 20 percent to physicians, 8 percent to nursing homes, and 6 percent for drugs.

These data suggest that there are great pressures in the health care system to maintain the status quo, since some health care industries and professionals are reaping high profits. This pressure to maintain the status quo may contribute to the relative lack of attention to health promotion and preventive health care.

Although there is not a direct relationship between health care spending and the health status of U.S. citizens, the age-adjusted death rate has dropped 69 percent from 1900 to 1982 and life expectancy at birth has reached an all-time high for males (71.0 years) and for females (78.3 years). There are two ways that life expectancy is usually examined: at birth and at age 45. Until 1950, the proportionate gain in life expectancy at birth was greater than the gains at age 45. For example, from 1900 to 1950, life expectancy at birth increased by 38 percent while life expectancy at age 45 increased by 15 percent. The major factors leading to the larger increase in life expectancy at birth have been attributed to nutrition, sanitary measures, immunizations, and the use of antibiotics (McGinnis, 1982).

Since 1950, however, a dramatic shift has occurred in that the proportionate gain in life expectancy at age 45 exceeded the gain at birth. From 1950 to 1980, for example, life expectancy at birth increased by 8 percent while life expectancy at age 45 increased by 13 percent. This shift has been attributed largely to a drop in cardiovascular disease, which in turn is related in large part to improvements in the control of blood pressure, reductions in the incidence of cigarette smoking, lower consumption of food high in fat and cholesterol, and increases in exercise (McGinnis, 1982). The shift is also related to a slowing of the decrease in infant mortality rates.

Health status varies on the basis of sex and ethnicity. In the case of sex, males have a higher rate of mortality than females for the top 15 causes of death. Similarly, blacks have a higher mortality rate than whites for 13 of the top 15 causes of death. The age-adjusted death rate for homicide was almost four times higher for males than for females and almost six times higher for blacks than for whites. While genetic and ethnic differences in health status do exist, these data as well as data reported below point to the important effects of lifestyle as well as environmental influences on health status. Moreover, these data portray a mixed picture. Thus, there is reason for being optimistic about the nation's health as long as it is tempered by the reality that many people are suffering and do not have adequate access to health care services. The lack of attention given to prevention, coupled with rising health care costs, is perhaps most troubling.

Health Knowledge and Behavior of the American Public

Several interesting insights into the health knowledge and behavior of the American public come from the 1985 Health Interview Survey, conducted by the National Center for Health Statistics (Thornberry, Wilson, & Golden, 1986). In some areas, health knowledge and practice of healthy behaviors was found to be quite high. For example, 91 percent of the U.S. public understood that smoking increases a person's chance of getting heart disease (although, as is discussed in chapters 2 and 5, the depth of knowledge about the ill effects of tobacco remains a problem), 77 percent knew that high blood pressure was related to strokes, 74 percent had had their blood pressure taken within the past year, and 98 percent knew that regular tooth brushing and flossing prevented dental decay.

While these data are encouraging, knowledge and behavior in other health areas were more discouraging — only 34 percent of women examined their breasts more than six times per year; 26 percent of respondents had on one or more occasions in the previous year consumed five or more drinks at one sitting; only 42 percent reported "exercising or playing sports regularly"; 41 percent did not have a working smoke detector in their home; only 32 percent wore their seat belts "all or most of the time"; and almost one third smoked cigarettes.

These data suggest that the amelioration of this country's health problems and the lowering of health care costs could be affected substantially by an increase in the practice of a variety of preventive health behaviors. Significant progress has been made in some areas over the past few decades, yet there remains numerous areas in which progress has been slow or nonexistent. The specific progress (or lack thereof) across several health problem areas is reviewed below.

Cardiovascular Disease

Cardiovascular disease (CVD), the leading cause of death in the United States, resulted in 986,400 deaths in 1984, over 70 percent of which were due to heart attacks or stroke deaths. This death rate is about the same as all other causes of death combined. This means that approximately one of every two Americans will die of CVD. The American Heart Association (AHA, 1987) reported that over 63 million of the 230 million Americans (or 30 percent) suffer from some form of CVD. Among the risk factors for

CVD are high blood pressure, cigarette smoking, high blood cholesterol and to a somewhat lesser extent obesity, type A behavior pattern, and physical inactivity. Almost 58 million people have high blood pressure, with the prevalence higher among black males and females than white males and females. Over 34 million Americans are obese, 27 million Americans have plasma cholesterol levels in the high range (i.e., over 239 mg/dl), and about 50 million smoke cigarettes.

Data on cardiovascular operations and procedures are also staggering. In 1984, physicians performed 202,000 coronary artery bypass grafts and 570,000 cardiac catheterizations. The total number of cardiovascular operations and procedures, excluding hemodialysis, was over 2 million. It should be noted that some people have questioned the need for many of these medical procedures (e.g., bypass surgery, which in many cases does not improve overall life expectancy). Regardless, CVD and its treatment represent a huge outlay of resources for this country: The total societal cost of CVD in 1987 is estimated to be $85 billion (AHA, 1987).

While these data are discouraging, there are several reasons for optimism. From 1964 to 1984, total CVD age-adjusted deaths dropped 37 percent. Middle-aged American men and women, compared to people in 26 other industrialized countries, experienced the steepest decline in coronary mortality for this 20-year period. This decline is in part attributable to changes in health-related behaviors such as cigarette smoking, nutrition, and blood pressure control. Califano (1986) noted that a majority of the decline in deaths from CVD were due to a drop in plasma cholesterol levels (contributing about 33 percent to the decline) and to a reduction in cigarette smoking (contributing about 25 percent). Interestingly, coronary care units contributed only 14 percent, hypertension medications 9 percent, and cardiopulmonary resuscitation 4 percent to the decline in CVD deaths.

In terms of health knowledge and health behaviors, from 1972 to 1980 the percent of the U.S. population knowledgeable about the risks of elevated blood pressure increased significantly while the percentage of hypertensives who had controlled their blood pressure increased from 16.5 percent to 34.1 percent.

With regard to food consumption patterns, data from the National Health and Nutrition Exam Survey portray a mixed review of the dietary practices of Americans (Block, Dresser, Hartman, & Carroll, 1985; also see chapter 8 for an extensive review of the American diet). For example, white bread products comprise the largest percentage of the average American diet; beef and whole milk dairy products are the major contributors of protein; and hamburgers, meat loaf, hot dogs, whole milk beverages, doughnuts and other similar sweets, beef steaks, and roasts are the primary contributors of fat.

Additional data from a comprehensive literature review conducted by the

National Research Council (1986) are worth mentioning. They reported that most people (90%) eat regular meals (two or three meals a day for three consecutive days), but snack at least once every three days (75%), and do not eat a wide variety of foods (e.g., 80% of assessed nutrients came from fewer than six different foods). Furthermore, the percentage of money spent on away-from-home food is steadily approaching 50 percent.

As with other risk-related behaviors, efforts to change the nutritional practices of the American public are resisted by the considerable resources of institutions vested in maintaining the status quo. For example, efforts to encourage consumption of lower-fat food are limited in this country by counter efforts of the food industry. As a case in point, McDonalds spent over $450 million in 1984 on advertising and promotion; in 1985, the top five fast-food chains (McDonalds, Burger King, Kentucky Fried Chicken, Hardee's, and Pizza Hut) spent close to $800 million. This may be compared to approximately $160,000 (a 5000 to 1 ratio) spent on public service announcements and the like promoting sound nutrition (Greene, Rouse, Green, & Clay, 1984).

Such advertising appears to be successful. Since its inception, McDonalds has sold over 52 billion hamburgers. There are now over 8,000 McDonalds restaurants, with assets topping $4 billion. They serve 18 million customers each day. This means that approximately 6 percent of the U.S. population visits a McDonalds every day! Given the high caloric, fat, and sodium content of McDonalds food (e.g., a Big Mac has 563 kilocalories, 33 grams of fat, and 1,010 grams of sodium), and all fast food for that matter, it is no wonder that CVD is so widespread. The all-American lunch of a Big Mac, small order of french fries, and chocolate milkshake contains a whopping 1163 kilocalories, 54 grams of fat (mostly saturated), and 1419 grams of sodium. In other words, it is a ticket to the all-American health problem: cardiovascular disease.

McDonalds is not the only culprit. The San Francisco Chronicle (1987) reported that there are over 117,000 fast-food restaurants in this country. These statistics underscore the importance of understanding health-related lifestyle and behavioral factors within the environmental context in which they reside. Consequently, strategies for change will often require individual, organizational, and institutional foci.

Cancer

Cancer is second only to cardiovascular disease in mortality and morbidity rates in the United States. The American Cancer Society (1987a) estimated that approximately 30 percent of Americans (71 million people) living today will eventually have cancer. Moreover, three out of four families will experience the disease directly. Excluding nonmelanoma skin cancer and carcinoma in situ, which account for over 500,000 cases of cancer, about 965,000 people were diagnosed with cancer in 1987; about 483,000 will die. This amounts to 1,323 deaths per day or one cancer death every 65 seconds. Undeniably, this is a disease that affects a great many Americans. The economic effects of cancer are also astounding. The estimated direct and indirect costs of cancer in 1985 were $71.5 billion.

On the positive side, however, the treatment of cancer has improved dramatically in the past 50 years. In the 1930s, less than 20 percent of cancer patients survived five years following diagnosis. By 1987, the relative survival rate (i.e., the rate that takes into account normal life expectancy) was 49 percent. For some cancers (e.g., Hodgkin's disease, leukemia, childhood cancers, testicular cancer) the survival rates can approach 100 percent, while for others the rates are much lower (e.g., survival rate for lung cancer is 13%). Although the age-adjusted cancer death rate has risen since 1930, most of this rise is attributed to lung cancer deaths attributed to cigarettes. If lung cancer is excluded, age-adjusted death rates for many cancer sites have leveled off or are declining.

Preventing Cardiovascular Disease and Cancer

Most of the premature morbidity and mortality due to CVD and cancer is preventable. Many more people would survive cancer if they detect and treat the illness earlier. The American Cancer Society (ACS) estimated that 170,000 more would have survived in 1987 with earlier diagnosis and prompt treatment. There are several health-related behaviors that prevent cancer. In relation to primary prevention (i.e., prevention efforts occurring prior to the onset of any symptoms), these behaviors are related to smoking, nutrition, sun exposure, alcohol, smokeless tobacco, estrogen use, radiation exposure, and occupational hazards.

The Surgeon General has written that cigarette smoking is "the single most preventable cause of death" (Surgeon General, 1979, p. 7). Overall, smoking is related to approximately 320,000 deaths each year, accounting for 30 percent of all cancer deaths, 85 percent of lung cancer in men, and 75 percent of lung cancer in women (ACS, 1987). Moreover, the cancer death rate for male smokers is double that of nonsmokers while for females it is 67 percent higher in smokers than in nonsmokers. Other risk factors being equal, the average smoker is two to four times as likely to have a heart attack than a nonsmoker (AHA, 1985). In the case of lung cancer, two-pack-a-day smokers have lung cancer mortality rates that are 15 to 25 times higher than those for nonsmokers (ACS, 1987).

The percentage of smokers during the past 30 years has dropped over 38 percent among men and over 33 percent among women. Even so, about 50 million Americans still smoke and it appears that heavy smokers (over 25 cigarettes per day) are not quitting as much as light or moderate smokers. The Centers for Disease Control (1987b) reported that in 1986, 26.5 percent of the U.S. population still smoked (29.5 percent of men and 23.8 percent of women). These figures are the lowest they have been since data were collected.

In 1984, the percentage of high school seniors who smoked daily was 18.7 percent, with 20.5 percent of the girls and 16 percent of the boys reporting daily smoking (McGinnis, Shopland, & Brown, 1987). There was, however, a 35 percent reduction between 1976 and 1984, with a 12 percent reduction between 1983 and 1984. These data suggest that the widespread smoking prevention and cessation programs conducted in school settings as well as the emerging social norm against smoking may be having positive effects, even though the rate of smoking among teenage girls is of concern to many people.

Before too much optimism is expressed, however, rates on the use of smokeless tobacco must be considered (Boyd et al., 1987). In an extensive review of the literature, Boyd and associates reported that typically between 40–60 percent of males had tried smokeless tobacco and 10–20 percent of older male youths reported recent use. Rates of use vary based on geography (e.g., 7 percent of 6th grade males in New York City reported ever having used smokeless products, while in Montana the rate was 68 percent), ethnic group (e.g., Native Americans have the highest utilization), sex (e.g., males are more likely to use), and age (e.g., use is correlated positively with age).

As was illustrated before with fast-food establishments, antismoking advocates are up against some stiff institutional competition. In 1983, the U.S. Public Health Service spent about $24 million in smoking control programs while the tobacco industry spent over $2 billion on advertising and promotion (in 1988, the tobacco industry is expected to spend close to $3 billion). The efforts of the cigarette industry were partially successful. In 1984, over 600 billion cigarettes were consumed in the U.S. (down from 640 billion in 1981) and the five largest tobacco companies had revenues of $25 billion and after-tax profits of $2.8 billion. Moreover, federal subsidies to the tobacco industry totalled $100 million in that same year while the federal government proceeded to collect $4.7 billion that year from cigarette taxes. These figures point to the complex issues and competing forces that are associated with implementing widespread smoking control programs (Hanlon & Pickett, 1984).

Nutritional factors, particularly obesity and diets high in fat and low in fiber, are associated both with CVD and with breast, uterine, colorectal, and prostate cancers (ACS, 1987). Foods rich in vitamins A and C may also help lower risk for cancers of the larynx, esophagus, stomach, and lung (ACS, 1987). Overall, dietary factors are estimated to cause 35 percent of all cancer deaths (Doll & Peto, 1981). For skin cancer, most cases are related to sun exposure. Excessive use of alcohol is also related to some forms of cancer, particularly oral cancers and cancers of the larynx, throat, esophagus, and liver. The effects of alcohol are magnified considerably if a person also smokes.

In addition to primary preventive lifestyle changes, cancer can also be prevented through secondary (i.e., early detection) measures. These include obtaining screenings for colorectal cancer (e.g., digital rectal examination, stool blood test, proctosigmoidoscopy examination). It is estimated that the practice of these secondary preventive behaviors will increase the survival rate for colorectal cancer from 55 to 85 percent (ACS, 1987). Similarly, PAP tests to detect cervical cancer and the practice of breast and testicular self-examination can result in earlier detection, diagnosis, and treatment and lower morbidity and mortality.

Substance Abuse

For all age groups, alcohol abuse and alcoholism cause major health problems. These include cirrhosis of the liver (the ninth leading cause of death in the United States), injuries and accidents (e.g., motor vehicle accidents, suicide, homicide), cancer, nutritional deficiencies, and fetal alcohol syndrome. Over 500,000 Americans are receiving treatment for alcohol-related problems, approximately 40 percent of emergency room admissions and 25 percent of inpatient admissions are estimated to be caused by alcohol problems, and about 18 million Americans over the age of 18 experience problems as a result of alcohol abuse (Alcohol, Drug Abuse, and Mental Health Administration—ADAMHA, 1987; Califano, 1986). Heavy drinking is a particularly serious problem, as 10 percent of all drinkers account for 50 percent of the total amount of alcohol consumed (ADAMHA, 1987). Consumption of alcohol in the 1980s seems to be declining slightly; the period from 1981–1984 marked the first three-year decline since Prohibition. However, in terms of overall costs, alcohol problems cost the United States $117 billion in 1983 (ADAMHA, 1987).

Though less prevalent than alcohol, drug abuse is another major national problem, one that has recently been widely publicized. Data from national surveys (ADAMHA, 1987; Polich, Ellickson, Reuter, & Kahan, 1984) indicated that 32 million Americans have used marijuana, cocaine, or another illicit drug in the last year, and over 23 million have used them at least once per month. Each year, cocaine is used by over 12 million people (Polich et al., 1984); each month it is used by 5 million people; and each day 5,000 Americans try cocaine for the first time (Lieber, 1986). Millions more use hallucinogens, stimulants, sedatives, and tranquilizers (ADAMHA, 1987).

Among high school seniors, 23 percent smoke marijuana at least once per month, and 5 percent have used cocaine. When queried about accessibility,

88 percent of high school seniors indicated that marijuana was "easy to get." Almost half (47 percent) noted that cocaine was readily available (ADAMHA, 1987; Lieber, 1986).

According to the National Organization for the Reform of Marijuana Laws (reported in Lieber, 1986), growing marijuana, a $16.6 billion-a-year industry, is probably the largest cash crop in the nation! Obviously, the drug problem is not simply a problem caused by individual abusers. A number of environmental and regulatory factors — such as the widespread availability of tobacco and other drugs; the proliferation of outlets that sell alcohol; laws allowing concurrent sales of alcohol and gas at service stations; the absence of alcohol and tobacco warning signs at points of purchase; the absence of warning labels on alcoholic beverage containers; ineffective strategies to ban the import of illegal drugs; and false advertising of tobacco and alcohol products — influence the actions that individuals take.

Preventing Substance Abuse

It is not surprising that the widespread problem of substance abuse has been met with diverse prevention and treatment strategies. In very general terms, there are two broad strategies to address substance abuse: reducing supply or decreasing demand. Examples of supply-side tactics include limiting production (by working with foreign governments and domestic farmers and producers) and using a variety of law enforcement techniques to limit production and availability (e.g., raids on farms, border patrols, sting operations on manufacturing plants, controlling street sales). Supply-side strategies are typically used by governmental agencies.

Strategies to lower the demand for substances include those focusing on both prevention and treatment. Preventive strategies include those directed at individuals or small groups (e.g., school health education, social resistance training for adolescents, counseling for those at high risk such as children of alcoholic parents) and those directed at the larger social context (e.g., banning tobacco advertising, enforcing laws that limit minors' access to alcohol and tobacco). These and other strategies will be reviewed in subsequent sections of this book.

Accidents and Injuries

According to the National Safety Council (1987), in 1986 94,000 Americans died from accidents and 8.9 million experienced disabling injuries. This amounts to one accidental death every six minutes and one injury (disabling and non-disabling) every 4 seconds! Overall, accidents are the fourth leading cause of death in the United States (behind heart disease, cancer, and cerebrovascular disease) and the *leading* cause of death for both males and females up to the age of 37. Nineteen-year-old males and females suffer more lives lost due to accidents than any other age group. One of the reasons that injuries have such an impact on public health is that relative to other health problems (with perhaps the exception of AIDS), injuries contribute much more to potential years of life lost. Obviously, this is due to the fact that injuries strike younger populations in the prime of their lives.

In 1986, most accidents occurred in motor vehicles, with 47,900 lives lost and 1.8 million disabling injuries. Consumption of alcohol is related to at least half of all motor vehicle accidents. Moreover, males are much more likely than females to drive while intoxicated (e.g., males in the 20 to 24 age group were 14 times more likely to be involved in fatal alcohol-related accidents than same-aged females). Death rates were higher for nonpedestrians, residents in rural areas, and during the evening hours. Also, higher fatality rates occur during the summer months (June–September) and during weekends (Friday–Sunday).

Fully 35 million work days were lost in 1986 due to accidents. This is expected to balloon to 100 million future days lost if the long-term effects of 1986 accidents are projected into the future. The National Safety Council (1987) estimated that the cost of accidents in 1986, including lost wages and loss of productive life, was $118 billion. Motor vehicle losses alone totalled $58 billion.

There is some encouraging news about accidents — from 1976 to 1986 the percent change in standardized death rates for all accidents dropped by 18 percent. Deaths from motor vehicle accidents dropped a net of 8 percent from 1976 to 1986, although they increased by 4 percent from 1985 to 1986.

Preventing Motor Vehicle Accidents

Many deaths and injuries due to accidents are preventable. In the case of motor vehicle accidents, the major types of prevention are occupant restraints, prevention of drinking and driving, and reduction of speed. For example, seat belt use would save from 12,000 to 15,000 lives each year if occupants used their belts at all times, and installation of air bags would save from 3,000 to 7,000 per year. Presently, just 34 percent of U.S. citizens wear their seat belts regularly, even though seat belts are from 50 to 65 percent effective in preventing fatalities and injuries (National Safety Council, 1987). It is encouraging to note that in recent years, many states have passed mandatory safety belt use laws although the interests of the insurance and automobile industries have at times collided on this and related issues.

Preventing individuals from driving motor vehicles while they are under the influence of alcohol or drugs would save thousands more lives each year. In 1986, for example, alcohol was a factor in at least 21,000 fatal accidents, 320,000 injury accidents, and over 1 million property damage accidents (National Safety Council, 1987). Similarly, enforcing the speed limit of 55 miles per hour limit on the nation's highways would significantly reduce injuries and fatalities. Since 1973, when the 55 mph limit was enacted because of the OPEC oil embargo, between 22,000 and 40,000 lives have been saved. If the limit is raised to 65 or 70 mph, as is occurring in areas across the country, a 10 to 15 percent annual increase in motor vehicle fatalities would occur in many of these areas.

Adolescent Pregnancy

Teenage pregnancy in the U.S. is now considered to be an epidemic and one of the most pressing public health problems of this century. More than 1 million teenagers become pregnant each year while over 400,000 have abortions (National Research Council, 1987). Greater than 80 percent of these pregnancies are unintended, and 20 percent result in low-birth-weight babies. In 1985, American families started by teenagers cost society an alarming $16.5 billion (Mitchell & Brindis, 1987). Currently, 80 of every 1,000 girls aged 15 to 17 and 155 of every 1,000 girls aged 18–19 become pregnant (about 10 percent overall) and over 1.3 million children are living in households headed by teenage parents (Mitchell & Brindis, 1987).

The consequences of teenage childbearing are staggering: When teenagers become pregnant, their social and economic problems escalate at an exponential rate. Compared with adult mothers, teenage mothers have lower-status occupations; earn less money; are less educated; are more likely to be separated or divorced; have more children during their lifetimes; are more likely to have daughters who become teenage mothers; have more complications from pregnancy and childbirth; report more stress; and are five to seven times more likely to live below the officially designated poverty level (Mitchell & Brindis, 1987; National Research Council, 1987).

Preventing Adolescent Pregnancy

An integrated psychology and public health perspective can lead to a broad understanding of the multitude of problems associated with early pregnancy. A comprehensive discussion of teenage pregnancy and its prevention from this perspective is discussed in chapter 7. In brief, there have been no well-designed evaluations of teenage pregnancy prevention programs. While there are examples of programs that illustrate effectiveness, the majority of prevention programs aimed at reducing the incidence of adolescent pregnancy have generally failed.

SUMMARY: A CASE FOR PSYCHOLOGY AND PUBLIC HEALTH

The data reported above on AIDS, CVD, cancer, substance abuse, injuries, and adolescent pregnancy, as well as similar data for other health problems, suggest that integrating psychology and public health would further our understanding of health and illness. Much of the morbidity and mortality in this country is due to lifestyle. Behaviors related to tobacco use, alcohol consumption, drug use, sexual activity, seat belt use, nutrition, and physical activity, to name a few, comprise the "lifestyle" that health professionals must address. Health behaviors, however, do not occur within a vacuum. To understand such behaviors, one must also understand the context in which behavior occurs. This context, comprised of a constellation of personal, interpersonal, environmental, and institutional factors, includes such things as public policies, the physical and social environment, institutional practices, and interpersonal influence. The dual consideration of individual behavior and the context in which behavior occurs is a theme covered throughout this book.

Psychologists, who are trained to understand and change behavior, can extend the effects of small-scale interventions to society at large by working with professionals in the field of public health. Public health professionals, expert in epidemiology, systems analysis, and large-scale social change, can further their impact on the health system by incorporating principles of psychology into their work. Given the enormity of the health problems facing this nation, reliance must be placed on designing and implementing approaches that incorporate the best educational, behavioral, environmental, and regulatory technologies that the fields of psychology and public health have to offer, while at the same time recognizing that the technologies must be generalizable to larger populations.

In the next section of the chapter, the fields of health psychology and public health are reviewed in order to provide a springboard from which an integrative perspective can be proposed. The final section of the chapter outlines a vision for integrating psychology and public health.

Health Psychology: A Subspecialty Coming of Age

Psychologists have been interested in health issues since the early 1900s (Rodin & Stone, 1987; Stone, 1979). Psychologists such as G. Stanley Hall in 1904 and William James in 1922 addressed health issues in their writing. In addition, discussion of the relationships between psychology and medical school education and practice began in 1911, with a panel at the annual meeting of the American Psychological Association (APA) (Stone, 1979). Research interest and professional affiliation with this area, however, grew at a relatively slow rate until the early 1970s. In a scan of *Psychological Abstracts* during 1950 and 1960, Rodin and Stone found just 136 articles in 1950 and 257 articles in 1960 that could be considered in the area of what is now known as health psychology.

The beginning of the current period of development of health psychology is usually connected to the 1969 publication of an article in the *American*

Psychologist by William Schofield. In this article, Schofield conducted a content analysis of *Psychological Abstracts* in 1966 and 1967 and found very few articles dealing with health psychology. He noted:

> Psychology is presently anemic vis-a-vis the other health professions; we are weak in numbers and in technology. . . . We may become robust. Whether psychology achieves a more significant and productive role as a health profession depends in part on the decisions (and interests) of individual psychologists (p. 579).

As a result of this article, APA appointed Schofield head of the Task Force on Health Research in 1973. For the period from 1966 to 1973, the Task Force conducted a content analysis similar to Schofield's previous one. They came to the same conclusion as Schofield: Psychologists had not to date been attracted to studying physical health and illness.

The growth of health psychology from the mid-1970s to the present time has been astounding. Indeed, a national survey conducted in 1974 found that only 52 psychologists considered themselves health psychologists. Just six years later in 1980, however, the number had grown to 1500. By 1988, the number of health psychologists was over 3500.

This burgeoning interest in health psychology is reflected along other dimensions as well. These include formal recognition of health psychology as a division of the American Psychological Association in 1978; the appearance of a landmark (and first) book on the subject in 1979 (Stone, Cohen, & Adler, 1979) as well as many other subsequent books on the field; the founding in 1982 of a journal devoted solely to the topic (*Health Psychology*); a national conference in 1983 on the education and training of health psychologists (Stone, 1983; Stone, Weiss, Matarazzo, Miller, Rodin, Belar, Follick & Singer, 1987a,b); the development of graduate training programs in health psychology (Belar, 1987); special health psychology tracts at annual meetings of the American Psychological Association; and a rapid increase in the number of manuscripts focused on health psychology. Schofield was clairvoyant when he wrote in 1969:

> We might decide (and wish) that we be allowed simply to go on with our presently established and circumscribed role as a limited health profession. We are unlikely to be permitted that option. Our decision, upon careful review, will result in action or inaction — and we will either move ahead or regress (p. 583).

Health psychology has 'moved' ahead and is now firmly established as a robust, rather than an anemic, subdiscipline within psychology. Moreover, current leaders in the field are optimistic about the field's long-term viability and its ability to contribute to diverse issues of concern to humankind (Stone et al., 1987b). The extent to which it becomes recognized by and contributes to disciplines beyond psychology is dependent upon whether health psychologists obtain adequate content knowledge and process skills relevant to other disciplines, base their interventions on empirical findings rather than ideology alone, and are able to communicate effectively with professionals from these other disciplines (Evans, 1988; Weiss, 1987).

Defining the Field

What is health psychology? Psychologists have gone to great lengths to define health psychology and to distinguish it from other related fields, such as behavioral medicine, behavioral health, and psychosomatic medicine. Although the perspective we have taken in this book is to examine the interrelationships between psychology (broadly defined) and public health, it is useful to define the unique territory of the fields related to psychology and health, beginning with the health psychology field.

The most widely cited definition of health psychology is

> . . . the aggregate of the specific educational, scientific, and professional con- tributions of the discipline of Psychology to the promotion and maintenance of health, the prevention and treatment of illness, the identification of etiolog- ic and diagnostic correlates of health, illness and related dysfunction, and the analysis and improvement of the health care system and health policy forma- tion (Matarazzo, 1980).

Behavioral medicine has been defined as:

> . . . the interdisciplinary field concerned with the development and integration of behavioral and biomedical science knowledge and techniques relevant to health and illness, and the application of this knowledge and these techniques to prevention, diagnosis, treatment, and rehabilitation (Schwartz & Weiss, 1978).

Behavioral health has been defined as

> . . . an interdisciplinary field dedicated to promoting a philosophy of health that stresses individual responsibility in the application of behavioral and biomedical science knowledge and techniques to the maintenance of health and the prevention of illness and dysfunction by a variety of self-initiated individual or shared activities (Matarazzo, 1980).

Finally, psychosomatic medicine

> . . . . studies the impact of emotional states and responses to stress on the development of somatic symptoms and illness . . . and assumes that all dis- eases have psychological components and that all of medicine should be en- compassed by psychosomatic medicine (Adler, Cohen, & Stone, 1979).

Thus, behavioral medicine is the most general of these fields of inquiry in that it involves multidisciplinary investigation in prevention, diagno- sis, treatment, and rehabilitation (cf. Altman & Green, 1988). Behavioral health is similar to behavioral medicine in its multidisciplinary orientation, although its primary focus is health promotion and disease prevention rather than treatment. Both of these fields emphasize the study of, and intervention on, individual behavior. The development of behavioral medicine over the past 20 years can be traced in part to the field of psychosomatic medicine. Psychosomatic medicine grew out of attempts, beginning in the early 1920s, to identify the specific psychological factors believed to play a major role in the development of specific somatic complaints. Investigators in psychosomatic medicine were also interested in studying the relationships between social, psychological, and biological factors and health outcomes. Unfortunately, the psychoanalytic approaches taken by professionals from a psychosomatic medicine paradigm did little to point the way to the development of specific interventions. Attempts to link personality types to specific disease states or to demonstrate that procedures stemming from psychosomatic theories were efficacious have in general been disappointing. The dearth of controlled intervention studies in this field points to the lack of a firm association between clinical practice and research, which some have suggested to be a result of its lack of success in achieving widespread effects on the medical and health fields (Agras, 1982).

Health psychology grew out of the behavioral medicine movement and is distinguished from behavioral medicine and behavioral health by its principal focus on a psychological perspective. As with other areas of psychology, health psychology is traditionally viewed as a science "intended to predict the behavior of conscious individuals (p. 29)" (Stone, 1987). Thus, health psychology is not an interdisciplinary field. In reality, however, there is quite a bit of overlap between all of these social science disciplines studying health.

Health psychologists conduct multidisciplinary research and intervention, and behavioral medicine professionals use health psychology theories and interventions (Bloom, 1988). Moreover, some professionals from these fields focus on the societal causes of illness and health, traditionally the purview of public health and medical sociology. The point here is that these disciplinary boundaries are often artificial, and there is often more overlap than separation. There is growing recognition in health psychology (which we hope will be followed by the development of theory and empirical research) that to understand complex phenomena such as health behavior one must consider factors in the larger system or context that may be beyond the specific variable of interest (Taylor, 1987; Stone, 1987).

So as not to clutter the literature with yet another label, we have selected a general title for this book, *Health Psychology and Public Health: An Integrative Approach.* Our intent is to operationalize Engel's (1977) call for cross-disciplinary investigation in health (often referred to as a biopsychosocial perspective).

The Contributions of Health Psychology

The perception that psychology can contribute to the prevention and treatment of physical illness is a result of at least three factors. First, and perhaps most important, was the recognition that the major causes of illness in modern times, i.e., chronic diseases, were strongly influenced by behavior (as reviewed extensively earlier in this chapter). Examining the risk factors of the four leading causes of death in the United States — heart disease, cancer, cerebrovascular disease (primarily strokes), and accidents — bring this point home. With such data in hand, psychologists realized that their discipline was uniquely qualified to improve the understanding, prediction, and change of health-related behaviors.

The second factor influencing the development of health psychology was the prevailing philosophy that the field should help ameliorate pressing social problems. Given the economic burden of illness on society, psychologists felt responsible for helping to improve the health status of citizens and decrease skyrocketing health care costs.

The third factor was the realization that federal and foundation grant money for health-related research and intervention was increasingly more available than funding for traditional areas of psychology. Along these lines, funding of the social and behavioral sciences from the National Institutes of Health grew from $42.4 million in 1976 to $100.4 in 1980 (Weiss, 1982). Similarly, the job market for students trained in health psychology offered optimism in a time of concern about placing psychology students (Altman & Cahn, 1987) and federal funds for training students in health-related research increased substantially (Weiss, 1982). Employment data suggest that there was a basis for this optimism — health psychologists are competitive for jobs in diverse settings (Altman & Cahn, 1987). Thus, psychologists devoted more of their collective resources to health so as to foster continued prosperity for the field.

In summary, health psychology has virtually exploded onto the current psychology scene, generating a great deal of research activity. Nonetheless, most of the research being conducted in health psychology remains clinical in nature, focuses on small samples of individuals, and generally does not use community and public health approaches. Stone (1987) suggested that a large majority of research conducted by health psychologists focuses on professional health care processes and on the "person whose health is at issue." He found few examples of health psychologists studying environmental hazards, symptom recognition and appraisal, and the psychological processes of the people and organizations that influence health care environments. Similarly, psychologists have generally not been interested in or effective at influencing public policy (DeLeon & Vandenbos, 1987). We hope that the perspective and concrete examples offered in this book will help move health psychology research and application to such new frontiers.

PUBLIC HEALTH: A MAJOR FORCE IN KEEPING OUR NATION WELL

In contrast to the relatively young field of health psychology, the public health field has long established itself as a major force in the health arena. Unlike health psychology, public health has traditionally subsumed a variety of professions and a diversity of perspectives reflective of its ever-changing and expanding focus. Among those things which historically have distinguished public health from other disciplines concerned with human health and disease are: the strong sense of social responsibility and justice to which it is tied; emphasis on the larger community and society as a whole, with a resultant concern for the social and environmental contexts of disease and health (a concern which has been traditionally overlooked or ignored by individuals utilizing a primarily medical/clinical perspective); development and utilization of epidemiological methods as a means of quantifying and tracking patterns of disease; a focus on prevention as a critical area of concern; and a view of health not simply as the absence of disease but as a tool for achieving human well being and potential (Hanlon & Pickett, 1984; Foege, 1987). The broadened viewpoint of public health that has evolved over the past century is perhaps best summed up in Winslow's definition of the field in 1920 as

the Science and Art of (1) preventing disease, (2) prolonging life, and (3) promoting health and efficiency through organized community effort for

(a) the sanitation of the environment,
(b) the control of communicable infections,
(c) the education of the individual in personal hygiene,
(d) the organization of medical and nursing services for the early diagnosis and preventive treatment of disease, and
(e) the development of the social machinery to insure everyone a standard of living adequate for the maintenance of health,

so organizing these benefits so as to enable every citizen to realize his birthright of health and longevity. (Winslow, 1920).

Additionally, public health has come to embody efforts aimed at marshalling local, state, national, and international resources and concerns to improve health on a community (or larger) level (Detels & Breslow, 1984; Foege, 1987).

The subject matter of public health has been, and will continue to be, vast. A variety of domains — including population policy, biostatistics, sanitation, injury control, health promotion, health services administration, nutrition, environmental health, health education, communicable disease control, and health policy — fall within its purview (Faden, 1987). To obtain an understanding of the number and scope of the problems to which the public health field has dedicated its efforts, one need only look at the recently published policy statements adopted by the governing council of the American Public Health Association (APHA, 1988). Major themes tying together the diverse group of professionals working in these public health areas include a primary focus on population groups rather than individuals as the unit of interest, study, and intervention, and an explicit commitment to social responsibility and the public welfare.

An Historical Perspective

Evidence of societal efforts to control disease predate the Roman Empire. Most of these efforts focused on increasing sanitation and sewage disposal, although the Romans in addition utilized other fairly advanced public hygiene methods, including ventilation systems and hospitals for the ill. In this country, the earliest public health efforts, beginning in the seventeenth century, focused on preventing the introduction of diseases from other countries (through such means as isolation of patients and ship quarantine) and limiting to some degree the widespread insanitary conditions which accompanied the growth of the population. America's strong ties with Great Britain allowed it to benefit from the number of important developments in public health that had been occurring in England over the course of several centuries (Rosen, 1958). Indeed, following the enactment of sanitary reform legislation introduced in Parliament in the mid-nineteenth century, cities such as London were rapidly transformed from disease-infested areas strewn with "nastiness and stinking dirt" (George, 1925) to centers where sanitation and hygiene became standard (Chave, 1984). Such ideas accompanied the colonists settling the North American territories, although, as was the case in Europe, they did not keep pace with the rapid expansion of the American population during the eighteenth and nineteenth centuries. Repeated epidemics of such diseases as smallpox, typhoid, cholera, and yellow fever ravaged the United States during that time; the average life expectancy in U.S. cities at mid-nineteenth century was found to be less than that for their British counterparts, which was approximately 36 years for the upper classes and 16 years for laborers (Richardson, 1887). This curtailed life expectancy was due in particular to a tremendous rate of infant mortality.

While the establishment of the germ theory of disease during this century provided public health and medical professionals with a clearer understanding of disease etiology and contagion, displacing the miasma or "bad air" notion of environmental forces in disease development, attention continued to be focused on sanitation as the primary means of protecting the public's health. In relation to the miasma theory, it is interesting (and unfortunate) to note that we can today find evidence supporting at least some of its suppositions in the forms of such environmental contaminants as air pollution and passive smoking—albeit with an understanding of the mechanisms underlying these factors, which was notably lacking in earlier musings surrounding miasma.

A turning point for American public health came in 1850, with the publication of the *Report of the Sanitary Commission of Massachusetts*, penned by Lemuel Shattuck (Shattuck, 1850). This insightful document addressed current as well as prospective health needs—not only those of Massachusetts but of the country as a whole. Included in its numerous recommendations were the collection of vital statistics, the establishment of state boards of health, training of health professionals in relevant aspects of public health and preventive medicine, and the control of smoking. Twenty-five years later, the far-reaching implications of this document began to be appreciated.

Movement toward stronger personal as well as public health practices during the nineteenth century increased on the local level with the advent of local boards of health. With the growth of urban areas, control of public health matters, largely in the form of stemming the outbreak of epidemic diseases, expanded to the state level. Massachusetts is generally credited with establishing the first formal state board of health in 1869 (Hanlon & Pickett, 1984), followed during the next fifty years by California and then the remaining states. Today these boards of health consist of the state departments of health, which are concerned with public health, sanitation, and the state hospital services, and departments of welfare, responsible for a wide range of social problems, including the care of deprived children, the mentally ill, and the financially indigent.

National initiatives developed as well, at first in forms such as those of the National Quarantine Conventions (Cavins, 1943), and the birth of American Public Health Association in 1872 (Bernstein, 1972). These developments led to the further recognition of public health matters as a national concern, with reorganization in 1902 of previous services at the national level into what is now the Public Health Service. The research arm of the Public Health Service—the National Institutes of Health—was expanded during the early 1900s as well, from a one-room bacteriology laboratory to what has become one of the most substantive public health and medical research centers in the world (Hanlon & Pickett, 1984).

During World War II the present-day National Centers for Disease Control (CDC) in Atlanta was added to the United States' public health armamentarium. The CDC today serves a variety of functions in addition to its epidemiologic function, including a health professional training center and a leading source of health communications and educational methodology (Hanlon & Pickett, 1984).

The combined efforts of these powerful national health agencies have culminated recently in the production of the far-reaching 1990 *Objectives for the Nation*, a national "blueprint" for initiating major and sweeping changes in disease prevention and health promotion in this country (U.S. Dept. of Health and Human Services, 1980). Congressional support in recent years, particularly in the 1960s, has allowed additionally for the continued expansion of medical care in this country, notably through the Medicare and Medicaid systems. Yet the American health care system, unlike many of its European counterparts, remains driven by an emphasis on personal responsibility for health care as part of the nation's free enterprise system (Chave, 1984).

The public health profession can be largely credited with the near eradication of this country's most deadly contagious diseases, among them smallpox, tuberculosis, and yellow fever. In doing so, the public health field has proven itself to be, perhaps more than any other medical or social science, a major champion of environmental and social influences in the understanding of disease prevention and health promotion. Yet, as noted earlier in this chapter, many of the greatest challenges we face in the health arena today come not in the form of infectious disease, but from chronic diseases (e.g., cardiovascular disease; cancer) associated most strongly with behavioral and lifestyle factors. Battling such diseases requires an increased understanding not only of important environmental and social factors involved in maintaining deleterious lifestyles, but of the myriad of behavioral, interpersonal, and psychological variables which may also influence the etiology and exacerbation of disease, as well as health promotion.

The public health field's recognition of the importance of personal health habits in influencing our nation's major causes of morbidity and mortality has been reflected in its growing focus during this century on public education as a major preventive strategy. Indeed, C. E. A. Winslow (1923) described this increased emphasis on education as the "keynote of the modern campaign for public health" (p. 55). In the past, public health concerns have moved from doing things *for* individuals, in the form of sanitation, food inspection, and rodent control during the eighteenth and nineteenth centuries (i.e., "passive prevention" strategies), to doing things *to* individuals, in the form of vaccinations, starting around the turn of the twentieth century. In contrast, the current health promotion emphasis focuses on the need to do things *with* people, along with inducing individuals to do things for themselves (Hanlon & Pickett, chapter 18, p. 296). Green and Anderson (1982) have described health promotion as "health education for voluntary change . . . which may include certain regulatory and environmental control strategies designed to channel and support behavior conducive to health" (p. 82). As they point out, the "health promotion era" of public health represents the current zeitgeist in a series of paradigm shifts that have helped to shape this expanding field, beginning with the miasma phase (1850-1880) described earlier and extending through the disease control (1880-1920), health resources (1920-1960), and social engineering (1960-

1975) phases. Notably, the health promotion definition used by Green and Anderson suggests a focus on multiple levels of intervention that is particularly germane to the current discussion concerning the interface of psychology and public health.

Public health education has historically recognized the importance of institutional, economic, and environmental influences on health behavior in addition to individual motivation, knowledge, and skills (Green, 1984; Nyswander, 1942). Yet, in recent years many health educators have, in response to at times restrictive health policies (Allegrante & Green, 1981; Faden & Faden, 1978) as well as to the burgeoning health intervention research emanating from the field of psychology, turned an increasing amount of attention to interventions directed at individuals and small groups (Green, 1984; Wallack & Winkleby, 1987). In this respect, "blaming the victim" has become a danger for public health educators in a similar manner as it has been for psychologists (Winett, 1983). Many public health professionals have noted that, while health education is typically an important dimension of public health, it is the environmental, institutional, and population-based emphases in conceptualizing health problems and health care that comprise public health's major contribution to the health field. Given the relevance of both perspectives in addressing the challenges currently facing the health field, a balance between the two would appear to be particularly useful.

Over the past two decades, the passage of the Consumer Health Information and Health Promotion Act of 1976, as well as several important documents on disease prevention and health promotion (most notably, the Lalonde Report from Canada in 1974; Lalonde, 1974, and the Surgeon General's 1979 Report; U.S. Dept. of Health, Education, & Welfare, 1979), has served to renew interest in and increase awareness of the complex factors influencing health behavior. While the themes found in both of these reports focus largely on individual, rather than environmental, influences, they have nonetheless sparked an increased flurry of activity and discussion among a variety of professionals in health care and health-related fields, including such emerging fields as preventive medicine. While recognizing the importance of preventive efforts on the part of the individual and the health professional, preventive medicine's major focus on the individual and his or her health practices serves to differentiate it from the environmental and institutional emphasis championed by the public health field.

The Need for Integration

The Individual

While educational efforts focused on the individual have made an important contribution in many areas of health (e.g., child health), it has become increasingly apparent that public education alone, in the absence of a thorough understanding of the behavioral, learning, communication, and marketing principles which have been increasingly documented over the past forty years (e.g., Rice & Paisley, 1981; Winett, 1986), can lead to efforts which may fall far short of their desired objectives (e.g., Robertson, Kelley, O'Neill, Wixom, Eiswirth, & Haddon, 1974; Ross, 1982). This is particularly the case with the more complicated types of health behaviors — such as cigarette smoking, dietary change, and weight loss — that health professionals are faced with altering today (McAlister, Puska, Salonen, Tuomilehto, & Koskela, 1982). Such observations indicate the need to integrate psychological and behavioral science principles with larger-scale approaches aimed at the individual.

Society at Large

As suggested above, ameliorating today's complex health problems requires initiatives combining perspectives, tools, and methodologies from health-related professions which have traditionally, with few exceptions, remained relatively isolated from one another. Public health and health psychology represent two such fields. As pointed out, the public health field can offer to psychologists a rich understanding of the environmental, social, legal, and economic contexts of health and illness, epidemiologic methods for identifying and tracking disease patterns and trends, and a commitment to social responsibility and to health promotion and enhancement that extends beyond individuals and disease. It brings an understanding of the importance of "passive" strategies (i.e., those measures which protect individuals automatically without requiring any action on their part, such as fluoridation of water) in addition to more active measures requiring individual action (e.g., buckling a seat belt; vigorous activity) (Williams, 1982). As stated earlier, the focus on populations rather than on individuals is a hallmark of the public health approach, as is the use of epidemiologic methods in the delineation of health and disease in entire populations. Such methods are used largely to observe systematically and describe disease phenomena and their relationship to potential causal agents (e.g., the association between use of the drug DES during pregnancy and cervical cancer in the resulting offspring), rather than to identify basic disease mechanisms themselves (Runyan et al., 1982). This can be contrasted with theoretically derived experiments with smaller samples, which are typically used by psychologists in attempting to establish causality between an agent or condition and an outcome (e.g., Barlow & Hersen, 1984).

In contrast to traditional psychology, public health's exclusive focus on health problems and the development of strategies for preventing them, along with the practical bent governing public health issues and concerns, has resulted in a field whose research base is largely empirically rather than theoretically driven. The model that has traditionally been applied to the understanding of health problems in the public health arena is referred to as the host–agent–environment model (Runyan et al., 1982). This model underscores the important interactions between individual susceptibility (i.e., "host" considerations), sources of disease and disability (i.e., the "agent"), and broader environmental forces which are key to public health. It can be contrasted with the traditional medical model of disease which focuses on one-to-one relationships between agent and host, leading to interventions typically applied to the host (individual). The latter model tends to ignore the interactional and contextual nature of disease while ignoring potential methods for intervention, such as environmental strategies. It often leads to intervention attempts focused on changing something about the patient, rather than looking beyond the individual to other health-related influences (e.g., other individuals, settings). As such, the patient is treated as an isolated (and often passive) entity. Medicine also differs from public health in its emphasis on curative rather than preventive targets. Preventive efforts that are undertaken by medical professionals tend to be tertiary in nature (i.e., focused on minimizing the effects of current disease). The alarming increase in health-related expenditures over the past two decades, coupled with a startling lack of changes in many of our nation's health statistics for the same period of time (e.g., infant mortality), suggests the limitations of a largely curative approach. Similarly, the notable decline in deaths from coronary heart disease over the past twenty years or so may be better explained by lifestyle changes than by technologic advances brought into play once the individual is ill (e.g., coronary artery bypass surgery; angioplasty) (Kannel, 1983). These comments aside, given American infatuation with technology of all sorts, medical technology included, it is not surprising that we as a society continue to focus most of our media attention and economic resources on expensive medical treatments rather than on less "heroic" preventive efforts.

In contrast to current medical efforts, public health efforts are often aimed at primary prevention (i.e., avoidance of disease prior to its occurrence) rather than secondary (early detection and treatment of disease to slow or eliminate its development) or tertiary prevention. The former type of prevention typically requires that the individual be recruited as an active participant in his or her health program at a time when he or she is *not* ill. Primary prevention continues to represent a stance which, with relatively few exceptions, runs counter to medicine's prevailing approach to intervention (i.e., focus on disease states and cures; the patient as the passive recipient of medical advise or treatment).

While formally a much younger discipline than public health, the health psychology field brings with it a rigorous scientific method for understanding human behavior, a tradition of delineating the individual contexts of health and disease, and a burgeoning armamentarium of techniques and approaches for modifying behavior and enhancing motivation and learning. As discussed earlier, much of psychology's previous influence in the area of health and disease, reflected in the psychosomatic medicine and behavioral medicine movements, has been focused largely on a curative rather than preventive approach. The emergence of the recent behavioral health movement (Matarazzo, 1980) has helped to increase psychologist involvement in primary prevention concerns as well. Noted earlier, psychology's behavioral, individual-based orientation to intervention would seem to fit quite well with current discussions focused on the important impact lifestyle factors can have on chronic disease risk (Belloc & Breslow, 1972; Lalonde, 1974). Indeed, a rapidly growing amount of psychological research over the past several decades has pointed to the role that sound behavioral principles and strategies can play in enhancing individual health (Agras, 1982). The emergence of such an orientation in the United States during the 1970s and 1980s fits, not coincidentally, with the political and economic milieu of that time, with its increased focus on individualism and reduced governmental intervention in the face of the problem of increasing health care costs.

Yet, while it is clear that health behaviors are a major factor in chronic disease progression, it has become less clear that the major strategies used to combat this problem should be in the area of individual behavior change (Williams, 1982). It seems reasonable that health promotion strategies focused largely on the individual will continue to be appropriate and/or necessary for some risk factor areas for which passive prevention approaches are at present largely lacking (e.g., physical activity). However, continued underattention to "agent" variables (Runyan et al., 1982), particularly of an environmental nature, can only serve to limit the speed with which major gains in disease prevention and control in this country can be fully realized.

Exclusive or near exclusive focus on individual behavior can further result in "blaming the victim" or "sickness as sin" attitudes, with the attendant ethical questions that such orientations raise (Crawford, 1978; Faden, 1987). It becomes particularly critical to explore fully the veracity of such a position when it drives policy decisions having a major impact on the lives of our citizens; for instance, in the case of reduced availability of subsidized health services for more indigent individuals on the basis that all individuals are fully responsible for and in control of their health-related behaviors and patterns. In this regard, it is of interest to note that experts such as J. H. Knowles, often quoted in the context of advocating individual responsibility in the area of health, actually emphasized the importance of both individual *and* environmental conditions in disease onset. As he notes:

> Over 99 per cent of us are born healthy and made sick as a result of personal misbehavior *and* [italics added] environmental conditions. The solution to the

problem of ill health in modern American society involves individual responsibility, in the first instance, and *social responsibility* through public legislative
and private volunteer efforts in the second instance. (1977, p. 58) [italics added]

While health psychologists have currently applied their expertise primarily to preventing or ameliorating health problems on an individual level, the
as yet untapped potential for expanding this expertise to other areas and
levels of intervention (e.g., control of hazardous wastes, allocation of health
resources, intervention with health policymakers) is striking (Faden, 1987).

Psychologists and public health professionals have, during the past six to
eight years, increasingly explored ways in which they may interact more
intensively (Matarazzo, 1984; Palinkas & Hoiberg, 1982; Green, 1984). The
potential success of such a liaison has been indicated by, among other
things, the promising outcomes to date of community-based efforts to decrease coronary heart disease (Farquhar, Fortmann, Wood, & Haskell, 1983;
Puska et al., 1983). Interest in an increasing cross-fertilization between the
two fields has been demonstrated by professionals in both fields, as shown
by devotion of a recent issue of the *American Psychologist* to the psychology–public health relationship (vol. 37(8), 1982) around the same time that an
issue of *Health Education* was being devoted to this question (vol. 12(3),
1981). There is evidence that such discussion is being accompanied by a
growing amount of active collaboration between the two disciplines as well.
For instance, a survey of schools of public health in 1981 revealed that 75
psychologists were on the faculties of the 22 schools (Matthews & Avis,
1982). While this number, in terms of the actual percentage of the faculty it
represents (i.e., 5 to 6%), is not large and the role of psychologists in such
settings remains at present somewhat limited, it suggests that the skills and
interests of professionals in these two disciplines overlap and that mutually
beneficial relationships are possible. Moreover, as our understanding of
health and illness continues to grow, the necessity for connections between
the two fields will be more fully appreciated. Additional evidence that this is
already occurring has been shown by the development of graduate programs
focused on attempts to formally combine aspects of the two disciplines
through the presence of a multidisciplinary faculty and set of course requirements (e.g., the graduate programs at the University of Alabama at Bir-
mingham). The formal addition, by the Association of Schools of Public
Health in 1983, of the behavioral sciences area to the other four core areas
of study (biostatistics, epidemiology, environmental health, and health services administration) required to attain the Master of Public Health (MPH)
degree serves as an additional testament to that field's growing interest in the
knowledge base being developed by psychologists and other behavioral
scientists.

Clearly, future efforts to enhance the health of our nation must be undertaken by health professionals cognizant of the complex and multi-level factors involved in disease etiology and which must come to play in the development of viable and comprehensive interventions. This is not to say, however, that such a coupling of different professions and disciplines will be achieved without some amount of friction or tension. Given our society's pluralistic foundations, complex socioeconomic structure, and often competing interests, health professionals engaged in such an effort will have to grapple with such issues as the sovereignty of individual free choice versus societal protection; corporate versus public interests; economic versus social concerns; class differences; and the benefits of planning for the present versus the future. Growing tensions in areas of primary importance facing this nation, such as the allocation of health care resources, will require increasing energy from health psychologists and public health professionals alike.

It is the thesis of this book that through more systematic explication and integration of the knowledge and experience that both psychology and public health have to offer to the health field, prospects for achieving important changes in a variety of health areas currently threatening our nation can be significantly enhanced. It is our goal to discuss and explore further how such an integration may occur. Chapter 2 will focus primarily on the description of a conceptual framework representing one approach for arriving at an integration of the two fields. This dynamic, levels-oriented framework emphasizes the particular strengths that each field brings to the understanding and enhancement of health in this country. Various aspects of the framework will then be applied in the description and discussion of nine areas of particular current interest to the health field, presented in the subsequent chapters. Chapters 3, 4, and 5 represent descriptions of three major intervention strategies which can have a potentially powerful influence on health-related efforts. These strategies include the application of incentives (chapter 3), the use of media (chapter 4), and the utilization of community-based techniques (chapter 5) in the development of effective programs. Points and perspectives from these three chapters, as well as from chapter 2, will be included when relevant in the subsequent discussion of six problem areas (chapters 6 through 11). These six areas, including community mental health, maternal and child/adolescent health (with a particular focus on teenage pregnancy), nutrition, worksite health and safety, environmental problems, and aging and health, were chosen based on their particular timeliness given the United States' current health needs and agenda. While obviously there are other health issues of similar importance facing our nation, the topics covered offer a broad sampling of the array of current problems which we believe lend themselves well to an integrated health psychology–public health perspective. The book concludes with an epilogue summarizing the more salient themes, tensions, and opportunities that exist in relation to the challenge afforded by the integration of these two perspectives.

Our original plan in writing this book was to develop a conceptual framework that could be uniformly applied to the topic areas discussed in the subsequent chapters. In delving into the individual content areas being covered, however, we quickly found that this approach was less fruitful than we had first imagined. This was due in large part to two things: the diversity of the topics chosen, which we felt compelled to present in order to give the reader the most accurate flavor of the promise offered by integrating psychology and public health perspectives; and our goal of attempting to break new ground for each of the topics examined, leading to discussions that are by necessity variable, depending upon where the "state of the art" resides for each topic under investigation. Due to these concerns, and the subsequent importance of determining the theories and methods of most relevance to the particular topic at hand (as underscored in chapter 2), the book is in some ways less uniform or cohesive than what may be typical for nonedited books; i.e., there are few formal linkages between chapters. We have instead striven to present a new way of looking at each topic area under the broad umbrella of the framework presented in chapter 2, with the goal of advancing discussion concerning linkages between health psychology and public health and how the two fields might most profitably interact.

2
A Conceptual and Strategic Framework for Integrating Psychology and Public Health

OVERVIEW

Chapter 1 presented the histories of health psychology and public health and the rationale for integrating both disciplines as one approach to understanding, preventing, and intervening with health problems. The purpose of this second chapter is to take that integration one step further by detailing a framework which synergistically combines psychological and public health concepts and strategies.

We believe that a framework is useful in establishing a common set of concepts, principles, procedures, and guidelines with which to organize any endeavor. Therefore, the framework for this book attempts to describe and then integrate these critical steps for planning any intervention:

- *Defining the problem* through an investigation of relevant data sources;
- Identifying different *theories* and *value stances* useful for understanding and framing the problem;
- Analyzing pertinent theories, influences, programs, and data in relation to *multiple levels* of understanding (e.g., personal, societal);
- *Specifying goals* for change;
- *Designing an intervention* with an eye to the practical considerations involved;
- *Implementing the intervention*;
- *Assessing* the variety of *impacts* which accompany the intervention.

While each of these steps is important, at the core of the framework is *multilevel analysis*. Such an analysis entails a wide-scope view of a problem from diverse perspectives.

It is important to recognize that we are *not* proposing a new discipline of "public health psychology" with this framework. Rather, we believe that psychology and public health will remain distinct and viable scientific disciplines. Because both disciplines have overlapping areas of interest, however, we believe that the strengths of each can be synthesized to further our

32

understanding of health and illness and to develop more effective interventions. As Sutherland (1973) observed: " . . . we have partitioned our science into parochialized segments even though the phenomena we collectively study are not so segmented" (p. 4).

With this as a backdrop, we now move to a detailed discussion of the framework. We first begin by differentiating the framework from other similar frameworks. Next, the framework is presented in its entirety in overview fashion. We then examine each component and the linkages between components. In order to illustrate how the framework functions, we use the core of the framework, multilevel analysis, to discuss programs and policies for curtailing adult cigarette smoking. A final section reviews the plan for subsequent chapters and how the framework will be used throughout the book.

OTHER APPROACHES: DIFFERENCES

The framework is different from a number of other viable and useful approaches for understanding and changing health-related practices. We are proposing a general and encompassing framework. This is quite different from describing, for example, where specific psychological theories may be useful in the health arena (e.g., Singer & Krantz, 1982). We are also not proposing that only one psychological position, such as social cognitive theory (Bandura, 1986), be the core of the framework, although that particular theory and specific methods (Kazdin, 1984) will be heavily drawn from and clearly have shown their value for analysis and intervention. We are additionally not proposing an approach which primarily centers on one strategy, e.g., health belief change (Janz & Becker, 1984), or even community health (Green and Anderson, 1982), although the mix of community psychology and public health approaches is evident in this book (Iscoe, 1982; see also chapter 5).

Rather, our purpose is to develop a conceptual and strategic framework that can synthesize a number of different theories, perspectives, and principles on the conceptual side, and techniques, procedures, and methods on the strategic side, in order to formulate multiple assessment and intervention approaches. The framework follows a 'process' — a series of steps and operations leading to a pragmatic and potentially effective health program or policy.

There are other frameworks that have been used successfully in health promotion. The social marketing and health education approaches are two of them. Social marketing attempts to adapt the perspective and key variables of product, place, price, and promotion from commercial marketing to the world of ideas, social causes, and behavior change (Fine, 1981; Kotler, 1982; Manoff, 1985). A product refers to a specific program (e.g., Mr. FIT) or even idea for behavior change (e.g., eating a diet low in fat reduces the risk of heart disease). Place is the point of distribution of a product, e.g., a well baby clinic or a shopping mall. Price includes all effort, time, and social costs, as well as monetary costs for procuring a product (i.e., participating in a program), while promotion refers to "delivery channels" used to induce product acceptance (e.g., interpersonal or media-based strategies for instilling health behavior changes).

At the heart of social marketing is a variety of formative research strategies (surveys, focus groups, pilot studies) used to design a particular program, at particular costs, delivered in specific ways and through certain delivery channels (e.g., cable TV; paraprofessionals), to specific population segments. The two key concepts are *segmentation* of a population into relevant subgroups and then *tailoring* or fitting the program to the beliefs, behaviors, settings, and constraints of one or more subgroups.

We see the identification of key analysis and programmatic variables as the major strength of social marketing. Genuine adherence to social marketing means attending to the interaction of product, place, price, promotion, and positioning (the "niche" of a product) variables in both assessment and intervention stages. This book incorporates these variables into the overall framework, particularly in the intervention design and implementation steps.

The PRECEDE model, developed by Green (1984), has also received extensive application in health programs. PRECEDE and this book's framework share certain similarities. The model discerns individual, setting, organization, or community factors which inhibit or facilitate change of key health behaviors. It is a multistage model based on a functional analysis of health problems.

The process in PRECEDE starts with a general assessment of quality of life in target populations. This assessment may pinpoint more specific health problems that may enhance or detract from the quality of life. Some relative ranking can be given to health concerns with particular regard to the appropriateness of allocating resources to that concern. The next step entails specification of health behaviors germane to high-priority health concerns and delineation of nonbehavioral factors (economic, environmental, genetic) which influence the specific health behaviors. An additional step analyzes "predisposing factors," or personal factors (e.g., beliefs, values) restricting or enhancing the potential for change. Analyses of "enabling factors," societal and systemic barriers to change along with skill and knowledge deficits, and "reinforcing factors," incentives and disincentives to change, continue the process. This step leads to consideration of the relative weight of predisposing, enabling, and reinforcement factors, the probability of change, and potential approaches in light of available resources. The final stages entail intervention design matched to administrative capabilities and resources, followed by intervention implementation, and evaluation.

The PRECEDE model is a comprehensive approach to health problems, and particularly to health behavior change. Of key importance is the emphasis by Green on organizational, community, and institutional factors. Throughout Green's extensive writings, he points out that most health promotion efforts focus only on individual factors, health education, or psychological interventions, while for Green, health promotion involves social and environmental support plus health education.

We agree in principle with the points (i.e., multilevel intervention) made by Green (and others) in the fields of community health, public health, and health promotion, and are indebted to him for the conceptualization of the PRECEDE model. Indeed, the steps in this book's framework resemble those in PRECEDE. Thus, our framework can be seen as the "next generation" approach, building on PRECEDE and social marketing.

One addition to these approaches is the focus on the theoretical underpinnings of interventions. At the beginning, when a problem is being defined, it is important to articulate and examine different theories that may guide subsequent analyses and program design. For example, a number of chapters rely heavily on developmental and ecological theories. These theories have much to offer as far as pointing toward critical times and events, cognitive and behavioral skills, and settings germane to particular population groups.

With this conceptual foundation, a problem can be analyzed more coherently from a multilevel (i.e., personal, interpersonal, organizational, institutional) perspective. The theoretical and subsequent multilevel analysis can suggest interventions which typically will combine individual change strategies (i.e., psychological) with system change strategies (i.e., public health). This will frequently mean that a number of methods, settings, and diverse personnel will be involved in an overall intervention. Likewise, evaluations of impacts will most often involve examining multiple outcomes at multiple levels. Thus, the results of a well-planned and implemented intervention can have conceptual, policy, and practical significance. Further, the framework should be generally useful for program design, implementation, and evaluation *across* problem domains.

PRESENTATION OF THE FRAMEWORK

Figure 2.1 presents the framework in its most simple form. Following the flow of the figure takes the reader through its conceptual and strategic steps. We have found (to jump ahead a bit) that these key steps were useful for organizing the content of particular chapters (e.g., see chapter 7 on teenage pregnancy). Perhaps, though, most importantly, we have also found that

Conceptual and Strategic Framework

Conceptual Steps

- Problem Definition

  - Explication of Theories and Values

    - Multilevel Analysis

      Strategic Steps

      - Specification of Goals

        - Design of Intervention

          - Implementation of Intervention

            - Assessment of Impacts

FIGURE 2.1. An Overview of the Book's Conceptual and Strategic Framework

these steps are central to formulating, designing, and implementing interventions.

The figure also suggests a linear process of conceptualization, design, and intervention—i.e., one step follows another in a step-by-step way. In our roles as researchers and interventionists, we have found, not surprisingly, that the process is actually a highly *interactive* one. Different theories and value stances often compel problem definition from different perspectives, perhaps also pointing toward alternative levels of analysis. Likewise, formative and pilot research used to design interventions may lead to unexpected findings and thus require a reconsideration of various theories, perspectives, and data, and renewed awareness of the sometimes neglected implementation steps, e.g., the fit of a program with organizational and community resources. Thus, by interactive, we mean that effective program design and implementation—the overall objective of the framework—will often involve back-and-forth movement between steps.

Because the interventions we are proposing will have a firm conceptual foundation and, where possible, will follow rigorous methodological guidelines, the results (impacts) of an intervention will feed back and serve as subsequent input for defining problems and for theory confirmation or disconfirmation. While it is easier, as in Figure 2.1, to show a linear process, as noted above, the framework is interactive within and between major (conceptual, strategic) steps and substeps (e.g., design of intervention).

Figure 2.2 presents another general overview of the framework. The conceptual and strategic bases of two different disciplines, psychology and public health, which have emphasized different levels of analysis—i.e., psychology stressing largely personal and interpersonal issues, and public health those that are organizational/environmental and institutional/societal—will be integrated to define health problems, study appropriate theories, analyze problems at different levels, specify goals for change, design and implement interventions, and assess impacts.

More specifically, once a level(s) and appropriate theory are finalized as a focus for potential intervention, additional assessment is performed to define targets (population segments), products (programs), and goals (e.g., specific behaviors to be changed to a specific degree). The next step involves intervention design with particular methods, settings, personnel, and a timeframe prescribed by a review of theory, the foregoing analyses, and formative research. Prior to implementation of an intervention, it is recommended that additional formative research and pilot studies are conducted, the fit of an intervention with organizations and communities is assessed, and an evaluation system (measures and design) is developed and pretested. Assessment of impacts is the final step and includes program component ('process') and effects analyses ('outcomes') across levels (Flay & Cook, 1981) and, where possible, cost-effectiveness and cost–benefit analyses (Levin,

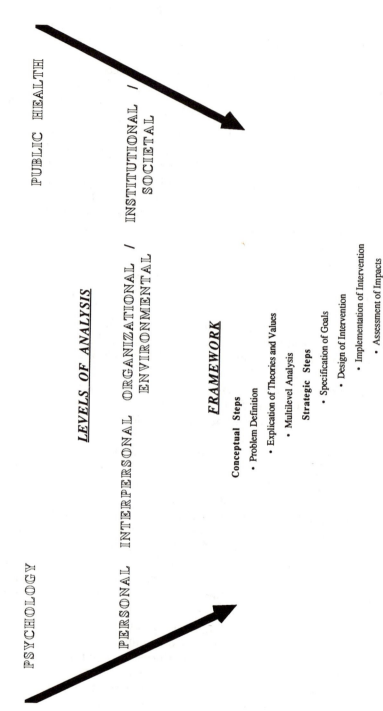

FIGURE 2.2. The Contributions of Psychology and Public Health and Levels of Analysis to the Book's Framework

1983). Cost-effectiveness analysis compares two or more approaches to a problem, e.g., the usual methods and the new program, on outcome and cost variables. Cost–benefit analysis focuses on program's costs compared to program's savings.

These analyses of a program then become part of the knowledge base for subsequent efforts. Thus, we are advocating a systematic, empirical approach for problem solving, with such efforts adding to scientific theory and practice.

A unique contribution to theory and practice of such a framework is the synthesis of psychological and public health principles and methods. At this point, we will more thoroughly examine each part of the framework with particular attention to the contributions of psychology and public health.

CONCEPTUAL STEPS

Problem Definition

Defining a problem most often starts with incidence data (number of new cases in a specified period) and prevalence data (number of existing cases; Hanlon & Pickett, 1984). Incidence and prevalence data inform us about the increase or decrease of a problem and suggest its relative seriousness. For example, knowing the prevalence of teenage mothers and the incidence rate by age across the last 10 years seems to paint an alarming picture (see chapter 7). Social indicators (e.g., rates of employment, crime, age distribution) also are used to define problems. Incidence and prevalence data and social indicators present a societal description of the problem.

Both psychological and public health approaches use these data as a starting point. Most frequently, however, as shown in Figure 2.3, a psychological approach will attempt to further define a problem by almost exclusively examining host factors—e.g., cognitions, emotions, behaviors, biochemical–physiological substrata. Public health (Figure 2.3) is more likely to focus on agents external to the individual and environmental factors correlated with the problem. Clearly, a more sophisticated approach to defining problems will examine the intersections of host, agent, and environmental factors, with each set of factors having pertinent theory and levels of analysis.

An overall objective for "problem definition" entails moving beyond incidence and prevalence data and behavioral-risk factors. That is, the problem definition stage should start to achieve a reasonably coherent picture of a chain of behaviors leading to exposure to the agent; the relative risk of each behavior(s) pertinent to the incidence and prevalence of a health problem; the settings in which these behaviors more frequently occur; and organizational, community, and institutional factors influencing such behaviors.

PSYCHOLOGY ------------------------------------ PUBLIC HEALTH

PERSPECTIVE

COGNITIVE
AFFECTIVE
BEHAVIORIAL
BIOCHEMICAL / GENETIC
SUBSTRATE

(Host Factors)

INCIDENCE
PREVALENCE
SOCIAL INDICATORS
RELATIVE RISK

(Agent, Environmental Factors)

GOALS

BEHAVIORS → SETTINGS → ORGANIZATIONS → COMMUNITY → INSTITUTIONS

AGENT

HOST ←→ ENVIRONMENT

FIGURE 2.3. The Contributors of Psychology and Public Health to Defining Health Problems

Defining the scope and behavioral and environmental correlates of AIDS (see chapter 4) is a good example of what is entailed in this step. And clearly, this step is also meant to be interactive, e.g., community norms and settings influence the frequency of the risk behavior.

Explication of Values and Theories and Multilevel Analysis

As shown in Figure 2.4, health may be seen as a function of 'lifestyle,' on the one hand, and of public policies and distribution of resources on the other—i.e., different levels of analysis. We use the word *values* to note that these divergent positions have not only theoretical importance but strong political and economic connotations (e.g., see Fuchs, 1975; Knowles, 1977; Matarazzo, 1982; Navarro, 1976). Approaching problems in certain ways can have great impact on societal priorities, policies, and resource expenditure. Defining a problem and placing the problem in a value and conceptual context brings a continual and unending tension to the field. There is no one correct position. For example, for every problem there are likely to be individual, interpersonal, organizational, environmental, and institutional mechanisms. Focusing on one level—one definition of the problem and a set of theories and values—may undermine the viability of other analyses (Rappaport, 1981). Thus, where feasible, a central part of using the framework entails attention to different levels of analyses.

One objective of noting theories and values associated with the different disciplines is to make more explicit the processes and assumptions of choosing where and how to analyze and act. A second objective is to meld, when appropriate, theories and strategies of different disciplines, i.e., multilevel analyses.

One of psychology's major contributions to health concerns and problem definition is theory. There are theories of beliefs (Janz & Becker, 1984), attitudes (Bauman, 1987), and behavioral analysis (Milby, 1982) which have been applied to health concerns. Other predominantly psychological perspectives have included an eco-behavioral approach (Winett, 1985) and Bloom's (1988) recent synthesis of the biopsychosocial model. In addition, systems theory, particular models (such as PRECEDE), and social marketing are used at the individual level. However, Bandura's (1986) social cognitive theory is becoming an inclusive perspective and will be used often in this book.

Bandura's theory rests on the consideration of the triadic influence operating among cognition, behavior, and environment, and how these three sets of factors reciprocally influence key mechanisms of change (e.g., self-efficacy). Particular strategies of behavior change (e.g., behavioral modeling) can also be derived from the theory. Bandura's theory encompasses other "minitheories" (e.g., theory of belief change) at the personal and interper-

PSYCHOLOGY

PUBLIC HEALTH

PERSONAL INTERPERSONAL ORGANIZATIONAL / ENVIRONMENTAL

INSTITUTIONAL / SOCIETAL

VALUES *HEALTH AS A FUNCTION OF:*

PERSONAL LIFESTYLE

SOCIAL NETWORKS

ORGANIZATIONAL / ENVIRONMENTAL FACTORS

ECONOMIC / POLITICAL / LEGISLATIVE SYSTEM

THEORIES / PERSPECTIVES

BEHAVIOR ANALYSIS

COMMUNICATION THEORY

COMMUNITY ORGANIZATION

PUBLIC POLICY

MULTILEVEL ANALYSIS   SYNTHESIS OF DATA, THEORIES, AND VALUES FROM DIVERSE PERSPECTIVES

FIGURE 2.4. The Contributions of Psychology and Public Health to Explication of Theories and Values and Multilevel Analyses

sonal levels as well as, to a somewhat lesser extent, higher levels of analysis (e.g., diffusion of innovations).

For certain problems, a lifespan developmental perspective can be used (see chapter 7 on teenage pregnancy, and chapter 6 on community mental health). Social, psychological, and biological changes reciprocally influence each other at different ages and clearly affect health issues and concerns. Of particular importance are difficult life transitions or "milestones" (Kobasa, 1985). Such transitions also frequently engender stress because they involve role changes and entail movement to new settings and circumstances. As noted before, this last point suggests that developmental theory needs to be coupled with conceptualization from a higher level of analysis, i.e., ecological theory. Thus, a developmental or ecological perspective can aid in identifying populations at risk and help in the design and delivery of programs in specific settings for specific population segments (see also Green, 1984).

Social cognitive theory, systems theory, social marketing, and developmental theory are also useful at the interpersonal level, and continue to have relevance at higher levels of analysis. However, for consideration of interpersonal factors in health, network, and social support theories (e.g., Rogers & Kincaid, 1981) as well as group dynamics (Yalom, 1985) and communication theory (Solomon & Maccoby, 1984) are most useful. Theory at this level may be considered "social psychological."

Figure 2.4 suggests that a focus beyond the interpersonal level begins to move conceptualization away from traditional psychology and toward territory more familiar to sociology, theories of organization and community change, "hybrid" disciplines such as environmental psychology, and attempts at interdisciplinary approaches such as social ecology. This province, as suggested by the figure, has traditionally been more the domain of public health. At the highest level of analysis, the institutional/societal level, conceptualization may come from economic theory, political science, and public policy analysis. Often, the attainment of the goals of public health have been sought in redistributions of resources and changes in regulatory policies (e.g., excise taxes on alcohol and cigarettes). These domains have in general been the furthest removed from psychology.

A major purpose of this book and framework is to integrate these different theories and concepts, often offering some synthesis of diverse positions for understanding problems and for designing interventions. This process is at the heart of the framework and the culmination of the conceptual steps.

An important caveat is that all three authors are behavioral scientists whose expertise is primarily at the individual and interpersonal level of theory and action. The authors are conversant with theory in communication, community organization, microeconomics, and social ecology, but are less well versed in macroeconomic and legal and regulatory policy analyses. Thus, our attempts to apply some theories will be assuredly less than expert.

Hopefully, some shortcomings may be overcome by the relatively unique integrations of positions and theories.

STRATEGIC STEPS

Specification of Goals

Figure 2.5 indicates that psychological and public health approaches are likely to specify goals in different ways. Typically, psychological programs have the objectives of changing cognitions and behaviors. This, of course, fits with the micro-focus on individuals. At the other extreme, a public health intervention is more likely to attempt changes at the macro level — e.g., changes in laws, regulations, and resource distribution. Micro-goals have sometimes been referred to as *'proximal'* goals, and macro-goals as *'distal'* goals.

It can be argued that in the absence of environmental change, the likelihood of maintaining individual behavior change is low (Brownell, Marlatt, Lichtenstein, & Wilson, 1986). Therefore, from a rather strict public health perspective, the many programs of individual health behavior change which do not include some emphasis on the environmental context seem relatively futile.

However, it can also be argued that many laws and regulations that are enacted do not have reliable behavioral effects — even though such behavior change is the ultimate goal of most legal changes. For example, the passage of a law in various states requiring that children be properly restrained when riding in automobiles showed, overall, some positive impacts but did not reliably result (given data using between-state comparisons) in substantially more parents buying car seats for and properly restraining children under five years old (Seekins, Fawcett, Elder, Jason, Schnelle, & Winett, 1988).

Further, Figure 2.5 indicates that between the extremes of micro and macro changes there are other workable and potentially worthwhile goals — e.g., specifiable and replicable structural change within organizations. These points suggest that debates about "better" goals can be vacuous. Indeed (looking ahead, since many recommended interventions in this book are multilevel), there are also frequently *multiple goals* for interventions. For example, programs in public schools with overall goals of reduction of the incidence and prevalence of teenage pregnancy have specific goals related to resource expenditure (space, money, and staffing for a school-based clinic), community acceptance (e.g., marked reduction of verbal and written objections to a clinic), interpersonal changes (e.g., increases in parent–adolescent discussions about sexual behavior), and personal behavior changes (an increase in safer sexual practices by adolescents). An effective program, there-

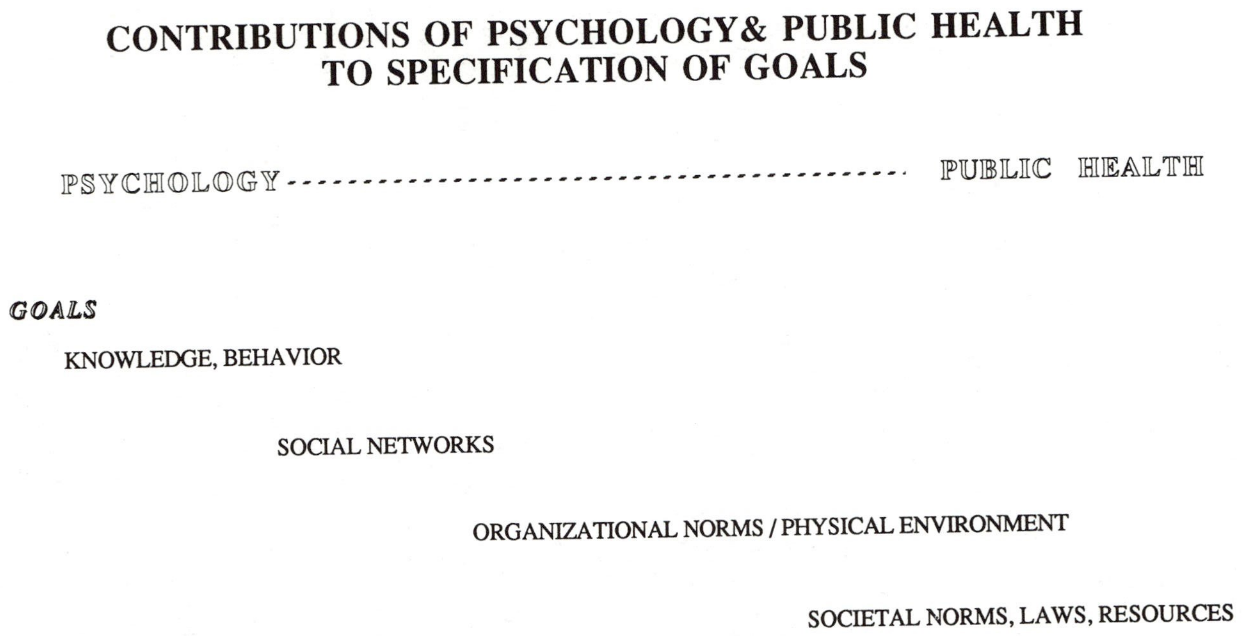

CONTRIBUTIONS OF PSYCHOLOGY & PUBLIC HEALTH TO SPECIFICATION OF GOALS

PSYCHOLOGY .... PUBLIC HEALTH

GOALS

KNOWLEDGE, BEHAVIOR

SOCIAL NETWORKS

ORGANIZATIONAL NORMS / PHYSICAL ENVIRONMENT

SOCIETAL NORMS, LAWS, RESOURCES

FIGURE 2.5. The Contributions of Psychology and Public Health to the Specification of Program and Policy Goals

fore, will often specify goals at different levels that are interrelated and which ultimately have an impact on the risk behaviors.

Design of Interventions

Figure 2.6 notes the contributions of psychology and public health to the design of interventions. Most psychologically based health programs will include one or more of these programs or products: self-help materials, instruction by experts or lay facilitators, use of print or visual media in varying formats and channels, group interaction and support, and individual motivational strategies, e.g., public commitments and contracts. These programs and products are geared primarily to changes in individual knowledge and behavior, e.g., knowledge of proper nutrition and maintenance of altered dietary and activity patterns.

Individually focused interventions have the potential advantages of being tailored to specific population segments and making use of network, family, peer, and other social influences. A major disadvantage is the lack of reach of many individual interventions, particularly when delivered within the traditional "waiting" mode—i.e., a professional, generally charging a high fee for service, literally waits for clients in distress. Some of the problems with individual interventions are circumvented when relatively inexpensive interventions are delivered in a more active "seeking" mode (Rappaport, 1977), although in both cases the likelihood of permanent individual change in the face of a nonsupportive environment is not substantial.

Public health–inspired health programs often involve organizational or institutional change—i.e., new policies or laws—and have as their target changes in resource allocations and societal and organizational norms. Traditionally, such interventions have been called "passive." The term means that once an intervention is in place, it does not require constant human vigilance and activity. Of course, the term passive belies the controversy and effort often entailed in instituting community or legal and regulatory change! One example of a public health intervention in worksites is the banning of smoking by legislation across many kinds of work settings (Fielding, 1986). It often is hoped that such legislation also will produce a positive "no smoking" norm in many settings and occupations. However, the question of how particular organizations and individuals deal with this health regulation (i.e., of the process of change stemming from this intervention) is often beyond the scope of the programs at this level of intervention and analysis.

Again, the example suggests that much may be gained by the synthesis of psychological and public health targets and interventions. For example, a five-year lead-in period (prior to prohibition of smoking at select worksites) could coincide with a bevy of individual and group programs to aid cessation efforts. Measures of individual and organizational levels of smoking

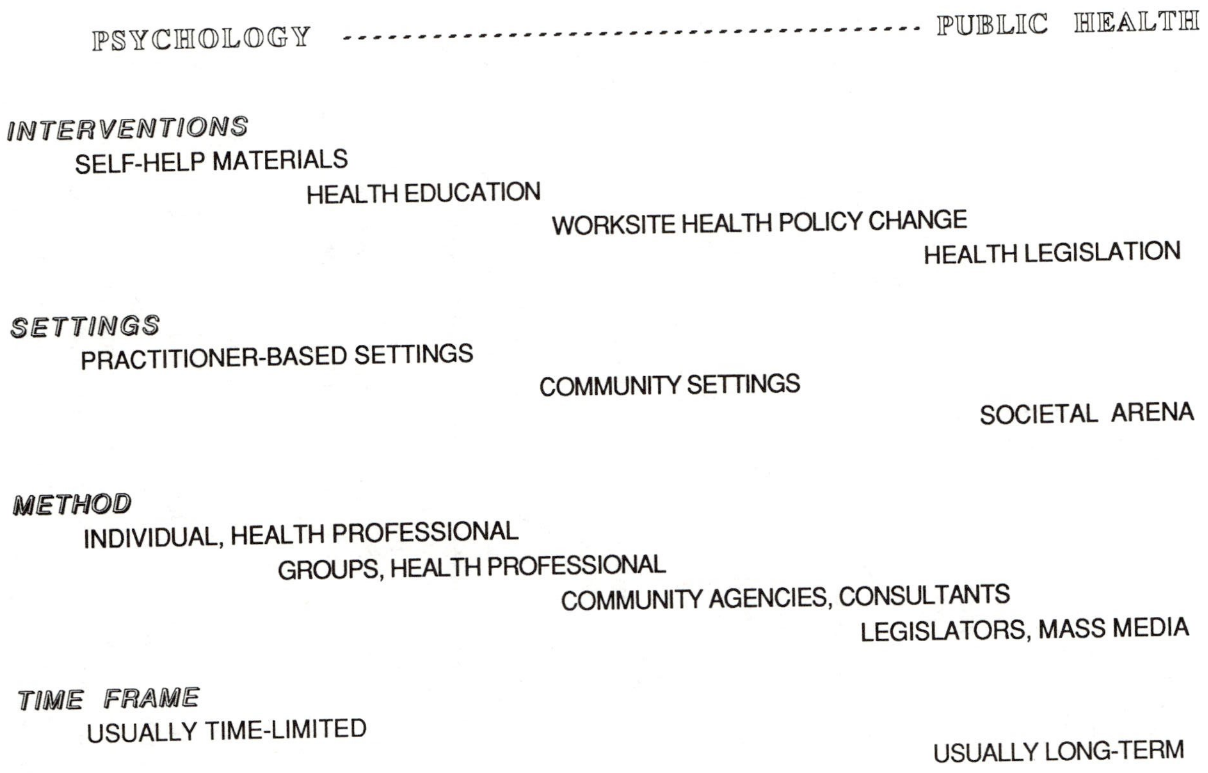

PSYCHOLOGY - - - - - - - - - - - - - - - - - - PUBLIC HEALTH

INTERVENTIONS
SELF-HELP MATERIALS
HEALTH EDUCATION
WORKSITE HEALTH POLICY CHANGE
HEALTH LEGISLATION

SETTINGS
PRACTITIONER-BASED SETTINGS
COMMUNITY SETTINGS
SOCIETAL ARENA

METHOD
INDIVIDUAL, HEALTH PROFESSIONAL
GROUPS, HEALTH PROFESSIONAL
COMMUNITY AGENCIES, CONSULTANTS
LEGISLATORS, MASS MEDIA

TIME FRAME
USUALLY TIME-LIMITED
USUALLY LONG-TERM

FIGURE 2.6. The Contributions of Psychology and Public Health to Designing Interventions

patterns and decrement over this and subsequent time periods would help to interpret future organizational stances toward other health promotion efforts (i.e., organizational norms). In addition, changes in disability and medical expenditures, measures pertaining to organizational and societal costs, would be better understood, and valuable predictive data obtained, *if* individual measures of smoking behavior were also collected. These points will also be addressed in the section on impacts.

Figure 2.6 also shows the different settings, methods, and time-frames typically used by psychological and public health approaches. The figure indicates that on these three dimensions there are likely to be substantial differences between approaches. Psychological interventions are most often conducted in homes, private practice settings, community mental health centers, hospitals, schools, churches, and work settings. Such interventions most often are delivered by psychologists, physicians, and nurses, or paraprofessionals and "mediators" under supervision. The method of intervention is usually instruction, training, or therapy on an individual or group basis. An important consideration is the time-frame, which is usually time-limited. That is, the structures of intervention are usually of limited duration, with the supposition that the effects of intervention will be relatively enduring.

Public health interventions also may take place in schools, work settings, health agencies, and churches, but also more generally within any community setting (e.g., toxic waste clean-ups). In addition, interventions often have a component that may be enacted in legal, economic, and political arenas (e.g., regulations on toxic waste). The method of intervention may entail consultation to public agencies, political lobbying, expert testimony, and development of regulations and laws. Interventions are designed to be (relatively) permanent — e.g., an institutional change, such as the DRG regulations, or a law (e.g., seat belt use), with the supposition (as noted above) that such "passive" interventions rectify the health problem (e.g., health care expenditures) or otherwise induce necessary behavioral changes (e.g., compliance with seat belt laws).

Thus, at their extreme, psychological and public health approaches are based on different assumptions and use quite different settings, methods, personnel, and time-frames. Clearly, for many health problems, a more ideal approach may attempt integrations across these various dimensions, a strategy demonstrated with some success by community psychologists (Heller, Price, Reinharz, Riger, & Wandersman, 1984). For example, psychologists can train paraprofessionals who, in turn, can help certain populations, such as the homeless, support themselves within alternative community settings developed by public health activists (e.g., an extension of the Fairweather Lodge program; see Heller et al., 1984).

Implementation of the Intervention

Over the last decade, some unofficial guides have been developed for effective program implementation that nicely blend some of the perspectives of psychology and public health. From the more individual level (primarily social marketing) comes the notion of conducting extensive formative research studies to identify receptive target populations and how interventions can be purposely designed to best meet the values and behaviors of select target groups (Rice & Paisley, 1981). Unfortunately, at this point, this intriguing and seemingly critical step in implementation does not have a scientifically sound set of methods (Winett, 1986). Indeed, many methods are borrowed from advertising (e.g., focus groups) and have questionable reliability, validity, and, hence, utility. We have previously suggested that developmental and ecological theory can be one conceptual basis of social marketing, and many of the points we will shortly make about measurement and impact assessment pertain to formative research.

Formative research also should be related to many of the points noted above about the various options for the design of an intervention, i.e., types of materials and settings. Ideally, an intervention's design will (relatively) uniquely fit a target population. More frequently, an existing type of program is fitted to the target population. Clearly, one major point from Figure 2.6 (above) is that there are many different potential combinations of materials, settings, methods, and personnel, many of which have yet to be fully explored.

Another essential step in successfully implementing an intervention is conducting a series of pilot studies. The series refines the preliminary program and measures so that a final program and set of measures is optimal. Unfortunately, few larger-scale programs have conducted adequate formative research, and fewer have conducted pilot studies. Many such programs, lacking such groundwork, have failed; this has been the case in particular for media-based programs (see chapter 4, and Winett, 1986). Unfortunately, such failures have often led to sweeping generalizations, e.g., "these kinds of behaviors cannot be changed by these techniques," rather than the more discriminating conclusion that appropriate formative and pilot research was never done to refine and optimize the approach.

A public health perspective, however, also adds much to effective program implementation by pointing toward organizational, community, cultural, and institutional barriers and facilitators of change. This point is nicely illustrated by the second generation of community health promotion projects discussed in chapter 5. In these projects, the long-range objective is to eventually have the sponsor's resources and staff withdraw from the community, while the community itself supports the program. In order to accomplish this objective, the program must be designed so that it can become embedded within the community's organizations and without draining those organizations of their resources.

Therefore, at the outset of intervention design and implementation steps, it is important for program planners to assess ethnic beliefs and behaviors in a community pertinent to a program. Likewise, it is equally important to understand the resources and operations of organizations that will house particular programs.

These points suggest a collaborative intervention model (in contrast to a professional/technical approach) that involves active citizen and organizational participation throughout the design, implementation, and follow-up phases of an intervention. This approach also has been articulated and demonstrated by community psychologists (Heller et al., 1984).

These various points about intervention implementation, and the relative contributions of psychology and public health, are shown schematically in Figure 2.7.

Assessment of Impacts

Figure 2.8 shows that psychology and public health have traditionally tended to rely on different measurement strategies, each with their relative strengths and weaknesses. However, as stated previously in this chapter, regardless of the level of analysis and intervention, appropriate conceptual and strategic steps will almost always start with an examination of epidemiological data (Hanlon & Pickett, 1984). That is, what person (host) and situational (environment) characteristics are predictive of health risk in a population? Further, what is the relative risk (the degree of the problem) afforded by such characteristics and what is the probability of affecting change in individual behavior and/or situational variables? Thus, regardless of level and subsequent measurement and intervention strategies, epidemiological data should form a primary rationale for targeting particular people, behaviors, and settings followed by estimations of the potential for change. Indeed, it can be cogently argued that the "bottom line" of an intervention will be provided by incidence and prevalence data and social indicators.

Clearly, however, the conceptual steps in a framework need to indicate behavioral links to health, social, and economic risk reduction. Thus, measuring behavioral change is critical. A major contribution of psychology to the measurement of effects is a more sophisticated approach to individual assessment. For example, a technology for surveys and interviews exists (e.g., Warheit, Bell, & Schwab, 1977) that can enhance or replace such techniques as 'needs assessment' (variously defined and conducted; Warheit et al., 1977). However, our preference is to rely less on self-report measures and more on direct observation and other tangible indicators of behavior in specific situations. This is because for a variety of reasons self-report measures, particularly general ones, often do not correlate well with behavior in

CONTRIBUTIONS OF PSYCHOLOGY & PUBLIC HEALTH TO IMPLEMENTING INTERVENTION

PSYCHOLOGY ---------------------- PUBLIC HEALTH

FORMATIVE RESEARCH

PILOT RESEARCH

ORGANIZATIONAL RESOURCES

CULTURAL / INSTITUTIONAL FACILITATORS AND BARRIERS

FIGURE 2.7. The Contributions of Psychology and Public Health to Implementing Interventions

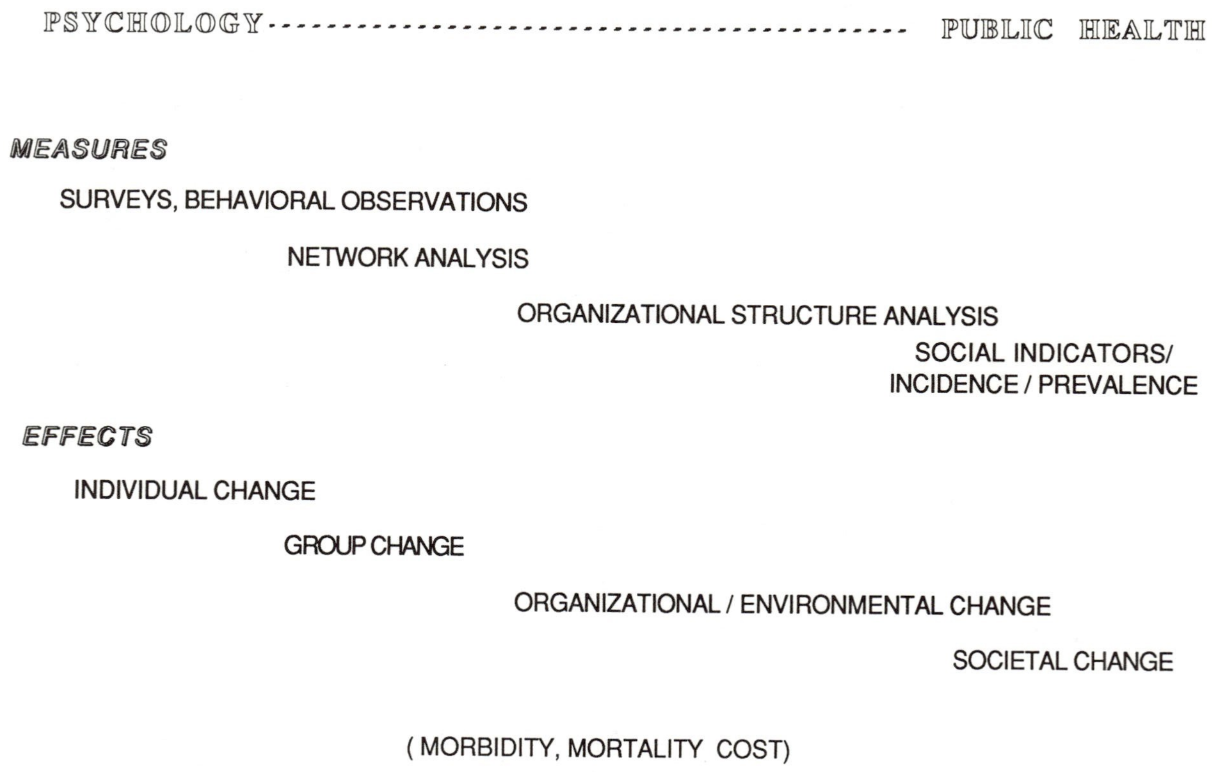

PSYCHOLOGY ------------------------ PUBLIC HEALTH

MEASURES

SURVEYS, BEHAVIORAL OBSERVATIONS

NETWORK ANALYSIS

ORGANIZATIONAL STRUCTURE ANALYSIS

SOCIAL INDICATORS/
INCIDENCE / PREVALENCE

EFFECTS

INDIVIDUAL CHANGE

GROUP CHANGE

ORGANIZATIONAL / ENVIRONMENTAL CHANGE

SOCIETAL CHANGE

(MORBIDITY, MORTALITY COST)

FIGURE 2.8. The Contributions of Psychology and Public Health to Assessing the Impacts of Interventions

important situations (Bandura, 1986). For example, actual observations of food choices in a cafeteria and activity in fitness programs are usually far more accurate (though sometimes more expensive) indicators of food preferences and activity than general survey items or even food diaries. Psychology can make a major contribution to measurement of impacts through its direct observational methods (Kazdin, 1984) which are being enhanced by computer technology (Walker, 1987).

An insistence on more direct behavioral data can lend more confidence to various kinds of measurement strategies directed at different levels of analysis. As a case in point, network analyses have most often depended on retrospective reports of interactions (Rogers & Kincaid, 1981). More fine-grain and timely methods yield more reliable data (Wahler & Graves, 1983). For example, covariations between observational (mother and child interactions at home) and highly specific self-report measures (of the number and valence of community contacts) have revealed how limited and negative social contacts can further undermine already problematic home interactions (Wahler, 1980). Such data help pinpoint network influences and suggest a specific network intervention.

Likewise, assessment of organizational change should not just be based on employer and employee reports of those policy changes (although some valuable methods exist here; e.g., Moos, 1985). Rather, at a minimum those data should be supplemented by specifications of the policies, job descriptions, and *actual observations* of the organization. Archival data and other nonintrusive data can also aid organizational assessments (e.g., see Fisher, Bell, & Baum, 1984). Similar strategies should be used to analyze public policies. For example, questions concerning the quality of care and current payment caps (limits on charges and third-party reimbursement based on diagnosis–DRGs) should not be answered just through reports of medical staff and patients, or even solely through archival data (e.g., diagnoses and utilization patterns such as days of inpatient care). The questions may be better answered by *defining* 'quality care' and then observing practices under payment caps and, if possible, also somewhere where caps do not exist.

The unique contribution of psychology to the assessment process is the insistence on more direct information-gathering techniques. Public health forms a foundation for this process by having epidemiology guide assessments but with more direct assessment techniques also applicable for higher levels of analysis and larger scale programs.

Interestingly, no matter what level(s) of intervention is involved or what other sets of measures used to assess impact, a program's societal impact can be evaluated when particular public health and cost data are also used. For example, an individually based intervention program (e.g., MRFIT) can reflect societal impacts when outcome measures track morbidity and mortality data of program participants and controls. Morbidity and mortality rates are individual data, but also indicate costs to society (i.e., loss of employment, disability payments, hospitalization costs).

Cost-effectiveness data of programs designed and delivered in various ways and for various objectives can further address the issue of societal resource allocation when, in particular, a common outcome measure, e.g., "well years" achieved, is used (Kaplan, 1985). Likewise, various programs can be subjected to "societal" cost–benefit analyses, wherein there is a full accounting of all gains and losses (Levin, 1983; Russell, 1985). The pressure on providers to justify all resources allocated to treatment and prevention indicates that in the future most programs will be subjected to multilevel assessments and more sophisticated cost-effectiveness and cost–benefit analyses.

The impacts of existing and ongoing evaluations comprise one complete iteration of this conceptual and strategic framework. Presumably, the impacts of relevant policies and programs are examined prior to finalizing an intervention strategy. In turn, the results of a newly developed initiative based on this framework also become part of the knowledge base (and conceptual steps) for subsequent use of the framework. Hopefully, the conceptual and strategic steps and the feedback afforded by the impacts of interventions will not only attest to the value of the framework, but more generally advance the field.

FRAMEWORK SUMMARY

Table 2.1 provides a more detailed summary of all the different elements of the process framework. While it is clear the framework is not singularly elegant, as for example one theory (e.g., health beliefs model; Janz & Becker, 1984), or more focused frameworks (e.g., PRECEDE; Green, 1981), we note these advantages:

1. Multiple sources of information are considered.
2. Different value positions are made explicit.
3. Various relevant theories can be used.
4. Multilevel assessments and multilevel interventions in different settings, using varied strategies and combinations of personnel, can be conceptualized and implemented.
5. Multiple impacts, including costs and benefits, can be ascertained.

We view our approach as an evolving framework and *one way* to integrate psychology and public health.

To illustrate the processes and utility of the framework, we next examine a major health concern—the continuation of cigarette smoking by a large number of adults. However, rather than conduct a more comprehensive use of the framework, as sometimes will be the case when other health concerns

Table 2.1. Conceptual and Strategic Framework*

Level	Problem Definition	Theories & Concepts	Values	Multilevel Analysis	Specification of Goals
Personal	Epidemiological data & biological & behavioral data	Systems Theory Social Cognitive Theory PRECEDE Model Attitude Change Behavior Analysis Health Belief Model Social Marketing Life-Span Development	Health and illness primarily a result of personal lifestyle	Integration of data, theory, and values from individual level with other levels	Individual Change
Interpersonal	Epidemiological data & social influence data	Systems Theory Social Support and Network Theory Communication Th'ry Group Dynamics Social Marketing Social Cognitive Theory	Health and illness is influenced by family, friends, and other social groups	Integration of data, theory, and values from interpersonal level with other levels	Individual and Group Change
Organizational/ Environmental	Epidemiological data & organizational/environmental influence data	Systems Theory Organizational Th. Community Organiz. Social Change Th'ry Social Marketing Social Ecology Alternative Settings Environmental Psych	Health and illness is influenced by organizational factors and by the environment	Integration of data, theory, and values from organizational/ environmental level with other levels	Organizational/ Environmental Change
Institutional/ Societal	Epidemiological data & legal, economic, regulatory, & policy data	Systems Theory Economic Theory Law Public Policy Political Science Social Marketing Epidemiology	Health and illness is influenced by societal resources, priorities and policies	Integration of data, theory, and values from institutional/ societal level with other levels	Legal, regulatory, policy change

(continued)

*Processes between and within steps are often interactive with an overall goal of formulating multilevel conceptualizationtions and interventions.

are reviewed in subsequent chapters, the focus here will be on the central element of viewing the problem from multiple levels. The multilevel analysis includes different theoretical perspectives and data sources, which in turn will suggest different kinds of policies and interventions. The critical health problem of smoking will also be addressed again in more detail in chapter 5.

CURTAILMENT OF ADULT CIGARETTE SMOKING: A MULTILEVEL ANALYSIS

As discussed in chapter 1, cigarette smoking is the number one health risk factor in the U.S. There are more than 320,000 preventable deaths each year in this country associated with cigarette smoking (Addiss, 1985). This figure is seven times greater than the number of persons killed annually in motor vehicle accidents, with the accident area recently receiving long-awaited,

Table 2.1. (Continued)

Program	Design of Intervention			Implementation of Intervention	Assessment of Impacts
	Settings	Personnel/ Method	Timeframe		
Self-help, media-assisted instruction, health education, counseling	Home, mental health center, hospital, private practice, churches, schools, work settings	Individual, therapist, physician, other health professional, facilitator, media	Usually time-limited	Formative research on beliefs, behaviors & response to prospective program	Individual data & cost data
Self- or mutual-help groups, group and family therapy, media-assisted group instruction, health education	Home, mental health center, hospital, private practice, churches, schools, work settings	Group, therapist, physician, other health professional, facilitator, media	Usually time-limited	Formative & pilot research on social factors & program acceptability & preliminary effects	Individual, group data & cost data
Changing worksite health policy, altering environment, changing norms; mass media	Work settings, health agencies, schools, other community settings, environment	Government, community agency, consultant, media, private sector	Usually long-term	Assessments of organizational/ environmental settings & optimal placement of an intervention for longevity	Organizational, environmental, data & cost data
Economic incentives/ disincentives, health legislation	Legal, political, economic, policy arenas	Government, politician, business, mass media, legislator, consultant, lobbying, expert witness	Usually long-term	Assessments of community, cultural, institutional barriers & facilitators and optimal placement of an intervention for longevity	Epidemiological & social indicator data & cost data

though perhaps disproportionate, attention (e.g., campaigns regarding drunk driving, child restraints). More women today are dying from lung cancer than breast cancer, and these morbidity data reflect sex-related changes in smoking patterns during the last 40 years (Addiss, 1985).

While the tobacco industry may argue that the facts about smoking remain to be proven, medical and epidemiological data create an almost irrefutable case. Coronary heart disease, other cardiovascular disease, certain site cancers, and obstructive pulmonary disease account for much of the excess mortality attributed to cigarette smoking (Kuller, Meilahn, Townsend, & Weinberg, 1982). Cigarette smoking increases the risk of lung cancer to a greater degree than other cancer sites, i.e., from 9 to 25 times greater risk, partly dependent on the amount and chronicity of smoking, a dose-morbidity relationship (Kuller et al., 1982). However, the risk of cancer of the buccal cavity and pharynx is increased 3 to 18 times by smoking; cancer of the larynx, 6 to 13 times; and cancer of the esophagus, 4 to 9 times (Kuller et al., 1982).

Cessation of smoking for several years can greatly decrease risk. Some residual risk remains and is related to the cumulative exposure to cigarette smoke. Further, while there is some permanent lung function damage attributable to smoking, cessation terminates continual damage, with lung function subsequently approaching that of nonsmokers (Kuller et al., 1982).

The monetary costs of smoking to the individual, organizations and corporations, and our country are staggering. According to Syme and Alcalay (1982), smokers have a 33% higher absenteeism rate than nonsmokers, 15% higher disability rates, decreased work productivity, and twice as many accidents and fires. Milo (1985) has estimated that the total annual cost of smoking, including direct costs from health care and indirect costs from productivity losses, is $47.5 *billion* (1980 dollars). More than two thirds of that cost was estimated to be attributable to lost earnings from illness and death.

In the face of such massive evidence of health risk, about 26% of adults, totalling approximately 65 million people, continue to smoke (Declining smoking rates, 1987). How can such seemingly self-destructive behavior be understood, and what can be done to sharply curtail cigarette smoking? The answers to these two questions will be examined at the four levels of analysis of our framework.

Personal Level

This level of analysis is concerned with biological, cognitive, and behavioral variables. Relevant theory includes psychobiology, social cognitive theory, health belief models and communication models, and behavior analysis. Importantly, it still can be shown that certain segments of smokers either do not really know about health risk or do not personally feel vulnerable. Warner (1986) has detailed how cigarette advertising attempts to undermine scientific evidence of the harmful effects of smoking. In part, this has resulted in a surprising and dangerous situation where the specific and profoundly harmful effects of smoking on the individual and society remain unknown by large segments of the population. Thus, most interventions, regardless of level, need an effective public information component to inform, persuade, and counter the massive expenditures for cigarette advertising.

However, other data do suggest, at a minimum, that many smokers feel that continued smoking is unhealthy. For example, Orleans (1985) has reported that 90% of U.S. smokers indicate they would like to quit, 60% have tried, and at least 60% are concerned about health risk. One parsimonious explanation of continued smoking is that nicotine is extremely addicting, cigarettes are readily available, and the method of medication (inhalation) greatly contributes to the maintenance of the addictive behavior (Russell,

1976). While there is clearly a psychological "habit" aspect of smoking, and certain facets of smoking (e.g., relapses) may not perfectly fit an addiction model (Benfari, Ockene, & McIntyre, 1982), it is difficult to conceive of most adults continuing to smoke nicotine-free cigarettes. In sum, most adults know at least something about the dangers of smoking; many want to quit, but remain addicted and unable to do so.

Investigations at the personal level during the last 30 years have attempted to find singular or multimethod strategies to help smokers quit. The assumption is that current smokers lack skills and motivation — i.e., that the problem is individually based. Approaches have typically followed different prominent paradigms of the period. For example, in the 1960s a number of methods were derived from classical conditioning and operant conditioning. In the 1980s methods were more likely to be multimodal and have biological, cognitive, and behavioral components. Most recent work is more focused on maintenance and relapse prevention (Brownell et al., 1986).

However, reviews (e.g., Leventhal & Cleary, 1980; Lichtenstein, 1982) consistently report only modest success (e.g., 30% long-term abstinence) for treatments usually administered to self-selected individuals or groups. No one method appears demonstratively superior, and the critical elements of successful long-term cessation remain largely unknown. Research on particular methods, often delivered in small groups, continues despite much evidence that most people who have quit have done so on their own, and most smokers do not want to go to organized smoking cessation programs (Schacter, 1982).

In addition, recent efforts have also emphasized simpler, more portable methods (e.g., Foxx & Brown, 1979); nicorette gum in conjunction with coping strategies for relapse prevention (Kozlowski, 1984; Killen, Maccoby, & Taylor, 1984); better programming and targeting based on "stage" of cognitive and behavior change (Prochaska & DiClemente, 1983); the concerns of segments of smokers (e.g., weight gain in women who stop smoking; Rodin & Wack, 1984); systematic involvement of physicians to promote cessation for their patients (Orleans, 1985); and mass delivery of self-help smoking cessation techniques via print and video media (Jason, Gruder, Martino, Flay, Warnecke, & Thomas, 1987). In a similar vein, use of worksite and community-based quit-smoking contests, developed as a means of making available potentially powerful incentives for the large number of individuals intent on quitting on their own, have had some success (King, Flora, Fortmann, & Taylor, 1987).

Interestingly, when individual smoking cessation strategies are compared in cost-effectiveness and cost–benefit analyses, those data indicate the impacts of individual interventions at other levels of analysis (e.g., impacts on work settings, resources, and public policy expenditures; Altman, Flora,

Fortmann, & Farquhar, 1987). However, note that many such efforts still focus primarily on individual factors (e.g., deficits in coping techniques) and are individually delivered. Other levels of analysis focus on additional mechanisms maintaining smoking and concomitant approaches to curtailing smoking.

Interpersonal Level

While many of the previously mentioned strategies have been delivered within group or organizational settings, for the most part those interventions target individuals. There has been minimal involvement of peers, groups, families, or other social factors (Syme & Alcalay, 1982). For example, and in contrast, Evan's (1984) approach to the prevention of teenage smoking rests heavily on the assumption that the peer group is a major impetus for initiation and maintenance of smoking. Accordingly, a major strategy of Evan's approach involves teaching young teenagers how to resist peer pressure to smoke (see review by Best, Thompson, Santi, Smith, & Brown, 1988).

While there are few interpersonal approaches to (adult) smoking cessation, some potential causal mechanisms and approaches to curtailment at this level appear identifiable. Smoking rates differ between different age, SES, and ethnic groups (Syme & Alcalay, 1982). Teenage females now smoke more than teenage males; blue collar workers smoke more than white collar workers; and blacks smoke more than whites (although SES contributes to this difference; Addiss, 1985). An important task involves understanding different beliefs, norms, functions, behaviors, situations, and reinforcers that contribute to differential smoking rates between segments. An assumption is that such understanding will delineate causal mechanisms which can be used to develop approaches to cessation tailored to different segments.

A compatible approach could entail training families and employee groups to help members quit smoking. For example, training could focus on ways to ease withdrawal systems and prevent relapses. Likewise, buddy systems within employee groups could instigate positive social support mechanisms, which have been related to long-term maintenance of cessation (Janis, 1983). More generally, appropriate social support appears to be an important element in cessation of addictive behaviors (Brownell et al., 1986).

Yet another approach, which has elements of higher levels of analysis and intervention, involves attempts to modify the social climate pertaining to smoking. For example, smoking has most often been seen as an individual's "right to choose." Such a stance continues to be actively promoted by tobacco corporations, and at least one leading feminist, Gloria Steinem, a founder of *Ms.* magazine, defends women's smoking with this posture. The right-to-choose philosophy most often negates influences other than "rational" choice (e.g., Friedman & Friedman, 1979). For example, extensive, well-targeted, and seductive advertising plays a part in smoking initiation (Breslow, 1982; see chapter 5 for relevant data on these points). The addictive qualities of nicotine maintain smoking in the face of reported desires to quit. It appears difficult to argue for individual freedom and choice when youngsters are lured by powerful influences into the use of a readily available addictive substance (Warner, 1986a).

The social climate may be changed through health education efforts in schools and through the media. Identification of economic, social, behavioral, and physiological maintainers of smoking may help to dispel the right to choose ideology. Further, it appears equally important to document that a smoker's behavior affects other people, and therefore is not merely a matter of individual freedom. Documentation of the effects of passive inhalation of smoke is one major, though controversial, issue (Eriksen, LeMaistre, & Newell, 1988; Haglund, 1986). Delineation and public communication of the economic costs of smoking as it pertains to each nonsmoking individual and our society may also contribute to a social climate that makes smoking less acceptable.

Organizational/Environmental Level

This level of analysis for curtailment of adult smoking emphasizes theory and action at the organizational and community level. Smoking behavior is seen as highly influenced by settings, rules, organizational policy, community norms, and substance availability. Change in these factors (e.g., organizational policy) usually constitutes the target for this level, with individual change following organizational/environmental change. A prime, though controversial, example of this approach is the policy, recently adopted by some organizations, which precludes hiring smokers. More moderate, though still controversial, organizational changes can include limiting smoking designated areas and removing cigarette vending machines from buildings. How such policies are developed — i.e., by decree or mutual agreement between labor and management — can have much to do with their acceptance (Fielding, 1986). Comparable methods for limiting teenage smoking can include banning smoking by faculty and students on school grounds and enforcing age requirements for purchase of cigarettes. A caveat is that mutual agreements between faculty, students, parents, and business people must be forged for this approach to work.

Note that with these types of strategies, the approach that has historically been the province of public health has been entered. That is, these strategies will require negotiation to establish and enforcement to maintain them, but they are instituted across the board. Such rules and organizational policy changes are designed to affect all present and potential smokers. Once in place, this approach does not require individual, voluntary action.

There has been considerable recent interest in worksite health promotion (see chapter 9), and such programs inevitably have smoking cessation as a prime focus (Feldman, 1984). Worksite programs also usually are designed for the well, adequately functioning, worker. Program providers have a reasonably captive audience and workers are given a convenient way to improve their health (Nathan, 1984b). Employers have become particularly interested in worksite health promotion programs because:

> Employers bear a major portion of illness costs. They pay the lion's share of the health insurance costs. They also absorb the productivity losses including those resulting from premature retirement and death. According to estimates by the President's Council on Physical Fitness, premature deaths alone cost American industry more than $25 billion and 132 million workdays of lost production each year. (Fielding, 1984, p. 239)

Worksite smoking cessation programs appear particularly promising from a cost–benefit perspective, whether they are entirely paid for by employers or cost-shared (Fielding, 1984). At least several worksite programs which focus on multiple risk factors, despite problems (e.g., modest, sustained participation rates), report promising health behavior changes (e.g., "Live for Life;" Nathan, 1984a; Wilbur & Garner, 1984; "Staywell;" Naditch, 1984).

However, it is important to note that the centerpiece of such programs is usually small-group instruction, even though considerable organizational resources and top management commitment are generally required to implement the programs (Fielding, 1984). What theory guides these efforts appears more characteristic of individual level analysis, e.g., health education models and social–cognitive theory. The point is that the burgeoning interest in small-group worksite health promotion may not be matched by organizational policy changes to increase, support, and maintain more individually based changes within these organizations.

An interesting augmentation of the small-group approach is the use of incentives contingent on smoking cessation and maintenance. The incentives — cash, prizes, or holidays — are usually provided by the participating organizations. Little evaluation work has been done on these programs. However, one controlled study (Klesges, Vasey, & Glasgow, 1986) showed that an incentive approach resulted in a greater level of participation in organizations for smoking cessation programs than when the same program was offered without incentives. Although the success rate at six months was about the same between incentive and no incentive conditions, because of the greater participation level, the incentive condition resulted in more quitters within the worksite than the no-incentive approach. While this appears to be a positive finding, there is also a "hidden" cost to this approach. That is, by inducing more people to participate in the program, the incentive condition also resulted in more failures. Such an outcome can be costly in the long term for individuals and firms. As will be argued in chapter 3, various health promotion programs purporting to use "incentives" beg for an appropriate and contemporary theory of incentives and motivation.

A number of community health promotion programs share similar characteristics to many organizational efforts. While the early forerunners have been criticized by some for insufficiently emphasizing organizational elements in the community, this appears to be less the case for the second generation of community programs (e.g., Farquhar et al., 1985). These multiple risk reduction programs, targeted to the general population, now have a stronger community organization element (see chapter 5). For example, in the Stanford Five City Project, local print, radio, and TV media are used for instructional purposes (i.e., knowledge change). Programs for health behavior change are conducted at local settings and within various organizations.

A basic goal of the Stanford Five City Project is that as a particular educational program matures, an increasing proportion of the media products and activities will rely on local community resources for collaborative production and distribution. From the outset, those programs involving interpersonal contact depend heavily on community resources. However, the entire process of program development is seen as a collaborative effort between Stanford University and the community, with the community eventually operating the programs while maintaining links to Stanford.

Perhaps the Five City Project and other similar projects are best seen as resting within *locality (resource) development* and *social planning* models. They involve much less social action, with fewer attempts to drastically modify community values, priorities, and ordinances (Rappaport, 1977). However, to the extent that communities modify, refine, and maintain such programs, and to the extent that community programs positively influence large numbers of citizens, the designation "community" certainly seems warranted.

Institutional/Societal Level

The basic assumption of the institutional/societal level of analysis is that organizational and community structures, interpersonal processes, the social milieu, and individual choice reflect institutional, societal policies. That is:

> Public policy is part of and a creator of modern environments. By intent or neglect, it affects not only our socially-created but also our natural worlds. In our communities, workplaces, schools, and homes, it sets the odds for what we, through organizations and as individuals, are likely to produce and consume in the form of goods, services, and information. Its influence pervades

the spectrum of ordinary activity—in food and housing, health care and education, transportation and communication, leisure and security. And policy assures how equitably these options for choice making—and thus for life styles—are dispersed among social and economic groups, organizations, and regions. (Milio, 1985, p. 603)

However, individuals are not powerless in the face of policy. Real or perceived changes at the personal level and the social and economic climate (e.g., disapproval of smoking; declining sales) can influence policy makers to enact policies which " . . . provide incentives to producers and consumers to make more healthful choices than they do today" (Milio, 1985, p. 603). Despite this notion of reciprocity, the overriding assumption is that efforts at lower levels will be best only minimally successful if policies still favor nonhealthy behaviors.

For smoking, the major problem in public policy involves the conflict between short-term economic interests and long-term health costs (Breslow, 1982). The parallel conflict between individual and corporate rights on the one hand and societal protection on the other is also prominent in policy debates on smoking control (Syme & Alcalay, 1982). Relevant frameworks include political science theory, constitutional law, policy analysis, and economic theories of demand.

A major focus and debate involves how to phase out tobacco production (and subsidies) and help diversify the tobacco industry. Such steps are buttressed by declining U.S. sales (although this is offset by the opening of markets in less developed countries), cheaper imported tobacco, increased operating costs, and a decreased need for labor (Milio, 1985). However, those representing health and related economic concerns face obstacles due to the industry's large contribution to the GNP and revenue from sales and taxes (Milio, 1985) and the continual existence of a strong tobacco lobby for cigarette manufacturers, allied with those in the mass media (through advertising revenue; Warner, 1986a), the sports world, and political representatives (mostly from the Southeast) (Bell & Levy, 1984; Milio, 1985). Long-term policy change must be comprehensive and deal with land use, manpower retraining, and alternative products. At the most basic level, policies must help to insure that different crops and products are profitable (Breslow, 1982).

Somewhat similar conflicts have involved cigarette advertising and promotions. Does government have the right to limit the advertisement of a legal product? Do corporations have a right to advertise an addictive substance with advertisements directed at teenagers? Do advertisements simply change brand preferences (the corporate position), or do they help to initiate new smokers (expand the market) by portraying smoking as socially acceptable, glamorous, sports-related, and masculine or feminine (Warner, 1986a)? Such conflicts are not presently resolved, although Warner (1986a) has shown how cigarette corporations must depend on the enlistment of new smokers to replace those smokers who have died or quit.

For the last 25 years, there has been a history of actions by the Federal Trade Commission involving health warnings on cigarette packages, counter ads on TV and radio via the structures of equal time and the Fairness Doctrine, and eventual banning of cigarette advertising on TV and radio (and, unfortunately, antismoking ads) under the Public Health Cigarette Smoking Act of 1969 (Breslow, 1982). These efforts have had an uncertain impact. For example, the 1969 Act was apparently favored by the tobacco industry because antismoking ads appeared to have some impact on sales (Breslow, 1982). Advertisement monies by cigarette firms, totalling over $1 billion per year, are now focused in other mass media (Milio, 1985). It appears that with increased deregulation of the media and the Federal Communication Commission's "free market" policies under former Chairman Fowler, access to the mass media for smoking cessation and other health promotion messages has been limited (Winett, 1986).

The issue of cigarette advertising and promotions is fraught with philosophical and legal conflicts. However, the case has been made that in consideration of the costs to individuals and society, as well as the inability to garner resources for effective counter campaigns, cigarette advertising and promotions should be banned (Warner, 1986a).

Another set of policies also directly affects smoking behavior. The price elasticity of demand for cigarettes is about $-.4$, meaning that a 10% price increase results in a 4% decrease in demand (Warner & Murt, 1984). Decreases appear to result both from decisions to quit smoking and not to initiate smoking (i.e., adolescents). However, in countries where excise taxes have kept pace with inflation, decreased demand has also been shown for blue collar workers (Warner & Murt, 1984). Additional economic levers include differential insurance rates and savings for companies with differential rates of smoking (risk ratings) and allowing individual (or organizational) costs of smoking cessation and other health promotion programs to be tax deductible (Warner & Murt, 1984). However, these measures may have less clear impacts.

Summary

This brief overview of several policy issues indicates the influence of such policies on individual and organizational choice. While change in higher level policies can promote health behaviors, change at lower levels can also set the proper social climate, whereby policy changes become more probable. Taken optimistically, this point indicates a reciprocity of influence (and synergism) between levels and the value of analyzing and understanding a health problem from multiple perspectives.

However, on balance, this brief overview also indicates tht the concerns at the policy level are quite diverse (e.g., agricultural and communication policy) and the conflicts long standing (e.g., individual and corporate rights versus societal protection). It becomes apparent that change at the policy level needs to be comprehensive, but will probably take many years to reach a state of acceptable compromise, let alone fruition.

USE OF THE FRAMEWORK

The prior section illustrated some of the different data sources, theories, concepts, assumptions, values, and courses of action pertinent to different levels of analysis. Presumably, all points could be considered before deciding upon a specific level for further investigation and action. In practice, depending upon one's position and resources, it is expected that most users of the framework probably would focus on only two levels — e.g., interpersonal and organizational. However, after picking levels of analysis, it behooves wise practitioners and researchers to understand processes and influences below and above their levels of focus (Winkler & Winett, 1982). For example, developers of small-group smoking cessation programs in organizations need to be cognizant of recent literature on addictive behaviors, as well as policies which may increase or decrease organizational commitment to health promotion.

Once settling on levels of analysis and intervention, and investigating diverse literature primarily pertaining to those levels (but also being cognizant of influences at other levels), the processes of program design and implementation begin. This process includes setting specific goals; weighing the advantages and disadvantages of differential emphases of the levels; and selecting appropriate targets, "products" (types of materials and procedures), settings, and personnel. Implementation processes include conducting formative and pilot research and assessing how to optimally place a program in organizations and communities prior to a full-scale operation. The final steps pertain to assessing the multiple impacts of a program. However, new conceptual or empirical input, e.g., a different theoretical perspective, unexpected formative or pilot research data, could mark the point for a full or partial reuse of the steps in the framework.

PLAN AND OVERVIEW OF THE BOOK

The conceptual and strategic framework and the "recurrent themes and tensions" noted in chapter 1, which primarily revolve around the choice between an individual or societal emphasis, form the core for the chapters in this book. The "technique" chapters, "Incentives," "Media," and "Community Health Promotion," take a particular perspective on how a major strategy can be most effectively used for health promotion. For example, the incentive chapter makes the case that the use of incentives in various realms of health promotion has been conceptually and procedurally simplistic. More than likely, this has resulted in less than optimal impacts. Social–cognitive and process-of-change theories form the cornerstone of a new, and seemingly more promising, approach to motivation. Concepts and procedures from this approach are then used to construct a specific community health promotion program. The overall program design and evaluation rests on the process framework.

The "content" chapters often will build on the technique chapters, and more explicitly follow the conceptual and strategic framework. However, as discussed below, the content chapters generally emphasize one aspect of the framework and, secondarily, other parts of the framework. Thus, the chapters illustrate use of the framework but do not use every step in a definitive way.

These chapters also take a particular perspective or problem focus, and do not attempt a completely comprehensive review of an area. However, all these chapters will generally follow the same outline which mirrors the framework. The problem will be stated, usually in both historical and contemporary content. Incidence, prevalence, and other assessment data will be presented and interpreted. The usual theoretical and practical approaches to the problem, and their successes and failures, will be noted, and some assessment of these prior efforts will be made, with pointed conclusions drawn.

A major task of each content chapter, and the pivotal part of the framework, is conducting the multilevel analysis. Theory, data, procedures, and outcomes from different levels will usually be presented. An assessment will be made of the conceptual and practical strengths and weaknesses, and benefits and costs, of different levels of conceptualization and action. Often this overview and assessment will bring into play the recurrent themes and tensions. For example, worksite health and safety has been viewed quite differently by management and labor. Management has tended to view problems in occupational health and safety as residing in the individual and, thus, solvable through individual interventions, e.g., stress management. Labor, in contrast, perceives that health and safety problems are inherent in the organization and environment of work, and solvable through system change, i.e., the conditions of work.

These different perspectives will most often suggest that a problem can be redefined in a multilevel way. For example, occupational health and safety problems are attributable to individual, host factors, peer group norms, job tasks and the work environment, and economic, legal, and regulatory influences.

From this analysis and conclusion, at least one exemplar multilevel intervention will be designed. Its development will rest heavily on the multilevel analysis, pertinent theories, principles and procedures, and consideration of appropriate targets, settings, personnel, time-frames, and impact assessment strategies.

The content chapters in this book discuss the following topics: community mental health, maternal and child health with a focus on teenage pregnancy, nutrition change, worksite safety and health, environment and health, and aging and health. A brief epilogue overviews the framework, the content covered in this book, and the potential for future development of the integration of health psychology and public health.

Our framework, focused reviews, and exemplar multilevel intervention plans are not presented as the final or only perspectives and methods on what are extremely complex problems. None of our plans are offered as 'a panacea.' Rather, each review, the framework, and the plans are examples of work towards more optimal integrations of psychology and public health.

SECTION II

TECHNIQUES FOR PROMOTING CHANGE: DISCUSSION AND APPLICATION

This section focuses on the explication of three potentially powerful techniques for promoting change that are applicable across a number of health problems and, in the case of incentives and media, a number of levels of analysis. The application of relevant theory as well as other salient aspects of the framework described in chapter 2 are used in discussing how these techniques might best be utilized in order to maximize their impact on the change process. It is not a goal of the book that these chapters serve as a comprehensive review of the techniques discussed. Rather, the chapters attempt to incorporate methods and viewpoints from health psychology and public health in offering a perspective that represents a departure from what has typically occurred in the two fields.

Chapter 3 focuses on the use of *incentives* in health promotion. Contemporary social cognitive theory is formally applied as an alternative to the more typical operant or economic approaches used in understanding how incentives might better be applied to promote health-related change. In addition, the chapter stresses the importance of differential application of incentives depending upon what point in the change process is being focused on (e.g., behavioral acquisition versus maintenance). A discussion of how incentives might be used in fostering exercise in a community serves to illustrate the points being made.

Chapter 4 focuses on the effective use of media in health promotion, using the contemporary AIDS epidemic to illustrate what are often the problems as well as strengths involved in applying media to promote health changes. As with the other chapters that comprise this book, particular emphasis is placed on higher levels of analysis (e.g., institutions, the community) than are traditionally focused on by psychologists, with application of relevant psychological theory often absent in public health intervention approaches.

Chapter 5 offers a selected review of community health promotion strategies and those elements comprising the more successful community campaigns to date. A combination of theory and observations based on experiences from the field is presented along with attendant caveats concerning application of a community approach. The systematic application of community strategies in response to the problem of smoking is subsequently presented. Suggestions for designing future community interventions are presented, using the framework presented in chapter 2 as an organizational tool.

3
Incentives in Health Promotion: A Theoretical Framework and Applications

OVERVIEW

The use of incentives for health promotion purposes represents a particularly engaging area of research and application for psychology and public health. On the one hand, psychology offers theories on incentives and reinforcement, while public health suggests the domains and avenues through which incentives can be widely applied. Then, too, it is apparent that incentives, intentionally or unintentionally, have been and will continue to be broadly used to influence certain behaviors and practices. And, indeed, there is ample evidence for their effectiveness.

For example, rates and amounts of insurance deductibles (cosharing) markedly influence health care service utilization; tax policy encourages expensive treatments that can be listed as itemized deductions, and discourages prevention activities that cannot be deducted; health maintenance organizations (HMOs), which receive a prepaid fee, attempt to limit expensive inpatient treatment; and the amount of excise taxes on cigarettes affects demand, particularly among younger persons contemplating or experimenting with cigarette smoking (Warner & Murt, 1984).

The purpose of this chapter is not to thoroughly review current impacts of incentives, but rather to serve a more general function. That is, we note that the substantial interest in using incentives, e.g., at worksites (Fielding, 1986), is not marked by application of more contemporary theory. We need to know what incentives are, how they work, when they should be used, and what other types of processes and procedures may be used with incentives, or can be effective alone. Most succinctly, we need to understand motivation.

The major contention is that while there is evidence that "incentives work," their present applications are far from optimal and are not based on contemporary theories of motivation. Further, incentives are often instituted to promote behavior change in the absence of serious consideration of concomitant and requisite skills, beliefs, and environmental supports essential to institute and maintain behavior change.

Most uses of incentives by individual firms and government, wittingly or unwittingly, follow the operant paradigm in psychology or classical (rational) economic theories. In the first instance, individuals tend to be portrayed as automatons responding to external stimuli — antecedent and consequent events. For example, the use of money rewards, contingent on participation and eventual cessation in a worksite smoking cessation program, is believed to operate by signaling the occasion for reinforcement to be delivered contingent on emitting specific responses, i.e., participation and cessation. Presumably, when the magnitude of reinforcement, its timing, and its schedule are appropriate (e.g., reinforcing cessation over time), many smokers will cease smoking.

Classical economic theories at first appear at odds with the operant paradigm, because such theories assume some individual or collective evaluation of the costs and benefits of different courses of action. However, the rational person is assumed to always choose to maximize outcomes (utilities). Thus, behavior can be predicted by an analysis of external events, i.e., reinforcement contingencies. The rational economic person is also an automaton.

Operant and classical economic theory do not place enough emphasis on cognitive processes, beliefs, symbols, and self-regulation, and, hence, personal agency for affecting behavior change (Bandura, 1986). This is not to say that all emphasis should be focused on personal agency. That would be an error of overcorrection. Rather, incentive and motivational processes and procedures must consider the triadic relationships of cognitive, behavioral, and environmental influences.

The first part of this chapter briefly overviews Bandura's social cognitive theory as a basis for understanding motivational processes. The second part of the chapter will delineate effective incentive variables partly derived from Bandura's theory. The third section will apply these principles and strategies to current and potential interventions at personal, group, organizational, and institutional levels. The final section will contain an extended example of a community intervention which is based on more contemporary motivational theory.

SOCIAL COGNITIVE THEORY

People act on their judgements of what they can do, as well as on their beliefs about the likely effects of various actions. There are many activities which, if done well, guarantee cherished outcomes, but they are not pursued by persons who doubt they can do what is needed to succeed. Self-perceived inefficacy can nullify the most enticing outcome expectations. Conversely, a strong sense of personal efficacy can strengthen and sustain efforts in the face of uncertain outcomes. (Bandura, 1986, p. 231)

Theory

The above quote from Bandura is central to understanding a contemporary theory of motivation. Behavioral response often cannot be predicted by only analyzing external events. Rather, cognitive mediators — i.e., beliefs pertaining to self-efficacy and outcome expectancy — and self-regulatory processes must be carefully considered, as well as social determinants such as modeling influences. In addition, it is important to differentiate the stage of change for which different processes and procedures are relevant. For example, the *acquisition* of knowledge and skills about personal health behaviors will usually precede adoption of a personal health ethic in which healthy behaviors are performed in a range of settings and time (*generality*), for a sustained period of time (*stability*). Monetary incentives may be useful for programs focusing on acquisition, but may perhaps be less useful for generality and stability (i.e., maintenance), which may depend more on self-regulatory processes.

In a social cognitive theory of motivation, self-regulatory processes are critical components. Self-regulatory processes depend on beliefs, self-evaluations, internal standards, and perceptions of the external environment. *Beliefs* refer to personal values, the saliency of particular behaviors to the individual, and their perceived malleability. *Self-evaluation* processes focus on assessments of personal skills as they relate to particular beliefs and alternative paths of action and contingencies. *Internal standards* include codes of behavior, proximal and distal goals, and personal standards used to guide and evaluate performance. *Perceptions of the external environment* are influenced by an individual's weighing of the valence of anticipated outcomes for different behavior-contingency relationships.*

As these points suggest, beliefs, values, standards, and perceptions are not construed as broad dispositions or traits. Rather, cognitive mediators are relatively specific to clusters of behaviors and settings.

Further, in this conceptualization, internal processes do not replace external events as the causal explanation of behavior. Rather, internal processes and external events are interactive causes of behavior, with persons seen as active agents exercising some influence over motivations and actions.

Note also that it is possible to subsume neoclassical economic positions under social cognitive theory. That is, in neoclassic economics the central

---

*Contingencies are events (internal or external to a person) which follow behaviors and serve to reinforce or punish preceding behavior.

assumption of utility (i.e., outcome) maximization through a thorough analysis of costs and benefits is replaced by notions of limits on information processing (e.g., Simon, 1979) and of the "nonrational" influences of information format, presentation, and stimulus configuration (Kahneman & Tverskey, 1984). Most generally, neoclassic economics emphasizes beliefs, perceptions, expectations, and information processing abilities as cognitive mediators of external contingencies.

Uses

Social cognitive theory is particularly applicable to health promotion efforts because it identifies multiple avenues for particular motivational procedures that appear useful at different stages in a process of change. For example, incentives may facilitate enlisting initial participation in activities that are not of immediate interest or may be arduous. However, generality and stability, as noted, may require more attention to modifying self-regulatory processes. Partial evidence to support this contention comes from an analysis of recent worksite smoking cessation programs that have used monetary incentives (e.g., Klesges, Vasey, & Glasgow, 1986; see also chapter 2). It is apparent that incentives in these instances markedly increased participation rates but did not alter long-term cessation rates. Thus, one unfortunate result of such programs is that they produce more failures than programs not using monetary incentives. Perhaps this is also the case because such programs have not focused enough on self-regulatory processes involved in generality and stability.

Schedules and Reinforcers

With regard to incentives and payment systems, both operant and social cognitive theory alert us to several key variables infrequently addressed in health promotion efforts. Schedules of reinforcement influence behavior, if not so much in exact accord with animal models, at least in ways that are readily extrapolated from the early work done in this area (Kazdin, 1984). For example, intermittent schedules of reinforcement are likely to yield more persistent behaviors. Focusing more reinforcement on behavioral maintenance may be one aid to long-term behavior change (Brownell et al., 1986).

Using an "incentive" does not mean that it is a reinforcer, i.e., has an impact on behavior. Operant theory defines a reinforcer in a circular way, i.e., by its effects on behavior. A consequent event that does not modify a preceding response (e.g., change its frequency) is not a reinforcer. Social cognitive theory also examines how potential incentives are perceived and valued by potential recipients. For example, relatively small payments for weight loss may be seen as demeaning, while additional unpaid vacation time for smoking cessation may actually be perceived as a punishment.

To date, most health promotion programs have made unverified assumptions about incentives and have used relatively unsophisticated schedules of reinforcement. For example, payments or enticements are generally chosen in a seat-of-the-pants way, and such "incentives" are frequently not scheduled in a manner meant to promote maintenance. The logistics and constraints of applied settings do not seem the problem here, but rather the excuse. The development of proper incentives may only rely on asking potential recipients what they are willing to work for and then delivering the incentives in ways conducive to behavioral maintenance.

However, incentives may be more critical in instituting initial efforts, if only because most incentive programs eventually end. This simple point may explain an apparent anomaly. For example, if Warner and Murt's (1984) analyses are correct, then (dis)incentives such as excise taxes on cigarettes predictably affect the behavior of many people over long time periods. In contrast, personal-level behavioral programs using incentives, such as response cost deposits (i.e., lose part of a deposit if smoking is resumed), at best, have shown maintenance for only several months (Bowers, Winett, & Frederiksen, 1987). The typical health behavior program has a termination point. Taxes, as all readers know, are interminable; but perhaps variables other than incentives, different procedures, and as-yet-undiscussed processes become particularly critical at different stages of behavior change.

Beliefs, Values, and Standards

Beliefs, values, and personal standards may be more important to long-term change if they are transsituational and lead to commitments. Beliefs and public and private commitments about the importance of personal health habits (i.e., strong outcome expectancies), and one's ability to implement and control personal health-related behaviors (self-efficacy beliefs), may help maintain health behaviors in the face of adversity and the absence of strong incentives. For example, a belief in the central role of good nutrition and exercise may lead to practices such as bringing food or searching out special stores and restaurants and gyms while on business trips. In this example, nutritional and exercise patterns become highly salient and barriers perceived by others to be difficult (i.e., finding proper meals) become surmountable. If a nutrition change program does not also instill strong beliefs, it is doubtful that behavior will be maintained when real or perceived barriers are reached.

Self-evaluation processes assess skills with regard to certain beliefs and alternative courses of action and consequences. *Self-efficacy evaluations* are one example of the outcomes of such assessments. *Self-efficacy* refers to beliefs about the ability to effectively enact certain behaviors under specific conditions. For example, a former smoker's probability of staying abstinent may greatly depend on his or her beleifs about his or her ability to cope with withdrawal symptoms and particular social situations. Enhanced beliefs about coping may be generated over time by systematic exposure to troublesome situations, with exposure aided by the teaching of coping techniques (e.g., relaxation training). Such exposure and practice may take place early in a program, perhaps while incentives are still in use, and successful enactment may forge efficacy beliefs which will sustain efforts in the future (Brownell et al., 1986).

However, self-efficacy beliefs are only one type of essential belief for many behavior change efforts. *Outcome expectancies* refer to the belief that adherence to a course of action will lead to specific outcomes — for example, the belief that lowering the fat content of the diet results in reduced cancer and cardiovascular disease risk, or that regular aerobic exercise results in better weight control and increased longevity. While self-efficacy refers to belief in the ability to perform specific behaviors, outcome expectancies are beliefs that performing the behaviors results in desired ends. For many health promotion efforts, both sets of beliefs are required (Stretcher, DeVellis, Becker, & Rosenstock, 1986).

Internal standards involve codes of behavior which relate to personal standards and proximal and distal goals. Internal, personal standards may evolve over time, be modified by precepts (e.g., new nutritional or exercise guidelines) and, modeling procedures, or change through social comparison or social evaluation processes. Personal standards and goals can generate and maintain considerable amounts of diverse behaviors. For example, in the case of exercise and athletic performance, few individuals, by definition, can match the performance of champions. Yet personal standards of excellence are developed that serve as a reference point. In addition, most effective training programs and their persistent adherents make use of proximal and distal goal setting, with consistent feedback on progress toward goals (Winett, 1988). Interestingly, while goals may be far removed from championship level, the key to success is they are challenging and interesting. Such goals and feedback reflect personal standards. They serve to motivate a considerable amount of behavior, often in the absence of strong external contingencies but in the presence of self-evaluations and self-incentives. Clearly, one task of health promotion programs is to help individuals develop standards, goals, and simple (self) feedback systems which motivate and sustain behavioral changes.

An overall explanation for the maintenance of self-directed efforts resides in the interplay of cognitive, behavioral, and environmental variables. That is, self-directed behaviors are maintained by efficacy beliefs, outcome expectancies, personal standards, self-evaluation, goal setting, feedback, self- and externally generated benefits, social rewards, modeling, fear of negative sanctions or self-punishment, and a supportive environmental context.

PROCESS OF CHANGE SCHEMA

Figure 3.1 is an attempt to present in one schema a systematic procedural process of change—one that follows from social cognitive theory and the foregoing discussion and whose procedures may be enacted programmatically. While a stage model assumes some linearity, as with other stage models (Brownell et al., 1986; Prochaska & DiClemente, 1983), it is also assumed that some movement can occur bidirectionally. For example, unsuccessful attempts at generality may warrant a return to incentive and modeling strategies.

In addition to Bandura's basic approach, we emphasize a greater delineation of contextual factors. These factors include prevailing beliefs and values, the availability of alternative behaviors and settings (or conversely, obstacles and barriers), and the degree of positive feedback and reinforcement accruable for adoption and maintenance of new practices. It is assumed that contextual factors are important at every stage. However, they may be critically important when behavioral acquisition is just beginning, when program incentives are not that strong, and certainly when program participation terminates, i.e., for generality and stability.

The process begins with incentives. As noted, incentives may be particularly useful in instigating initial participation and other preliminary attempts at change, if incentives are valued and salient, and are properly scheduled and contingent on appropriate behaviors. A key strategy during *acquisition* of new behaviors is modeling. The effectiveness of modeling depends on its type (e.g., video modeling, face-to-face modeling, participant modeling), how well characteristics of the models fit observers (program participants), and the outcomes experienced by models contingent on appropriate performances.

Effective modeling procedures should lead to appropriate outcome expectancies (e.g., the specific benefits of a modified diet or smoking cessation) and increased self-efficacy about abilities to perform new behaviors (e.g., new dietary practices at home; first attempts at coping with reduced nicotine intake and subsequent withdrawal symptoms). The next step entails setting specific goals, performing the behaviors, and receiving feedback. Considerable social support may be necessary for these early, often difficult, steps. The initial performance and feedback resulting in satisfaction or some dissatisfaction affects self-efficacy and modifies performance (e.g., continue to reduce fat in meals; take one step back and smoke a slightly higher nicotine cigarette). A number of iterations of the process (as signified by the returning arrow) may be necessary to reach a final goal for the first part of the

Stages

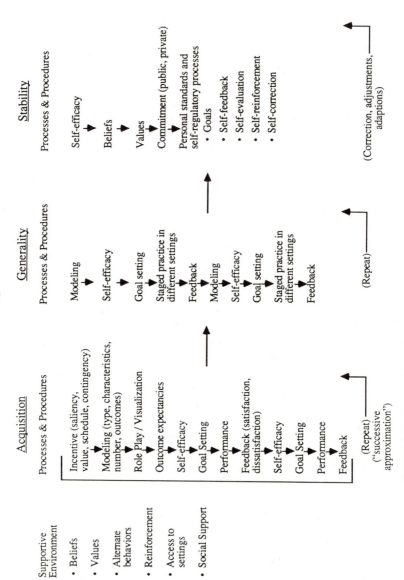

FIGURE 3.1. A Process of Change Schema Emphasizing a Supportive Environment and Different Procedures for Different Stages of Change

change process (e.g., home meals average only 20% fat; initial smoking cessation). Social support continues to be important.

The *generality* of the newly acquired behaviors is the next stage. The use of modeling to teach different coping strategies for multiple settings is enhanced when staged practice is used. For example, the neophyte ex-smoker must learn and practice ways to be in tense social and business situations while controlling anxiety, not accepting offers of cigarettes or engaging in other health-detrimental practices (such as overeating). The use of modeling and staged practice increases self-efficacy, and leads to appropriate goal setting, enhanced performance, and feedback. It is also assumed that a number of iterations of this stage are needed.

Success with generality increases self-efficacy and sets the occasion for *sustained* (or *stable*) behavior change. Transsituational beliefs and values about particular sets or codes of behaviors emerge, resulting in public and private commitments about these behaviors. Over time, internal standards and goals pertinent to new practices are developed and are modified and maintained through programmatic and self-evaluation processes. This final step may also entail a number of iterations.

This schema fits best with programmatic change, such as might be attempted in worksite health promotion programs. As a heuristic, the schema suggests a number of points where health promotion programs may be lacking. For example, programs may emphasize initial change at the expense of generality training. Appropriate outcome expectancies (e.g., the benefits of stopping smoking) may be assumed when, in reality, specific knowledge of outcomes is often superficial (e.g., as in the case of smoking; Warner, 1986a). Or efforts to instill a "health ethic" may receive too much attention at the beginning of a program, while rudimentary skills are neglected.

Much of this process may also hold for individual change efforts instigated alone or with peers. For example, ominous results from a medical screening may serve as an impetus to seek graphic information about exercise and dietary practices, leading to initial but tentative efforts at change. These tentative steps become expanded upon when gradual enactment leads to positive feedback.

Quite obviously, strong contingencies, such as high prices or stiff penalties, can lead to different behavioral paths. For example, high taxes on liquor and strong penalties for underage drinking can result in abstinence, but often only under certain conditions. Empirical and conceptual support is available for this contention. For example, teenagers who cross state lines to drink less expensive liquor in states with fewer restrictions or penalties for drinking manifest a degree of stimulus control and motivation predicted by the operant paradigm (Kazdin, 1984). In this example, the teenagers in question have neither the skills to refuse alcohol nor the beliefs or values. The major point is that the effects of laws, and in this case disincentives, depend on the context in which they are enacted and whether or not other facets of behavioral influence and self-regulation are emphasized in a campaign.

However, strong external pressures may in other instances result in appropriate beliefs and values when a supportive context exists. For example, considerable peer pressure may be reduced (i.e., negative reinforcement) when a person joins a subculture such as a religious group. Once in the subculture, particular skills and more general values and beliefs may be easily and lastingly acquired.

The schema may be particularly helpful in assessing and designing individual, organizational, and institutional efforts at health behavior change. This is because it forces a focus on necessary processes and steps and those critical procedures and stages that may be weakly planned and implemented. In particular, it is clear that most programs do not consider the many procedures and steps often necessary for sustained behavior change. However, before illustrating how this schema can guide program development and implementation and fit with the overall process framework from chapter 2, parameters of effective incentives and delivery systems will be examined.

EFFECTIVE INCENTIVES

Table 3.1 attempts to summarize the points from the prior sections, and some additional ones, so that noneffective and effective incentive variables and processes are delineated. Briefly, the table indicates that:

1. Incentives should be perceived positively, not demeaningly or coercively.
2. Incentives need a supportive context — i.e., supportive beliefs and values and readily available and reinforceable alternative responses — to be maximally effective.
3. Incentive procedures need to be clear in relation to where the focus and contingency are, i.e., on the process (e.g., smoking cessation) or outcome (e.g., decreased utilization of health care services), or both, and the incentives should appear to be direct and contingent (e.g., smoking cessation is accurately monitored).
4. Symbolic incentives (e.g., "Fitness Employee of the Year") must have a valued and suitable meaning to the target audience. Price changes and procedures which reduce the response cost (e.g., time and effort) of certain behaviors should be highly perceptible.
5. The schedules for the delivery of incentives should attempt to follow research data on the effects of schedules of reinforcement. That is, initial reinforcement should be immediate, and, where possible, subsequent incentives should follow an intermittent, variable schedule which is thinned out over time.

Table 3.1. Noneffective and Effective Incentive Variables and Processes

	Incentive Variables and Processes	
	Noneffective	Effective
Perception/Belief	Incentive appears demeaning or coercive	Incentive appears positive and in best interests
Context	Nonsupportive beliefs and values and alternative behaviors difficult to enact and/or not likely to be reinforced	Supportive beliefs and values and alternative behaviors readily available and likely to be reinforced
Focus	Unclear if focus on process or outcome and incentive appears indirect or subject to change	A clear focus on process or outcome, or both, and incentive appears direct and contingent
Type	If symbolic, has ambiguous meaning; if tangible, not useable; price change or response cost reductions are not highly perceptible	Must have suitable valued meaning if symbolic; if tangible, must be useable and suitable; price changes and reduction in response cost must be highly perceptible
Schedule	Delayed, one-shot, fixed schedules; abruptly ending schedules	More immediate, periodic, variable schedules; thinning schedules
Magnitude	Inappropriately low or high	Appropriate
Delivery	Private, impersonal channels; appears unintentional; no goals or feedback	Public, interpersonal channels; appears intentional; incentives coupled with goals and feedback
Stage	Inappropriately delivered, e.g., for stability rather than acquisition	Appropriately delivered, e.g., for acquisition
System/Program	Incentive used alone	A comprehensive approach is taken, i.e., awareness and consideration of related behaviors and an overall program

6. The magnitude of the incentive should be sufficient to promote the behavior change. However, overly large incentives may create a situation where subsequent, more appropriate incentives will be perceived as too minimal.

7. Care should be taken to maximize the delivery of incentives so that receipt of incentives does not appear subject to chance (i.e., as with some lotteries). A feedback system can track performance toward meeting goals, and incentives can then be linked to fulfillment of these specific goals and objectives. Additionally, incentives should be delivered through public

and interpersonal channels, thus optimizing the vicarious reinforcement of others.

8. Incentives should most often be used for the acquisition stage, as depicted in Figure 3.1.
9. Incentives should be developed and delivered with the consideration of interrelated behaviors, practices, and settings (e.g., smoking policies at the workplace) and should comprise only one part of an overall program and comprehensive approach.

Table 3.2 delineates types of incentives and disincentives — i.e., direct payment, price reduction, reduction of response cost, price increase, and increased response cost — and the level and source of delivery. For example, at the organizational level, employees can receive direct payment for participation in health promotion activities; an HMO may offer reduced membership payments for families or groups; a business concern can markedly

Table 3.2. Types of Incentives

Level of Delivery (Source)	Direct Payment	Price Reduction	Reduce Response Cost	Price Increase	Increase Response Cost
Individual	Self-contracting, e.g., for weight loss	Voluntary pre-payment which reduces price, e.g., membership, insurance	Procure equipment, facilities; change schedule of work	Self-contracting, e.g., penalties and fines	Self-control strategies, e.g., stimulus control for smoking
Interpersonal	Family, group contracting, e.g., for weight loss	Group procurement and payment so that each member pays less	Reciprocity arrangements, e.g., buddy systems	Family, group contracting, e.g., penalties and fines	Mutually agreed restrictions, e.g., stimulus control for smoking
Organizational	Participation incentives; payment for changed behavior	Subsidize participation; reduced fees for family/group participation	Procure facilities; flexible schedules; open access	Fines, penalties for health/safety violations	Restrict behaviors; restrict terms of employment
Institutional	Federal funds for enacting health and safety standards	Itemized deductions; deductible rates; decreased insurance rates for lower risk	Allow deductions for preventive services	Excise taxes; effluent taxes	DRG; no federal funds if no health and safety standards

reduce the response cost for exercise by building its own facilities; fines and penalties may be used in settings where safety practices are critical; and organizations can increase the response cost of smoking by limiting it to certain times and places.

Table 3.2 also needs to be integrated with the points on Table 3.1. For example, using the example of fines and penalties for violations of safety practices, the system must be set up for the best interests of employees and be positively presented; alternative (safe) behaviors and practices should be easily performed; contingencies need to be clearly directed to the process (particular behaviors), outcomes (e.g., rate of accidents), or both; the behaviors and outcomes should be, where possible, publicly monitored, with particular goals. The achievement of such goals should be valued by all members of the organization. Reasonable fines and penalties should be used, with infractions detected quickly and contingencies also quickly applied. Unless the system is to be kept indefinitely, reinforcement schedules should be thinned and, eventually, other fading (from reinforcers) procedures need to be considered.

As noted, safety records should be public information, with public goals and feedback. However, the fine and penalty system should be construed as only an initial aspect of learning to work in a safe and efficient way, and only as part of a comprehensive employee safety program.

Table 3.2 also suggests a key point emphasized in this book. Many optimal programs will operate on multiple levels. For example, the possibility of lower insurance rates if there are fewer smokers may spur a large corporation to subsidize participation in smoking cessation programs and pay successful employees. Such programs would probably be bolstered by buddy systems which can help to reduce the physical and psychological costs of withdrawal and maintenance, and by restrictions on smoking which provide environmental supports. Individual participants will probably also be aided by learning self-contracting and other self-control strategies.

However, it is unclear from Table 3.2 which type of incentive or disincentive is more effective. Most likely, the type of incentive is less important than the points addressed in Table 3.1.

Table 3.3 indicates that regardless of the level of focus, four different general health promotion goals are perceivable. Practices and behaviors can be eliminated (e.g., smoking), decreased (e.g., absenteeism), established (e.g., through regulations) or replace other practices and behaviors, or increased (e.g., exercise). Most often, programs will focus on multiple goals and multiple processes. However, from the perspective of developing a science of health behavior change, the recognition and study of the effectiveness of different approaches and procedures for different behavioral goals, e.g., to eliminate a behavior or increase a behavior, seems very much needed (Kazdin, 1984).

Table 3.3. Goals for Incentive Programs

Level	Eliminate	Decrease	Establish	Increase
Personal	Smoking	Fat consumption in diet	Birth control practices	Exercise
Interpersonal	Incorrect health communication	Peer support for health-detrimental practices	Family planning practices	Social support mechanisms
Organizational	Excessive health care expenditures	Absenteeism	Preventive health programs	Participation in preventive health programs
Institutional	Inefficient use of resources	Overuse, inappropriate use of health services; individual and collective health risk practices	Laws, regulations, contingencies	Alternative practices at all of above levels

Additionally, an integration of the points from Figure 3.1 and Tables 3.1 and 3.2 suggests that different goals and concomitant behaviors may represent different points on a process of change continuum. Specific goals may be more optimally approached at certain levels with selected incentive procedures, but each goal and set of behaviors requires attention to effective variables and processes. It appears necessary prior to program implementation to assess target populations with regard to points relevant to the process of change continuum. Such assessments can provide a basis for segmenting a population and offering specific, germane programs.

For example, establishing exercise practices in a sedentary population is different from enhancing already existing practices. In the first instance, rudimentary instructions, modeling, simple goals, self-control strategies, incentives, and feedback may be particularly important. In the second instance, where practices are already established, providing access to facilities and more flexible work schedules may be all that is required to optimize fitness. However, the provision of facilities and alternative schedules suggests an organizational ethic and commitment to fitness.

Establishment of practices in the above example entails more attention to individual beliefs, information, strategies, and incentives. Maintenance and enhancement (i.e., generality and stability) revolves more around removal of barriers and a supportive organizational context.

While many of the points made in this section appear intuitive and obvious, it is our contention that many health promotion efforts have not carefully considered the specific behaviors and goals of their efforts, how these goals may be best monitored and approached (i.e., level), where different target populations are on a process of change continuum, how far a program wants to take participants—i.e., acquisition, generality, or stability—and what procedures need to be stressed and optimized based on these considerations. We are suggesting a degree of specificity often lacking in such enterprises. In addition, these planning, design, and implementation steps can be incorporated into the overall framework previously presented in chapter 2.

FRAMEWORK

The foregoing points and discussion on incentives and motivational mechanisms and strategies fit with the overall framework for this book. The problem definition pertains to what practices need to be changed, in what way, at what levels of intervention, and by what incentive or disincentive procedures. Table 3.3 expresses these points. Then, too, Figure 3.1 indicates that part of the problem definition entails assessing where target populations are situated on a process of change schema.

Figure 3.1 also provides a theory, mostly based on Bandura (1986), about motivational mechanisms and appropriate strategies. Consistent with the perspective of this text, we have added more of a consideration of contextual variables to Bandura's theory. Value considerations enter into the analysis when questions are asked about which health and safety practice, of which individuals, changed by what means. Tables 3.2 and 3.3 partly address these questions.

Multilevel analysis requires attention to all the points made above. Such analyses require that the interaction of person, setting, and institutional variables be analyzed as they contribute to particular health problems. Often such analyses will require the collection of general and more specific assessment data. For example, considerable data are accumulating about what kinds of worksite programs can address particular problems (O'Donnell, 1986), but local assessment data are needed to bolster general findings and fit local needs within the general context of effective programs. Again, such assessments need to pinpoint problems and address questions as to a target population's standing on a process of change model.

The advantages and disadvantages of different intervention alternatives as they relate to the findings of the assessment data are next considered. Tables 3.2 and 3.3 provide alternative approaches. However, any incentive/motivational program needs to fit the tenets of Table 3.1 (effective processes). Finally, the goals of the program will need to be seriously considered as the goals relate to settings that are required, types of personnel needed, and a relevant time-frame for the effort. Evaluation measures also need to coincide with the goals of the program and the pertinent steps in a process of change continuum. For example, a program that is focused on early initiation of a health behavior should focus on assessing efficacy beliefs and outcome expectancies.

In the next section, an extended example is developed that proceeds through all these initial steps and then uses the analyses for program design, implementation, and evaluation.

EXTENDED EXAMPLE

This extended example, which will illustrate the points made throughout this chapter and use aspects of the process framework, is focused on one simple health behavior practice, exercise, and develops a strategy for instilling, increasing, and maintaining the simplest type of exercise, brisk walking. From a practical public health perspective, brisk walking is the exercise of choice because it can be done by most of the population with minimal preparation or risk, requiring no special equipment or facilities, and yet can provide adequate fitness benefits and risk reductions.

The basic fitness criterion is about 10–12 miles per week, performed in three to five sessions, at a pace of somewhat less than four miles per hour — i.e., rapid, brisk walking. This amounts to about two and one half to three hours of walking per week.

The caloric expenditure for such an effort is between 800–1000 calories per week. This is about half the caloric expenditure per week for physical activity that Paffenbarger, Hyde, Wing, & Hseih (1986) found to be health protective (longevity) in their well-known study of male Harvard alumni. However, several key points still recommend this duration and intensity of exercise because:

1. As noted, it can be achieved by a large segment of the population.
2. It represents a base level of fitness which may be expanded upon with the addition of other kinds of exercise (e.g., cycling), activities (e.g., gardening), or leisure pursuits (e.g., dancing).
3. Once one basic health practice is established, interest and commitment toward other practices may be spurred.
4. Even this relatively low level of activity would burn in a year's time the equivalent of 12–15 lbs.

Thus, for practical reasons, a health promotion program can start with this one basic health behavior.

The community level, which in our example will also encompass the personal and interpersonal levels, is chosen as the locus of intervention so as to potentially activate the behavior of many people (King, Haskell, Houston-Miller, & Blair, in press). In addition, this level is chosen because quite similar information (perhaps delivered somewhat differently) can be provided to different population segments. Despite trying to activate many people, we do not see a large structure or many personnel required to implement this program. A volunteer group, a public health department, university staff or faculty, a local TV or radio affiliate, or another commercial concern might all be possible planners and implementers, alone or in collaboration. The necessary skills for this program (e.g., design, promotion) may be held by any of these groups and staffs.

We also envision this program operating in several ways that can serve to differentiate it from a number of other community programs. They include the following:

1. Use of preassessments and formative research based on the process of change model, in order to structure different types of "subprograms" for different segments — e.g., the occasional walker versus the completely sedentary person.
2. Since walking is a public behavior, actual observations can be made to ascertain baseline levels for particular age groups. Criteria for walking may be developed so that it is differentiated from "strolling" (pace), walking to a vehicle (duration), or unhealthy walking (i.e., smoking while walking).
3. Based on these observations, graduated programmatic goals can be set for different population segments, with results observed. Other simple measures can be used that are pertinent to the process of change continuum (e.g., outcome expectancies) for different segments (e.g., the elderly).
4. Incentives, media presentations, use of models, community goals and feedback, while starting on a rich schedule, would be thinned but sustained over time.
5. Individual and group feedback and goals can be meshed with community ones.
6. The largest emphasis would be on generalizing and sustaining brisk walking through specific procedures and through contextual changes.

Figure 3.2 presents a schema for the community walking program which follows the process of change model in Figure 3.1. We note that this campaign can represent the concerted efforts of public and private sector interests (although, as noted above, a large structure is not needed). Public interests can include university departments, public health departments, and relevant community organizations (e.g., YM-YWCAs), while private sector involvement could best include sports and shoe stores and companies and HMOs. The most basic element is one of reciprocal reinforcement, i.e., a mutuality of benefits. For example, the project can include an evaluation component so that publishable results are accruable to the academicians; the public health department can use the campaign as a way to better position itself as a prevention agency; organizations and HMOs can utilize it to enhance favorable public relations; and private concerns can receive free "image" advertising, while at the same time increasing sales (through sports apparel and shoes).

A Step-By-Step Walking Campaign

Acquisition

Supportive
Environment +

Assessment and formative research and observations
▼
Segmentation
▼

• Public and
private sectors

Subprograms for different target groups
▼

• Mutuality of
benefits

Information, prompts, and modeling (media) and incentives *
▼
Positive outcome expectancy and self-efficacy beliefs
▼

• Media, HMO,
volunteer group,
university, public
health agency,
shopping malls

Specific individual and commmunity goals
▼
Performance alone and special events; participant modeling
▼
Feedback, individual and community (media)
▼

• Groups and
buddy systems

Revise goals, reset performance
▼
Repeat (successive approximation)

• Business settings
(facilities, flexible
hours)

Generality

Continue individual and community goal setting and feedback
▼
Thin reinforcement schedule
▼
State-of-the-art programs
▼
Aperiodic modeling and new personal standards
▼
Staged practice for different conditions
▼
Revise goals, reset performance
▼
Repeat

Sustained

Continue goal setting, feedback, and varied performance
▼
Community, individual health/athlete identification
▼
Standards, guidelines, and practices of healthy/athletic
▼

+ Continues in all phases
* Lotteries, giveaways,
challenges and competitions;
Individuals and group

Maintain walking campaign and phase in another

compatible health behavior

FIGURE 3.2. A Step-by-Step Walking Campaign Based on the Process of Change Schema

The campaign might start the way a number of community health promotion programs have commenced (see chapter 5). The media can provide general information about the campaign and specific information about walking, pertinent to different segments. However, we see the media performing a more specialized motivational set of purposes, which we group under antecedent and consequence strategies. For example, we envision the media systematically providing repeated prompts and graphic models. We also see the media being used to provide community feedback (e.g., number of walkers, relationship to goals).

Incentive procedures can also follow a number of strategies that most generally increase early participation. These strategies can include giveaways to individuals for participation in community walks, lotteries, and organizational challenges and competitions, which can have individual and group reinforcers. These are direct payment strategies occurring in a social context to increase their saliency and vicarious reinforcement processes. Lotteries can be based on walkers wearing a sign with their license plate number or other visible identification. This information, when spotted by observers, can be entered into a pool for relatively frequent drawings (see Rudd & Geller, 1985). Organizations and businesses could also develop internal and external challenges and competitions. However, these procedures should only be of a sufficient magnitude to promote increased participation levels to predesignated goals. High magnitude incentives may result in very high initial participation, with a large drop-off and a large contrast to nonincentive conditions.

Modeling procedures are also particularly important in the acquisition stage. A usual array of known, high-status models could participate in public events, though their appearance at more informal occasions may be more beneficial. Then, too, particular (but ordinary) models representing different population segments can be enlisted and followed as they progress in their walking program (see Jason, Gruder, Martino, Flay, & Warnecke, 1987). In particular, how such models overcome some obstacles (e.g., a tight schedule), pitfalls (e.g., doing too much too soon), and receive positive outcomes would be emphasized. Participant modeling can be performed by more experienced and fit walkers who can appear at formal events or informal settings and offer advice, encouragement, companionship, and feedback. These sets of modeling and information procedures, plus incentives, should instill appropriate outcome expectancies and high self-efficacy beliefs and initiate behavior changes.

As noted, the media can provide frequent feedback on citizens observed walking, perhaps by segment. Most certainly, however, comparisons would be made between numbers of present walkers, numbers at baseline, and goal figures. Supplementary information could be presented related to frequency of walking, duration, and intensity (i.e., pace).

The media can also be particularly valuable in providing people with basic information on fitness walking (Sweetgall, 1985). In addition, the media can instruct individuals on simple ways to monitor and chart their efforts, how to set goals, self-contract, and involve other supportive individuals. Unlike a number of other community health promotion projects, this project would also emphasize state-of-the-art information about fitness and training that should be important to more advanced exercisers and aid the long-term maintenance of all participants. For example, individuals can be instructed on setting proximal and distal goals; how to make these goals interesting, challenging, and achievable; how to introduce variety into their walking routines (e.g., by terrain and pace); and use of other more sophisticated methods (e.g., training cycles and periodization), providing a more varied and suitable training stimulus (e.g., as with interval training).

As we noted, the need to make fitness activities progressive, challenging, variable, and goal-directed (in a word, more enjoyable) appears to be overlooked in many community health promotion efforts (King et al., in press). These aspects are not just important physiologically, but clearly fit within our schema (Figure 3.1) as critical to behavioral maintenance. For example, as two experts have noted:

> Boredom kills more fitness programs than any other villain — more than injuries, more than lack of time, more than lack of equipment. People get tired of doing the same things all the time, whether it's working on an assembly line or running laps around a small indoor track. (Todd & Todd, 1985, p. 109)

Environmental supports during the acquisition stage can include the promotion of group and buddy systems and safe and welcome access to a number of settings (i.e., various methods to reduce response costs). For example, a number of large shopping malls might open early in the morning for walking groups and individuals. Group walking in parks at night can be more enjoyable and safer than solo expeditions. Business organizations could also develop minimally flexible scheduling that could more easily accommodate morning or lunchtime walking. However, note that unlike other fitness activities, a walking program would require virtually no resources or facilities.

The program components just described, with the exception of the training components, are not very different from any number of community health efforts (chapter 5). However, three major points are emphasized in Figure 3.2. Environmental supports and procedures are developed, implemented, and work in concert with each other throughout all phases of the campaign. Several variations and iterations of procedures are probably necessary to enlist more walkers and to reinstruct and motivate initial walkers who were only partially successful or unsuccessful. This is both a successive approximation strategy and a method to reduce dropouts. Then, too, differ-

ent segments can be "plugged into" the program at different phases (e.g., an occasional walker may start at the generality stage).

Our third major point is that too much of the focus in many community health programs remains at the acquisition stage. Maintenance components that do exist are often minimal in contrast to the scope and effort of initial efforts, and may not be systematic. In a number of ways, the present proposal's generality stage differentiates it from those programs by:

1. Maintaining some activities on a thinned schedule. For example, community observations, goal setting, and feedback should be continued, with feedback given intermittently. Modeling activities, particularly through aperiodic media reports and events, should be maintained. Seasonal changes requiring changes in clothing may also present new opportunities for lotteries and giveaways.
2. Using models to demonstrate overcoming obstacles and barriers. Again, seasonal changes provide such opportunities, as well as demonstrating simple ways to maintain walking on business trips, holidays, or when buddies are not available. Staged practice should accompany the systematic, but aperiodic, modeling. For example, demonstrating that wearing layers of lightweight clothing makes winter walking comfortable and easy can precede the first real winter day. The media can then feature short spots on the many walkers who successfully negotiated the colder weather. Note that such modeling can help to create new personal standards, i.e., outdoor walking *can* be done in virtually any weather.
3. Maintaining all other environmental supports such as mall access, business organization programs, and aperiodic community events.
4. Emphasizing how individuals can continue to monitor progress, add variety, and reset goals so that walking remains interesting and challenging. Additional emphasis can be placed on making private and public commitments.
5. Maintaining all supports and procedures in a systematic way and also allowing for iterations of the generality stage (see Figure 3.1).

However, a generality stage is not sufficient. We envision a number of approaches to making walking a sustained activity for many members of the community. These include maintaining environmental supports, such as mall access, more flexible work schedules, and intermittent media prompts; information emphasizing the benefits of walking; modeling and feedback; and incentive programs conducted by the private sector. However, another evolution in the overall campaign is needed. Media and other promotional activities can identify the community as healthy, energetic, and fit (i.e., social evaluations). Media can also emphasize that individuals who have maintained walking at the minimum criteria can think of themselves as fit, healthy, and perhaps even athletic (self-evaluations). Media messages and modeling can then portray how fit and healthy individuals behave, through their own standards and precepts, in a wide variety of settings and circumstances — i.e., standards, guidelines, and practices of a "healthy life style."

Finally, using a refined version of the walking campaign (i.e., based on feedback about effective and noneffective procedures in that campaign), another health promotion campaign that builds on the success of the first one can be orchestrated. For example, this second campaign can emphasize the synergistic combination of good nutrition and exercise to good health. The nutrition campaign would, of course, have nutrition in the foreground but maintain walking and exercise in the background. Again, the brackets and a two-way arrow in the schema signify the comprehensive and varied dimensions of this approach (see Figure 3.1).

Consistent with the process of change framework and our overall framework, evaluations should focus on a number of facets of the campaign and walking behavior. For example, particularly early in the campaign, tapping knowledge, outcome expectancies, and self-efficacy beliefs can not only signify if the campaign is meeting its early objectives but also provide one vehicle for feedback to refine and adjust the campaign. Measures of walking behavior (as described above) may also be obtained over time in the general population and, perhaps, also for predesignated samples of people representing different population segments. Evaluations must be intermittently continued so that generality and stability can be assessed. Measures can also assess benefits to collaborating firms — e.g., image ratings of hospitals and records of sales of walking shoes. Finally, if warranted, cost evaluations could be performed.

Thus, our extended example of a campaign to increase walking makes use of a variety of assessment and motivational strategies, while unfolding through a process-of-change approach relevant for different population segments. Incentives are merely one tool to be used at first to initiate and increase walking. Multiple strategies are orchestrated for generalizing and then sustaining those initial steps toward fitness and wellness.

4

Concepts, Principles, and Strategies to Effectively Use Media for Health Promotion: Altering the Course of the AIDS Epidemic*

There are a number of compelling quotes from the landmark Institute of Medicine, National Academy of Science report entitled *Confronting AIDS* (Baltimore & Wolff, 1986) which set the stage for this chapter concerning the use of media in health promotion. First, there is the urgency to act because of the great potential for reducing human suffering and the resulting costs to society if the number of new cases of AIDS can be reduced.

> Because of the lag time—up to four years or longer—in the development of AIDS after HIV infection, approximately 50 percent of the AIDS cases diagnosed in 1991 will be in persons who are infected now but do not yet have AIDS . . . Thus, about half of the AIDS cases diagnosed in 1991—and a growing proportion after that—can potentially be prevented. It is in this course of action that the greatest opportunities for altering the course of the epidemic lie. (Baltimore & Wolff, 1986, p. 95)

Second, there is the recognition that public education to achieve large-scale behavior modification is the primary course that must be immediately followed.

> For at least the next several years, the most effective measures for significantly reducing the spread of HIV infection are education and voluntary changes in behavior . . . public education about HIV infection is, and will continue to be, a critical public health measure, even if a vaccine or drug becomes available. Education in this instance is not only the transfer of knowledge but has the added dimension of inducing, persuading, and otherwise motivating people to avoid the transmission of HIV. While it would be unrealistic to believe or claim that the spread of HIV infection is likely to be stopped by education efforts to induce behavioral change, the efforts can be entered into with a strong degree of conviction and hope. (p. 96)

---

*We acknowledge the thoughtful feedback and editorial help provided by Anne Riley on this chapter.

93

Third, there is the recognition of the conceptual, technical, ethical, and regulatory barriers that must be surmounted if public education campaigns are to be effectively designed and delivered so as to change the course of the AIDS epidemic.

> Forces that shape human behavior, and the best approaches to influencing behavior to protect health, are among the most complex and poorly understood aspects of society's response to the AIDS epidemic (p. 230).

> Deliberate efforts to use the media to influence behavior have not necessarily achieved their desired result (p. 231).

> If an educational campaign is to change behavior that spreads HIV infection, its message must be as direct as possible. Educators must be prepared to specify that intercourse — anal or vaginal — with an infected or possibly infected person and without the protection of a condom is very risky. They must be willing to use whatever vernacular is required for that message to be understood. Admonitions to avoid "intimate bodily contact" and the "exchange of bodily fluid" conveys at best only a vague message (p. 10).

> Demographic features and social dynamics related to HIV infection should be thoroughly studied in order to develop effective means to reach people at risk, to delineate the obstacles to behavioral change, and to determine effective language and styles of communication among various population groups (p. 27).

> One page of advertising in a major newspaper can cost around $25,000 per day, and a minute of national television time can cost between $60,000 and $400,000. Consequently, to influence the behaviors affecting HIV transmission, policy makers must begin to contemplate expenditures similar to those made by private sector companies to influence behavior — for instance, $30 million to introduce a new camera, or $50 million to $60 million to advertise a new detergent. Furthermore, advertising campaigns at these levels are judged successful even when they produce relatively modest shifts in behavior. The efforts needed to influence the behaviors that spread HIV will have to be greater and more sustained (p. 132).

> The total educational effort is the combined responsibility of all levels of government, and the private and philanthropic sectors must also participate significantly in this activity (p. 111).

And finally,

> AIDS education should be pursued with a sense of urgency and a level of funding appropriate for a life-or-death situation (p. 112).

These quotes indicate the dilemmas and promises for using media for large-scale health promotion and, specifically, for preventing the spread of AIDS. To summarize:

- Enormous health problems exist or are in the making which can be ameliorated or prevented.

- Mass media are one of the few ways to reach large audiences.
- However, the conceptual and technical bases for developing media efforts that activate broad and durable behavior change—i.e., a public health impact—are not clear.
- Reliable access to the media is most often limited to commercial interests with sufficient money to buy time or space.
- Specific content needed for particular health promotion efforts may be constrained by tradition, competing interests, or regulation.
- Various health problems, and particularly AIDS, demand immediate action.

The objectives of this chapter are to develop an approach for the design of effective media—a second potentially powerful weapon for achieving health-related changes—and to delineate a number of strategies pertinent to addressing monetary and regulatory barriers to media access. If effective media can be developed and barriers at least partially transcended, we can seriously consider what may be accomplished by media-based health promotion efforts, alone and in conjunction with interpersonal and community organization approaches. A final, extended section will synthesize the conceptual and technical material and demonstrate how a media approach, in conjunction with some aspects of the book's framework (e.g., multilevel analyses for planning multilevel interventions), may be used to alter the course of the AIDS epidemic.

BRIEF HISTORICAL OVERVIEW

Certainly, the idea of using media for promoting large shifts in a population's beliefs and behaviors is not a new one (e.g., Laswell, 1948). However, during the last 60 years several different and often opposing perspectives on media effects can be discerned (Winett, 1986). The advent of radio and its apparently effective use for propaganda purposes in totalitarian countries in the 1920s led to an extreme "strong effects" model, i.e., the "hypodermic needle" perspective. That is, the audience was seen as passive recipients of media messages who more or less automatically changed beliefs and behaviors. This was a simple input–output model which may indeed have fit the context of totalitarian countries, where there were no competing messages in other channels or media and where particular beliefs and behaviors were modeled and rigidly enforced. Not surprisingly, this perspective was inappropriate for democratic countries.

Indeed, some pivotal studies in the 1940s suggested that media, primarily radio and newspapers, had little effect on beliefs and behaviors (see Winett, 1986). At best, media could support the status quo, but they could not alter existing mores or behavioral patterns. This was known as the *weak effects* model (Lazarsfeld & Merton, 1971). Interestingly, this pessimistic model was dominant in the behavioral sciences until the 1970s, despite the fact that the data base supporting the model was developed prior to the advent of television (McLeod & Reeves, 1981). In addition, and in contradiction, most behavioral scientists accepted findings about the strong negative impacts of television (Liebert, Sprafkin, & Davidson, 1982). Thus, some basic contradictions and inconsistencies existed, points to be shortly explored.

By the 1960s and 1970s, a different approach, stemming from different literature, suggested a more proper role for media than the weak effects model. Research from studies in the diffusion of innovations (e.g., use of new farming implements or strategies, adoption of birth control practices; Rogers & Shoemaker, 1971) pointed toward a "two-step model" of communication effects (Katz & Lazarsfeld, 1955). Media was seen as potentially able to influence key innovators, i.e., "opinion leaders" or "gatekeepers." These individuals adopted new practices, and through interpersonal contacts the practices were eventually passed on to the general population in a relatively orderly and predictable way. This model instigated considerable work (Rogers, 1983; Rogers & Kincaid, 1981) and, recently, closer scrutiny (Bandura, 1986; Winett, 1986).

Bandura (1986) has emphasized that the diffusion of innovation can be better explained as an example of the process and efficacy of modeling. That is, particularly vivid media, i.e., TV, can have relatively powerful modeling effects on certain individuals. These individuals publicly adopt the innovation or practices and are modeled by others, based on such key variables as perceived status of the model and reinforcement contingent on the adopted innovation. Bandura has also noted that since media variables and target behaviors are diverse and complex, it is simplistic to assign particular effects to particular media. He takes exception to the frequent claim that TV will only affect beliefs and attitudes, not behavior.

Further, Winett (1986) examined data from a large diffusion-of-innovation study on birth control practices conducted in Asia. Rogers and Kincaid (1981) had concluded that their data from this study supported the two-step model and the key role of interpersonal contact. Winett's examination of the study indicated that media—particularly contact with a birth control campaign on television—appeared to have strong effects and explained more of the variance associated with the decision to adopt birth control practices than did interpersonal influences. Winett's interpretation of the results supported a stronger media effects perspective and the key role of behavioral modeling.

As noted previously, much of the evidence for the weak effects model accrued prior to the widespread adoption of television. Television is particularly salient to the discussion at hand because of its pervasiveness and ability to clearly and vividly demonstrate particular behaviors. In addition, as noted, by the 1960s a strong effects position was held by many behavioral scientists when the focus was on the depiction of violent and aggressive behavior on television and subsequent aggressive behavior in viewers (Liebert et al., 1982). While the strength and generality of such effects have been debated over the years (e.g., Freedman, 1984), and the original position has been modified (e.g., Singer & Singer, 1983), the belief in the efficacy of television to influence negative behaviors stands in contradiction to conclusions that the medium is not an effective one for positive behavior change!

A partial answer to this paradox is found when the concepts, content, format, and delivery of prosocial and health messages, spots, and programs are examined (e.g., Wallack, 1981). Not only have such efforts in the past usually failed to follow sound conceptual paradigms and marketing plans, but they have most often suffered from very low dosages and duration (Lau, Kane, Berry, Ware, & Ray, 1980). That is, exposure was most often not intense or prolonged, and, hence, media reach was minimal. It is, therefore, not surprising that many such efforts failed. In contrast, the reach (intensity, frequency, duration) of many television programs graphically depicting violence is often quite substantial. Further, the formal features of much violent television fare includes rapid pacing and other communication strategies to maintain attention. Often, prosocial spots and programs have not used such strategies. Thus, the content *and* context of positive and negative messages have been different (Wright & Huston, 1983). The apparent paradox of weak effects for prosocial television and strong effects for negative depictions on television is resolved when differential communication strategies and audience reach are investigated.

Perhaps a starting point for present-day perspectives can be traced to Mendelsohn's (1973) often-quoted article entitled "Some reasons why information campaigns can succeed." Mendelsohn noted that communication campaigns generally were neither based on social science research nor research in the process of change, and that therefore both the substance of the campaigns and their evaluations were often of poor quality. According to Mendelsohn, campaigns can succeed if middle-range and reasonable goals are established and if basic marketing principles—i.e., audience segmentation and tailored messages—are used in planning and orchestrating the campaign. Mendelsohn concluded at that time that " . . . very little of our mass communication research has really tested the effectiveness of the application of empirically grounded mass communication principles, simply because most communications practitioners do not consciously utilize these principles" (p. 51).

These points and perspectives raise the following questions: What are appropriate principles? How can they be integrated into one framework? And how can the framework be used as a starting point for developing campaigns of sufficient efficacy to make a difference in the course of health problems with the magnitude of AIDS?

PRINCIPLES AND APPROACH: STRENGTHS AND LIMITATIONS

In several recent publications, the first author has attempted to delineate principles of the effective use of media (i.e., belief and behavior change) and to use these principles within one framework for the design, implementation, and evaluation of media-based efforts (Winett, 1986; Winett, 1987; Winett & Kramer, 1988; Winett, Kramer, Walker, Malone, & Lane, 1987). Clearly, both the principles that have been identified and the framework are similar to principles described and organized by others (e.g., Solomon & Maccoby, 1984). However, the process of discerning these principles has primarily consisted of (a) a distillation of prominent communication and psychology theory and research and (b) the verification of these principles through a review of those prosocial media efforts that have been most effective, as well as (c) testing the efficacy of these principles in empirical work involving change in consumer behaviors (Winett et al., 1987).

Table 4.1 provides a succinct summary of particularly effective elements and variables for information campaigns. The variables and elements partly follow classic communication variables (McGuire, 1981). The points made in the table also provide many initial caveats about the efficacy of campaigns designed to stem the tide of a serious health problem. For example, messages must be high quality, very vivid and specific, and well targeted to particular audiences. In the case of behaviors that put a person at high risk for AIDS and audience segments performing these behaviors, the ability to verbally and graphically depict high-risk practices and to reach key segments is, at best, limited.

Considerable formative and pilot research must be done to carefully match messages with target audiences. While such a point appears to be intuitively obvious, a consensus exists that few information campaigns have performed any sophisticated formative research (Rice & Paisley, 1981). Further, unlike much "message testing" for products, or in some instances health campaigns, which rely on verbal reports of message acceptance and comprehension, the formative research emphasized in this approach (below) rests on pilot testing for behavior change.

The Table also stresses that effective messages will be those where (a) considerable research has been undertaken to understand personal and environmental inhibitors and facilitators of behavior change; (b) conceptualizations focusing on behavior change (e.g., social cognitive theory; Bandura, 1986) are the basis for message or program strategies and formats; and (c) the emphasis is on change in simple but key behaviors.

Table 4.1. Elements and Variables Related to Ineffective and Effective Information Campaigns*

	Ineffective	Effective
Message (format & content)	Poor quality decreases attention	High quality to enhance attention (e.g., comparable to commercial ad)
	Overemphasize quantity vs. quality	High quality may overcome some problems in limited exposure
	Vague or overly long messages: drab, e.g., "talking head"	Highly specific messages; vivid, e.g., behavioral modeling
Channel	Limited exposure (e.g., late night PSAs)	Targeted exposure
	Inappropriate media (e.g., detailed print for behavior change)	Appropriate media (e.g., TV for behavior change)
Source	Not well attended to	Trustworthy, expert or competent; may be also dynamic and attractive
Receiver	Little formative research to understand audience characteristics	Much formative research to target message to audience
Destination	Difficult or complex behaviors resistant to change	Simple behaviors, or behaviors in a sequence, changeable and where long-term change can be supported by the environment
Conceptualization	Inappropriate causal chain (e.g., early events as predictors of later ones)	More appropriate causal chain and emphasize behavior change
	Little analysis of competing information and environmental constraints	Analysis of competing information and environmental constraints used to design messages
Goals	Unrealistic, i.e., expect too much change	Realistic, specific, limited

*From Winett, 1986

For example, messages about AIDS may focus on misbeliefs about the use of condoms (i.e., a reduction in spontaneity and sexual pleasure), show their ready availability, and, within present constraints, dramatize their effective use. As also noted in Table 4.1, the goal of such a campaign needs to be realistic, specific, and limited. For example, an increase in condom sales by 10–15% for the target population segments may be reasonable.

Thus, unlike other reviewers of health information campaigns who have concluded that such efforts are usually predestined to failure (e.g., Wallack,

1981), we take a more optimistic view. However, this is only the case when all the caveats suggested by the prior discussion and Table 4.1 are considered. Another central point is the consolidation of the concepts, principles, procedures, and stages of testing and enactment into one coherent approach which serves as a basis for orchestrating the campaign.

Figure 4.1 shows one approach, known as the *behavioral systems* approach, for delineating and organizing concepts, principles, and stages. Not surprisingly, this framework, which has evolved over a number of years, is also similar to the framework used throughout this book. For a media-based approach to behavior change, as depicted in Figure 4.1, a multilevel analysis is particularly important so that we may consider facilitators and inhibitors of change at various levels, how various supports can be combined with a media effort, and identify key resistance points, both for message delivery and behavior change, that must be overcome. Such analyses lead

BEHAVIORAL SYSTEMS APPROACH

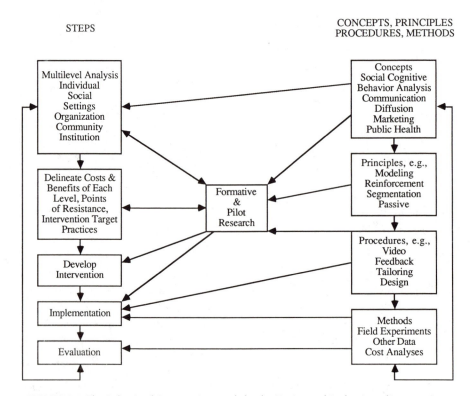

FIGURE 4.1. The Behavioral Systems Approach for the Design and Evaluation of Interventions

to working hypotheses which then must be further assessed in formative research and analyzed in pilot studies which emphasize behavior change.

However, of equal importance is the use of theory to guide initial analyses and research. For example, both social cognitive and diffusion theory suggest that one way to instigate change is for key individuals to publicly model innovative behaviors. This perspective suggests that media interventions could be combined with community organization approaches wherein respected individuals lead (innovate) by example. In addition, a public health approach suggests that a media intervention needs to be combined with a passive strategy, e.g., greater availability of condoms.

In the next stage, the process becomes more specific. It is here that the costs and benefits of different types of intervention combinations should be considered and where particular strategies are devised based on principles from the foregoing theories. For example, different types of models and messages may be considered for particular segments and a reinforcement procedure sketched out for procurement by targeted audiences of certain products. In a further step toward specificity, these program principles and ideas can be fitted into particular procedures. It is these procedures which then need to receive final pilot testing and refinement prior to a large-scale trial of a major intervention. Thus, the approach emphasizes an orderly flow from theory to intervention, with formative and pilot research central to each step.

Most often, an attempt will be made to introduce the intervention in a way that would lend itself to a sophisticated evaluation, i.e., a quasi-experiment. Evaluations include analyses of process, outcomes, and cost effectiveness for various subgroups of individuals as well as organizational and community impacts (Flay & Cook, 1981). The results of the trial will contribute to refinements of other efforts; also, given that the interventions are based on theory, the results may verify the utility of different theories or suggest particular modifications in theory or action. For example, chapter 3 on incentives noted a particular set of steps for initial and long-term change that can be verified in a media campaign which either uses media as the sole intervention method or combines media with other types of strategies.

The behavioral systems approach, when juxtaposed with the effective variables and elements noted in Table 4.1, indicates specific points, steps, and strategies which need to be adhered to in developing media campaigns. When all these steps are carefully followed, some modest success may be expected in reaching some limited, but significant, public health goal.

Thus, we feel that the behavioral science technology for effective campaigns is, if not quite apparent, at least evolving. However, a major dilemma is not technology specification but the difficulty in gaining access to the media, particularly to network television, which reaches large audiences.

MEDIA ACCESS

Problems

Television and other media in the United States are unusual when compared to their counterparts in other Western countries. From the outset, television was clearly to be a free enterprise system with minimal governmental control. This has resulted in many positive developments, e.g., extensive programming, largely unshackled news reporting. At the same time, it has meant that access to the networks is primarily achieved through one means — money. Those with money, and lots of it, buy time for commercials that support the airing of particular programs. When programs receive wide viewership as judged by Nielsen, Arbitron, or other, newer rating systems, it means that many people will see a commercial and a network can charge more for a commercial during the program. In this analysis, the program has one major purpose: to hold a large number of viewers so they will see different commercials. Thus, network fare is dominated by comedy, other entertainment, and sports.

And because of the tremendous amount of money at stake, the medium becomes very conservative, primarily in two ways. Most new programs resemble formerly successful programs, i.e., the "spin-off." Thus, the seemingly endless offerings of the networks and the many cable stations are belied by the fact that most programs fit into a few categories, and that within those categories programs closely resemble one another. In addition, the number of companies capable of producing quality television programs is also limited. This also has restricted the diversity of available programming.

A second point of conservatism is that the networks will attempt to have offerings that appeal to a mass audience, while offending virtually no one. A frequent result is that controversial subjects may be avoided or only presented in certain ways. More will be discussed shortly about this particular point.

One result of the network and free enterprise systems has been enormous influence and profits for a few concerns at the cost of any serious sustained use of the medium and the public airways for public education and societal enhancement. Again, the starkest purpose of the medium is to be sufficiently entertaining so that viewers will continue watching a particular program in order to view particular commercials. Since many viewers may turn off an hour program that seriously discusses AIDS or other urgent health topics, few such programs appear in prime time. As will be noted, however, there are some excellent exceptions to this rule (e.g., an NBC program on AIDS in January, 1987, hosted by nightly news anchor Tom Brokaw).

It is also important to note that in recent years regulations that at least in spirit required programming responsive to community needs or presentation of different sides of issues have been rescinded — or simply not enforced — by the Federal Communications Commission. The commission has taken the stance that a free market approach allows for the most diversity of content in television and other media. This stance has been challenged by others based on historical analyses of gradual centralization of control of media (Bittner, 1980), and contemporary analyses of program diversity (Bagdikiam, 1985; Le Duc, 1982). Thus, critics of the "free enterprise" system for particular media do not believe that the product of that system has been diversity and competitiveness. Rather, the result is seen as producing a narrowing of both players in the field and program content.

A final and certainly germane point for any large-scale media campaign to change risk behaviors for AIDS is current restrictions that still hold for language and visual content on television. Thus, presently, while all manner of violence and mayhem prevail and sexually explicit content is used to hold audience interest in programs and to pitch products, certain other words and products cannot be used. For example, it is doubtful that the term "anal intercourse" will be used in a prime-time program (although by 1987 this had been done in news and talk shows), while at this point condoms and other contraceptives have just begun to be advertised on the networks. However, it is unclear if these commercials will explicitly address disease prevention issues, as has been done in other Western countries.

Overall, we conclude that while behavioral scientists and prevention professionals now have a reasonable technology with which we can use television and other media for large-scale health promotion, access is most often highly restricted. The next section outlines some strategies for accessing the media in light of these restrictions.

Strategies

Strategies to gain access to broadcast or print media with wide viewership or circulation can be broadly included under three cateories: *confrontation, bypass,* and *reciprocity.* Included under confrontation strategies are various activist approaches, used alone or in combination with efforts within the legal system to institute regulatory change. For example, various groups have sought in recent years to alter the content of children's television programs (i.e., violence) and commercials aimed at children, and other groups have focused on the broadcasting of sexually explicit videos (such as those on MTV) and language. The purpose of these groups has been to spark enough public interest so that pressure is brought to bear on legislatures, who in turn can convene public hearings. Such hearings also can become media events and thus, if effective, further arouse public interest. The end result of the process should be an enactment of a new standard or regulation.

At best, the results of such reformist efforts appear to be time-consuming and may only slightly alter media content. That is, the time involved in all the steps noted above is lengthy and the results may not be that discernible; in some instances, perhaps, the results are even counterproductive. For example, in the opinion of some (Warner, 1986a), cigarette companies acquiesced to (and, perhaps, even initiated) a ban on advertising cigarettes on television and radio, because it allowed the companies to pour their advertising dollars into less expensive, and in some cases better targeted, print and billboard media. The ban on advertising also meant that effective antismoking spots were also banned.

Other proposals have called for radical reform. For example, Manoff (1985) has described a more drastic set of strategies which entails having networks and sponsors set aside ten percent of their advertising budgets and commercial time for public services uses. Warner (1986a) has also recently outlined a similar plan so that an effective antismoking media campaign can be mounted. These proposals are different from current policies for public service announcements (PSAs). PSAs are put on at the discretion of the networks and affiliates, which means that they are chiefly aired during periods when commercial time has not been sold. In addition, PSAs are rarely of the technical quality of most commercials. Thus, the ability to effectively target high-quality spots is largely lost with PSAs.

Under Manoff's proposal, an independent, non-profit corporation would oversee the time bank process to assure a proper degree of fairness and control. While this idealistic system could result in a number of excellent and sustained national health promotion campaigns, the realization of this and similar proposals is many years in the future, by the most optimistic account.

A basic tension exists between efforts which may eventually provide the most change in media policies in the future, with perhaps the stongest outcomes, versus using the resources available to yield less pronounced changes but more immediate outcomes. In the case of AIDS, the costs of waiting will be too dear (Baltimore & Wolff, 1986). Therefore, attempts to use bypass and reciprocity strategies should be given the highest priority.

Strategies which bypass the networks focus on less expensive ways to reach particular target audiences. A number of possibilities exist, including gaining access to local cable stations and using inexpensive videotapes or relying on print and pictorial media. More sophisticated but still local media can also be developed. For example, in chapter 8, dealing with nutrition change, interactive information systems for malls and supermarkets will be described. Presumably, such systems could be developed with a range of content.

The bypass strategies, unless replicated in numerous localities, sacrifice audience reach for practicality and manageability. That is, rather than being broadcast approaches, they are "narrowcast" strategies. Although these efforts can certainly be worthwhile at a local level and can have great value through replication, the urgency of the AIDS epidemic suggests that at a minimum other media strategies need to be used in concert with the bypass approach.

A martial arts metaphor suggested to the first author by Robert Hess is the basis for the reciprocity approach. In martial arts, one of the trainee's first lessons is to use an opponent's superior force rather than trying to futilely combat it. In the present discussion, the power of media corporations to resist attempts at reforming them, to overwhelm the influence of "smaller" media, must be acknowledged. What the health campaigner wants is the power and reach of the larger media. A number of imperfect but intriguing possibilities have already been demonstrated within this approach.

Leonard Jason and his colleagues (Jason, Gruder, Martino, Flay, Warnecke, & Thomas, 1987) are developing a general approach to working with local affiliates in health promotion campaigns. In these Chicago-based programs, affiliates have been willing to use expensive air time (though primarily during newscasts) to develop a sustained campaign. Typically, a campaign uses segments several minutes long, at least several times per day, to verbally and visually instruct viewers on the rudiments of a health behavior change approach. Instruction is provided by experts and model program participants and unfolds over periods up to a month. There has also frequently been an interpersonal, group support element activated at worksites and other community settings, which tries to adhere to the televised segments (i.e., similar to "media forums;" Rogers, 1983). Additional cooperating service agencies and companies have underwritten the costs of producing and distributing instruction booklets which individuals can use to follow the campaign in both a prescriptive and tailored fashion. For example, particular strategies which the literature suggests are effective for smoking cessation are programmatically synthesized, as are ways to individualize the strategies.

In this approach, everyone appears to benefit. The companies receive free publicity and enhance their public image. The affiliate receives these benefits plus, perhaps, increased viewership. The health promoters gain use of a powerful medium and accompanying community support systems. The public gains the most up-to-date health information and motivational strategies. Further, and most importantly, Jason (personal communication, February 1988) reports that four separate campaigns have shown long-term changes in smoking patterns, nutrition, exercise habits, and reported stress.

Obviously, this approach is similar to a number of community health promotion campaigns described in chapter 5. We, however, see the model evolving from Jason and his colleagues' work as more focused on the use of television and the importance of particular behavior change strategies, and perhaps more representative of the key concept of "reciprocal reinforcement," i.e., the idea that the actions of each person or organization in a relationship are mutually reinforcing.

Another intriguing possibility involves altering the content of current network programs and specials so that a public health impact may be achieved without sacrificing the entertainment and audience appeal of programs. For example, a possibly large public health impact was lost during the 1985–1986 television season in the *Miami Vice* series, when the leading character, Sonny Crockett, stopped smoking: His efforts at cessation were never depicted in any of the shows. Part of the persona of the character, who particularly appealed to teenagers and young adults, involved a trail of cigarettes. Weaving the character's cessation methods and efforts into a series of shows as a subplot could have yielded, at a minimum, wide exposure and audience identification and knowledge gain.

Some of this potential was possibly reaped by a program in the *Cagney and Lacey* series which dealt with the conflicts involved in the decision to have an abortion and by a special during the 1985–1986 season (*An Early Frost*) which portrayed one family's attempt to come to grips with their grown, homosexual son's affliction with AIDS. This type of program, as will be discussed in a later section, may have good potential for fear reduction in the general population. Other entertainment programs are also, albeit sporadically, beginning to address pertinent issues and behaviors for contraception and prevention of pregnancy. However, much more is needed on a sustained basis to provide persuasive information on prevention strategies for high-risk behaviors.

One vehicle for such an effort is a highly popular program wherein creative control exists within one or only a few people. *The Cosby Show*, which every week features a black upper-middle-class family where the husband is a doctor, the wife a lawyer, and four of the five children are teenagers or young adults, is one example. The potential of this type of program to allay the fears about AIDS of millions of viewers, while retaining its sparkling humor, seems enormous.

Yet another approach could follow the lead of the successful collaborative campaign mounted by the National Cancer Institute (NCI) and the Kellogg Company (Warner, 1987b). This elaborate and expensive campaign resulted in the Kellogg Company increasing its sales of high-fiber cereals, while the NCI apparently effected a healthful shift in dietary practices. Perhaps it is possible for the Public Health Service to institute a similarly broad and sustained campaign with corporations that manufacture and distribute condoms.

At this juncture, concepts, principles, procedures, and a framework for developing effective media have been outlined. The limits and potential of different approaches to delivering messages and programs have also been discussed. In the next section, we delineate public beliefs, practices, and preventive behaviors and processes, for the general public and for targeted populations, that are integral to the AIDS epidemic. The final sections of this chapter will assess and synthesize what beliefs, behaviors, and processes can be best approached by what methods, and then we will provide one exemplar AIDS prevention campaign that uses both this synthesis and the framework of this book.

RISK AND PROTECTIVE BEHAVIORS FOR AIDS

According to Baltimore & Wolff (1986), five basic elements are involved in the transmission of an infectious agent: (a) an infected source; (b) a vehicle or mechanism of spread; (c) a susceptible host; (d) an appropriate site of exit from the source; and (e) an appropriate site of entry into the susceptible host. In recent years (see also Osborn, 1988), a considerable amount of epidemiological data has investigated these five elements for AIDS and has concluded that

transmission of HIV is limited to sexual, parenteral, and maternal–infant (possibly including *in utero*) routes. It has been postulated, but not proven, that adult infection may require direct blood exposure and may be enhanced by coincident damage to skin or mucous membranes to facilitate viral entry. . . . There is no evidence for other routes of HIV transmission. In fact, there is now substantial evidence against transmission through so-called casual contact, including regular close contact (such as that occurring in sharing accommodations, eating utensils or even toothbrushes), that does not involve parenteral or sexual exposure, despite the fact that HIV has been reported to have been occasionally isolated from saliva and tears in small amounts. (Baltimore and Wolff, 1986, pp. 50–51)

Table 4.2 summarizes information about the two main modes of transmission, particular target groups, and risk and protective behaviors. Epidemiologic study has identified receptive anal intercourse with ejaculation of semen between homosexuals as a major risk behavior for AIDS. Risk appears to be increased by rectal douching because of trauma to normal protective barriers and rectal mucosa, and increased risk is associated for homosexuals with recreational drug use of amyl and butyl nitrates ("poppers") and the practice of sex with multiple partners (thereby increasing the probability of contact with HIV). Risk is also increased by frequent attendance at bars and bathhouses, also because in these settings there is likely to be contact with multiple, often anonymous, sexual partners. To put into perspective how such practices can dramatically spread exposure to HIV, it has

Table 4.2. Most Frequent Mode of Transmission, Target Groups, Risk Behaviors, and Protective Behaviors for HIV

Mode of Transmission	Target Groups	Risk Behaviors	Protective Behaviors
Sexual Transmission	Homosexuals	Receptive anal intercourse with ejaculation of semen	Abstention or use of condoms
		Rectal douching	Use of condoms
		Manual-rectal intercourse	Abstention or use of condoms
		Recreational drug use (especially amyl or butyl nitrates, "poppers")	Abstention
		Multiple partners	Monogamy
	Heterosexuals	Vaginal intercourse	Use of condoms
		Multiple partners	Monogamy
IV Drug Use (Parenteral)	Frequent & Occasional Users	Shared syringes and needles	Use of new or clean syringes and needles; abstention
	Sexual Partners of IV Drug Users	Anal, vaginal intercourse	Abstention, monogamy, or use of condoms

been noted that " . . . some homosexual men reported hundreds or even thousands of sexual partners during their lifetime" (Baltimore & Wolff, p. 59).

Although there does not appear to be increased risk associated with casual contact, oral-genital sex, or mutual masturbation, increased risk through sexual transmission is spreading to other target groups. For example, bisexual men can spread HIV through vaginal intercourse.

Table 4.2 also notes protective behaviors for sexual transmission. At present, only three practices appear to lower risk: abstention, monogomy, and use of condoms. Abstention is not practical for most members of the target group, monogomy may be difficult to achieve, and there are still some questions about the protective capabilities of condoms in anal intercourse. The situation is also more complicated by the fact that even with the adoption of a protective behavior, e.g., limiting the number of sexual partners, risk may still not be abated; and, indeed, risk may continue to increase because the proportion of HIV carriers in the population is increasing.

On a more positive note, in some communities (e.g., New York, San Francisco), homosexuals are well organized. This means that there are channels for information and influence. While this positive picture is clouded by the fact that a large percentage of homosexuals do not identify with an organization (Baltimore & Wolff, 1986), and that homosexual practices are still illegal in most states, recent analyses of various studies of homosexuals do indicate a decrease in high-risk sexual practices (Becker & Joseph, 1988; see this chapter's postscript).

As also shown in Table 4.2, the major mode of parenteral transmission is through IV drug use. Other target groups (with their own risk practices) include those individuals who receive blood transfusions (e.g., hemophiliacs). However, the blood supply has been increasingly made safer by excluding as donors individuals involved in risk-related practices and through a screening test for the presence of HIV in the blood of potential donors.

The major risk behavior associated with IV drug use is the sharing of syringes and needles. Sharing of equipment occurs because of lack of availability (it is illegal to possess drug paraphernalia) and the rituals and "bonding" associated with the practice. Since there is frequent sharing across social and friendship groups, e.g., as dramatized in "shooting galleries," the probability of rapid and geometric spread of HIV readily exists.

Another prime target group is the sexual partners of IV drug users. These partners cannot be easily classified. Partners can be male or female and come from many walks of life (as is also the case for homosexual men). Thus again, the chilling insight is quickly obtained that in the future AIDS will probably not be as restricted to particular target groups.

Protective behaviors for IV drug users mostly pertain to the use of new or clean syringes and needles and abstention from sex, or, more realistically, monogamy or use of condoms. As will be discussed shortly, the strategy of freely disseminating syringes and needles is fraught with legal and other problems. In addition, IV drug users are not an organized subculture and often lead unstable lives, furthering the difficulty in reaching this target group (Drotman, 1987).

ISSUES AND CONCERNS

Table 4.3 provides a list of current, diverse issues and concerns related to curtailing the AIDS epidemic while protecting individual civil liberties and the general public. Of major importance is that knowledge about the modes of transmission and modes of protection still remains somewhat unclear for a significant proportion of the population, policymakers, and even members of high-risk groups. One result of limited knowledge has been some unwarranted fear and resultant discriminatory policies—e.g., excluding children with AIDS from schools or adult AIDS victims from work settings. However, it is critical that this point is underscored. While a media campaign can increase knowledge about transmission and protection, such a campaign may legitimately sensitize other fears. For example, proper warnings about AIDS may conclude that this disorder is no longer confined to restricted

Table 4.3. Current Issues and Concerns in the AIDS Epidemic in the United States*

Issue	Concerns
Modes of transmission	Accuracy of knowledge; fear of public, opinion leaders, policymakers, and groups at risk
Modes of protection	Accuracy of knowledge about protective practices across population
Explicitness of educational programs	Violations of media and local regulations and customs
Availability of condoms	Violations of local regulations; increase in sexual activity
Distribution of needles, syringes	Legality and increase in drug use
Use of drug treatment facilities	Current overcrowding and costs
Regulation of places for high-risk behaviors	Violations of civil rights versus containing the spread of HIV
Safety of blood supply	Fear of contamination and spread of HIV
Discrimination in the workplace	Violations of civil rights and fear of employees
Involuntary testing	Violation of civil rights and coercion
Voluntary testing	Uncertain results
Media reporting	Inaccuracies; sensationalism
Program design and evaluation	Difficulty in evaluating changes over time in high-risk behaviors

*Based on Baltimore & Wolff, 1986.

groups, but that rather the incidence of AIDS is spreading throughout the general population. And that, indeed, *is* frightening.

However, a major barrier to proper instructions for adults and youth about risk and protective behaviors consists of pictorial and language restrictions in the media and in public schools. Such limitations appear to be diminishing within newspapers and TV. Baltimore and Wolff (1986) reported on the Diamond and Bellitto (1986) study which has traced editorial language in newspapers. For example, an August 1985 editorial spoke of transmittal "through the exchange of bodily fluids." One month later, the term "anal intercourse" was used. As noted above, condom ads are appearing in some affiliate areas, and a few TV programs have explicitly discussed and modestly shown risk and preventive behaviors. By 1988, most newspapers and magazines, certainly, were frankly discussing the modes of transmission of the AIDS virus.

This evolution in the media may, however, be offset by policies that have been mandated for the Centers of Disease Control. These policies revolve around the "dirty words" issue and emphasize local control, via review boards, of explicit AIDS educational material.

Barriers also limit the widespread distribution of condoms. Their sale or free distribution in certain settings (e.g., schools, bars) may violate local custom and/or result in protests by interest groups, including those who can expect financial losses from free distribution (i.e., pharmacists). In addition, an argument can be made that ready availability of condoms will promote sexual promiscuity. Of course, similar arguments have been made when wider distribution of condoms was advocated for only contraceptive purposes. In that instance, data have suggested that many teenagers are sexually active before using contraceptives and that availability of contraceptives appears not to increase sexual activity (see chapter 7).

Freely providing syringes and needles further dramatizes barriers to possibly effective action. Sale or possession of this equipment, except for medically prescribed purposes, is illegal. While fear of AIDS may have altered IV drug use patterns, it is conceivable that freely providing unused equipment could remove such fears and *increase* drug use. It is likely that such programs will be tried on a limited experimental basis to more accurately ascertain outcomes (Dortman, 1987).

Another approach to reducing the spread of AIDS is to increase the availability of drug treatment facilities. Presently, such facilities are stretched to the maximum in serving clients. However, as noted by Baltimore and Wolff when arguing for increasing drug treatment services, the cost for treating an addict for a year can be as low as $3,000, while the costs for treating an AIDS victim for a year can be $50,000 to $150,000 per year. These alluring cost comparisons are moderated by the sobering practical and ethical issues involved in prioritizing drug treatment of HIV afflicted and nonafflicted addicts. Perhaps, though, preventive drug programs may have a more central role to play in curtailing the AIDS epidemic.

Other approaches more consistent with a public health model entail restrictions on places where high-risk behaviors occur and mandatory screening and testing. Thus, closing down or otherwise restricting use of bathhouses and certain bars is one way to reduce multiple, gay, sexual contact. Mandatory screening and testing can more immediately pinpoint and track victims and, perhaps, reduce the spread of the disease. These approaches particularly underscore a theme of this book—i.e., the protection of individual rights versus the protection of the general public good. If restrictions were done selectively—i.e., not limiting the right to congregate in places for social purposes—then violations of civil rights would be less of an issue. Indeed, such restrictions have already been enacted in New York and San Francisco. As for closing down "shooting galleries," it would be hard to make the case that civil rights were being violated.

Involuntary testing and surveillance programs and discriminatory policies at the workplace more clearly do violate civil liberties. Involuntary testing programs are a highly coercive approach which is under fire in other realms (e.g., testing for drug use). Discriminatory policies at work in some instances are attributable to fear based on incomplete or inaccurate information, e.g., how HIV is spread. The alteration of such formal and informal policies might be achieved if victims of AIDS were classified as disabled individuals and, therefore, protected under more general laws.

Voluntary testing presents another set of related problems and issues. For example, even with more sophisticated testing protocols, many individuals will be falsely labeled seropositive. Testing services also may be swamped with requests. However, knowledge about health status may lead some individuals to adopt health-protective practices. For example, some who test negative for HIV may be motivated to remain infection-free, and some who test positive may be willing to limit health-risky behaviors. Of course, testing HIV-seropositive also can have devastating psychological effects (Osborn, 1988). As an overall perspective on actions to take that restrict behaviors, possibly stigmatize individuals, and otherwise limit civil rights, a guideline of "least restrictive alternatives" has been outlined (Gostin and Curran, 1987a; 1987b). That is, at a minimum, less coercive methods should be favored and tried first.

Yet another major issue pertains to accuracy in media accounts. Cases in point are the seemingly weekly reports of new "effective" AIDS treatments. While it can be argued that the public has a right to know the latest information, it can also be argued that claims for treatment efficacy should only be reported cautiously in the absence of scientific peer review. Obviously, cautious statements do not sell newspapers or attract television viewers. In this instance, however, there is the need for greater accountability and less sensationalism on the part of the media.

The delineation of risk and protective behaviors, and the issues, concerns, and barriers related to effective action for AIDS underscores the myriad of legal, ethical, and strategic problems asociated with altering the course of the epidemic. Only a strong, pervasive force can seemingly attempt to deal with and overcome these many obstacles. As Baltimore and Wolff noted:

> The most fundamental obligation for AIDS education rests with the federal government, which alone is situated to develop and coordinate a massive campaign to implement . . . educational goals. (p. 104)

As noted in this chapter's introduction, policies and actions toward AIDS must be approached as a life-and-death struggle. In the 1980s, federal actions on AIDS have been stymied by two sets of circumstances. The Reagan administration emphasized state and local direction in education and health policy, and only in the latter part of 1987 started to take a more affirmative (though troubled and controversial) stance toward AIDS research, treatment, and prevention. This was a long overdue step by the federal government, which is the only entity that can implement the necessary large-scale effort. The federal government, for example, is in the best position to initiate policies so that air time is available for explicit spots and programs on AIDS. And only the federal government can generate the one billion dollars in funds that Baltimore and Wolff estimated are needed annually to fight the AIDS epidemic on many fronts.

The second set of circumstances limiting action may have been the apparent general confinement of AIDS during the first part of the 1980s to homosexuals and drug addicts. Clearly, the AIDS afflictions of these groups were seen by some as a fitting epitaph for immoral behavior, and perhaps even as evidence of divine intervention. However, if AIDS spreads to the overall population and claims so-called "innocent" victims, such beliefs may change. A clamor may then develop for federal action.

Even if the federal stance will radically change, the last issue noted on Table 4.3 alerts us to a point that is most critical and central to the perspective of this book. It is extremely difficult to conceive of ways to accurately evaluate changes in risk-related and protective behaviors over time since those behaviors are private and, in many states, illegal. Further, contact with HIV does not automatically equate to AIDS or AIDS related complex (ARC), a series of symptoms that may or may not result in AIDS. Infections can also incubate for years. Finally, risk behaviors may decrease and protective behaviors increase, but the number of new cases (incidence) may continue to rapidly increase. This is because higher prevalence rates increase the probability of contact with HIV despite salutary behavioral changes.

Thus, while every health problem and related behaviors and policies discussed in this book have presented complexities to the understanding and barriers to effective action, perhaps in no other area is this more apparent than in efficacious policies and programs for AIDS. What then may be realistically done using media as the primary programmatic vehicle?

BASES OF AN EFFECTIVE CAMPAIGN

A review and integration of the following—the points made on Table 4.1 about effective elements and variables of media campaigns; key aspects of the behavioral systems approach; our framework; and the process of change model developed in chapter 3 on use of incentives in health promotion—can provide the bases for delineating necessary facets of a media approach to altering the course of the AIDS epidemic. Starting with Table 4.1 (page 99), several points are apparent. Messages, spots, and programs need to have high quality, be specific, vivid, and explicit, and model desired behavior changes to targeted audiences. Video media is particularly recommended for its modeling potential. Considerable formative and pilot work must be done so that language, scenes, and prescribed behaviors closely fit the target audience. Further, messages must be delivered by sources that are seen as trustworthy and competent by the target audience.

However, prescribed behavior changes must be simple to enact, with few obstructions to performance, and where reinforcement or at least no punishing contingencies will follow the performance of the prescribed behaviors. When barriers exist for behavior changes, such barriers must be realistically depicted, with strategies given for overcoming them. Finally, there is a major caveat for program development and evaluation — focus on realistic, specific, and limited goals.

The behavioral systems approach more clearly delineates the conceptual, principle, and procedural bases for programs, and further suggests that multilevel analyses can pinpoint the costs and benefits of interventions at different levels. Once concepts, principles, and procedures are tied to the decision to act at specified levels, then formative research is conducted to design an intervention and pilot research is undertaken to pretest the efficacy of a program and further refine it.

The framework (presented in chapter 2) emphasizes steps similar to those in the behavioral systems approach. Indeed, we feel that a major value of the book's framework and the media approach is to underscore the careful step-by-step process needed for designing and evaluating health programs. The framework, however, has a greater delineation of theories, assessment data, and settings, as well as of the methods, personnel, and time-frames appropriate to different levels of analysis.

Finally, the process of change schema from chapter 3 emphasizes these critical points. There are different stages of change and these stages may require the emphasis of different procedures. For example, incentives may be particularly necessary during the behavioral acquisition stage, while the fostering of commitments, beliefs, and internal standards may be more important for sustained change. In addition, the schema indicates that programming and behavioral change efforts do not occur in a vacuum. Alternative behaviors should be readily apparent and easy to perform, with a high probability of reinforcement.

MEDIA ACCESS STRATEGIES
AND GENERAL INITIATIVES

In earlier sections of this chapter, problems in gaining access particularly to network prime time were described. A number of strategies for confronting, bypassing, or attempting to cooperatively work with media industries were also detailed. We believe that the scope and urgency of the AIDS epidemic requires that major emphasis be placed on federal involvement and action so that at least a minimum amount of prime time becomes available for AIDS-related spots and programs. Such initiatives need to go beyond opening the airwaves to condom ads, as has occurred via network affiliate policy in a number of cities. This is a good and necessary first step. However, a more concerted campaign can both broadly educate the public about AIDS and at the same time direct prescriptive messages to particular population segments. In addition, local efforts following the reciprocity model developed by Jason and his colleagues can supplement and sharpen any overall federall initiative. Clearly, local strategies can and should be used in order to effectively narrowcast media to particular target groups.

The discussion of model programming starts with reasonable targets for a federal initiative — conveying correct information and allaying of fear.

Information gain and fear reduction can be achieved on a population basis with an orchestrated array of spots, segments within ongoing programs, and programs which entirely focus on AIDS. Considerable formative research needs to be conducted to assess information and misinformation of particular target groups and trustworthy sources for these diverse target groups. A general plan entails using the formative research data to construct spots and programs that are tailored to different segments, and thus — just as with commercials and regular TV fare — are fitted into particular time slots to increase the probability of being viewed by target audiences.

We feel that for conveying information and allaying fears, two basic psychological strategies are important. The first is the classic two-sided approach to message delivery (Hovland, Lumsdaine, & Sheffield, 1949). For example, any spot or program can acknowledge that not everything is known at this point about AIDS, new information is constantly being gathered, but at this point in time, the facts are the following. . . .

A second major strategy is the use of modeling. Knowledge and fear about contact with persons with AIDS at work, school, and the community may best be met by models who interact with AIDS victims in these settings. It must be shown that nothing negative happens to the model. Indeed, there can be some positive outcomes, such as the admiration of others and the internal rewards and feelings associated with being compassionate.

It would appear relatively simple to weave complimentary segments into ongoing programs. For example, Bill Cosby, in his role as Dr. Huxtable, can be shown interacting with an expectant mother whose husband has AIDS. Considerable new information would come from this segment. Dr. Huxtable could discuss and show how the demographics for AIDS have changed. The program could also depict Dr. Huxtable confidently interacting with, and touching, the expectant mother, showing that AIDS is not transmitted by casual contact.

Alex and Mallory, characters on the *Family Ties* program, can be shown as doubting and fearful models who gain information and reduce their fears and interact with persons with AIDS at school or work. Note that this example nicely combines drama with an effective psychological strategy, that is, the coping model (Bandura, 1986). Similarly, other prime time special programs and made-for-TV movies can, as has been done before, focus on AIDS.

However, as has been noted, we feel that the focus of spots and programs needs to follow and be cognizant of psychological strategies and accompanying formats that will best serve the goals of information gain and fear reduction. While few psychologists and health professionals are creative experts — e.g., in choreographing particular scenes — we do know what has a good probability for affecting information and behavior change. Such points may not be considered by media professionals.

For example, programs, in the interest of dramatic appeal, will too often model positive and negative behaviors and leave the resolution of conflicts unclear. Table 4.4 shows three major formats that have been used in presenting prosocial programming and the advantages and disadvantages of each format. The first format only entails having models display the appropriate behaviors and receive positive outcomes. This format is very clear and has

Table 4.4. Presentation Formats for Prosocial Programs: Advantages and Disadvantages*

Presentation format	Advantages	Disadvantages
1. One model or several models only display prosocial behavior and no portrayals of antisocial or conflicting behaviors.	• Very clear • Most support from social learning theory • Can be very effective in classroom and therapy and easily supplement with interpersonal activities	• Not very dramatic • Few commercial programs in this format • May not hold attention • Most of research on captive audience and assessment in artificial settings • May have generalization problem when viewer encounters negative situations
2. One or more models exhibit prosocial behaviors while the same people or others display antisocial or inappropriate behaviors which *receive negative consequences.*	• Provides drama • Most similar to usual TV fare • *Sesame street* and *Mr. Rogers* appear to successfully use	• Antisocial and inappropriate behaviors may be modeled • May need interpersonal supplement to sort out positive and negative behaviors
3. One or more models exhibit prosocial behaviors while the same people or others display antisocial or inappropriate behaviors, *but no final resolution presented.*	• Provides drama • May provoke post-viewing problem solving to solve conflict • May be effective when coupled with post-viewing interpersonal activities	• Antisocial and inappropriate behaviors may be modeled • Viewer may not generate post-viewing problem solving

*Based on Lovelace and Huston, 1982.

been shown to be effective (see Winett, 1986), but lacks dramatic appeal. In the second format, some models display appropriate behaviors which are reinforced, while models who display inappropriate behaviors receive negative consequences. This format can provide drama and has been used successfully in some prosocial programs. It is, however, important that it is very clear by the end of the program which are the appropriate behaviors. Finally, as noted, the third format, where both appropriate and inappropriate behaviors are displayed and there is no final resolution, is not recommended. Indeed, this format has the potential for conveying the wrong message.

As we have stressed, it is also critical that spots and programs use explicit language. For example, the terms "being cautious" and "using protection" need to be replaced by specific statements about condoms. This means that the ban on "dirty words" needs to be relaxed. Expressions such as "the exchange of bodily fluids" or "sexual contact" need to be replaced by explicit and specific ones, e.g., anal intercourse.

It is equally important that spots, segments, and programs be pretested on measures of knowledge about and fear of AIDS. Similar assessments should be made as the spots and programs are actually shown. In addition, more behavioral measures can attempt to monitor such indicants of programmatic effects as the number of discriminatory instances at work and school.

We envision spots and programs proceeding over a period of several months, with assessments also ongoing and continuing after such an effort. As noted also, more local efforts could supplement these extensive and general federal efforts. Overall, as suggested by the prior points, this effort would be staffed by psychologists, health professionals, and marketing and media experts. However, this first layer of effort is primarily directed to the general public. Its major goals are information gain and fear reduction. Attempting to modify specific health risk and protective behaviors is the more difficult task to which we now turn.

MODIFYING HEALTH-RISKY AND PROTECTIVE BEHAVIORS

As shown previously in Table 4.2, the two primary modes of transmission of HIV are sexual (anal and vaginal) intercourse, and through sharing of needles and syringes for IV drug use. A media approach alone may have some impacts on sexual behavior. We are less sanguine about media impacts on IV drug use, although ironically the acquisition of HIV through sharing of equipment may receive wide network exposure, as we will discuss later.

For modification of sexual practices, we envision a campaign where programs and messages are sufficiently diverse and well targeted to appeal to men and women of different ages, sexual persuasions, and social strata, but one in which the common denominator is use of explicit language and graphic depiction of alternative practices. Note that the health protective behaviors here are restricted to abstention, monogamy, and use of condoms. More realistically, the focus can be on monogamy and condom use — "safer sex" — with the latter practice indirectly verifiable. The same points concerning formative research, two-sided communications, and use of modeling, as noted in the section on the general campaign, pertain here. For example, models may initially be skeptical about the use of condoms because they reduce spontaneity and pleasure. However, after appropriate segues and scenes, the same models can now say how using condoms enhances spontaneity and pleasure because they know they are safer.

Spots, program segments, or entire programs can be developed in much the same way as noted for the general campaign. The use of the format (Table 4.4) where appropriate behaviors are reinforced and inappropriate ones punished is clearly the most suitable one.

However, major additional strategies are also advocated pertaining to evaluation, the campaign's unfolding, and use of local media. The media program can be tested alone and in areas where condoms are freely distributed. In the first instance, self-reports of condom use and sales data can serve as outcome measures. In the second case, self-reports of condom use and numbers of condoms freely distributed can be dependent measures. Obviously, increased design sophistication, such as comparison communities and the strategic introduction of condom sales in target communities, additional measures (e.g., rates of teenage pregnancies; community acceptance), and extensive follow-ups can also better indicate immediate and long-term individual and community impacts (Flay & Cook, 1981).

Since it is also envisioned that such a campaign would take place over an extended time period, an attempt should be made to pattern the campaign after the process of change model developed in chapter 3 (see p. 78). For example, in communities where condoms may be freely distributed, some numbering system could be used so as to create a lottery. The general idea is to use incentives early in the acquisition stage. Explicit instruction and counseling on use can also be provided through print and interpersonal channels, available in places where condoms can be distributed (e.g., schools, community sites). Such instruction and counseling must also deal with the ambivalence that males and females may have toward condom use. When orchestrated with the previously described "modeling spots," the incentives and print and face-to-face information should maximize positive outcome expectancies and efficacy beliefs and initial trials of condoms.

Latter parts of the campaign can emphasize that individuals should always have condoms available (generality) and explore the particular beliefs and commitments associated with a healthier life style (sustained change). While throughout all phases of the campaign we envision that a positive, straightforward tone is maintained, the use of fear tactics does seem warranted (Leventhal, Safer, & Panagis, 1983). This is because very specific steps to obtain protection will be shown, and, in most instances, the product needed to ensure safety will be readily available. That is, there are simple, readily available ways to reduce fear.

This overall campaign, using network television, interpersonal and print channels, and local distribution points, can obviously be enhanced by local television and print media. Clearly, the approach developed by Jason et al. (1987) can be an excellent adjunct. Different segments can also be devoted during proper time periods to different subgroups, e.g., heterosexual teenagers and homosexuals. Locally recognized leaders and local models can increase information flow, source credibility, and identification with models.

Since this chapter focuses on a predesignated specific intervention strategy — i.e., media-based interventions, with attendant concepts, principles, and procedures — the overall framework only marginally served as a basis for developing the approach. However, a further articulation of the media campaign does necessitate closer examination of personnel, settings, and other persuasive methods for presenting information. These facets of the campaign may be best particularized at the local level. For example, the provision of extensive face-to-face information and/or the free distribution of condoms would greatly increase the need for personnel, settings, and resources, as compared to those required for a media campaign alone. However, regardless of the specifics of a local campaign, ongoing and sophisticated process and outcome evaluations pertinent to meeting the initiative's objectives will be emphasized.

If all parts of the campaign were used in concert, perhaps even without the free distribution component, we feel that while this campaign would be costly, it can be reasonably effective. Process evaluations would assess the campaign's effectiveness in reaching certain "guideposts," e.g., media reach and knowledge change. Such ongoing data feedback can help alter and refine campaigns, if necessary, in midstream. Outcome evaluations would assess attainment of the overall campaign objectives. For example, we predict that a campaign of this sophistication and magnitude could at a minimum increase the use of condoms, slow the exponential trend for the increasing rates of incidence and prevalence of AIDS, and most likely reduce teenage pregnancy. Sales data and hospital records can serve as indicants of meeting these goals, particularly if comparison data are available from communities not receiving the campaign. Whether or not such a campaign increases promiscuity can also be evaluated although, perhaps, only from self-report measures.

Cost analyses can also be done so that estimates are obtained for the costs of informing population segments, increasing condom sales to a specified degree, and preventing a case of AIDS (Levin, 1983). The relative costs and benefits of prevention of AIDS compared to treatment could also be estimated (Russell, 1985).

Thus, we are optimistic about the probability of relative success of this campaign. However, a campaign for modifying IV drug practices would probably meet with less success.

The difficulty of obtaining air time may on the one hand be compounded; however, the possibility may also be perhaps enhanced for spots and programs dealing with IV drug use, because the topic does have dramatic appeal. That is, ironically, the spread of AIDS through sharing equipment could become more widely known than transmission through sexual behaviors simply because the specific behaviors associated with sharing equipment can be vividly depicted on network television! However, it is less likely that these same behaviors can be the subject of spots.

All the foregoing points about formative research, two-sided messages, use of models, proper presentation formats, interpersonal and print channels, and other local media productions also are relevant here. However, two other key points are recommended. We would advocate a heavy tone of fear, since there is some anecdotal evidence that fear of contracting AIDS has resulted in altered IV drug use patterns (Baltimore and Wolff, 1986). Entrance into a drug rehabilitation program can be offered as the available alternative response for fear reduction (Leventhal et al., 1983).

On a more limited basis, we also recommend small-scale experiments where the media approach is combined with free distribution of syringes and needles. However, the possibility that free distribution could lead to increased drug trafficking and use must be seriously entertained and evaluated, lest the effort ameliorate one problem and worsen another.

Such plans for a media approach to modify health risk and health-protective behaviors for the transmission of HIV only provide a sketch of what can be done. Hopefully, the sketch suggests that what needs to be done from a large-scale communication perspective is relatively clear and achievable. The conceptual and technical tools are available to alter the course of the AIDS epidemic. What remains to be seen is whether at local and federal levels there is the will to do so.

POSTSCRIPT

By the late spring of 1988, the issues concerning the modification of risk behaviors for AIDS had come into sharper focus in some respects. In other respects the issues became even more muddled. Furthermore, in at least one way, the scientific literature on communication and risk behavior change came full circle to where this chapter began.

During 1987 and 1988, two major communication efforts were launched. The Surgeon General's excellent brochure on AIDS was made available in large numbers to various organizations. In June of 1988, a simplified version of the brochure was sent to every U.S. home. Of course, a caveat is that, at best, a one-time mailing of a brochure can probably only hope to inform part of the population about the causes and prevention of the disease and keep salient points about AIDS high on the national agenda.

A TV campaign, "America Responds to AIDS," was produced by the public health relations firm of Ogilvy and Mathers for the U.S. Department of Health and Human Services, through the Public Health Service and Centers for Disease Control. At least one of the networks relaxed their usual standards so that *relatively* explicit 10- to 120-second spots could be viewed by the general public. However, the ad campaign, though precedent-setting, primarily used fear arousal, with viewers able to obtain more verbal and written information through calling an "800" number. While the notion of focusing on a specific, simple behavior (call an "800" number) is a recommendation of this chapter, the advantages of fear arousal as a strategy in this context are not that clear. More could be gained, perhaps, if fear was used as an attention-getting cue, followed by explicit depictions of risk-reduction behaviors. Most important, the links between viewing an ad, fear arousal, calling and receiving information, and then following through and changing high-risk behaviors appear tenuous. Finally, the ads and overall campaign were apparently *not* tested in a formative and pilot research stage for behavioral impacts.

On the positive side, the campaign can be seen as a "small win" (Weick, 1984) — i.e., the federal government and TV networks have taken one step in the right direction. On the negative side, the degree of explicitness of content and prescriptions for behavior change pale in contrast to much stronger TV efforts mounted in European countries and Australia. The "America Responds" campaign runs the risk of following a history of inadequate U.S. public media campaigns (Winett, 1986). Campaigns that are impotent from the outset are mounted, and their weak impacts are used to confirm the self-fulfilling prophecy that "media cannot affect behavior change."

The public during the early part of 1988 was also exposed to highly conflicting information through newspapers, magazines, and TV. The *New York Times* ran a number of front-page stories where leading public health officials in the Northeast were quoted as indicating that the epidemic was being contained and that the spread of AIDS to the heterosexual population was extremely negligible. Within a few weeks of these reports, which were reprinted in newspapers across the country, *Newsweek* magazine published excerpts from an alarmist book by well-known sex therapists Masters and Johnson (Masters, Johnson, & Kolodny, 1988). Using dubious sampling and interpretive methods, the authors claimed that the modes of transmission for AIDS are more numerous (e.g., deep kissing, and even more casual contact) than previously thought and that the incidence and prevalence of AIDS in the heterosexual population was far higher than previously reported. These claims and *Newsweek's* role in widely presenting them were quickly labeled as irresponsible by the medical and public health establishments.

Nevertheless, such conflicting and bewildering reports were bound to diminish the credibility of authoritative sources and leave the public perplexed.

These conflicting reports aside, some excellent studies did appear in the early part of 1988 (e.g., see Osborn, 1988). These studies have started to paint a clearer picture of the extent of the epidemic, its impacts now and in the future, and strategies, targets, and likely outcomes for behavior change efforts. For example:

1. By the end of 1987, about 50,000 cases of AIDS had been reported, with about 21,000 of these cases reported in 1987 alone. Blacks and Hispanics still had rates of reported AIDS cases 3 to 12 times greater than whites, with the differential rate attributable to IV drug use. However, there has been great variation of HIV infection in IV drug users by region of the country (e.g., 0%–70% of a sample infected). Samples of heterosexual men have shown ranges of 20% to 50%. Samples of heterosexual men and women (done at STD clinics) who do not use IV drugs and who have not had contact with persons of known risk for AIDS have had infection rates of 0% to 2.6% (Curran, Jaffe, Hardy, Morgan, Selik, & Dondero, 1988). Of course, these were the rates disputed by Masters and Johnson.

2. There was also ready acknowledgment from public health professionals that the dynamics of the modes of transportation of AIDS require more understanding. Further, more local epidemiological studies are needed to pinpoint populations at risk for HIV infection (Allen & Curran, 1988). State and local public health services have rapidly increased during the last four years to meet the demands of the epidemic (Rowe & Ryan, 1988), but expenditures, services, and impacts vary widely by region (e.g., compare expenditures, services, and impacts in New York or San Francisco to a midwestern city). In any case, health departments are responsible for surveillance and control of the HIV epidemic and are expected to provide free HIV testing and counseling, HIV services in drug abuse and STD clinics, notification to individuals unknowingly exposed to HIV, local information and education efforts, restrictive measures for some HIV patients, regulation and closure of public settings associated with high risk of HIV infection, and monitoring and reporting of all HIV tests (Judson & Vernon, 1988). In other words, public health departments are responsible for an array of costly community and individual services.

3. Interest started to become focused on two other risk groups in addition to bisexual men. Prostitutes, because of multiple partners, some unprotected sex, and IV drug use, have shown relatively high prevalence rates of HIV infection, and can be conduits for spread to other populations (Rosenberg & Weiner, 1988). Heterosexual adolescents also appear to be a high-risk group. They already have high rates of STD and multiple sexual partners (see chapter 7). Even more significantly, while knowledge of AIDS appears to be increasing in this population, condom use apparently has not (Kegeles,

Adler, & Irwin, 1988). Particular misperceptions about condom use and personal feelings of invulnerability have been linked to the low use of condoms (Kegeles et al., 1988).

4. A number of provocative articles (e.g., Brandt, 1988a; 1988b; and see Brandt, 1987) drew important historical parallels between the current AIDS epidemic and the much longer history of the syphilis and gonorrhea epidemics. Several major points are particularly informative to the present dilemma. Moral outrage, fear campaigns, and calls for abstinence were all strategies that failed to control syphilis. Modifying sexual practices (e.g., providing condoms to soldiers in World War II) proved effective, but even behavioral changes and the development of a vaccine have not eradicated syphilis and gonorrhea. Indeed, rates are once again increasing. The lessons of these epidemics appear to be the need for a state of constant vigilance, effective and continual behavioral changes, and the recognition that any disease is a complex biological, behavioral, social, and cultural phenomenon, requiring multiple levels of analysis and intervention.

5. On an optimistic note, Becker and Joseph (1988) provided an extensive review of community and media-based efforts to change behaviors related to reducing the risk of HIV infection. There was reasonably good evidence that homosexual and bisexual men have "rapidly and profoundly" altered their sexual practices. These behavior changes include decreasing the number of sexual partners, decreasing the frequency of unprotected anal intercourse, and more general increased use of condoms and spermicides. However, Becker and Joseph (1988) also indicated that changes in homosexual men may be attributable to educational levels and the organization of communities. Similar responses have not been seen in minorities and for drug abusers, although there is some evidence that IV drug abusers have been attempting to disinfect needles and syringes. Thus, progress has been made along the lines suggested by Brandt (1988a; 1988b) — modification not elimination of risk behaviors.

6. Becker and Joseph (1988) also reported two sobering points. There is little documented change for vulnerable adolescent and young adult heterosexuals. Further, most health behavior changes entail a series of lapses and relapses (Brownell et al., 1986), and lapses and relapses in consistently following safer sexual practices appear to frequently occur (Becker & Joseph, 1988). With AIDS, such lapses and relapses can lead to more spread of the disease throughout the society. For the individual, a lapse or relapse can be lethal. Thus, Becker and Joseph (1988) noted that campaigns must emphasize lifetime change.

7. Fineberg (1988) expanded on this sobering perspective. Again, an historical approach was valuable in showing that it has taken about 25 years (since the 1964 Surgeon General's report) for our society to seriously discuss the possibility of a smokeless society. Even with that movement and atten-

dant actions, smoking rates for population segments remain disappointing (e.g., adolescent females). Likewise, the widespread adoption of safer sexual practices may take many years to achieve; even then, certain segments may not follow the larger culture's mores and practices. Fineberg (1988) also developed a quantitative risk reduction model which yielded another disquieting finding. He showed that switching from many sexual partners (e.g., 50 in a 2- or 3-year period) to monogamy dramatically reduced the probability of infection. However, reducing from 50 to 5 (an extremely effective behavior change for any campaign) resulted in very marginal changes in risk. Thus, campaigns need to be incisive and emphasize continual change.

8. Fineberg (1988) also identified key obstacles to effective AIDS education:

a. the social complexity of sexual and drug abuse behaviors and their biological bases;
b. the long period of virus incubation before visible signs of disease appear;
c. a lack of clarity about risk to the heterosexual population;
d. confusion about approaches to education — i.e., moralistic approach and abstention, fear, or promotion of safer sexual and drug use practices;
e. conflicting messages from medical, public health, and political officials; and
f. the extreme behavioral changes needed over lifetimes.

In the end, we have apparently come full circle in once again noting both the obstacles and potential for behavioral changes to alter the course of the AIDS epidemic. These obstacles include not only the need for more technical refinement of effective communication strategies but the economic, regulatory, and normative barriers that prevent effective health promotion messages from being delivered to diverse population segments. When obstacles can be at least partially overcome, the potential for further altering the course of the AIDS epidemic seems substantial.

This final, extended quote from Brandt (1988a) indicates both where we have been and where we need to travel:

> Today calls for better education are frequently offered as the best hope for controlling the AIDS epidemic. But this will only be true if some resolution is reached concerning the specific content and nature of such educational efforts. The limited effectiveness of education which merely encourages fear is well-documented. Moreover, AIDS education requires a forthright confrontation of aspects of human sexuality that are typically avoided. To be effective, AIDS education must be explicit, focused, and appropriately targeted to a range of at-risk social groups . . . If education is to have a positive impact, we need to be far more sophisticated, creative, and bold in devising and implementing programs. (Brandt, 1988a, p. 364)

5
Community Health Promotion

INTRODUCTION

As underscored in chapter 1, disease patterns in the United States have changed significantly since the turn of the century. Concerns over infectious and communicable diseases have since been replaced (with the exception of AIDS) with increasing alarm over today's major killers—the chronic diseases (USDHEW, 1979; USDHHS, 1980). With this dramatic shift in the pattern of health problems and the increasing cost of health care, there has also been increased attention paid to understanding and changing the constellation of behavioral and environmental factors influencing the development and progression of these problems (Matarazzo, 1984). As a consequence, national standards and goals for the prevention of illness have been proposed (USDHEW, 1979; USDHHS, 1980; USDHHS, 1984), reaffirming prevention as a public health, as well as an individual, issue.

As reviewed throughout this book, there are many strategies available to decrease health problems. These strategies range from intensive individually focused programs (e.g., biofeedback) to large-scale community- or policy-based programs. The latter approaches, the focus of this chapter, attempt to reduce health problems through a variety of informational, educational, behavioral, organizational, environmental, legal, and economic interventions.

The first part of this chapter will summarize the rationale, both theoretical and practical, for community-based efforts. The second section will review exemplary community interventions. It will focus predominantly on heart disease prevention efforts, though we recognize that there are numerous other social and community interventions that have been implemented (see Gesten & Jason [1987] and chapter 6 of this volume for an excellent review of these). The final section of the chapter will take a single health-related behavior, cigarette smoking, and analyze it using the framework outlined in chapter 2, with community intervention as a focus.

Rationale for Community Intervention

Community-based interventions are distinguished from other strategies by the methods used to reach program recipients (i.e., mass media, community organization, environmental change) and the target of these methods.

These interventions usually have as an ultimate target the behavior of individuals—they are designed to increase health knowledge, the practice of healthy behaviors, the utilization of health services, and the environmental supports conducive to healthy behavior. Additional targets of change include organizational (e.g., implementing worksite health programs), environmental (e.g., inclusion of exercise facilities in a community park to encourage and support physical activity), and public policies (e.g., passage of a community ordinance banning smoking in public places). Consideration of these macro-level factors, which encourage or support individual behavior change, typifies a successful community-based effort.

Community programs have been developed and funded in large part because of the belief that sole reliance on individual approaches when attempting to combat illness and promote health was likely to fall short of national and local health status objectives. The primary limitation of individual, group, and even some organizational programs is cost relative to effectiveness. Clearly, there are highly effective individually based health promotion programs. Unfortunately, the extent to which they can be disseminated to large groups of people is limited by their cost, labor intensity, and generalizability. In contrast, the advantages of community interventions include their relevance to the everyday environments of people, potential for diffusion of effects to large numbers of people, generalizability, utility to health policy, and potential for cost-effectiveness (Farquhar, 1978; Farquhar, Fortmann, Wood, & Haskell, 1983; Puska, Salonen, Nissinen, et al., 1983).

In addition, the validity of broad-based community intervention is increased because health is influenced by factors at multiple levels of analysis (Eisenberg, 1977) and because risk factors are prevalent throughout the population (Blackburn, 1972) (see also chapter 6 on waiting vs. seeking mode interventions). Limiting the targets of health interventions to individuals who explicitly seek assistance obviously omits those who could benefit from preventive measures and those who do not seek help from the traditional avenues currently available. Evidence suggests that most Americans fall into this latter group (Matarazzo, 1982).

While community-based efforts hold great promise, there are many challenges associated with their successful implementation. One of these is that long-term behavior change is usually a key objective and message of these programs. The consequences of non-adherence with many preventive behaviors are, at least in the short-term, not severe. For example, eating a diet high in fat has relatively few immediate, discernible negative health effects. This is one reason for the high degree of non-adherence with preventive regimens. For many individuals, a major illness or disability must occur for them to consider a health behavior change. In clinical settings, health professionals can often circumvent this problem by attending to those cognitions, emotions, and behaviors of an individual that support nonadherence and developing a regimen focused specifically on obviating such behaviors. In contrast, community programs often rely on demographic and epidemiologic indicators to guide program development resulting in regimens that cannot be tailored easily to individual or even group needs.

Thus, one major impediment to the effective delivery of community programs is the inability to obtain feedback from the target audience. While community programs reach a large number of people (often through mass media), program effectiveness may be limited by the difficulty in delivering messages tailored to specific audiences that allow for immediate feedback. Such constraints may result in increased difficulty in reaching the people most in need of assistance. Social marketing techniques, however, can help implementers tailor messages to the desired audience.

If the appropriate audience can be reached, other challenges exist. For example, in terms of understanding and remembering information, we know from clinical research that over half the information presented to individuals in a health care setting is typically forgotten within minutes of being presented (Green, 1979). This percentage is likely to be much higher for messages communicated as part of community intervention, for the reasons stated above. In addition, the intensity (strength) of messages delivered through community interventions, compared to clinical interventions, is usually lower, thereby decreasing the potential for behavior change. Moreover, the messages delivered to communities through print and electronic channels often compete with communication from "illness" industries (e.g., advertisements urging people to drink alcohol, purchase high-fat foods, engage in casual sex, smoke, and the like). At times, it is evident that messages promoting health pale in contrast to messages promoting ill health. However, there is evidence that the antismoking advertisements that appeared on radio and television during the 1960s and early 1970s were twice as effective as smoking ads, even though they were played much less frequently (Hamilton, 1972). Thus, as discussed in chapter 4, gaining access to expensive media is an ongoing problem for community health promotion programs.

The previous section has outlined briefly some of the reasons why community-based intervention programs have been attempted and reviewed the challenges associated with doing so. The next section examines in more detail what actually is meant by community intervention.

What is a Community?

When we use the term *community*, what specifically are we referring to? Community is a catch-all term without clear boundaries. We can, however, identify common features of all communities. In the most general sense, communities are: settings in which activity takes place; collections of individuals; vehicles through which interactions occur among and between individuals and institutions; and social systems that pose problems and afford opportunities to individuals and institutions within them (Cox, 1979; Sanders & Brownlee, 1979). Chavis and Newbrough (1986) suggested further that a community can be viewed as a set of social relations bound together by a common sense of community. An ideal community, then, is "one that maximizes citizen input by providing opportunities for individuals to participate and contribute to the welfare of the group" (Heller & Monahan, 1977, p. 382).

As reviewed below, there is a rich theoretical literature in the social sciences that helps to clarify the important influence of the community context on behavior (Kuhn, 1975; Stokols, 1980; Wicker, 1979). For purposes of this discussion, this literature will be characterized as the contextual or ecological perspective.

It is important to state here that most community health promotion efforts to date have not drawn on contextual/ecological theoretical perspectives. Rather, current programs typically utilize principles from communication–behavior change theory, community organization, and social marketing (as reviewed in a later section of the chapter). A contextual/ecological perspective is presented here as an approach that could complement the predominant theories guiding current health promotion efforts and presumably help to improve program effectiveness. A contextual/ecological perspective will be highlighted throughout the chapter and is consistent with the framework outlined in chapter 2.

The philosophical underpinning of a contextual/ecological perspective is the concept that behavior does not occur within a vacuum. Behavior and the settings in which behavior occurs are viewed as *interdependent* rather than as *independent* (Wicker, 1979). As early as the 1940s, for example, Egon Brunswick and Kurt Lewin discussed ecological concepts in terms of individual perceptions of environments (Wicker, 1979). Until the work of two of Lewin's students — Roger Barker and Herbert Wright — was published in the 1950s and 1960s, psychology and other social sciences were generally uninfluenced by ecological thought.

Barker developed his ideas on ecological thought from a variety of systematic observations he and his associates made of human behavior in various settings (Wicker, 1979). These observations can be summarized as follows: (a) the variance in an individual's behavior is better predicted by knowing the setting in which the behavior takes place than by knowing something about the individual's knowledge, attitudes, motives, intelligence, or personality; (b) in similar surroundings, different people (i.e., in terms of intraindividual factors) often behave in similar ways; (c) behavior is often restricted to conform to the setting in which the behavior occurs; (d) the behaviors of individuals are coordinated with the objects in their environments; and (e) the regularities in environments may not always be apparent to the people in them.

These observations led to the philosophy that settings are *ordered*. They do not influence behavior or experiences through luck or chance, or serve as passive backdrops to behavior; rather, they are active, organized, and self-regulating. Wicker (1979) captures the essence of this "behavior-settings" approach:

> If people enter and remain in a setting, they will behave in ways that are compatible with its program. They will not show the many other behaviors of which they are capable if those behaviors are not compatible with the program. This prediction can be made with confidence, because we know that the self-regulating processes in a setting act to assure this result. People in drugstores 'behave drugstore', for example; they do not behave 'post office', or 'swimming lesson'. (p. 18)

Trickett (1987) outlined an ecologically based rationale for community health interventions. Drawing on the work of James G. Kelly and students, he described four underlying principles that guide ecological theory and intervention: (a) adaptation (i.e., characteristics of social settings affect attitudes and behaviors, thereby requiring people and settings to adapt); (b) interdependence (i.e., social settings have interdependent relationships such that behavior in one setting is partly a function of the influence of factors in other settings); (c) cycling of resources (i.e., the resources available to social settings — technological, social, and so forth — affect the development and survival of communities and therefore must be understood); and (d) succession (i.e., the past, present, and future affect communities and people in communities). With these principles as a guiding perspective, Trickett argued that the sociocultural context defines the meaning of health-related behaviors, the design of successful interventions hinges on an understanding of this sociocultural context, and the norms of settings, such as schools and health care agencies, should ideally coincide with the views and norms of their consumers (i.e., person–environment fit).

While ecological theory can help account for influences beyond the immediate (i.e., micro/meso) environment, there is little empirical research examining meso- and macro-environmental influences, a topic area in which public health professionals could contribute significantly. In addition, there is very little research on the temporal qualities of environments. A systems orientation, as described in chapter 2, can help extend the contributions of a contextual perspective.

A systems approach implies that communities cannot be understood adequately through a reductionistic approach. That is, separating the components that make up a system from the system as a whole provides an incomplete and usually invalid picture of the phenomena under the study.

Understanding and accounting for the community social context in which health behaviors occur is essential to the success of community programs. Unlike most curative or individually based adherence efforts, community programs are not typically delivered within a medical or clinical setting but are disseminated to people in the everyday environments in which they live (e.g., homes, workplaces, schools, restaurants, community centers, grocery stores, shopping centers). An inherent difficulty of these sites of intervention is that most people do not regard health as a salient topic; this affects the way in which health information may be delivered, attended to, processed, remembered, and acted upon. Without viewing health interventions within the context of a complex social system, a system with a set of rules and values separate from those of individuals residing in it, the likelihood of developing a successful intervention is diminished. For example, the interventions in supermarkets described in chapter 8 require a knowledge of the design of such settings and consumer, employee, and management norms and behaviors pertinent to that setting. In the absence of such an ecological perspective, supermarket interventions will be less effective.

Attempting to influence the social context in which health behaviors occur in the ways noted above has implications for the time course in which an impact is expected to occur. When individual behavior change is the outcome of interest, it is often reasonable to expect change within days or weeks. When organizational, environmental, legal, or economic changes are among the desired outcomes, however, change cannot be reasonably expected in such a short period of time.

Influencing the community context in which health behaviors occur, then, is in many ways more difficult than changing an individual's behavior in a clinical or small group setting. On the other hand, if changes in the community context can be achieved, the impact on behavior change is likely to be much greater and longer-term than individual approaches because of the basic tenet of ecological theory that states that the interaction between individuals and settings, most influences behaviors. The ability to foster communities that promote health is dependent upon stimulating opportunities for group membership and influence, meeting group needs, and promoting the sharing of social support (Chavis & Newbrough, 1986). In summary, successful community interventions will be sensitive to the synergistic relationships between individuals and the social context in which they are immersed.

The previous sections provided a general background to the theoretical and practical issues involved in designing and implementing ecologically grounded community interventions. In addition, characteristics distinguishing an "ideal" community were reviewed. The next section reviews some of the community-based programs that have been implemented to date and then describes typical intervention components of these programs.

REVIEW OF COMMUNITY-BASED HEART DISEASE PREVENTION PROGRAMS

Beginning in the early 1970s with the Stanford Three Community Study and the North Karelia Project, large-scale community-based disease prevention programs were begun with the expectation that broad-based community intervention would result in lasting and cost-effective individual and community change. Internationally, there now exist at least ten large-scale community-based heart disease prevention programs (Farquhar et al., 1983; Weiss, 1984). Examples include the Stanford Three Community and Five City Projects in California (Farquhar et al., 1983; Maccoby & Altman, 1988; Maccoby & Alexander, 1980; Meyer et al., 1980; Stern et al., 1976); the Minnesota Heart Health Project (Blackburn et al., 1984); the Community Health Improvement Project in Pennsylvania (Cohen, Stunkard, & Felix, 1986; Stunkard, Felix, & Cohen, 1985); the Pawtucket Heart Health Project in Rhode Island (Lasater et al., 1984; Lefebvre, Lasater, Carleton, & Peterson, 1987); the German Heidelberg Study; the Finnish North Karelia Project (McAlister, Puska, Salonen, Tuomilehto, & Koskela, 1982; Puska, 1984; Puska, Salonen, Nissinen, et al., 1983; Puska, Nissinen, Salonen, et al., 1985; Puska, Salonen, Tuomilehto, et al., 1981; Puska, Salonen, Tuomilehto, et al., 1983); the Australian North Coast Project (Egger et al., 1983); and the Swiss National Research Program (see Table 5.1). In general, these programs receive most of their funding from government sources.

The target populations for these programs range from about 30,000 to over 430,000, in several intervention and control towns, and they typically last from three to fifteen years. Results from these studies have been promising both in terms of impact and cost-effectiveness (Altman, 1986a; Farquhar, Fortmann, Wood, & Haskell, 1983; Puska et al., 1983). Because many of these programs have not yet published outcome data, only a few are discussed in detail below.

Stanford Studies

The Stanford Heart Disease Prevention Program (SHDPP) was established in 1971 to conduct the Three Community Study (TCS), which occurred from 1972–1975, and later the Five City Project (FCP), which started in 1978 and will continue through the mid-1990s. Each of these studies, as well as other similar studies carried out in Minnesota, Rhode Island, and Finland, will be referred to throughout the chapter.

Three Community Study

Three comparable small communities (approximately 15,000 residents in each) in Northern California were selected for the study—one control and two intervention. Both intervention communities received a mass media

Table 5.1. Prominent Community-Based Multifactor Health Promotion Programs*

Program	Country	Sites
Stanford Three Community Study	United States	Three towns, two treatment; n = 45,000
Stanford Five City Project	United States	Five cities, two treatment; n = 330,000
North Karelia Project	Finland	Two counties, one treatment; n = 433,000
Swiss National Research Program	Switzerland	Four towns, two treatment; n = 40,000
North Coast Project	Australia	Three towns, two treatment; n = 70,000
South African Study	South Africa	Three towns, two treatment.
Community Health Improvement Program	United States	Two counties, one treatment; n = 224,000
Heidelberg Study	Germany	Two towns, one treatment; n = 30,000
Minnesota Heart Health Project	United States	Six communities, three treatment; n = 356,000
Pawtucket Heart Health Project	United States	Two cities; one treatment; n = 173,000

*Adapted from Farquhar, Maccoby, & Solomon (1984).

campaign which was facilitated by the fact that they shared some media channels (e.g., television and radio). Residents at high risk for cardiovascular disease in one of the intervention communities also received intensive behavioral face-to-face instruction. Survey and medical data were obtained from a cohort of individuals in each community (35–59 year old men and women).

The goals of the TCS intervention program were to raise awareness of cardiovascular disease (CVD) risk factors as well as to equip individuals with the behavioral skills necessary to alter risky behaviors. Diverse and integrated media strategies were developed in both Spanish and English. These included TV spots, bus cards, newspaper ads, billboards, pamphlets, booklets, radio programs, and so forth. The TCS was one of the first community interventions to explicitly combine mass media with interpersonal behavioral strategies to affect the behavior of entire communities.

Data from the TCS indicate that after three years of intervention, participants in the intervention communities achieved a 9 to 15 percent decreased risk of cardiovascular disease while participants in the control community had a 3 percent increased risk (Maccoby & Alexander, 1980). The findings bolstered the Stanford's group belief that broad-based community intervention was feasible and potentially effective. The researchers recognized further that employing a stronger community organization and development perspective could enhance the effectiveness of a media and face-to-face intervention program and lead to the maintenance of effects at both the individual and the organizational level of analysis. In essence, then, the Stanford researchers recognized that interventions sensitive to the vast array of ecological niches in communities were needed. To test this hypothesis (among others), a subsequent larger-scale study, the Five City Project, was designed and begun in 1978.

Five City Project (FCP)

The FCP differed from the TCS in the following ways: The communities were larger (117,000 in the two intervention communities) and more socioculturally complex; the interventions were more extensive and directed at the entire population; the intervention period ran for six years; community ownership was encouraged so that changes would be maintained; effects were assessed in a wider age range (e.g., 12–74) and by both cross-sectional and longitudinal measurement; and morbidity and mortality were assessed. The selection of the five communities (two were intervention communities) was done based predominantly on apriori criteria for size and available media channels.

The education program attempted to increase health-related knowledge, skills, and behaviors, decrease death and disease among individuals, and encourage institutions (e.g., worksites, schools, local government) to promote health through environmental and policy changes. As with the TCS, a variety of strategies were implemented to achieve the desired changes. These included using broadcast media (e.g., TV spots and programs, news series, radio shows), print media (e.g., newspapers, pamphlets), community interpersonal programs (e.g., classes, lectures, incentive-based contests, use of community opinion leaders), and environmental programs (e.g., food labeling in restaurants). In most instances, different intervention strategies were used in conjunction with each other, capitalizing on the synergistic effects that occur when multiple strategies are used in an integrated fashion. The intervention components of community interventions will be reviewed in detail in a later section of the chapter.

As of early 1988, only interim results are available. The data suggest, however, that the FCP achieved many of its goals. Compared to the comparison communities, residents of the intervention communities showed increases in knowledge of cardiovascular risk factors and decreases in systolic and diastolic blood pressure, resting pulse rate, smoking rate, and overall risk of CVD as measured by the multiple risk logistic.

Conclusions from the TCS and the FCP are strengthened by similar findings from the North Karelia Project implemented in Finland. Ten-year follow-up data from the North Karelia Project showed that men in the intervention community, compared to men in the reference area, achieved net reductions of 28 percent in smoking, 3 percent in serum cholesterol, 3 percent in systolic blood pressure, and 1 percent in diastolic blood pressure. The net percent reductions for women were 14 percent, 1 percent, 5 percent, and 2 percent, respectively (Puska, Salonen, Nissinen, et al., 1983). Over a five year period, the age-standardized net percent reduction in heart disease mortality among men in the intervention community, as compared to men in the rest of Finland, was 11 percent (Puska, Nissinen, Tuomilehto, et al., 1985).

Taken together, data from current community-based heart disease prevention programs suggest that community intervention is (a) possible, (b) acceptable to community residents, and (c) effective in changing some indices of health knowledge, behavior, and (in the case of the Finnish project) actual health status. Until data assessing the maintenance of these changes are collected, definitive conclusions about the efficacy of community intervention is probably best delayed. On the other hand, it is evident from a variety of sources that continued research and application of community health promotion programs is justified. All researchers in this field recognize that there are limitations to their efforts. They also recognize that their accomplishments in changing individual and community health provide adequate justification for fine-tuning and expanding their efforts.

As noted previously, these community programs were developed with the explicit intent of generalizability and cost effectiveness (Farquhar et al., 1983). Some data addressing this question come from the Finnish project, in which it was estimated that about one percent of smokers in Finland achieved at least a six month cessation rate with a cost of approximately $1.00 for each six month "success" (McAlister, Puska, Koskela, Pallonen, & Maccoby, 1980). A cost analysis comparing alternative smoking cessation strategies in the Stanford Five City Project supported the greater cost-effectiveness of community-wide approaches (Altman, Flora, Fortmann, & Farquhar, 1987). Additional cost analyses of community interventions are a necessary prerequisite to adequately interpreting their merits and potential for generalizability (Altman, 1986a).

COMPONENTS OF COMMUNITY-BASED INTERVENTIONS

Community interventions have been influenced by a variety of theoretical perspectives. As noted previously, however, these programs have not been guided by an ecological/contextual perspective. Later in the chapter, the potential advantages of this perspective will be elucidated. The most prominent theories or perspectives guiding community interventions to date include community organization and development, social marketing, communication–behavior change theory, and diffusion theory (Farquhar, Maccoby, & Wood, 1985; Solomon & Maccoby, 1984). The specific interventions developed by these programs have been diverse and innovative, drawing on both psychological and public health approaches. The typical intervention components include mass media, screening, behavioral strategies, community activation, and environmental policy strategies. Each of these are reviewed briefly below.

Mass Media

Most community programs use television, radio, newspapers, pamphlets, and other media to provide community members with basic information on relevant risk factors and methods for making behavioral changes to reduce their risk (Farquhar et al., 1983; Blackburn et al., 1984; Lasater et al., 1984). In addition, informational and behavioral print materials distributed through direct mail and at points of purchase (e.g., supermarkets, restaurants, libraries, worksites) have been utilized to complement broadcast messages and to advance behavioral skills in these areas (Davis-Chervin, Rogers, & Clark, 1985).

The reliance on mass media in community prevention programs is predicated on some intriguing figures on media utilization. For example, in the typical U.S. home, the television is on over seven hours per day (*San Francisco Chronicle*, 1985), and on any given day, 65 percent of the population will watch television (Lau, Kane, Berry, Ware, & Ray, 1980). Upon graduation from high school, students will have had an average of 12,000 hours of formal education and 22,000 hours of watching television (Lau et al., 1980). Along these lines, Ulene (1980) has argued that media-based health programs can be both informative and commercially successful. The six-minute segment he had on TV twice per week achieved two million patient contact hours and was equivalent to one quarter the amount of time all obstetricians and gynecologists in the country (approximately 20,000 at that time) spend in one year of teaching patients.

One of the limitations of community media campaigns is that an individualized, interactive approach (i.e., one in which information is discussed, written down, repeated, and tailored) often cannot be used. Media-based interventions may also be limited by the following: (a) they may reinforce, rather than change, beliefs or behavior (Budd & McCron, 1981); (b) they may be more effective when opinions are not well established (Budd & McCron, 1981); (c) they may be attended to primarily by people who already believe the message (Tones, 1981); (d) it is difficult to obtain the necessary feedback from the target audience in order to assess impact (Tones, 1981);

(e) most people use mass media for entertainment, not for education (Lau et al., 1980); (f) mass media programs must compete against numerous other programs and commercials taking opposing viewpoints (Lau et al., 1980); and (g) health promotion programs cannot usually have the reach of commercial programs because of difficulties in garnering media access and may have to dilute health messages to satisfy the needs of collaborating organizations (e.g., a dairy council) (see chapter 4).

A strategy used in the Stanford Five City Project to increase the interactiveness of electronic media was to use television and radio programs that allowed (and encouraged) people to apply the information presented to their own particular situation. For example, an hour-long television show ("The Heart Health Test") incorporated a self-monitoring component by allowing time for viewers to assess and record their own health-related behaviors. The show then provided viewers information with which to evaluate and change, if necessary, their lifestyle. Thus, a potentially sterile television show that only provided information was transformed into one that was proactive, by allowing viewers to immediately apply the information provided to their particular interests and concerns.

Another strategy used by the Stanford group was to combine electronic and print interventions to increase the likelihood that tailored information was provided. For example, a self-help quit smoking workbook ("Cool Turkey") was developed to help smokers quit. To increase the reach and effectiveness of this program, a parallel radio series was developed which helped smokers run through the "Cool Turkey" course and provided additional information on quitting (presented by an expert on smoking cessation). The program generated a great deal of interest because a popular disk jockey worked with the smoking cessation expert, on the air, for one week in an effort to quit smoking himself with the "Cool Turkey" course. Moreover, listeners of the radio program were provided a phone number to call to receive additional information on smoking cessation. Thus, the effectiveness of a simple self-help print media program was bolstered by including a radio series, modeling opportunities, and personalized feedback over the telephone (cf. McAlister et al., 1980).

A final strategy worth mentioning is a telemarketing procedure implemented in the Pawtucket Heart Health Program (Schwertfeger, Elder, Cooper, Lasater, & Carleton, 1986). In this effort, 4000 residents of the intervention community were contacted over the telephone by volunteers (using random digit dialing procedures) and asked if they were interested in receiving self-help behavior change materials or in attending health behavior change groups that were being organized. This effort resulted in about 400 people participating in the heart health program. In addition, an important side effect was that the community volunteers who made the calls learned about the program and would probably be future community health opinion leaders. This telemarketing approach, like the Stanford strategies described above, are effective in recruiting program participants who might not be recruited using traditional strategies. In addition, the approach of combining intervention strategies used in these projects can improve the ability of mass media to provide personalized attention and feedback.

Social Marketing

Social marketing is a way of bridging the gap between community prevention approaches, with their increased potential for reaching large numbers of people, and individually based programs, in which tailoring can be accomplished. As discussed in chapter 2, a social marketing approach emphasizes the tailoring of programs to specific needs of targeted population segments through careful delineation of the "product" (e.g., regimen requirements and complexity), place (e.g., convenience factors), price (i.e., psychological, physical, and financial), and promotion (Kotler, 1975). As a consequence, the health professional increases the possibility of health behavior change by developing and delivering the 'right' information to the 'right' people at the 'right' time and place. This differs from a strict information dissemination approach, in which the focus is typically on saturating the community with general health information. Most of the large-scale heart disease prevention programs use social marketing as a central element in program design and implementation (Lefebvre, Harden, Rakowski, Lasater, & Carleton, 1987).

Screening for Risk Factors

Some community-based programs use screening and health monitoring systems as a conduit for directing individuals into more formal health care systems, where education and instruction can take place. Although screening programs which are unintrusive and located in high volume settings have the potential for reaching large numbers of people, they often suffer from the problem of reaching individuals who are already "converted" (i.e., who have healthy lifestyles) while not reaching those individuals at highest risk. The Minnesota Heart Health Program, however, has been successful in screening a majority of the residents in their intervention communities. It is important to recognize that screening is effective only to the extent that those screened take a follow-up action (e.g., maintain current behavior, change current behavior, seek professional assistance, inform others of screening opportunity, and so on). Thus, screening should be viewed as a preliminary step in improving the health of community residents.

If successful, community screening, with follow-up, can be a very effective educational tool with which to instruct community residents on achieving a healthful lifestyle. Its cost-effectiveness relative to other interventions is yet to be assessed adequately. Community screening programs can also be effective in advertising dates and locations of health programs, providing information to residents about where to obtain information they desire, and triaging individuals to specialized health services.

One alternative to infrequent, nonsystematic, and incomplete screening programs is the use of fairly continuous self-monitoring systems involving low-cost, easy-to-use procedures which the individual can carry out (Levin, 1976) with or without the aid of specific equipment: For example, in the area of smoking, portable alveolar carbon monoxide ecolyzers can be located at the worksite or in other community locations (Scott, Denier, Prue, & King, 1986). In recent years, this health screening strategy has become more prominent — for example, blood pressure meters in supermarkets and pharmacies, heart rate meters in shopping malls, and three-minute cholesterol screening machines (i.e., reflotrons) provided in physician offices, at health fairs, and at a variety of community events. Even with these technologies, the issue of referral follow-up remains an important challenge.

Behavioral Strategies

Behavioral approaches offer useful tools for enhancing adherence to individually focused curative and preventive regimens (e.g., Epstein & Cluss, 1982; Martin & Dubbert, 1982). With appropriate modification, at least some of these strategies can be applied to community efforts.

Given the utility of immediate consequences in aiding long-term behavior change, it is important to develop methods of increasing positive consequences immediately surrounding a behavior and decreasing any positive consequences experienced as a result of non-adherence. By the same token, bringing negative consequences of long-term non-adherence into the person's immediate environment can aid in motivating continued adherence to regimens for which major health consequences may only be experienced in the future. On the community level, as on the individual level, this can be accomplished through repeated provision of health information emphasizing both the immediate positive consequences for adherence (e.g., in the area of smoking cessation, emphasis on better-smelling breath and clothes, reduction in coughing, monetary savings), and the immediate negative effects of non-adherence (e.g., serving as a poor role model for one's children). In addition, it appears that individuals may in fact be less aware of all the long-term consequences of their health-related behavior patterns than currently thought by many health professionals, particularly in the area of smoking (Warner, 1985). Given this, messages which clearly define the potential hazards associated with a given health practice, coupled with suggestions for making changes, are warranted.

In addition to self-control techniques such as self-monitoring and feed-back, a variety of other behavioral strategies found to be useful in clinic-based adherence programs can be applied successfully to community settings. These include stimulus-control techniques (e.g., increased salience of the appropriate behavior via personal as well as community signs, announcements, and other prompts), and reinforcement control methods (Epstein & Cluss, 1982). Provision of individual and organizational incentives (i.e., reinforcement) for the practice of healthy behavior has also been tried at the community level. For example, some worksites have instituted contests and other incentive-based programs for enhancing adherence to such preventive behaviors as smoking, weight control, and exercise (King, Birkel, Carl, Lovett, & Flora, 1985; King et al., 1987; Kiefhaber & Goldbeck, 1984). The number and variety of potential incentives that worksites can utilize in promoting behavior change makes them particularly attractive (see also chapter 9 on worksites and chapter 3 on incentives). Limitations in using worksites as places to carry out health programs include the potential lack of generalizability from worksite behaviors to behaviors in other settings, the fact that some segments of the population are not often found at worksites (e.g., children, elderly, non-working or self-employed adults), and the difficulty in conducting well-designed evaluation studies that do not disrupt worksite routines. Several community-based contests and incentive programs have, however, been implemented for smoking as well as exercise, with promising short-term results (Brownell & Felix, 1987; King et al., 1987). The long-term impact of such programs on maintenance remains to be seen.

An alternative to implementing behavioral programs directly in community settings is the systematic dissemination of behavioral programs through the mail. Such programs can achieve individual behavior change and also promote behavioral modeling that can lead to diffusion effects (e.g., early adoption of a behavior change by opinion leaders in the community who then serve as role models for later adopters). The use of step-by-step kits and correspondence courses for such behaviors as smoking, weight control, dietary change, and exercise maintenance has been tried, with some success (Sallis et al., 1986).

For example, the Stanford Heart Disease Prevention program has developed a series of self-help kits on smoking cessation, weight control, nutrition, walking, and jogging. These materials provide people with a step-by-step discussion of what needs to be changed, why it needs to be changed, how to maintain change, and what to expect if changes are made. They come with magnets so that "tipsheets," diaries, goals, and so forth can be posted in a prominent place (e.g., refrigerator) to cue individuals to take an action. While "minimal" interventions of this kind can be effective alone, their effectiveness has been increased by combining them with other, more extensive interventions in an overall campaign. A quit smoking kit, for instance, can be offered as part of a community-wide smoking cessation campaign which includes quit smoking classes, incentive-based quit smoking contests, access to physicians prescribing nicotine chewing gum, and a media blitz outlining the dangers of smoking. In short, the effectiveness of a single intervention such as a self-help kit is typically enhanced if it is provided within a larger smoking cessation effort (i.e., synergistic effects among interventions are possible; Jason, Gruder, Martino, Flay, Warnecke, & Thomas, 1987).

Finally, social support has been found to be a significantly potent factor in obtaining adherence to a variety of preventive regimens (Colletti & Brownell, 1982; King & Frederiksen, 1984) in part through the provision of social validation or modeling of appropriate preventive measures (Sensenig & Cialdini, 1984) and through rewards provided by significant others (Levine & Sorenson, 1984). Methods of expanding the influence of social support to the community level merit attention. The SHDPP, utilizing diffusion of innovation theory, has worked to diffuse prevention information and strategies from individuals who are social opinion leaders, and who have been successful in maintaining preventive behaviors, to members of their own social network (Cirksena et al., 1985). This approach offers the possibility of supplying ongoing and personal feedback, advice, and motivational support to individuals who otherwise might not be reached.

Community Activation

Researchers and community leaders recognize that the effectiveness of mass media and behavioral interventions can be enhanced by attending to issues surrounding community organization and development (i.e., understanding and utilizing the community context). Encouraging the active involvement of community groups in the design and implementation of interventions can enhance program delivery and reach, improve the likelihood that individual and organizational behavior change will be maintained, and encourage the ownership and eventual control of interventions by the community, leading to maintenance beyond the formal period of research funding. All community interventions commit significant time and resources to community activation. While there are different methods of achieving activation, the goals of activation — collaboration, feedback, and eventual community ownership — all influence the efforts of community interventionists. Because of the importance of long-term maintenance of interventions (i.e. ownership), this issue is discussed fully later in the chapter.

A variety of theorists and practitioners have proposed models of community organization and development (see Pentz 1986 for a review). A systematic approach to community organization has been proposed by Pentz (1986): (a) identify the target population; (b) conceptualize the community unit (i.e., demographically, ethnographically, and socially); (c) identify community leaders (i.e., gatekeepers and opinion leaders); (d) convene a meeting of community leaders to achieve a consensus on problem definition and to adopt a strategic plan; (d) establish a program coordinating committee; (e) conduct program planning and train program implementers; (f) implement program; and (g) maintain program efforts through process monitoring a feedback to implementers. While there hardly exists a single way to activate communities for health promotion, Pentz' model illustrates that there can be a technology of community organization that is systematic — that is, community organization is not necessarily dependent upon the unique artistic or speaking abilities of individual(s) savvy to community politics.

Another community activation approach involves instruction of volunteers and non-health professional community members (e.g., teachers, clergy) in the dissemination of health information and programs (Lefebvre, Lasater, Carleton & Peterson, 1987). As a result of their occupations, these people often have access to individuals who might otherwise not seek out information on lifestyle management. The Pawtucket Heart Health Program has developed a comprehensive and innovative system for using volunteers (Lefebvre, 1987). In the first three years of their intervention, for example, they recruited almost 900 volunteers who invested over 30,000 hours of their time. Volunteers are used in a variety of roles: administration, behavior-change counselors, and heart health coordinators in community organizations. By recruiting volunteers, the Pawtucket program has greatly extended its ability to promote healthy lifestyles and environments in the intervention community.

Environmental and Policy Approaches

Given the burden of the costs of a treatment-laden health care system, environmental and policy interventions fostering the practice of positive health-related behaviors (DeLeon & Vandenbos, 1984) are relevant and timely to community interventions. The argument for this stems from the observation that behavior is affected as much by political, economic, legislative, and cultural influences as by personality, behavioral, and medical (i.e., individual) factors. As a result, the focus of intervention must be multifaceted (Levine & Sorenson, 1984; Williams, 1982). As was noted in chapter 1, public health approaches (e.g., economic and social change, environmental controls, immunizations, health education), rather than medical advances, have been the primary force lowering morbidity and mortality in the past

100 years (Terris, 1981). It should be noted, however, that some health behaviors may be difficult to change because they are deeply embedded within the sociocultural context (Levine & Sorenson, 1984).

The significance of including environmental and policy issues in community health promotion, largely lacking in recent community-based health promotion programs, is evident when practices on the part of the federal government that encourage unhealthy behavior are examined. This is perhaps best illustrated by the disparity between the contribution of behavior to morbidity and mortality (around 50%) (USDHEW, 1979) and the amount of money spent on prevention (about 2.5% in 1978; Cormier, Prefontaine, MacDonald, & Stuart, 1980). Although federal funding for health promotion and disease prevention has increased since 1978, there still seems to be a disparity between the key contributors to health status (i.e., behavior) and where most of the federal money is applied (i.e., expensive technological treatment).

Although some policies may only be implemented on state or federal levels (e.g., food labeling, automobile safety devices in cars, regulations concerning third-party payments, taxation policies), others are amenable to implementation on a community level. Examples of environmental and policy strategies relevant to community prevention programs include point of choice or point of purchase information focusing on the potential health effects of a product (e.g., food items, tobacco products); availability of safe, convenient, and attractive places to perform healthy behaviors such as exercise (King, Haskell, Houston-Miller, & Blair, 1988; Martin & Dubbert, 1982); smoking policies in public places; worksite safety regulations; environmental policies facilitating health-related behavior (e.g., bicycle paths); and inclusion of relevant health promotion information and strategies in educational curricula.

Although it is sometimes difficult to implement strategies that automatically protect people (i.e., passive prevention), the obstacles to implementing these are usually cultural, social, economic, and political rather than technological. In the case of air bags in cars, for example, it has been determined unequivocally that air bags would dramatically reduce injury and death from car accidents (Williams, 1982). Unfortunately, few cars are equipped with this protection, due primarily to economic concerns of the automobile industry.

It is clear that environmental and policy approaches to promoting health can be used in community health promotion programs. To date, however, these programs (with some exceptions, particularly in worksites) have relied more on mass media and educational approaches to promoting health behavior change. The next generation of community studies would benefit from incorporating macro-level interventions. The case study on smoking presented later in the chapter describes specifically how this incorporation might be accomplished.

LIMITATIONS OF COMMUNITY INTERVENTION

There are a variety of limitations with existing community-based interventions (Altman, 1986a). These include the dependence on quasi-experimental research designs, the fact that investigators are not blinded to the experimental conditions, the small numbers of intervention communities, baseline differences between intervention communities and comparison communities, the limited cost analysis data, and the limited knowledge pinpointing the specific effects of interventions as isolated from the effects of other interventions that occur (i.e., component analyses). In addition, there are few qualitative analyses (e.g., through observation, ethnographic strategies, or non-obtrusive measurement) of these interventions. Likewise, additional information on the effects of community interventions on the larger community structure is needed. For example, such interventions could influence the structure and delivery of community health services; the community traditions influencing individual community structure; involvement of community decision makers in health services; the amount of distribution of illness across social or cultural strata; the availability of health services; the political milieu; the physical environment in which health programs operate; and the social norms about health. Thus, a broad-based orientation at multiple levels of analysis would advance the field.

Increased exploration of the constraints of using community approaches to promote healthy behaviors should be undertaken. Aside from financial constraints, it is possible that programs at this level may be more effective for some behaviors (e.g., dietary changes) than for others (e.g., seat belt use). It is also apparent that some behaviors are strongly influenced by environmental factors (e.g., dietary practices) while others may be less so (e.g., dental practices). This is due primarily to the saliency of pressures to engage in unhealthy behavior. In the case of smoking, nutrition, alcohol use, or even sexual activity, for example, there are numerous, if not overwhelming, influences (at all levels of analysis) encouraging people to adopt what health professionals would classify as unhealthy behaviors. This point will be made clear in the final section of this chapter in the discussion on smoking. In contrast, there are few industries that attempt to keep people from exercising. Thus, a campaign to increase the physical activity of community residents is not burdened with many counter-messages, although clearly there are other barriers to increasing physical activity! It is important, then, to understand how community approaches vary based on variables such as targets, methods, and outcomes.

WHAT MAKES COMMUNITY HEALTH PROMOTION SUCCESSFUL?

Based on experiences derived from the TCS, the FCP, and other similar community research, the Stanford group has developed a general set of guidelines with which to evaluate whether community health promotion efforts are likely to succeed (Health Promotion Resource Center, 1987). These guidelines stress that community interventions should attempt to be *comprehensive* and *integrated* for maximal effectiveness. To be comprehensive, a program must address:

• multiple health problems;
• multiple health change goals (e.g., awareness, knowledge, beliefs, motivation, skills, behaviors, maintenance, and environmental and policy change);
• multiple targets of change (e.g., individuals, organizations, environments);
• multiple channels of communication (e.g., face-to-face, mass media);
• multiple strategies for change (e.g., educational, community organization and development, environmental, regulatory);
• multiple evaluation methodologies (e.g., formative, process monitoring, summative, cost analysis).

An effective program must also integrate interventions within the community and combine the efforts of diverse community organizations. *Integration* refers to coordinating interventions, collaborating with existing community organizations, and sequencing implementation plans to take advantage of community events or social norms relevant to the intervention. In short, integration increases the potential effectiveness of interventions by forcing implementers to take into account community-level factors and the potential synergism that multiple interventions can produce.

INSTITUTIONALIZING HEALTH PROMOTION PROGRAMS IN THE COMMUNITY

One of the most important goals of community-based intervention is the long-term maintenance of effects and the collaboration between researchers and community leaders that is at the heart of maintenance. In individually based health promotion efforts, the key players are typically health professionals in a single setting (e.g., hospital or clinic-based physicians, psychologists, dieticians, nurses). In contrast, the success of community programs is often dependent upon the collaboration of professionals, paraprofessionals, and volunteers from various community settings. A community program, because it is often just one of many health programs offered at any given time, must pay particular attention to the social and political milieu in which it is delivered and attend to what marketers call "positioning," or determining a program's distinct niche.

Community-based health research and intervention has matured in the past two decades, from a period characterized by excitement, innovation, and exploration through a period characterized by skills development and increased awareness of its effects on others. These programs now face the tensions associated with adolescence—assumption of responsibility for emerging programs and transfer of programs developed in experimental settings to community controlled programs. One of the challenges is ensuring that interventions designed in research projects are incorporated in the community (Altman, 1986b; Murray, 1986). In the Lewinian tradition of action research, Pekka Puska, a community health researcher from Finland, captures this point (personal communication): "All the scientific work is nothing if nothing happens in the community."

Investigators from these programs have become increasingly concerned about the long-term effects of their programs. Their concern stems from the realization that in many other research areas, termination of research funds for community intervention results in termination of the relationship between researchers and communities and of the programs they have designed, implemented, or administered. It would be unfortunate to develop a program that reduces the cholesterol levels, smoking, obesity, or blood pressure of community residents, for example, only to have the same health problems reappear once the program was terminated. Thus, community researchers need to confront two questions regarding the worth of their efforts to society at large: (a) How can long-term relationships be fostered between researchers and the communities which they study and in which they intervene? (b) How can community interventions designed and implemented by research organizations be useful after the formal phase of research ends? Although there are compelling reasons for community health researchers and professionals to be concerned about incorporation, there has been little discussion in the scientific literature about what this entails and how it can be achieved (Altman, 1986).

Simply stated, incorporation is the *replication* by community organizations of interventions that were originally designed or implemented in research settings; *adaptation* of these interventions to meet specific community needs; and the *innovation* by community organizations of interventions that are, in part, stimulated by a relationship between researchers and the community (Altman, 1986b). Thus, an outcome of incorporation is the exchange of knowledge, resources, strategies, and programs among research organizations and community organizations. In turn, this leads to the implementation of effective and lasting programs in communities and to the development of new scientific questions. Incorporation, however, transcends "mere continuation" of interventions (Huberman & Miles, 1984). As these authors note, structural, procedural, and organizational change supporting the adoption of an innovation is central to the definition of incorporation, as is the process of adaptation and reinvention.

Although it is reasonable for researchers to "do-for or do-to" communities during the research and development phase of a community intervention, a more collaborative orientation (i.e., "doing-with") is necessary for incorporation to occur. Viewing researchers as instruments of community change, rather than as facilitators of community change through empowerment processes, inhibits researchers' contributions to meaningful and long-term community change.

Achieving this change in orientation is certainly no easy task; for most researchers, it will require a paradigm shift (Kuhn, 1970). As noted in the next section, there are numerous barriers to achieving this change, not the least of which is limited funding for comprehensive community programs. On the other hand, successful incorporation would certainly advance the field and make generalizability and social action valid goals of community interventions.

A few psychologists have discussed the issues surrounding incorporation. Miller (1969) called for "giving psychology away" to nonpsychologists as a means of promoting human welfare, Rappaport (1981; 1987) discussed the concept of "empowering" community groups so as to increase their self-determination, and Bales (1970) suggested that " . . . there is no such thing as community research apart from community practice" (p. 271). An empowered community is likely to be committed to assuming responsibility for program delivery thereby increasing the potential for interventions having long-term effects as well as affecting the "hard-to-reach" populations through diffusion of innovations (Rogers, 1983). Research on self- and mutual-help groups (Riessman, 1985), perceived personal control (Janis & Rodin, 1979), learned helplessness (Seligman, 1975), and on self-efficacy (Bandura, 1986) points to the important effects of self-determination. Moreover, empowering communities may engender a stronger sense of community (Sarason, 1974) and could result in communities being more apt to work toward collective goals. Likewise, Wandersman (1981) argued that citizen participation in the research and intervention process has the potential for improving the lives of individuals and communities as well as increasing the quality of data collected by researchers.

In an ideal world, empowerment of a community would include community ownership of all dimensions — of the problem, of the resources to resolve the problem, and of the short-term and long-term solutions to the problem. Empowerment also implies knowledge of when assistance is needed and the ability to access assistance. Researchers certainly could provide some types of technical assistance needed by community groups mounting health promotion programs. Rappaport (1987) articulated the potential of empowerment:

> Empowerment is a pervasive positive value in American culture. The concept suggests both individual determination over one's life and democratic participation in the life of one's community, often through mediating structures such as schools, neighborhoods, churches, and other voluntary organizations. Empowerment conveys both a psychological sense of personal control or influence and a concern with actual social influence, political power, and legal rights. It is a multilevel construct applicable to individual citizens as well as to organizations and neighborhoods; it suggests the study of people in context. (p. 121)

Challenges to Successful Incorporation

The incorporation of research-based programs in the community often challenges the relationships that exist between researchers and communities (Altman, 1986b). These challenges center around the resolution of (a) ownership and control issues; (b) the research focus of investigators versus the service delivery focus of community representatives; (c) different time orientations on the part of researchers and community representatives; (d) the difficulty of ensuring program integrity when ownership is turned over to communities; (e) the tendency to maintain the status quo rather than develop innovative or improved programs; (f) obtaining broad-based community support for incorporation; (g) community reliance on scientific expertise and scientist identity as "the expert"; and (h) limited community resources to carry on programs. The relative importance of these factors will vary for each community–researcher partnership. As noted throughout this book, trying to identify the single explanatory variable or intervention does not account adequately for the complex and multilevel relationships that exist. In the current day and age, however, economic factors certainly restrict many communities' intentions to incorporate community health promotion programs.

Dialectical Perspective on Incorporation

At the root of the relationship between researchers and communities is a conflict characterized by dialectical properties (Altman, Vinsel, & Brown, 1981; Rappaport, 1981). For the researcher concerned with incorporation, a dialectical tension exists between maintaining control over the interventions and empowering the community to assume control. Similarly, there is a dialectical tension for the community between the desire for autonomy and the community's dependence on researchers for their expertise. These tensions continually affect the extent to which incorporation is achieved in complex social environments and are necessary for change to occur. Without recognizing and coping with these tensions, successful community incorporation is difficult to achieve.

The long-term relationships between researchers and communities and the incorporation of interventions developed within a research context are areas ripe for inquiry. It is time once again for the research community to confront the issue of the extent to which research makes a difference to society. This issue has both practical and empirical ramifications. The practical ramifications are perhaps more easily identified and can be summarized under the rubric of the social relevance and utility of science. Scientists, however, must believe that participation results in more valid empirical research and theory. Communities and community researchers need to develop symbiotic relationships. Community researchers should be given the same message that Peace Corps volunteers are given before they embark on community work: "It is important to remember that someday you will no longer be there and the community will have to find the answers to their own problems."

USING THE FRAMEWORK TO ANALYZE SMOKING CONTROL PROGRAMS

Despite some limitations of community-wide approaches to health promotion, there seems to be a general consensus that such approaches complement and supplement individual- and policy-focused health promotion strategies. The purpose of this final section of the chapter is to illustrate how smoking control might be addressed through a comprehensive and integrated community approach. The section uses the framework described in chapter 2 and augments the smoking example provided at the end of that chapter. As noted previously, the framework allows for examination of health-related issues from different perspectives, theories, methods, and data sources, and facilitates a thorough assessment of their benefits and drawbacks.

Problem Definition

Perhaps more than any other health topic, tobacco use has generated a great deal of interest among researchers from numerous disciplines, practitioners, government officials, and, of course, tobacco industry representatives. Psychologists and public health professionals typically approach the smoking and health issue from very different perspectives. Generally speaking, psychologists have directed their attention more to the cessation and prevention of smoking through individual and interpersonal strategies. There is a large literature in psychology on individual factors predicting cigarette use (e.g., personality, behavior pattern, peer pressure). In contrast, public health professionals have focused most of their attention on the policy, regulatory, legislative, and political ramifications of tobacco use. In

1987, for example, the American Public Health Association (APHA) issued policy statements on the taxation, advertising, and promotion of tobacco products (APHA, 1987). They proposed increasing the import duty on tobacco products, increasing federal taxes on tobacco by at least a factor of five, increasing state taxes on tobacco products, and indexing the tobacco tax rate to inflation or to increases on the wholesale price of tobacco products. They also proposed a ban on all media advertising and promotion of all tobacco products.

As noted in a later discussion of intervention strategies, the way in which the smoking problem is defined and the theories and values that emanate from a definition certainly affect how one chooses to intervene. The value structure of the public health community is consistent with being proactive and activist. The APHA, representing public health professionals throughout the country, is outspoken about the smoking issue. In contrast, the American Psychological Association (APA), representing American psychologists, has not taken as strong a public stand on the smoking issue. In fact, *Psychology Today*, a magazine that was owned by the APA with a subscription of close to 1 million readers, accepts a significant amount of tobacco advertisements. Not surprisingly, many members of the APA have protested vehemently about this practice, resulting in lengthy discussions among APA policymakers about how to reduce and eventually phase out tobacco advertising. The magazine was sold by APA in 1988. The point here is that the value structure of psychologists and public health professionals is different and, as a result, the way in which the problem is defined — theoretically and conceptually — is also different.

Levels of Analysis

There are a variety of factors which potentially influence the adoption and maintenance of smoking. With the individual as the fulcrum, these factors range from proximal to distal and can be subcategorized as micro-, meso-, and macro-level factors. For purposes of this discussion, four specific factors are discussed: (a) personal (micro), (b) interpersonal and social (micro/meso), (c) organizational and environmental (meso/macro), and (d) regulatory and policy (macro). To prevent the following case study from being unnecessarily complex, no distinction is made between adoption, cessation, and sustained abstinence of smoking.

The ultimate goal of micro-, meso-, and macro-level interventions is to improve the health status of individuals, since individuals, not systems or environments, experience illness and health. The goals of macro-level interventions (e.g., increasing the tax on cigarettes) can influence the actions that individuals take (e.g., not purchasing cigarettes). Similarly, a goal of many micro-level interventions (e.g., teaching individuals how to get their employer to provide nonsmoking sections in public areas) is to influence actions taken at meso- or macro-levels of analysis (e.g., implementation of a worksite smoking policy). As such, there are interactional and synergistic connections between levels of analysis. The means by which individuals are reached and influenced, however, can be quite different based on the level at which one intervenes. In more cases than not, there is a reciprocity of influence between levels of analysis (see related discussion in chapter 2). There are few examples of programs that focus exclusively on a single level of analysis (Green, 1986). In fact, Green suggested that individuals and systems are not "mutually exclusive or opposite ends of a political or theoretical continuum (p. 29)."

However, there are few multilevel analyses in the smoking literature. Even analyses of smoking behavior from a sociocultural perspective do not carry the multilevel analogy to its fullest (e.g., Syme & Alcalay, 1982). In a review article on relapse with addictive substances, for example, Brownell, Marlatt, Lichtenstein, and Wilson (1986) proposed an organizing framework for understanding the determinants and predictors of lapse and relapse. They classified variables on the basis of individual and interpersonal factors, physiological factors, and environmental and social factors. Environmental and social factors, however, were defined narrowly as social support and immediate environmental stimuli and external contingencies (e.g., social pressure, cues from situations previously associated with the addictive behavior). Their conceptualization does not account for meso- and macro-level factors as defined earlier.

A similar perspective is evident in the 1987 report on smoking and health submitted by the U.S. Department of Health and Human Services — to Congress (USDHHS, 1987a). In this national status report, four factors affecting smoking behavior were outlined — physiological, psychological, cognitive, and social-demographic. The social and demographic factors discussed were social support, socioeconomic and occupational status, age, race, and sex. Later in the volume, community-wide and worksite smoking programs were reviewed. On a more positive note, Schwartz (1987) wrote what is probably the most comprehensive review of smoking cessation methods ever written. Although he did not review macro-level strategies very much, the report otherwise provides a comprehensive discussion of the literature on smoking cessation methods and should be included in the "must read" category for professionals interested in antismoking efforts.

For the most part, however, the dominant perspective on smoking control among the federal government and the scientific community (with the exception of many public health professionals) does not give meso- or macro-level variables very much attention in terms of their direct and indirect contributions to the adoption and maintenance of smoking. A notable exception to this is a review article by Iverson (1987) in which he summarized, using a general multilevel perspective, factors influencing smoking behavior.

He reviewed worksite, school, community, physician, policy, and economic smoking control programs and argued that all must be considered in a comprehensive smoking control effort.

Because analyses of meso- and macro-level influences on smoking behavior have not been as common as analyses of micro-level influences, more attention in this section will be directed toward macro-level variables. A true multilevel analysis considers each level as equally important—that is, each level defines and is interdependent with all other levels.

Two schematic representations of smoking behavior are presented in Figure 5.1. The top schematic suggests that smoking behavior can be influenced by each level of analysis directly and through interactions between levels. It also suggests that variables within a level of analysis can influence other variables within that level and variables at other levels. The bottom schematic represents an ecological interpretation of smoking behavior. The ribbon signifies the multiple and synergistic effects on smoking behavior of variables at multiple levels of analysis. As will be noted in the sections to follow, we argue that smoking behavior is influenced by factors working together at multiple levels of analysis. As one brief example, if adolescents are taught social resistance skills in a school program but can easily purchase cigarettes from local stores, the effectiveness of the school program will be diminished significantly. On the other hand, if adolescents get consistent messages from multiple sources that smoking is undesirable, it is less likely that they will smoke. This multilevel/ecological orientation to smoking control will be discussed throughout the rest of the chapter.

Personal Level

There is a large literature on the relationship between personal-level variables (e.g., occupational status, personality, stress, mood, self-efficacy, age, sex, knowledge, attitudes toward smoking, and degree of nicotine addiction) and smoking behavior (Brownell et al., 1986; USDHHS, 1987a). These variables can act synergistically with variables at other levels of analysis to influence smoking.

One personal-level variable that has received a great deal of attention from both smoking and antismoking advocates is the public's knowledge about smoking. The conventional belief is that both smokers and nonsmokers are well aware of the dangers of smoking. How can they not be, when each package of cigarettes is labeled with a warning describing some of the dangers? This point is made vivid in the following excerpt from a letter received in 1987 by an antismoking advocacy group from a smoking advocate who was upset about negative statements made about the tobacco industry:

> You disparage kids' and parents' intelligence, making them seem stupid dupes of your targets, the tobacco companies. People are smarter than you think—

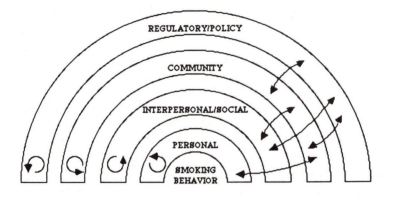

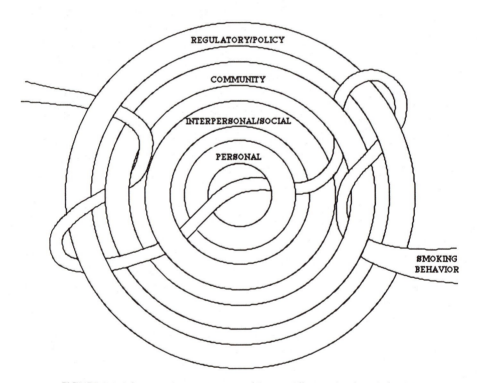

FIGURE 5.1. Schematic Representations of Factors Affecting Smoking Behavior

they can make up their minds about smoking, balancing advertising and your kind's hysteria.

Survey data about the knowledge of smoking, however, suggest an alternative viewpoint (Warner, 1986a). It seems clear that most people recognize that smoking causes cancer. This knowledge appears to be superficial—

many do not realize that smoking reduces life expectancy, is the principal cause of lung cancer, and that lung cancer is typically fatal. Moreover, knowledge that smoking is related to heart disease, chronic obstructive lung disease, and problems during pregnancy is "soft" (Warner, 1986a). Perhaps most disturbing is the misunderstanding of the hazards of smoking low-tar and nicotine cigarettes. The idea that the tobacco industry has developed a "safe" cigarette is accepted by some people. For example, when R. J. Reynolds announced they had developed the "cleanest" cigarette (one in which the smoke is not visible to the human eye), it resulted in confusion among the general public about the effects of smoking. It is likely that many people equate "clean" with safe and will smoke the R. J. Reynolds "smokeless" cigarette for health reasons. This would be unfortunate because this cigarette emits the same amount of addicting nicotine, carbon monoxide, and a host of other unknown, possibly harmful constituents as does any other cigarette.

Warner (1986a) summarized the evidence on the public's knowledge of smoking as follows:

> . . . the public ranks smoking as a hazard in the same category as toxic dumps, saccharine, EDB in muffin mix, moderate overweight, and so on. That is, there is little differentiation of the degree of hazard, and hence the importance of not smoking becomes diluted by the perception that smoking is simply one more ingredient in an environmental soup of risks to health. Finally, careful research has revealed that smokers do not personalize the risks of smoking. They acknowledge them, but they perceive them to be 'other people's problems.'

Interpersonal/Social Level

Research on the effects of interpersonal and social factors related to smoking behavior has also attracted considerable research attention (USDHHS, 1987a). Variables in this domain include peer pressure, family stress, social reinforcement to adopt smoking, the attitudes and behaviors of authority figures such as physicians (e.g., many physicians do not advise their patients to quit smoking), teachers, athletes and peers, and factors related to the home environment (e.g., single-parent families, student employment, and latchkey children). Overall, the research evidence suggests clearly that some of these variables are important determinants of smoking behavior. Perhaps the most widely studied variable in this regard is peer pressure (Botvin, 1986; Evans, 1980; Harkin, 1987; Klepp, Halper, & Perry, 1986). A variety of programs that increase the ability of adolescents to practice social resistance skills have been designed and implemented with some success (Schwartz, 1987).

Organizational/Environmental Level

Factors at the community level of analysis as they relate to smoking have received considerably less attention than variables at the personal or interpersonal/social level of analysis. Examples of organizational/environmental variables include workplace smoking policies, access to cigarette vending machines, restaurant policies regarding smoking sections, warning labels at the point of purchase of cigarettes, billboard advertising, cigarette advertising, free distribution of cigarettes, the importance of smoking control vis-à-vis other community concerns, and behavior settings conducive to smoking. Many of these variables (e.g., cigarette advertising in community settings) overlap with the discussion to follow on variables in the regulatory/policy level, and therefore will not be reviewed here.

Regulatory/Policy Level

The next section, drawn from Altman (in press), reviews cigarette advertising and promotion, censorship in the popular press, taxation, access to cigarettes by youth, public events surrounding smoking and health, smoking in public places, and government support of the tobacco industry. These variables, in synergistic relationships with variables at other levels of analysis, affect the adoption, cessation, and sustained abstinence of smoking. Table 5.2 summarizes policy factors, their potential effects on smoking rates, and the pro-health position on each factor.

Cigarette Advertising Practices. The tobacco industry spent $2.5 billion dollars in 1985 on advertising and promotion expenditures while public and private counteradvertising totalled about $5 million, a 400-fold difference (Federal Trade Commission—FTC, 1986; Warner, 1986b). In 1988, the to-

Table 5.2. Summary of Regulatory/Policy Factors Affecting Smoking Behavior

Factor	Health Promotion Position	Potential Effects on Smoking Rates
Advertising and Promotion	Total ban	Substantial
Self-Censorship in the Press	Increase coverage of ill effects of tobacco and of tobacco industry practices	Moderate
Taxation Policy	Increase taxes	Substantial
Access to Tobacco by Minors	Increase compliance with existing laws and promote stronger laws	Substantial
Media Practices and Modeling	De-glamorize tobacco use	Moderate
Public Events re: Smoking and Health	Fund a comprehensive antismoking campaign	Moderate
Regulations re: Smoking in Public Places	Strive for a smoke-free society	Moderate

bacco industry figure is expected to be close to $3 billion. Expenditures have increased considerably in the past few decades, climbing from about $261 million in 1964 to its current level. Among all products, expenditures for cigarette advertising are first in outdoor media, second in magazines, and third in newspapers (Davis, 1987). One of the outcomes of the 1971 ban on radio and television advertising of cigarettes was the removal of the equal time requirement for antismoking advertisements (i.e., the Fairness Doctrine). This is significant since the antismoking ads were quite effective (Hamilton, 1972; Teel, Teel, & Beardon, 1979; Warner, 1986a). One analysis (Hamilton, 1972) suggested that the antismoking ads were twice as effective as the smoking ads. The effectiveness of an antismoking PSA and advertising campaign is enhanced if a variety of novel ads are aired, the ads are disseminated broadly, saturation is high, and ads are aired over an extended period of time (Flay, 1987).

People are barraged with cigarette advertisements each and every day. In the case of billboards, over 40,000 in this country contain ads for cigarettes (Lippman, 1986). And an analysis of eight popular magazines found that in 1985, the average number of tobacco advertisements in each issue was approximately six (Albright, Altman, Slater, & Maccoby, 1988). The targets of magazine tobacco ads have changed since 1960, with more attention in recent years to youth, women, and minorities (Albright et al., 1988; Davis, 1987; Ernster, 1985). In addition, the tobacco industry targets different demographic groups with customized, and inherently appealing, ads. Magazines with large youth readerships, for example, receive disproportionately more ads with recreation and risk or adventure themes, while women's magazines receive disproportionately more ads with romantic and erotic themes (Altman, Slater, Albright, & Maccoby, 1987).

Citing data from the FTC, Davis (1987) noted that promotional expenditures (e.g., promotional allowances, sampling distribution, distribution bearing name, distribution not bearing name, public entertainment, and so on) have increased rapidly compared to advertising expenditures (from 26 percent in 1975 to 48 percent in 1984). These data may represent a subtle change in the tactics of tobacco advertisers away from manifest (obvious) promotional strategies to more latent strategies.

The tobacco industry continues to maintain, despite a great deal of public and professional protests to the contrary, that their advertising strategies are designed to influence current smokers to switch brands rather than to attract nonsmokers, such as women and youth. Examining the brand switching argument of the tobacco industry by using simple mathematical logic raises questions about the intent of cigarette advertisers (Warner, 1986a). Each year, about 1 million smokers die and 1.5 million quit smoking. Therefore, the tobacco industry must recruit about 2.5 million new smokers each year just to maintain (not increase) the current smoking prevalence rate. Since 60 percent of smokers begin smoking by the age of 14 and 90 percent by the end of their teenage years, 5000 children and teenagers would have to start smoking each day of the year for the tobacco industry to maintain the smoking prevalence rate (Johnston, 1986; Warner, 1986a). Moreover, the six million-plus teenagers who smoke cigarettes spend nearly $1 billion each year on tobacco products (Joe B. Tye, personal communication, February, 1988).

There are additional facts that negate the tobacco industry position: (a) only 10% of smokers switch brands each year (FTC, 1985); (b) over two thirds of existing cigarette brands are owned by Phillip Morris and R. J. Reynolds, indicating that most brand switching occurs between brands owned by the same company; (c) assuming a brand switching argument, in 1983 the tobacco industry would have spent about $346 for every smoker who switched brands at the same time that the after-tax profits generated by the average smoker was about $80.00, thereby resulting in significant monetary losses (Tye, Warner, & Glantz, 1987); and (d) expenditures for cigarette advertising in magazines with large young male and female readerships is high (Hutchings, 1982). In addition, one Australian study (Chapman & Fitzgerald, 1982) and one British study (Ledwith, 1984) report data indicating that adolescents are in fact aware of specific cigarette advertisements and of the promotional tactics used by tobacco companies to support sporting events.

Thus, to understand smoking behavior, we must consider the powerful influences of tobacco advertising.

Self-censorship in the Popular Press. Popular women's magazines that accept cigarette advertisements, on average, publish from 12–63 times as many articles on nutrition, contraception, stress, and mental health as they do on smoking (Warner, 1985; Whelan, Sheridan, Meister, & Mosher, 1981). An analysis of 12 women's magazines during a 12-year period from 1967 to 1979 found that the mean number of antismoking or smoking cessation articles published was 2 (range 0 to 11). The one magazine that did not accept cigarette advertising, *Good Housekeeping*, ran a total of 11 articles during this time period. In contrast, the 12 magazines containing cigarette ads ran an average of 4.5 articles on stress, 8.6 on nutrition, 9.3 on contraceptives, and 21.5 on mental health (Whelan et al., 1981). The blatant inattention to the hazards of smoking was clearly evident. One of these articles was entitled "The ABC's of Preventive Medicine" and ran through the alphabet providing health advice for each letter. Smoking or tobacco was not mentioned! It must be noted here again that the popular psychology magazine sold in 1988 by the American Psychological Association (*Psychology Today*) accepts a significant amount of tobacco advertising. Notwithstanding the necessity of this policy vis-à-vis economic factors, it is an unfortunate and ironic situation for the discipline of psychology whose mission is to improve the health and well being of people.

The important point of this discussion is how censorship may affect consumers' smoking-related knowledge, attitudes, and ultimately behaviors. As reviewed earlier in the chapter, survey data indicate that in fact the typical citizen in this country does not know about the specific health risks of smoking (Warner, 1986a). In an environment of responsible media coverage of the health risks of smoking, it is probable that fewer people would adopt smoking and more people would quit smoking (Warner, 1985).

Taxation of Cigarettes. The taxation of cigarettes is regulated federally and in each state (USDHHS, 1987a). As of 1987, North Carolina had the lowest tax rate per pack (2 cents) while Maine had the highest (28 cents). The tax rates on cigarettes and their effects on the retail price of a pack of cigarettes are strongly related to smoking behavior. Warner (1986c) noted that an 8 cent *decrease* in the federal cigarette excise tax would result in about one million young people ages 12–25 and several hundred thousand adults adopting smoking (i.e., elasticity of demand is high). Conversely, an 8–16 cent *increase* in the tax would encourage 1–2 million young people and 800,000 to 1.5 million adults to either quit smoking or to not take up the habit. Sensitivity to cigarette prices (i.e., elasticity of demand) is inversely related to age, due in part to the fact that young people tend to be less addicted to nicotine and on average have less disposable income than older adults (Warner, 1986c). Thus, increasing the price of cigarettes through increasing taxes on tobacco is one of the most effective ways to prevent or stop smoking among large groups of people, especially those under the age of 25. This strategy is a persuasive example of the effects that macro-level variables have on individual behavior.

Income generated by taxes on tobacco can be earmarked specifically for health-related research or for school health education programs. Unfortunately, however, only six states use money generated from taxes on tobacco to support health-related programs (Alaska, Idaho, Kentucky, Louisiana, Nebraska, and New Jersey). Moreover, it is unfortunate that only 18 states require elementary and secondary schools to instruct students on the dangers of tobacco and just 3 states implement in-service training programs for school staff on the effects of tobacco.

The authors are unaware of empirical data examining the effects on either smoking behavior or social norms of earmarking tobacco taxes to health-related research or school health education programs. The topic seems ripe for investigation. Our interpretation of the current state policies toward this issue is that the minimal state support for health concerns sets a tone that could influence social norms. Moreover, it would be interesting to examine whether states that use tobacco tax revenue for health research and intervention programs would, overall, be committing more money to negating the negative health effects of tobacco than states that do not use tax revenue for these purposes.

One policy alternative is to earmark a few pennies of the federal excise tax on tobacco for a media antismoking campaign. One penny would generate about $300 million in annual revenue, enough for a sizeable campaign. For the typical smoker who consumes a pack and a half a day, this would add about $5.50 more each year. If five cents were earmarked, $1.5 billion would be generated and each smoker would pay about $27 each year (Warner, 1986a). Warner (1986b) noted persuasively:

> The beauty of this proposal, in addition to its independence from tobacco advertising per se, is that the revenue to combat tobacco use would shrink automatically as the campaign worked and hence as the need for it diminished: as tobacco use fell, the tax yield would decrease proportionally. The campaign would self-destruct as Americans ceased their self-destructive tobacco habits.

Federal income tax policy also relates to smoking (at least under tax laws in the early 1980s). An interesting medical tax deduction allowed by the Internal Revenue Service is for meals and lodging provided during treatment for substance abuse (drugs, alcohol). The IRS does not allow, however, deductions for smoking cessation programs or other preventive measures (Syme & Alcalay, 1982).

Access to Cigarettes and Legal Age of Minors. Obviously, access to cigarettes is a critical determinant of whether people (particularly children and adolescents) experiment with or maintain smoking behaviors. Ten states (20%) do not regulate the sale to or use of tobacco by minors (Colorado, Georgia, Kentucky, Louisiana, Montana, New Hampshire, New Mexico, Virginia, Wisconsin, and Wyoming) and two states permit its towns, cities, and municipalities to enact such ordinances (Missouri, South Dakota). Only 21 states prohibit the sale or furnishing of cigarette wrapping papers and related paraphernalia to minors. There is wide variability in how states define minors. Hawaii defines a minor as anyone under the age of 15, while Utah and Alabama are the most restrictive, defining minors as those under the age of 19.

Access to cigarettes for adults has been treated by states in some rather strange ways. For example, in South Carolina, cigarettes confiscated from dealers who failed to pay taxes are donated to mental patients residing in state facilities. And as a measure of the power of nicotine addiction (or of prison officials), prison officials in Pennsylvania and Kentucky have the authority to grant or withhold smoking privileges from inmates so as to control inmate behavior (USDHHS, 1987a).

Enforcing existing laws that regulate access to cigarettes among underage youth has recently become a key strategy in the armamentarium of tactics used by antismoking advocates. The need for this strategy is evident in an incident told to the third author (DA) by Joe B. Tye, Executive Director of Stop Teenage Smoking of Tobacco (STAT) (personal communication, March, 1987). Joe took his 14-year-old babysitter, braces and all, to 38 retail stores that sold cigarettes in Santa Clara County, California. California law states that no person under the age of 18 can purchase cigarettes. Almost unbelievably, 95 percent of the stores (36 of 38) sold cigarettes to the 14-year-old. Similarly, in nine communities throughout the state of Massachusetts, an 11-year-old girl was successful in purchasing cigarettes in 75 of 100 stores (DiFranza, Borwood, Garner, & Tye, 1987). Only 4 percent of the stores had a copy of the law posted and 36 percent either were unaware of the law or could not identify the legal age for purchasing cigarettes. Clearly, the social norms surrounding smoking facilitate, if not encourage, the adoption of this behavior among underage youth.

Promotion of Cigarettes at Social, Educational, Artistic, and Athletic Events. Promoting cigarettes at various public events is a major strategy of the tobacco industry. Examples of such promotion includes the Virginia Slims tennis tournaments, the Winston rodeo series, the Marlboro country music series, the Kool Jazz Festival, John Player Special motor racing, Kool Achiever Awards (for adults who improve the quality of inner-city communities), Phillip Morris sponsorship of a nationally shown Turkish art exhibit in 1987, and the omnipresent cigarette billboards in stadiums and public arenas. There have even been reports of cigarette companies distributing free cigarettes to youth at rock concerts (Whelan et al., 1981).

The effects of this type of promotion on the knowledge and attitudes of children and adolescents were examined in the United Kingdom (Aitken, Leathar, & Squair, 1986). The authors reported that most children understood the concept of sponsorship, and many were actually able to associate specific brands with sponsored sports by the time they were in late elementary or early junior high school.

In a 1987 column in the *San Francisco Chronicle*, Glenn Dickey noted cogently some of the economic, political, and ethical challenges that the Women's International Tennis Association (WITA) faces as it considers divorcing itself from cigarette company sponsorship. The issues he raises with regard to women's tennis certainly apply to other athletic, musical, and social events:

* The contract. The cigarette company has the right to match any other offer that is made for sponsorship, which makes it very difficult for the tennis association to sell to another company. It's an exercise in futility for another company to make an offer, knowing it will be matched . . . The directors (promoters), especially, are not eager to change the deal. The cigarette company provides an easy source of money.

* The fragile nature of the women's tennis association. Women's tennis has prospered partially because their organization, unlike the men's, has been very

tightly organized. . . . They have put together strict rules about participation in tournaments, and they have prohibited players from participating in exhibitions at the time of a sanctioned tournament. . . . There is nothing that requires players to belong to the tennis association. The younger players, who did not go through the period when the women's game was suffering, do not necessarily have the same loyalty to the group. So, if the WITA decided to take a stand and drop the cigarette sponsorship — which would mean lower purses, at least in the beginning — the younger players could break with the WITA and play exhibitions for quick money, which would be devastating to the tournaments.

* Loyalty. Those who have been involved for a long time with women's tennis, either playing or in an executive role — or both — remember that the cigarette company financed the tour at a time when no other sponsor would touch it. . . . Cigarette advertising has long been banned on television, but the company banners are plastered everywhere in arena, so those watching televised matches see the company logo on almost every shot. The winners reinforce the image by thanking the company in the public presentations after the matches. The cigarette company is so tied to women's tennis that people refer to the tournament by the company's name. What sponsor would willingly give up that kind of identification? (Dickey, 1987, p. 51)

Media Practices Relative to Modeling of Smoking. The modeling of smoking behavior occurs widely in television and movies. While the prevalence of smoking actors now is less than it was during the period from the 1930s to 1960s, it is still an issue to many antismoking advocates. Cruz and Wallack (1986) conducted a content analysis of routine prime-time television shows in the fall of 1984 (116 hours of programming) and found that there was about one act of smoking during each hour of programming. Almost two-thirds of the smokers were lead characters, males were three times more likely to be smoking than females, and 70 percent of smokers were in "strong or enduring roles" (as opposed to "bad or outside the law"). Moreover, there was only one instance in which the potential desire to quit smoking was portrayed. The rate of smoking acts per hour varied by the type of television show as follows: situation comedies (.36), movies made for TV (.83), dramas (1.01), and movies made for theatres (1.62). This study illustrates vividly the social norms surrounding smoking among television writers, producers, and actors.

In the movie industry, related incidents have been reported. Evidence that consumer products advertised implicitly in movies results in increased sales is evident in the movie *E.T.,* in which the promotion of Reese's Pieces candy resulted in an 85 percent increase in sales. In the movie *Superman II,* Philip Morris paid to have Marlboro displayed prominently throughout the movie. In *Beverly Hills Cop,* there was a great deal of attention given to Lucky Strikes, Kent, and Pall Mall cigarettes. In one scene, the star, Eddie Murphy, steals a truck filled with Lucky Strikes and Pall Malls. When he tries to sell them, he proclaims, "These are very popular cigarettes with the children. I don't smoke Lucky Strikes. I smoke king-size Kent" (*Tobacco and Youth*

Reporter, 1986, p. 11). These examples of the promotion of cigarettes in movies are planned and strategic, rather than coincidental.

The promotion of cigarettes also appears in *Moviegoer* magazine, a free magazine distributed throughout the nation's movie theaters (*Tobacco and Youth Reporter*, 1986). Paid for entirely by R. J. Reynolds and published by the 13–30 Corporation, which edits it for "the young film buff" (quote from *Advertising Age* magazine, cited in *Tobacco and Youth Reporter*, 1986), a recent issue of the magazine had 24 total pages and 5 full pages of cigarette advertisements. As summarized in the *Tobacco and Youth Reporter*:

> Since more than 40 percent of people who attend movies today are under the age of 21 and teenagers are three times as likely as adults to be frequent moviegoers, it would seem that Reynolds has not chosen a very good audience if its only interest is in adult smokers. . . . Practically every issue includes a popular young star on the cover and reviews of movies that are geared toward adolescent audiences. (p. 13)

As an aside, after publication of this issue of the *Tobacco and Youth Reporter*, RJR stopped publication of *Moviegoer* magazine (probably because of the anticipated bad press it would have received from antismoking groups, parent groups, and the like).

Major Public Events Surrounding Smoking and Health. Since the early 1960s, antismoking campaigns, events, and messages have been present in numerous ways — in broadcast media, in narrowcast media, and in community events. In an analysis of the effects of the overall antismoking campaign (with the beginning of the campaign being 1964, with the publication of the Surgeon General's report), Warner reported an econometric analysis showing that in the absence of the campaign, per capita consumption of cigarettes would have been 20 to 30 percent higher by 1975 and 40 percent higher by 1978 (Warner, 1981).

Experiences in Norway lend credence to the idea that a total ban on cigarette advertising as one component to a larger effort may be an effective strategy for preventing the adoption of smoking (Lochsen, Bjartveit, Hauknes, & Aaro, 1983). The campaign in Norway included a ban on all advertising as well as other strategies designed to restrict smoking (e.g., establishment of governmental bodies dealing with smoking, intensification of public education efforts, use of mass media). The data indicate that in the absence of this national effort, smoking rates would have been 23 percent higher over, approximately, a 20-year-period.

Regulation of Smoking in Public Settings. The regulation of smoking in public places is becoming an increasingly popular strategy to protect the health of smokers as well as nonsmokers. There appears to be widespread support for such regulation. In a nationwide Gallup poll conducted in the mid-1980s, 88 percent of all respondents and 80 percent of respondents who smoked thought that some type of worksite smoking policy was advantageous, although only 12 and 4 percent respectively thought that smoking should be banned altogether (Bureau of National Affairs—BNA, 1986). Other examples include the Interstate Commerce Commission restricting smoking to the back 30 percent of buses, the Civil Aeronautics Board requiring airplanes to provide nonsmoking areas (as well as recent legislation banning smoking on domestic flights under two hours), and many cities and counties banning smoking in public places (e.g., by 1986 in California, over 73 had passed ordinances restricting smoking in workplaces) (BNA, 1986; McManus, Taylor, & Patrick, 1987). The Americans for Non-Smokers' Rights (ANSR), an advocacy group in California, estimated that almost 50 percent of the population in California live in areas that protect the rights of nonsmokers (BNA, 1986). To date, no non-smokers' rights bill has been repealed.

The tobacco industry has been aggressive in its attempts to influence public opinion about smoking. In 1983, the tobacco industry spent over $1 million in an effort to prevent passage of a San Francisco ordinance regulating smoking in the workplace. This was 15 times more than what was spent by groups supporting the ordinance (Martin & Silverman, 1986; McManus et al., 1988). The tobacco industry lost the battle as the ordinance passed narrowly (50.4% to 49.6%).

By this point in the discussion on smoking, it should be evident that obtaining an adequate understanding of smoking behavior requires careful assessment of the multiple factors that affect an individual's decision to adopt or maintain smoking. With the previous discussion serving as a general introduction, the next section of the chapter applies the framework explicated in chapter 2 to the design of a comprehensive community health promotion program to prevent smoking.

A Model Community Smoking Control Program

Analysis of the smoking control efforts of community-based health promotion programs illustrates diverse selection of interventions, particularly within personal and interpersonal levels of analysis and to a lesser extent within an organizational/environmental level of analysis. The predominant focus of intervention to date has been on increasing the skills of smokers (e.g., to quit, resist urges, prevent relapse) and the skills of nonsmokers at risk of smoking (e.g., social resistance skills training to decrease the effects of peer pressure to smoke). Few researchers doubt the efficacy of these approaches, which should certainly be part of any community-based smoking control effort.

Noticeably absent from current community-based programs is a strong focus on reducing the policy level influences on smoking behavior. That is,

few programs have addressed the fact that youth have ready access to cigarettes in vending machines and stores; worked with store merchants to en-
force access laws already on the books; put pressure on their local newspapers, magazines, and billboard companies to ban tobacco advertising;
pressured local government to pass nonsmokers' rights bills or ordinances;
pressured worksites to establish a norm of nonsmoking; and so on. The
skills required to engage in community advocacy are not usually within the
repertoire of scientists currently involved in community health promotion.
On the other hand, data suggest that learning these skills would increase the
effectiveness of other more traditional approaches. The American Cancer
Society (1987b,c) has published the first manuals to specifically help people
learn these advocacy skills.

As just one example, when a large worksite in the northwest passed a
smoking ban, eight percent of smokers quit, consumption of cigarettes
among smokers decreased by six cigarettes per day, and the percentage of
smokers attending smoking cessation programs at the worksite increased by
13-fold (Martin, 1987, personal communication). It is unlikely that the cost-
effectiveness of a skills training worksite intervention would be better than a
smoking ban. However, the ban worked synergistically with personal and
group smoking cessation interventions, with the overall effect being greater
than those for a ban or smoking classes alone. This synergism between levels
of analysis has been, and will continue to be, highlighted throughout this
book (see Figure 5.2 for a specific example).

In short, the way in which the smoking problem is defined by community
health promotion interventionists could benefit from expansion. The eco-
logical/contextual model described in the early part of this chapter might
help guide program designers and implementers to approaches that have the
most potential for community activation and change (Trickett, 1987). For
example, recognizing that behavior and the settings in which behavior occurs are interdependent would help programs designers attend to the settings
in which tobacco use is most encouraged and salient (e.g., free distribution
of cigarettes at neighborhood events, tobacco billboards in settings fre-
quented by children, cigarette vending machines near schools, and so forth).
This is in contrast to the approach which assumes that the environment is a
background variable to the beliefs and behaviors of individuals.

Incorporating multilevel interventions into community intervention and
using contextual/ecological theory to guide such efforts will undoubtedly
require some retooling of the staff of these programs and, as noted in the
next section, some careful thought as to how to operationalize the policies
and regulatory strategies that will produce the intended effects. Along these
lines, Flay (1987) reviewed mass media smoking cessation programs and
concluded that while they can be effective, the knowledge necessary for
achieving their maximum impact is seriously lacking. Specifically, he suggested that future generations of mass media programs should use more sophisti-

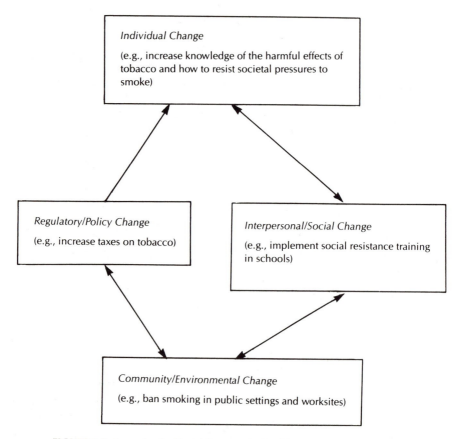

FIGURE 5.2. Example of a Model Community Health Promotion to Prevent the Adoption of Tobacco Smoking

cated evaluation designs and obtain knowledge about what program components were central to program effectiveness (cf. Altman, 1986).

Employing a multilevel contextual approach poses a number of challenges to people involved in designing community health promotion programs. First, it is difficult to parcel out the relative contributions of each level to smoking-related behaviors. Similarly, assessing the relationships and potential synergistic effects between levels is extremely difficult. While there are multivariate data analytic strategies that can model complex relationships such as these (e.g., path analysis, LISREL), it is more than a statistical problem. The critical issue is how behavior is influenced by (and influences) multiple levels in a configuration of place (setting) and time. That is, smoking occurs in a complex web of place and time. It cannot be understood as a behavior influenced by personal-level variables alone, irrespective of where and when the behavior occurs. If this assumption is accepted, then interventions designed to prevent the adoption or promote the cessation of smoking should ideally be designed with consideration to temporal and spatial dimensions and lifespan and developmental variables. Interventions that are effective at certain times, in certain settings, and with certain people of specific ages may not be effective at different places, times, or with different people.

An example of this orientation is in the study of peer pressure to smoke (Evans, 1980). While there is a great deal of research on this topic, most of it is done within the interpersonal/social level of analysis and with little consideration to temporal qualities. One way to increase our understanding of adolescent peer pressure to smoke is to consider the effects that regulatory and policy variables have on peer pressure. For example, easy access to cigarettes (i.e., no enforcement of minimum age purchase laws), low tax rates (and therefore cheaper cigarettes), and advertisements portraying positive interpersonal relationships resulting from smoking may all increase the opportunities for children and adolescents to adopt smoking and may enhance their ability to serve as influences to others. In the case of smoking, peer pressure can only succeed if the substances around which pressure is exerted (e.g., tobacco) are available at a certain time and place and if the resistance to peer pressure among others is low. It is not simply an issue of equipping individuals with resistance skills. The temporal and spatial qualities of peer pressure (i.e., when and where it occurs) and the developmental stage of pressured individuals are also important to consider. It is likely, for example, that the opportunities to exert peer pressure are enhanced after school and before parents return home from work, during social events (e.g., school dances or football games), on weekend nights, and during summer months. To date, the primary research strategy has been on increasing social resistance skills rather than on decreasing availability and access. A multilevel perspective would treat these two levels of influence as potentially synergistic and would examine them within a time/place configuration.

Thus, an "ideal" community-based smoking control program would define the problem comprehensively, address the fact that smoking is influenced by factors at multiple levels of analysis and therefore requires multilevel interventions that work together synergistically, and recognize that the community context and the individuals residing in the community exist in an interdependent relationship.

SUMMARY

Community-based approaches to health promotion and disease prevention hold great promise for improving the health of individuals and communities at large. Some psychologists and public health professionals have contributed to the development of current community health promotion efforts. With the innovative use of public health and psychological theories, intervention methods, and evaluation strategies described in this chapter, there is great potential for developing even more effective programs.

As is evident in our review of smoking control efforts, the more that a community health promotion program can address the smoking problem from multiple levels of analysis, the greater the likelihood that it will counteract the broad range of influences on smoking behavior. Clearly, a multilevel intervention program can be costly and requires skills that many program implementers do not have. On the other hand, one explanation for the lack of multilevel interventions is the narrowness in problem definition.

If the public health community better understood the psychological and behavioral sequelae of smoking (and other health problems) and if the psychology community had a better appreciation of the powerful influence of regulatory/policy variables on smoking (and applied their knowledge of individual behavior change when working with policymakers and social institutions), the high smoking prevalence and incidence rates in this country would likely be reduced significantly. Application of more comprehensive frameworks, such as that described in chapter 2, can help designers and implementers of community health promotion programs move beyond traditional disciplinary constraints and view health problems in a broader context.

SECTION III

SELECTED PROBLEM AREAS

STRIVING FOR AN INTEGRATION OF HEALTH PSYCHOLOGY AND PUBLIC HEALTH PERSPECTIVES

The following section presents a discussion of six problem areas, chosen because of their particular current relevance to our nation's health. As stated previously, our goals in writing each chapter were to attempt a unique or innovative integration of theory, methods, and perspectives offered by the health psychology and public health fields. Thus, while we have tried as much as possible to sample from the broad array of literature currently available for each problem area, the chapters should not be construed as comprehensive reviews of any of the problem areas presented.

Chapter 6 focuses on a discussion of prevention in *mental health*, utilizing what is termed as a developmental (drawn largely from psychology)/ecological (i.e., reflecting the emphasis on environmental factors representative of a public health approach) perspective. This perspective is used in concert with the framework presented in chapter 2, to design an intervention program to meet the challenges and stresses currently facing dual-earner families in this country.

Chapter 7 presents a general overview of the issues and trends found in the *maternal and child/adolescent health* field, with a subsequent in-depth analysis of this nation's current *teenage pregnancy* problem. A developmental/community-based perspective is subsequently applied in exploring the types of intervention strategies that might profitably be brought to bear in stemming the tide of pregnancies occurring among our nation's adolescents.

Nutrition and health is the focus of discussion in chapter 8. Given the relevance of this topic area for all Americans, the framework presented in chapter 2 is extensively applied in describing strategies that involve multiple levels of analysis as well as in designating particular targets and settings for intervention.

Chapter 9 discusses health in the *workplace*. Trends from both public health and health psychology, in relation to health initiatives occurring at and around work, are highlighted. Using the framework as a jumping-off point, the needs and potential opportunities for workplace-based health programming are explored.

Chapter 10 focuses on *environmental health*. The wide range of issues subsumed under this heading, from noise pollution to nuclear war, is staggering. The issue of hazardous waste is used to highlight ways in which health psychology and public health may join forces in advancing solutions. More than any other topic area discussed in the book, the integration of behavioral/psychological processes, environmentally based approaches, and potentially conflicting value systems to enhance intervention efforts in the environmental sphere are seen as vitally critical, not only to the health of our nation but to other nations as well.

Chapter 11 presents discussion focused on health and *aging*. The major dimensions of disability facing individuals as they age — including those involving sensory, somatic, cognitive, and social spheres — are discussed in relation to the types of programming efforts that can occur at different levels of analysis. Theories drawn from clinical psychology are meshed with a preventive perspective in describing how morbidity and dependence can be decreased while quality of life is enhanced in the older years. A multilevel approach is subsequently applied in discussing intervention methods for Alzheimer's disease.

While focusing on different issues and conceptual points, the chapters described above are organized along similar lines. They begin with a description of the current epidemiological data available on the general topic under consideration. For those chapters representing a broad, diverse, and well-researched topic area (e.g., mental health, maternal and child/adolescent health, environmental health), this general epidemiological description is supplemented with an in-depth epidemiological analysis of a specific sub-area of interest (e.g., teenage pregnancy; the hazardous waste problem). Epidemiological discourse is followed by a discussion of the types of trends in conceptualization and intervention represented by traditional psychological and public health efforts in the field. The types of theory and methodology which appear to be particularly relevant for the development of intervention strategies are identified, along with appropriate levels of analysis. These approaches are then applied in the delineation of an innovative program for combating the problem. Because of our strong belief in the critical importance of public health-oriented (as opposed to medical or clinical) conceptualizations of the health issues presented in the book, discussion will be focused largely on solutions involved in the *primary prevention* of the problem.

6

Prevention in Mental Health: A Proactive, Developmental/Ecological Perspective*

INTRODUCTION

Most of the content of this book documents a keen commitment and emerging progress by health professionals and psychologists in mounting an array of health promotion and prevention programs. These programs seriously address host and environmental factors that can enhance health and prevent disease.

There also has been some long-term parallel interest in preventive mental health theories and interventions (e.g., the Vermont series of conferences and books). However, with some exceptions (e.g., Felner, Jason, Moritsugu, & Farber, 1983; Rappaport, 1977; Rappaport, 1981) and more recent interest (Edelstein & Michelson, 1986; Jason, Felner, Hess, & Moritsugu, 1987), conceptualization, commitment, and activity by psychologists in preventive mental health has not had center stage. Indeed, some most recent debate and recommendations have left psychologists' role in prevention in very limited quarters, e.g., the effects of psychotherapy services on patients' use of other health services (Ware, Manning, Duan, Wells, & Newhouse, 1984).

Such roles and issues are hardly trivial, yet as noted essentially stick to prevailing conceptualizations and delivery modes. Further, it may even be the case that the expansion of third-party payments for psychological services, i.e., restorative therapy for established disorders, may on the one hand have brought psychologists long-sought parity with psychiatrists and clear monetary gain, but on the other hand exacted the cost of conceptual and strategic retrenchment into the "medical model" (Mechanic, 1978).

Of course, there is a long history of bold pronouncements of milestones and even of revolutions in mental health, with (as we will shortly see) some consistent flaws. These major markers have included:

---

*We appreciate the advice and feedback we received on earlier versions of this chapter from Lenny Jason, Tom Ollendick, and Anne Riley.

1. Pinel's dramatic unchaining of incarcerated, mentally disordered individuals in the 1790s in France, and the eventual, more humane treatment of mental patients in hospitals. While this was undoubtedly a critical step, one effect of the movement to hospitalize mentally disordered individuals, led by Dorothea Dix in the United States, was the demise of the moral treatment era (1800–1850) in the United States. This approach emphasized community-based treatment along more behavioral, social, and religious lines. It was replaced by the medicalization of "mental" problems and treatment in large hospitals (Heller, Price, Reinharz, & Wandersman, 1984).

2. The mental hygiene movement, whose start was marked by Clifford Beers' 1908 publication of *A Mind that Found Itself*. The movement focused on public education about mental health and reform of institutional treatment. Although a preventive stance was part of the movement's call for public education, its main thrust was more humane treatment of the seriously mental ill.

3. The Freudian psychoanalytic revolution in the conceptualization and treatment of neurotic disorders dominated psychology and psychiatry for at least 50 years (1915–1965), with remnants of the approach still being influential today. While fostering a more psychological conceptualization of mental disorders, psychoanalytic conceptualization and treatment parodied the medical model (i.e., intrapsychic causality; expensive one-to-one treatment), excluded ecological analyses, and neglected preventive activities.

4. The passage of The National Mental Health Act by the United States Congress in 1946, and the creation of the National Institute of Mental Health. In the main, these early developments focused on improving hospital care and the start of more extensive research on major mental health disorders. An emphasis on these more serious disorders continues to exist today.

5. The 1963 passage in the United States of the Mental Retardation Facilities and Community Mental Health Centers (CMHC) Construction Act, with subsequent amendments in the 1960s and 1970s. The CMHC Act was to be a bold new approach to treatment and prevention, by emphasizing innovative intervention and personnel, research, and community consultation and education. A quarter of a century later, the results of the CMHC movement can be seen as mixed. Its major accomplishments have been providing more direct services to a wide spectrum of people (particularly the underserved) and becoming a fulcrum for more effective after-care for former mental patients. Such care has been facilitated by follow-up capabilities, but perhaps more so by the advent and widespread use of psychotropic drugs (Hanlon & Pickett, 1984). The shortcomings of the CMHC movement have included a failure to conduct innovative research

and maintenance of minimal preventive consultation and education activities (Heller et al., 1984). CMHCs have mostly become outpatient therapy clinics supported by third-party payments.

6. During the same period as the CMHC movement, another conceptual revolution took place. This was the advent of the behavioral paradigm in psychology, i.e., behavior analysis, behavior modification, and behavior therapy. By basing therapy and other interventions on laboratory-derived and empirically tested principles, it was believed that a science of behavior change could have dramatic impact within a short time on virtually all developmental, educational, social, health, and psychiatric problems. While there have been successes with heretofore untreatable populations and problems (Kazdin, 1984), and intriguing extensions to organizational and community interventions (Greene, Winett, Van Houten, Geller, & Iwata, 1987), there have also been major disappointments, e.g., in maintenance of treatment effects (Brownell et al., 1986). In addition, although earlier efforts emphasized training paraprofessionals and natural behavior change mediators, along with working in the natural environment, it is apparent that today a good deal of behavior therapy is conducted by professionals within office settings—i.e., the medical model (O'Leary & Wilson, 1987). Thus, it can be argued that the behaviorist revolution has been more a conceptual and procedural innovation than a movement with a lasting impact on service delivery modalities or primary prevention.

7. The splintering away from the CMHC movement by disappointed, though perhaps more zealous, psychologists, psychiatrists, and social workers, whose orientation was more community and action-oriented. In psychology, this group called themselves community psychologists. For the last 20 years, this group has searched for a value, conceptual, and research stance consistent with such themes as social justice and welfare, citizen participation, empowerment, and prevention (Heller et al., 1984). Thus, as compared to behavior therapy, community psychology is not so much a technical revolution as a call for a different set of rules, emphases, and values. However, surprisingly, rarely have community psychologists made close connection with the methods of public health (e.g., Catalano, 1979).

This chapter is written within the spirit and basic tenets of community psychology and public health. It is our belief that an integration of community psychology and public health can form a basis for a revolution in mental health. This may be particularly the case when the values, perspectives, and strategies of community psychology are meshed with the behavioral and social cognitive paradigms, as well as salutogenic, ecological, and developmental perspectives. Preventive mental health theory and action can become center stage in psychology and public health.

However, the history of prior revolutions suggests more guarded pronouncements, the recognition and advisability of more evolutionary steps (e.g., Weick, 1984), more serious questioning and study, and careful investigations before manning the barricades. These questions and areas of study form the backbone of this chapter and include:

1. Is there a convincing need for the prevention of mental health disorders?
2. What different stances for psychological inquiries have to be taken when the goal is prevention rather than treatment of mental health disorders?
3. What conceptualizations and strategies are critical for constructing such preventive interventions?
4. What are appropriate targets for preventive interventions?

NEEDS

For over a quarter of a decade, most significant reports about the incidence and prevalence of mental health disorders have noted that needs far outstrip resources and services as constituted at the time of the study (e.g., Joint Commission on Mental Illness, 1961; Gurin, Veroff, & Field, 1960; also see Gesten & Jason, 1987). For example, Munoz, Glish, Soo-Hoo, and Robertson (1982) reported that while the prevalence rate for severe affective disorders is about 6%, a relatively high percentage in itself, mild to moderate depressive symptomatology rates range from 9–26%. Although it appears that a sizeable percentage of mildly to moderately depressed individuals will improve without treatment, a reasonable proportion in the mild to moderate range will become worse and require extensive intervention or become dysfunctional (O'Leary & Wilson, 1987).

In another domain, a recent Psychology in the Public Forum series in *The American Psychologist* (Garrison, 1987; Hart & Brassard, 1987; Melton & Davidson, 1987; Rosenberg, 1987) focused on an emerging set of concerns and problems grouped under the term psychological maltreatment of children. According to Hart and Brassard (1987), psychological maltreatment appears to be more prevalent and destructive than other forms of child abuse and neglect. In particular, long-term social and emotional dysfunction is associated with early treatment. The condition (which is fraught with definitional difficulties) can occur in isolation or as a concomitant of child abuse and neglect. In 1984 (as cited in Hart and Brassard), there were 1.7 million reported cases of child abuse and neglect. One implication of the series was that even with a stringent definition of psychological maltreatment, it is likely that the incidence and prevalence rates for various forms of child abuse, neglect, and maltreatment are much higher than 1.7 million cases. Further, legal, resource, conceptual, and technical limitations (see below) hamper approaching this problem in a concerted and effective way.

Kiesler (1985) has estimated that at any given time 15–35% of the population needs mental health services. Even at the low end of the estimate, the number of individuals represented far surpasses the capabilities of mental health services as presently constituted and delivered. Gesten and Jason (1987) also cogently noted that although 3.2 million children show evidence of major emotional problems, only 10% receive treatment. In addition, half of the seven million children with major learning problems never receive any help.

Using data from Kramer (1982), Gesten and Jason (1987) made some sobering predictions about mental health problems at the turn of the twenty-first century:

1. The number of persons with mental health disorders will be about 40 million, up from 33 million in 1980.
2. This estimate may be too modest because of potential increases in mental health needs as a result of people living longer, sick and/or dependent elderly, and an increase in children from single-parent households.
3. Shifts to high technology, which for some population segments may cause physical relocations and periods of unemployment, may result in increased mental health disorders (Brenner, 1973; Catalano & Dooley, 1983; Dooley & Catalano, 1980; Liem & Ramsay, 1982).

Thus, even if these estimates of current and future incidence and prevalence rates are halved, they suggest an overwhelming number of troubled individuals who do not, or will not, receive mental health services. More to the point, it is almost impossible to imagine the complementary number of mental health service providers who can deliver effective restorative therapy. This is the case, when, on the one hand, paraprofessionals are considered integral to treatment programs (Hattie, Sharpley, & Rogers, 1984), but, on the other hand, it is realized that chronic problems often require sustained and extensive treatment. Even with high-level, intensive intervention, many problems are not reliably responsive to treatment.

The situation within the mental health system is put into further perspective when it is realized that the mean number of sessions attended by clients at mental health centers is only about four (Wagner, 1985). Thus, many clients who may profit from intensive extended therapy do not consistently stay long enough in the system to receive benefits.

It is also difficult at this juncture to imagine huge increases in federal or state funding for mental health services so that service reach and potency are magnified. What increases there may be seem more likely to be directed to hospital-based treatment, which now accounts for 70% of funds for mental health care (Gesten & Jason, 1987).

Thus, it appears that millions of people, now or in the future, will show evidence of major health problems. However, as presently constructed, and even with a large increase in funding, it is difficult to discern how the mental health system of private practitioners and delivery persons in mental health centers can possibly make substantial inroads into this enormous set of problems. While not denying that a place will always exist for psychotherapy services, and that some therapy procedures are becoming remarkably effective (e.g., O'Leary & Wilson, 1987), the solution (if any) to these problems appears to demand reconceptualizations and reorientations along the lines of prevention. More of the same in mental health is not appropriate.

STANCES AND CONCEPTS

The foregoing points and discussion make the case that the CMHC and behavioral revolutions of the 1960s and 1970s in mental health conceptualization and service were, in actuality, only part of an evolutionary process. There is some agreement that during the last 25 years significant strides have been made in extending services to wider population segments, e.g., poorer people and the developmentally disabled (Heller et al., 1984). However, the product offering has remained essentially the same, the proverbial old wine in a new bottle. Indeed, it can be said that confusion exists within the field as to what constitutes innovation.

Perhaps, more importantly, there has been a basic shortcoming in failing to separate three facets of psychological intervention—timing, conceptualization, and service delivery (Rappaport, 1977). By timing it is meant whether an intervention is primary, secondary, or tertiary prevention. These forms of prevention were noted in chapter 1 and constitute a temporal continuum for intervention.

Considerable effort, energy, and debate in psychology has focused on the conceptualization of interventions, but not on service delivery modalities or their timing (e.g., Goldfried, 1980). Often, such debates and new conceptualizations are thought to represent marked innovations. For example, as noted above, this was the case with the ascendance of the behavioral paradigm in the 1960s and 1970s. It is true that behavioral concepts and principles formed the basis for interventions for previously untreated or untreatable people, e.g., severely retarded, and effective, relatively short-term treatment for specific problems, e.g., anxiety disorders (Kazdin, 1984). However, most often in the case of behavior therapy, the new treatments were fitted into the prevailing delivery system—i.e., one-to-one psychotherapy. Thus, what innovation there was pertained mostly to conceptualization. The delivery system and the timing of interventions often remained the same.

It can further be said that debates about the efficacy of different treatment often amount to debates about relatively minor differences in approach. For example, even when cognitive treatment is offered compared to behavioral treatment for depression, there are strong similarities in the treatments. Both treatments are usually provided by experts within the confines of weekly or twice-weekly hourly sessions occurring in an office. Both treatments tend to focus on individual deficits, thought patterns, or skills, and both treatments, on a procedural level, may actually not be that different. For example, both treatments may try to provide clients with feedback on present behavioral patterns and set up corrective experiences or outside sessions for clients to test out new behavioral patterns (Goldfried, 1980).

Rarely have sustained debates by mental health professionals examined the service delivery component; as we have seen, it has been taken as a given. Service delivery can most basically be addressed within the context of two critical aspects—stance and level (Rappaport, 1977). By stance it is meant whether an intervention style can be described as "seeking" or "waiting." The waiting mode is characterized most strongly by professionals physically remaining within a service system and, indeed, waiting for clients, generally with chronic problems, to come to them. This is the most prevalent mode of operation for psychologists and, not surprisingly, it is in this mode that psychologists receive third-party payments. The seeking mode describes a style where professionals are usually physically operating outside the service system and seeking to intervene in problems before they become chronic. However, in practice, it is acknowledged that waiting/seeking is best thought of as a continuum, and less as a dichotomy.

In addition, the waiting mode is usually associated with restorative therapy, while seeking is generally associated with prevention. This, however, need not always be the case. For example, a psychoanalytic psychologist may offer advice to many troubled individuals through a newspaper column or TV show.

The level of intervention has been repeatedly discussed throughout this book. Suffice it to say that for the most part psychological interventions are focused on the individual or interpersonal levels. As we have noted, such interventions have the disadvantages of being expensive and limited in reach into a population or community. Thus, we characterize most mental health services as individual-level, waiting mode interventions.

Table 6.1 shows examples of waiting and seeking mode interventions at different levels, with the waiting mode emphasizing late preventive activity and the seeking mode more primary prevention. While it is obvious that those examples in the waiting model are most familiar and acceptable, it should also be apparent that seeking mode interventions represent relatively untapped, potentially highly efficacious avenues. Further, it is possible to describe mid-way interventions, e.g., when consultation to organizations on stress management emphasizes individual and organizational change pro-

Table 6.1. Level and Mode of Mental Health Interventions

Level	Mode	
	Waiting	Seeking
Individual	Therapy for chronic problems	Consultation on mental health to leaders, "gatekeepers" for stressful life events
Interpersonal	Therapy for families	Support groups for impending divorcees
Organizational/ Environmental	Provide consultation for worksite human resource professional where there is high prevalence of mental health problems in settings	Provide consultation on organizational structures associated with mental health problems prior to high prevalence rates
Institutional	Provide documentation of the mental health effects of mass layoffs and unemployment and provide organized help	Design and deliver programs for new job skills; testify on the effects of economic recessions during nonrecession periods

cesses. Those interventions in the seeking mode at the organizational/environmental and institutional levels are in most accord with public health interventions. However, while we are emphasizing integrations of community psychology with public health, as is discussed in the next section, there are problems in trying to mirror public health approaches for conceptualization and intervention in mental health.

TARGETS AND APPROACHES

Many successful public health efforts have followed a relatively orderly pattern of identifying, through epidemiological research, specific agents and environmental and host factors contributing to specific diseases or injuries. After these factors are identified for populations at risk, specific interventions can be mounted that may focus on host, agent, or environmental factors alone, or in combination. For example, chapter 4 discussed epidemiological research and showed how AIDS was initially spread in homosexual men through sexual contacts and by IV drug users through the sharing of needles. It was also possible to identify high-risk places such as bathhouses and shooting galleries. Note that the focus is on a specific agent, specific sexual and drug-related behaviors, and particular settings, whose confluence clearly marks a greatly increased probability of disease for target populations. While such analyses do not necessarily assure that successful programs can be mounted, i.e., given political, legal, social, and technical constraints and limitations, the emphasis is definitely on prevention of specific diseases.

Epidemiological methods can identify populations at risk for mental health problems, but such analyses are not likely to be able to pinpoint specific agents, environments, and host characteristics leading to specific psychological problems. For example, the same set of conditions, high stress and social isolation, can result in alcoholism, child abuse, depression, or none of these problems (Cassell, 1976).

The picture is further clouded by changes over time in diagnostic categories and continued problems in reliable diagnoses (Albee, 1986). For example, with regard to the first issue, the diagnostic system introduced in 1980 (and recently revised) no longer denotes homosexuality as a psychological disorder, and the general category of neurosis was dropped. Thus, a variety of psychological disorders appear to 'come' and 'go' as a result of reclassification, which may have less to do with scientific discovery and more to do with changes in the political and social fabric.

The Ecological Approach to Intervention

At least three major perspectives have emerged that attempt to mesh public health and mental health methods and goals. The first perspective, with a more ecological stance, makes the case, as noted above, that the same psychological conditions can result in a variety of psychological problems (Cassell, 1976). It is the conditions, and to some extent host factors, that are readily identifiable as risk-producing; specific disorders cannot be predicted. From this perspective, it makes sense to mount general intervention programs aimed at common stressors. For example, common stressors for children occur at such 'milestones' or 'life transitions' as school transfer (Jason, 1987) or divorce (Bloom, Hodges, Kern, & McFaddin, 1985).

General programs can be developed to help negotiate these milestones without the aim of preventing specific pathologies in specific individuals. It is also apparent that large-scale environmental changes such as economic recessions (Liem & Ramsay, 1982), or indeed, even seemingly moderate economic changes (Catalano & Dooley, 1983), or natural or man-made disasters (Heller et al., 1984), set the stage for a range of psychological problems. Proactive efforts which combine individual and higher level interventions can lessen the psychological impacts of such environmental changes (Felner et al., 1983).

Early Intervention in Selected Cases

However, to some (e.g., Lorion, 1983), this approach is too amorphous and difficult to justify on scientific grounds. The emphasis of the second perspective is on identifying specific social psychological and host factors that result in specific (DSM-III) disorders. For example, specific family patterns may be related to childhood schizophrenia. If this is the case, early intervention programs can be mounted with families at risk. Presumably, such efforts would eventually lower the incidence and prevalence of schizophrenia.

This was the approach adopted by the Office of Prevention at the National Institute of Health, a program recently disbanded (Goldston, 1986). The specificity of assessment measures, target populations, and disorders called for by this perspective is appealing, as is its attendant aura of scientific rigor and manageability. It is also easier to see this focus (e.g., on pathological family patterns) gaining popular and political support compared to approaches which smack of social engineering (e.g., specifying criteria that must be met before firms can abandon communities).

Most recently, this perspective has been somewhat modified so that the emphasis is on identifiable, high-risk populations—i.e., those at risk for a variety of psychological disorders. An example of a high-risk group is that of young, unmarried, female parents with minimal psychological and financial support or education.

The Medical–Biological Approach

A third perspective attempts to more closely follow a medical–biological approach. Though debated for many years, there is evidence that a number of major mental health disorders and psychological problems may have genetic and biochemical substrata—e.g., manic–depression, schizophrenia, alcoholism (Edelstein & Michelson, 1986; Lamb & Zusman, 1974). The notion here is that the emphasis of research needs to be focused more clearly on identifying and understanding the biological determinants of mental illness. Once these determinants are marked, appropriate medical interventions (e.g., drugs) can be prescribed. Further, if it is firmly believed that the bases for major health disorders are biological, then social psychological preventive interventions, particularly of the more general kind, are seen, at best, as misdirected and futile, and, at worst, as wasteful efforts. However, even with effective medical treatment for mental health problems, programs would still be needed to help in the long-term adjustment and coping processes.

Quite obviously, this perspective turns back the clock about 100 years to the emergence and then deification of the medical model of psychopathology. Yet there is certainly enough substance to this approach to give even the staunchest environmentalist pause. It is difficult to deny that there are genetic and biological factors associated with the most costly disorders. A major caveat, though, with a long conceptual and research history, is that these are *predispositions* which probably require stressful circumstances to manifest themselves into full-blown disorders. Thus, interventions on one side of the equation, i.e., reducing stressors in at-risk populations, are one fruitful approach even if it is shown that most major mental health disorders have a biological basis. Further, our knowledge at this point of the biological determinants of mental health disorders is unfortunately quite modest (Edelstein & Michelson, 1986).

RESEARCH AND INTERVENTION: GOALS

Repeatedly, demands for action, whether in the treatment or prevention arena, have called for a focus on major mental health disorders such as schizophrenia and at times, for a more optimistic search for cures. It is undoubtedly true that these disorders exact an enormous toll on individuals, families, communities, and the mental health and health system. For example, the cost of a public psychiatric hospitalization for one year can exceed $30,000. Thus, the focus appears warranted because that is where savings can be made.

However, two points need to be made. First, it is not clear if any cures will be forthcoming within the near future. That is because, as noted, our knowledge about biological bases of mental disorders is still modest. Second, the focus on major mental health disorders and hospitalization obscures the personal, community, and societal costs of more common and pervasive problems in living that have primarily environmental causes. For example, as noted above, psychological mistreatment of children appears far more pervasive and costly than childhood schizophrenia. The origins of psychological mistreatment are seen as residing within interactions of individual psychopathology, disturbed families, community structures, and institutional practices (Rosenberg, 1987).

On another front, only recently have the costs of economic recessions been examined (Catalano & Dooley, 1983). In the past, it was assumed that the effects of unemployment were relatively benign and short-term. However, as unemployment becomes the more permanent lot of particular workers, the psychological and health effects have been studied and shown to be substantial—e.g., major depression, alcohol abuse, and family disturbance, coupled with loss of medical benefits (Liem & Ramsay, 1982). Likewise, even milder economic downturns appear to have general negative impacts on individual indicants of mental health for some population segments (Catalano & Dooley, 1983). Interestingly, neither the costs of psychological mistreatment or some rather direct effects of unemployment or economic recessions have typically been considered under such rubrics as "the cost of mental illness."

It is important at this juncture to clarify what we are and are not proposing. We do not propose the abandonment of medical treatments, or of the search for cures for schizophrenia, autism, and other apparently genetically based disorders. Nor should medical efforts be deemphasized for disorders such as alcoholism, which appear to have a biological (predisposition) component. We also do not devalue careful assessment and intervention research directed toward understanding and reliably preventing specific DSM-III disorders. We are not proposing far afield societal engineering projects that may or may not have preventive mental health outcomes. Further, we are not ignoring the role that individual deficits play in provoking problems in living. However, we are proposing a balance in the research and intervention agenda. This balance includes more value of and focus on investigations of common stressors, the modification of conditions resulting in such stressors, and the strengthening of individuals to effectively negotiate common stressors through a variety of individual and collective action.

If we turn once again to the psychological maltreatment of children, we can find some insight into different conceptualizations and strategies that appear necessary to understand and ameliorate the problem. Both conceptualizations and courses of action are quite different from prevailing mental health frameworks and treatment strategies. Indeed, they are even in contrast to theory and intervention associated most often with preventive mental health measures, although they are consistent with and expand upon public health concepts and strategies.

ECOLOGICAL AND DEVELOPMENTAL PERSPECTIVE

Two useful approaches for understanding psychological maltreatment are the ecological and developmental perspectives (Bronfenbrenner, 1979). The ecological perspective is, in part, embedded in the book's framework, i.e., levels of analysis and their interactions. Psychological maltreatment can be examined as it relates to child characteristics and parental beliefs and behaviors, family characteristics and patterns, neighborhood parameters (e.g., degree of stability), subculture and community norms and values, and prevailing cultural conditions. Catalano (1979) has shown that the ecological perspective actually has a long history in sociology and, to some extent, psychology. Besides presenting individual problems within context, the perspective is useful for examining causality at multiple levels which then suggest multiple avenues for interventions.

The developmental perspective points toward different issues and problems that will be manifested by the child and family at different points in time. The developmental perspective links with the ecological perspective because different issues and problems unfold in different settings. In addition, maltreatment at different stages of development may have different effects in later life. The combination of these perspectives also indicates that effectively approaching individual cases and problems in their entirety entails multilevel assessments and congruent interventions aimed at different kinds of families. For example, parent education, support groups, and public education conducted in easily accessible settings may be appropriate for certain kinds of psychological maltreatment. Such conceptualizations and strategies are in contrast to providing intensive and expensive psychotherapy to parents or children only within a mental health facility.

THE COMPETENCIES/RESOURCE PARADIGM

Melton and Davidson (1987) and Rosenberg (1987), however, in their analyses and recommendations, go several steps further than more typical preventive interventions. For example, Rosenberg cites research on stress resistance and invulnerability (e.g., Garmezy, 1981). That is, many children exposed to extreme stressors do not manifest present or later difficulties. This intriguing body of research shifts our attention toward examining competencies, resources, and coping abilities. Key questions become " . . . what combination of protective factors at what level(s) are necessary to offset particular vulnerabilities at other level(s)?" and " . . . how would these particular combinations vary according to the developmental stage of the child and family?" (Rosenberg, 1987, p. 169).

Melton and Davidson (1987) detail the historical and present-day issues, both legal and psychological, entailed in family intervention. They note in conclusion that many usual preventive and intervention strategies (e.g., protective services and foster or institutional care) are not likely to be workable. They recommend as a more fruitful course investigating and promoting positive entitlements (e.g., clean, safe neighborhoods) for children and policies that strengthen families.

Thus, Rosenberg and Melton and Davidson are calling for a paradigm shift that combines salutogenic, ecological, and developmental perspectives, and in theory and practice will focus on competencies, strengths, coping, and resources. This perspective, is, indeed, far afield from paradigms requiring specification of particular psychological pathology or genetic deficits resulting in specific mental health disorders. However, the approach is also one step beyond the call for more general interventions aimed at common stressors, though it is congruent with other attempts at developing comprehensive salutogenic models (Antonovsky, 1979; 1987). At this juncture, it is important to examine recent work which has attempted to follow the strengths, competencies, and resource paradigm.

Recent Studies

Table 6.2 is primarily a distillation of the comprehensive review provided by Gesten and Jason (1987) of recent preventive work based on the competency, coping, and resource perspective. An attempt is made in the table to

Table 6.2. Categorization of Recent Preventive Mental Health Efforts

	Competence Building	Social Support	Mutual Help	Behavioral Community	Empowerment
Agent	Assess What are Critical Skills/Behaviors	Pinpoint Individual, Social, and System Barriers to Social Support	Identifying Individual, Social and System Barriers to Mutual Help	Ascertain System Parameters Related to Detrimental Behaviors	Assess Multilevel Sources of Powerlessness[45]
Host	• Increase Cognitive and Social Skills of Children at Risk, e.g., Low SES, Disturbed Families[1-8] • Teach Problem Solving and Communication Skills Early in Marriage[9-11] or Shortly after Divorce with Parents and Children[12-16] • Teach Skills to Prevent Depression[17] • Teach Skills to Prevent Child Abuse[18,19] • Teach Social Problem Solving Skills[20-23]	• Teach Skills to Gain Social Support[25-26]	• Provide Groups for Mutual Help with or without Professional Facilitators[32-35]	• Change Diverse Detrimental Behaviors using a Variety of Behavioral Strategies[36-40]	• Teach Skills to Gain Access to Resources[46-48]

• Teach School Transition Skills24

Environment

Modify Environments so that Competent Behaviors are More Probable	*Increase access to Supportive Environments27–31 / Modify Environments so that Social Support Behaviors are More Probable	Modify Environments so that Mutual Help Behaviors are More Probable	*Provide Assessments of Environmental Change, Mobilize Community Systems41–44	Modify Institutionalized Disenfranchisement
1. Berrueta-Clement, 1984	13. Warren et al., 1984	25. Guerney, 1985	37. Winett et al., 1985	
2. Johnson & Breckenridge, 1982	14. Stolberg & Garrison, 1985	26. Taylor et al., 1984	38. Tartinger et al., 1984	
3. Johnson & Walker, 1985	15. Pedro-Carroll & Cowen, 1985	27. Henninger & Nelson, 1984	39. Van Houten et al., 1985	
4. Jordan et al., 1985	16. Pedro-Carroll et al., 1986	28. Unger & Wandersman, 1985	40. Rudd & Geller, 1985	
5. Pierson et al., 1984	17. Munoz et al., 1982	29. Felner et al., 1982	41. Elder et al., 1986	
6. Slaughter, 1983	18. Olds, 1984	30. Wright & Cowen, 1985	42. Jason et al., 1986	
7. Ruth-Lyons et al., 1984	19. Harvey, 1985	31. Roskin, 1982	43. Winett & Neale, 1981	
8. Goodman, 1984	20. Shure & Spivack, 1982	32. Videka-Sherman, 1982	44. Seekins et al., 1986	
9. Giblin et al., 1985	21. Feis & Symons, 1985	33. Hinrichsen et al., 1985	45. Rappaport, 1977	
10. Guerney, 1986	22. Mannarino et al., 1982	34. George & Gryuther, 1985	46. Fawcett et al., 1984	
11. Markman, 1986	23. Gesten et al., 1982	35. Rappaport et al., 1985	47. Glidewell, 1986	
12. Bloom et al., 1985	24. Elias et al., 1985	36. Yokely & Glenwick, 1984	48. Thorsherm & Roberts, 1986	

classify the various studies (noted by reference numbers at the bottom of the table) within specific categories (e.g., social support) and then by its focus on agent, host, or environmental factors. Across the table, an asterisk indicates work that has been done and appropriate reference numbers. Those entries without asterisks indicate work that has generally *not* yet been emphasized in this perspective.

Examination of the table indicates that except for omnipresent (i.e., poverty) and particular (e.g., specific public school policies) sources of powerlessness, which were treated extensively in Rappaport's (1977) classic book, much work still remains to be done. For example, there is still a need for more understanding of which social skills are important at different developmental periods in specific settings, and which are significant for later adjustment (Ollendick, 1987). Analyses of social support and mutual help need to provide more than descriptive studies attesting to the role of such help in promoting mental health; individual, social, and environmental barriers to mutually positive interactions must be discerned (e.g., Fisher, Bell, & Baum, 1984).

It is apparent from the table that most of the recent studies and projects have attempted to change host factors—i.e., cognitions, behaviors, specific skills, coping strategies, or problem-solving approaches. Since most of the work noted on the table has been performed by psychologists, this emphasis is not surprising. Rather than lamenting this point, we note quite positively that those techniques being developed are effective in modifying critical host factors and, most importantly, appear to yield preventive outcomes. For example, a special, comprehensive intervention program after separation or divorce has resulted in better psychological adjustment four years after the intervention (Bloom et al., 1985).

It is also apparent in examining Table 6.2 that much more needs to be done in designing environmental (setting) changes so that positive behaviors are more likely to occur. Strategies such as mobilizing community systems for mental health promotion in ways congruent with community health programs (described in chapter 5) and moving more into the realm of political action, in order to eventuate a more equitable distribution of resources, have received only scant attention. Thus, we see that the task at hand, for prevention in mental health, is that of creative integration of ecological and developmental perspectives into an approach which allows for understanding of critical agents related to positive mental health, and where such understanding and appropriate theory can form the underpinnings for multilevel change strategies entailing host and environmental modifications.

PROACTIVE/DEVELOPMENTAL/ECOLOGICAL PREVENTION PARADIGM

In this section, we integrate several different points and perspectives noted in this chapter into one overall paradigm for prevention in mental health. We see this paradigm as appropriate for analyses and intervention directed toward populations at risk as well as for more general quality of life concerns. We first review these points again here.

1. Mental health interventions should take a *proactive* approach, i.e., emphasize the seeking mode, and not be just reactive, or work in the waiting mode (Ollendick & Winett, 1985; Rappaport, 1977).
2. Mental health interventions should focus on building strength and competencies and not only on treating deficits (Gesten & Jason, 1987). Carrying this idea one step further suggests an emphasis on positive mental health through different empowerment strategies including more access to resources (Rappaport, 1981).
3. A *developmental* perspective entails focusing on successfully negotiating life transitions, milestones, and their attendant stressors (Felner, Farber, & Primavera, 1983). Transitions and milestones are relatively predictable, and it is believed that general skills helpful for successfully transversing stressful encounters at one point in life can be useful at later points (Danish, Galambos, & Laquatra, 1983). In this respect, coping with stressful conditions can be strength-producing.
4. An *ecological* perspective involves careful analyses of immediate settings (e.g, interactions at a child day care center), organizational structures (e.g., the physical and social environments of day care settings), interactions of one setting (e.g., day care settings rules) with another setting (e.g., work schedules), and institutional policies (e.g., maternal and paternal leave policies). The basic thrust is an examination of multilevel influence and change in appropriate structures to promote mental health (Bronfenbrenner, 1979; Cowen, 1980).

Table 6.3 is an attempt, albeit a static one, to illustrate the proactive/developmental/ecological perspective for two different life transitions, parenting with young children and adapting to retirement. For this table, we have broadly defined competencies as skills or insights of individuals, and resources as both tangible, i.e., time and money, and relatively intangible, i.e., respect and caring from others. Settings include a wide spectrum of places where interactions and care occur and where consideration (i.e., specific policies) for population segments and cultural norms (i.e., mass media) emerge.

The table does not depict well the sense of interactions and, indeed, synergistic possibilities among levels, as well as between competencies, resources, and settings, that is central to ecological/system perspectives. For example, parental leave policies and more flexible work schedules can enhance family support and child care competencies by allowing more time for family interactions and reducing stress engendered by coordination of work and home life (Winett & Neale, 1981). It is possible that in general a better home life may result in more productive behavior at work, thus further

Table 6.3. Proactive/Developmental/Ecological Prevention Paradigm as Illustrated by Two Different Life Transitions and for Different Levels of Analysis

	Parenting with Young Children			Adapting to Retirement		
	Competencies	Resources	Settings	Competencies	Resources	Settings
Personal	Appropriate parenting behaviors and development of loving relationships	Enough money for basic home and child care needs	Adequate home setting	Suitable interests and commitments so that time and activities are valued; engagement in basic health practices	Enough money for basic home needs and outside interests	Adequate home setting which may need modification for physical decline
Interpersonal	Family communication skills; mutual support skills; problem solving abilities; preventive health practices	Relatively stable family existence; supportive social network; access to prevention and medical services	Adequate home setting and proximity to supportive others and their settings; prevention and medical centers	Attachment to social relationships and networks which may or may not be immediate family's; social support and problem solving skills	Relative family stability; minimally supportive social network	Adequate home setting and proximity to supportive others and their settings
Organizational/ Environmental	Child care workers to adequately care for children; general positive regard and value of children in immediate settings; emphasis on preventive health care	Access to child care settings; work schedules to facilitate home and work life without undermining income; preventive health care facilities; general community value	Adequate child care settings; facilitative work environment and general community settings supportive of children; prevention health centers	Regard and value for elderly by various individuals in immediate work, social, and health settings	Access to settings which provide meaningful interactions with other individuals	Settings which provide access to others, suitable roles, and value the elderly
Institutional	Institutional policies which hold children in the highest regard	Specific policies which promote children and families—e.g., parental leaves, subsidized child care at worksites	Promotion of family and child health and welfare through state and federal legislation, corporate sector, mass media	Institutional policies which promote the continual involvement and wellness of the elderly	Specific policies which enhance quality of life for the elderly, e.g., part-time work, full, comprehensive health care coverage	Promotion of health for the elderly through state and federal legislation, corporate policies, depictions in mass media

promoting more flexible work hours in the world of work. An adequate home (setting) and income (resources) can set the stage for emergence of appropriate parenting behaviors. Adequate problem-solving abilities stabilize a family's existence and its access to social and material resources. And, of course, the combination of a more stable and relaxed home life and satisfying and financially rewarding work can have synergistically positive impacts on child development.

Not surprisingly and as suggested by others (Albee, 1986; Danish et al., 1983), some of the same competencies (e.g., problem-solving skills), resources (e.g., social support), and settings (e.g., adequate housing) emerge as important at different points in the life cycle. It is the fine points and particulars of the skills and settings which change over time. If this is indeed the case, it suggests that preventive mental health interventions can be fit into more general finite categories (e.g., those that teach people to increase their social support) and tailored to particular points in the life cycle (i.e., retirement).

Perhaps, also, Table 6.3 does not suggest the proactive nature of the paradigm. That is, once the parameters of competencies, resources, and settings are more fully understood (although assuredly many parameters are, e.g., adequate health coverage and appropriate post-natal care), the goal is to promote positive mental health through particular interventions. A range of possible strategies follow those that were previously shown in Table 6.1. For example, mutually supportive parenting and babysitting groups can be developed with only very minimal paraprofessional help. Workers can and have banded together to bargain for changes in their work conditions, a collective empowerment strategy. Other interventions, however, more clearly call for policy change at state and federal levels (e.g., personal leave policies). Without such higher level intervention, substantial barriers will remain for some positive organizational, group, and individual initiatives.

WORK AND FAMILY LIFE: APPLYING THE PARADIGM

Background

In the following sections, we will develop background information and empirical support for approaching the problems of many dual-earner families with young children (for more details, see Aldous, 1982). Later, we will use the material in these sections, in concert with the book's framework, to design an integrative intervention for helping families with young children, consistent with the proactive/developmental/ecological perspective.

Our approach is not directed toward particular critical incidents (e.g., returning to work after the birth of a child), but rather is focused on one pervasive problem. That is, when children are young (arbitrarily less than 10 years old), it is difficult to coordinate work and family life, particularly for single parents or when both parents are working full time outside the home. Children must be given their breakfast, sent or taken to a child care situation or school, and later in the day picked up, or have a responsible person home when the children arrive from school or the child care center (i.e., to avoid the "latchkey syndrome"). In the evening, there is dinner to prepare, chores to be done, and children to be cared for, as well as time needed for spouses or partners. In between all these activities, the person must fit in eight to nine hours at the worksite and additional time for commuting, which can be substantial.

This brief overview suggests two problems with the resource of time. Time must be closely regulated so that home, child care, and work responsibilities are coordinated. However, there simply may not be enough time to manage these diverse activities.

In the 1970s, there was considerable interest in alternative work schedules, particularly in flexible work hours or "flexitime" (Winett & Neale, 1980). The original interest pertained to flexitime as a mechanism to allow workers greater control over their work life. Under flexitime systems, workers were usually allowed to alter their arrival and departure times within set parameters (e.g., arrive between 7:00–9:30 a.m.) as long as they worked during core hours (e.g., 11:00 a.m.–3:00 p.m.) and put in eight hours per day. In other systems, hours per day could be altered if a designated number (i.e., 40 hours) was accrued by the end of the week.

Evaluations of such systems suggested that flexitime increased worker morale, decreased absenteeism, and in some instances appeared to increase productivity (Nollen, 1982). Another interesting byproduct of the system was that in areas where many business establishments worked on flexitime, typical rush hour traffic was alleviated (Nollen, 1982).

At the same time, a number of experts on family life saw that flexitime could be particularly helpful for families with young children (Bronfenbrenner, 1977). For example, by arriving early at work and thus leaving early, parents could be home when their child arrived, thus avoiding the latchkey syndrome. Overall, flexitime was seen as one simple way to help a large segment of the population coordinate work and family life and, hence, also reduce stress.

Empirical Support for Flexible Work Schedules

This general hypothesis has been tested out in research studies (Bohen & Viveros-Long, 1981; Winett & Neale, 1981; Winett, Neale, & Williams 1982). For example, in the first author's work, two quasi-experiments were performed with two large federal agencies in Washington, D.C. For these studies, a measure was developed using a time/event log system (Robinson,

1977) where all study participants monitored their use of time about twice per week for about two months prior to flexitime and then for periods up to seven months after flexitime. Several different checking methods showed that the time logs were reliable instruments. In this way, for example, it was possible to track time spent with family members before and during flexitime. Additional measures included evaluations of the quality of time spent and weekly measures that examined the stress involved in typical daily activities, e.g., preparing dinner in the evening.

The flexitime systems were quite limited — i.e., two-hour leeways in arrival and departure time — but typical of systems developed in the United States. The studies compared individuals who elected to alter their work schedules, and similar individuals who decided to remain on their same work schedules. Generally, all participants were from two-parent families where both parents worked full-time and where there was at least one child at home less than ten years old. Participant's mean age was about 33 and the average gross family income in 1988 dollars was about $41,000.

The results of the second study are depicted in Figure 6.1. The figure shows that participants using flexitime were able to increase their time with their family by about one half hour per day, which was rated as good quality time. In addition, reported stress involved in daily activities was reduced. Participants sticking to the regular schedule showed no appreciable changes in time use or stress levels.

Although the results of the studies were positive, it was apparent that flexitime was hardly a panacea. For example, there is still much reported difficulty in managing work and family responsibilities. This was made more apparent when all time at the work site (about nine hours) and commuting time (about two and a half hours per day) was accounted for. There simply was not much time for other activities, which could only be engaged in at a high personal cost. For example, few people in the study took the time to exercise, and participants' exercise time averaged less than 10 minutes per day. Thus, it appeared that while flexitime was helpful for parents with young children, it was obviously not a complete solution.

Individual Level

The prior studies with flexitime primarily evaluated the effects of an organizational intervention on individual behavior. In addition to the individual measures, indices focusing on the organization suggested that the system was implemented with few problems and at virtually no cost to the organization (Winett et al., 1982). However, as noted, flexitime did not alleviate all problems associated with time management. To some degree, time management problems for parents who have young children and are employed outside the home require other kinds of organizational and institutional changes to be discussed later. These same problems also require indi-

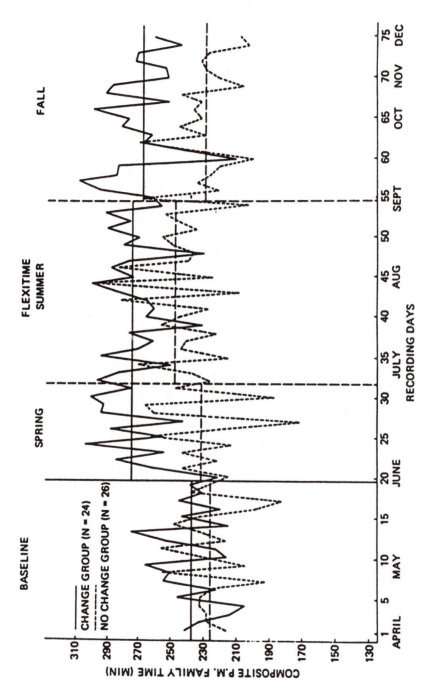

FIGURE 6.1. Composite Family Time in Minutes for Persons Who Changed or Did Not Change Their Schedule Under Flexitime Across Phases of the Study (from Winett & Neale, 1981)

vidual level change. For example, individual skills and competencies in personal management and parenting come into play. That is, it does not make sense to totally "blame the system."

King, Winett, and Lovett (1986) undertook another project in family life that had a more individual focus. Consistent with the book's framework, this project was preceded by considerable formative and pilot research (King & Winett, 1986). The formative research included interviews and questionnaires with female clerical staff, female faculty, and administrators at a large university who were mothers of younger children. The research revealed that the time management problems and stress from coordinating home and work life were major difficulties. However, much to our surprise, more flexible work schedules were not highly endorsed by these women as a favored way to alleviate time and stress problems. Perhaps it was the case that within the conservative climate of this university, flexible hours were not seen as that viable an alternative; perhaps other problems with flexitime (e.g., not being available for the boss) were envisioned; and perhaps also, the short commute of most of the employees obviated some of the need for flexitime. In any case, these female employees strongly endorsed learning about time management skills within a supportive group situation (i.e., with similar women, no men included) as their preferred mode of help.

In this study, the major focus became using time management and social support as ways to increase priority time. Priority time was defined individually by each participant as behaviors in her life that were important and for which she wanted to spend more time (e.g., time with the children in the evening; time to be alone and read; time to exercise). Such time was reliably tracked by each individual in a way similar to the time logs used in the flexitime studies.

Participants were randomly assigned to small groups that met twice per week for four weeks. The groups differed in that one condition entailed directly teaching time management skills to participants within a group that was also interactive and emphasized mutual help and support. One group only received time management, one group only followed the precepts of social support, and there was a waiting-list control condition.

The results of this study for the priority time measure are shown in Figure 6.2. It is quite apparent that the combination of the time management and social support was the most efficacious approach, and, indeed, this finding was later replicated with the waiting list control participants. Further, it may also be noted that the results appeared to maintain in the follow-up phase. The combination condition also showed some (marginal) reductions in reported stress.

Note also from Figure 6.2 that while time management alone led to increases in priority time, this was *not* the case for social support alone. At least within this context and using our priority time measure, even though

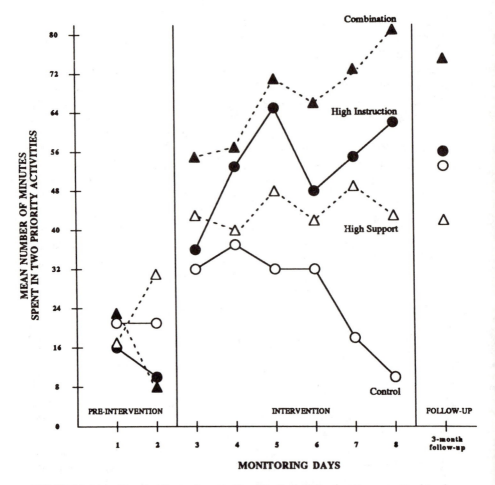

FIGURE 6.2. Mean Time in Minutes Spent in Two Priority Activities by Women in Combined,
High Instruction, High Support, or Control Conditions Across Phases of the Study
(from King, Winett, & Lovett, 1986)

the social support alone condition was reported as highly valued by participants, it was ineffective. The amorphous concept of social support undoubtedly needs to be unraveled (Heller, Swindle, & Dusenberg, 1986).

Clearly, this study, to better fit our developmental/ecological perspective,
could have (a) defined its transition point more clearly – for example, working more exclusively with employees who were new parents and/or just returning to full employment status; and (b) tracked how altered behavior
(i.e., priority time), which usually took place in the home, affected other
family members and behaviors on the job.

Neither the selection/targeting or management across settings strategies
were followed. However, the study did show that individual interventions

that teach specific skills can be of considerable immediate and enduring value (Danish et al., 1983).

Conclusions

Within the general domain of interventions aimed at the problems encountered in coordinating work and home life, a multilevel approach is favored. For example, the two sets of studies reported in this section certainly suggest that if flexitime, an organizational intervention, could be combined with the time management instruction delivered in supportive groups, a particularly effective combination should emerge.

However, the flexitime studies, which were conducted in a large city environment, showed that when large blocks of time committed to commuting were added to work time, time for other activities became a very precious resource. Thus, it would appear that one other intervention to help parents with young children entails part-time work (e.g., 66%, 75%) that maintains status on a job or career ladder and where full benefits are accrued, albeit on a prorated basis. Also, at certain points, such as the birth of a child, leaves for men and women need to be available which guarantee the same or similar position on return to work. A recent Supreme Court case has guaranteed this right. These other kinds of interventions in the work world have required, and will continue to require, changes at the institutional level.

A COMPREHENSIVE APPROACH USING THE BOOK'S FRAMEWORK

Defining the Problem and Multilevel Analyses

In these last sections, we will use the prior empirical findings and conclusions to illustrate a more comprehensive approach to the problems of parents working outside the home. The example will make use of the proactive/developmental/ecological perspective and flow through the book's framework.

The specific problem can be defined at multiple levels. At the individual level, the problem of being a parent with a young child(ren) and also working full time outside the home is manifested by a general difficulty in coordinating home and family life activities. More specifically, there is a shortage of time for home and child care activities, resulting in high levels of stress for a substantial percentage of parents working full time outside the home. The supposition is that for a subset of this population segment, high levels of stress may contribute to a range of mental health (e.g., marital discord) and health (e.g., substance abuse) problems. The word *may* is underscored since this chain of events is not well documented in the literature. In addition, the goals of the intervention to be described are primarily health enhancement and improved quality of life, rather than preventing pathology.

From a developmental perspective, though, it is likely that individual manifestations of the general problem are relatively more intense at certain points. For example, following the birth of a child, returning back to work full time may be particularly stressful.

From an ecological perspective, certain environmental impediments and changes can heighten stress. For example, child care using home-based individuals may break down or terminate. Or the transition from a day care center, which extended to 5:30 p.m., to public school, which ends at 3:00 p.m., can result in considerable problems for parents working outside the home. Thus, life transition and ecological considerations are important aspects of defining the problem and designing programs.

At the interpersonal level, there also is some evidence that because of time constraints and role conflicts, working parents with young children may not have strong social network affiliations or social support (Hopkins & White, 1978). If more time is made available for social activities, stronger network affiliations may develop. As noted in King et al. (1986), there appear to be at least some indirect benefits that accrue from regular group interactions with individuals in similar work and family group situations.

At the organization/environment level, it has been noted that work hours have rarely been established with the family needs of workers as a prime or even secondary consideration. Indeed, within the corporate and labor world, work and family domains have been separated and therefore, not surprisingly, have infrequently been cojointly studied in the behavioral sciences (Kanter, 1977). At the level of work organizations, a number of interventions, such as flexitime, can help working parents. In addition, for some individuals (e.g., those with long commutes), being able to partly work at home also may be helpful. However, there are some obvious tradeoffs for individuals working at home—e.g., social isolation, part of a home which must be devoted to work space, interruptions and distractions versus saving time—as well as organizational problems (e.g., supervision), and institutional dilemmas (e.g., tax deductions for home work space).

It has also been noted that other organizations and settings, particularly those involved in child care, can help or hinder the working parent. It still is the case that most of the care of preschool children is done by informal or more formalized means in the children's home or the homes of others (i.e., babysitters). The advantages of such care are that it can be more personalized and provide more attention to individual children. Unfortunately, such care can also be haphazard and unsupervised. The effects of center care on child development have been studied for years. At a minimum, it has been found that high-quality center care is not harmful and may, indeed, have some developmental benefits (Twardosz, 1987). However, quality in state and federal regulation is generally defined by particular aspects of the child care setting (e.g., fire safety; ratio of staff to children at particular ages) and has less to do with specific interaction styles or environmental parameters that may enhance activities (e.g., Twardosz, 1987; Twardosz, Cataldo, & Risley, 1974). Although it is possible to inform parents what the research literature suggests as a more optimal form of center care, a center may more likely be chosen because it is conveniently located and has better hours of operation (e.g., will care for children until 6 p.m.). Because there is not an unlimited number of centers, choice may be more a product of fit with immediate needs and scheduling.

A specific problem for families with school-aged children is the latchkey syndrome. The basis of the problem from an ecological perspective is that the school day ends too early and work ends too late. Thus, the child may arrive home from school and be alone for two to four hours. As we noted above, part of the solution for this problem rests with extending care in the school setting until the late afternoon and with flexible or part-time work schedules.

Extensions of school-based care and the provision of part-time work with full job or career ladder consideration and prorated health benefits are primarily institutional issues. That is, while any school district or work organization might develop innovative programs in these domains, such benefits are unlikely to become universally available without state and federal initiative. At a time of fiscal conservatism, innovations that appear to be expensive are most unlikely to garner support. However, modification of the school day and part-time work may provide benefits to diverse population segments. For example, after-school programs could be separately paid for by working parents, thus providing additional jobs for others. Likewise, the option of protected part-time work may provide a predictable pool of hours and work so that additional people can be hired—i.e., new jobs will be created. A caveat, as noted, is that such innovations require change at the institutional level.

In a number of cases where flexitime was adopted on an experimental basis, labor and management negotiated so that certain regulations were temporarily suspended. Thus, for example, with flexitime systems where more than eight hours could be worked on a particular day, overtime provisions were dropped (Nollen, 1982). Similar stances can be taken so that small-scale experimentation is conducted with after-school programs and part-time work.

This overall review and our work described in prior sections suggest that the problems of time and stress for working parents with young children are the result of combinations of individual, interpersonal, organizational, and institutional factors. The problems may be heightened at difficult transition points and by ecological variables. The discussion also outlined a number of alternative steps and programs. At this juncture, the conceptual and strategic underpinnings of the proposed interventions will be described.

Goals, Concepts, and Strategies

It has already been underscored that the interventions to be designed will fit within a proactive/developmental/ecological perspective. In this chapter, these three terms have been described at length and will not receive further explanation here. The general goal of the intervention is to provide parents working outside the home with the skills and environmental mechanisms to better coordinate home and work life at particular transition points, such as school entry of a child. The focus in this section is on the concepts and strategies which underlie different parts of the intervention.

As was noted, there appears to be a need for teaching individual skills in time management, handling critical situations, (e.g., the loss of a babysitter), negotiating new family arrangements such as the division of labor for child and home care, and giving and receiving social support. In addition, more straightforward information needs to be imparted on such topics as choosing a mode of child care. These diverse skills, as well as more specific information, present a good fit with social cognitive theory, particularly behavioral modeling techniques (Bandura, 1986). For example, different scenarios in a short lesson plan format can be videotaped with alterations in the characters and situations encountered (e.g., single female parent in a large city) designed for specific population segments. These videotapes can be made generally available through mass market distribution (about two thirds of American homes now have VCRs) and through hospitals, pediatricians, libraries, worksites, and rental stores.

The videotapes can use an interesting storyline and the strategies and formats described in detail in chapter 4. Consistent with social cognitive theory, each particular topic (e.g., time management) should have demonstrations, instruction in goal setting, and step-by-step individual assignments. A recommendation for the videotapes is that they be viewed with spouses or partners and friends or acquaintances in small groups and then discussed afterward, specifically with regard to carrying out particular steps. This idea follows the notion of a media forum successfully used in the dissemination of innovations (Rogers, 1983). Additional material on later segments of a tape can focus on maintaining skills through varying and trying circumstances and discuss developmental hurdles the child will pass and their respective and particular problems. It also is possible to conceive of a series of such tapes covering different childhood periods, e.g., school entry.

Thus, through behavioral modeling which should increase self-efficacy, goal setting, and social support, and through practice and maintenance exercises, the videotapes would be designed in a way that encapsulates what is known about initial and longer-term behavior change (Bandura, 1986; Brownell et al., 1986).

The more didactic information can also be presented in an effective visual manner. For example, actual depictions of optimal and suboptimal child care situations can be shown. Key points that differentiate such settings can be emphasized.

Clearly, the second conceptual notion which underlies the individual level intervention is *personal control*. That is, the general goal of teaching time management, parenting, and other family skills is to help individuals gain a measure of control of their behavior and settings. The perception and gaining of control is a legitimate goal in its own right, since perceptions of noncontrol have been identified from a variety of perspectives as a key component of ill-health (e.g., Antonovsky, 1987). The notion of personal control is also a basis of interventions at organizational and institutional levels.

Alternative work patterns such as flexitime, flexiplace (i.e., work at home), and part-time work allow individuals more choice on when, where, and how long they want to work, and how work will fit together with other responsibilities. Granted that not everyone relishes the idea of such control, but for those who do, alterations in work patterns provide a vehicle for control. Note, however, alternative work patterns are *not* being mandated for working parents. The different work patterns are simply one possible choice.

Extensions in school hours also provide an important degree of control by allowing parents to work more routine hours with the assurance that their child is in a suitably supervised situation. Likewise, extended school days are an option and not mandated.

As was noted above, ecological interventions also nicely fit public health ideals of creating structural, passive interventions. However, adhering to the notion of personal choice means that such structures and resources are available, and not required, as are some other public health interventions. Thus, it is anticipated that the choice dimension would be emphasized and resistance and, indeed, backlash, diminished.

Intervention Design Issues

Consistent with a proactive, developmental, and ecological perspective, the interventions to be designed should be most appropriately targeted to parents just prior to and during a transition point. Thus, for example, before the birth of a child, some planning and practice should occur, with the most intense part of the intervention (individual instruction) occurring at a critical juncture such as the return to work. A period for trying new work patterns and individual skills and resources (which could be creatively combined) can also be used. A commitment can be obtained to a particular pattern after this time, with the commitment to last for at least several months.

An ecological perspective recommends interventions at multiple levels — i.e., individual instruction plus group support plus organizational change. Optimistically, it can be expected that this strategy will result in interactive and synergistic benefits. For example, more skilled and less stressed parents should be more productive workers, and more optimal work conditions should enhance family life.

Intervention Implementation Issues

In some respects, this overall program appears to be exceedingly complex because it involves multiple strategies in multiple settings. While by no means dismissing the difficulty in implementing such an effort, it should be noted that in the spirit of public health, parts of the overall intervention are relatively passive. For example, once the rules and supervisory systems for alternative work patterns are in place (by no means a simple task, since part-time work and flexiplace, as noted, require institutional actions), except for periodic review and some revisions, it is not an intervention that requires constant prompting and surveillance for behavior change. Likewise, once an after-school program is established, it can also continue with routine supervision and administration. Further, such programs can be used by successive waves of parents and children. Thus, these interventions also fit Cowen's (1980) notion of prevention through structural change.

The individual-level intervention, while made relatively permanent by use of videotape, does require diverse and considerable person power in the design and revision phases (Winett, 1987). For example, an array of production professionals (from scriptwriters to camera people and tape editors) is needed. In addition, marketing professionals using formative research strategies can help in capturing the nuances of critical behaviors and situations for different people (e.g., middle-income but single parent living in a large city) at different points in the life cycle.

These subtle yet important differences between target audiences can be studied and then important points used by behavioral scientists, working in concert with scriptwriters and other production personnel. Relevant scenarios need to be created for the videotapes, with these scenarios adhering to the structures of social cognitive theory for story line, modeling, and format (Winett, 1986). It is also apparent that effective segmentation and targeting would require permutations of basic videotapes by person, place, and life-cycle variables. Differential marketing plans may be required for different segments. It was noted above that the videotapes would be "relatively permanent." In order to continue to be effective, it is likely that the videotapes would have to be periodically updated and altered to reflect changing conditions and mores. Thus, it is clear that the individual part of the intervention would require considerable resources and personnel to design, produce, and market the videotapes and implement the overall program.

The group part of the intervention, however, is seen as informal, although the videotapes can include pointers for mutual help and feedback in practice assignments, topics for discussion, and so on. Except for opportunity costs, this part of the overall program should be neither cumbersome nor expensive.

As with all the exemplar programs described in this book, it is recommended that any larger-scale efforts be preceded by a series of small-scale pilot studies. For example, several cooperative firms could test out the feasibility of alternative work schedules with parents returning to the work force after the birth of a child. The individual and group components emphasizing information dissemination, skill development, and mutual help and support would also be enacted. And a detailed and comprehensive measurement system (below) can examine multiple impacts and program areas in need of change.

Additional pilot studies can help refine an overall program. However, it is likely that a series of pilot studies would need to be undertaken for programs aimed at different target groups at different points in the life cycle. It is important at the end of a series of pilot studies not only that refined programs emerge, but that there is a good sense of the relative costs and benefits to individuals, organizations, and communities of alterations in family patterns, child care settings, and work sites.

Assessment of Impacts

As noted, the general goal of the intervention is to provide parents working outside the home with specific skills and environmental resources to better coordinate home and work life at particular transition points. This general goal should be manifested by self-reports of more feelings of control over scheduling and responsibilities and less stress; more quality time spent with children and spouse or partner; better child adjustment and development; and more satisfaction and productivity at work. Thus, measurement must consider a person's cognitions, affect, and behavior in multiple situations and in the face of particular critical incidents; the effects of the person's interactions on others (spouse, child, coworkers), and how individual, group, and setting processes and changes affect each other.

In addition, it appears important to carefully document the costs and benefits for work and school settings, beyond those estimates made in the pilot studies. For example, measures of all employees' satisfaction and productivity with the introduction of alternative work patterns, which may only be used by a minority of employees, can be ascertained. The questions of the effects of flexitime and part-time work on supervisory efficiency and additions to the work force and attendant costs (e.g., for training) need to be determined. More briefly, evaluation needs to be pinpointed, yet comprehensive. In addition, and consistent with the book's framework, the entire assessment of the impacts phase needs to adhere to the basic tenets of the proactive/developmental ecological perspective, so that the evaluation is a test of components of the perspective and overall orientation.

CONCLUSION

The multifaceted intervention described in the last sections of this chapter is certainly more extensive than those more individual-based "Strength and Competency" programs described in Table 6.2. The intervention is also quite far removed from programs that are designed to prevent a particular DSM-III disorder, and seemingly from a different world than a medical model orientation seeking to cure major mental health disorders by finding their biological bases. The intervention proposed in this chapter will not cure major mental health illnesses, although it is likely that if effective, the intervention may reduce the incidence and prevalence rates of DSM-III disorders. The intervention is, therefore, in no way seen as a panacea—i.e., as a means to eliminate all individual pathology and all life's problems. Overall, however, the goals and operation of this type of exemplar, comprehensive approach should demonstrate the benefits of proactive interventions based on developmental and ecological considerations and the framework of this book.

7
Prevention in Maternal, Child and Adolescent Health: A Developmental, Multilevel Approach to the Problem of Teenage Pregnancy

INTRODUCTION

Maternal and child/adolescent health is among the most important of health care fields. A major reason for this is the potential twofold impact of health efforts in this area — both on the mother as well as the child — during what are considered to be the most critical stages of human development. Because of this impact, the field of public health has paid particular attention to the health care concerns of pregnant women and their infants. Considerable time and effort has been directed toward identifying and preventing a range of diseases and conditions influencing the health of the mother and her child.

The focus and scope of this book obviates an extensive review of this field. The interested reader is directed to other sources for such a review (e.g., Hanlon & Pickett, 1984). Instead, the current chapter presents a brief overview of major trends stemming from both public health and psychology-based efforts in the field. This is followed by an in-depth analysis of a problem of particular importance to the maternal and child health arena — teenage pregnancy. The framework described in chapter 2 is applied in discussing the integration of theoretical approaches, stemming from psychology, with epidemiological and health education approaches from the public health arena.

Current Epidemiologic Trends

Significant advances have been made in the maternal and child health care field over the past fifty years. During that time, maternal mortality in the United States has declined nearly one hundred percent, while infant mortality has declined about seventy-five percent (Hanlon & Pickett, 1984). The factors influencing these improvements include improvement in maternal nutritional status, increased effectiveness and availability of medical technology and services, and improvement in methods of early detection, screening, and intervention. For instance, it has been pointed out that the percentage of women receiving prenatal care during the first trimester of pregnancy has continued to increase, from 68 to 74 percent during the 1960s and 1970s (U.S. Public Health Service, 1983).

Many of the hazards to pregnant women and infants in this country have been brought under control over the past seven to eight decades. This has been accomplished with the advent of measures such as disposal of human wastes, purification of water, sanitation of milk and food, and improved prenatal management of a host of infectious diseases (e.g., tuberculosis, diphtheria, whooping cough, measles) and genetic disorders (e.g., Rh reaction). Current hazards are found instead in the increasing amount of toxic substances existing in the environment (Messite & Bond, 1980); the present organization and uneven availability of health services for pregnant women (with strong ethnic, socioeconomic, and geographic differences in maternal and infant mortality continuing to exist in this country; Hanlon & Pickett, 1984); and the mother's own health behaviors (e.g., alcohol, tobacco, and drug abuse during pregnancy; Cushner, 1981).

In addition to these risks, an increasing amount of discussion has taken place over whether pregnancy and childbirth should continue to be treated as a medical problem or, instead, as a natural process. Proponents of the "demedicalization" of maternal care point to the large proportion of medical and technical procedures currently being performed in the United States (including electronic monitoring of the fetus, induced labor, and Caesarian sections), which may in many cases be unnecessary, as well as potentially risky and costly. For instance, a study of live births in the state of Arkansas showed that medical interventions were distributed disproportionately by day of the week, suggesting that more than simply medical considerations were involved (Mangald, 1981). This is in the face of evidence suggesting that 70% of all pregnancies are perfectly normal, and thus could, if accompanied by accessible medical backup, occur in a more natural setting with fewer medical interventions, risks, and significantly reduced costs (Hanlon & Pickett, 1984). As the American public becomes increasingly savvy concerning consumer issues in the health care arena, debates concerning such issues are expected to intensify. Examples of recent consumer preferences in the area of childbirth include alternative birthing centers, increased involvement on the part of the husband and family, and a shorter hospital stay following delivery.

Conceptual Approaches

Given the remarkable physical and psychological changes that occur for the mother and child from the point of conception through the birth and rearing of the child, it makes sense to apply a developmental approach in studying maternal and child health. Health professionals have typically focused on several discrete physiologic phases in delineating potential problems that could threaten the mother and/or her child. They include the preconceptional period, when issues of birth control, sexual activity, and family planning are important; the antepartum (pregnancy) phase, when prevention-oriented health care and health behavior are critical; the intrapartum (delivery) phase, when the focus is primarily on access to proper medical and health services; the postpartum period, typically composed of the first year of life, when congenital problems, issues related to feeding, respiratory difficulties, accidents, battering, and homicide comprise the types of hazards typically faced; and the preschool (ages 2-4), childhood (ages 5-12), and adolescent (ages 13-19) periods of development. Of the latter three phases, the preschool phase is considered to be a particularly important period of physical and emotional growth. Although death at this point in development becomes more infrequent, morbidity, in the form of communicable diseases, accidents, and psychological or emotional trauma, is often high (Hanlon & Pickett, 1984). During all three of these phases, the psychological and intellectual development of the child becomes an area of major concern.

Trends from Public Health and Psychology

As has been noted for other health topics presented in this book, the work of professionals in public health and in psychology has advanced relatively independently.

Public Health

The targets for intervention by public health professionals have traditionally been the pregnant woman and young children, particularly infants. An extensive amount of effort has been directed toward improving health care during pregnancy, delivery, and the postnatal period, along with delivering preventive health care services (i.e., screening). Such efforts have been increasingly supplemented with programs aimed at aiding decision making during the preconceptional period as well. These programs include state-administered genetic counseling services and a burgeoning of family planning and contraceptive services (National Center for Health Statistics, 1982). For the period following conception, an array of programs has been developed in such areas as maternal and child nutrition, as well as programs dealing with sexually transmitted diseases, alcohol and tobacco use, and drug abuse during pregnancy. Medical techniques such as amniocentesis for high-risk pregnant women (e.g., those over 35, or with a prior history of congenital difficulties) have been increasingly perfected. Following birth, health departments and other public health agencies currently offer a variety of services, including newborn and infant feeding programs, well-child clinics, and services for handicapped children. Health departments are typically involved as well, in collaboration with social services and similar agencies, in child abuse reporting and case-finding activities. With the increase in family-oriented childbirth, a growing effort has been made to include family members in many of the programs mentioned above. Such developments have paralleled the changing attitude in recent years toward the use of professionally trained nurse-midwives and out-of-hospital deliveries (American Public Health Association, 1980; Bennetts & Lubic, 1982). These types of efforts underscore the growing focus on "rehumanizing" what has become an increasingly technological and sterile approach to the childbirth process.

To aid programming efforts in areas related to pregnancy, childbirth, and child care, the American Public Health Association has published a book of guidelines and standards in a variety of areas, including family planning, prenatal and postpartum care, health education, teenage pregnancy, and nutrition programs (Committee on Maternal Health Care and Family Planning, 1978). In addition, professionals have in the past called for a five-part approach to the area, including: formation of a maternal–child national health service, which would provide family planning services, prenatal care, obstetric services and postnatal care, well-child services, immunizations, pre-school screening, and school health programs; a public feeding program; community-based family support centers; national housing reform; and continued effort to develop performance standards and guidelines for health departments and private providers (Miller, 1975). In our current period of political conservatism and fiscal uneasiness, it is doubtful whether such programs will occur on a national level, although some states and cities have taken the lead in enhancing maternal and child health programming for their populations (e.g., Porter, 1981).

In addition to programs offered by health agencies, women's health groups have become increasingly active in informing women about ways to take better care of themselves, physically as well as emotionally. Self-help books such as *Our Bodies, Ourselves* (Boston Women's Health Book Collective, 1976) have provided an array of information on issues of specific relevance for women, such as gynecological care, pregnancy, and rape.

These and the other public health programming efforts described above have been largely empirically, rather than theoretically, driven. As is the case for most public health endeavors, the primary target has been prevention of problems through methods that are typically applicable on a large scale and which include higher levels (i.e., institutional, environmental, organizational) of analysis and intervention. Such efforts have generally been primarily service-oriented.

Psychology

In contrast to public health efforts in the field, a major focus of psychological study of maternal and child health has been on childhood development, particularly on psychological, emotional, and intellectual fronts. In these areas, theory-building and application have been particularly strong (e.g., Piaget & Inhelder, 1969; Erikson, 1968; Bandura, 1977; Jessor, 1984). Theoretical formulations of cognitive, emotional, moral, and behavioral developmental patterns have been described, and, in some cases (e.g., the work of Piaget and Bandura), applied directly to the development of educational curricula and remedial learning programs.

Areas of childhood development where psychologists have made contributions of particular note, in terms of increased understanding as well as intervention, include: developmental disorders (e.g., infantile autism, developmental dysphasia, developmental dyslexia, attention deficit disorders; Ornitz, 1986); achievement deficits (Lloyd & Bettencourt, 1986); and childhood behavior disorders, such as school refusal or depressive behaviors (Gelfand, Ficula, & Zarbatany, 1986). Other areas of increasing interest include the influence of family interaction patterns on childhood development and prevention of crime and delinquency (Nietzel & Himelein, 1986).

Aside from a few recent efforts to consider these issues in light of a preventive orientation (e.g., Edelstein & Michelson, 1986), much of the focus of psychologists remains on developing methods for identification and treatment of distressed children and families. With some exceptions (e.g., achievement deficits, some types of developmental disorders), a significant proportion of such intervention efforts occurs outside of typical child or family settings (i.e., in clinics or mental health centers). One area in which primary prevention efforts by psychologists and other health professionals have been growing, with promising outcomes thus far, is school-based health promotion programming. In areas such as alcohol and drug use (Perry & Jessor, 1983), smoking (Telch, Killen, McAllister, Perry, & Maccoby, 1982), and dietary intake (King et al., 1988), recent evidence suggests that children and adolescents can be taught a set of cognitive–behavioral skills for implementing preventive health behaviors.

In addition to the school setting itself (Rutter, Maughan, Mortimore, & Outston, 1979), some psychologists have focused on the effects of environmental influences such as media (Bandura, 1973; Rychtarik et al., 1983) on childhood development and behavior. Yet most efforts by psychologists to date have remained within personal and interpersonal levels of analysis.

Convergence of Psychological and Public Health Perspectives

It is clear that both psychology and public health fields have much to offer in responding to the health challenges presented in the maternal and child health arena. As has been discussed in chapter 1, the public health perspective brings with it a rich source of epidemiological data and methods, as well as a focus on preventively based and higher-order approaches to intervention. In contrast, psychology offers a diversity of developmental, cognitive, and behavioral theories along with empirically based intervention strategies of potential relevance to the maternal and child health field. In addition, it offers particular insights into mental health issues. The rest of this chapter focuses on the blending of psychology and public health perspectives in discussing one of the major challenges currently facing the maternal and child health field, as well as the nation as a whole—the problem of *teenage pregnancy*.

TEENAGE PREGNANCY—THE EXTENT OF THE PROBLEM

In its social, scientific, political, and economic makeup the United States is a country of startling contrasts. Perhaps nowhere is this more evident than in the statistics which define the magnitude of the problem of teenage pregnancy in this country. Despite the position of the United States as one of the richest and most advanced countries in the world, it continues to lead all other Western developed countries in rates of teenage pregnancy, abortion, and childbearing (The Alan Guttmacher Institute, 1986). This is particularly the case for teenagers under 15 years of age. The United States has also earned the peculiar distinction of being the only country in which the rates of teenage pregnancy have actually been increasing in recent years. In 1988 alone, more than one million teenage pregnancies occurred, which translates into a ratio of roughly one pregnancy per every 10 teenage girls (Foster, 1986). This teenage pregnancy rate is more than twice that of countries such as Canada, England, and Wales (Jones et al., 1985). For the two million girls turning fourteen during the next year, approximately forty percent can be expected to become pregnant at some point during their teenage years (The Alan Guttmacher Institute, 1981). The vast majority of these pregnancies will be unplanned (Jones et al., 1985).

While the teenage pregnancy rates in the United States differ drastically relative to other Western nations, research suggests that patterns of premarital sex and the proportion of teenagers engaging in sexual activity in the United States are similar to those of other developed countries (Dryfoos, 1985). Approximately half of 15 to 17-year-old males and one third of 15–17-year-old females are sexually active (Foster, 1986). Given the current low rates of teenage marriage in the United States (about 4 percent of teenagers), most teenage sexual activity takes place outside of marriage (The Alan Guttmacher Institute, 1981). The declining rate of teenage marriage in this country since the 1960s is a consequence of a number of factors, including growth of extended educational opportunities, poor job prospects for young adults, women's increased entry into the workforce, and a greater acceptance of nonmarital sex and cohabitation (Furstenberg & Brooks-Gunn, 1986). If young people today were to continue their parent's tradition of delaying intercourse until they were of marriageable age, they would need to wait until they were in their early to middle twenties, rather than late teens, as was the case in the 1950s. Given this, it is not surprising that the relationship between marriage and sexual activity has been attenuated (Furstenberg & Brooks-Gunn, 1986).

Although teenage marriage rates declined as the rates of teenage sexual activity rose during the "sexual revolution" of the 1960s and the decade following it, the issue of teenage sexual activity and pregnancy is actually quite an old one. In fact, teenage sexuality has been considered a problem as far back as the turn of the century (Furstenberg & Brooks-Gunn, 1986). Kinsey and colleagues (1953) estimated that during the 1950s a significant percentage of all marriages were to pregnant teenage girls. In contrast to earlier times, fewer teenage pregnancies today result in marriage; for instance, in 1978 only 31 percent of pregnant teenagers electing to give birth opted for marriage (The Alan Guttmacher Institute, 1981).

While the number of teenage pregnancies increased during the 1970s, the number of births to teenagers of all ages has actually shown a decrease between 1970 and 1984 (National Research Council, 1987). This decline has been attributed to the diminishing size of the teenage population since 1977 and the increased use of contraception among teenagers, as well as an increased number of teenage abortions starting in the late 1970s (National Research Council, 1987). Approximately 30 percent of all abortions performed in the United States each year—approximately 443,300—involve adolescents (National Research Council, 1987). This is despite the fact that teenagers account for only eighteen percent of sexually active women capable of becoming pregnant (The Alan Guttmacher Institute, 1981). For girls between the ages of 15 and 19, forty percent of their pregnancies end in abortion. For younger girls, the number of abortions has outnumbered the number of births since approximately 1974 (National Research Council, 1987). It is frightening to realize that the U.S. teenage abortion rate alone equals or exceeds the teenage pregnancy rate in other Western nations (The Alan Guttmacher Institute, 1981).

As indicated above, there has been an increase in use of contraceptives in the teenage population in this country, beginning in the 1970s, although this increase leveled off in the early 1980s (National Research Council, 1987). Despite this increase, level of contraceptive use among U.S. adolescents remains poor relative to use in other industrialized nations (Furstenberg & Brooks-Gunn, 1986). This is not surprising given the mixed messages American youth receive concerning contraception and the haphazard way in which birth control services are delivered to many teenagers (Jones et al., 1985). Of those stating that they use some form of birth control, many are inconsistent users (National Research Council, 1987). Because approximately half of all premarital pregnancies occur during the first six months following initiation of sexual activity, early contraceptive use is particularly crucial (Zabin, Kantner, & Zelnik, 1979). Unfortunately, between one third and two thirds of individuals use no contraception at first intercourse (Morrison, 1985).

Despite the decline in the rates of teenage parenthood since the mid-1970s, parenthood does occur in over half a million teenage girls each year (comprising almost fifteen percent of all births in the United States), and thus remains a serious national problem (National Center for Health Statistics, 1985). The birth represents a second or third delivery for well over ten percent of teenagers (Foster, 1986). In addition, despite the overwhelming number of teenage births which are unintended, it appears that extremely few teenagers elect to give their babies up for adoption (National Research Council, 1987).

The Cost of Teenage Pregnancy

The economic, social, and psychological costs of teenage pregnancy to this nation are staggering. Pregnant teenagers who give birth have a substantially lower probability of finishing high school, have reduced job prospects, and are more likely to rely on public assistance than other groups (Foster, 1986). Approximately sixty percent of teenage mothers receive welfare, with almost half of all Aid to Families with Dependent Children (AFDC) outlays going to households containing women who are or have been teenage mothers (Burden & Klerman, 1984).

Pregnant teenagers, particularly young teenagers, also face an increased number of serious health risks. For girls age fifteen and younger, pregnancy is associated with an increased risk of conditions such as anemia, toxemia, and birth complications (Rosenbaum, 1985). While adequate prenatal care, particularly during the first trimester, is considered to be crucial to minimize complications during pregnancy and birth, less than half of teenagers typically receive prenatal care during that period (National Center for Health Statistics, 1984). As a result, the pregnant teenager may unknowingly subject her infant and herself to a variety of health hazards, including those brought on by deleterious health behaviors such as malnourishment, alcohol consumption, smoking, and caffeine intake (Randolph & Gesche, 1986). While abortions are associated with fewer health risks than childbirth, the moral, psychological, and legal tensions often surrounding the decision to abort cannot be ignored (Interdivisional Committee on Adolescent Abortion, 1987). Abortions are also more costly to society than is prevention of the pregnancy itself. For the sexually active teenager, the risks of becoming pregnant are compounded further by the potential risks of contracting sexually transmitted diseases (STD)—a hazard of major proportions facing young people in this country. Eighty-six percent of the over ten million cases of STD which occur annually are found in 15- to 29-year-olds (U.S. Public

Health Service, 1983). The recent increase in AIDS poses a potentially serious additional threat to sexually active teenagers.

In addition to the teenage mother herself, babies born to teenagers face an increased number of health risks, including low birth weight and premature birth (Foster, 1986). Both of these conditions are associated with heightened risks of birth defects or disability. Compared to normal weight infants, low birth-weight infants are 20 times more likely to die in the first year of life; those who survive face a one in four chance of sustaining a chronic disability (Foster, 1986). With the stress of teenage motherhood comes an increased risk for the child of inadequate health care, inadequate nutrition, accident, or injury (Rosenbaum, 1985; Spivak & Weitzman, 1987), and abuse and neglect (Bolton, Laner, & Kane, 1980). The few studies conducted in the area of cognitive development to date also suggest that preschool- and elementary school-age boys born to teenage mothers show poorer cognitive functioning than boys born to older mothers (the reasons for the sex difference are currently unclear) (Furstenberg & Brooks-Gunn, 1986). Decrements in school achievement in children of teenage mothers have been noted through adolescence (Brooks-Gunn & Furstenberg, 1985; Spivak & Weitzman, 1987).

Alarmed by the above trends, the Committee on Child Development Research and Public Policy within the National Research Council established, with support from five foundations, a study panel in 1984 on adolescent pregnancy and childbearing. The panel ended its two-year review of trends, research, and policy and program alternatives in the area with a statement defining six general conclusions. Briefly, the conclusions consisted of the following (National Research Council, 1987): (a) In relation to a future course of action, *prevention* of adolescent pregnancy should receive the highest priority. This conclusion has been echoed by other professionals as well, including the Council of State Policy and Planning Agencies, which has stated that "preventing teenage pregnancy could be the single most important measure . . . that could be taken in avoiding both short-term and long-term costs, both to the teenagers themselves and to the taxpayers" (Foster, 1986, p. 29); (b) Contraception is currently the surest strategy for achieving pregnancy prevention — in particular, the panel identified the contraceptive pill to be the safest and most effective means of birth control for sexually active teenagers; (c) Conceptualizations of the problem and relevant solutions must include teenage boys; (d) Teenagers are a heterogeneous group; thus, a variety of approaches, tailored to specific needs, will need to be developed; (e) If it becomes necessary to set priorities within the adolescent population as a whole, then greater attention should be focused on those teenagers for whom the consequences of pregnancy and birth are likely to be the most serious — namely, young teenagers and those from economically and socially disadvantaged backgrounds; and (f) Given the magnitude and nature of the problem, responsibility for developing solutions should be shared across a number of levels, including individuals, families, voluntary organizations, communities, and governments.

Implications of the above conclusions, in relation to the types of intervention strategies currently proposed in this area, will be discussed later in the chapter.

Factors Associated with Teenage Pregnancy

From our preceding discussion, it has become apparent that, rather than being confined to one behavior, the road to teenage pregnancy is comprised of a chain of behaviors and decisions embarked on by the adolescent, any one of which could be used as a focus for study and intervention. These decisions include the decision — albeit often unplanned and arrived at hastily (Chilman, 1983) — to become sexually active; once active, the decision to use some form of contraception or not; if pregnancy occurs, the choice as to whether to carry the child to term or not; and, finally, the decision to keep the child or give it up for adoption (Flick, 1984). Obviously decisions occurring later in this sequence, because they are dependent on the outcomes of earlier decisions, will necessarily affect a smaller number of individuals. Interventions focused on later decisions (e.g., decisions to continue a pregnancy or not, or to keep the child once born) also, for the most part, necessitate greater societal involvement and costs (Moore & Burt, 1982). All of these decisions are influenced, to a greater or lesser extent, by a host of environmental factors (e.g., the family, neighborhood and community norms).

Similar to other areas discussed throughout this book, much of the effort that has gone into the teenage pregnancy area currently has focused on intervening with the teenager *after* she has become pregnant (e.g., Canada, 1986; Davis et al., 1986; Elster, Lamb, Tavare, & Ralston, 1987; Sugar, 1984b). Yet, in contrast to other areas, a growing amount of attention has also been given to influencing the decisions having a direct impact on prevention of pregnancy, i.e., decisions to become sexually active and to use contraception (Foster, 1986). As has typically been the case, efforts undertaken in the area of prevention have been spearheaded mainly by public health professionals, although psychologists have added some notable research in areas such as those assessing the influence of knowledge and attitudes toward sex and contraception on sexual activity and contraception use (e.g., Allgeier, 1981; DeLamater, 1981). In addition, psychologists have developed a number of theories, particularly in the area of child development, which have helped to shed light on the reasons underlying adolescent sexual behavior and may continue to be useful in aiding intervention. These will be discussed later in this chapter.

To increase the potential efficacy of intervention efforts, public health professionals and psychologists alike have searched for the factors having a major influence on sexual behavior in adolescents. In doing so, practically all working in this area have been struck by the incredible complexity of the behaviors under study, and the fact that variables spanning all levels of analysis, from intrapersonal through societal, are significantly involved. Suffice it to say that the web of causation is extremely complex, and we are currently far from having a solid understanding of how factors interrelate and interact with one another. Given this, research has typically focused on explicating single factors that appear to be associated with teenage sexual activity, contraceptive use, and pregnancy. Some of the more potent demographic and social variables are discussed below, using categories adapted from those proposed by Flick (1984). While most work to date has gone into explicating the characteristics of teenage girls at risk for becoming pregnant, the necessity of putting more effort into understanding the role of the teenage boy in all aspects of the behavioral chain has been increasingly stressed (Foster, 1986).

Factors Associated with Sexual Activity

Demographic Variables. Not surprisingly, the older the teenager, the more likely it is that he or she is sexually active. Average age at first intercourse is currently 16 for girls and 15 for boys, with mean age continuing to drop steadily with time (National Research Council, 1987). Ethnicity is also associated with sexual activity. Black teenagers are currently forty percent more likely to be sexually active than whites, although sexual activity in whites appears to be increasing more rapidly, and includes having more sexual partners and more frequent intercourse than blacks (Foster, 1986). A more potent predictor than ethnicity is poverty, with poorer teenagers much more likely to become sexually active at an early age (Randolph & Gesche, 1986; Salguero, 1984). Added to this is the effect of the living environment, with urban teens more active than nonurban teens and those living in ghettos more active than those who are not. Additionally, low educational attainment is related to sexual activity in both teenage boys and girls (Foster, 1986).

Family Variables. A host of family factors have been suggested to be linked with increased teenage sexual activity. They include weak parental involvement in the life of the teenager and poor parent–child communication; large family size (independent of poverty and educational factors); engagement in sexual activity on the part of an older sister; less involvement in religious activities on the part of the family and the teenager him or herself; and being part of a single-parent family (Flick, 1984; National Research Council, 1987). The evidence concerning some of these factors (e.g., the effect of parental communication about sexual matters) is currently mixed (Fursten-berg & Brooks-Gunn, 1986). While teens with working mothers also appear to be more sexually active, they are also more likely to practice contraception (Flick, 1984).

Individual Variables. Sexually active teenagers tend to have lower aspirations and expectations for achievement and success coupled with a high value placed on independence, are more inflexible and confused concerning what is appropriate gender-role behavior, and, for males, report higher self-es-teem than their less active counterparts (Foster, 1986). Because the majority of the data in this area are cross-sectional, the temporal nature of the association is unknown. In addition, sexually active teens tend to engage more frequently in other risk-taking behaviors (e.g., use of marijuana, alcohol), and, for males, behave more aggressively than other teenagers.

Interpersonal Variables. As is the case for other behaviors of teenagers, such as drug abuse and smoking (Johnson, 1983), sexual activity is strongly influenced by the teenager's peer group. For both sexes, strong involvement with peers is related to earlier engagement in sexual activity. For younger teens, sexual activity often begins in conjunction with friends or acquaintances, rather than with steady dating partners (Zelnik & Shah, 1983). Teenagers engaging in sexual activity or using contraception tend to have friends who are also engaged in these activities (Furstenberg & Brooks-Gunn, 1986). In addition to the influences of friends, the influence imposed by the male partner of a couple can be quite potent (Flick, 1984; Fursten-berg & Brooks-Gunn, 1986). Recent studies suggest that for girls, sexual behavior is influenced more by social factors than by biological factors such as physical maturation; the latter has, in contrast, been found to be a strong influence for boys (National Research Council, 1987; Udry, Billy, Morris, Groff, & Raj, 1985).

Factors Associated with Contraceptive Use

Factors that have been found to be associated with teenage contraceptive use share a significant amount of overlap with those related to teenage sexual activity. They include the following:

Demographic Variables. Teenagers of lower socioeconomic status (SES), as well as those coming from larger families, are less likely to use contraceptives than other teenagers. In addition, blacks and Hispanics are less likely to use effective contraception than whites (National Research Council, 1987). This is despite the fact, pointed out earlier, that close to ninety percent of sexually active teenage girls do not want to become pregnant.

Girls who have become pregnant in the past are also more likely to use birth control than those who have never become pregnant (Foster, 1986).

Family Variables. As is the case for initiation of sexual activity, teenagers from families engaging in positive communication may be more likely to use contraception compared to those without such communication channels, although current evidence on this is mixed (Furstenberg, Herceg-Baron, Shea, & Webb, 1984; Morrison, 1985). Similarly, knowing about the contraceptive experiences of parents or siblings may increase the likelihood of early use of contraceptives (Flick, 1984). However, in general, parents are typically rated as the least important source of contraceptive information (Morrison, 1985). More frequently rated informational sources include peers, books and other media, and, for some teenagers, medical professionals (Morrison, 1985).

Individual Variables. Age (and the wisdom that typically accompanies it) is a strong predictor of contraception use. Other individual factors related to the use of birth control include belief in one's risk of becoming pregnant, perceived convenience of contraception, higher academic achievement, holding a more flexible view of female roles, having accurate knowledge about sex and birth control, a good self-concept, and sense of personal control (Flick, 1984). It has also been noted that women typically know more about contraception than men (Morrison, 1985).

Interpersonal Variables. Those teenagers who practice contraception appear to be less influenced by their peers than those who do not. For those who are in a steady relationship, teenage girls who are able to communicate effectively with their partners, and who feel that they have some influence in the relationship, are more likely to use contraception, even when their boyfriends are against it (Foster, 1986).

Other Environmental Variables. Among other environmental factors influencing use of contraception are the availability and confidentiality of contraceptive services, with family planning services that do not require parental consent showing a larger amount of use than those that do (Foster, 1986). In contrast, sex education classes have often been mentioned relatively infrequently as a source of knowledge about contraception (Morrison, 1985).

The Role of Media

A potentially powerful environmental influence on young people in relation to all aspects of sexuality is that of the mass media. As a researcher in the field stated in 1985:

> American teenagers seem to have inherited the worst of all possible worlds regarding their exposure to messages about sex: Movies, music, radio and TV

tell them that sex is romantic, exciting, titillating; premarital sex and cohabitation are visible ways of life among the adults they see and hear about; their
own parents or their parents' friends are likely to be divorced or separated but
involved in sexual relationships. Yet, at the same time, young people get the
message good girls should say no. Almost nothing they hear or see informs
them about contraception or the importance of preventing pregnancy . . .
Such messages stifle communication and expose young people to increased
risk of pregnancy, out-of-wedlock births and abortions. (Jones et al., 1985, p.
61)

From lyrics of popular music through MTV and nighttime "soaps," teenagers receive a daily barrage of sexual messages; so much so that it would be
surprising if their attitudes and actions were *not* affected accordingly. While
it is clear that the media can exert a powerful influence in focusing attention
on topics such as sex and in affecting the attitudes and beliefs of teenagers in
relation to sexual activity (Chilman, 1983; also see chapter 4), there has to
date been a dearth of information available through mass media sources
focused on the problems of unprotected sex and the costs that can accompany it. In the wake of the growing AIDS crisis, increasing pressure is being
applied by health professionals and other groups to disseminate information
broadly on safer sex practices, through both print and broadcast media
sources, to the American public. While we remain hopeful that this will
indeed occur, with potential positive consequences seen in the area of teenage pregnancy as well, federal and network response thus far has been
painfully slow (Holden, 1987). It is unfortunate that, with the wealth of
media channels and resources available to us, we have as yet been unable to
fully harness its enormous potential to positively influence the health of our
society.

Factors not Associated with Sexual Activity or Contraceptive Use

From the above brief review, it is clear that factors such as poverty,
influences from peers and other environmental sources, and ambiguous
parental involvement or modeling exert a powerful effect on the lives of
adolescents as they attempt to negotiate a path toward adulthood. The
accumulating literature in the field has also made clear those factors that do
not seem to be associated with teenage sexual activity or contraceptive use.
These factors include receiving public assistance, such as Aid to Families
with Dependent Children (AFDC), which does not appear to induce teenagers to become pregnant (Flick, 1984; Jones et al., 1985). In fact, Jones and
colleagues (1985), in a study of thirty-six developed countries, found that all
countries distributing even greater welfare benefits to pregnant teenagers
than the United States actually had lower adolescent pregnancy rates. Similarly, available research suggests that sex education courses do not have the
effect of increasing the amount of sexual activity among teenagers that some
individuals have accused them of having (Foster, 1986). While it remains

unclear whether or not sex education courses actually reduce teenage pregnancy rates, there is some data suggesting that involvement in such courses may foster more conservative attitudes among students toward premarital sex (Kirby, 1984). Finally, peer popularity in and of itself appears to have little bearing on the age of initiation or the amount of sexual activity in which a teenager engages (Flick, 1984).

APPLYING THE CONCEPTUAL/STRATEGIC FRAMEWORK TO UNDERSTANDING TEENAGE PREGNANCY— CONCEPTUALIZATIONS OF THE PROBLEM

While the epidemiologic data presented above help to identify those populations at greatest risk for becoming pregnant as teenagers, it is left to theoretical discussion to explicate some of the possible interrelationships among factors and to explore the motives (the "whys") underlying these relationships. Unfortunately, despite the large amount of effort that has been spent on increasing our understanding of teenage pregnancy, the field has suffered from a lack of a clear, comprehensive theoretical foundation (Reppucci, 1987).

Past attempts to explain the causes of teenage pregnancy have been largely unidimensional, focusing on the influence of one or two factors as the reason for the problem while excluding other variables known to play a role (Reppucci, 1987). A brief discussion of some of the more popular of these approaches follows, with subsequent description of the most recent multicomponent intervention efforts in the field. Finally, we will present suggestions, based on the model presented previously, for developing a more comprehensive framework for understanding, and intervening on, the behaviors leading to early pregnancy.

Psychological Conceptualizations

Intrapsychic and Psychodynamic Postulations

Early efforts on the psychological front (not necessarily by psychologists) have in particular been quite reductionist. Energy was put toward the development of a psychological "profile" to explain what was hypothesized to be a pathology shared by teenage girls who became pregnant (Abernathy, 1974; Curtis, 1973; Schinke, Gilchrist, & Small, 1979). The variety of psychological deficiencies and abnormalities proposed by professionals in the field has covered the gamut from attention seeking and depression through character disorder and psychosis (Sugar, 1984a). The act of becoming pregnant has been hypothesized to be, respectively, an escape from or reaction to conflict with the mother (Bonam, 1963; Fisher, 1984), a means of meeting oral dependency desires (Khlentzos & Pagliaro, 1965), a way of fulfilling deep narcissistic needs due to a poor self-concept (Fisher, 1984), a representation of a syndrome of failure (Webb, Briggs, & Brown, 1972), and a symbol of gross denial mechanisms (Schaffer & Pine, 1972; Shopper, 1984). Shopper (1984) has discussed adolescent sexuality and pregnancy in the context of what she terms the struggle over "vaginal ownership." Interestingly, in some cases teenage pregnancy in whites was attributed to psychopathology while pregnancy in nonwhites was proposed as being due to sociological factors (Sugar, 1984a).

Other researchers, however, have found no evidence of psychological disorder prior to pregnancy in pregnant, relative to nonpregnant, white and black teenagers (Gottschalk, Titchener, Piker, & Stewart, 1964; Kinch, Waring, Love, & McMahon, 1969). Suffice it to say that most research undertaken in this area has been uncontrolled, limited (e.g., based on retrospective reports from already pregnant teens), or biased in a number of other ways (Sugar, 1984a). Much of it smacks of a "blaming the victim" posture, while ignoring the potent environmental factors present. In addition, intrapsychic conceptualizations of the problem offer little direction in terms of intervention, save for an intensive, drawn-out process of psychotherapy. Needless to say, such an approach is expensive and highly impractical given the scope of the problem, and particularly problematic given the needed focus on prevention.

Current Psychological Conceptualizations

More recent approaches to the understanding of teenage pregnancy from a psychological perspective have focused on psychological and educational factors related to the behaviors preceding pregnancy, i.e., sexual activity and contraceptive use. In relation to teenage attitudes, beliefs, and knowledge in the area of contraceptive use — variables that have traditionally been popular sources of study for psychologists in general — there have been surprisingly few studies reported (Morrison, 1985). Knowledge about contraception appears to vary over time and with the age of the teenager, with younger and less sexually experienced teenagers knowing less than others (Morrison, 1985). While knowledge and beliefs concerning contraception vary across samples studied, findings in the area of human reproduction itself, particularly in younger teenagers, are fairly homogeneous; they suggest that many teenagers know relatively little about the facts surrounding becoming pregnant (DeAmicis, Klorman, Hess, & McAnarney, 1981; Freeman, Rickels, Huggins, Mudd, Garcia, & Dickens, 1980). While those who have participated in sex education classes know somewhat more than those who have not participated, the overall impact of sex education classes in these areas appears to be weak (Morrison, 1985). Possible reasons for this are discussed later in this chapter.

While a number of studies have found a correlation between attitudes held toward contraception and contraception use (e.g., Furstenberg, Shea, Allison, Herceg-Baron, & Webb, 1983; Gerrard, McCann, & Fortini, 1983), a causal relationship between such attitudes and contraceptive behavior cannot be directly inferred. In fact, other studies have found no relationship between attitudes toward contraception and contraception use (e.g., Jorgensen, 1980). For both sexual activity and contraceptive use, the role of attitudes, beliefs, and knowledge remains clouded, because these variables are often measured after sexual initiation has already occurred, resulting in the potential confounding of sexual experience in relation to these variables (National Research Council, 1987).

Several individual difference or personality variables have been studied in relation to contraceptive use. Studies focusing on locus of control (Rotter, 1966) have found mixed results, depending on how contraceptive use was defined (i.e., dichotomously, or by consistency of use). Studies using a dichotomous scale have generally found an association between use and a greater internal locus of control (Lundy, 1972; MacDonald, 1970). In contrast, no relationship has been found when contraception consistency or efficacy were used as independent variables (e.g., Herold, Goodwin, & Lero, 1979). Similar to locus of control, research findings on the relationship between contraceptive use and self-esteem have been mixed (Morrison, 1985).

It has been suggested that, given the reportedly unplanned nature of a teenager's initial forays into the sexual arena, formal decision-making processes become a less relevant approach to apply to the initiation of sexual activity (Furstenberg & Brooks-Gunn, 1986). A possibly more applicable area for the study of decision models concerns the decision to use contraception. One widely known model that has been applied to the contraception area is Ajzen and Fishbein's theory of reasoned intentions (Ajzen & Fishbein, 1980). This model postulates that an individual's behavior is best predicted by his or her behavioral intention, which in turn is influenced by the person's attitude toward performing the behavior coupled with his or her normative beliefs about the behavior.

Application of Ajzen and Fishbein's model and similar attitudinal and decision models to contraception behavior has thus far yielded promising results. Studies using this type of model have been able to explain over half the variance in women's intentions to use contraception (Jaccard & Davidson, 1972; McCarty, 1981), as well as providing a method for helping to identify particularly important beliefs and attitudes related to contraceptive use. The strong associations found between attitudes and behavior using such models underscore the importance of using specific definitions of the behaviors under study in investigating associations among variables, rather than the more common approach of using definitions of attitudes and behaviors which are vague, general, and imprecise (Morrison, 1985). However, most studies of this type have focused on older women (i.e., college students) rather than younger teens, a group at especially high risk for engaging in unprotected sex.

Similar to the Ajzen-Fishbein model, the few empirical applications of the Health Belief Model (Janz & Becker, 1984) to the study of behaviors associated with teenage pregnancy have in general yielded promising, albeit preliminary, results (Eisen, Zellman, & McAlister, 1985). Further research, undertaken in a controlled fashion, is necessary before a determination of actual utility of this approach for predicting and modifying behavioral outcomes can be made. As for the attitudinal models discussed previously, discussions of the Health Belief Model have focused largely on potential applications to decisions concerning contraception use (Katasky, 1974; Nathanson & Becker, 1983).

Decision making and similar approaches to the problem have more recently been supplemented with other techniques based on a cognitive–behavioral or social learning theory perspective (Schinke, Gilchrist, & Small, 1979). While such a perspective offers potentially useful methods for formulating intervention strategies in this area, it has to date often been applied in a haphazard or unsystematic fashion, or as part of a more general intervention package in which its relative contribution to outcome is blurred.

Environmental Conceptualizations

In addition to the types of unidimensional psychological approaches discussed above, health professionals have focused on one or two environmental factors, such as lack of ready access to contraceptives or lack of appropriate sex education, as the principal reasons for the teenage pregnancy problem (Furstenberg, Masnick, & Ricketts, 1972). Notably, over half of white and black individuals now in their twenties, and close to half of Hispanic individuals of that age, participated in a sex education course sometime during their teenage years (Dawson, 1986; Marsiglio & Mott, 1986). As many as eighty-five percent of current American teenagers have received some form of instruction related to sexual activity (Sonenstein & Pittman, 1984; Zelnik & Kim, 1982). Furthermore, approximately eighty percent of school districts in large U.S. cities currently offer some form of sex education (Sonenstein & Pittman, 1984).

While there is strong support for school-based sex education courses among teachers and the general public (Marsiglio & Mott, 1986), findings from evaluations of sex education courses are mixed, due in part to the great variation in goals and content of such courses (Furstenberg & Brooks-Gunn, 1986). While increases in short-term knowledge, and in some cases attitudes about sexuality and sexual relations, have been demonstrated, such programs have had less success in showing changes in sexual activity, effective contraception use, or incidence of pregnancy (Kirby, 1984; Marsiglio & Mott, 1986).

In addition to the variability in defining what is indeed a "sex education course," much of the confusion in the field is a function of the less than optimal study designs and procedures that have been typically employed. This has been due, at least in part, to the constraints on data collection imposed by many school systems (Scales, 1981). While some surveys of teenagers have found an association between involvement in sex education and a lower incidence of intercourse (Furstenberg & Brooks-Gunn, 1986; Zelnik & Kim, 1982), as well as greater likelihood of using contraception (Marsiglio & Mott, 1986; Zelnik & Kim, 1982), the sequence of these events is currently unclear, making it impossible to state the nature of any causal relationship. It is also possible that involvement in sex education classes could affect teenagers' willingness to report their sexual activity, artificially altering associations between these two factors (Dawson, 1986). As mentioned earlier, the one observation that appears to be relatively stable across studies is the lack of an association between sex education courses and an increased amount of sexual activity (Furstenberg & Brooks-Gunn, 1986; Kirby, 1984; Marsiglio & Mott, 1986). Researchers have suggested that for many teenagers, such courses may be "too little, too late," occurring after they have already had their first sexual encounter (Marsiglio & Mott, 1986). Until a consensus is reached concerning what the focus and breadth of such courses should be, it is doubtful that they will have a substantial effect on the teenage pregnancy problem (Scales, 1986).

Similarly, while family planning and birth control became increasingly available to teenagers during the 1970s, rates of teenage pregnancy remained high (Furstenberg & Brooks-Gunn, 1986). Such programs continue to face major difficulty in getting teenagers to use contraception in a consistent and appropriate fashion (Morrison, 1985). In addition, effective evaluation of such programs is often lacking (Jones, Namerow, & Philliber, 1986). Such problems underscore the observation that it appears to be more than simply exposing teenagers to these services that is the critical factor. As Dryfoos (1984) and others have pointed out, despite the controversy that continues to surround the offering of these and other preventive interventions to teenagers, such programs are in fact currently available in many parts of the United States. Thus, perhaps not surprisingly, simple access to relevant programs and services does not in and of itself appear to be enough to effectively curtail the teenage pregnancy problem.

The Medical Approach

We would be remiss if we did not include the medical approach to understanding teenage pregnancy in a list of unidimensional frameworks for conceptualizing the problem. The medical community has traditionally viewed teenage pregnancy as principally an obstetrical problem (Johnson, 1986). The focus has thus been on the identification and control of fertility rates, as well as perinatal, neonatal, and maternal mortality and morbidity rates. Yet little attention has been paid to understanding the psychosocial or environmental factors influencing each of these rates. In addition, as has typically been the case, medical conceptualizations have focused largely on interventions occurring after the individual has been "afflicted" (in this case, once the teenager has become pregnant) rather than on primary prevention efforts (Hanlon & Pickett, 1984). Such an approach can be costly, both in terms of the medical costs incurred by higher-risk pregnant teens and the psychosocial costs experienced by individuals who in most ways are still children themselves.

Moving from Static to Dynamic (Developmental) Approaches

The types of approaches described above generally ignore the contextual (Reppucci, 1987) and developmental influences that shape the lives of adolescents during what is typically an extremely tempestuous period of remarkable physical, social, and psychological change. Placing the teenage years into a developmental context can help to enhance our understanding of these influences, both internal and external, and aid in the increased tailoring of approaches throughout this period.

Adolescence, rather than viewed as a more or less uniform (and, from many parents' perspectives, incomprehensible!) period of life, has been described by many developmentalists as having its own series of progressive stages or levels (Proctor, 1986; Tietze, 1981). While the presence of qualitatively distinct stages of development proposed by Piaget and others has been challenged (Flavell, 1984), it does appear that there are continuous cognitive developmental trends which are seen clearly as an individual moves from middle childhood through adolescence. These trends include an increasing capacity to process information and movement from concrete to formal operational thinking (Flavell, 1984). When such notions are combined with similar observations on adolescent development, a general template of adolescent development emerges.

Early adolescence has been identified as beginning around age 11 or 12, and lasting through approximately age 14. Physically, the young teen is beginning to experience pubertal changes, including rapid growth and development of secondary sexual characteristics. In contrast to these striking physical changes, the young teen's intellectual processes have been described as remaining largely concrete (Piaget & Inhelder, 1969). There is little future-oriented forethought or planning, with decisions based largely on the individual's past or present experience. Consideration of longer-term outcomes of present decisions is relatively absent. During this period of development the teen is just beginning to form a stronger sense of self, along with separating his or her identity from others, although these processes are in a relatively nascent form. Eriksen (1968) and others suggest that this identity formation extends to the individual's sexual identity and sexuality.

Given the pronounced changes being experienced physically, along with attendant changes in body image, feelings surrounding sexual identity and sexuality are often confused and unclear at this time (Proctor, 1986). As teenagers begin to internalize societal values and mores concerning sexual identity and behavior, mixed emotional reactions, including guilt, may accompany initiation of sexual activity (Reppucci, 1987). It has been suggested that such emotional reactions, while not preventing sexual activity, may instead discourage *premeditated* sexual activity (i.e., sexual activity in conjunction with contraception) (Fox, 1977). In the throes of these changes and responses, it is not surprising that young teens may turn to their peer group, as well as to parents, to obtain reassurance and normative information concerning the changes they are experiencing (Johnson, 1986). As such, conflicts with parents over issues of independence and control remain relatively limited at this age.

Given their difficulty in connecting present behavior with future outcomes, their uncomfortableness with sexuality (often associated with delayed prenatal care for those who become pregnant; Proctor, 1986), the mixed societal messages they receive concerning sexuality, and their ignorance concerning the importance of contraception and how it works, young teenagers are particularly vulnerable to the risks of pregnancy (Miller, 1981). Conflict between parental beliefs and values and peer values have been noted to lead to further confusion and behavioral inconsistency, for younger and older teens alike, in areas such as contraception use (Morrison, 1985). As the age of first sexual intercourse among female teenagers continues to decrease (National Research Council, 1987), younger teenagers become an extremely important target for prevention effort.

During middle adolescence (i.e., 14 to 15 through 16 years of age), the teenager continues to work toward accomplishing the variety of developmental "tasks" which comprise adolescence (Mercer, 1979). These include an increasing acceptance of body image, separation and independence from parents, and formation of an adult identity in sexual, intellectual, and work-related spheres. Information to help him or her accomplish these tasks is gleaned from a variety of sources, including the home, school, peer group, and the media, as well as the teenager's continuing assessment of his or her own abilities (Johnson, 1986). With physical development largely completed at this point, cognitive development continues, with the beginnings of more abstract thinking becoming increasingly apparent. The teenager begins to better understand the effects of current behavior on future outcomes, although this capacity is often applied variably. While body image begins to stabilize, conflicts with parents and other authority figures over control and independence issues typically come to the forefront. At this point, peer group influence is often noted to be particularly strong, as the teenager struggles to develop his or her identity apart from parents and family (Johnson, 1986). A significant part of this identity development is played out in the sexual sphere, as the teenager attempts to define whom he or she is.

Jessor and Jessor (1977) have discussed this teenage behavior pattern within the context of what they refer to as Problem-Behavior Theory. Briefly, their research suggests that certain adolescents are particularly prone to engaging in a variety of problem behaviors, with precocious sexual activity identified as one of those behaviors (others include use of alcohol and drugs, cigarette smoking, and aggression). Jessor and Jessor identify "problem behavior proneness" within the context of three theoretical systems: the Personality System (e.g., independence, lower academic achievement, alienation, external control, tolerance of deviance, less religiosity); the Perceived Environment System (e.g., limited support from parents and friends, lower perceived influence of parents relative to friends, friends who serve as models for problem behavior); and the Behavior System (e.g., lower involvement in conventional behavior, higher involvement in a variety of other problem behaviors).

Taken together, the three systems delineate a theoretical pattern or profile which identifies those teenagers who might have an especially rough time during this particular period of teenage development. In fact, as discussed earlier, many of the factors noted above have indeed been linked with teenage sexual activity and pregnancy (National Research Council, 1987). The Jessors' work suggests that, in addition to early pregnancy, these teenagers are susceptible to a variety of other health-compromising behaviors. It further suggests the potential utility of formulating prevention approaches which include three systems of influence specified above, and which focus on the individual's general *lifestyle* rather than (as has been the more typical intervention approach to date) on a single problem behavior (Jessor, 1984). The Jessors have stressed the reinforcement of alternative behaviors which serve functions similar to the risk-taking behaviors (i.e., which reinforce independence from parents, strengthen identity with a peer group, help the teenager cope with stress and avoid boredom) as an important intervention approach. The introduction and/or strengthening of health-enhancing behaviors such as appropriate dietary choices, regular involvement in physical activity, social skills development, and regular use of contraception can provide teenagers with more positive health behavior alternatives. In addition, finding ways to minimize teenage involvement in harmful behaviors, protect the adolescent from the negative consequences of such behaviors, and delay onset of those behaviors are also suggested as viable intervention strategies (Jessor, 1984). The latter suggestions reflect the awareness that experimentation with different risk-taking behaviors is, to some degree, simply a part of normal adolescent development (Jessor, 1982).

As late adolescence is reached (approximately 17 through 21 years of age), conflicts with adults typically recede as the individual's identity as an emerging adult is confirmed (Erikson, 1968). At this point the individual is typically capable of formal operational thinking (Piaget & Inhelder, 1969), with the ability to plan in a responsible fashion. Sexual concerns become more strongly tied with concerns about establishment of more stable, long-term relationships. As such, a sense of commitment begins to replace the focus on exploration and romanticism driving previous sexual activity (Johnson, 1986). While in at least some cases problem behaviors continue, as the individual enters young adulthood such behaviors are typically supplanted by an increasing tendency toward conventionality and conformity (Jessor, 1984). Clearly, it is at this latter stage of development that individuals are most likely to heed messages and warnings concerning safe sexual practices and pregnancy prevention.

A summary of these developmental theories is found in Table 7.1. As with all theoretical approaches, the developmental conceptualizations presented are aimed at adolescents in the aggregate. As a consequence, potential shifts in cognitive, social, and sexual development due to differing cultural, social, and economic contexts are overlooked. As in the application of any theory, it behooves the researcher or practitioner to assess the particular developmental patterns seen in the specific group being targeted for study and/or intervention. In doing this, theoretical structures can be tailored to form a better fit with observations from the field. This point aside, developmental theory offers clear reasons as to why many of the unidimensional approaches described previously have had less than encouraging results. Expecting many teenagers, particularly younger ones, to easily understand and utilize information concerning current sexual behavior and future outcomes, and as a consequence automatically use available family planning and contraceptive services, becomes a questionable activity at best. The problem is compounded when the functional basis and meanings of sexual activity for the teenager (i.e., as much more than simply the sex act itself) are taken into account. Developmental theory also underscores the point, made in the recent report by the Committee on Child Development Research and Public Policy described earlier, that adolescents are a heterogeneous group. In particular, differences in age of only a few years can nonetheless translate into major disparities in cognitive, physical, and social development.

CURRENT INTERVENTION APPROACHES TO TEENAGE PREGNANCY AND ITS PREVENTION

The general conceptual approaches described above have been applied in various ways in developing the types of intervention methods employed currently to combat the teenage pregnancy problem. Using the conceptual

Table 7.1. Contributions of Selected Developmental Theories to
Understanding the Teenage Years

Theories	Young Teens (11–14 yrs.)	Mid-Teens (14–17 yrs.)	Older Teens (17–21 yrs.)
Piaget & Inhelder (1969)	Concrete operational; little future-oriented planning, abstract thought.	Beginnings of formal operational thought, but variably applied.	Formal operational; ability to plan in a responsible manner.
Eriksen (1968)	Identity vs. identity diffusion stage of development; early beginnings of development of an independent identity and an adult sense of self.	Continued formation of adult identity in a number of areas; increasing acceptance of body image, separation and independence from parents.	Confirmation of emerging adult identity.
Jessor & Jessor (1977)	Beginnings of adolescent problem behaviors; proneness toward behaviors predicted by presence of personality, perceived environment, and behavior systems variables.	Increase in problem behavior proneness, including precocious sex, smoking, problem drinking, illicit drug use.	Continuation of problem behavior proneness; with entry into young adulthood, increase in conventionality, proneness toward conformity.

model presented in chapter 2 as an organizing schema, these major intervention approaches are outlined in Tables 7.2 and 7.3. The tables are not exhaustive; rather, they are used to underscore the major current trends in teenage pregnancy intervention. It should be noted that in truth there is overlap (at times substantial) between the different categories of programs shown in the table, as professionals in the field have attempted to enhance program outcomes. In discussing these categories subsequently, it is important to recognize that all categories of programs currently suffer, in one degree or another, from problems in evaluation. Rarely have evaluations involved a control group or a comparison of different programs "head to head" (Foster, 1986). Thus any conclusions drawn concerning those factors which appear to be effective must be seen as preliminary. The major types of intervention approaches are discussed in more detail below.

Programs for the Pregnant and Parenting Teen

Given the potentially powerful consequences of primary prevention efforts as the major route for intervention in this field, programs for already pregnant and parenting teenagers will be discussed only briefly. Not surprisingly, the major thrust of such programs has been a medical one, although in recent years attempts to supplement adequate medical and health care with information that will enhance the socioeconomic outcomes for such teenagers has been growing (Anastasiow, 1984; Canada, 1986; Davis et al., 1986; Hardy, King, & Repke, 1987; Polit & Kahn, 1985; Salguero, Schlesinger & Yearwood, 1984; Stuart & Wells, 1982; Timberlake, Fox, Baisch & Goldberg, 1987). As such, multidisciplinary expertise is being brought to bear in increasing the opportunities for pregnant and parenting teenagers to enhance their life options, as well as increasing those for their children.

Most programs in this area continue to take place in medical settings, such as hospitals and clinics, with the health professional or counselor serving as the major intervener. Such programs have been recently augmented, albeit to a relatively small extent thus far, with school-based approaches to helping pregnant teenagers (e.g., DeRose, 1982). One of the goals of these types of programs is to prevent the pregnant teen from leaving school. However, program outcomes are currently sparse. More comprehensive approaches have attempted to include a focus on education, job training, family support, and contraception use in addition to medical and health services (Foster, 1986); however, such programs still comprise the minority. Major programming efforts remain on the personal and interpersonal levels of analysis. While better-controlled efforts have shown promising results (Polit & Kahn, 1985; Hardy et al., 1987), at least in the short term, the majority of programs still suffer from poor evaluation and minimal follow-up. It is unclear what type of support (both fiscal and social) such programs will continue to receive amidst the current conservative wave of opinion sweeping the nation (Scharf, 1984). One thing that is clear, however, is that the problem of pregnant and parenting teenagers shows few signs of going away, and, as pointed out previously, will continue to present current and future generations with complex economic, social, and moral issues.

Primary Prevention Efforts

Sexuality Education Programs

As noted earlier, the area of sex education is comprised of a mix of diverse programs containing a variety of contents, formats, and goals (Dryfoos, 1984; Marsiglio & Mott, 1986). Such interventions span the range from two-hour seminars to comprehensive courses that incorporate peer teaching and parent participation. While targeted levels of intervention have been largely personal and interpersonal, sex education programs have increasingly supplemented personal and interpersonal approaches with an organizational focus, contributed largely through involvement by a growing number of our nation's schools. While a large proportion of sex education programs occur in schools, an increasing number of other institutions and settings have begun to be utilized as well. They include adolescent organizations such as Girls' Clubs, as

Table 7.2. Placing Current Intervention Approaches to Teenage Pregnancy
in the Context of a Conceptual Model: Stage One*

Problem Definition		System Analysis	
Strategy	*Level*	*Theories, Concepts*	*Assessment*
Pregnant Teen Programs			
(1–6)	Personal	Medical/health,	Clinical, diagnostic
(7)	Interpersonal	education, Social	Surveys
(8)	(Organizational)	support network Communication	
Sex Education	Personal,	Health education,	Surveys, question-
(9–12)	Interpersonal,	Communication,	naires; vital statistics
	Organizational	Decision making	(e.g., birthrate)
Contraceptive/ Family Planning Services (13–19)	Personal, Interpersonal, Organizational	Medical/health education, communi- cation, Health belief model, Decision mak- ing, Social learning theory	Medical chart data, surveys, question- naires, vital statistics
Life Skills/Options Training (20–22)	Personal, Interpersonal, Organizational, Environmental	Health education, Communication, Values clarification, Social welfare focus	Surveys, questionnaires
Community-wide Programs (23, 24)	Personal, Interpersonal, Organizational, Environmental, Institutional	Medical/health education, Communi- cation, Decision making, Social learning, Diffusion theory	Surveys, question- naires, community and county trends

(*continued*)

*Numbers refer to references, below.
Pregnant Teen Programs:
1. Hardy, King, & Repke, 1987
2. Timberlake, Fox, Baisch, & Goldberg, 1987
3. Canada, 1986
4. Davis, Fink, Yesupria, Rajegowda, & Lala, 1986
5. Polit & Kahn, 1985
6. Anastasiow, 1984
7. Salguero, Schlesinger, & Yearwood, 1984
8. DeRose, 1982

Sex Education:
9. Marsiglio & Mott, 1986
10. Harris, 1986
11. Dawson, 1986
12. Kirby, 1984

well as a variety of social service agencies. Teachers, health professionals, and nurses, as well as teenagers themselves, have been used to disseminate relevant information.

Most programs, regardless of format, have typically been successful in increasing participants' knowledge, and in some cases attitudes, about sexuality. Yet their impact on what have been considered to be useful or necessary behavioral skills (e.g., problem solving, decision making, communication

Table 7.2. (Continued)
Stage Two

Goal Specification		Intervention
Targets	*Products*	*Settings/Methods*
Knowledge, behavior related to pregnancy, birth, child care	Counseling, health education, referral	Clinics, hospitals, schools, health professional, couselor, parent
Knowledge, attitudes, behavior related to sexual activity, birth control, pregnancy	Comprehensive or short program, conferences, peer education, parent–child programs	Schools, clinics, teen organizations (YWCA, Girls' Clubs; teacher, health professional, nurse
Knowledge, beliefs, attitudes, behavior related to birth control, pregnancy	Long or short sex education program, counseling, referral, comprehensive health services	Clinics (free-standing, school-based), M.D. office, teen centers, hospitals, health departments; educator, health profession-al, nurse, peer
Knowledge, beliefs, attitudes, behavior related to sexuality, life planning	Courses, workbooks, counseling	Youth agencies (Girls' Clubs), schools, health clinics; educator, health professional
Knowledge, beliefs, attitudes, behavior related to sexuality, general problem solving	Sex education, medical services, community awareness & support (media, health fairs)	Schools and colleges, clinics, churches; educator, counselor, health profession-al, student instructor, community leader, clergy, parents

Contraceptive/Family Planning Services:
13. Jones, Namerow, & Philliber, 1986
14. Harris, 1986
15. Morrison, 1985
16. Eisen, Zellman, & McAlister, 1985
17. Withington, Gimes, & Hatcher, 1983
18. Edwards, Stienman, Arnold, & Hahanson, 1981
19. Thornburg, 1972

Life Skills Training:
20. Schecter, 1986
21. Dryfoos, 1984
22. Cooper, 1982

Community-Wide Programs
23. Apte, 1987
24. Vincent, Clearie, & Schluchter, 1987

skills) as well as on "bottom line" outcomes (e.g., sexual activity, contraceptive behavior, pregnancy) have been, at best, mixed (Kirby, 1984). A potential problem with the teaching of skills such as the ones just mentioned may be that, while teenagers may be able to use them in a classroom setting, methods for enhancing generalizability of their use to real-world settings has not been sufficiently attended to (Kirby, 1984). In fact, those programs attempting to increase parent–child communication skills surrounding sexuality by including both parents and children (particularly younger ones) together in the classroom have typically shown the most promising outcomes (Kirby, 1984). Such situations allow for more realistic rehearsal of relevant behaviors, enhancing the probability of generalization to settings other than the classroom. Kirby has suggested the utility of similar techniques for teenage couples. Such suggestions aside, it has become apparent that current sex education programs will need to supply teenagers with more than knowledge if they hope to have a significant impact on teenage pregnancy rates. Efforts to combine such programs with clinic services have been promising, albeit require further systematic evaluation. Currently, relatively little theoretical thought has been systematically applied in the development of such courses.

Contraceptive and Family Planning Services

Family planning services currently exist in a variety of settings, including physicians' offices, hospitals, and clinics housed in local health departments, as well as school-based and free-standing clinics run through the auspices of Planned Parenthood affiliates, family planning councils, and neighborhood family planning centers (National Research Council, 1987). Studies have revealed that the most important factors influencing the use of such services by teenagers include confidentiality, the presence of staff competent in dealing specifically with teenagers, and proximity (Ralph & Edgington, 1983; Zabin & Clark, 1983). Yet, as noted earlier, simply having access to family planning services is not enough, in and of itself, to lead to an increased use of contraception and other family planning strategies by adolescents. Programs that have been particularly successful have offered family planning, with consistent and frequent follow-up, within the context of a comprehensive health care clinic located in a school setting (i.e., including an organizational level of intervention) (Ralph & Edgington, 1983; Foster, 1986). Within such an organizational focus, the techniques used to promote behavior change and positive outcomes have been largely personally and interpersonally based (i.e., contraceptive counseling, pelvic exams, follow-up on prescription use). Professionals in the field have noted that unless such clinics make prevention of teenage pregnancy a particular priority, reflected in the amount of effort placed in family planning activities, their impact on pregnancy rates will remain relatively minor (Foster, 1986).

While some family planning programs have incorporated aspects of theoretical approaches, such as the health belief model and social learning theory, into their counseling and education programs (e.g., Eisen et al., 1985), many currently do not. As such they fail to take advantage of the growing base of behavior change strategies that psychologists and other professionals have been developing over the past four to five decades.

Life Skills/Options Training Programs

A growing number of health professionals have urged us to look beyond teenage pregnancy itself to the web of economic and social factors which they suggest are the principal reasons for it (Dryfoos, 1984; National Research Council, 1987). One of these factors is educational attainment. Contrary to what many think, while pregnancy is the single most cited reason for dropping out of school among teenage girls, less than half of girls dropping out do so as a consequence of being pregnant; a much greater number become pregnant *after* they have dropped out (Foster, 1986). Teenage dropouts who are unemployed are at particularly high risk for becoming pregnant (National Research Council, 1987). Dryfoos and others have stressed the importance of putting increased efforts into finding ways to prevent dropout, which in turn could have a significant impact on the teenage pregnancy rate. They argue that simply giving teenagers the *capacity* to control their fertility, through sex education and family planning programs, is not enough. What is missing in many of these programs is an additional focus on increasing the teenager's *desire* to avoid pregnancy. For those adolescents coming from disadvantaged backgrounds, where economic prospects are generally bleak, the consequences of giving birth during adolescence on future life choices are at best nebulous, and at worst of little functional impact whatsoever. Proponents of life skills training programs suggest that until the disadvantaged teenager's social and economic needs are met, more traditional approaches such as sex education and family planning will be of minimal usefulness for them (Dryfoos, 1984).

It is argued that a crucial aspect of meeting the disadvantaged teenager's welfare needs is keeping them in school through graduation. While current job prospects for minority youth, particularly women, are far from rosy, those prospects become substantially worse for individuals who do not graduate from high school (U.S. Bureau of the Census, 1984). Several strategies have been used to help at-risk youth obtain a base of educational experience in the hopes that it will pay off in the job market. These include tracking and counseling of marginal students prior to dropout, provision of remedial education for basic academic skills (i.e., the "three Rs"), enrollment of at-risk students in alternative schools with the goal of obtaining a diploma, provision of in-school work experience to make school more relevant and meaningful to students, and vocational training focused specifically on skills needed to increase immediate employability (Foster, 1986).

While each of the above approaches has demonstrated some success in increasing scholastic achievement and, in some instances, influencing employment outcomes for disadvantaged youth, their effect on teenage pregnancy is much less clear. Although data suggest that employed teenage girls are less likely to become pregnant than unemployed teenagers, the actual nature of the relationship between teenage employment and pregnancy prevention is currently unknown (Wehlage, 1982). It is possible that other factors (e.g., emotional maturity) may be associated with both of these outcomes. In addition, it has been argued that pushing adolescents into the adult world of work, without first allowing them the opportunity to mature adequately in a positive, supportive school environment, is doing them a strong disservice (Foster, 1986). Those programs which might have the greatest potential for affecting adolescent pregnancy rates are the ones which combine school, career, and pregnancy planning information in one curriculum. Currently some of the more innovative of these sorts of programs have been developed under the auspices of youth organizations (e.g., Girl's Club, the Junior Leagues), and Planned Parenthood affiliates, often working in tandem with local schools (Dryfoos, 1984).

In addition to academic and work-related training, what such programs can offer teenagers, similar to successful sex education and family planning programs, is the opportunity to interact frequently with positive adult role models in a safe, supportive environment (Dryfoos, 1983). Consistent, one-on-one contact between the teenager and a supportive adult has been suggested to be a particularly potent influence for disadvantaged or isolated adolescents.

As the above discussion indicates, life skills (or "life options") training programs focus on teaching adolescents a set of skills that goes beyond traditional sexuality education or family planning. Involved in such programs is an identification of the types of social and environmental factors that may play a role in teenage pregnancy, among them social and economic deprivation. As such, the program orientation can be seen as expanding to the environmental level of analysis, even though the interventions themselves currently reside principally at personal, interpersonal, and organizational levels. While still in many ways in its infancy, the life skills training program concept has been receiving increasing support from individuals and agencies working in the adolescent area. It is possible that future programs of this type will include an increased community focus, as agencies and organizations interested in reproductive health care and youth social and employment services collaborate in developing programs for teenagers which meet a variety of needs (Dryfoos, 1984).

Community-wide Programs

While engendering an increasing amount of interest, pregnancy prevention programs utilizing the resources of an entire community are currently scarce. As discussed in chapter 5, community-based efforts typically feature community organization activities and use of "big" media resources (e.g., television, radio, newspapers) largely absent in other intervention efforts.

Given the number and variety of factors influencing teenage pregnancy, many of them woven within the social, economic, and institutional fabric of a community, a community perspective may be critical if significant progress is hoped to be made.

One of the better evaluated community-based adolescent pregnancy prevention programs to date has been undertaken by Vincent and colleagues (1987). The focus of intervention was the resident population of the western half of a county in South Carolina, where the population is largely black and rural, with low income and limited education. Applying principles from social learning theory and diffusion theory (Rogers, 1983), the program developers (professionals from a school of public health who have received federal funding for the project) have succeeded in institutionalizing aspects of the pregnancy prevention program throughout the county's school systems and among important community organizations and groups. These groups include clergy, church leaders, and parents. Program information is disseminated through the local radio station and newspaper, as well as via statewide television. Messages focus to a great extent on problem solving, and at times have been broadened to include health areas in addition to sexual behavior (e.g., alcohol and drug abuse, smoking, nutrition, weight control). Evaluation has included use of trend data collected by the South Carolina Department of Health and Environmental Control. The data collected thus far are encouraging; the intervention portion of the county showed a decline in number of teenage pregnancies (from 60 per 1000 females to 25 per 1000 females) in comparison with other counties in the area. This decline has apparently been sustained for three years after the implementation of the community-wide program.

Such efforts, while quasi-experimental, represent in many ways a comprehensive, state-of-the art approach to intervening with a population to reduce teenage pregnancy on a large scale. A variety of resources and persons are called on, not only to participate in the program but to help shoulder responsibility for it. While community-wide approaches hold promise, there are still many unanswered questions concerning the ease with which some communities can be organized around certain problems or themes; the ability for the communities themselves to maintain programs often initiated by academic institutions who in many ways see themselves (and are often seen) as being outside of the central community structure; and the actual cost-effectiveness of such large-scale, resource-laden approaches. In addition, getting communities to place a morally controversial and socially complex issue, such as teenage pregnancy prevention, at or near the top of a typically extremely long list of urgent community concerns can, in many cases, be extremely difficult. Whether the political and economic climates of many communities will support these types of efforts remains to be seen.

TOWARD A MULTILEVEL, MULTIPROCESS CONCEPTUALIZATION OF TEENAGE PREGNANCY PREVENTION

Our brief review of the intervention strategies being applied to the teenage pregnancy problem indicates that, in contrast to prevention activities in many other areas, a great deal of thought and energy is currently being directed toward the problem. In addition to the continued honing of efficacious intervention strategies across multiple levels of analysis, interventionists in the field will be required to better define the best mix of strategies and approaches most relevant for teenage subgroups (i.e., program tailoring), and which involve the most efficient utilization of resources (Mitchell & Brindis, 1987). To do this, we suggest that more systematic application of developmental theory, in terms of both cognitive development and risk-taking behavior, is relevant. In addition, in the face of major influences on the part of a variety of institutions, such as the family, schools, religious organizations, and the media, a higher-level, community-based approach appears to be warranted.

The developmental formulations described earlier can be combined with the conceptual model presented in chapter 2 in developing a more comprehensive approach to the teenage pregnancy prevention problem. An example of this approach is presented in Table 7.3. Adolescence has been divided into three general phases, per discussions by a number of researchers (Johnson, 1986; Proctor, 1986). As noted earlier, the boundaries separating such phases are in reality somewhat more indistinct than is indicated. For each general phase of development, potential intervention strategies have been noted for the four levels of analysis described in the conceptual model—i.e., personal/interpersonal, organizational/environmental, and institutional/societal.

As we have described previously, the early teen years (from approximately eleven or twelve through about fourteen years of age) are a time of tremendous physical changes which can be frightening for many teenagers. On the personal level, it is critical that the young teenager receive accurate information concerning what he or she can expect during adolescence, physically, emotionally, and socially. Structuring of expectations during this early period may help to diminish feelings of insecurity that frequently accompany such major changes, and provide a context within which the adolescent can compare his or her own experiences, as well as the experiences of peers. Given that young adolescents are still by and large in a concrete operations stage of cognitive development, it may be difficult for them to use the specter of future consequences for current behavior to guide their decisions. Instead, information should be given to help dispel myths concerning sexual activity (e.g., "everyone is doing it"; "a person won't get pregnant the first time"; and so forth), and to place sexual activity within the context of an array of personal health-related decisions which the adolescent will be facing over the following years. Reassurance should be given concerning the appropriateness of delaying sexual activity, though young adolescents should also be introduced to family planning service methods and providers, who, ideally, are located close to the school.

It is recommended that interactive, small-group approaches to learning be utilized, to allow the teenager to interact freely with both peers and adults without the embarrassment that typically accompanies discussions of sexuality in the United States (Dryfoos, 1985). Within this context the adult educator needs to be someone who is comfortable and knowledgeable about sexuality and adolescence (National Research Council, 1987). Such educators ideally would be certified to teach in the area following a standardized training program.

In addition to small-group teaching methods, learning should be made as experiential as possible. Role-playing of age-appropriate situations can enhance learning by allowing teenagers to actually practice responses and receive feedback from peers and adults. Appropriate responses (including saying "no") can be identified by the group. Participants can be encouraged to use such responses outside the classroom through structured homework assignments that involve peers as well as parents. Because young teenage girls often experience their first sexual encounter with older, rather than same-age, boys, discussion of this should be included. Ideally, having older teenage boys (as well as girls) help with the instruction and discussion could also help to generalize responses on the part of the younger teenager to individuals of that age group.

Early adolescence is also an important time to identify those teenagers who, due to life circumstances, may be at particular risk for early sexual activity and pregnancy. These include teenagers coming from broken homes where parental guidance may be reduced or negligible; those appearing to be isolated socially from peers; teenagers having academic difficulties or poor school attendance; those involved in other forms of risk-taking behavior (e.g., substance use or abuse); and those having an adult role model (mother, sister, grandmother) who experienced pregnancy as a teen (Proctor, 1986). It has been suggested repeatedly that these teenagers in particular can benefit from frequent one-on-one contacts with a caring adult who, in many instances, can function as a surrogate parent (Dryfoos, 1984; Foster, 1986; Proctor, 1986). While it is obviously not feasible to give all adolescents this sort of personalized attention, the schools may be able to target those teenagers who could benefit most from such attention. Linkages could then be made within the school itself as well as with other institutions in the community (e.g., churches, youth organizations) who could aid this endeavor.

Table 7.3. A Developmental, Multilevel Approach to Teenage Pregnancy Prevention

Levels	Young Teens (11–14 yrs.)	Mid-Teens (14–17 yrs.)	Older Teens (17–21 yrs.)
Personal Physical	Information on sexual development, dispelling myths; emphasis on delay of sexual activity; discussion of family planning services and methods; sexuality as one of an array of health-related behaviors; method-trained educator	Continued information on reproduction, birth control methods (pill, condom), STDs; use of family planning services; connection between sexual activity and future outcomes; discussion of sexuality in the context of health-enhancing behaviors; method-trained educator, peers	Same
Cognitive/Affective	Values clarification; structuring expectations *re* adolescence, sexuality; promote staying in school	Focus on meeting independence, self-concept needs in alternate ways; making choices *re* sex; emphasis on taking responsibility, particularly on the part of males; career path development; continued values clarification; promote staying in school	Responsible relationships, marriage; emphasize and expect pre-planning
Behavioral	Role-play of hypothetical situations; meet family planning service providers; communication skill training (including saying "no")	Decision-making/ problem-solving skills training; conflict resolution training; role-play; experience-oriented homework assignments; training, remediation for job-related skills; teach ways to minimize effects of risk-taking behaviors	Continued focus on decision making, problem solving, conflict resolution; continued job skill training

(*continued*)

Table 7.3. (Continued)

Levels	Young Teens (11–14 yrs.)	Mid-Teens (14–17 yrs.)	Older Teens (17–21 yrs.)
Interpersonal	Small group, interactive approaches to learning; link with consistent adult role-models; allow time for one-on-one adult/teen interactions, particularly for at-risk teen; include parents in programs; teach parent–child communication skills	Use of peer teaching and counseling; continued interactions with adult role models; continued time for one-on-one adult–teen interactions	Continued peer & adult counseling on issues related to sexuality, birth control, job-related decisions
Organizational/ Environmental	School-based curriculum; family planning services close by; linking of congruent messages by churches, youth organizations; messages delivered by media (TV; relevant radio stations); organization of school, other youth groups around themes appropriate to pregnancy prevention	Continuation of a consistent school-based curriculum; programs through social service agencies to reach dropouts; incentive-based job training, academic remediation programs; continued use of media, other community organizations; family planning services close to school	Continuation of school-based curriculum, extended through college level; incentive-based job training, academic remediation programs; media; targeting of young adult social organizations
Institutional/Societal	Laws ensuring access, confidentiality of minors in relation to family planning services; mandated standardized, comprehensive health programs (including sexuality) for schools, beginning in elementary school (development of a curriculum spanning all grades); certification training of educators, counselors in the field	Same	Same

Though these issues often present a challenge for even the most intact families, parents should, whenever possible, be included in the young teenager's sexuality program (Mitchell & Brindis, 1987). This can be accomplished through discussing issues of adolescent sexuality and development, along with values clarification, with parents separately, as well as including them in classroom discussions focusing on communication training and conflict resolution. The goal is to optimize the relationship with the parent as much as possible during a period when most teenagers are still amenable to direct parental control and guidance.

On the organizational level, having family planning services that are close by and that maintain confidentiality will enhance efforts to get teenagers of all ages to utilize such services. In addition, development of a school sexuality curriculum which is standardized across school districts in a community can aid efforts to present a standard message from a number of different community resources to all community teenagers. Efforts to institutionalize such a curriculum will in many communities require, or at a minimum benefit from, the types of interorganizational discussion and planning described in chapter 5. An additional institutional-level strategy for enhancing current pregnancy prevention efforts includes the development of community (or state) training and certification procedures for educators and counselors in the field. This would allow for a level of standardization of content and format throughout a community that would most likely aid adolescent learning as well as evaluation efforts.

Efforts to coordinate the variety of messages on sexual behavior and teenage pregnancy being carried by community institutions, organizations, and media sources is considered to be an extremely important, albeit challenging, task. A recommended first step is to compose a community-based task force (including school officials, church leaders, parents, youth organization and Planned Parenthood representatives, and so on) to spearhead discussion on methods for introducing consistent messages and information on these topics throughout the community. While it may not be possible in at least some (perhaps most) communities for such a task force to come to a firm agreement as to the types of messages teenagers should be exposed to, such meetings may at least provide community segments with a basis for beginning discussions about the problem.

From an institutional and legal perspective, confidentiality for minors, particularly under age 15, in relation to family planning services continues to be a decidedly thorny issue. Attempting to include parents in a more active way while at the same time seeking to protect the privacy of the adolescent are goals that will necessarily be in conflict at times. In addition to the issue of unrestricted access to contraceptive services, debate has become particularly heated over confidentiality issues related to the decision on the part of the teenager to have an abortion. Although the Supreme

Court held in 1976 that a minor has a basic right to privacy that prevents a third party, even a parent, from overriding the minor's abortion decision, many legislatures have since tried to limit access by teenagers to such services (Paul & Schapp, 1982). While the Supreme Court has currently stood firm on the fundamental right of minors to privacy, access to abortion has been increasingly limited by legislation (i.e., the Hyde Amendment), sustained by the Court, which has severely curtailed the use of federal funds for such services. Other legal and societal issues involving the adolescent include consent to medical care on the part of the minor, financing of the minor's medical care, financial support for the minor and her child, legal rights of the illegitimate child, custody issues concerning the child, including termination of parental rights to custody, and paternal child support (Paul & Schapp, 1982). Of continuing importance to debates concerning these and other issues relevant to adolescence is ongoing representation by adults whose primary responsibility lies with playing an advocacy role for the teenagers themselves.

Programs relating to the young teenager should blend, conceptually and structurally, with those devised for the midteen years (generally ages 14 to 17). Of major importance to teenagers at this point are the struggle to separate oneself intellectually and emotionally from one's parents, and the increased influence of the peer group. Strategies should thus incorporate in a strong fashion the use of peer teachers while perhaps diminishing the ostensible role of the parent, at least in the classroom. In particular, information should emphasize the role and responsibilities of the male (Pitt, 1986), especially in regards to younger females. There are some data to suggest that targeting the male adolescent can lead to an improvement in the use of contraceptives (Withington, Gimes, & Hatcher, 1983). Yet, in general we remain largely uninformed concerning male attitudes, motivations, and experiences related to sexuality and pregnancy and the best methods for reaching young men on these issues (National Research Council, 1987; Finkel & Finkel, 1981). Much of what has been written concerning adolescent boys has focused largely on their role once pregnancy has occurred (e.g., Herzog, 1984). Research available on attitudes and behavior prior to pregnancy suggests that, for many teenage boys in this country, sexual experience continues to be perceived as a critical "rite of passage" into manhood, with sexual decisionmaking viewed largely as the males' prerogative (Scales & Beckstein, 1982). Myths among males related to sexuality (e.g., "men always want and are always ready for sex", "sex equals intercourse"; Zilbergeld, 1978) continue to run rampant (Scales & Beckstein, 1982).

Several researchers have suggested that through mid-adolescence many boys are operating at a level of moral functioning focused on social conformity rather than on societal responsibility (D'Augelli & D'Augelli, 1977). Thus it might not be surprising that many of them choose behavioral paths reflecting stereotypical "macho" sexual roles rather than mutual decision-making with one's sexual partner. Such suggestions aside, it is clear that young men are bombarded with messages concerning male sexual roles that run counter to what they need to be taught to behave responsibly sexually. Rather than simply blaming them, methods of conveying more beneficial sex roles to young men (as well as women) need to be developed. Programs which utilize males (both adults and peers) who can consistently model more appropriate sexual attitudes (e.g., positive attitudes toward contraceptives, the importance of caring, honest relationships and mutual decisionmaking) may help in this regard.

The media is also a potentially powerful purveyor of sex-role messages, though one that to date has been used largely to continue to promote macho images among males. The National Urban League has attempted to alter this somewhat, by launching recently its "Male Responsibility" media campaign directed at black adolescent males. The focus of the campaign is to increase awareness among adolescent males of their responsibilities in sexual relationships and parenting (Pitt, 1986). The most effective (and cost-effective) ways of analyzing the impact of such campaigns remain unclear. Yet the number and variety of media products currently being geared toward youth (e.g., youth magazines, television shows, radio stations) make this a prime method for helping to change the social norms surrounding sex-role behaviors.

In addition to the use of effective adult and peer models, programs for this age group should provide specific information on contraceptive methods and a clear link with nearby family planning services. The connection between sexual activity and future outcomes should be emphasized; this should include not only pregnancy but sexually transmitted diseases. Programs in this and other health areas which stress the concepts of choice, personal decisionmaking, and the development of a set of personal values may be particularly useful for this age group (Dryfoos, 1984). The training of specific decisionmaking and problem-solving skills, with opportunity for structured rehearsal, feedback, and extramural practice, is recommended. To increase the likelihood that such approaches will be incorporated and used, their application should extend to the variety of health-related areas of particular relevance for adolescents. These include alcohol and drug use, smoking, and dietary intake. They can also be applied to decisions concerning dropping out of school and future employment. Because teenagers at risk for teenage pregnancy are likely to engage in other types of risk-taking behaviors as well, strategies focused on risk-taking in general need to be developed. One approach involves promoting an overall lifestyle that is health-enhancing, rather than singling out one behavior (sexuality) as the primary focus for intervention. Within such a focus various options can be laid out for teenagers, with the goal of teaching them to make educated choices concerning health, employment, and other relevant topics. Choices may range from abstaining from different behaviors to engaging in behaviors with an eye to reducing their negative consequences (e.g., if the choice is to drink, then someone else drives; if the choice is to be sexually active, then contraceptives are used).

Teaching social resistance skills to teenagers has been shown to be a promising approach to preventing increases in risk-taking behavior as well (Johnson, 1983). Teenagers are taught methods to resist influences (from peers, older individuals, the media) for the risk-taking behavior. In addition, preparing teenagers for potentially difficult transitions (e.g., the move from elementary to junior high school, or from junior to senior high school), as well as providing special support to those lacking adequate family relationships, may help to keep risk-taking behaviors at a level considered normal for adolescents generally (Foster, 1986). Those teenagers targeted as being at particular risk should continue to receive, if at all feasible, one-on-one attention and support from a caring adult. While face-to-face contact may be most efficacious, it may also be useful to maintain contact through less intensive strategies (e.g., telephone and/or mail contacts). Such forms of contact have been found to be helpful in maintaining health-enhancing behaviors in adults (King, Dreon, Frey-Hewitt, Terry, & Wood, 1987; King, Taylor, Haskell, & DeBusk, 1988). High-risk teenagers could in addition benefit greatly from a case management approach, which has been surprisingly absent from the pregnancy prevention field (Mitchell & Brindis, 1987).

Added to the largely personal and interpersonal approaches described above is the necessity for developing organizational strategies for reaching those teenagers who have dropped out of school. It is clear that such strategies will need to involve community agencies and organizations beyond the schools themselves. In lieu of more typical approaches requiring that the adolescent come to the service provider, methods for bringing programs to the neighborhoods where at-risk teenagers reside are indicated. An increasing number of organizations have begun to incorporate mobile-based services (e.g., bookmobiles; blood pressure testing van services) as an alternative to more conventional service delivery modes. It is possible that a similar concept could be applied in reaching out-of-school adolescents concerning health-related issues. Obviously, to be effective such units would require staffing by individuals savvy to the culture of the neighborhood and knowledgeable concerning adolescent development and potential academic and job-related opportunities.

Programming for older teenagers should continue to emphasize and expand on themes related to taking responsibility for decisions concerning sexual and other relevant activities. Discussions should include the structuring of expectations concerning long-term relationships and marriage.

Continuing communication and conflict resolution skills training is seen as useful. The potential influence of their behavior on those of younger individuals who may be using them as role models should also be discussed.

Summary

A major goal of the developmentally based multilevel approach described above is to extend current pregnancy prevention methods, by focusing more systematically on the *tailoring* of strategies to adolescent subgroups and on the incorporation of multiple levels of intervention. While only adolescent age groups were discussed it is obvious that children's questions concerning sexuality do not begin in adolescence. It therefore makes sense that a comprehensive approach to sexuality and pregnancy prevention, focused largely in the schools, would start with elementary school-age children and continue through junior high and high school (using age-appropriate messages and strategies geared to each age group's specific level of comprehension, cognitive development, and interests). The development of such a curriculum requires collaboration from a variety of professionals, including sexuality educators, teachers, and developmental psychologists. Inclusion of information, from an early age, that highlights more flexible sex-role behaviors could greatly aid efforts to enhance mutual decisionmaking and trust concerning sexual behavior later on. It is clear that sex-role learning occurs at an extremely early age, and is influenced to a great extent by modeling of appropriate sex-role patterns by others (Maccoby & Jacklin, 1974). It therefore makes sense to include discussions of sex-role typing among educators and other adults having frequent contact with children (e.g., pediatricians, guidance counselors, coaches) in the development of curricula that touch on such issues with the children themselves.

The diversity of messages and extensive number of channels through which sexuality information and normative behaviors are communicated calls for multilevel, larger-scale approaches to intervention. Unlike health behaviors such as smoking and drug use, where messages to the public from a variety of community sectors are relatively homogeneous, messages related to sexual activity continue to be varied, contradictory, and controversial. Perhaps for no other behavior is the American public more sensitive or emotionally and morally uncomfortable than with the issue of sexuality. Already charged emotions become even more intensified when children are made the focus of interest and concern. Given this, it becomes that much more important, and difficult, to adopt a community approach to the problem.

Investigators in the field have suggested the following strategies in the successful promotion of a community-wide teenage pregnancy prevention effort (Dryfoos & Brindis, 1987):

1. Public commitment to pregnancy prevention and support for intervention by local officials, community leaders, and parents. Coordination can occur through organization of a community-based coalition, task force, or advisory committee.
2. A consistent message to young people, through the media and other channels, that choices other than early childbearing are available. (See chapter 4's discussion of media applications.)
3. A focus on the schools, where many young people spend a substantial amount of their time.
4. Access to programs convenient to the school setting that increase the young person's capacity to prevent pregnancy (i.e., sex and family life education, birth control and comprehensive health clinics, condom distribution).
5. Access to pregnancy counseling and related abortion and maternity services (through settings such as the schools).
6. Training of relevant personnel in a variety of sexuality-related areas (e.g., sexual identity, sex-role behaviors, sexual abuse, sexually transmitted diseases [including AIDS], abortion). Such personnel should receive continuous supervision and feedback.
7. Priority given for serving high-risk youth (including programs that enrich life options as well as give young people the capacity to prevent pregnancy); case management approaches that involve one-on-one individual attention may be particularly useful, as well as those approaches which bring programs and services to the young person (rather than vice versa).
8. Teaching a variety of skills to enhance outcomes (e.g., methods to help delay initiation of sexual intercourse; effective use of contraception when intercourse is initiated).
9. Availability of crisis intervention and referral services related to sexual activity, pregnancy, and so on.

Dryfoos and other professionals in the field stress the importance of making sexuality and birth control information and services accessible to young people as early as possible, preferably *before* they become sexually active. In tailoring efforts to meet important community needs and enhance community acceptance, formative evaluation, including a needs assessment, is strongly recommended. At this early stage, available and potential community resources should also be identified, along with sources of data providing the intervention team with, among other things, a demographic, economic, and social profile of the community. Vital statistics can also be obtained to aid program evaluation.

It is apparent that the marshalling of resources and support for such an effort will undoubtedly take a substantial amount of time, effort, and perseverance. Yet the growing number of individuals and services throughout this country being dedicated currently to efforts in the adolescent pregnancy area are a testimony to the critical importance of the problem both to our nation's present interests and future prospects. The importance of directing a greater percentage of the present effort in the field toward more systematic investigation of potentially powerful influences — i.e., adolescent boys, both parents of a family unit, the media, public policies — will increase as the United States continues its efforts to meet this challenge.

8
Steps to Make North American Diets Health Protective

INTRODUCTION

This chapter continues the focus on contemporary health concerns with rich histories in both public health and health psychology. In particular, this chapter illustrates how multilevel analyses can help to pinpoint targets and settings for interventions that synthesize public health and psychological approaches toward modifying the dietary practices of the general population.

Health Risk, Disease Prevention, and Diet

Dietary change has a rather unique history in public health and in health psychology. Legislation on safe food production, spurred by Upton Sinclair's book *The Jungle*, an exposé of the meat industry, but also through industry's goal of self-protection, culminated in the Pure Food and Drugs Act of 1906 (Barkan, 1985). This was one of the most publicized, if perhaps not completely effective, public health campaigns undertaken at the turn of the century (Schultz, 1981). Adequate nutrition for mothers and children has also been a prominent concern throughout the history of public health and remains so today (Hanlon & Pickett, 1984). Psychologists also have a long history, albeit of modest success, in weight control, overnutrition, and dietary change (Wilson, 1984). Additionally, most recent psychological work has attempted to unravel the puzzle of eating disorders such as bulimia and to develop effective treatments (Love & Ollendick, 1986). Both sets of psychological efforts mostly focused on self-selected overweight or distressed individuals, in contrast to the population-focused public health programs.

Public health and psychological traditions and expertise coalesce around contemporary concerns in developed countries about the linkages between typical Western diets and the prevalence of coronary heart and cardiovascular disease (CVD) (Cummings, 1986; Simopolos, 1986) and certain site cancers (Cummings, 1986; Greenwald, Sondik, & Lynch, 1986). Note, however, that the traditional public health concern of undernutrition and contaminated food has been replaced by the focus on overnutrition and chronic disease (Surgeon General, 1988).

THE EPIDEMIOLOGICAL EVIDENCE

Cancer Risk

Clearly, what was once considered speculative, part of the fringe, zealot sector of the health movement, has now come center stage, as illustrated by this recent statement from National Cancer Institute (NCI) professionals:

> Poor dietary practices, including inadequate intake of fiber and important micronutrients, are probably as significant as tobacco smoking in causing cancer. The consensus of scientists is that as much as 25 to 35% of cancer mortality is related to dietary factors. This estimate is based on a large number of studies, although uncertainty surrounds the exact magnitude of the association and the biological mechanisms involved. (Greenwald et al., 1986, p. 271)

According to Greenwald et al. (1986), the role of dietary factors in cancer incidence receives support from four types of epidemiologic studies:

1. International correlation studies that have compared dietary intakes to cancer rates
2. Studies of migration from areas with low cancer rates to or from areas with high cancer rates
3. Comparison of certain low-risk U.S. populations (e.g., Seventh Day Adventists) to the general U.S. population
4. Case control and cohort studies that compare dietary patterns in cancer patients to controls in the study population.

In addition, epidemiologic evidence is further supported by experimental animal studies and other test systems. Overall, the evidence indicates the following:

1. A diet high in fat, particularly saturated fat, is associated with cancer of the breast, colon, rectum, uterus, prostate, and possibly several other sites. A caveat is that the data base and attendant associations are more suggestive than definitive (e.g., compared to smoking and lung cancer; Miller, 1986).
2. A diet high in fiber is associated with a lowered risk of colon and rectal cancers. A caveat here also is that since dietary fiber and fat are usually inversely related in the diet, it is difficult to estimate the relative contribution of each factor to the risk of cancer at those sites. However, the epidemiological evidence for a diet low in fiber and increased colon cancer risk appears strong (Greenwald, Lanza, & Eddy, 1987).
3. The possibility exists of micronutrient (vitamins, minerals) involvement

in cancer risk, with much additional research being presently conducted to verify relationships.

The overall evidence of increased cancer risk from a high-fat, low-fiber diet is substantial enough for NCI to develop dietary goals for the general population for the years 1990 and 2000 specifically designed for cancer prevention. The 1990 dietary goals include:

1. Increasing fiber in the diet from the present per capita average of 11 g per day to 20 g. This is to be accomplished by increased consumption of grains, fruits, and vegetables.
2. Decreasing the daily average of fat consumption (percent of calories) from about 37 percent to 30 percent. This can be accomplished by decreased consumption of high-fat dairy products, eggs, and meat, with the concomitant increase in grains, fruits, and vegetables.

In the year 2000, dietary goals entail an increase in per capita fiber consumption to 30 to 35 g per day, with fat consumption being reduced to 25%. There are also specific strategies noted to reach these goals, including having by 1990:

1. 75% or more of the population able to identify the principal dietary factors known to be — or strongly suspected of being — related to cancer;
2. 70% or more of the adult population able to identify foods low in fat and high in dietary fiber;
3. labels on packaged foods which contain useful calorie and nutrient information so that consumers can select more healthful diets, with similar information displayed where nonpackaged foods are obtained or purchased;
4. all states include nutritional education as part of a required comprehensive school health program at both the elementary and secondary school levels;
5. most routine health contracts with health professionals include an element of nutrition education and counseling; and
6. all managers of institutional food services understand and actively promote healthy dietary patterns.

These goals indicate the increased probability of cancer risk that NCI has attached to high-fat, low-fiber diets, and cancer prevention afforded by dietary change. This increased probability is also disputed by some professionals (e.g., Harper, 1984) who claim the evidence is neither clear nor demanding of action. Two camps appear to exist. The activists stress the dietary–disease links and call for public intervention. The traditionalists question the empirical basis of such claims and continue their efforts to ameliorate undernutrition. The debate is highly emotional because of the absence of incisive (human) data, the reportedly different corporate ties of the activists (e.g., cereal companies) and traditionalists (e.g., the egg industry), and the change in funding clout for nutrition research over the years from the Department of Agriculture to the National Institutes of Health.

In addition, while the larger percentage of health professionals appears to concur with the NCI position, the evidence that does exist may also be interpreted differently by corporate interests. Demand for their products may rise or fall dependent upon the degree of certainty and publicity given to the dietary–disease link data (e.g., the recent NCI–Kellogg Company campaign for high-fiber cereals; Warner, 1987b). However, the approach to dietary change, as exemplified by the NCI goal statements, appears to rest heavily on education and knowledge gain. For example, school programs, product labels, and aware professionals are seen as favored intervention strategies, rather than seemingly more potent approaches in the public health tradition — e.g., reducing the fat content of select foods through regulatory policy.

As discussed in various chapters in this book, those particular and usually individual- and group-level approaches may at best be only modestly effective when used alone for promoting large population changes. Part of this chapter will discuss efforts at dietary change launched from different perspectives and levels of analysis. We also will use our framework to outline one potentially efficacious multilevel approach. Prior to this point, dietary factors related to cardiovascular disease will be discussed.

Cardiovascular and Coronary Heart Disease

Although data indicate about a 30% decline during the last 20 years in mortality from cardiovascular and coronary heart disease (CHD) (Matarazzo, 1984), these diseases remain the number one cause of premature death in the United States and other industrialized countries and the number one contributor to health care costs (Matarazzo, 1984). Hypertension, high blood cholesterol levels, and overweight, aside from genetic predisposition, are the major risk factors for these diseases. Evidence indicates that these risk factors also have an important link to diet, linkages seemingly less disputed than those for cancer.

Kaplan (1986), using a stringent criterion of systolic pressure greater than 160mm and/or diastolic pressure above 95mm, estimated that there are 30 million hypertensive individuals in the United States. Despite great efforts expended during the last 25 years to control hypertension, the disease frequently remains untreated and infrequently well controlled. About 55% of hypertensives are not on treatment, 21% are not controlled, and only about 24% are controlled (Kaplan, 1986). In addition, since a number of hypertension medications also pose other risks, interest in dietary change is increasing, although evidence here is not conclusive.

Sodium restriction, highly touted until recently, is receiving more discerning investigation. More moderate restrictions of sodium in the diet, 75mm to 100mm per day, seem to provide benefits with no harm, and only take several months for individual adjustment. However, " . . . the reported benefits of a reduced sodium intake may reflect an increased potassium intake, since whenever sodium is deleted from the diet by the substitution of natural foods for processed foods, potassium intake will increase" (Kaplan, 1986, p. 510).

The role of fat, particularly saturated fat, has received better and more recent empirical support. While warning that it is difficult to determine the effects of a single nutrient, Puska et al. (1985) and Tuomilehto et al. (1985) working in Finland have provided good support for the health-protective benefits of a lowered fat diet. In these experimental studies, normals, borderlines, and mild hypertensive individuals have been monitored (e.g., blood pressure, cholesterol level) during a baseline period in which they adhered to their usual diet. In an experimental phase of 6 to 12 weeks, individuals followed a low-fat diet (25% of calories from fat), with additional manipulations focusing on the polyunsaturated/saturated (P/S) fat ratio. After the intervention phase, participants in the studies switch back to their usual diets.

Across studies and phases, the clearest results showed that a low-fat diet reduced systolic and diastolic blood pressure, reduced total and LDL cholesterol, and increased serum HDL. Less clear results pertained to the different P/S ratios. Thus, based on this research, the one health-protective recommendation for reducing risk of cardiovascular disease is to reduce fat in the diet. However, research continues to examine the separate roles of monosaturated, saturated, and polyunsaturated fats. It appears that the recommendation to reduce saturated fats will continue to receive the most support.

Note also that the diet recommended for cancer-risk reduction fits these same guidelines (i.e., reduced fat, increased complex carbohydrates). However, there is conflicting evidence on how easily individuals can switch to and maintain a low-fat diet (Reeves, Foreyt, Scott, Mitchell, Wohlleb, & Gotto, 1983) and which population segments would most benefit from resource expenditures that may be required to promote such dietary change. One relevant population would appear to be overweight individuals.

As Hubert (1986) has recently noted:

. . . optimal preventive strategies will require modification of early markers for the development of CHD, hypertension, and hyperlipidema. The accumulated evidence strongly suggests that overweight or obesity is such a precursor to disease development and that prevention of CHD can be greatly prompted by control of this attribute in overfed and sedentary populations such as those in North America. (Hubert, 1986, p. 493)

Hubert noted that although the pathogenic mechanisms through which obesity operates for CHD are not proven to a definitive degree, the evidence includes the temporal sequence of cause and effect, the strength of association, the consistency of findings across studies, and the biologic plausibility. There is a strong relationship of excess weight or weight change to systolic and diastolic blood pressure change and the development of hypertension. Indeed, " . . . early prevention of weight gain may be an important key to the reduction of hypertension and its sequelae in the general population" (Hubert, 1986, p. 495). Measures of obesity and changes (gain) in weight are also associated with undesirable low-density lipoprotein cholesterol (LDL-C) and inversely related to high-density lipoprotein (HDL-C) levels, which are important predictors of future coronary events in population groups. Indeed, more recently, increased diagnostic focus has been on the HDL/LDL ratio than on the overall cholesterol count, although the overall count is still predictive of health risk.

As also reported by Hubert (1986), weight loss in borderline hypertensives can be an effective treatment, while with controlled hypertensives, weight loss may allow withdrawal from drug therapy. Although considerable debate still revolves around the role of weight reduction in the prevention of CHD (e.g. there are many different types of studies and measures), prospective longitudinal studies conducted in North America mostly with men provide reasonably good evidence. In studies where observations have continued for four to five years, there is a linear relationship between some measures of obesity and CHD morbidity and mortality. These data have led Hubert and others to conclude that " . . . the accumulated evidence strongly suggests that obesity is an important risk factor for premature CHD in the general population" (p. 500).

While such epidemiological research has made it more clear *what* risk factors should be the focus of intervention, it is not clear *how* this can be accomplished. For example, weight control regimes — from individual therapy to group programs to self-help and worksite programs — show minimal success (Brownell, 1986), albeit in highly self-selected, perhaps "hard-core" samples of individuals (Schacter, 1982). However, one sound, although until recently not frequently tried, strategy for weight control entails moderate increases in activity and exercise and an emphasis on a high-complex carbohydrate, high-fiber, low-fat diet, which often is also a lower calorie diet (Brody, 1985). Although such a diet and activity regime may not be the singular strategy for the highly obese, for the moderately overweight and the general population this type of diet may be the weight control diet of choice. However, dietary pronouncements and goals are clearly not enough, as we will shortly discuss, to overcome psychological and social barriers to dietary change.

On the other hand, what is most striking about the conclusion concerning weight control is that a high-complex carbohydrate, high-fiber, low-fat diet is the same dietary prescription, whether for cancer prevention or cardiovascular disease prevention (Cummings, 1986; Surgeon General, 1988). Further, there are apparently no accounts of harm to individuals or populations who follow this kind of diet (although some recent work with population segments continues in order to further clarify this point).

The major purpose of this chapter is to examine—primarily through different levels of analysis, concomitant intervention strategies, and overall use of the framework—how large-scale dietary change can be achieved. However, prior to those sections of this chapter, it is important to examine how North American diets have evolved in this century and what products and meals constitute today's typical North American diet.

THE TYPICAL NORTH AMERICAN DIET

Because of changes in production (e.g., more processing of foods) and distribution (e.g., the rise of fast-food establishments), most reviewers of dietary changes in North America during the last century conclude that from a health-protective perspective, diets have become worse! For example, according to Greenwald et al. (1986):

1. Fiber intake since 1909 has declined 20% to 8 to 12 g per day.
2. The proportion of calories from carbohydrates has fallen since 1909 from 56 to 46%, while the number of calories contributed by sugar increased, and those calories from starches and plant foods rich in fiber have decreased.
3. Although exact analyses are not available, during this same period there have been decreases in per capita consumption of fruits, vegetables, dried beans, peas, nuts, fiber, and cereal products.
4. During this century, processed fruit consumption, mostly consisting of citrus fruit juice, has increased ten-fold and consumption of processed vegetables has increased four-fold, while since 1909 consumption of fresh fruits has declined 36% and consumption of fresh vegetables has decreased 23%.
5. Per capita consumption of dietary fat has increased 31% since 1909, from 32 to 41% of calories (although some experts believe that total fat consumption is about 37%).
6. The increased consumption of fats appears explainable by a two-fold increase in the use of fats and oils used in the commercial processing of foods, especially fast foods, snacks, and convenience foods.

Two important questions are whether these trends have asymptoted for the general population and whether widely publicized changes in dietary practices still largely pertain to a relatively small population segment. One way to answer these questions is to examine the current content of the North American diet.

The National Health and Nutrition Exam Survey has studied dietary intake data as reported by 11,658 black or white adults, ages 19–74, who represented 132 million U.S. adults (Block, Dresser, Hartman, & Carroll, 1985). The data are suitably extensive and can only be given a capsule summary here, which nevertheless provides one picture of the typical U.S. diet:

1. The major contributors of calories are white bread, rolls, and crackers, 9.6%; hamburgers, cheeseburgers, meat loaf, beef steak, and roasts, 8.5%; doughnuts, cookies, and cake, 5.7%.
2. The major contributors of protein are beef steaks and roasts, 12.6%; pork, hot dogs, ham, and lunch meats, 9.4%; hamburgers, cheeseburgers, and meat loaf, 8.9%; and whole milk and whole milk beverages, 6.3%.
3. The major contributors of carbohydrates are wheat bread, rolls, and sugared crackers, 15%; soft drinks, 9%; doughnuts, cookies, and cake, 7.5%; all fruits and juices, 6.6%; and all cereals, 3.2%.
4. The major contributors of total fat are hamburgers, cheeseburgers, and meatloaf, 7.0%; hot dogs, ham, and lunch meats, 6.4%; and whole milk and whole milk beverages, 6.0%, with approximately 50% of the total of saturated fat contributed from hamburgers, cheeseburgers, meat loaf, whole milk and whole milk beverages, cheese, beef steaks and roasts, hot dogs, ham, lunch meats, eggs, and pork.

According to Block et al. (1985), beef products should be the first object of personal and societal intervention because beef is by far the most important single contributor to fat in the U.S. diet. Beef also contributes 18 to 20% of total saturated fat and 16 to 18% of total cholesterol. In comparison, butter and ice cream only contribute 2.4 and 2.1% of total fat, respectively.

In addition, Block et al. noted that while there was some dietary variability by regions, there was not great variability of foods by demographic groups. One conclusion from the data from Block et al. is that while, perhaps, diet has changed in recent years in certain population segments, across the entire U.S. most individuals consume a high-fat, high-meat, low-complex carbohydrate, low-fiber, high-simple sugar diet.

Additional surveys and monitoring of food purchases across demographic samples have substantiated this position (e.g., Winett, Kramer, Walker, Malone, & Lane, 1987). For example, food product choices and meals differed little between lower-middle and upper-middle class samples. From these same data, focus groups, and observations, a composite "exemplary" dinner for an adult was constructed. The main part of the meal consisted of a six-ounce steak, a small baked potato with two pats of butter and sour cream, and a small salad drenched in dressing. The meal contained 1400 calories, and was 70% fat, 13% carbohydrates, and 17% protein.

The conclusion is that the typical North American diet is in need of a "major overhaul" (Kaplan, 1986, p. 515). The question as noted in the prior section is how, and we add here, to what degree and lengths? The next sections will examine these questions from the perspectives of different levels of analysis.

MULTIPLE LEVELS OF ANALYSIS

As we have noted, the most critical aspect of using the framework entails a thorough overview of multiple levels of analysis. That overview allows examination of the problem from different perspectives, theories, and data sources, narrows the focus for further review, and leads to more assessment of the advantages and disadvantages of intervention design, implementation, and evaluation steps.

The personal level of analysis stresses that current dietary practices are a result of personal choice, primarily based on knowledge, beliefs, and habits. Therefore, change efforts, for example, directed at knowledge and beliefs, based on the health beliefs model (Janz & Becker, 1984) and targeted for individual citizens, is a preferred strategy. The strategy may be articulated in self-help materials, health education programs, and media-assisted instruction, or perhaps through counseling.

The interpersonal level of analysis assumes that nutritional practices are largely influenced by family, peer, and social groups. Change efforts at this level will usually attempt to encapsulate the influence group within a program — e.g., family health programs or worksite social support groups — or will be directed to the assumed source of influence. For example, an interpersonal or media-assisted program may teach parents how to model and reinforce better dietary practices for their children. Psychological and communication theories are applied at this level.

The organizational/environmental level points toward settings and their norms, rules, and design as the major influence on dietary practices. Attempts to alter nutritional information provided in cafeterias and supermarkets, as well as the array of meals and products offered in these settings, fits within this level of analysis. The assumption is that a redesigned setting will influence many individual consumers; thus, the perspective of this level of analysis is more similar to public health than are those of the prior levels.

The institutional/societal level assumes that current dietary practices have accrued from a series of policies that have determined national priorities and resource expenditures. For example, massive farms, certain methods of breeding and agriculture, particular market advantages, and mass distribution systems have favored certain products. Such institutional arrangements, coupled with traditional preferences, aggressive marketing, and ready availability and convenience (e.g., fast-food establishments) explain current practices. Change efforts at this level entail legislative, regulatory, and economic interventions to expedite market forces and are most congruent with public health initiatives.

In the following section, we review in more detail the conceptualization, strategies, advantages and disadvantages, and outcomes of efforts at these different levels. Each level provides particular insights and methods for approaching nutritional change, with multilevel efforts capitalizing on the strengths of each level.

A MULTILEVEL APPROACH

What makes the study of food intake so interesting is that, unlike sleep, the effects of cognition, environment, and culture, all extrinsic to biological state, are nonetheless its major determinant. People eat what they like, at times and in ways that are most convenient or socially mandated; they tend to eat what others whom they perceive as similar to them eat; and frequently they eat too much or too little, depending on the influence of environmental cues and social pressure. (Rodin, 1984, p. 549)

The quote from Rodin makes the case that understanding and modifying current dietary practices entail analyses beyond that of the individual. Simply focusing on taste preferences or knowledge of nutrition will result, at best, in an incomplete picture. Nevertheless, understanding personal factors — i.e., beliefs and behaviors and their relationship to group, organizational, and institutional influences — is important, and provides a starting point for this analysis.

Personal Level

According to Rozin (1984), there is surprisingly little research about the development of food preferences. Much attention has been focused on physiological aspects of overweight (Brownell, 1986), but much less on everyday preferences of normal weight individuals. However, there is research pointing toward biological preferences for certain substances, e.g., sweets, and evidence of genetic predisposition or ethnic group membership influencing preferences, e.g., lactose intolerance.

Rozin indicated that biological and cultural factors establish constraints or predispositions within which an individual develops a unique set of preferences and attitudes. For example, biological preferences for sweets can be satisfied by innumerable sweet products. Those individuals with lactose intolerance now have wide choice in yogurt products. Likewise, the availability and successful harvesting of particular crops, e.g., corn, led to a wide variety of products and meals based on corn.

Preferences in food have sensory and affective aspects, perceived consequences, and ideational aspects (e.g., appropriate–inappropriate, pleasing–disgusting). All these factors are important for public health efforts. For example, new food or alternative, healthier offerings should have a pleasing look, smell, and taste. To achieve these qualities, it may be necessary to prepare new products and meals in ways that appear most similar to usual products and meals so that new offerings are not rejected. This also is important because repeated exposure to a food and the perception that respected others value the food figures prominently in food preferences (Rozin, 1984).

These points were substantiated in a recent attempt to promote the selection of low-fat, high-complex carbohydrate entree selections in student cafeterias (Miller, 1987). Low-fat entrees were usually only selected if they were most similar to typical offerings and were presented in a pleasing way. Offerings with which these students had little prior experience, e.g., broiled fish dishes, were infrequently chosen unless incentives were offered. This study suggested that a "passive" strategy, i.e., reducing the fat content in highly preferred entrees, would be more efficacious than attempts to markedly alter entree preferences. In addition, it may be possible to develop a "successive approximation" strategy to modifying current products so that products can retain their market share.

Additional support for this position is found in Rozin (1984) who concluded his article on food habits and preferences with this sobering quote:

> Attempts to change cuisine, often in the direction of providing a more balanced or economical diet, have met with failure more than success because of the basic conservatism of cuisine. The conservatism is clearly seen within our own culture in the fact that the ethnic origins of Americans are more clearly revealed in their kitchens and their dining room tables than in other aspects of their behavior. (Rozin, 1984, p. 602)

The quote from Rozin underscores the need to understand the context of eating and the role of a cuisine and culture as a prerequisite for planning dietary change. That is, " . . . people eat food, not nutrients" (Rozin, 1984, p. 603). However, this position may be changing, as reflected in general observations. Dietary concerns are receiving more media attention. For example, recent high-fiber breakfast cereal commercials have been couched in NCI recommendations (Warner, 1987b). Eating patterns also appear more homogeneous. For example, on surveys, few people indicated any ethnic preferences in dinner choices (Winett et al., 1987). These points indicate that within the constraints of past preferences and product availability, the time may be optimal for attempts to change dietary practices. One important question is: How knowledgeable about nutrition are individuals?

Part of the answer comes from frequent surveys done by the Food and Drug Administration (FDA) in conjunction with its food labeling program. Food labels, which most often simply list ingredients in descending order of amount in the product, will have minimal impact on purchases if consumers understand neither the terms nor their relevance to nutrition. Unfortunately, these surveys (Heimbach, 1981; Schucker, 1983) suggest that:

1. Labels tend to be most understood by higher SES segments.
2. Consumers tend not to know the difference between terms such as saturated and polyunsaturated fat.
3. Terms such as sodium are understood, but it is not known how much sodium is required per day.
4. There appears to be more interest in specific consumer segments in risk avoidance (e.g., high-calorie food) than in health benefits (e.g., fruits and vegetables).
5. Specific knowledge of nutrition is poor.

Focused surveys across SES groups support these points (Winett et al., 1987a). For example, while virtually all respondents displayed general knowledge ("Nutrition is related to heart disease and cancer"), few respondents were aware that a high-complex carbohydrate diet was preferable. Further, few respondents could identify complex carbohydrates; more importantly, key myths of nutrition prevailed. For example, most respondents indicated that "starch," such as that in potatoes, was "fattening" and that for weight loss reducing starch was a basic strategy.

These data indicate that a prominent task which remains is mass nutritional education of consumers. Mass individual efforts will, at least in part, need to be accomplished through use of the media, particularly television. Such efforts may additionally require regulatory and programmatic changes, as discussed in chapter 4 and in a later section of this chapter, so that nutritional messages can compete with commercials. To preview here the enormity of the task and the countervailing force that will be necessary, it may be noted that children see an average of 10,000 TV commercials a year for food. Most of these commercials are for sweetened cereals, candy, gum, cookies, crackers, and fast foods (Wadden & Brownell, 1984). "There is little doubt that these commercials influence what children want and what they eat" (Wadden & Brownell, 1984, p. 613), and empirical study (e.g., Gorn & Goldberg, 1982) supports this contention. Further, it is estimated that advertising expenditures for the items noted above have approximately a 5,000-to-1 ratio to nutritious advertising (Greene, Rouse, Green, & Clay,

1984)! For example, in 1984, McDonald's alone spent over $250 million on TV advertising.

However, it is important that when nutritional messages and programs do have wide exposure, social-psychological influences supporting current practices and related to success and failure of change efforts are given prominent consideration. For example, while Brownell et al. (1986) have focused on physiological, cognitive, behavior, and environmental factors associated with lapses and relapses in eliminating addictive behaviors (including overeating), some of their major points pertain to population-based efforts. These include aiming proper messages at suitable segments (e.g., those segments interested in dietary change receive more specific instructions), increasing motivation for change, and developing coping strategies for inevitable lapses. Thus, public health efforts using large-scale methods such as mass media still must base strategies for (mass) individual change on psychological concepts and methods.

To summarize individual level factors, on the positive side, data on food preferences suggests that shifts can be made if attention is paid to presenting healthier foods in more familiar contexts. However, this point also suggested that an efficacious passive strategy entails alteration of products and meals, a task involving organizational and institutional change. Likewise, while the public has gotten the message that nutrition is important to health, more specific knowledge about nutrition is missing. It was suggested that mass education is needed. These efforts need to incorporate psychological principles and strategies, but such an approach also necessitates organizational and institutional change. Before turning to those levels, interpersonal factors will be examined.

Interpersonal Level

As noted previously, intervention for dietary change at this level will most often attempt to encapsulate a family, peer group, or network within an intervention. The approach not only offers some potential for reduced costs of intervention; it makes sense conceptually. A family, group, or network at times share the same environment and can shape that environment, and members can differentially reinforce each other.

The work of Baronowski and his colleagues (Jaycox, Baronowski, Nader, Dworkin, & Vanderpool, 1983; Nader, Baronowski, Vanderpool, Dunn, Dworkin, & Ray, 1983) on the Family Health Project illustrates both the promise and problems inherent in this level of intervention. Nader et al. (1983) cogently pointed out that community approaches to risk reduction change often require complex and extensive programming, albeit for modification of multiple risks in populations. The Family Health Project only focused on reducing dietary sodium and saturated fat, and increasing aerobic exercise with a program conducted in a weekly group format. Nader et al. also noted that body weight, blood pressure, and serum lipoproteins have been shown to be highly related within families. These relationships reflect not only genetic factors but also the similar dietary and exercise practices of family members, and provide empirical justification for family interventions.

The program featured eight hour-and-a-half meetings, with part of that time devoted to aerobic exercise. The sessions were constructed within a cognitive–social learning framework and included, in addition to aerobics, activities which were to be extended to the home to enhance recognition of high-sodium and high-fat foods — filmstrips on appropriate dietary choices; social inoculation (i.e., role playing resisting offers of inappropriate foods), the making of healthy snacks by parents and children within the sessions, and role playing solutions to anticipated problems to be faced when sticking to new dietary practices.

Twenty-four families, representing three ethnic groups — Anglo, Black, and Mexican-American — met in three separate homogeneous ethnic groups. Parents were generally in their mid-thirties, and children were in the third to sixth grade. However, most meetings were only attended by mothers and children. This point underscores that often members of a group or family will not attend project meetings, may be disinterested or uncooperative, and even undermine others' efforts. On the positive side, the materials used were not expensive, and meetings could be led by a paraprofessional. However, again on the negative side, the program did report dropout problems and problems in recruiting participants. Each group of eight families also re-quired about 12 hours of group meeting time.

Unfortunately, the primary data reported for this project was based on self-reports of consumption of high sodium and saturated fat foods, plus some self-monitoring of dietary selection and amount of aerobic exercise. These data suggested some minimal dietary changes, but no change in aero-bic exercise. In addition, there were no pre–post differences in weight, blood pressure, serum lipoproteins, or fitness as measured on a bicycle ergometer. Intensive programs such as this one require more intensive evaluations (e.g., observations of meals or evidence of food purchases) and also require sub-stantial outcomes to warrant the time and expense that are generally asso-ciated with intervention at this level. Moreover, Nader et al. suggested that this program may be more effective if it focused on actual dietary-related behaviors, e.g., food shopping and meal preparation. The entire effort does underscore this point: changing nutritional practices is a difficult task.

Food shopping and meal preparation were part of an experimental media-based effort to promote nutritious and economical food purchases (Winett, Kramer, Walker, Malone, & Lane, 1988). The media aspects will be reported in the last section of this chapter. As a comparison to media-based proce-dures, some participants received an interpersonal component ("participant modeling") developed for adults in a household (Kramer, 1987). First, the adults viewed a 30-minute videotape where a rationale and appropriate food purchases and meals for a low-fat, high-complex carbohydrate diet were explained and modeled within a storyline. In addition, strategies were shown that could result in monetary savings. Next, about 45 minutes were taken by a staff member to discuss how the adults would implement these dietary practices, with specific meals, purchases, and obstacles discussed and, where possible, resolved. Several days later, the primary shopper in the household was taken by the same staff member on a planned shopping trip which adhered to the video's guidelines on planning nutritious meals and using a detailed shopping list.

Each week, participants submitted on a special form a detailed list of all food purchased, which was also subjected to reliability testing. The data were acceptably reliable (Kazdin, 1984), but did require substantial participant and staff time to obtain and interpret. These data were converted in a nutritional analysis for each participant to percent fat and saturated fat, protein, and complex and simple carbohydrates, as well as an analysis of costs. Participants generally had as their goals having weekly purchases approximate 58% total carbohydrates, 48% complex carbohydrates, 30% fat, and only 10% saturated fat and 12% protein, as well as reaching a monetary goal of reducing food costs by 15%.

For a mean of six weeks after the shopping trip, participants received feedback via a telephone call on their nutritional analysis, progress toward goals, and advice on how to reach those goals. Comparison conditions (see pp. 276–278) included ones where project participants saw the video and only received a general discussion with no weekly feedback; video viewing alone or with written weekly feedback; a lesser quality (no storyline or modeling) video alone or with feedback; and an untreated control condition.

The results of this study showed that adding the pointed discussion, shopping trip, and personal feedback to the video modeling resulted in about 15% appropriate shifts within carbohydrate and fat nutrient categories of food purchases, as well as yielding about an 8% cost savings. Seeing a video alone was not effective for nutritional or monetary change. The outcomes for participant modeling also tended to show better results for specific nutritional changes (e.g., reduction in saturated fats), but seeing the modeling video with feedback was generally as effective as the seemingly optimal interpersonal condition. As in the Family Health Project, the time and effort expended on the interpersonal intervention did not appear justifiable.

Thus, at this point the rationale for family-based dietary interventions remains intuitively appealing. However, as illustrated by these quite different efforts, at this point a technology for such interventions seems lacking. It does appear that effective family-based interventions may require more focused *in vivo* training and feedback. Such intensive efforts will require substantial dietary shifts to warrant their apparent costs.

Organizational/Environmental Level

There is now considerable work in dietary change at this level of analysis. Efforts include projects located at the worksite, in schools, in cafeterias and supermarkets, and those which have focused on entire communities. The results from cafeteria and supermarket studies are particularly encouraging in suggesting a common and simple set of effective procedures. Worksite-based and school-based projects remain diverse, while most community-based efforts have more or less followed the Stanford model (Solomon and Maccoby, 1984; see chapter 5).

Worksite and School Programs

To date, most worksite dietary programs have focused on overweight and obese employees (Brownell, 1986; Wadden & Brownell, 1984), with much less attention directed toward dietary change in all employees (Fielding, 1984). This emphasis is partly the result of controversy (until most recently) on the role of diet in cancer and CHD, and the greater perceived risk (and visibility) of overweight employees to the organization. Where nutrition education and modification of cafeteria offerings have been part of a comprehensive wellness program, as in the Johnson & Johnson "Live for Life" program, it is not clear what effects these interventions have had on dietary practices (Nathan, 1984a). At worksites, interventions for weight loss are becoming more effective (e.g., by using monetary incentives and competitions; Brownell, 1986; Jeffrey, Forster, & Snell, 1985). It is probable that as dietary bases of ill health receive more empirical support and publicity, recent encouragement about dietary change resulting from more innovative worksite efforts with the overweight will diffuse to programs for all employees.

Two recent projects (Coates et al., 1985; Walter, Hofman, Connelly, Barrett, & Kost, 1985) demonstrate both the potential and pitfalls in designing, implementing, and evaluating school-based health promotion programs. According to Coates et al., while there were more than two dozen reported empirical nutrition education studies, only a handful met criteria for quality investigations, including specification of treatment components, adequate and reliable dependent measures, and adequate follow-up. With these points as presumably a focal concern, Coates et al. developed a school-based program to target high blood pressure through early diet modification.

Coates' prior work (Coates, Jeffrey, & Slinkard, 1981) had suggested that a structured school-based program with motivational components for predominantly middle-class children could result in changes in knowledge of nutrition and food preferences in school. The project reported here attempted to replicate this program with black, inner-city high school students and also analyze the contribution of different aspects of the program including a parental involvement component and school-wide media. A final objective involved trying to predict which students responded to the program. This objective was based on Jessor's (1984) social psychological position that health-compromising and health-enhancing behaviors are best viewed as a syndrome, not as separate behaviors. Thus, in this project other health-related practices (i.e., smoking, drinking, physical activity) were also assessed to ascertain who responded and if other health practices not targeted by the program were affected.

Two different high schools, including grades 10, 11, and 12, were involved in the project. All students were enrolled in a mandatory one-semester health education course; about 45% of the enrolled students were male and 55% were female. Virtually all students were from low-income black families. About 25% of adults in the catchment area reportedly had diastolic blood pressure greater than 90 mm Hg or maintained a blood pressure below 90 mm Hg while on antihypertensive medication.

The study used a two-by-two design in one school with eight health education classes randomly assigned to treatment. The design compared class instruction to no class instruction, and parental involvement to no parental involvement. The entire school also received media that sought to popularize the program. The control school also had eight classes. Assessments were conducted before the program, immediately and one month after, and then at the start of the next school year.

Six 45-minute classes were taught by research staff with regular teachers present. The classes emphasized eating only certain snacks (e.g., fruit) and not others (e.g., potato chips); setting specific dietary goals; overcoming barriers to change; role playing resisting peer, media, and family pressure; reducing salt in the diet and the connection of salt to hypertension; contracting in the class to share messages with parents; and understanding food labels. Thus, the program attempted to model desired behavior, role play those behaviors, set specific goals, and provide feedback and reinforcement for change.

The objectives of parental involvement included informing parents about the program and securing their support for it; encouraging parents to make heart-healthy snacks available and to decrease the availability of high-salt snacks; and teaching parents to read labels and the comparative costs of heart-healthy snacks. Unfortunately, the extent of the parental part of the program was confined to three brochures sent home and two five-minute structured telephone calls.

School-wide media followed a "Great Sensations" theme. Posters with the project's objectives including attractive models eating appropriate snacks, point-of-sale flyers in the cafeteria lines suggesting low-salt snacks, and verbal reinforcement from cashiers for purchasing low-salt snacks all comprised the "media" component.

The apparent weakness of the parental and media components was unfortunately matched by the weakness of the dependent measure. The main measure was a questionnaire which listed high-salt, high-sugar, high-fat, and heart-healthy snacks. Students checked off what they ate at breakfast, midmorning, lunch, mid-afternoon, and after dinner. Scores were derived for percent of salty snacks consumed, percent of target snacks consumed, and percent of other snacks consumed. Additional questions tapped other health behaviors. Thus, there apparently were no actual observations of food purchases or aggregate sales data. In defense of Coates et al., collecting such data is not simple, requiring collaboration with food service providers and possible monitoring of students eating lunch off campus.

The results of this study based on the self-reported checklist suggested that students in the intervention school compared to the control school slightly reduced their consumption of salty snacks. However, only students receiving classroom instruction showed any evidence of replacing salty snacks with appropriate snacks. Not surprisingly, the weak parental involvement component showed very minimal impacts. It did appear, however, that health behaviors clustered so that it was possible to (weakly) predict responsiveness to the program. Thus, it appears that the Coates et al. program may have had some effective components, such as classroom instruction, but minimal development of the other media and parental components, as well as a weak measurement system, precludes any definitive conclusions.

This type of work, however, warrants subsequent research development. For example, it may also be interesting to attempt to have teenagers influence their parents, instead of targeting the parents. In addition, King, Saylor et al. (in press) demonstrated that in-school programs with more specific procedures can impact on student lunch choices. This project used in-school monitoring of actual lunch choices and, thus, improved the Coates et al. study. However, King et al. did find that gaining cooperation from school food service providers presented some problems, and that many students ate lunch off campus and could not be monitored (see above).

A far more ambitious project is being conducted by Walter et al. (1985). The objective of this program is to demonstrate over a five-year period the feasibility and effectiveness of the primary prevention of chronic disease among a cohort of school children. In particular, these objectives include reducing the incidence of cigarette smoking and favorably shifting the distributions of blood pressure, blood lipid levels, body mass indices, and cardiovascular fitness. Walter et al. noted that the present project represented a natural evolution of school-based programs which have appeared successful in modifying knowledge, attitudes, and risk-related behaviors. However, as the above review of Coates et al. and King et al. suggested, a number of problems, including further development of behavior change strategies and objective measurement of change, remain in this area.

In the first year, the Walter et al. project involved 2,283 fourth graders in one school district in the Bronx, New York. The mean age of the students at the start of the program was nine years; about 50% of the children were black, 24% were white, 23% were Hispanic, and 3% were Asian. The median 1983 family income was $22,000 (lower-middle class). Fourteen schools were randomly assigned to intervention conditions, and eight schools were controls.

The major part of the intervention consists of the "Know Your Body" curriculum developed by the American Heart Association. The curriculum includes sections on nutrition, fitness, and cigarette smoking prevention and is conducted for about two hours per week over the entire school year by regular teachers. These teachers had, however, received special training, and they were monitored and given feedback based on classroom visits and their adherence to the curriculum.

According to Walter et al.:

> The overall curriculum objective is to provide children with the skills required to adopt behavioral patterns consistent with the program goal of changes in chronic risk factor distributions. The curriculum was developed using social learning techniques. Each activity is designed to incorporate five social learning strategies to encourage behavior change; namely, modeling of desired behaviors, behavioral rehearsal, goal specification, feedback of results, and reinforcement for favorable behavioral change. (Walter et al., 1985, p. 774)

The nutritional component of the program follows the American Heart Association's "prudent diet" which emphasizes maintenance of ideal weight, decreased consumption of total fat and saturated fat, cholesterol, sodium, and refined sugar, and increased consumption of complex carbohydrates and fiber. The basics of cardiovascular fitness are being taught, and smoking prevention training mainly entails learning how to resist pressures to smoke. The entire program is delivered within a multimedia format.

Yearly measures for the program include systolic and diastolic blood pressure, cholesterol and high-density lipoprotein, serum thiocyanate (for smoking), a ponderosity (height–weight) index, triceps skinfold thickness (for percent body fat), and a post-exercise pulse recovery rate. Thus, this is one of the few school-based studies to employ measures that truly reflect health risk. While these measures are laudatory and extreme care is being taken to standardize them, it appears equally important to gather information on actual behavior changes—e.g., dietary choices and aerobic activities—to understand what aspects of the program appear effective and what behavioral processes are reflected in the "hard" measures. These data are apparently lacking.

The first-year program results showed small changes, including a reduction of systolic blood pressure by 1.9 and diastolic blood pressure by 1.8; a reduction of total cholesterol by 3.1, an increase in HDL by 1.0, and a reduction of a total cholesterol/HDL ratio by .10; a reduction of serum thiocyanate by 3.3; a reduction of the ponderosity index by .09 and the triceps skinfold by .06; and an increase in the recovery index by .3. Thus, the first-year results are quite modest.

However, on the positive side, the school-based program was very acceptable to students, parents, and teachers, and was feasibly conducted. Walter et al. attributed the positive receptiveness of the program and its smooth operation to the considerable care and time put into preparing the school, parents, and medical community for the project, and to the attention given to teachers to overcome any resistance to the curriculum.

Walter et al. noted that for blood pressure and cholesterol measures, the first-year results compared favorably to community and even clinic-based efforts. That is, about half the effect of those programs was found by the first year of this program. There was also some indication that program students were initiating smoking at a lower rate than controls. First-year results were less conclusive for the ponderosity index, triceps skinfold thickness, the recovery index, or HDL. These results suggest that physical activity was not affected.

Walter et al. modestly concluded that

> The magnitude of the effect of school-based programs of chronic disease prevention is likely to be small. Such programs cannot be expected to have a favorable influence on all of the multitudinous determinants of risk-related behavior patterns, such as societal custom, economic necessity, family practices, media influences, peer pressure, psychologic predisposition. . . . Nevertheless, the importance of small shifts in population distributions of risk factors in the prevention of chronic disease has been underscored repeatedly in the literature. (Walter et al., 1985, p. 780)

However, these modest results need not be seen as conclusive for all school-based programs. Indeed, the development of these programs seems to have followed a less-than-optimal process. That is, entire programs have been instituted prior to assessing particularly effective procedures. Interestingly, supermarket-based programs for altering food purchase choices at first followed this more molar approach and showed essentially no changes. More recent efforts have emphasized testing specific and simple procedures and have yielded some encouraging results. A similar and "fruitful" approach has been followed in cafeteria studies. These efforts underscore a general point made throughout this book—the need for a social marketing framework and formative and pilot research for the design and pretesting of programs.

Supermarkets, Cafeterias, and Restaurants

There are two prominent supermarket projects, both conducted with the Giant Foods chain, which further illustrate the importance of field testing specific procedures. The first program can be described as "amorphous" in that a number of different and rather elaborate procedures were instituted with apparently no impact on food purchases. In the second program, a much simpler, more specific procedure was used alone and had demonstrated impacts.

The "Foods for Health" program was a joint effort involving Giant Foods, Inc., and scientists at the National Heart, Lung, and Blood Institute of the National Institutes of Health (National Heart, Lung, and Blood Institute, 1983). It serves as a good example of private and public sector cooperation. The project was based on pilot work (Zifferblat, Wilbur, & Pinsky, 1980) showing that prompts at the point of food selection in a cafeteria and vending machines could alter food selection of Institute employees to a significant (i.e., statistical and health criteria) degree. The Institute scientists were interested in seeing if this approach could work on a large scale. At the same time, Giant Foods believed that helping shoppers make more nutritional purchases would benefit their shoppers and the firm (e.g., by increasing customer loyalty and attracting new customers).

The project, conducted from October 1978 to October 1979 in 90 Giant Food stores in the Washington, D.C. (experimental) and Baltimore (control) areas, had these basic assumptions:

1. Knowledge of nutrition is somewhat limited, thus resulting in less than optimal purchases.
2. If consumer awareness and knowledge of nutrition is increased, then consumers will implement purchase and dietary changes, following a hierarchy of effects model (McGuire, 1981).
3. Point-of-purchase information is an effective way to increase awareness, knowledge, and, eventually, behavior.

Unfortunately, it appeared that, other than the pilot studies, little formative research was done to assess typical consumer beliefs and knowledge, their connection to actual food purchases, and the efficacy of the particular strategies used in the project.

The central theme of the project was that given the facts, "you decide." The primary information vehicles were the *Eater's Almanac*, a series of four-page brochures distributed every two weeks within supermarkets, and companion supermarket shelf tags called "Shelf Talkers." In the 26 issues, the Almanacs provided facts about heart disease, cardiovascular risk factors, and nutrition. They identified research questions that remained unanswered but gave seasonal suggestions for food selection and preparation, such as holiday and summer meals. Thus, the almanacs may be ineffective because their information was complex and vague (Winett, 1986). However, the shelf tags were placed directly below designated products to provide information at the point of selection. Presumably, the almanacs would be taken home and read.

Other promotional devices included radio spots, newspaper ads, in-store banners, window signs, and in-store posters, all tied into the almanacs. Over the course of the project, over two million almanacs were distributed. However, most aspects of the program focused solely on awareness and knowledge.

The evaluation assessed the feasibility of the approach—i.e., in-store nutritional education and private–public sector cooperation; awareness and use of the program by shoppers; reported nutritional knowledge and food habits; actual food purchases in the supermarket; and general interest in and dissemination of the program to other organizations. Evaluation instruments included telephone surveys and questionnaires with representative samples of Giant Food store shoppers and food purchase data generated by the computer-assisted checkout system in 10 Washington, D.C., and 10 Baltimore stores matched on demographic and sociological characteristics. There were also some unobtrusive observations made of shoppers.

Overall, the findings indicated great public and professional interest in the project; extensive and smooth cooperation between the representatives of the private and public sectors; and some small but significant changes in knowledge. However, there was no actual change in purchase pattern.

A closer examination of the project description and data in the rest of the report showed the following:

1. At the outset of the project, only one (i.e., Giant) of 20 food retailing chains contacted would meet all the requirements of the project, e.g., the experimental design and extensive promotional materials.
2. The use of radio spots, newspaper ads, window signs, and banners was also quite extensive and strategic and continued throughout the program.
3. The almanacs did not merely emphasize general nutrition, but instead focused on reducing fats, cholesterol, and calories in the diet (a positive aspect of the almanacs).
4. The computer-assisted checkout system monitored 246 items that were eventually reduced to nine categories (e.g., eggs, milk, salt). The categories did represent ones frequently noted in the almanacs, although fruit and vegetable purchases were not monitored.
5. Although 45% of the Washington, D.C., sample indicated they read the

project materials, so did 35% of the Baltimore sample—i.e., either there were problems with the self-report measures or there was contamination in the Baltimore stores.

6. At the outset, over 70% of both samples could correctly answer key items about the fat and cholesterol content of food and relationship of dietary fat to serum cholesterol.
7. It was not clear what percentage of people actually read the almanacs.
8. The gain in knowledge was only about 8% to 10%, and education level was related to knowledge.
9. At the end of the program, about 90% of all survey respondents (including controls) endorsed nutritional beliefs highly consistent with the project's goals.

The results of this program warrant some discussion. In the history of health promotion programs, this program was developed at the "first dawn." That is, it is easy to criticize the project based on the informative experiences of this one and other projects, and in light of more recent emphases on social marketing and behavioral outcomes. It is clear that additional formative research was needed to assess the knowledge, beliefs, and behaviors of the target population. More attention needed to be directed to strategies to promote behavior change, given already adequate knowledge. In addition, an analysis of food shopping behavior suggests that in-store prompts and displays (unless very specific, targeted to certain items, and intrusive) will probably not be an effective behavioral intervention in supermarkets.

The need to focus and simplify the approach taken in the "Food for Health" project is captured by this quote by the National Heart, Lung, and Blood Institute (1983):

> . . . in the 26 Eater's Almanacs and 23 shelf signs, a great deal of information and general food selection and preparation principles were presented. This information was illustrated by specific foods, but the consumer then had to apply this information among the 10,000 to 40,000 grocery store items and individualize the messages to their own food preparation techniques. (p. 49)

However, it may be the case that a simpler and much more focused approach could be effective. Some recent evidence to support this position comes from an evaluation of the effectiveness of more specific shelf tags used in Giant Foods stores to indicate foods low or reduced in sodium, cholesterol, or calories. According to Dr. Alan Levy (personal communications, September 1984; November 1986), a psychologist who performed the evaluation for the Food and Drug Administration (FDA), the program solely consisted of the specific shelf tags. There was no other persuasive, promotional materials. The FDA allowed Giant Foods to experiment with the special labels. The approach was based on the evidence from the first project that many consumers are aware of dietary-health links. Because knowledge was not the issue, it was decided to merely help an *informed segment* choose the right products.

Levy, Mathews, Stephenson, Tenney, and Schucker (1985) reported that in about half of the targeted items, there were statistically significant shifts in the rate of product purchases in Washington, D.C., stores (experimental) compared to Baltimore stores (controls) of about 4% to 8%. Levy et al. indicated that this change was about what might be expected from pricing or other promotional strategies. Obviously this is a very simple, portable approach. And, indeed, the success of this program has encouraged other food concerns to adopt more consumer-oriented policies.

However, emphasis should not just be placed on in-store approaches. Collaborative work with supermarket chains has the advantages of saliency and immediacy (of behavior) for point-of-purchase prompts and other media and a ready dissemination system. In-store approaches have the disadvantages of softening messages about certain products (e.g., meat), competing with an array of existing stimuli in the supermarket, and having to be processed by fast-moving and inattentive shoppers. In addition, as noted before, out-of-store video modeling and feedback procedures which focused on simple shopping and nutrition guidelines were effective in shifting shoppers' choices to lower-fat, higher-complex carbohydrate products, while reducing overall food expenditures (Winett et al., 1988). Such approaches, however, require creative access to the media to have large-scale impacts. The costs and benefits of in-store and out-of-store approaches clearly warrant more study, and the advantages and disadvantages of the different approaches are summarized in Table 8.1. These points will be addressed again in the chapter's final section.

Interestingly, efforts in cafeterias to alter meal selections have had a fairly

Table 8.1. Advantages and Disadvantages of In-Store and Out-of-Store Nutrition Campaigns

In-Store	
Advantages	*Disadvantages*
More salient	Limited time for consumer consideration
More immediate (to choices)	Less comprehensive
More specific (to products)	Less interactive
Ready access and dissemination	Less incisive

Out-of-Store	
Advantages	*Disadvantages*
More time for consumer consideration	Less salient
More comprehensive	Less immediate (to choices)
More interactive	Less specific (to products)
More incisive	Access and dissemination problems

similar history to supermarket studies. Rather general programs have had marginal or no success (Mayer, Dubbert, & Elder, 1987). More specific programs appear to affect customer choice. For example, in a recent project conducted in a public cafeteria, Mayer et al. (1986) only used a general prompt (a large sign) to inform customers of reasons to eat lower-calorie and lower-fat meals, and specific, small prompts which identified those meals. Using a reversal design, they were able to demonstrate shifts in choice for low-fat meals of about 20%. This study also employed a seemingly more accurate approach to data collection than relying on inventories by staff of meals served (which can be problematic; Miller, 1987). Unobtrusive observers kept track of meal choices. Similar prompts and data collection procedures can be used in school-based studies such as in Coates et al. (1985), with the observational data having more value than self-reports of prior practices and purchases.

However, efforts which follow Mayer et al. need further refinement and expansion. In that study, no effort was made to monitor or prompt how cafeteria patrons added to their basic entree or chosen dessert. A low-calorie, low-fat entree can quickly change composition with the addition of butter, sauces, and other fatty add-ons. Likewise, the nutritional content of the entire meal can be radically altered by a lavish dessert. It may be that similar, specific prompts can be used for more appropriate add-ons and desserts.

Another major setting for intervention is restaurants. Presently, families spend over a third of their food dollars outside the home (Wadden & Brownell, 1984), and presumably many of these dollars are spent at fast-food establishments. The typical burger, french fries, and shake meal is very high in calories (about 1,000) and fat (about 40%), although some fast-food meals (e.g., pizza without a meat topping) do come close to meeting optimal nutrition guidelines. Some establishments have attempted to capitalize on signs of market shifts away from typical fast-food fare. For example, a number of restaurants promote their new salad bars, and others promote their offerings as low in calories and fat. A caveat here is that for the most part new offerings and their promotion represent market expansion strategies. There is not really an attempt to shift current customers to healthier choices.

However, Wagner and Winett (1988) capitalized on these marketing trends while working with a national fast-food chain. Formative and pilot research had indicated themes (low-fat; fitness) and strategic places (just under the large, wall-size menu) for large signs urging customers to eat salads. Tent cards placed on tables carried the same theme as the large sign. Thus, this study closely followed Mayer et al. (1986).

Using an ABAB design, a comparison site, and the restaurant's computer recording system, it was clear that the simple intervention resulted in increases in salad purchases of about 13% for a month. Most of the salad increases were actually side salads, probably additions to a meal, and not salad bars, a possible substitution for another meal.

The study also did not track which customers choose salads or dressings used on salads. Thus, the health benefits of this particular intervention are unknown. However, the intervention increased sales for the restaurant. Therefore, health promotion programs may, in some cases, prove to be profitable for commercial concerns, a key point that should influence commercial acceptance of such efforts.

While studies in this section show a number of positive signs, a few caveats are in order. In addition, and as noted in the prior section, what customers have with and add to their salads and low-calorie meals can markedly alter the nutritional composition of a meal. Moreover, not all foods promoted as low calorie or low fat fit those qualities. For example, an examination of the offerings from one fast-food chain which positions and labels its products as low fat and low calorie indicated that a number of the products were moderately high in calories, fat, and sodium. In addition, for at least one chain that will reveal to customers the nutritional content of their fast food, the information and brochures appear (not surprisingly) one-sided. For example, it is difficult to discern the calorie and fat content of a typical meal.

While these points should not dampen enthusiasm for ongoing efforts at this level, it does suggest that changes at the institutional/societal level may be necessary if work within settings such as supermarkets and restaurants is to have more integrity and clout. For example, specific terms such as "low fat" and "lean" need to have particular meaning through regulatory policy (see below). More active governmental efforts could also better guide consumer choices. Consumers need to understand what the terms mean.

Before turning to work at that level, community studies, which form a midpoint between change in specific settings and organizations and change in laws and institution practices, will be briefly examined. Attention to community studies is limited in this chapter, since that body of work was addressed separately in chapter 5.

Community Studies

Community studies have a relatively recent history in that the first large-scale efforts were mounted in the early 1970s in California by the Stanford University group (Farquhar, Maccoby, & Wood, 1977) and in Finland with the North Karelia project (Puska, 1984; Puska, Nissinen, Tuomilehto et al., 1985). Each project was conducted for a considerable length of time, with follow-ups, so that more definitive conclusions about their impacts took 5 to 10 years to consolidate. In addition, data from more extensive and refined efforts—i.e., the second generation of community projects (e.g., Farquhar, Fortmann, Maccoby, Haskell, Williams, Flora, Taylor, Brown, Solomon, & Halley, 1985)—are just becoming available (chapter 5).

These first projects focused on multiple risk factors, primarily those pertaining to CVD—i.e., smoking, serum cholesterol, and blood pressure. While evidence was available in the 1970s about the links between these risk factors and CVD, the stronger evidence on diet and cancer risk was not yet a cornerstone of these programs. It is, therefore, possible that current programs which emphasize dietary modification to a greater extent may show more change in related behaviors and risk factors.

The early community programs attempted to link together media, small-group and other interpersonal service efforts, and to some extent community organization, in one concerted effort. The conceptual and strategic bases included communication, diffusion theory, social marketing, and social learning theory (Solomon & Maccoby, 1984), and used multiple channels for delivering information and provided multiple opportunities to enact new behaviors. These programs can be seen as community locality and resource development, and are much less in the social action mold (Rappaport, 1977).

The strength of these first efforts was their pioneering attempt to integrate a number of concepts and procedures so as to deliver a preventive, population-focused program. Their weakness is that except for rather molar variables (e.g., media versus interpersonal channels), it is difficult to discern effective and noneffective procedures, and, by necessity, such efforts were quasi-experiments.

Both the first Stanford and Finnish programs showed small population-wide changes in serum cholesterol and blood pressure and self-reported changes in dietary practices (e.g., reducing egg consumption), beyond changes shown in comparison communities. In addition, there is some accumulating evidence for decreases in CVD-related morbidity, mortality, and resultant health care costs in target communities (Puska et al., 1985). However, at least in these early efforts, most risk reduction seems attributable to changes in smoking rate, not dietary change.

Current efforts reviewed in chapter 5 include more of a strategic emphasis on community organization and targeting of dietary change. In addition, more attention to social marketing and media access appear to have made messages better targeted and more effective than in the prior project. These programs seem promising for risk reduction, but may also profit from greater input from studies evaluating specific procedures. That is, at present most community studies bear some similarity to the first NHLBI–Giant Foods project, which used an assortment of general procedures. The second study with Giant Foods showed that a much simpler, less expensive, more specific approach worked better. Some additional refinement, streamlining, and attention to more passive procedures (as opposed to reliance on interpersonal processes) may also make community efforts more effective.

Such an emphasis is represented by the work of LeFebvre et al. (1986), who demonstrated that highly specific and well-targeted interventions may have pronounced impacts on the dietary practices of large groups of people. In particular, the availability of new technology that can feed back cholesterol and other important blood assay measures (HDL, LDL), now within minutes, portends the beginning of effective, low-cost procedures useable with many individuals (see LeFebvre et al., 1986). Other community intervention studies were detailed in chapter 5.

Institutional/Societal Level

The objectives of changes at this level are to make certain food products more or less available, more or less expensive, and more or less desired by the public. These objectives may be accomplished by legal/regulatory or free-market approaches, or by some combination of these approaches. Legal/regulatory approaches generally attempt change by decree. Free-market approaches more generally attempt to use incentives and disincentives, with present-day free-market approaches requiring some government intervention. Institutional change of the food cycle can focus on production, distribution, promotion, and sale, singularly or in any combination. These considerations lead to the simple matrix shown in Figure 8.1.

Examination of the matrix suggests that in the present conservative, deregulatory era, it is unlikely that strong laws and regulations will be promulgated to change the production, distribution, promotion, and sale of foods. Instead, there have been, and probably will continue to be, a series of relatively weak regulations. For example, better definitions and terms for grades of meat have been developed—e.g., "lean" means 85% fat-free, and "extra lean" means 95% fat-free—to reflect concern with the fat content of meat. However, it is unclear if these terms will be properly promoted to the public. There are also other quirks in the labeling system. Terms such as "lite," "lower fat," or "leaner" can be used if the product contains 25% less fat than usual. However, the word "lean" can still also be used in a brand name if the product if 25% lower in fat.

There will be more experimentation by the FDA with conventional food labels; however, as noted in a prior section, such food labels have yet to demonstrate a marked impact on consumer behavior. It is doubtful that food labels will be required to much more prominently display fat, calorie, or cholesterol content, and very doubtful, indeed, that foods will display warnings such as "Continued Consumption of This Product MAY CAUSE CANCER." Further, it is not part of the FDA's mandate to be actively

Method

Phase	Legal/Regulatory	Free Market
Production	Prohibit, limit, or change certain crops, livestock, or products, e.g., require production of lean meat or low-fat dairy products.	Provide supports only for certain crops, livestock, e.g., price supports for lean meat.
Distribution	Prohibit, limit distribution to certain times and places, e.g., prohibit supermarkets from stocking certain products.	Make distribution easier or harder, e.g., allow unrestricted growth of new products.
Promotion	Designate how promoted, e.g., labels, warning statements, commercial statements.	Competitively exploit particular markets and segments, e.g., low-calorie foods.
Sale	Prohibit, limit sale of a product, e.g., cereals over a specified sugar content.	Reduce or increase costs of a product, e.g., by competitively exploiting markets, mass production, and price reductions.

FIGURE 8.1. Legal/Regulatory and Free-Market Approaches to Modify the Production, Distribution, Promotion, and Sale of Food

involved in public education (Schucker, 1983). Thus it is unclear, given labels that are potentially effective but not very demonstrative, who will actively promote their salience to the public.

Another avenue of acton, also under the purview of the FDA, is for coalitions of public interest groups (such as the Center for Science in the Public Interest) and legislators to press for changes in the *standards* of certain products (Schultz, 1981). For example, if all dairy products were required to be low in fat content to a specified degree, then such a "passive" strategy could have a substantial population impact.

Quite obviously, this is a politically and economically controversial path, particularly because low-fat products are currently available and new standards would restrict some consumers' "freedom of choice." In addition, product standardization and availability does not automatically equate to lowered consumption of health-detrimental substances. For example, some smokers of low tar and nicotine cigarettes may smoke more cigarettes and change their smoking typography (e.g., inhale more deeply) so as to maintain an acceptable nicotine level (Russell, 1976).

Despite these many problems, more incisive product labels and new standards are important institutional/public health change strategies deserving more attention. Minimal action and weak regulations also suggest to the public that an area is of little concern or danger. More action and stronger regulations present a very different message to the public.

Other regulatory policies could be promulgated by the Federal Communication Commission (FCC) and Federal Trade Commission (FTC). For example, the FTC could designate certain food commercials which depict enjoyable, healthful consumption of certain foods as "deceptive." There is some history of FTC action with deceptive food commercials in the 1960s and 1970s. In a few instances, corporations were required to develop and broadcast corrective commercials (Wilkie, McNeill, & Mazis, 1984). Such actions are highly controversial and appear unlikely to occur in the 1980s and 1990s. Likewise, it appears doubtful in the near future that certain food products will be prohibited from advertisement, as are cigarettes and liquor from TV and radio advertisement. The slow and rather unsuccessful campaign to limit the advertising of highly sugared cereals and other junk food during children's TV programs suggests that this will not be the most efficacious path to follow.

In part, these problems revolve around the unique tradition of American media, particularly radio and TV networks, as commercial enterprises (Le Duc, 1982; also see chapter 4). The major purpose of radio and TV is to deliver an audience to the sponsor. The programmed entertainment is the vehicle of deliverance. Numerous commentators (e.g., Manoff, 1985; also see chapter 4) have noted how the commercial network system has primarily served corporate interests at the expense of the public interest. Eras where there have been efforts to reform the system, e.g., to provide more access for public interest concerns or counter positions as with the "fairness doctrine," have been quickly followed by eras such as the present one which have sanctified the free-market approach to communication (reviewed in Winett, 1986).

As a result, it is difficult to have strong, consistent, and timely counter-messages on the most powerful and expensive medium, TV. For example, there are few, if any, expertly produced commercials or public service announcements (PSAs) during prime time showing viewers healthier alternatives to often high-calorie, high-fat fast-food lunches. Some approaches to regulatory change, particularly for delivering health messages, have been described elsewhere, but without much optimism for near-future implementation (Winett, 1987). Instead, the present era is much more supportive of free-market approaches.

A major basis for a free-market approach to changing food choices is that there is presently a small, but potentially much larger and receptive, market for healthier foods. As this market becomes exploited, consumer demand will reciprocally affect production, distribution, promotion, and sales. It then becomes advantageous for all players in the food market to coalesce around healthier foods. Government may seek to expedite and channel this process (e.g., price supports for particular products), but in essence the market must be allowed to work.

Currently, we are seeing the rapid expansion of products and markets for healthier foods. On the positive side, new products (e.g., high-fiber cereals) and services (e.g., salad bars at restaurants) are appearing. On the negative side, in the absence of some regulatory control, the health concerns of segments of the public are being deceptively manipulated. For example, the term "natural" is attached to a plethora of products; and some products promoted as low calorie are actually moderately high in calories or fat. In other words, allowing the corporate sector both to educate (via commercials) and exploit the public has resulted in some predictable problems.

It would appear more beneficial to have government do the educating and directing of the public, and the corporate sector exploit these presumably more accurate beliefs and expectations. In the absence of regulatory reform mandating greater access to the media to deliver nutritional messages, collaborations between government and the corporate sector may allow a degree of control and influence by government of commercial messages. For example, this appears to be the case for the Kellogg Company's high-fiber cereal commercials which begin by stating the NCI's position on this type of food. Reportedly, this $28 million campaign was quite successful in increasing the sales of Kellogg and other brand, high-fiber cereals (Warner, 1987b). These commercials and the approach are, however, controversial. When a health claim is made for a food, it turns the food into a drug, and the efficacy of drugs must be approved by the FDA.

However, in the winter of 1988 (Shapiro, 1988) the FDA proposed to dismantle its rules against health claims on labels. The agency intends to develop guidelines to regulate the content of messages. In the interim period, the FDA will allow food corporations to use their new labels and compete for the "health-conscious" consumer segment.

Proposed future guidelines will call for truthful and not misleading information on the label; the information must be based on scientific evidence and follow recognized nutritional principles. Since, as this chapter indicates, there is controversy and vested interests on all sides of nutrition questions, tracking food labels during the next several years, and concomitant industry, government, and consumer response, will be, indeed, a very interesting endeavor. Thus, Freimuth, Hammond, and Stein (1988) conclude that because this precedent-setting campaign was remarkably successful, it has potentially opened a Pandora's box of concerns, e.g., deceptive advertising and manipulation for tremendous profits.

Yet another free-market media strategy would entail collaboration between government and the producers and writers of particular TV programs (Winett, 1987). For example, even as a minor, but consistent, subtheme, the discussion and modeling by a popular TV family of their efforts throughout a year to change their dietary practices could have a marked impact on millions of viewers (Bandura, 1986). Thus, a collaborative, not adversial, relationship between government and business would appear to be one element of success.

Summary

At this juncture, considerable space has been devoted to examining the problem of promoting a healthier diet from the perspectives of different levels of analysis. These analyses are at the core of the book's framework. It is apparent that virtually any intervention will require some intervention at the person level (i.e., correct information), but that interventions at the person or interpersonal levels appear to require higher level support for wide-scale efficacy and impact. Likewise, in the present era, nutritional change will likely not be mandated through regulation, but be more a product of market forces.

Thus, multilevel interventions that provide incentives to individuals, firms, and the government are preferred. At this point, one such multilevel approach will be developed with the use of elements of the entire framework. It is important to note that this is, indeed, only one example of many potential approaches.

EXEMPLAR MULTILEVEL INTERVENTION

Rationale and Pilot Work

This exemplar intervention will combine person and organizational/environmental levels. The rationale for choosing this particular intervention rests on data supporting its potential efficacy and the manageability of the effort at the supermarket level. These plans can be mounted by government and industry or, quite conceivably, by industry alone, and are designed so that individual consumers and a participating firm will mutually benefit.

The review of the personal level in a prior section indicated that there is still a considerable lack of knowledge and a number of misbeliefs concerning diet–health links, diets that are both health-protective and enjoyable, and appropriate meal preparations. In addition, there are personal (e.g., taste preferences), interpersonal (e.g., family member reactions to new meals), and cultural (e.g., men's beliefs about appropriate meals) barriers to dietary change that must also be the focus of an intervention.

The exemplar project is an extension of the work of Winett et al. (1988) partly described in prior sections (pp. 258–259) of this chapter. That project continued a long series of studies in consumer behavior (Winett, 1986) and demonstrated that video modeling, feedback, and goal setting were effective strategies for helping consumers alter the nutritional content of their food purchases, while at the same time saving money.

The overall results of that project are shown in Table 8.2. Examination of that table clearly shows the efficacy of feedback and goal setting and suggests that modeling, feedback, and goal setting can be almost as effective as similar procedures with an interpersonal element, and indicates that information content alone (the lecture video condition) is not very effective. However, the results failed at this point to show the efficacy of modeling alone. Note, though, that the effect size for modeling–feedback is reasonable. The 6.7% reduction in total fat represented about a 16% reduction within the fat category and more than a 50% reduction in fat toward the 30% total fat goal.

Program Conceptualization and Components

The exemplar project extends this research by refining the modeling component, automating procedures, and housing them in the supermarket setting. In this way, the aspects of saliency, immediacy, specificity, access, and dissemination are amplified (see Table 8.1).

For this intervention, it is proposed that mass media, particularly television, promote knowledge, belief, and minimal behavior change. Through extensive formative research and pilot tests, which proceed from local, to regional, and then, perhaps, national efforts, we envision the development of a campaign of sufficient intensity and duration to build from an initial rationale of dietary change to highly specific points about food shopping, meal preparation, and strategies for family resistance. The objective is to move a mass audience from a stage representing marginal interest to enhanced efficacy beliefs and outcome expectancies and then to at least initial active behavior change (Prochansky & DiClemente, 1983; see chapter 3). Ideally, the audience would be segmented with regard to present dietary practices and propensity for change, with appropriate messages delivered to each segment. Since this may not be possible within one campaign, the notion of an evolving or "unfolding" approach is introduced. However, compared to the prior study, much more specific formative and pilot research will be conducted on acceptable, new meals. This new content and greater exposure of the messages could now make "modeling alone" effective.

One conceptual base for health promotion campaigns has been detailed by Solomon and Maccoby (1984). Their model entails an integration of communication, social marketing, and social cognitive principles. For example, it is important that credible messages are developed in ways in which visual and auditory features assure attention, memory, and later cues for action (Wright & Huston, 1983). Messages must use terms that are readily

Table 8.2. Percent Change in Nutrient Content and Dollars Spent Weekly for Food Purchases During Intervention[a]

	Control	Modeling No FB	Modeling FB	Lecture No FB	Lecture FB	Participant Modeling FB	Modeling Discussion No FB
Complex Carbohydrates	-1.2	-2.9	+5.4**	+1.9	+2.9	+1.5	-1.0
Simple Carbohydrates	+1.2	+1.3	+0.1	-1.3	+0.6	+5.1*	+0.3
Total Carbohydrates	0.0	-1.6	+5.5*	+0.6	+3.5	+6.6**	-0.7
Protein	-1.6	-1.0	+0.8	+0.6	-1.1	-1.7	+1.2
Saturated Fat	+0.9	+0.4	-0.9*	-0.4	-1.2*	-2.2*	+0.7
Total Fat	+1.3	+1.8	-6.7**	-0.8	-2.6	-5.5*	-0.7
Dollars	-8.7	-12.5	-26.4*	-2.0	-15.6	-12.0	-2.7

[a]Only includes dollars spent on food
*p < .05 when compared to control condition
**p < .01 when compared to control condition

understood and settings that are easily recognizable; barriers to change must also be realistically presented (Manoff, 1985). Throughout the messages, particularly salient behaviors must be modeled (Bandura, 1986). In addition, it is important that the entire approach have a unifying theme and "brand" name (Manoff, 1985). As detailed in chapter 4, all these salient points about message design and implementation can be fitted into one approach called "behavioral systems."

The format for the messages is 30-second commercial spots in the case of an initiative by a firm alone, or 30-second commercial spots and well-placed PSAs in the case of a firm–government partnership. It is important that the unfolding process follow an ideal pace so that there is wide audience exposure to the different stages of messages (e.g., the rationale), without undue repetition and concomitant audience boredom.

The unfolding approach and the number of messages can allow for the more specific presentation of at least several strategies for nutritional change that can be used separately or in combination. For example, to reduce fat intake and increase that of complex carbohydrates and fiber, product substitutions can be made (e.g., fish for beef, whole-grain breads for white bread), and/or the proportions in meals can be changed. The typical steak and potato dinner can now consist of only three ounces of steak, a large potato with two pats of margarine, two pieces of toast, and a large salad with a low-fat dressing (750 calories, 25% fat, 21% protein, 54% carbohydrates). In addition, complex carbohydrates, such as spaghetti, can become the centerpiece of more dinners. As noted before, for many viewers, it is necessary to carefully depict the purchase of new products, or smaller proportions of products, meal preparation and presentation, and verbal replies to surprised, chagrined, or annoyed family members (Winett et al., 1987).

In the prior section, it was also noted that arguments against a legal/regulatory approach to nutrition change were the ready availability of appropriate food products and the potential to profit from expanding the market for healthier foods. Thus, a supermarket that aggressively enters into the health promotion business may find a better niche in a highly competitive field (Schultz, 1981). Such positioning is not without its costs as evidenced by, for example, the opposition from the meat and dairy industries encountered by NHLBI and Giant Foods during the first project (Curt Wilbur, personal communication, June 1984). However, certain meat and dairy products may represent declining markets, so that a supermarket chain promoting other products may exploit expanding markets and make up losses in sales in one product class by increases in other product classes. Thus, health promotion in the supermarket may provide one instance where consumers and some firms can mutually benefit.

Supermarket interventions have primarily relied on antecedent strategies, i.e., general information, point-of-choice information, and specific prompts. At this point, evidence only supports the efficacy of specific prompts. In this proposed intervention, we include the specific shelf tags found effective by Levy et al. (1985) that identified products high in fat, sodium, and calories. We would also separately and prominently tag low-fat and high-fiber products (as is being done in a current Giant Foods project).

The out-of-store media and in-store prompts can also be augmented by another antecedent strategy using "electronic mechanizing." Short, 30-second to two-minute segments paralleling the out-of-store media, but focusing more on products and substitutions in the supermarket, can be available at one or more locations in the supermarket. These "new media," videodisc systems can be minimally interactive, but still allow several shoppers to enter the system at the same time and at selected points. Messages on the system can also be unfolding and recycled over time. A caveat is that such systems can be expensive and have as yet received few sound evaluations concerning customer use and individual and aggregate impacts (Winett, 1987).

One recent effort, for example, used a touch screen microcomputer software program, which gave supermarket customers access to eight nutrition modules, each of about a one-minute duration. However, only about five percent of the customers used the system during a four-week test period, and impacts on purchases were not assessed (O'Malley, Heger, Trudgett, Mayo, & Gardner, 1987).

Thus, even the supermarket interventions using electronic, point-of-purchase merchandising still rely on antecedent strategies. Aside from usual supermarket promotions entailing various price reduction tactics, another consequence strategy has apparently not been tried. That strategy is feedback and goal setting, and there is, as was seen in Table 8.2, some evidence of its effectiveness for nutritional change (Winett et al., 1988).

We envision two points of feedback in the supermarket. On entry into the supermarket, customers can receive feedback on main items that they intend to purchase. This can be accomplished by providing customers "opscan" shopping lists (with the store name and promotion theme prominently displayed) upon exiting the store. These lists can then be completed at home and fed into a stand-up reader when entering the store. Within seconds, a customer can receive simple written statements about the nutritional content of their choices, suggested alternatives, daily special alternatives, and suitably positive statements about appropriate selections. Specific goals should also be employed (Bandura, 1986). For example, the feedback should be presented in relationship to the NCI 1990 goals. Specific individual goals in a successive approximation format can also be employed where the systems have sufficient memory. Therefore, customers will have definitive points to meet. Feedback and goal setting on intentions can be coupled with feedback and goal setting on actual choices.

Feedback on choices can rely on a refinement and expansion of detailed, computerized receipt and inventory systems presently operative in a number of chain stores. Figure 8.2 presents a schema showing four items on a presently existing receipt and the same items on the feedback receipt. Specific food items (yogurt) can receive specific labels ("low-fat"). In addition, a goal-setting system can be devised for this point of feedback.

Quite obviously, developing the software and optimizing the logistics and mechanics of the feedback systems will require considerable formative and pilot research. Regular feedback *from customers*, e.g., on their success or nonsuccess with alternative meals, must also be obtained. In addition, *all* terms used on shelf tags, intention and choice feedback, and goal-setting and TV messages would need to be matched and briefly explained in the messages. In these ways, the campaign can represent an integrated, orchestrated effort with a high probability of success.

Figure 8.3 shows an overall schema of the in-store component of this intervention. A variation of this basic plan is being designed and implemented by the first author with funding from the National Cancer Institute (Winett, 1988). While it is too early to report any results, we do note that the in-store video and feedback/goal-setting systems will closely follow the definitive points for effective media delineated in chapter 4 and the process of change model depicted in chapter 3.

Although the major conceptual base for this program is social–cognitive and behavioral theory and the approach requires individual action, the overall intervention also has some important public health elements. The use of TV and the supermarket setting represents strategies to reach populations. Likewise, the media, prompts, and feedback system require minimal interpersonal interaction. Thus, these are psychologically based procedures adapted to be used on a population basis. However, unlike passive measures, where presumably effects can be sustained almost indefinitely, approaches such as the one we have outlined here probably have a more limited life. To maintain interest and enlist new converts, it is likely that the components of this intervention will need to be frequently refined and updated. For example, feedback messages can routinely and frequently be rephrased and points added or deleted. However, although there is good evidence for the initial effectiveness of the modeling, feedback, and goal-setting procedures we have

Standard Computerized Receipt	Modified Computerized Receipt
Plain Dannon Yogurt – Qt.	Plain Dannon Yogurt – Qt. – Low Fat
Hamburger – 2 lbs.	Hamburger – 2 lbs. – High Fat
Corn Bran – 1 lb.	Corn Bran – 1 lb. – High Fiber
Apples – 2 lbs.	Apples – 2 lbs. – High Complex Carbs.

FIGURE 8.2. An Example of How Specific Feedback and Labels Can Be Used in Supermarkets Providing Detailed Receipts

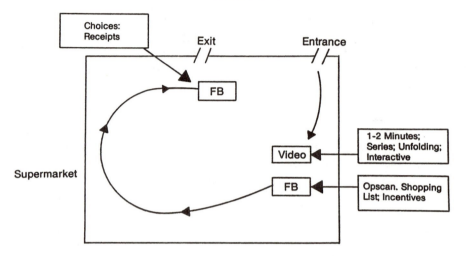

FIGURE 8.3. A Schema of a Project Using Video and Feedback–Goal-Setting Strategies Within Interactive Information Systems in a Supermarket (Based on Winett, 1988)

outlined, at this juncture we cannot present any evidence suggesting long-term effectiveness. Certainly, this point mandates pilot tests to ascertain if impacts can be discerned for periods of six months to a year. In addition, it is quite likely that various prompting and incentive procedures (e.g., providing coupons) will be necessary to initiate and *sustain* active consumer use of the systems. These procedures would also need to be investigated in pilot studies.

Temporal, Personnel, and Evaluation Issues

For this example, we have spent a considerable amount of time detailing the concepts, principles, procedures, and settings for the proposed intervention. The book's framework also indicates that we need to attend to temporal, personnel, and evaluation issues. As noted previously, it is unclear for how long this modeling–feedback approach using mass media and in-store systems can be effective. At a minimum, it was suggested that the messages need to be frequently changed to maintain interest. We must modestly admit that this critical part of the proposed intervention also needs to be studied in pilot research.

As with other multilevel interventions described in this book, a number of different kinds of professionals and personnel are required. For example, in addition to health psychologists and public health professionals who can provide expertise on psychological procedures, nutrition content, and evaluation (see below), expertise is needed in both mass media and the special in-store media. Indeed, these two kinds of media will involve different media professionals. Coordination of the media campaign and in-store promotions will call for advertising personnel working with national and local professionals from the supermarket chain. Overall, these diverse professionals and personnel must be managed and coordinated to work in concert with each other, clearly not an easy task (Winett, 1987).

An optimal evaluation plan attempts to integrate health psychology, public health, corporate, and policy concerns. For example, from the psychological perspective, we would want to track samples of consumers so as to better understand the process of change and know when and where system and procedural refinements are needed (see chapter 3). Thus, examining linkages between viewing and attending to TV messages, knowledge, change, understanding of terms, use and understanding of feedback and goals, specific self-efficacy beliefs, short- and long-term changes in food purchases, and satisfying and nonsatisfying meals reported by customers represent data of general interest to the field and to the particular interest of fine-tuning and more effectively marketing this mass intervention. In addition, to understand the efficacy of components of this overall mass media and in-store system, a quasi-experimental design can be used, with some areas receiving the whole program, the store part only, or media only, and some areas serving as comparison areas. It is also important to assess the kinds of in-store promotions that are necessary to sustain consumer participation.

Analyzing shifts in aggregate sales of product classes and overall sales can also provide data relevant to public health impacts and the benefits accrued to the firm. For example, good estimates can be made for population shifts in percent total fat intake based on individual data and aggregate store data (using select items). It is possible that the special in-store systems can attract new customers or have original customers more regularly shop in the same supermarket chain. It is also important to assess how shifts in sales between product classes (e.g., meat and fish) affect the overall profit figures for the supermarket chain. Finally, more sophisticated cost-effectiveness and cost-benefit analyses can be used to examine the relative costs and outcomes of the whole program and its components, and the costs and benefits to consumers, the participating firm, nonparticipating firms, and to government (Levin, 1983). It is hoped that such detailed individual, setting, and cost analyses would precede any very large-scale implementation, thus allowing for refinement, fine-tuning, and predictable impacts.

CONCLUSION

The current proposal is but one example of the potential amalgamations of health psychology and public health for nutritional change. More imaginative and far-reaching interventions should accrue from combining instituional efforts with organizational, interpersonal, and individual change strategies. Hopefully, approaches similar to the one offered in this chapter will start the steps toward reaching the goals enunciated by the NCI for the years 1990 and 2000, as well as for goals pertinent to cardiovascular risk reduction and weight control.

9
Health in the Workplace

INTRODUCTION

In recent years, health in the workplace has received increasing attention from health professionals, workers, employers, and the government, due to concern about rising health care costs; an increased understanding of the relationship between behavior, working conditions, and health; and the fact that many people spend more time at work than they do at home. In examining these trends, we will utilize principles from psychology and public health and the framework described in chapter 2 to better our understanding of how the workplace can help promote health and prevent disease.

Work, either paid or unpaid, is central to most Americans' perceptions of themselves and of society at large. This is perhaps most evident when strangers meet for the first time. The first question they usually ask one another is: "What do you do?" (i.e., What is your occupation?). People spend most of their waking hours at work. Indeed, the fibers of society—interpersonal relationships, economics, and health—are affected profoundly by work. Work even influences recreation and leisure opportunities to the extent that such opportunities are dependent upon work-generated income and are scheduled around work time (Robinson, 1977; also see chapter 6 on mental health). Moreover, individual and social well being are in large part affected by work, not just the availability of work but also its quality (Hamburg, Elliot, & Parron, 1982; Kahn, 1981).

The structure and content of work is changing rapidly. A report commissioned by the federal Office of Disease Prevention and Health Promotion (ODPHP) and the National Institute of Occupational Safety and Health (NIOSH) provides a glimpse of what the future might hold (Bezold, Carlson, & Peck, 1986). Prepared by the Institute for Alternative Futures in conjunction with the Washington Business Group on Health, this report noted several profound changes in the type of work people do and the ways in which they do it. For example, automation and artificial intelligence have eliminated many jobs, particularly those in the manufacturing and service sectors; almost 10 percent of the workforce share a job and the average workweek has declined to about 32 hours per week; the number of women and elderly seeking work is increasing rapidly; through advances in information technology, more work is being conducted at home; and people are increasingly attempting to balance their careers with concerns about family and self-fulfillment.

Cover articles in the March 1987, issue of *Ms.* ("Whose Job is Child Care?"), the February 16, 1987, issue of *Fortune* ("The Number 1 Cause of Executive Guilt: Who's Taking Care of the Children—and How Will They Turn Out?"), and the June 22, 1987, issue of *Time* ("Who's Bringing up Baby?") reflect the profound changes that have and will continue to occur (Rubin, 1987; Chapman, 1987; Wallis, 1987, respectively). Men and women will try to influence the policies of corporate America by demanding such benefits as longer maternity and paternity leave, options for part-time work, on-site day care centers, child care as part of their benefits package, and job or income protection at the time of childbirth (see also chapter 7).

This issue has also been addressed in the popular scientific press. The December 1986 issue of the American Psychological Association's monthly newspaper, *The APA Monitor*, had as the lead story an article entitled: "Latchkey Kids" (Landers, 1986). It noted that in 1985, more than 60 percent of single parent mothers and married women with children under the age of 18 were in the labor force (i.e., 33.5 million children had mothers who worked). While there are conflicting viewpoints on the effects of being a latchkey child (see also chapter 6), it is clear that families and the society at large must consider critically how their children will be educated and raised outside of the home environment.

A model program in this regard is being developed at Stanford University. The university has planned an extensive day care center for children of its employees. The center will initially handle 100 children from birth to five years of age and has the capability to take care of children who are ill. This center will provide comprehensive care and education for children and reflects the university's recognition that recruitment and retention of quality employees requires bridging the gap between work and home. This worksite program and others like it illustrate clearly how societal norms can influence the content, structure, and meaning of work, the health and well being of employees who work, and the intersection between work and home demands.

Work-Related Health Problems

Public health professionals, more than psychologists, have examined the effects of work on health and have been actively involved in reducing work-related health problems. Some of the contributions of public health to health in the workplace will be reviewed below.

For centuries, the relationship between work and illness has been generally recognized, although even to this day it is often difficult to clearly link health problems to work-related conditions, because of long latency periods between "exposure" and ill health, overlap between work- and non-work-related causes of illness, and inadequate reporting systems (Froines & Baker, 1985). The best available data suggest that the magnitude of the problem, particularly in industrialized countries, is monumental. Citing data from the government, Froines and Baker (1985) reported that the ten leading work-related diseases and injuries in 1982 were lung diseases (e.g., asbestosis, lung cancer, coal workers' pneumonconiosis); musculoskeletal injuries (e.g., back or neck problems); occupational cancers (e.g., bladder, liver); amputations and other injuries (such as fractures, eye loss, lacerations); cardiovascular disease; reproductive disorders (e.g., infertility, spontaneous abortion); neuro-toxic disorders (e.g., toxic encephalitis, personality changes); noise-induced loss of hearing; dermatological problems; and psychological disorders (alco-holism, neuroses). The agents that cause these problems are diverse and in-clude biological, chemical, physical, and social hazards. Approximately 50,000 chemicals evident in the workplace have known toxic effects, over 2000 are suspected human carcinogens, and 18 are known carcinogens (Levy, Hopkins, Chesney, Ringen, Nathan, & MacDougal, 1986; USDHHS, 1980).

Each year, 100,000 Americans die from occupational illnesses, 400,000 new cases of work-related diseases are observed, over two million workers experience disabling injuries, and thousands of lives are lost due to "acci-dents." Homicide in the workplace, recently brought to the attention of the public health community, is an alarming problem and will require a concert-ed effort to protect workers at highest risk (i.e., police, security guards, taxi drivers, and those in retail trades with frequent public contact in which money is exchanged) (Davis, 1987; Kraus, 1987).

The direct and indirect costs of these work-related health problems — $35 billion in 1986 — is substantial (National Safety Council, 1987). Many em-ployees are at risk for chronic diseases. For example, it has been estimated that among the workforce, there is a 15–25 percent prevalence rate for high blood pressure; from 30 to 50 percent of employees smoke (with higher prevalence rates among blue collar workers and those in the service indus-try); fewer than half of employees (at best) exercise regularly; and about 14 percent of male workers and 17 percent of female workers are at least 20 percent over ideal body weight (Fielding, 1984).

These personal health behaviors add to the health problems experienced by workers, both directly and synergistically with hazardous agents. A re-port by the Surgeon General (1985) suggested that smoking causes more deaths and disability among workers than factors in the workplace environ-ment, although the combined effects of smoking and occupational expo-sure, because of synergistic processes, cause more health problems than the sum of their separate effects. For example, the risk of lung cancer among asbestos workers is 87 times greater for workers who smoke over one pack of cigarettes per day compared to nonsmokers.

Understandably, some union groups have reacted negatively to this report. They believe that reports such as these, which tend to attribute primary responsibility for health to the individual, obviate the important contributions that the environment and public policies make to the health and well being of employees. This tension between individuals and institutions will be discussed in detail later in the chapter, as it is important to our understanding of how principles of psychology and public health can be brought together to better understand work-related health and illness.

The Meaning of Work

Many people joke about wanting to win a lottery or horse race so they can quit their job early and retire. Survey data suggest, however, that most people would continue to work even if they had enough money to stop. That is, for most adults, there is no satisfactory alternative to work, even with the stress and dissatisfaction that work can bring. Interestingly, it appears that the attachment to work in general is stronger than the attachment to a specific job (Kahn, 1981). After reviewing the literature on work and health, Kahn (1981) stated two policy directives: (a) the provision of work is necessary for individual and social well being; and (b) the quality of a job is almost as important as the availability of a job.

As illustrated by the unemployment rates in the United States, the availability of employment continues to be a problem, particularly in poor communities or among disadvantaged populations. What is often not considered, however, are the problems associated with the quality of a job and working conditions and the differences in the quality of jobs in different population segments (Kahn, 1981). Differences in the perceived quality of work is evident in surveys of blue and white collar workers. White collar workers are more likely than blue collar workers to report that they would choose a different career path if they had the choice. Also, because there are differences in the types of workers in particular industries, work-related health problems are often experienced disproportionately by different demographic groups. Minority workers and workers in blue collar, industrial, and service jobs are much more likely than others to be exposed to environmental toxins and to experience work-related health problems. They also run a higher risk of unemployment (Kahn, 1981).

Health Care Costs and the Workplace

The skyrocketing cost of health care is one of the most popular topics of conversation in America today. Corporate managers complain about how sick employees cut into their profit margin. Families talk about how much money they have to pay for unreimbursed medical care expenses or insurance deductibles. Politicians anguish over how much the government pays for health care. And health care professionals are becoming increasingly concerned about their ability to maintain or develop profitable practices. An examination of health care costs in the United States validates these concerns. In 1986, health care costs comprised approximately 11 percent ($400 billion) of the gross national product. In other words, we spent over $1 billion dollars each day on health care.

Citing data from the President's Council on Physical Fitness, Fielding (1984) noted that premature deaths in a single year cost the private sector $25 billion and 132,000,000 days of lost production. The Health Insurance Association of America (1986) reported that in 1984, businesses and the public sector paid almost $100 billion for employee health problems. As further examples of this problem, consider the following: more than one penny of each first-class stamp pays for the health care of postal workers and dependents; three cents of every dollar spent on a fast-food hamburger goes to the health industry; in the late 1970s, when Blue Cross/Blue Shield was the largest supplier to Chrysler Corporation, health care costs were one-tenth of the cost of each Chrysler K-car produced; and the U.S. auto industry had to sell 500,000 cars in 1984 just to pay for its health care bills (Califano, 1986). In 1985, General Motors spent over $2 billion for employee health benefits or about $5000 for each active employee each year (Demkovich, 1986). Obviously, a company the size of GM (550,000 active employees, 280,000 retirees, and 1,400,000 dependents, or about 1 percent of the U.S. population) is acutely aware of health care cost containment. The direct and indirect costs of health care for employers has been estimated to be as high as 25 percent (House & Cottington, 1986). Now more than ever, worksites are struggling to bring the costs of health care under control. The next section reviews some of these efforts.

HISTORICAL PERSPECTIVE

For generations, work has been associated with well being and with illness. House and Cottington (1986) suggested that since World War II, there have been two primary historical periods of interest in work and health (see Table 9.1 for an overview). The first, labeled the occupational safety and health movement, had as a primary goal the reduction of work-related injuries, illness, and death. Interest in occupational health and safety peaked during the period of the "Great Society" programs of the Democratic-controlled Congress (late 1960s and early 1970s) with the passage of federal legislation protecting workers. Foremost among the laws passed during this period was the Occupational Safety and Health Act of 1970 that created the National Institute of Occupational Safety and Health (NIOSH) in the Department of Health, Education, and Welfare and the Occupational

Table 9.1. Key Movements in Worksite Health

	Goals	Strategies	Locus of Responsibility
Occupational Health and Safety Movement	Reduce work-related health problems that occur as a result of factors not under the control of individual employees	Protect workers from biological, physical, chemical, and environmental hazards in the worksite; promote the active participation of labor unions in the decision-making process	Management, regulatory policies
Health Promotion Movement	Improve the quality of work; improve the health of employees by encouraging the practice of healthy employee behaviors, in the workplace as well as other life domains	Implement individual behavior change programs; modify the worksite environment to support healthy behaviors; provide incentives to healthy employees	Individuals and worksite policies that impact on individual employees

Safety and Health Administration (OSHA) in the Department of Labor. This movement, illustrating the political strength of labor unions and the working class, focused its attention on environmental, physical, chemical, and biological hazards in the workplace. The focus of efforts to address work-related health problems, therefore, was placed predominantly on regulatory processes (i.e., factors outside of the individual worker and his or her behavior). Stressful components of working life (Hamburg et al., 1984) focused on included factors related to the physical environment (e.g., chemicals, noise, temperature, odor, glare) and to a lesser extent mass production technology (e.g., repetitive or machine-paced jobs, shift work, accessibility of the job).

The public health community was a key in the initiation and implementation of this movement. Psychologists, while involved in treating workers experiencing mental health problems as a result of work problems, were not visible players in the occupational health and safety movement. Perhaps as a result of the lack of involvement of psychologists and other social scientists in this movement, stressful conditions related to the lack of work (e.g., unemployment and retirement) were not a primary focus of the occupational health and safety movement, nor were qualities of work that could influence mental and physical health. These qualities include such things as task content (i.e., the job activities), autonomy and control (i.e., degree of free-

dom), supervision and resources (i.e., the extent to which adequate information and support is provided), relations with co-workers, wages and rewards,
promotions, working conditions, and organizational context (i.e., characteristics of the worksite such as size and managerial philosophy) (Kahn,
1981).

By the late 1970s and early 1980s, the Democratic Party and organized
labor were losing political clout. Coupled with dissatisfaction from employers who had to pay for health care expenses, this political context led to a
weakening of the occupational health and safety movement and increased
attention to the responsibility of workers for their own health. Employers,
as well as taxpayers, felt the effects of these worksite regulations on the
"bottom line." The theme here was one of getting the government "off the
backs" of business. These costs and the pressures on companies to contain
health care expenditures led to a strongly held feeling among many in the
private sector that part of the problem was attributable to regulations and
policies developed during the occupational health and safety movement of
the previous decade.

During this period, there were also significant changes in the theories
and concepts guiding mainstream psychology. Relevant here was the increased interest in behavioral approaches (e.g., coping, self-control) and on
the relationship between the environment and behavior. In effect, mainstream psychology began to accept an "outer" model as one explanation of
personality.

In conjunction with these changes in society at large and in academic
disciplines, a second movement in work and health emerged and grew substantially during the late 1970s and into the 1980s. House and Cottington
(1986) referred to this movement as the workplace health promotion movement. The health promotion movement is distinctly different from the occupational health and safety movement. Worksite health promotion focuses
primary attention on general health and well being rather than only on
work-related health problems. It also focuses on individual responsibility
for health and illness rather than on external or environmental factors
(House & Cottington, 1986). Even so, House and Cottington suggested that
additional attention should be directed at the role of the psychosocial environment in workplace health promotion: Researchers should examine the
level and scheduling of work loads, interpersonal relationships, fit or misfit
between work and non-work, job satisfaction, and so forth. We will return
to this topic later in the chapter.

Unlike the occupational health and safety movement, it appears that
the worksite health promotion movement has brought together public
health professionals and psychologists. Professionals from both disciplines
are involved in designing, implementing, and evaluating worksite health
programs.

WORKSITE HEALTH PROMOTION

Why the Worksite?

The interest in worksite health promotion stems from the inherent (yet often unproven) advantages that worksites offer for health behavior changes and more "passive" interventions. These include an accessible population for programs, convenience for employees, the opportunity for capitalizing on group social support and influence, the availability of existing communication and health care delivery channels, and the potential for replication and generalizability across worksites and employee populations (Behrens, 1983; Chesney & Feuerstein, 1979; Cohen, 1985; Conrad, 1987; Nathan, 1984a; Roccella, 1982). There are a variety of specific outcomes that can potentially be influenced by worksite programs. For workers, these include reduced health care costs, sick leave and increased social support, morale, and quality of life. For employers, the potential advantages are reductions in health insurance costs; disability and death claims; treatment-related costs; absenteeism; on-the-job accidents; and turnover (and thus replacement costs), while employee productivity, job satisfaction, morale, health status, and the community image of the worksite improve. Finally, potential societal advantages of health promotion programs include reduced health care costs and improved health and quality of life for the citizenry (Hollander, Lengermann, & DeMuth, 1985), although there are few examples of the cost-effectiveness of worksite health promotion programs.

Proclamations about the efficacy of worksite health promotion, particularly with respect to its cost–benefit and its effect on morbidity and mortality, are made with scarce and at times conflicting empirical evidence (Warner, 1987a). A typical viewpoint about the efficacy of worksite health promotion programs comes from a representative of United Technologies Corporation:

> As a businessman, I'm concerned about the ability of American industry to compete in a tough global business environment. The most important ingredient in our success will be the quality of our workforce. Also vital will be our ability to control costs and improve productivity; health is fundamental to both of these. (Gray, 1983, p. 657)

Similarly, Robert N. Beck, Executive Vice President for Corporate Human Resources of the Bank of America, wrote:

> . . . the most important reason for doing health promotion is that American industry has realized that their major competition is international, and that the other countries of the world have been able to be more cost-effective. . . . Putting a few investment dollars into prevention has a great big payoff on the end for cost containment. It's just good sound business. (Beck, 1987, p. 5)

As Warner (1987a) noted, however, advocates of health promotion programs should be careful in their statements about program efficacy:

> The point here is simply that workers who are "saved" by health promotion are unlikely to go through the rest of their work careers free of any illnesses or any diminution in their work capacity. Thus any such later costs, made possible by the successes of health promotion, must be recorded as debts on the employer's health promotion financial balance sheet. (p. 47)

Examples

Worksite health promotion programs usually employ two general approaches: (a) *passive* health promotion programs that protect employees from health risks without an employee engaging in a specific behavior (e.g., non-smoking sections to limit exposure to second-hand smoke, environmental modification of plants or offices to protect workers from injury or exposure to toxins, reduction of fat in foods offered in worksite cafeterias), and (b) *active* health promotion programs that require employees to engage in behaviors that protect or optimize their health (e.g., exercising, quitting smoking, wearing hard hats, not drinking alcohol on the job). Within these approaches, a variety of specific strategies have been employed. These include traditional educational and informational strategies; screening of health-related behaviors and risk factors; use of incentives to promote and reinforce behavior change; environmental manipulation to support the practice of healthful behaviors; and policy and regulatory changes. The majority of worksite health promotion programs employ informational and educational approaches directed at individuals. Some worksites use multiple strategies. An example of this is a worksite that passes a policy restricting smoking, disposes of on-site cigarette vending machines, and makes smoking cessation programs available to those employees currently smoking.

The targets of worksite programs can, theoretically, be quite varied. Targets could include current employees, their spouses and children, retired employees, management, insurance carriers, and the community at large. Most programs are narrowly focused on current worksite employees (i.e., a more traditional psychological model) and are disease, rather than wellness, driven. That is, there is more interest in preventing disease than there is on promoting job satisfaction, reducing stress, improving working conditions, improving interpersonal relationships among workers, and designing work environments that are challenging and rewarding. These latter outcomes are generally characterized as "wellness" rather than disease prevention outcomes.

In a review of the early worksite health promotion literature, Fielding (1979) suggested that six programmatic efforts were warranted: (a) hypertension screening and follow-up, (b) smoking cessation programs, (c) exercise programs, (d) diet modification, (e) alcoholism groups, and (f) auto safety programs. Although the literature on worksite health promotion has burgeoned since this review, Fielding's recommendations are probably still appropriate. Additions might include drug as well as alcohol prevention and treatment programs, AIDS education programs, general injury prevention programs, and programs that educate employees about appropriate utilization of the health care system.

While there is insufficient space here to review worksite health promotion programs in detail, a few exemplary programs will be highlighted. In a national survey of worksites with more than 50 employees (USDHHS, 1987b), it was found that 66 percent had at least one health promotion activity (with smoking control cited most frequently). Larger worksites (over 750 employees) were more likely than smaller worksites to sponsor health promotion activities. The reader is referred to other sources for more detailed descriptions of worksite health programs (cf. Cataldo & Coates, 1986; Damberg, 1984; Fielding, 1979, 1984; Hallett, 1986; Michigan Department of Public Health, 1986; O'Donnell & Ainsworth, 1984; Parkinson & Associates, 1982; USDHHS, 1987b).

The most widely recognized and cited worksite health promotion programs occur at large worksites. Examples include the "Live for Life" (LFL) program at Johnson & Johnson (Wilbur & Garner, 1984) and the "Staywell" program at Control Data Corporation (CDC) (Naditch, 1984). These programs, as described below, are comprehensive health education efforts which combine individual education with group support and sophisticated behavior modification techniques.

Live for Life (LFL)

In 1978, Johnson & Johnson, a company that carries its own health insurance (i.e., it is self-insured), began a comprehensive health education program for its employees. The company undertook this program because: (a) health care costs were increasing dramatically; (b) the scientific evidence linking lifestyle to health had reached a point at which a health behavior change program could be justified; and (c) the company perceived itself as an industry leader in health care.

The LFL program includes screening of risk factors and risk-related behaviors, seminars, focused behavior change programs in a variety of areas (e.g., nutrition, smoking, stress management, physical activity, weight control) and modification of the work environment to promote health. In short, it is focused primarily on individual behavior change (i.e., a psychologically based model).

Early evaluation data from a controlled study of four Johnson & Johnson worksites (and five comparison worksites) suggested that it successfully attracted employees to participate (e.g., 76 percent of the employees were

screened and 65 percent attended lifestyle seminars) and resulted in significant health attitude and behavior changes (Wilbur & Garner, 1984). It is still
unknown whether this program will be able to achieve long-term changes or
whether it can be replicated in other organizations. A cost analysis of the
LFL program is presented later in the chapter.

Staywell

The Staywell program was initiated in 1979 and is now offered to over
20,000 CDC employees and spouses (Naditch, 1984). Like the LFL program, Staywell focuses primarily on smoking, weight control, fitness, stress
management, and nutrition. The program includes a general orientation,
behavioral health screening and completion of health hazard appraisals,
group workshops during which appraisals are interpreted, behavior change
courses in each risk factor area, and programs to help employees modify
their work environment for optimal health. A controlled study found that
participants in Staywell, compared to matched non-participants, reported
greater changes in health behaviors. The most impressive results were for
smoking cessation. Perhaps the most innovative aspect of the Staywell program is the computer-managed program of health behavior change. In this
program, individuals are matched to interventions and are given health
information that best fits their needs. The program adapts information provided based on changes made (or not made) and compliance rates.

Other Programs

Other worksites have implemented health promotion–disease prevention
policies. Smoking prevention and cessation programs are the most common
target and there are now many model programs (see Eriksen, 1986, for an
excellent review of these).

Pacific Northwest Bell, with support by the two employee unions, for
example, banned smoking in company facilities. After six months, only a
few complaints about the policy had been received. Although the effects of
this policy on smoking adoption and cessation are unavailable, there is some
evidence that the policy, along with a program that reimbursed employees
for participating in a smoking cessation program, increased the number of
employees interested in quitting smoking (Martin, Fehrenbach & Rosner,
1986).

Likewise, employees working at Group Health Cooperative in Puget
Sound exhibited broad support for a policy prohibiting smoking in its 35
facilities. In fact, 85 percent approved of the decision, many noted improvements in their and co-workers' performance, and the reported rate of smoking decreased (particularly in the number of cigarettes smoked).

A similar experience occurred in San Francisco. In 1983, the San Francisco Board of Supervisors passed legislation requiring a ban on smoking in

the workplace if a compromise between smoking and non-smoking employees was not possible. After one year, very few complaints had been received and no legal actions were taken (Martin & Silverman, 1986). These examples of policy-level interventions suggest that such strategies can be quite effective, do not seem to raise many ethical or legal concerns, and may complement traditional health education programs in the workplace.

A more aggressive stance has been taken by USG Acoustical Products. In 1987, the company told its 1300 employees that they had two choices: quit smoking or quit their jobs. Company management noted that their decision was based on a concern about their employees' health rather than on reducing insurance rates. To assist smokers in quitting, the company is paying for each smoker to attend SmokEnders, a commercial program that helps smokers quit. To the best of our knowledge, the legal and ethical implications of this aggressive policy have not been tested in a court of law. The question that arises in this regard is who determines the policy boundaries. That is, is it ethical and legal for employers to require all employees who are diabetic, obese, inactive, and so forth to quit? Undoubtedly, civil libertarians will participate in these decisions.

Along similar lines, the Bonne Bell cosmetic company provides incentives to employees who make and maintain health behavior changes (Bergquist, 1986). They pay employees 50 cents for each mile run and five dollars for each pound lost (up to 50 pounds over a six month period). If employees gain back weight they lost, however, they are expected to contribute 10 dollars for each pound gained to a charitable organization.

Cost Analyses

The cost–benefit and cost-effectiveness of worksite health promotion programs are widely debated topics in the health field. Three general strategies to control health care costs have been used by businesses: (a) changing insurance coverage; (b) educating employees about the appropriate use of the health care system; and (c) encouraging employees to modify their health-related behaviors. There is strong evidence that the first two strategies lower health care costs. Evidence that the third strategy lowers health care costs is not as clear.

Changing insurance coverage of employees is perhaps the most common strategy of controlling health care costs. This includes raising employee contributions to insurance (e.g., increasing co-payments and deductibles, eliminating first dollar coverage), decreasing the extent of coverage, offering (or requiring) health maintenance organization or preferred provider organization options, and negotiating *a priori* rates for medical procedures with insurance providers or health professionals.

Another example of this strategy is simply monitoring health care expenditure patterns. Surprisingly, in previous years (and continuing to this day), many companies did not keep track of their health care utilization and cost data. General Motors, for example, discovered that employees in New Jersey were hospitalized more and stayed in the hospital longer than employees in other states. Moreover, almost one third of the costs and hospitalized days were questionable (Demkovich, 1986). Similarly, Chrysler discovered that its podiatry bills increased 133 percent in just five years and that its employees in Michigan were using podiatrists 10 times more than employees in Illinois and nine times more than Alabama employees. In 1979, Michigan podiatrists, comprising 4 percent of the surgeons in the state, performed 16 percent of surgery. After instituting a second opinion program to prevent unnecessary foot surgery, Chrysler reduced surgeries by 60 percent and saved over $1 million per year (Califano, 1986).

The second strategy, employee education on the use of the health care system, includes prior authorization programs, in which second opinions are required for many inpatient and outpatient surgical procedures; suggesting (or requiring) that generic drugs be used; educating employees about the appropriate use of emergency rooms (which are costly); and providing employees with information about what action to take in the event of a health problem. One of the more popular examples of the latter strategy is the distribution of the book by Vickery and Fries (1981) entitled *Take Care of Yourself*, in which readers are given specific guidelines about the seriousness of various symptoms and appropriate actions to take in the event that these symptoms are experienced. Distribution of this book to company employees along with other minimal interventions (e.g., health appraisals, short films) has reduced utilization of health professionals from 10 to 35 percent (Lorig, Kraines, & Richardson, 1985; Moore, LoGerfo, & Inui, 1980; Vickery, Kalmer, Lowry, Constantine, Wright, & Loren, 1983), a cost savings worth many times the price of the book (a few dollars).

The third strategy, encouraging employees to modify their health-related behaviors, is the primary focus of most worksite health promotion programs (e.g., Johnson & Johnson's LFL). There is limited empirical evidence that these programs are cost-beneficial, although the lay public and business managers usually promote their cost savings, as illustrated earlier in the chapter. Most programs to date have not collected quality cost data to allow for an adequate cost analysis. Marvin Kristein, one of the leading authorities on the economics of worksite health promotion programs, wrote in 1982:

> There is no hard evidence that one company with a health promotion program has saved money as compared to another similar company which does not have such a program. There is no clear-cut example of a company saving money, in the long or short run, in terms of medical care spending or insurance costs or any other category of spending. There is highly suggestive evidence that, in the

short run, spending on health promotion does promote health and improve the "quality of life" of participants and that it costs money. (Kristein, 1982, p. 27)

More recently, Louise Russell (1986), in a book entitled *Is Prevention Better Than Cure?*, suggested that prevention has risks and costs and usually adds to the cost of medical expenditures. She argues that it should not be viewed as the best or only alternative for dealing with some health problems. Dealing with most health problems requires a mix of prevention and treatment.

These cautions aside, there is aggregate national epidemiological data suggesting that preventive interventions are cost-beneficial. In a cost analysis, Kristein (1983) reported that pack-a-day smokers cost their companies between $336 and $601 more per year than nonsmokers (in 1980 dollars). In his estimation, more than half of these costs can be recaptured through smoking cessation programs. He concluded that it would be profitable for employers to spend up to $150 on each employee per year encouraging them to quit smoking. Interestingly, he did not discuss how smoking prevention programs would contribute to cost savings. Similarly, worksite programs focusing on the control of high blood pressure have been estimated to have a benefit–cost ratio of between two to one and four to one and would save worksites several billion dollars annually (Kristein, 1982).

One of the most widely cited cost studies comes from the Johnson & Johnson Live for Life program (LFL) which found that in comparison to those in control worksites, employees receiving the LFL program had significantly lower rates of increase in hospital admissions and inpatient hospital costs (Bly, Jones, & Robertson, 1986). It should be noted, however, that for hospital admission rates, only one of the intervention groups was significantly different from the control group. Other health-related costs, such as outpatient costs and days spent in the hospital, did not differ significantly between groups. Overall, women had higher medical utilization rates and health care costs than men, age was associated positively with costs and utilization, and salaried employees had lower costs and utilization than wage employees. Importantly, the cost savings obtained were not immediate — they took about four years to appear. In fact, in the second year, inpatient costs were significantly higher for employees receiving the program compared to employees not receiving the program. This reversed by the fourth year. The authors project savings of $245,000 per year due to the LFL program.

Thus, these data suggest that a well-designed, intensive, worksite health promotion program can approach acceptable cost–benefit ratios. What this study is unable to provide is whether less intensive (or well-funded) programs, which are the norm, can be as equally cost-beneficial. It should also be noted that there have been several highly critical reviews of this study

(Jones, 1987; Kuller, 1987) that caution health professionals from making too much of the data. Until additional cost analyses of worksite health promotion programs are completed, researchers and practitioners should remain cautiously optimistic and not entirely persuaded that such programs are cost-beneficial.

Similar findings are reported from a five year cost analysis of Indiana's Blue Cross and Blue Shield health promotion program (Gibbs, Mulvaney, Henes, & Reed, 1985). These authors found that after five years, employees who participated in the health promotion program averaged 24 percent lower health care costs than nonparticipants. As with the Johnson & Johnson LFL program, participants had higher health care costs early in the program but the trend reversed within a year.

Conclusions about the cost–benefit ratio of worksite programs must be evaluated with respect to two other factors. First, two thirds of corporate health care costs are attributable to the spouses and dependents of workers, most of whom do not participate in worksite health promotion programs. Second, a majority of health care costs are due to psychiatric problems, problems not typically addressed by worksite health promotion programs (Conrad, 1987).

Ethical Considerations

In recent years, throughout the health promotion field, there has been increased (although still inadequate) discussion of the ethical underpinnings of health promotion. In particular, cautionary notes about worksite health promotion have recently received needed attention (Allegrante & Sloan, 1986; Becker, 1986; Green, 1987; Hollander & Hale, 1987; Merwin & Northrop, 1982; Wallack, 1987). Ethical considerations center around tensions that exist between individuals and institutions: (a) individual vs. societal responsibility and (b) individual choice vs. social protection. There are no obvious solutions to these complex tensions. It is instructive, however, to examine how they influence the design and implementation of worksite health promotion programs.

"Blaming the victim" is perhaps the most frequently discussed ethical issue. Citing research in psychology suggesting that illness is more frequently (and easily) attributed to the individual and her or his behavior, Allegrante and Sloan (1986) noted that it therefore is easier to target health promotion efforts at individual workers (e.g., lifting boxes incorrectly) rather than at the workplace environment (e.g., loading boxes with too much weight, not providing employees with adequate training about correct lifting procedures). In some cases, this orientation may be associated with increased physical and emotional problems (e.g., guilt, lack of self-esteem, frustration, eating disorders, stress). Becker (1986) argued that this bias has led to the perception of good health as a sign of character and moral worth — in a sense, "the New Morality":

> Health promotion, as currently practiced, fosters a dehumanizing self-concern which substitutes personal health goals for more important, humane, societal goals. It is a new religion, in which we worship ourselves, attribute good health to our devoutness, and view illness as just punishment for those who have not yet seen the Way . . . If, indeed, avoiding health risks buys us a few more years, we should be worrying about the quality of the society and environment in which those years will be spent. (p. 20)

Focusing on the individual worker while excluding the workplace may also place health professionals in a tenuous position between workers and management who define the problem and potential solutions differently. This ethical dilemma has been coined "the dilemma of conflicting loyalties" (Allegrante & Sloan, 1986).

On the other hand, who is and should be responsible for the costs of health care, when the costs may indeed result from actions taken by individual workers? Employers have recently taken a stronger position on this and are asking employees to assume greater responsibility for health care expenses (e.g., higher deductibles, reduced coverage). A 1987 article in the San Francisco Chronicle ("Stop smoking or be fired, employees told") reported on the aggressive posture toward smoking taken by the Acoustical Products company. As mentioned previously, the company told its employees to either stop smoking or quit their jobs. The company made available free of charge to employees a commercial stop smoking intervention (SmokEnders) and gave employees who did not want to use this strategy an equal amount of time to quit. The director of public relations for the company justified this hardnosed policy as follows: "It's an across-the-board thing applying to workers and management. We already have a good safety record, so it is not being done to cut our insurance costs. It was a decision we've been thinking about to help make everyone healthier. It is not a smoking ban. It is a ban on smokers." While there are no simple answers to the question of who is responsible for health care costs, the correct answer and fair solution probably lies somewhere between the individual, the workplace, and society at large.

In an exchange of letters to the editor of *Health Education Quarterly* on victim blaming, Green (1987) and Wallack (1987) agreed that the term has often been used inappropriately as an argument against programs aimed at changing an individual's knowledge, attitudes, and behavior. They noted the need for a better understanding of *both* how the broader socioeconomic context affects behavior and how individuals can be encouraged to change unhealthy practices. That is, the debate on victim blaming should not be framed as an either–or question. As Wallack noted, " . . . let us provide individuals with knowledge, skills, and increased resources to better navigate a hazardous social and physical environment. But at the same time, let us focus serious attention on reducing the number and intensity of the hazards through which the individual must navigate" (p. 385).

A second ethical issue concerns the available evidence (or lack thereof) linking individual health behaviors with health status and the role that professionals should play vis-à-vis education and advocacy (Becker, 1986; Merwin & Northrop, 1982). Since basic research has not established clearly the relationship between certain behaviors and illness (Kaplan, 1984), there are ethical issues involved in suggesting certain lifestyles. There are situations in which the consumer is confused by the debates among "experts" who promote conflicting lifestyles. Witness the recent debates among experts on the efficacy of calcium supplementation, estrogen replacement therapy, exercise, breast self-examination, routine physical exams, fish oil, and monounsaturated fats, to name a few. It is understandable that consumers are confused about what they should be doing. It is incumbent upon health professionals to emphasize to the public that no "magic bullet" exists.

Becker (1986) argued further that scientists should present their work to the public as trends and probabilities (not as absolutes), emphasize that scientific information is usually accumulated incrementally, and give equal attention to the limitations, risks, and unknowns of science. In defense of the scientific community, it should also be stated that the popular press should be more responsible in reporting research data.

In short, Becker argued that health professionals involved in worksite health promotion should question their right to present health information to workers when it is unclear what effects (positive, negative, or neutral) the information will have. Along the same lines, Merwin & Northrop (1982) suggested that the appropriate role of public health educators is to educate rather than to advocate:

> Is it appropriate for a health educator to market a particular course of action aggressively, or should it be his or her primary responsibility to educate towards a better understanding of the complex issues and choices of action? (p. 73)

As discussed later in this chapter, this stance has broad implications for public health interventions and requires an understanding of communication and psychological research. A large body of research from psychology, for example, demonstrates that the provision of information alone often does not change attitudes, beliefs, or behavior. On the other hand, in practice there may not be much of a difference between educating and advocating. Both terms may simply be characterized as attempts to "influence" a person, an organization, or a larger social system.

In short, worksite health promotion programs are based in large part on the notion that health is (or should be) an important life value of workers. For many workers, however, there are other life goals (often in juxtaposition to health) with greater immediate priority. This begs the question: Whose right is it to determine life goals and priorities? Researchers and policymakers often assume wrongly that increasing life expectancy and decreasing morbidity is the worker's most highly desired and ultimate life goal. Ethically, this stance may lead health professionals to overstep the bounds of current knowledge in advocating a particular lifestyle whose goals workers may not value or desire. Such a stance also places excessive attention on individual responsibility and invades worker privacy and personal freedom.

USING THE FRAMEWORK TO ANALYZE WORKSITE HEALTH PROMOTION

The purpose of the next section of the chapter is to examine a variety of worksite health promotion efforts through use of the framework described in chapter 2. The framework allows for examination of these efforts from different perspectives, theories, methods, and data sources, and facilitates a thorough assessment of the benefits and drawbacks of current efforts. Four subtopics will be covered: problem definition, levels of analysis, intervention design, and impact analysis. It should be noted that in contrast to the other chapters in this book, the next section of the chapter uses a variety of topic areas as exemplars, rather than just one, to illustrate how the framework can be useful.

It is our opinion that current worksite health programs generally lack comprehensiveness in problem definition, intervention design and implementation, and program evaluation. Several people have noted the potential of comprehensive health promotion programs (Health Promotion Resource Center, 1987; O'Donnell, 1986) but there are few employers that have actually implemented such programs. In addition, it appears that participation in such programs is distributed unevenly across demographic groups. A model comprehensive worksite health promotion program proposed by O'Donnell (1986) has the following elements: (a) awareness and education components (e.g., newsletters, special events, flyers, posters, seminars, meetings); (b) health management processes (e.g., personal assessment, goal setting, skills building, leadership training); and (c) supportive environment (e.g., employee ownership, corporate policies, physical environment). Table 9.2 illustrates a comprehensive approach to worksite health promotion.

Table 9.2. A Multilevel Approach to Worksite Health Promotion

Personal

- Increase understanding of health risks and health-promoting activities
- Increase motivation to participate in health activities
- Increase behavioral skills to engage in health actions
- Increase participation in worksite health activities such as educational programs, health screenings, and environmental modification programs
- Provide treatment services to employees in need (e.g., substance abuse counseling)

Interpersonal

- Increase bonds between employees and between employees and the worksite
- Establish employee support groups
- Increase communication between employees and management

Organizational/Environmental

- Educate worksite decision-makers on worksite hazards and on health promotion
- Develop effective health communication campaigns for employees
- Develop policies to minimize accidents at the worksite
- Make available to employees health care services or referrals to services
- Implement policies that reward good employee practices and/or health status (e.g., insurance coverage, employee recognition program)
- Make available health promotion services to families of employees
- Design worksite environments and policies that promote health

Institutional/Societal

- Establish guidelines on acceptable levels of exposure to harmful substances in the worksite and maintain surveillance systems to ensure that exposure does not occur
- Establish policies that automatically protect employee health
- Provide economic protection for employees who are injured on the job or who are laid off
- Provide retirement and other benefits that contribute positively to employee health and well being

Problem Definition

Much of the research and intervention on worksite health promotion has dealt with the inherent tensions between workers and institutions by focusing efforts either at workers or at institutions. As noted in earlier sections of the chapter, the sociopolitical milieu has had profound influences on how health problems among workers have been defined. At the extremes, workers' health problems were viewed either as a function of their misbehavior or as a function of the work environment. Even to this day, there are few analyses or programs that view the problem as a function of both the individual and of the larger context. To bring this into sharper focus, the topic of stress in the workplace will be reviewed as an example of how a problem can be defined comprehensively.

For workers, management, and insurance companies, the stress associated with work has been and will continue to be a very popular topic

(Altman & Jackson, 1984; Byers, 1987; Cooper & Payne, 1980; Moss, 1981; Murphy & Schoenborn, 1987; Price, 1986; Veninga & Spradley, 1981). In fact, burnout, one of the more commonly used terms to describe the effects of stress, was coined by researchers studying occupational stress (Maslach, 1982). The implications of worksite stress are substantial: 8–10 percent of employees experience disabling emotional problems, work-related mental stress now comprise about 14 percent of stress claims under workers' compensation, and the costs of absenteeism, diminished work performance, and increased health care expenses is about \$150 billion each year (Byers, 1987; Landers, 1987).

As reported earlier, however, work also has many benefits (e.g., income, friendships, personal growth). Thus, it is a mistake to study stress in the workplace without also considering the positive aspects of work. Antonovsky (1987) has addressed this general issue through the concept of *salutogenesis*. In his view, we should study how people are able to cope with the unending demands of everyday life (in this case, the demands of work) rather than only looking at those people who are unable to cope. In a sense, he is calling for a wellness model approach rather than a disease model approach. A salutogenic approach to worksite health would probably increase our understanding of the key issues and improve our ability to promote health and prevent disease among employees. It should be noted, however, that Antonovsky's perspective stems from a psychological tradition in which the focus is on individuals' ability to cope with life demands.

There are a variety of stress management strategies available to implementers of worksite health programs. These range from those which help individuals cope better with job demands to those which alter the workplace environment. In general, programs with a focus on improving an individuals' ability to cope with stress are more prevalent than programs that alter the workplace environment (Byers, 1987; Landers, 1987).

Price (1986) has categorized stress management programs as follows: (a) individual level programs aimed at reducing stressors (e.g., stress inoculation, time management, assertiveness training, overload avoidance); (b) programs directed at diminishing or counteracting the stress response (e.g., deep muscle relaxation, meditation, physical activity); (c) programs focused on increasing one's ability to cope with task demands (e.g., task redesign, participative management); and (d) programs addressing role and interpersonal demands (e.g., goal setting sessions, social support groups).

In addition, there are a variety of environmentally oriented programs which could decrease the experience of stress among employees (e.g., flexitime scheduling; adding more frequent breaks to employees working in an assembly line operation; providing healthy food in the worksite cafeteria). Comprehensive or multimodal programs that utilize a variety of strategies are more likely than narrowly based programs to decrease stress in the workplace (Price, 1986). Our reading of the literature on stress management

programs in worksites, however, indicates that the most widely used programmatic format is directed toward enhancing coping responses in the face
of stressors — there are few programs that are multi-dimensional.

Although stress is widely discussed and experienced, there has been considerable confusion, and debate, about what stress is (Altman & Jackson,
1984). The variation in how stress is defined engenders confusion and hin-
ders communication among those who study it. The three primary ways in
which occupational stress has been defined are: (a) stimulus- or demand-
based (i.e., stress is a harmful or threatening condition); (b) response-based
(i.e., stress is a reaction to an adverse condition); and (c) transactional (i.e.,
stress is a perceived imbalance between demand and response capability). In
psychology, a transactional view has been adopted widely in the theoretical
literature and somewhat less so in the interventions used to manage stress. In
contrast, public health professionals are more likely to study stress from
either a demand-based (i.e., to examine environmental stressors such as
noise and toxic chemicals) or a response-based perspective (i.e., to examine
what stress management strategies patients used to cope with stress from an
operation).

A transactional perspective specifies that stress is a hypothetical condition defined by an imbalance or misfit between demands and coping resources, as mediated by cognitive, behavioral, and social factors (Lazarus,
1966; McGrath, 1970). That is, stress is experienced when the demands on a
person exceed his or her capacity to respond to the demands. Demands are
sometimes referred to as stressors and responses to demands as stress responses. Stress responses can be behavioral (e.g., alcohol abuse, smoking),
psychological or cognitive (e.g., distractibility, depression), medical (e.g.,
myocardial infarction, ulcers), or all three (Price, 1986). A transactional
approach emphasizes the interconnectedness of persons and environments
and also the importance of examining both subjective and objective characteristics of persons and environments. Temporally, work-related stress may
be conceptualized as an immediate, static event, as a long-term process, or
as something in between. Spatially, work-related stress may be conceptualized within the confines of the job or work setting or across various life
domains (e.g., work, home, leisure). It is important to keep in mind that
from this perspective, stress is not caused by either the work environment or
the employee alone. Rather, stress can only be understood as a relationship
between individuals and their environments (Price, 1986).

Recognizing the differences in how stress is defined is as important to the
practitioner as it is to the academician. Viewing job stress as the degree of
balance between demands and coping resources could enable practitioners
to make more accurate appraisals of the factors contributing to health problems (e.g., job dissatisfaction). With regard to treatment, this approach
would encourage the practitioner to go beyond dealing symptomatically

with stress responses by conducting a thorough and comprehensive analysis of the relationships between demands in the workplace, at home, and in other life domains, and a person's ability to deal adequately with these demands over time. A practitioner who utilizes this approach would view the relationship between persons and environments as interactive and mutually deterministic. This recognizes that accounting for subjective perceptions of work demands and coping resources is just as important as understanding objective indicators of demands and resources.

For example, to understand why an employee is "stressed" and not performing his or her job as expected requires a comprehensive analysis of life domains and environments and the extent to which synergistic relationships among domains exists. Life domains can be studied on a variety of dimensions (e.g., home, work, recreation, church) and require attention to developmental life stage and life goals.

Singer, Neale, & Schwartz (1987) reported a study with hotel workers that took into account the multiple influences on stress responses. Of interest here is their use of the "Occupational Stress Evaluation Grid" (OSEG). The OSEG assesses the following dimensions:

1. sociocultural (e.g., race discrimination, national labor relations climate)
2. organizational (e.g., labor negotiations, staffing and hiring policies)
3. work setting/interpersonal (e.g., management style, group norms)
4. job characteristics (e.g., unpredictable scheduling, time pressure, heavy lifting)
5. physical environment (e.g., poor ventilation, poor quality food)
6. family/social (e.g., child care, schedule interferences)
7. individual/psychological (e.g., mood or memory changes, helplessness)
8. biological (e.g., substance abuse, hypertension).

Through this comprehensive assessment, Singer et al. were able to understand the experiences of hotel workers and to suggest changes, at multiple levels of analysis, to improve the situation.

This discussion of stress in the workplace illustrates that problem definition is central to how interventions to promote health among a worksite population might be designed. As noted in the discussion on stress management (and this certainly applies to other workplace health issues), the theories and values guiding problem definition are typically narrow in focus. That is, health problems are infrequently viewed as a function of both individual and structural or societal factors. In fact, knowledge of the disciplinary training of program designers would be a good predictor of the type of intervention implemented. There are relatively few examples of programs that cross levels of problem definition and levels of analysis. The framework outlined in chapter 2 may assist researchers and interveners in the development of such strategies.

Levels of Analysis

Related to problem definition is the relative lack of comprehensive systems analysis of worksite health. That is, multilevel analysis and intervention is not that common. To illustrate the unique contributions that a systems analysis can provide, the issue of substance abuse and drug testing in the workplace will be used.

Screening employees for drug use is another example of the tension between collective interests and individual interests. One outcome of the Reagan administration's "war on drugs" has been increased interest among worksites in testing employees for drug use. In 1982, only 3 percent of employees were tested for drug use. Now as many as 30 percent of the Fortune 500 companies test the urine of current or prospective employees and the number is expected to exceed 50 percent in the next year (Grzelka, 1987; O'Keefe, 1987).

This policy has been opposed vehemently by many employee groups and civil libertarians (e.g., the American Civil Liberties Union—ACLU). Moreover, some psychologists have questioned whether testing is in fact a valid way of measuring job impairment (Bales, 1987). This issue is not a new one to worksite health programs, as it centers around the rights of individual self-determination versus the rights of organizations. Briefly, employee groups argue that broad-scale urine testing is degrading, intrusive, and has a high rate of false positives. In a study conducted by the Centers for Disease Control, for example, the average laboratory error rate (mostly false negatives) was 31 percent, with a high of 100 percent (O'Keefe, 1987).

Another major problem with the validity of drug testing is cross-reactivity. That is, some over-the-counter medications and foods produce false positive tests (e.g., Contac, Sudafed, diet pills, decongestants, asthma medications, cough syrup, some antibiotics and painkillers, poppy seeds, herbal teas) (O'Keefe, 1987). Moreover, some prescription medications (e.g., for epilepsy, anxiety disorders, narcolepsy, insomnia, muscle spasms) will result in positive tests. In such cases, employees taking legitimate medications would have to explain their situation, with the possible effect being embarrassment and humiliation. This is particularly salient in small worksites (where the majority of employees in this country work) in which confidentiality and anonymity are difficult to maintain (Bales, 1987).

As a result, employee groups argue that it is unreasonable to subject employees to testing unless impaired performance could endanger the lives of the public (Grzelka, 1987). This approach, adopted by many companies, allows testing for "due cause." There are still validity problems, however, with this approach. Since the effects of drugs on behavior can seldom be measured after about four to eight hours, an employee who has used drugs in the evening is unlikely to exhibit impaired work performance the next day (Bales, 1987).

The keen interest in testing comes at a time when drug use is actually lower than it was in the late 1970s (except for that of cocaine), suggesting that factors other than epidemiology are at the root of the drug testing movement (O'Keefe, 1987). These factors include the conservative sociopolitical environment, the sensational media coverage of drug use, and readily available technologies to test urine for substances.

As summarized by Bales (1987), some psychologists also wonder whether testing will result in employees switching to alcohol or refraining from seeking medical care for fear of punishment. In essence, the introduction of a drug testing intervention may cause reverberations in the social system that are more serious than drug use by a minority of workers.

In contrast, employers argue that testing can change the behavior of individuals who abuse or who are at risk of abusing drugs. In addition, they believe it is their right to protect their business interests. They reason that if employees who abuse alcohol or drugs cost the company more than employees who do not, it is their right to determine whether testing should be conducted. Employee groups and employers generally agree that testing alone will not solve the substance abuse problem. Preventive education and referral to treatment programs must also be made available to employees.

Obviously, preventing or treating substance abuse problems in worksites is complicated. In our view, a comprehensive systems analysis of the problem can lend insight into the most effective ways to address it. For example, individually based programs (e.g., Employee Assistance Programs, drug testing) are sometimes warranted, as there are people who need treatment and counseling and there are jobs in which use of drugs or alcohol would compromise the safety of others (e.g., air traffic controllers, train engineers). Many companies, however, stop their efforts at this point and do not offer programs at the interpersonal/social level (e.g., establishment of employee support groups; family-based intervention), at the worksite policy level (e.g., enactment of policies prohibiting the use of tobacco or alcohol on the job or in the cafeteria, discouragement of alcohol gift-giving, ban on reimbursement of alcohol as a business expense, availability of non-alcoholic drinks at social gatherings), and at the community level (e.g., support of alcohol warning labels at point of purchase, support of access laws prohibiting the sale of alcohol and tobacco to minors, free-ride programs during the holiday seasons, sponsorship of school health education programs, support of server intervention training programs). These different programs may have direct, indirect, or synergistic effects on the substance abuse problem in a worksite. For example, support of a school health education program, which on the surface seems removed from the worksite substance abuse problem, might convey a message to workers and the community at large that substance abuse is unacceptable to the company and, through the children of employees, influence the habits of workers. The point here is that multiple levels of analysis and intervention will usually be more effective than a narrowly focused effort.

Intervention Design

One of the distinguishing attributes of worksite health promotion efforts in recent years is the primary attention given to changing individual health behaviors rather than or in addition to aspects of the organizational context (Sloan, 1987). The balance between individual and higher-level responsibility, therefore, has shifted away from organizational and societal causes and toward individual causes.

The targets of many worksite health promotion programs are focused narrowly. As discussed previously, for example, individuals, rather than environments or policies, are the predominant targets of health promotion programs in worksites and a pathogenic approach (i.e., disease model focusing on risk factor identification and management) rather than a salutogenic approach (i.e., a wellness model focusing on the promotion of health through the enhancement of coping resources) has been the model of choice (Antonovsky, 1987). Moreover, many worksite health promotion programs are not connected to other aspects of employees' lives. This connection could take the form of allowing the families of employees to participate in worksite health promotion activities, scheduling activities that minimize interference with both work and family commitments, and providing incentives for participation (also see chapter 3). Each of these solutions, however, requires resources which for many companies do not exist.

The selection of specific intervention strategies for worksite programs follows from this focus on individuals. That is, the armamentarium of worksite health promotion interventions consists primarily of tools to either persuade individual employees to engage in healthy behaviors or to dissuade them from engaging in risky behaviors. As a rule, they do not focus on changing policies, regulations, or environments that either promote or reinforce unhealthy behaviors or present such formidable barriers that healthy behaviors are very difficult to practice. Moreover, they are typically conceived and conducted by psychologists, health educators, and human resource specialists. Exceptions to this bias include efforts by worksites to implement policies banning smoking at the worksite (e.g., Martin & Silverman, 1986; Martin, Fehrenback, & Rosner, 1986).

Along these lines, Pechter (1987) noted: "A . . . fundamental reason that blue-collar workers avoid fitness programs is that health promotion carries a 'let them eat cake' message. It is seen as a Band-Aid solution. It seldom addresses exposure to toxic chemicals, the dizzying effects of shift work, or the monotony of repetitive jobs. It doesn't question the organization of work" (p. 14). Similarly, Gordon (1987) has argued that the worksite is not a neutral site for health promotion. Within the worksite, there can be competing priorities that lead to a polarization of the worksite population. In her view, health promotion programs are often coercive in that they give workers a message that their boss wants them to participate and they tend to divert attention away from environmental hazards and toward individual behavior change. An example of a more environmentally focused perspective comes from David LeGrande, Director of Occupational Safety and Health for the Communications Workers of America:

> Our orientation deals with adapting the workplace to meet the worker. Specifically, we look at the work station and work equipment, the work environment, and work organization issues, such as input of workers into design aspects of the job, for example workload, work pace. We look at managerial style, and we also look at training . . . Nutrition, smoking, lifestyles I see as less significant a factor in terms of illnesses and injuries and well-being. (LeGrande, 1987, p. 7)

LeGrande's position must be balanced with existing knowledge about lifestyle and health. It also should be recognized that LeGrande's position, in its extreme form, can be just as oppressive as the position taken by the USG Acoustical Products company with regard to its stringent smoking policy (discussed earlier in the chapter).

There also tends to be a bias in terms of which employee groups have access to health promotion programs. It is more common for these programs to be made available to executive or white collar employees than to blue collar employees. The recognition of this problem has even made it into the popular press. The January 11, 1987, issue of the *San Francisco Chronicle*, for example, ran a major story entitled, "Corporate fitness and the collar barrier: Why company health programs fail blue-collar workers" (Pechter, 1987). The article noted that many of the high-tech facilities, equipment, and programs invested in by companies are used by employees who already believe in practicing a healthy lifestyle and who in many cases are already in good physical condition, rather than by the employees who could benefit more significantly. The *Chronicle* article quoted Charles Althafer, the assistant director for health promotion at NIOSH: "The company gym is now the place where boy meets girl. It's done mainly for the white-collar worker. We call it the 'carpet-floor syndrome,' because everybody who uses health promotion works on carpeted floors. This is the single biggest issue in health promotion today." In a poignant description of the problem, the following example was given:

> On a recent afternoon at L. L. Bean in Freeport, Maine, the chairman of the company was working out in the new mini-gym . . . It has bright fluorescent lighting and piped-in music and features stationary bicycles, a cross-country

ski machine and weight lifting apparatus. As the chairman worked on a rowing machine, four white-haired women, retirees in their 70's or 80's, pedaled furiously on the bicycles. A few hours later, the night-shift was on duty — overweight, middle-aged women, sitting for hours under gloomy light on obsolete, break-your-back stenographer's chairs, their eyes fixed on VDT screens. These workers complain of numerous chronic ailments, and as a group they run up bigger than average medical bills. They don't have time to ride the exercycles. What they need are chairs with better lumbar support and shift rotation schedules that don't scramble circadian rhythms. (p. 13)

Similarly, a March 25, 1987, article in the *Wall Street Journal* noted that blue collar workers are much less likely than white collar workers to have access to or interest in corporate health promotion programs (Rundle, 1987). Moreover, blue collar workers are often cynical about the motives of companies that sponsor such programs. This cynicism is based on a perception that health promotion often obscures other more serious health threats (e.g., toxic exposure) and health status data collected as part of risk-factor screening may influence promotions or dismissals (Rundle, 1987).

Thus, the absence of a wellness or salutogenic approach, the lack of comprehensiveness in intervention targets, and the narrow focus on individual behavior change has led, we think, to the development and implementation of worksite health promotion programs that fall far short of their potential.

Impact Analysis

Many worksite health promotion programs have not been evaluated with enough rigor to allow for adequate interpretation even of short-term effects. Although several of the larger worksite programs have been allocated adequate evaluation resources and expertise (e.g., the Live for Life and Staywell programs), the overall effectiveness as well as the cost–benefit ratio of programs that reach the majority of the worker population (i.e., those implemented in smaller worksites) is relatively unknown. Little, if any, data exist on the extent to which worksite health promotion programs have effects in the middle or long term or whether there are effects on ultimate outcomes (i.e., morbidity, mortality). Also, the amount of formative and process evaluation data collected is minimal. What is particularly troubling about this, from a scientific as well as a public health perspective, is that employee participation rates (i.e., reach) and adherence to healthy behaviors promoted by the programs appear to be low in many cases.

Thus, at this early stage in the implementation of these programs, very little data exist to suggest that the current direction being taken is efficacious or generalizable across diverse worksites or worksite populations. Moreover, most programs are implemented in a piecemeal fashion, with more attention to a medical model approach (early detection and treatment) than to a wellness or health promotion approach. Companies that adopt an extreme interpretation of wellness would in fact expand their efforts even further (e.g., to include spiritual health concerns). Not surprising, then, many of the "model" worksite health promotion programs reflect biases in the larger health field. Given that many designers and implementers of these worksite programs, as well as the corporate officials responsible for financing them, were trained in traditional approaches to health care, this is to be expected. Developers of worksite health promotion programs and the worksites in which their programs are implemented who are able to break from traditional models and approaches will be the ones to advance the field from its current position. There certainly is a need to break new ground in worksite health promotion. There is also a critical mass of human and corporate resources to do so. Achieving the potential will require innovative people who are willing to depart from tradition.

In addition, worksite health promotion programs are, in large measure, a product (or benefit) offered to employees of large worksites. Very little is known about the extent to which small worksites (less than 50 employees), which comprise the majority of the nation's workforce, can mount successful programs. Moreover, the unique aspects of small worksite health programs have not been documented adequately. For example, it is unclear whether employees from small worksites have different experiences based on the lack of anonymity that exists when everybody knows one another. From an organizational level, smaller worksites are less likely than larger ones to be able to fund comprehensive health promotion programs. Smaller worksites may, however, be better able to influence social norms surrounding health. Research in social psychology on group dynamics might provide some insight into this phenomena (Cartwright & Zander, 1968). These and other potential differences need to be studied since most people in this country work in small organizations.

SUMMARY

This chapter has reviewed past and current efforts to promote health and prevent disease in the workplace and has used the framework outlined in chapter 2 to assess the current state of the art. As the number of people who are employed increases and the quality and quantity of their work experiences change, new opportunities for maintaining and improving their health are possible, as long as a careful analysis of problems and potential solutions is undertaken.

It should be evident that psychologists and public health professionals bring different, although complementary, values, methods, and intervention strategies to the worksite health promotion field. Public health professionals have long been involved with workers and work environments. Their involvement has traditionally been with respect to occupational health and safety — assessing and controlling hazards in the worksite, establishing standards and regulations to protect workers, and, recently, developing health promotion programs for workers.

In contrast, psychologists have historically not been very involved in workplace health issues. For these psychologists that were involved, their roles were generally limited to serving a counseling function in employee assistance programs or participating in the selection of potential employees through administration of standardized tests. In recent years, however, psychologists have followed (and in some cases, pushed) the health promotion movement into worksites. In doing so, they have identified diverse research and clinical opportunities.

Although the disciplines of public health and psychology have become active participants in worksite health promotion, our assessment of the literature to date suggests that they have not capitalized on the potential contributions that each can make to the other. These contributions center around the application of sophisticated behavior change and environmental change strategies at the organizational level of analysis. Our hope is that utilization of the book's framework will help professionals from these two disciplines better understand how and when it would be appropriate to cross disciplinary boundaries.

As noted throughout the chapter, worksite health promotion programs pose a variety of tensions to workers, employers, and society at large. The most prominent of these are between the needs and demands of individuals and the needs and demands of institutions. This tension is readily apparent in how the problem of worker health is defined and later intervened upon (e.g., as a function of lifestyle vs. as a function of the worksite environment). In addition, there appears to be more attention to preventing physical illness than there is to promoting physical and/or mental wellness (with the exception of some stress management programs). For example, the most widely acclaimed worksite health promotion programs focus very little on enhancing the psychosocial environment or the quality of the work experience. Rather, they seem to be aimed predominantly at reducing specific risk factors or environmental exposure.

The tension between individuals and institutions also affects the way in which the worksite system is analyzed. It appears that comprehensive systems analysis does not occur much beyond academic circles. Moreover, the fact that worksite programs that provide automatic protection to workers (e.g., to control toxic exposure) are not often integrated with health promotion programs (e.g., to change lifestyle) suggests that comprehensive program planning and implementation is not the norm. Use of a framework underscores the variety of potential directions that health professionals can take in advancing the scope and effectiveness of worksite health programs and can lead, it is to be hoped, to a healthier workforce and work environment.

10
Environmental Health

INTRODUCTION

Dating back thousands of years, civilizations have been concerned about their surrounding environment — the air they breathe, their water supply, removal of wastes, drainage systems, and factors that influence personal hygiene. The study of how the environment affects health and how it can be altered to improve health is one of the hallmarks distinguishing the discipline of public health from other disciplines. Indeed, environmental health has a rich history in the discipline of public health. Defined traditionally, environmental public health is "the study of disease-causing agents that are introduced into the environment by humans, as well as the illnesses that are caused by these agents" (Blumenthal, 1985, p. 1). Public health concerns about the environment have expanded in recent decades and now include disease vectors (e.g., mosquitoes, lice, rodents), food, air resources, solid waste, radiation, occupational health, housing, noise and other environmental stress, marine biotoxins, accidents, and nuclear war (Purdom, 1980a; Trieff, 1980).

There also appears to be a small movement afoot in public health to conceptualize "environment" as inclusive of social psychological factors. For example, Lindheim and Syme (1983) view the environment as an interaction including natural and man-made forms, social processes, and relationships between individuals and groups. Their work has given credence to the idea that the social environment (e.g., social relationships, social support) has an important influence on physical and mental health. As is noted below, however, it has in general been psychologists, rather than public health professionals, who have developed theoretical and conceptual models that account for the richness of human relationships with the surrounding environment.

Although issues involving environmental health have not generated as much interest in psychology, some psychologists have attempted to understand the interrelationships between environments and behavior (I. Altman, 1975; Stokols & I. Altman, 1987a). Environmental psychology, the subfield of psychology with a primary interest in these issues, has been defined by Stokols and I. Altman (1987b) as "the study of human behavior and well-being in relation to the sociophysical environment" (p. 1). Recently, psychol-

314

ogists have become involved with applied environmental issues such as nuclear war (e.g., Fiske, 1987) and toxic waste (e.g., Edelstein & Wandersman,
1987).

The interest in environmental health extends beyond the scientific communities of public health and psychology. Individuals, organizations, communities, and nations around the world are consumed by concerns over the
environment. One need only examine newspapers or popular magazines to
realize how much interest the environment generates. In recent years, the
most salient concerns have been human-caused pollution and carcinogens
(e.g., air pollution, acid rain, radiation, PCBs in water supplies, pesticides,
depletion of atmospheric ozone, airborne asbestos, indoor air pollution,
hazardous waste), nuclear energy, and conservation or rationing.

Governments around the world spend considerable time and money on
environmental issues. In the United States, for example, major environmental
agencies include the Environmental Protection Agency (EPA), the Occupational Safety and Health Administration (OSHA), the Consumer Products
Safety Commission (CPSC), and a variety of state, county, and municipal
agencies. In addition, diverse public and private organizations are dedicated
to improving the environment. These include the Sierra Club, the National
Audubon Society, the National Geographic Society, the Environmental Defense Fund, American Peace Test, Greenpeace, the Natural Resources Defense
Council, and the Citizen's Clearinghouse for Hazardous Waste.

As reported in the *San Francisco Examiner* (Coates, 1987), worldwide
concern about the environment, for good reason, continues to grow: (a)
each year, worldwide, an area about the size of the state of Nebraska is stripped of every tree and many species of plants and animals; one
serious outcome of this is that 17,500 plant and animal species become
extinct annually; (b) in the last 50 years, about half the world's rain forests
have disappeared; (c) the buildup of carbon dioxide in the air is increasing
the atmospheric temperature (i.e., the "greenhouse effect") and may lead to
melting polar ice caps and increasing size of deserts; and (d) "natural hazards" due to floods and droughts have increased (often caused by growing
deserts, shrinking forests, and rising sea levels). There is no question that
humans are having a dramatic effect on the environment. In some cases,
these effects are irreversibly negative. In turn, man-made as well as natural
environments have dramatic effects on humans.

It is beyond the scope of this chapter to review comprehensively how
practitioners of public health and psychology have approached environment
health. Indeed, numerous books have been dedicated to this endeavor (e.g.,
I. Altman, 1975; Greenberg, 1987; Purdom, 1980a; Stokols & I. Altman,
1987a; Trieff, 1980; Turiel, 1985) and thousands of articles and chapters
have been written. Instead, we hope to discuss some exemplary intersections
between public health and psychology, assess how these fields have or could

come together around environmental health, and stimulate innovative ways to improve the health of humans and the environments in which they live. The specific examples reviewed will thus be illustrative rather than inclusive. While each discipline will continue to contribute uniquely to our understanding of the environment, we hope that the integrative perspective offered here extends the separate contributions that each discipline makes. It should be noted as well that the classification of a particular issue, perspective, or study as representative of public health or of psychology may not always be appropriate because the boundaries between the disciplines sometimes overlap. As is evident throughout this book, however, the dominant theories and methods of public health are generally different from those of psychology.

To lay the groundwork for a discussion of potential areas of intersection, it is important to provide a rudimentary overview of the principles and techniques of environmental public health and of environmental psychology (see Table 10.1 for an overview).

A Public Health Perspective on the Environment

Traditionally, environmental public health has focused considerable attention on environmental hazards and their effects. Hazards include infectious agents, irritants, respiratory fibrotic agents, asphyxiants, allergens, metabolic poisons, physical agents, mutagens, teratogens, and carcinogens (Blumenthal, 1985). The four basic ways in which a hazardous substance can reach humans is through direct exposure (e.g., ingesting paint containing lead), discharge into air or water supplies (e.g., carbon monoxide emitted through automobile engine exhaust), inadequate landfills (e.g., leaking

Table 10.1. Public Health and Psychological Approaches to Environmental Health

	Public Health	Psychology
Predominant Theories/ Concepts	Environment/host/agent; biological pathways	Behavior analysis; transactionalism; community empowerment
Primary Goal	Protection of physical health	Optimization of person–environment fit
Targets	Physical environment; environmental hazards	Physical and social environment; commonly used settings
Primary Level of Analysis	Community at large, institutional, societal	Individual, interpersonal, organizational
Intervention of Choice	Large-scale passive prevention	Enhancement of individual coping skills; alteration of environment to match knowledge and skills

substances through runoff, leaching, or travel through the food chain), or through dumping (Blumenthal, 1985). The extent to which a particular hazard causes a health problem and the magnitude of the problem is affected by characteristics of the host, the agent, and the environment (Blumenthal, 1985).

The public health literature is replete with detailed discussion of specific environmental hazards, potential routes through which exposure occurs, and policies and laws regulating hazards. The primary focus of this chapter is to explore individual and community behaviors in response to environmental hazards, a dimension of environmental public health that has received somewhat less attention relative to other dimensions (e.g., health effects of hazards). We believe that psychological theories, methods, and interventions can add new insights to research on environmental health. Likewise, we believe that public health has a great deal to bring to psychology, not the least of which is a sophisticated understanding of biological and environmental systems and their effects on physical health.

A Psychology Perspective on the Environment

Psychologists from a variety of perspectives (e.g., environmental, social, cognitive, and community psychology) have worked on environmental issues. Interestingly, health psychologists have generally not tackled this topic. Environmental psychology, the subfield of psychology most closely linked to environmental health, is generally concerned with the reciprocal relationships between persons and environments at multiple levels of analysis and with the utilization of this knowledge to improve the quality of life (Moore, 1987). Environmental psychologists conceptualize the environment as more than a physical entity. In their view, the environment is contained in the psychological experiences of individuals, in social relationships, and in a physical time–space dimension (Saegert, 1987). Environmental psychologists refer to the concept of embeddedness and mutual determinism to describe the environment. That is, to understand the environment you must understand how individuals define and shape it. Likewise, to understand individuals, you must understand how the environment influences them. Thus, environmental psychologists study how environments affect, and are affected by, cognition, personality, emotion, child development, aging, conservation, personal space, territoriality, crowding, stress, and crime (Stokols & I. Altman, 1987a). For interested readers, extensive reviews of the history of environmental psychology are offered by Moore (1987), Sommer (1987), and Proshansky (1987).

Community psychologists have also contributed to our understanding and alteration of the environment (Geller, Winett, & Everett, 1982; Holahan & Wandersman, 1987). The perspective of community psychology is generally characterized by a focus on assets (health) rather than deficits (illness), prevention rather than treatment, community systems rather than individuals, the ties between individuals and the surrounding environment, and on social and environmental change (Heller, Price, Reinharz, Riger & Wandersman, 1984; Holahan & Wandersman, 1987; Rappaport, 1977). In addition, behavioral community psychologists have contributed significantly to altering behaviors detrimental to the environment (e.g., Geller et al., 1982; Geller, 1987; Winett et al., 1982; 1985).

Before discussing specific areas of intersection between psychology and public health, it is useful to examine in depth how much risk the environment poses.

Environmental Risk

The Scientific/Quantitative Perspective

Quantitative risk assessment or risk analysis has become a standard source of information with which to make decisions about the environment (Brown, 1985; Lave, 1987; Russell & Gruber, 1987). Decisions about the environment may involve important tradeoffs between economics, conservation, and health. Quantitative risk assessment provides policymakers with information with which to evaluate the costs and benefits of a particular decision. Society is generally faced with either "risk–risk" situations (i.e., requiring a choice between the best of alternatives with some risk) or "how safe is safe" situations that require decisions about how much to sacrifice (e.g., programs, activities, money) in order to achieve a reduced risk (Lave, 1987).

There are four primary steps to quantitative risk assessment (Russell & Gruber, 1987): (a) assess the hazard, including its toxicity and the strength of the evidence linking it to health problems; (b) assess the dose–response characteristics (i.e., the magnitude) of the hazard; (c) determine the extent of exposure to the hazard among population subgroups; and (d) characterize the risk, including a description of the assumptions made and the uncertainties that remain. Data gathered from these steps will theoretically provide the background information necessary to make an informed policy decision.

Predictions generated by quantitative risk assessment can rarely be validated by direct observation (Brown, 1985). First, some risks are so low as to be undetectable (e.g., in the case of a chemical that causes 1000 excess deaths in a population of hundreds of million). Second, society usually reduces risks that are high, thus limiting a true examination of its effects. Third, eliminating alternative causal explanations for environmental risks that take years to materialize is difficult. For these and other reasons, quantitative risk assessment is not as "objective" and value-free as one might first think.

The General Public's Perspective

Obtaining or estimating quantitative measures of environmental risk — such as levels of carbon monoxide in the air or chemicals in the drinking water — is one way to understand the surrounding environment in which we live. The general public, however, is less likely than scientists to have access to or to rely on "hard" environmental risk data to make a decision about an environmental issue. The lay public typically uses intuitive judgments (or perceptions of risk) to make such decisions. Moreover, lay attitudes and beliefs are influenced predominantly by mass media, not by scientific data (Slovic, 1987; Slovic, Fischhoff, & Lichtenstein, 1980). For example, a common perception among the general public is that human-made substances in the environment are the strongest predictors of cancer. In contrast, the scientific community reports that pollution and industrial products cause only about 3 percent of tumors, while lifestyle factors such as tobacco (30 percent) and diet (35 percent) are actually stronger predictors (Doll & Peto, 1981).

The divergence of expert and lay perceptions of environmental hazards frequently leads experts to ask the question: Why is the public so uninformed? (Fischhoff, Svenson, & Slovic, 1987). Regardless of the 'facts' about risk, lay as well as expert *perceptions* of the facts are important determinants of individual and community responses to the environment and to the development of public policy. In addition, it is often erroneous to consider expert opinions as objective and lay opinions as subjective. As Fischhoff et al. (1987) noted, "Objectivity is a goal of good science, rather than a characteristic of its product. . . . A better description of public–expert disagreements would be as conflicts between two sets of (inevitably subjective) judgments" (p. 1097). Robinson (1987) suggested that, in fact, workers are aware of many of the hazards they face in the workplace and are willing to engage in actions to reduce their risk. Moreover, hazardous workplaces are associated with greater dissatisfaction, absenteeism, strikes, and quit rates.

The general public, in contrast to the scientific community, generally believes that the risk today is less than it will be in the future and greater than it was in the past (Slovic, 1987). Furthermore, while experts view riskiness as a function of expected future mortality, the general public views riskiness in terms of "dread risk" (i.e., perceived lack of control, dread, catastrophic potential, fatal consequences) (Slovic, 1987). Factors with high "dread risk" scores include nuclear weapons or war, nerve gas accidents, and nuclear reactor accidents. Slovic wrote:

> Perhaps the most important message from this research is that there is wisdom as well as error in public attitudes and perceptions. Lay people sometimes lack

certain information about hazards. However, their basic conceptualization of risk is much richer than that of the experts and reflects legitimate concerns that are typically omitted from expert risk assessments. As a result, risk communication and risk management efforts are destined to fail unless they are structured as a two-way process. Each side, expert and public, has something valid to contribute. Each side must respect the insights and intelligence of the other. (p. 285)

Along similar lines, the former head of the Environmental Protection Agency, William Ruckelshaus (1983), issued a call for more citizen participation and for a closer relationship between scientists, public policymakers, and citizens. He wrote:

To effectively manage risk, we must seek new ways to involve the public in the decision-making process. Whether we believe in participatory democracy or not, it is a part of our social regulatory fabric. Rather than praise or lament it, we should seek more imaginative ways to involve the various segments of the public affected by the substance at issue. . . . For this to happen, scientists must be willing to take a larger role in explaining the risks to the public—including the uncertainties inherent in any risk assessment. Shouldering this burden is the responsibility of all scientists, not just those with a particular policy end in mind. . . . In a society in which democratic principles dominate, the perceptions of the public must be weighed. Instead of objective and subjective risks, the experts sometimes refer to real and imagined risks. There is a certain arrogance in this—an elitism that has ill served us in the past. (p. 1028)

To achieve the vision that Ruckelshaus sets forth, attention to principles from both psychology (e.g., risk perception, group dynamics, and communication) and public health (e.g., community mobilization, systems analysis, and epidemiology) is necessary.

Biases in environmental perceptions may occur because of limitations in humans' abilities to process information (Baum et al., 1981). People create simplified interpretations of the world to cope successfully with diverse information and events. In risky situations for which evidence and information are lacking, people are likely to rely on estimates of danger to reduce uncertainty. With a primary goal being to reduce uncertainty, these estimates may lead to biased judgments about risk.

The availability of risk information and images also affects risk perception. People are more likely to believe that an event will occur if they can readily recall or imagine it (thus, frequently occurring events are more "available"). Baum et al. suggested that this availability bias is particularly germane to rare events like Three Mile Island (TMI) because of the conflict it generates for the public. On the one hand, the public is exposed to stark and frequent images of the nuclear holocaust in the media. Juxtaposition to this are the statements they hear from scientists and politicians who argue that nuclear power is safe. In this scenario, the perception of a high likelihood that a nuclear problem will occur (i.e., availability) clearly influences public opinion, even though the hard "facts" may indicate that the likelihood is actually quite low. Similarly, the risk of dramatic events occurring (e.g., being exposed to nuclear fallout) is often overestimated relative to common events (e.g., being in an auto accident).

As noted previously, the media have a lot to do with how risks are perceived. Singer and Endreny (1987) monitored 15 media outlets (e.g., newspapers, magazines, television) over a four-month period in 1984 (and a four-week period in 1960) for stories dealing with hazards. They found that media tend not to cover the risks with the greatest effects on morbidity and mortality: "A rare hazard is more newsworthy than an old one, other things being equal; a new hazard is more newsworthy than an old one; and a dramatic hazard — one that kills many people at once, suddenly or mysteriously — is more newsworthy than a long-familiar illness" (p. 13). They suggested further that media are more likely to report on harms (e.g., property damage, illness, injury, death) than on risks (e.g., the likelihood of the hazard occurring) and little attention is given to benefits and the ratio of benefits to costs. These findings have important implications for our understanding of risk perceptions and how to change them since most people get their information about environmental risk from media sources.

Germane to this issue is an analysis of how the news media reported on the nuclear accidents at Three Mile Island (TMI) in the United States and at Chernobyl in the Soviet Union (Friedman, Gorney, & Egolf, 1987; Rubin, 1987). In analyses of news reports and interviews with a variety of people involved in these events, Rubin concluded that official sources presented overly optimistic reports and tended not to confirm bad news, did not have adequate systems for communication, and withheld important information (e.g., amount of radiation, the relationship between radiation and risk) (cf. Friedman et al., 1987). Rubin concluded that from the perspective of information dissemination, TMI was out of control until three full days after the accident.

The situation at Chernobyl, according to Rubin, was even worse. At comparable stages, the accident at TMI was a major world event while the accident at Chernobyl was only known to Soviet officials, individuals directly at the plant, and to a small number of other people (e.g., ham radio operators monitoring communications). Rubin's analysis suggests that the news media (and therefore the public) have been systematically restricted from valid information about nuclear accidents. Further, it has been suggested that risk communication and journalistic news are at odds with one another (Wilkens & Patterson, 1987). This position is taken by Wilkens and Patterson because news is based on novelty rather than situational analysis, is event- rather than systems-centered, is focused on "humanizing" stories, and does not translate mathematical risk very well (i.e., in terms that the lay public can understand). They cite the December 1984 chemical accident at Bhopal, India, and the Chernobyl crisis as supportive of this position.

As is evident when one considers the case of exposure to radon gas, other factors affect public perceptions of environmental risk. Radon, a radioactive gas present in soil, is perhaps the most serious indoor air pollutant and is thought to contribute to about 10 percent of the lung cancer cases in this country (Ames et al., 1987). Serious problems can occur when radon gas and the radioactive decay products it produces are trapped inside homes. According to one estimate, one million homes in the U.S. have levels of radon that exceed those received by uranium miners (Ames et al., 1987). Survey data from New Jersey (Sandman, Weinstein, & Klotz, 1987; Weinstein, Sandman & Klotz, 1987) suggest that people tend to overestimate the risk of radon exposure when it is perceived as foreign to their community and underestimate its risk when it occurs "naturally" in their homes. Weinstein et al. proposed several factors that may have contributed to these risk perceptions: (a) because radon has no color or smell, people have a difficult time understanding its risk; (b) because naturally occurring radon does not affect every home on a given block, people believe that their individual homes are safe; (c) people are more frightened by human-produced risks (e.g., toxic waste dumps) than by naturally occurring risks and feel less sense of control over such natural risks (unlike a risk brought into their community); (d) people tend to be frightened of radiation and of lung cancer; (e) the risk extends to all family members; and (f) the value of homes exposed to radon can be decreased substantially. There are two key points raised by this research. First, risk perceptions are complex and require careful assessment to understand them. Second, a valid understanding of risk is dependent on obtaining both objective and subjective measurements.

Slovic (1987) also emphasized that risk analysis researchers and policymakers should consider the "higher order impacts" of environmental events, since the effects of an event may have inconsequential direct effects (e.g., few deaths, injuries, material damage, monetary loss) but important ripple effects on institutions or the larger social order (e.g., litigation, regulatory policy, investor uneasiness, community opposition). The 1979 nuclear power plant accident at Three Mile Island (TMI) is a case in point. Although no one died and few contracted cancer as a result of this accident, the accident caused substantial monetary losses for the utility company that owned the power plant, a decline in the worldwide nuclear power industry (as a result of increased construction and operating costs and reduced operation of reactors), reliance on more expensive sources of energy (e.g., oil), and increased public opposition to nuclear power.

The disparity between expert and lay perceptions of environmental risk poses problems for people responsible for setting environmental health policy (Ames et al., 1987):

Because of the large background of low-level carcinogenic and other hazards, and the high costs of regulation, priority setting is a critical first step. It is important not to divert society's attention away from the few really serious hazards, such as tobacco or saturated fat (for heart disease), by pursuit of hundreds of minor or nonexistent hazards. Our knowledge is also more certain about the enormous toll of tobacco — about 350,000 deaths per year. . . . Obviously prudence is desirable with regard to pollution, but we need to work out some balance between chemophobia with its high costs to the national wealth, and sensible management of industrial chemicals. (p. 277)

Thus, research on risk perception and the communication of risk information has begun to identify how people process risk information. Leading researchers have noted, however, that more data need to be collected on what people know, what they want to know, how to express risks and consequences, and what ethical, legal, and political ramifications of communication programs should be considered (Slovic et al., 1980).

INTERSECTIONS BETWEEN PUBLIC HEALTH AND PSYCHOLOGY: RESPONSES TO ENVIRONMENTAL THREATS

The next section of the chapter explores potential intersections between psychology and public health with particular attention to the responses of individuals, organizations, and communities to environmental threats or problems. This discussion will focus on why and how these responses are evoked and their effects at different levels of analysis.

As with the other chapters in this book, the framework presented in chapter 2 will guide this discussion. While exposure to toxic substances is the primary example used, topics such as environmental stress (Baum, Singer & Baum, 1981; Evans & Cohen, 1987; Lazarus & Cohen, 1977) and conservation behavior (Cone & Hayes, 1977; Geller, Winett & Everett, 1982; Pitt & Zube, 1987; Stern & Oskamp, 1987; Winkler & Winett, 1982) could also serve as good examples of potential integration.

Overview

Understanding and changing environmental behavior is the central issue in the intersection between psychology and public health. In this chapter, environmental behavior is defined as including actions taken by citizens (e.g., wearing protective gear when using pesticides), organizations (e.g., policies regulating exposure to toxic chemicals), communities (e.g., laws regulating the storage and transfer of hazardous chemicals), nations (e.g., establishment of national regulatory agencies), and the global community (e.g., World Health Organization guidelines on environmental health).

Thus, the behaviors of individuals and institutions affect, and are affected by, the environment. To fully understand environmental health issues, therefore, one must understand the underlying behavioral patterns that affect and are influenced by the environment. Moreover, it is important to balance, through this integration, a quantitative approach to the environment with people's perceptions of and responses to the environment. In sum, we are interested in how exposure to toxic substances influences community dynamics and structures — such as social relationships, community conflict, sense of community, empowerment, and solidarity. We also move beyond a treatment focus (e.g., how does toxic exposure affect behavior?) to a comprehensive prevention focus (e.g., how can individuals and communities influence the decisions made on toxic production, use, monitoring, and exposure?).

There are several recent examples of public health and psychology being integrated around environmental issues. The field of behavioral toxicology (Fein, Schwartz, Jacobson & Jacobson, 1983; Weiss, 1983), for example, attempts to identify the behavioral effects of environmental hazards. In this chapter, we hope to advance this integration to include not only individual behavioral responses and the mental and physical health effects of environmental hazards but also the responses of organizations and communities to these hazards.

Toxins and the Publics' Health

Environmental hazards may be carcinogenic (i.e., cause cancer), mutagenic (i.e., cause a change in a gene, cell, or organ system), or teratogenic (i.e., cause a malformation in a fetus) (USDHHS, 1980). As outlined in USDHHS (1980), toxic agents and radiation can cause a variety of specific health effects including acute poisoning, impairment in growth, infertility, skin disorders, cancer, neurologic problems, behavioral problems, immunologic damage, and various chronic degenerative diseases. They also affect communities by causing explosions, fires, air and water pollution, odors, noise, traffic safety, declining property values, and overall quality of life (Anderson, 1987).

Over 4,000,000 compounds have been synthesized or isolated from naturally occurring materials, over 55,000 are produced commercially (with about 1,000 new compounds introduced each year), and in excess of 30,000 toxic solid waste disposal sites exist in the United States alone. Moreover, over 13,000 substances currently used are potentially toxic to workers; over 2,000 are suspected of causing cancer in laboratory animals (USDHHS, 1980). The statistics for hazardous waste are just as staggering. Nearly 300 million metric tons of waste are generated each year in the United States (Harris, English, & Highland, 1985). While hazardous waste disposal technologies exist, each year improper disposal causes major health and environmental problems. Neighborhoods and communities around the country are routinely and often unknowingly at risk of toxic exposure because of the frequent transport of toxic and hazardous materials on highways and streets and by rail, barge, or pipeline.

There are four primary strategies for managing hazardous waste (Carden, 1985; Sherry, 1985); (a) modify the waste so it can enter the environment safely (e.g., incineration, detoxification, neutralization, reaction, solidification, encapsulation, biological degradation); (b) store the waste so that it cannot enter the environment; (c) recycle the waste so that it can be used in another, safer form; and (d) eliminate the production of the waste. The most common method of managing waste, accounting for about 80 percent of regulated hazardous waste disposal, is land disposal (e.g., landfill, land farming, surface impoundments, waste piles) (Harris et al., 1985). As of 1980, on the order of 13,000 active hazardous and nonhazardous waste landfills existed in the United States (Anderson, 1987; Harris et al., 1985). Although the technology for handling hazardous waste seems straightforward, many problems in fact exist.

Case Studies

Love Canal

The story of Love Canal began in the late 1800s when William Love began a major construction project to link the lower and upper levels of the Niagara River near the falls (Carden, 1985; Hess & Wandersman, 1985; Levine & Stone, 1986; Stone & Levine, 1985). The project was terminated well in advance of completion, leaving about 1000 meters of an excavated canal. In the 1940s, Hooker Electrochemical Company purchased the canal and 16 surrounding acres and began disposing, legally, its chemical waste there. The area was viewed as an ideal disposal site because of the lack of human population and the surrounding geology which served to contain the wastes to the canal. Over an 11-year period, 21,000 tons of chemicals were deposited in the canal. In 1953, Hooker Electrochemical Company sold the site for one dollar to the Niagara Falls School Board. According to Carden (1985), Hooker wanted the site to be used only for a park with the school built on an adjacent site. Because Hooker's request was overruled, they noted on the deed that chemicals were buried there, thereby relinquishing (so they thought) any responsibility for damage or injuries that might result. Before the school opened its doors, almost 13,000 cubic meters of the canal were removed and a sewer line was installed. By the mid-1970s, the caps and sides of the canal trenches were thinned or breached from construction and from the removal of fill. By 1976, these factors contributed to the leakage of chemicals. By the time that leakage was detected, about 1,000 families lived within a 10 block area surrounding the canal. A grass roots group was formed (Love Canal Homeowner's Association) to provide social support and information and to serve as an advocate for the concerns of local residents.

Three Mile Island

Three Mile Island (TMI) is a nuclear power station located near Harrisburg, Pennsylvania. In 1979, a partial meltdown of the radioactive fuel rods in one of the two reactors occurred unexpectedly and caused radioactive contamination of the reactor building, the containment building surrounding the reactor, and the atmosphere. These events led to the temporary evacuation of 144,000 residents and significant unrest in the community as well as the nation at large (Baum, Fleming, & Singer, 1982; Black, 1987; Davidson et al., 1986; Hartsough & Savitsky, 1984).

Jackson Township, New Jersey

In the Legler section of Jackson Township, New Jersey, Glidden Paint Company had historically mined minerals for its products (Edelstein & Wandersman, 1987; Gibbs, 1986). During the 1970s, the abandoned mine site was used as a toxic waste landfill. The landfill apparently was not very carefully monitored; by 1978, residents of the suburban community that had sprung up around the site were informed that their water supply was contaminated. For two years, 300 residents could drink only bottled water. A newly formed grassroots organization, the Concerned Citizens Committee, subsequently won an award of more than $15 million from the Township (which, as of 1987, was being appealed).

These three case studies will be used to illustrate how principles from psychology and public health can improve our understanding of environmental problems.

Responses to Environmental Hazards

Individual Level Responses

Considerable debate on the physical health effects of hazardous sites has and will continue to occur. There is little debate that Love Canal residents were exposed to a variety of chemicals. The health effects of this exposure, as collected through surveys and epidemiological surveillance, however, are equivocal. Surveys completed or commissioned by residents are somewhat more likely to detect health problems due to exposure than surveys completed by the government (Anderson, 1987). Taken together, the data suggest that some physical health problems were more common (e.g., low-birthweight babies, brain tumors) but for most reported health problems, statistically significant differences were not found. Anecdotal evidence indicates that widespread and diverse mental health problems were evident among Love Canal residents. Similarly, Gibbs (1986) surveyed residents of Jackson Township, New Jersey, several years after the toxic waste problem was identified. She reported that residents exhibited higher than normal levels of stress, external locus of control, health concern, generalized psychopathology, and depression. As with data from Love Canal and other toxic waste sites, it is apparent, and perhaps not surprising, that both mental and physical health problems are caused by environmental hazards.

Extensive data on the health effects in the aftermath of the accident at the TMI nuclear power plant (Baum, Fleming, & Singer, 1982; Davidson et al., 1986) show little evidence that chronic disease rates increased as a result of the accident. Other health effects, however, have been documented. For example, Davidson and colleagues reported that even two years after the accident, residents exhibited higher levels of stress responses (as measured by psychological, behavioral, and biochemical indices) than people living in control communities. They also reported that TMI residents perceived having less control over their environment and overall experienced more helplessness.

Davidson et al. (1986) and Baum et al. (1982) also reported data collected several days prior to, during, and several months after plant officials released radioactive krypton gas into the atmosphere through a controlled venting procedure (this occurred about 15 months after the accident). These investigators were asked by the Nuclear Regulatory Commission to provide a report on the potential effects on stress of venting radioactive gas into the atmosphere. Briefly, there was a paradox between the options available. The option that would achieve the quickest cleanup (venting into the atmosphere) was also the option most likely to be viewed by residents as a threat to health and safety. The options viewed by residents as the safest (e.g., absorption systems, gas compression, cryogenic systems), would require the most time for cleanup (up to four years).

Thus, Baum et al. identified the key issue in the selection of an option as a tradeoff between acute and chronic stress. They hypothesized that symptoms of chronic stress would be apparent among residents of TMI but that venting would likely result in an increase in acute (short-term and anticipatory) stress and not have an effect on chronic (long-term) stress. They based these hypotheses on the following: (a) risk perception research indicating that radiation generates significant emotional response among the general public; (b) risk perception research indicating that the general public generally believes that nuclear facilities are dangerous; and (c) survey research after the accident indicating that there was a great deal of uncertainty and confusion among the general public about the "facts" surrounding the incident (due to poor communication with the government, scientists, and public policymakers).

Across psychological, behavioral, and biochemical measures of stress, Baum et al. reported data confirming their hypothesis that venting increased acute levels of stress but not chronic stress. Even so, they also found that, overall, residents of TMI, compared to other communities, exhibited more symptoms of chronic stress. In several respects, this research is important to our exploration of the potential for integration of psychology and public health. First, it took into account some aspects of the social context of TMI by being sensitive to historical factors that took place in the community. Second, the evaluation included an assessment of effects at multiple levels and brought to bear research on social cognition, attitude change, and environmental policy. Even so, some of the effects on community-level variables were not assessed (e.g., effects on perceived quality of community life, citizen participation, sense of community, etc.).

Community Level Responses

Once a community recognizes that it has a toxic exposure or waste problem, a variety of attitudes, emotions, behaviors, and events are triggered. The typical response is, "not in my neighborhood." People recognize that toxic waste is produced in this country and that a place to dispose of it is necessary. However, they do not want it disposed near them. When the government selects a community for a waste site, more often than not the community response is negative, feelings of mistrust are common, and people perceive the decision as a threat to their well being (cf. Bachrach & Zautra, 1986).

Many communities around the country have formed citizen action groups to deal with such environmental threats. A survey of some of these organizations found that members were from diverse sociodemographic groups and generally believed that they could achieve social change, even against numerous obstacles (i.e., they were empowered). Moreover, these organizations were generally savvy about accessing diverse sources of information. These sources included, for example, direct observation, media reports, government reports, first-hand investigations, attendance at conferences and meetings, networking with other citizen action groups, and contact with scientific experts (Freudenberg, 1984).

A general process framework that explores community responses to toxic exposure has been proposed by Edelstein and Wandersman (1987) (see Figure 10.1). This framework is described below because it highlights the importance of viewing toxic problems from multiple levels of analysis and in terms of its ecological embeddedness in the community. The first stage of their model, community turbulence, is characterized by uncertainties about health risks, environmental damage, personal and community costs, foci of responsibility, and potential solutions. Because everyday life is disrupted by such turbulence, people begin to engage in coping strategies such as seeking

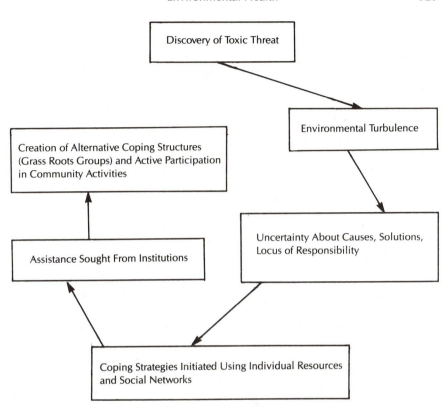

Adapted from "Community Dynamics in Coping With Toxic Contaminants," by M. R. Edelstein and A. Wandersman. In *Neighborhood and Community Environments: Human Behavior and Environment* (vol. 9), edited by I. Altman and A. Wandersman (pp. 69–112) (New York: Plenum, 1987).

FIGURE 10.1. Community Responses to Toxic Contamination

assistance from social networks of friends and family or from institutional networks such as local government. These networks are often of limited value to the victims. In seeking support from social networks, for example, victims may find that people outside of the situation have difficulty relating to what they are experiencing, are personally threatened by being close to the toxic waste problem, and may unwittingly engage in "blaming the victim" (e.g., you should not have moved into that neighborhood). Institutional networks also cannot meet all of the needs of victims. Institutions can lead victims to believe they have no control or power to make decisions and can prevent victims from gaining access to information by imposing on them complex bureaucratic structures and procedures.

Because of the deficiencies in social and institutional networks, victims may attempt to create alternative coping structures such as grass roots community organizations of victims. These grass roots groups tend to be developed on the basis of spatial boundaries (e.g., defined by the area of toxic exposure) and can provide residents with social support, a feeling of being connected to others in the community, trusted information, self-efficacy, and a sense of community empowerment, and may serve as a bridge between formal and informal community support systems.

Edelstein and Wandersman (1987) go on to propose a process of participation in community organizations formed in response to toxic contamination. Essentially, this process characterizes a community in terms of its environmental characteristics (e.g., density), ecological characteristics (e.g., size, geographic boundaries), and social characteristics (e.g., social networks, norms). These community variables, along with individual variables (e.g., demographics), affect the characteristics of the community organization developed (e.g., in terms of structure, function, relationships with formal community institutions, and so forth) and in turn the types of citizen participation fostered. Participation, through feedback loops and at multiple levels, affects the community organization as well as the community at large.

The beauty of Edelstein and Wandersman's characterization is its sensitivity to the complexities in communities exposed to environmental hazards and its facilitation of an analysis of effects and intervention possibilities at multiple levels of analysis. Thus, by creating turbulence in a community, environmental hazards contribute to the development of community organizations whose intent it is to create community stability and to help develop action plans to rectify the problem. Based on their experiences in Legler, New Jersey, Edelstein and Wandersman suggested that toxic incidents serve both to bring communities together and to split them apart (i.e., their effects are dialectical).

Public health professionals have identified a complementary process, the issue-attention cycle, to explain the actions taken to decrease or prevent environmental problems (Downs, 1972, as reported in Sewell, 1980). This process, which emphasizes societal responses more than the process outlined by Edelstein and Wandersman, has five stages: (a) pre-problem, in which only experts and special interest groups recognize that a problem exists; (b) alarmed discovery and euphoric enthusiasm, in which a problem becomes a legitimate social concern through a sensational event, disaster, or politics; (c) recognition of the cost of solving the problem in which society realizes that the problem requires significant resources to rectify and may come at the expense of doing something else; (d) gradual decline of interest during which time other issues grab the interest of the public; and (e) post-problem, during which time the problem is not of public concern.

This cycle was elaborated upon further by Sewell (1980) who proposed a heuristic model to help explain the pace and direction of action taken on environmental problems. In this model, Sewell proposed nine broad factors affecting the attention directed toward an environmental problem. These factors include (a) nature of the issue (e.g., the larger the scope of the problem, the more attention it will receive); (b) implications for the attainment of other social goals; (c) number of contending interests; (d) perceived threats to existing institutions; (e) the number of levels of jurisdiction (e.g., resolution of problems increases in difficulty as the number of levels of jurisdiction increases); (f) the distance of the decision-maker from the locus of the problem (e.g., action is more likely to be taken if the decision-maker(s) are close to the problem); (g) availability of technology; (h) urgency for action; and (i) division of scientific opinion.

In summary, these two perspectives on community response to environmental hazards suggest that community organizations are formed because of a common goal that serves to tie people together. As with any social group, intergroup conflict is bound to occur in community organizations. In the case of citizen action groups established to address environmental threats, several sources of friction can be identified: tensions between the needs of individuals or families and of the community (as represented by the community organization); lack of commitment to the organization beyond a narrow issue (e.g., legal action against the company owning the toxic waste site); differences in the activities of the organization; and mistrust among group members.

There is general consensus that for a community to deal effectively with environmental hazards, community activism (i.e., concerned, informed, and active citizens) is a prerequisite (Sherry, 1985). Sherry argued that citizens, as well as government and industry representatives, are essential components to an overall strategy. There are numerous examples of communities who have dealt successfully with environmental hazards by involving citizen groups who have questioned authority and taken an active interest in problem identification and resolution (Sherry, 1985).

Interviews with a sample of Love Canal residents illustrate the types of citizens who become active in such groups (Stone & Levine, 1985; Levine & Stone, 1986). Stone and Levine reported that activist families, compared to nonactivist families, tended to be younger and to have fewer children, higher levels of education, and higher incomes. Activist families were more likely to perceive their health being worse than it was a few years ago and to believe that their homes were unsafe. Interestingly, activists were less likely to report negative effects as a result of the crisis. It appeared that the social relationships of activists changed more than those of nonactivists (e.g., activists were more likely to report both a loss of friends and the development of new friendships as a result of the crisis). For all people interviewed, it was clearly evident that the toxic waste problem affected all aspects of their lives, including family and social relationships, perceived health, quality of life, and the property values of homes.

Once a toxic waste problem is identified, the first question confronted concerns what should be done to clear up the problem and to minimize its impact. The second question confronted concerns what people who may have been exposed should be told.

The Right to Know: What Should People Be Told About Toxins?

The public health and public policy communities have spent considerable time debating the merits and costs of notifying workers who have been exposed to toxic substances (Ashford & Caldart, 1985; Bayer, 1986; Cohen, Colligan, & Berger, 1985; Robinson, 1987; Ruttenberg & Powers, 1986). The issues raised in this debate could and should also be applied to toxic waste problems in communities at large. In short, the right-to-know issue refers to the sharing of information between those who have the information (usually manufacturers) and those who do not (usually company employees or citizens). The working assumption underlying the provision of risk information is that the health of people exposed will be improved (Ashford & Caldart, 1985). The key issues in this debate include questions about the locus of responsibility, what level of exposure warrants notification, when and how notification should occur, how much information and what type of information is sufficient, who has the inherent right to information, what remedies are available to workers who are notified, and whether notification could actually cause mental or physical health problems (Bayer, 1986). Grobstein (1983) argued that scientists would be remiss if they withheld information about risks because of discomfort about imperfections in their data. He suggested that data are never incontrovertible and that scientists' responsibility is to communicate the level of certainty and how the level can be increased — that is, to provide the best available advice recognizing that uncertainty will exist.

The integrative perspective promoted in this book would extend these points in that the issues surrounding risk notification are not only informational, political, ethical, and economic but also psychological (cf. Cohen et al., 1985; Fessenden-Raden, Fitchen & Heath, 1987). While the law requires that health risk information be communicated to workers at risk (Cohen et al., 1985), there seem to be minimal guidelines as to how this information should be presented. Moreover, most companies that communicate risk information to their employees are driven strictly by concerns about technical accuracy and legal liability and not with how people receive and process the information (Cohen et al., 1985; Fessenden-Raden, Fitchen & Heath, 1987). Ideally (and perhaps unrealistically), however, developers and implementers of risk communication strategies and messages would have a sophisticated understanding of communication science and psychology and recognize that community-level factors (e.g., attitudes toward local government and polluters, community structure) affect risk perceptions and subsequent actions

(Fessenden-Raden et al., 1987). Specifically, they should understand how information is processed, interpreted, and acted upon and what factors influence the efficacy of different communication strategies (Winett, 1986; see also chapter 4). Such an understanding would undoubtedly affect how and what information is actually presented to people exposed to toxins. The social psychology literature on the effects of information on patients' adjustment to medical procedures (e.g., Taylor & Clark, 1986) may be relevant to the provision of environmental risk information to workers and communities.

In a review of numerous studies on this topic, Taylor and Clark provided the following conclusions about what and how information should be given to patients undergoing medical procedures:

1. There is no risk in providing information to patients who are willing to receive information.
2. Information can be in the form of describing expected sensations, procedures, or both.
3. Additional benefits can be derived if coping techniques or behavioral instruction is combined with information.
4. Provision of some sensation information is beneficial to adjustment.
5. Information can be provided by various people, and is most effective when an empathic demeanor is taken.
6. Although there are limited data on the timing, length, and repetitiveness of information, there is some evidence that lengthy messages may be overwhelming and that repetition is desirable.
7. The way the material is presented (face-to-face, slide show, or other means) does not alter message effectiveness.
8. Effectiveness is increased if patients are given the opportunity to ask questions.
9. To evaluate the effectiveness of the provision of information, multiple evaluation measures are necessary.

The key point of this discussion is that individual and community responses to environmental hazards are dependent in large part on information (cf. Mattson, Pollack, & Cullen, 1987). If risk communicators do not communicate effectively or are not credible sources of information, individual and community responses will be affected adversely. We suggest that psychological research on the effects of information on cognitions and behavior and on the adjustment to threatening events would contribute substantively to the "right to know" movement in environmental public health by helping researchers and practitioners better understand how, what, and why certain beliefs and behaviors about toxic hazards are evident and what can be done to alter them (Winett, 1986). In addition, obtaining a better understanding of the role that media plays in the web of information dissemination is critical in this regard. Furthermore, risk communication should be viewed as a dynamic process of interactions between receivers and senders rather than a one-way transfer of information at a single point in time (Fessenden-Raden, et al., 1987).

To address some of the concerns about risk communication, the National Institute of Occupational Safety and Health (NIOSH) developed a set of 14 guidelines for the development of health risk messages (Cohen et al., 1985). They are good examples of the type of integration we have suggested (e.g., "integrating health risk messages with other information/educational activities"; "fitting messages to the demographic make-up of the target audience"; "designating credible sources of information"; "balancing fear arousal in hazard messages with actions that can control risk"; "enhancing the meaning of quantitative measures of health risk"; "directing messages through as many channels of the existing social/communications network as is feasible"; and "providing means for evaluating the effect of the message in meeting its intended goals").

A complementary perspective was offered by Bachrach and Zautra (1986), who suggested that psychologists could contribute significantly to the process of selecting the location of toxic waste sites. Specifically, they argued that psychologists could facilitate meetings between the government and communities, train government officials in human relations skills and conflict resolution, and provide alternatives to discussing these sensitive issues in large community forums. Such strategies could help to prevent from occurring some of the problems related to community responses to toxic waste. Bachrach and Zautra went on to suggest that involving psychologists in the environmental impact statement process has the additional potential for minimizing stress-induced health problems once the site becomes operational.

Hess (1985), however, expressed some doubts about the ability of psychologists to assist people who have actually experienced an environmental catastrophe. This viewpoint is based on the limited experience most clinical psychologists have with events that occur in the physical environment. He noted that many clinicians focus predominantly on intrapsychic issues (behavior therapy is of course one exception). Taken together, the work of Bachrach and Zautra and Hess suggest that while there probably is an important role that psychologists could serve in environmental health, additional training or concrete experiences would be beneficial for many psychologists.

USING THE BOOK'S FRAMEWORK TO ANALYZE ENVIRONMENTAL HAZARDS

The final section of this chapter uses the framework developed in chapter 2 and the discussion in this chapter of integrating psychological and public health perspectives to analyze the topic of environmental health.

Problem Definition and Levels of Analysis

The problem of environmental health is certainly on the minds of many people. The problem can and should be conceptualized at multiple levels of analysis. As reviewed throughout this chapter, the problems caused by environmental toxins are evident among individuals, in social relationships, organizations, communities, states, nations, and the world at large. The problems caused by environmental hazards are related to mental health, physical health, organizational functioning, economics, politics, and ultimately to the survival of the human race.

By and large, scientists and policymakers have directed most of their attention to how environmental hazards affect physical health rather than to how they influence mental health or the quality of life for individuals and communities (exceptions to this were noted previously). There also appears to be a bias toward conceptualizing environmental health in terms of secondary prevention or treatment rather than primary prevention. Primary prevention is certainly discussed in terms of technological innovations to prevent environmental problems (e.g., effective landfill technology) but there is considerably less attention directed at the development of strategies to equip individuals and communities with resources to prevent environmental problems from occurring in the first place. We believe that the study of environmental health problems could be advanced with a redefinition of the problem so as to incorporate a primary prevention orientation. Such a redefinition would mean that researchers, policymakers, and community activists would examine how environmental health problems could be prevented at multiple levels of analysis and not just through technological strategies.

The apparent bias toward a technological understanding of environmental hazards is important to consider; the accident at TMI is a case in point (Saegert, 1987). Saegert noted that the safety of TMI was guaranteed by engineers, with the blessing of government officials, through the technological design of fail-safe systems. Before the accident, nuclear power plant officials thought very little about how to deal with problems that extended beyond the actual facility. Apparently, they reasoned that fail-safe engineering would guarantee that problems beyond the grounds of nuclear facilities would not occur. As has been documented, however, the issues raised by nuclear power plant production extend beyond "hard" technology into quality of life. Nuclear power generated complex effects and issues (positive as well as negative): community distrust in government officials, fear among residents living near plants, public disapproval (or, at least, annoyance) about the nuclear power industry, community upheaval and disintegration, citizen participation, breakdown in social relationships, economic hardship for all parties involved, monumental changes in the worldwide nuclear power industry, safer designs and regulatory policies, to name several. Obviously, generating energy from nuclear power creates more than just engineering challenges.

As Saegert and others have noted, the events that transpired at TMI and other sites illustrate that environmental events, psychological responses, behavior, health, economics, history, ethics, and politics are intertwined and inseparable aspects of environmental issues. Saegert argued further that resolution of the complex issues raised by nuclear power is not likely to be easy, because our understanding of environmental issues changes regularly. She noted that the effects of environmental conditions on different constituencies result in competing goals and thus in both benefits and costs for any decision made. She went on to suggest that our focus should be an effort to understand the dimensions of uncertainty that underlie the relationship between individuals and environments.

As with many of the other health issues raised in this book, tensions among the competing goals of individuals, communities, and institutions often underlie how a particular health issue is defined and acted upon. For environmental health issues, these tensions center around individual vs. community vs. societal needs, community vs. institutional control, right-to-know vs. right-to-control-information, short-term gain vs. long-term costs, and health vs. economic goals. Economic tensions are particularly salient in environmental health. Because there are limitations in the amount of money that can be used to protect the environment as well as in the technology available to do so, society has difficult decisions to make relative to the tradeoffs between health and safety benefits and the cost for achieving such benefits (Seneca, 1987).

The point here is that environmental health issues must be viewed with respect to their embeddedness in complex environmental and social systems and in terms of the tradeoffs that are a part of any environmental decision. Embeddedness refers to the fact that a phenomenon is influenced by a surrounding set of events and circumstances (Stokols, 1987). For example, the risk perceptions and risk-related behaviors of individuals and communities are influenced by complex and multilevel factors. These factors include how the media and risk communicators shape and influence risk perceptions; how psychological and other "subjective" dimensions affect risk perceptions and responses; how historical factors (e.g., previous individual or community responses to hazards) affect responses to a current situation; and so forth. An environmental manipulation of one variable in an ecologically embedded system will have effects on other parts of the system. Thus, environmental events are best understood and intervened upon if professionals cross their traditional disciplinary boundaries (our interest here, of course, pertains to psychologists and public health professionals crossing boundaries). Doing so will increase the likelihood that valid detection of complex, multilevel, and ecologically embedded environmental phenomena will occur. An example of a multilevel intervention matrix incorporating this perspective is illustrated in Table 10.2.

Table 10.2. Strategies to Prevent/Control Exposure to Toxic Substances
By Levels of Analysis

Personal

- Increase understanding of environmental risks
- Increase behavioral skills to diagnose problem and to protect oneself from exposure to toxins
- Increase motivation to participate in community activities to prevent or limit exposure
- Increase control over environmental events

Interpersonal

- Increase bonds between community residents
- Increase participation in community organizations
- Establish environmental citizen action groups
- Educate scientists on public perceptions of environmental risk
- Increase communication between citizens and policymakers

Organizational/Environmental

- Educate the media on environmental hazards and their presentation
- Develop effective risk communication campaigns
- Develop policies to regulate exposure to toxins
- Establish procedures for cleaning up environmental hazards
- Develop emergency evacuation procedures
- Make available health care services for exposed individuals

Institutional/Societal

- Establish guidelines or laws on acceptable levels of exposure
- Conduct quantitative analysis studies to assess environmental risk
- Maintain environmental hazard surveillance systems
- Develop and implement technologies to prevent toxic exposure
- Earmark money to clean up toxic waste sites

Expanding the Conceptualization of Environmental Health

To achieve this expanded definition and multilevel analysis of environmental health, advancing currently used theoretical formulations is necessary. As mentioned previously, theory development in environmental psychology has contributed to our understanding of environment and behavior and therefore is reviewed below as it pertains to environmental hazards.

I. Altman and Rogoff (1987) reviewed four primary philosophical orientations that have influenced psychological research and theory. These orientations have been termed *trait* (i.e., a focus on intrapsychic processes); *interactional* (i.e., intrapsychic and environmental factors are viewed as separate but interacting entities); *organismic* (i.e., although intrapsychic and environmental entities are viewed as separate, the whole is seen as more than the sum of its parts); and *transactional* (i.e., entities are viewed holistically and as a confluence of people, space, and time).

The transactional orientation has particular relevance to this discussion for the following reasons. First, it focuses on events. Events are composed of the confluence of people (i.e., psychological processes), space (social as well as physical), and time. As Wapner (1987) noted, a transactional perspective considers the unit of analysis to be the person-in-environment system. By focusing on events in this way, environmental health researchers and practitioners would be more likely to understand the diverse aspects of a particular environmental event. To date, much of the work on environmental hazards has not incorporated such a systems perspective and instead has focused on the physical environment and its effects on physical health. In short, we are promoting here a theory that is sensitive to the context surrounding an environmental hazard. A contextual perspective would include consideration of psychologically relevant aspects of the environment, the temporal process of activities (e.g., activities, processes, and changes rather than states), and how the setting relates to other life domains of people.

Second, this perspective would foster attempts to understand an environmental hazard from the perspective of the people who are integrally a part of the hazard (i.e., from an insider's perspective). This would include not only the people exposed to the hazard but also officials responsible for regulating and managing systems related to the hazard. This orientation is consistent with some of the points raised previously on subjective risk analysis.

Third, transactional theory can guide the development of measurement strategies and research designs sensitive to the specific environmental hazard of interest. That is, the use of standardized instruments developed for cross-setting use would not typically be the most desirable choice. If one accepts an event as the unit of analysis, then measures of the person-in-environment must necessarily be tailored to specific events. This is not to say that standardized instruments and designs should not be used. Rather, they should be supplemented with those that are sensitive to the specific event of interest. The above discussion on transactional theory is an example of how one theoretical perspective could help in the reconceptualization of environmental health problems.

Goal Specification

As noted previously, communication of risk to the general public and to individuals at risk of environmental hazards and the resulting effect on risk-related behaviors have become key issues in the field of environmental health. Research on risk perceptions and communication would ideally provide decision-makers with information with which to design effective risk communication programs. The goals of this work should be multidimensional in the sense that changes in awareness, knowledge, behavior, social norms, and public policy could all be desired outcomes. The ideas on effective health communication presented in chapter 4 and in Winett (1986) are certainly relevant in this regard.

Intervention

A variety of strategies to prevent health problems caused by toxics have been proposed (see USDHHS, 1980, for an overview). The strategies include increasing the biologic and epidemiologic knowledge base; delivering educational programs to the general public and to individuals, organizations, and communities at risk; providing effective health care services; improving relevant technology; and adopting legislative, regulatory, and economic measures in the best interests of the public.

In terms of handling toxic waste, for example, the dominant paradigm seems to be focusing on technological solutions directed at the source of an environmental hazard. Psychologists who study toxic waste, in contrast, tend to focus their attention on how individuals and communities can develop or access resources to help them cope with the problem after it has developed (e.g., social support, financial assistance). The dual track of altering the hazard and helping equip individuals and communities with necessary coping skills is a strategy that emanates directly from an integration of psychology and public health.

Along these lines, one of the key factors that seems to be related to individual and community health is control and connectedness between individuals and their environments (Lindheim & Syme, 1983). Lindheim and Syme state:

> The findings . . . have as a common element the importance to health of being connected: being connected with others, being connected with one's biological and cultural heritage. . . . Thus, no matter how elegantly wrought a physical solution, no matter how efficiently designed a factory, no matter how safe and sanitary a building—unless people can, in some way, create, manage, change, or participate in activities that affect their lives, dissatisfaction, alienation, or even illness are likely outcomes. (p. 354)

Other factors related to successful coping and health status include perceiving a sense of control of one's destiny (Edelstein & Wandersman, 1987; Wallston, Wallston, Smith, & Dobbins, 1987), feeling empowered to cope with the problem (Rappaport, 1987), and feeling part of a larger community that can provide support (e.g., a sense of community) (McMillan & Chavis, in press). The point here is that too much attention on either the source of the problem (toxics) or on the response to the problem will result in a less than optimal response to program resolution. Thus, interventions directed at the stressor as well as at responses to the stressor are needed. For some environmental problems, one approach may be more appropriate than another. For example, if technology to reduce leakage of toxic waste into groundwater is not available, other non-technological solutions must be used. For many environmental problems, however, attention to one approach at the expense of another will likely result in the design of less than optimal interventions. To achieve this integration, psychologists (or other social scientists) and public health professionals must bring their strengths and collective expertise to bear on the issue. For instance, combining public health education strategies for supplying people with accurate information about environmental risks, as well as teaching people behavioral skills to reduce risk (e.g., routinely testing drinking water) might lead to more effective community responses than if either public education or behavioral skills training were used alone (cf. McGuire, 1980; Winett, 1986).

In particular, the use of behavioral strategies to prevent environmental problems (Geller, 1986, 1987; Winett et al., 1982, 1985) could advance the field of environmental health. A behavioral approach focuses primary attention on the specific target behavior of interest (e.g., littering) and attempts to manipulate environmental stimuli and response contingencies associated with the behavior. The goal is to either increase the frequency of the desired behavior or to decrease the occurrence of undesirable behaviors. Changing attitudes, beliefs, or values directly is not a primary focus although it certainly is an outcome.

Behavioral strategies typically focus on antecedent or consequence strategies or both (Geller, 1986). Antecedent strategies are those that occur prior to the target behavior and include the provision of information or education, modeling, goal setting or commitment strategies, and engineering and design technology. As reviewed by Geller, research on antecedent strategies has been successful across a variety of target behaviors (e.g., seat belt use, littering, energy conservation, recycling). Several key information and educational strategies associated with effectiveness have been identified. These include tailoring messages to the specific target behavior, offering convenient alternative desirable behaviors when the goal is to decrease the occurrence of undesirable behaviors, avoiding strategies that threaten perceived freedom, and delivering messages close in time to the target behavior of interest.

Consequence strategies, which provide pleasant or unpleasant consequences, serve as contingencies for the occurrence of particular behaviors (Geller, 1986). Contingencies may be in the form of contingencies or other tangible rewards (e.g., monetary rebate), opportunities to engage in positive behaviors (e.g., getting a preferred parking space), punishment (e.g., fines for littering), or negative consequences (e.g., information that energy use is unacceptably high). In a variety of settings, research has shown that the provision of specific and frequent feedback influences behavior (Winett et al., 1982; 1985). In addition, positive or negative consequences may be contingent on particular responses (e.g., installing insulation on a water heater) or on particular outcomes (e.g., reduction in amount of gas used to heat a water heater) (Winett et al., 1982; 1985). Although behavioral strategies to prevent environmental problems have a track record of success and hold great potential, evaluating their overall utility is limited by the lack of information about their long-term effectiveness, their applicability to certain environmental issues (e.g., toxic waste, air pollution, population explosion), and the relative lack of attention to systems and ecological concerns (Geller, 1986).

SUMMARY

Taken together, the work of both psychologists and public health professionals suggests that environmental problems are likely to be dealt with most effectively if they are conceptualized and intervened upon from an ecological and multilevel perspective. As reviewed throughout this chapter, the resolution of environmental problems has been conceptualized from a variety of theoretical and conceptual orientations including risk perception, behavior analysis, organizational change, community mobilization, systems analysis, and societal change. As with the other health issues reviewed in this book, there is no intervention or intervention strategy that is a panacea. The integrative perspective promoted here would argue for an approach that combined aspects of each of the available perspectives in a systematic, conceptually sound manner. Since environmental problems have diverse causes, the solutions applied to the problem must be equally diverse and attention to ecological embeddedness is critical. Our hope is that the use of this perspective will help alleviate current environmental problems and help to prevent future threats to the environment and thus to public health.

11
Processes of Aging: Enhancement of the Later Years

Contributed by Steven B. Lovett

INTRODUCTION

The elderly comprise one of the fastest growing segments of our society. Adults 65 years of age and older accounted for only 4% of the population in 1900. By 1980, there were over 25.12 million older adults comprising 11.3% of the country's population (Phillips & Gaylord, 1985). It is projected that older adults will account for 21.1% of the United States population by the year 2030 (Phillips & Gaylord, 1985). In contrast, the under-65 population will increase by only 15%. The notable increase in the population of older adults has had a tremendous impact on the health care needs and expenditures of this country. Expenditures for adults 65 years of age and older currently account for approximately 30% of the national health budget (Friedman & Haynes, 1985) and over 25% of the total federal budget. What's more, these expenditures will continue to increase.

In spite of these compelling reasons for focusing the efforts of public health and health psychology professionals on older adults, very little attention has been given to the population until relatively recently. As noted in chapter 1, the American Public Health Association has existed since the late 1800s but did not establish a section on aging until 1978. Most of the work done with the older population has focused on two major issues: (a) the financial stresses placed on the nation's health care system by the rising proportion of older adults in the population and (b) the need to provide supportive services to those older adults who are unable to meet their own needs of daily living. Considerable data collection and analysis have been done to predict the health care needs of older adults into the next century (Estes & Lee, 1986). In addition, an elaborate system of supportive services for older adults has been established as a result of the Older Americans Act and its amendments (Ruchlin & Braham, 1987) though relatively little evaluation of these programs has occurred. In contrast to other public health initiatives (e.g., the prevention of cardiovascular disease — Hanlon & Pickett, 1984), strategies emphasizing disease prevention and health promotion for older adults have been slow to appear. Phillips & Gaylord (1985) have stated that current public health efforts on behalf of older adults are fragmented, inefficient, and being pursued in an uncoordinated fashion. Currently available methods for preventing, delaying, or lessening the impact of disability associated with aging are not being used to their fullest extent.

Historically, psychologists have focused much of their attention on changes in perceptual and cognitive functioning related to aging (cf. Botwinick, 1984). Since the mid-1970s, there has been an enormous increase in both the amount and variety of research focused on older adults (Birren & Schaie, 1985). In response to the increased research activity on aging, the American Psychological Association initiated the journal *Psychology and Aging* in 1987. Unfortunately, the area of health psychology has not yet reflected this surge of interest in aging. Many of the interventions developed for such things as weight control, smoking cessation, exercise maintenance, and other health-related behaviors could be usefully applied to older adults. Additionally, work done with older adults in areas such as coping have potential relevance to health issues. As is true in public health, psychological efforts relevant to the health needs of older adults have been pursued in a fragmented, unsystematic manner.

Although the fields of public health and psychology have only recently formalized their interests in older adults, the fields of geriatrics and gerontology have been active for some time. The American Geriatrics Society was founded in 1942 by physicians interested in geriatric medicine. Three years later, an interdisciplinary group that has become known as the Gerontological Society of America (GSA) was formed. GSA currently has sections focusing on behavioral and psychological sciences, social science and policy, biological sciences, and medical sciences. These two organizations have provided a forum for individuals of many disciplines to pursue their interests related to gerontology. Although research and service programs germane to the health issues of older adults have grown out of this work, again no commonly accepted set of goals and objectives have been established. It is also our belief that the fields of psychology and public health could greatly advance current efforts in the field by joining with the professionals of other disciplines to identify a coherent and comprehensive strategy for addressing the health needs of older adults.

It is important to acknowledge the reasons why older adults have not attracted greater attention among public health professionals, psychologists, and other health professionals until relatively recently. Many of the reasons reflect a variety of inaccurate stereotypes and negative attitudes commonly exhibited toward the elderly (Butler, 1980). Some of these stereotypes, as they relate to health issues, include:

• Being sick is just part of growing old, so it is useless to try and prevent illness in older adults.
• Older people are "stuck in their ways" and would not engage in health-related programs anyway.
• Older people are depressing to work with (no one wants to be reminded that they will be old someday!).

Fortunately, these myths and misunderstandings about the aging process are beginning to be dispelled. For instance, recent survey data indicate that, contrary to popular belief, most older adults consider themselves to be in good or excellent health (Kovar, 1986). Medical research has shown that certain types of physiologic decline previously assumed to be part of normal aging are in fact related to controllable factors such as diet and exercise (Rowe & Kahn, 1987). This has led some investigators to hypothesize that strategies for "successful aging" can be developed (Rowe & Kahn, 1987).

The belief that older adults "are too set in their ways" to benefit from new and innovative health programs is also being proven to be inaccurate. The current cohort of older adults have joined and benefited from wellness programs (Promoting Health among Older Adults, 1987), participated successfully in psychoeducational interventions designed to alleviate depression (Gallagher, 1981), attended health education programs to promote self-care of disorders such as arthritis (Lorig & Fries, 1986), and are increasingly active in the political arena (e.g., through such organizations as the Gray Panthers; Gibbs, 1988). Clearly, older adults are as willing and able to participate in and benefit from programs designed to promote well being as are younger individuals.

Lastly, there is hope that the disinterest among various professional groups in working with the elderly is eroding. Most health-related disciplines are beginning to offer at least some training in working with older adults and it is hoped that the graduates of such programs will demonstrate a more positive attitude toward the elderly than those who never received such training.

Challenging negative attitudes about aging will not necessarily entice more public health professionals and psychologists to focus their work on the health needs of older adults. There needs to be a set of common goals and objectives to focus research and programming efforts and reduce the current fragmentation observed in both fields. A conceptual framework capable of integrating the different perspectives and theoretical orientations that public health and psychology bring to the study of older adults' health care concerns is one step in that direction. The present chapter will attempt to:

1. Apply the conceptual framework discussed in chapter 2 to the problems of the elderly. This framework will be used to identify general goals for

research and programs addressing the health concerns of older adults; specific target areas that need to be addressed to attain the general goals; and potential intervention strategies for the identified target areas.
2. Use the framework to examine the health care concerns associated with Alzheimer's disease and suggest a systematic approach for addressing them.
3. Suggest directions for future research.

CONCEPTUAL FRAMEWORK

The framework proposed in chapter 2 of this book provides a structure for integrating efforts that address the health concerns of older adults. Several components of the framework are particularly useful: establishing goals, selecting targets, and identifying strategies. The concept of levels of analysis can also be used to integrate a diversity of possible intervention strategies. Each component of the framework as it applies to older adults is described below.

Goals

An overriding goal in all public health efforts is to maintain or improve individuals' quality of life by preventing disease and alleviating the burdens of illness (Phillips & Gaylord, 1985). This same goal is obviously applicable to older adults. We would like to suggest, however, that an equally useful public health goal for the elderly would be to maintain or improve older individuals' quality of life *by preventing chronic disability and alleviating the dependency imposed by disability* (Hanlon & Pickett, 1984).

Disability is defined here as the loss of resources which interferes with an individual's ability to independently engage in activities needed to maintain his or her quality of life. The related concept of *dependency* is defined as the need to rely on other people to perform tasks important to an individual's quality of life. Although disability and dependency are far from ubiquitous among older adults, they do affect a significant minority of the population. The most comprehensive assessment of the prevalence of functional limitations of older adults in the United States has come from the Supplement on Aging Questionnaire (SOA) administered during the 1984 National Health Interview Survey (Dawson, Hendershot, & Fulton, 1987). The findings summarized here are based on a national probability sample of 11,497 community dwelling individuals 65 years of age or older.

Health problems made some home management activities (e.g. shopping, meal preparation, managing money, doing housework) more difficult for 26.9% of the sample. Difficulty performing personal care activities (e.g. bathing, dressing, walking) were reported by 22.7% of the sample. The personal care activity most often reported as difficult was walking (18.7%) and the most difficult home management activity was heavy housework (23.8%). Based on the survey findings, it was projected that approximately 7 million noninstitutionalized older adults suffer from some degree of functional limitation.

There are a number of reasons why we believe that goals of preventing chronic disability and dependency are as valuable as that of preventing disease. The major causes of mortality among the elderly are heart disease, cancer, and stroke (USDHHS, 1986). These disorders are responsible for the deaths of three out of every four persons 65 years of age or older. These diseases have received extensive attention in the public health field, although the population of interest has often been those under 65 years of age (Hanlon & Pickett, 1984). Current research indicates that the most successful intervention strategies for these diseases should occur as early in life as possible (Hanlon & Pickett, 1984). This does not imply that preventive efforts should not be attempted with older individuals. In fact, there is a great need for research exploring the potential benefits of lifestyle and health behavior changes initiated later in life. It is clear, however, that the best strategy for preventing such diseases is to intervene early.

Another factor limiting the utility of a disease prevention focus is the high prevalence of multiple, chronic diseases in the elderly (Estes, 1977). It is unclear at this point whether there is a coherent set of strategies which can prevent the combinations of illnesses frequently seen in the elderly.

Survey data indicate that the presence of a disease does not correlate highly with reports of disability and dependency. For example, two thirds of a sample of the elderly in Cleveland, Ohio, reported no limitations of their daily activities although almost all reported the presence of some chronic disease (U.S. General Accounting Office, 1979). Thus, strategies for preventing disability and dependency do not necessarily have to prevent the occurrence of disease.

There have been many advances in the development of life-sustaining technology, and these advances have contributed to the growth of the older population (Hanlon & Pickett, 1984). Extending life does not necessarily mean that quality of life will be preserved, however, if longer life simply means increasing disability and dependency. Methods are available to prevent or lessen the impact of disability associated with aging (Phillips & Gaylord, 1985). Even if the age of death is not modified, the length of time an individual must live with disabilities can be decreased by strategies designed to prevent disability. Fries and Crapo (1981) have referred to this as "flattening the morbidity curve." We propose, therefore, that the major goals of public health efforts for older adults include preventing disability and minimizing dependency.

More than general goals are required to devise interventions for minimizing disability and dependency among older adults. It is essential to determine:

- **What** type of disability will be the focus of the intervention?
- **Who** will receive the intervention?
- **When**, in the course of development of the disability, will the intervention be delivered?

Answering the questions of what and who will be the focus of an intervention actually provides a method for defining intervention targets, a key element of the conceptual framework described in chapter 2.

Defining Targets

What Types of Disability Should Be the Targets of Interventions?

As defined above, disability refers to a loss of function. The types of losses of greatest interest in the areas of public health are, of course, losses in physiological functioning. These include loss of sensory, physical, or cognitive function. In addition, public health treatises on older adults often discuss psychological losses, especially bereavement, retirement, and mental health disorders (Friedman & Haynes, 1985). We propose that these categories of losses be used to define targets for intervention. Each of these losses can result from a variety of diseases or other causes. The major etiologies of each type of loss are described below.

Sensory Loss. The two most debilitating forms of sensory loss are loss of vision and loss of hearing. The likelihood of occurrence of both of these problems increases with age. Approximately 7.8% of adults over the age of 65 are believed to suffer from low vision (Nelson, 1987), which is typically defined as best corrected acuity of 20/70 or worse or a visual field of 40 degrees or less (normal field = 180 degrees). Even among adults considered to be legally blind (best corrected acuity of 20/200 or visual field of 20 degrees or less), there is usually some amount of usable vision. There are four disorders of vision common among the elderly: macular degeneration, retinal damage, glaucoma, and cataracts.

Macular degeneration refers to a variety of disorders that affect a portion of the retina called the macula. The macula provides images of great clarity in the central part of the visual field. Consequently, macular degeneration leads to blind spots in the center of one's vision but can leave peripheral vision relatively unaffected. There is no effective treatment for macular degeneration.

Retinal difficulties are usually manifested as tears or detachments of the retina, the nerve-rich tissue at the back of the eye which transmits images to the brain. Visual difficulties caused by retinal damage are manifested as blind spots in the part of the visual field served by the damaged area of the retina. Microsurgery, lasers, and freezing techniques are used to repair tears and separations, but cannot restore damaged tissue.

Glaucoma is caused by a buildup of fluid pressure within the eye, which can eventually damage the optic nerve. Commonly, visual difficulties occur in the periphery of the visual field, resulting in tunnel vision. The onset of the disease is gradual and free of other symptoms. The disease may be quite advanced before an individual is aware of it. Treatment usually consists of medication in the form of eye drops and occasionally surgery. The treatment is usually effective in arresting the process but cannot restore damage already done to the optic nerve.

Cataracts are a disorder of the lens in which the lens becomes clouded, sometimes to the point of opacity. They typically develop gradually and cause losses in overall visual acuity. Cataract sufferers also become very susceptible to glare. Cataract surgery, often accompanied by a lens implant, usually provides an effective cure.

The exact etiologies of the above disorders are unknown. They sometimes arise secondary to other physical diseases, such as diabetes and hypertension. Treatment for secondary eye disorders typically involves treatment of the underlying physical disease.

Hearing loss affects approximately 25–30% of individuals aged 65–74 years and almost 50% of those 75 years of age and older (Anderson & Meyerhoff, 1982). Loss is usually gradual, and individuals will often deny they have a hearing problem (Corso, 1977). The most common hearing deficit among older adults is presbycusis, a bilateral loss resulting from neural degeneration (Olsho, Harkins, & Lenhardt, 1985). Presbycusis initially causes difficulty in hearing high-pitched sounds and gradually results in losses of middle and low range frequencies as well. Persons suffering from presbycusis have difficulty understanding speech, because the selective loss of reception for certain frequencies distorts sound and more time is required for the auditory centers to interpret speech sounds (Stone, 1987). Hearing aids are not always helpful because they magnify all frequencies equally, causing certain sounds to be much louder than normal (Stone, 1987).

Physical Loss. Physical loss is defined for our purposes as any decrease in an individual's physical strength, endurance, coordination, or dexterity which limits his or her ability to perform those activities which sustain quality of life. These activities range from basic ambulation to the fine motor skills needed to pursue an avocation such as painting. There are numerous reasons an older adult may sustain physical loss. Osteoarthritis, rheumatism, and other degenerative joint conditions are estimated to limit the daily activity of approximately 11.7% of the adults 65 years of age or older (Metropolitan Life Insurance Foundation, 1982). Heart disease and hypertension have a similar effect on another 16.6% of the elderly (Metropolitan Life Insurance Foundation, 1982). Acute illnesses result in more days of restricted activity for the elderly than for younger adults (Estes, 1977).

Accidental injury is a major source of disability for the elderly. Adults 65 years of age and older report almost three times more disability days due to injury than the next most afflicted group of 6–16 year olds (Friedman & Haynes, 1985). Automobile accidents and falls are the most commonly reported mishaps (Waller, 1985). Falls frequently result in fractures for older adults and are the leading cause of accidental death for individuals over 74 years of age. Osteoporosis exacerbates the injuries resulting from falls, especially in white females. It has been estimated that 25% of all white females have had at least one fracture caused by osteoporosis by the age of 65 (Marx, 1980).

Cognitive Loss. Cognitive loss refers to any decline in memory function, reasoning, language, judgment, or perception that interferes with an individual's ability to perform activities needed to sustain his or her quality of life. Cognitive loss has typically been considered an immutable result of the aging process. Epidemiological data fail to support such a broad assertion. Only 10% of the population over the age of 65 have significant cognitive impairment (National Institute on Aging Task Force, 1980). In general, loss of cognitive functioning results from specific disease processes such as stroke, Alzheimer's disease, Parkinson's disease, and other degenerative neurological conditions. Medical treatment may diminish or arrest the progress of certain disorders, such as Parkinson's disease, but there is currently no method of restoring damaged brain tissue. Potentially reversible cognitive loss can occur as a result of drug interactions or side effects, malnutrition, endocrine dysfunction, acute infections, episodes of depression, and other medical disorders (Office of Technology Assessment – OTA 1987). Appropriate treatment of these disorders may return cognitive functioning to normal.

Psychosocial Loss. Psychosocial loss includes losses in an individual's social network and general mental health problems. Social losses are common among the elderly. People retire from their jobs, thereby severing ties with co-workers and losing one of their major life roles. Many individuals relocate following retirement and are faced with the loss of old friends and neighbors. Perhaps most difficult of all, the incidence of death among spouses and friends increases with age. While psychosocial losses are not health issues *per se*, they have a very strong effect on elders' quality of life and possibly direct and indirect effects on individuals' health status. For example, individuals who have lost a spouse report more physical symptoms and men have higher mortality rates than do nonbereaved age-matched controls (Jacobs & Ostfeld, 1977). In addition, social support is often cited as a factor which protects people from stress and assists them in recovering from illness (Cohen & McKay, 1984). For these reasons, social loss is commonly considered to be an important target for public health efforts with the elderly.

It has been estimated that at least 10% of adults 65 years of age or older have cognitive or emotional problems severe enough to warrant professional attention (USDHEW, 1979). Depression is the most common disorder. The incidence rate has been estimated to be 3% to 5% (Blazer & Williams, 1980). Schizophrenia and other paranoid disorders are rare among older adults. Prevalence rates have been estimated to be between 1% and 2% for individuals 60 years of age and older (La Rue, Dessonville & Jarvik, 1985). Psychiatric disorders may be triggered by sensory, physical, or social loss (or all three) and may therefore contribute to the degree of disability experienced by an older adult. Pharmacological treatment of a disorder may also cause symptoms of depression, confusion, or anxiety (Ouslander, 1982). A little understood area of increasing importance is the aging of individuals who suffer from chronic psychiatric disorders or developmental disabilities (La Rue, Dessonville, & Jarvik, 1985). It is not known whether their level of functional independence deteriorates more rapidly than that of the general population.

Who Will Receive the Intervention?

Interventions can be developed for the older adult who is at risk of or is experiencing a disability. Interventions can be expanded to include the older adult's family and immediate social network or they can focus on organizational and community efforts to minimize disability and dependency. Finally, interventions can be designed to influence public policy and governmental spending relevant to the health needs of older adults. This hierarchy was described in detail in chapter 2 as personal, interpersonal, institutional/environmental, and societal levels of analysis. Combining the levels-of-analysis dimension with the type-of-loss categories described above, it is possible to delineate specific and integrated targets for intervention, all of which contribute to the general goal of decreasing disability and dependency among older adults. For example, targets in the area of sensory loss could include:

1. *Personal level:* Developing programs to train individuals to use assistive devices (e.g., hearing aids) to compensate for sensory loss.
2. *Interpersonal level:* Developing programs to educate spouses about the nature of their mates' sensory loss and what they can accomplish with the use of an assistive device.
3. *Institutional level:* Training health care professionals to organize and conduct the programs described above.
4. *Societal level:* Promoting government funding of the above programs so

that they can be made available to all older adults who could benefit from them.

Selecting targets based on the type-of-loss and the level-of-analysis dimensions answers the questions of what and who should be the focus of an intervention. The last dimension that must be considered when designing an intervention is when, in relation to the onset of a disability, it is to be implemented.

Timing of the Intervention: Primary, Secondary, or Tertiary Prevention

There are three points at which intervention strategies can be applied: before any disability has been experienced; at the first sign of pending disability; or after a certain degree of disability has developed. Traditionally, these three types of intervention strategies have been referred to as primary, secondary, and tertiary prevention. The focus on disability and dependency in older adults makes it useful to further delineate types of tertiary prevention strategies. An individual may experience a disability as a result of one or more of the losses described above; however, methods may exist for reversing, arresting, or delaying the progression of the disability or allowing the older adult to continue to meet his or her own needs in spite of the disability. We refer to such interventions as *rehabilitation* strategies, because they allow individuals to maintain their independence in daily functioning.

A disability may progress to the point where an older adult is forced to rely on the assistance of other people to manage activities of daily living. Strategies for providing an individual with needed assistance are referred to as *supportive service* strategies. Supportive service strategies are also a form of tertiary prevention.

Descriptions of the types of interventions possible at each time point are presented below. Note that all the examples represent personal level interventions (i.e., they focus on the older individual).

Prevention Strategies
Prevention strategies are those which may actually block the development of disability and dependency. The best examples of such strategies are the lifestyle changes found to prevent or limit the development of cardiovascular disease, including modification of diet, smoking cessation, and maintenance of sufficient physical activity (Kaplan & Stamler, 1983). Unfortunately, the etiology of many of the chronic, degenerative diseases which afflict elders have yet to be determined; thus, there are relatively few strategies known to completely prevent disability from these diseases.

Losses secondary to specific disease processes may be preventable if the disease is controlled. For instance, visual loss associated with diabetes may be prevented by aggressive strategies to control blood sugar level. There is increasing evidence that minor but measurable declines in cognitive functioning are more likely to appear in individuals whose hypertension is not well controlled (Wilkie, 1980). Clearly, the aggressive treatment of an ongoing disorder can be considered to be preventive only with respect to the secondary losses that the disorder might cause.

Early Detection and Treatment Strategies

Early detection and treatment strategies are those which emphasize the detection and treatment of potentially disabling conditions early in their course, thereby limiting or delaying their effects. An example of early detection strategies are health screening programs for older adults. These can be effective in detecting previously undiagnosed medical conditions (Furukawa, 1982). Health education programs may also provide useful strategies for teaching people how to perform their own screenings (e.g., breast self-exams) or conduct their own treatments (e.g., arthritis education and exercise programs – Lorig & Fries, 1986).

Prevention and early detection strategies are the preferred methods of approach to any disease or disabling condition (Hanlon & Pickett, 1984). However, developing such strategies requires basic knowledge about the etiology and course of the disabling condition being attacked; many of the chronic diseases associated with aging are still poorly understood (cf. Weiler, 1987). As medical research increases our understanding of these diseases, the possibility of developing truly effective prevention and early detection strategies will increase as well.

Rehabilitation Strategies

Rehabilitation strategies seek to restore lost function or eliminate dependency by teaching individuals new ways of accomplishing tasks necessary to maintain their quality of life. There are many potentially useful rehabilitation strategies available that have not been systematically applied to the problems of disability and dependency in later life (Phillips & Gaylord, 1985). The most promising strategies represent three approaches to rehabilitation: somatic approaches, skills training approaches, and cognitive/affective approaches.

Before describing each of these approaches, it is important to delineate more specifically the goals of rehabilitation strategies. The ultimate goal of restoring lost function and teaching new methods of accomplishing daily tasks is to maintain the older adult's quality of life. However, neither degree of disability or extent of dependency is perfectly correlated with individuals' perceptions of quality of life (cf. Zarit, Reeves, & Bach-Peterson, 1980). The same disability experienced by two different individuals may produce little change in one person's perceived quality of life but drastically lower that of the other. To be successful, therefore, rehabilitation strategies must preserve or enhance the older adult's positive perceptions of his or her quality of life. An understanding of the mechanisms by which such differences in perception of quality of life occur is a necessary perquisite for designing and evaluating rehabilitation strategies. Several psychological theories of stress and depression can be integrated to explain individuals' affective reactions to their disability. Such an integration provides a potentially useful model to guide the development and application of rehabilitation strategies. This model, described in greater detail below, represents a cognitive–behavioral theory of coping with disability and dependency.

A Cognitive–Behavioral (C/B) Theory of Coping with Disability

Lazarus and his colleagues (Lazarus, 1966; Lazarus & DeLongis, 1983; Lazarus & Launier, 1978) have argued that the distress experienced by an individual faced with a potentially stressful situation is directly related to the individual's appraisal of the event, rather than the objective nature of the event itself. An individual's appraisal of an event is a combination of two different judgments. The first judgment concerns the degree of actual or potential personal harm associated with the event. An event will cause stress only if it is perceived to be potentially harmful (physically or psychologically). The second judgment concerns the individual's estimate of whether he or she has the resources and skills needed to eliminate or minimize the harm resulting from the event. The fewer resources and skills the individual believes he or she can use to control the event, the greater the perception of stress.

The applicability of Lazarus' stress model to disability can be demonstrated with an example. Mr. Smith and Mr. Jones suffer the same degree of sight loss from macular degeneration. Mr. Smith enjoys spending much of his time in activities requiring high levels of visual acuity: repair of electronic equipment, keeping the financial records of his fraternal organization, and so forth. Mr. Jones spends his enjoyable moments in activities requiring far less visual acuity, such as listening to music and talking to friends. Mr. Smith is likely to perceive his visual problems as a greater threat to his quality of life than will Mr. Jones. If Mr. Smith is also unaware of optical aids and special training programs which might help him continue to pursue his enjoyable activities, he is even more likely to feel distressed. Additionally, if aids and training programs were offered to Mr. Smith, he might not perceive them as useful resources because they could not completely restore his vision or because he believes that he would be incapable of making effective use of them. Therefore, the existence of these rehabilitation options might not improve the quality of his life because his appraisals prevent him from using them.

Lazarus' stress model predicts that the level of distress associated with a disability will be reduced if the individual's perception of the harm resulting from the disability is reduced or the perception of available resources for managing the disability is increased. Three popular and well-researched cognitive–behavioral theories of depression suggest methods for altering these perceptions: Lewinsohn's social learning theory (Lewinsohn et al., 1986), Beck's cognitive theory (Beck, Rush, Shaw, & Emery, 1979), and D'Zurilla's problem solving theory (D'Zurilla, 1986).

Social Learning Theory

Lewinsohn's social learning theory of depression emphasizes the role of pleasant and unpleasant events in the determination of daily mood. He and his colleagues have demonstrated that the absence of positively reinforcing (i.e., pleasant) events leads to lowered mood and eventually depression (Lewinsohn & Libet, 1972). This can occur even in the absence of specific negative events. In addition, low mood tends to decrease a person's activity level, thereby decreasing pleasant events even further. Extrapolating to the experience of an older adult with a disability, daily mood (and, eventually, quality of life) declines if the individual is unable to engage in his or her usual pleasant activities. Lower daily mood may then result in increasingly fewer efforts to discover alternative pleasant activities in which the individual may still participate, resulting in further decreases in mood. The result of this downward spiral of mood and activities can be an unrealistically high appraisal of loss coupled with a low appraisal of ability to cope with the disability.

Cognitive Theory

Beck's cognitive theory of depression (Beck, Rush, Shaw, & Emery, 1979) emphasizes the role of automatic thoughts in the development of low mood and depression. He and his colleagues have demonstrated that depressed individuals have automatic thoughts that often reflect inaccurate and predominantly negative appraisals of the events they experience (Beck, Rush, Shaw, & Emery, 1979). For example, an individual experiencing difficulty in using a new hearing aid may automatically think "A hearing aid will never work for me!" Since he or she has had little or no practice in using a hearing aid, it is inaccurate to jump to the conclusion that it will never work. The automatic thought is also a negative one because it implies that it is useless to continue working with the hearing aid and that the hearing loss is destined to remain a permanent disability. Negative automatic thoughts may be associated with both appraisals of loss and appraisals of coping ability. In both cases, they are likely to result in a negative perception of quality of life.

Problem Solving Theory

The problems associated with the occurrence of a disability are often numerous and complex. Older adults are faced with the task of learning new information about the nature of their disability, estimating its effect on their daily lives, and developing plans for coping with these effects. Basic problem-solving skills are needed to accomplish these tasks. A deficit in problem-solving skills can be responsible for unrealistically negative appraisals of the losses caused by a disability and inaccurate appraisal of the potential for actively addressing those losses. D'Zurilla (1986) has reviewed and organized the diverse literature on people's ability to solve social problems and identified the skills needed to be an effective problem solver. They include the ability to: clearly define the problem and express it as a behavioral goal; brainstorm potential solutions; weigh the "pros" and "cons" of each potential solution; select and implement the best solution from the available options; evaluate the effects of the solution once it is implemented; and return to step 1 of the model if the initial solution does not produce the desired results.

In summary, the proposed cognitive–behavioral model of coping with disability states that decreases in quality of life following a disability are a function of an individual's appraisal of what important aspects of daily life have been or could be lost and whether the resources to restore or minimize these losses are available and useable. An especially useful concept for defining the losses imposed by a disability is that of pleasant and unpleasant events. The degree to which unpleasant events outweigh pleasant events in a person's schedule of daily activities determines, in part, his or her perception of quality of life. Additionally, the tendency to engage in negative automatic thinking can produce appraisals of harm and coping ability that are more negative than the objective reality of the person's situation seems to warrant. Lastly, appraisals of harm and inability to cope can be inflated for individuals who lack effective problem-solving skills, because they will have difficulty developing systematic plans for using available resources to maintain their quality of life. The C/B model of coping with disability presented above indicates that rehabilitation strategies can improve quality of life by both decreasing actual levels of disability and dependency and modifying unrealistically negative appraisals of loss and coping abilities.

Three approaches to rehabilitation are described below: somatic approaches, skills training approaches, and cognitive–affective approaches. The C/B model of coping with disability will be used to indicate how each approach may be able to maintain the quality of life of older adults.

Description of Rehabilitation Strategies

Somatic Approaches. Somatic approaches refer to medical procedures that can contain or reverse disability caused by disease. Treatments are available for controlling chronic disorders such as diabetes and hypertension. Physical therapy for individuals disabled by a hip fracture, joint disease, stroke, or other condition can help to restore muscular control. There are currently no effective medical treatments for some disorders associated with aging, such as Alzheimer's disease (OTA, 1987). Somatic approaches are designed to maintain quality of life by eliminating or containing the disabling effects of disease processes.

Skills Training and Education Approaches. Even when there is substantial loss of sensory, physical, or cognitive function, individuals can often be taught other methods of performing the activities that maintain their quality of life. For example, extensive training programs have been designed to teach people how to function independently with sight loss. D'Zurilla's (1986) review of the literature on social problem-solving indicated that training in general problem-solving skills is useful and effective in helping people cope with a variety of problems, such as depression, stress, smoking, and overeating. Skills training can help maintain quality of life through several mechanisms. Learning and applying new skills can reduce dependency, thereby lessening the older adult's appraisal of the degree of harm resulting from a disability; mastering useful new skills can also enhance an individual's appraisal of his or her ability to cope with whatever difficulties may arise from a disability (cf. Bandura, 1982).

Cognitive–Affective Approaches. Cognitive–affective rehabilitation approaches attempt to maintain quality of life in older adults by teaching individuals specific skills for controlling stress and maintaining their daily mood at a comfortable level, in spite of the difficulties experienced as a result of a physiological or psychosocial loss. In terms of the C/B model of coping with disability, these approaches attempt to modify appraisals of harm and coping without necessarily changing the actual degree of disability or dependency experienced. Some of the most promising techniques are those based on the work of Lewinsohn and Beck, presented earlier.

Lewinsohn and his colleagues (1986) have devised treatment strategies to counteract the downward spiral of mood and activities described above. These treatment strategies have been used effectively with older adults (Thompson, Gallagher, & Breckenridge, 1987). The strategies teach a series of skills that allow the individual to monitor mood and activity level, determine which activities have the most positive effect on mood, and develop and implement a self-change plan to increase the frequency of daily pleasant events. In addition, treatment can involve training in very specific skills that the individual needs in order to increase pleasant events. Social skills training, assertiveness training, and relaxation training are perhaps the most common adjunct skills included in treatment (Lewinsohn et al., 1986).

Beck and his colleagues have developed strategies for controlling negative automatic thoughts that involve teaching an individual how to monitor his or her mood and thoughts, how to challenge inaccurate thoughts, and methods for replacing inaccurate negative thoughts with positive thoughts that more accurately describe the events experienced (Beck, Rush, Shaw, & Emery, 1979). These strategies have been adapted and used successfully with older adults (Thompson, Gallagher, & Breckenridge, 1987).

Supportive Service Strategies

It is not always possible for an older individual afflicted with a disability to maintain functional independence in all the activities important to his or her quality of life. Limitations can occur in many areas: transportation, access to legal, financial, medical, and recreational services, household maintenance, shopping, and personal care activities such as food preparation, personal hygiene, and grooming. The most recent data on the number of older adults requiring assistance with activities of daily living were obtained from the Supplement on Aging (SOA) survey of the 1984 National Health Interview Survey described above (Dawson, Hendershot, & Fulton, 1987). The survey assessed only community-dwelling older adults and not those in long-term care facilities, all of the latter presumably requiring some assistance with activities of daily living. The findings indicated that 22.2% of the respondents required assistance with one or more home management activities such as doing housework, preparing meals, and shopping. Only 9.6% required assistance with one or more personal care activities such as bathing, dressing, or walking.

The majority of supportive services are provided by the families of older adults. Unfortunately, when older adults must go outside the family for services, the range of available community services frequently fails to satisfy their needs (Dawson, Hendershot, & Fulton, 1987). Deficits in personal care activities often lead to institutionalization, even though the same services could be provided by home health aides. However, home health aide services are often nonexistent outside of cities and are both expensive and sometimes nonreimbursable in areas where they are offered (Ruchlin & Braham, 1987). The greatest challenge to this nation's system of social services is to provide a diverse and accessible array of services to disabled older adults.

Summary

Establishing categories of interventions based on their status as primary, secondary or tertiary prevention efforts answers the final question needed to define an intervention approach "When, in the course of a loss, is the intervention to be applied?" Historically, public health initiatives have focused on primary and secondary prevention efforts. Currently, the lack of medical knowledge about chronic diseases in older adults limits the number of effective prevention and early detection strategies available. The tertiary prevention strategies emphasizing rehabilitation are an area of untapped potential, however. As indicated above, many strategies developed for younger adults in the psychological and behavioral sciences are simply waiting to be modified for use with older adults. Supportive service strategies, also a form of tertiary prevention, are designed to minimize dependency rather than disability. Providing these necessary and important services presents a challenge to communities and the nation as a whole; it is in this arena that public health professionals have been most active.

USING THE CONCEPTUAL FRAMEWORK

Identifying Intervention Strategies Relevant to Public Health Initiatives for Older Adults

The conceptual framework described above classifies an intervention strategy on the basis of answers given to three questions: (a) **What** type of disability will be the focus of the intervention? (b) **who** will receive the intervention? and (c) **when,** in the course of development of the disability, will the intervention be delivered?

The framework provides categories for 96 types of interventions. If a comprehensive survey of public health, psychology, and the general field of gerontology were conducted, work relevant to each of these 96 types of interventions would undoubtedly be found. Such an undertaking is clearly beyond the scope of the present chapter. An attempt has been made, however, to illustrate the utility of the framework in identifying and integrating interventions in Tables 11.1 through 11.5.

Table 11.1 lists examples of personal-level interventions for each type of loss at each stage of prevention. The listing highlights the vast range of intervention strategies relevant to the goal of maintaining quality of life in older adults by preventing disability and minimizing dependency. It is also obvious that the interventions involve many disciplines, including medicine, psychology, and public health.

Table 11.2 presents interpersonal-level interventions at each level of prevention. Social services interventions were divided into two types—informal and formal. Informal services are those provided by family and friends. Typically, most of the needs of a disabled older adult are met by one primary caregiver; however, the table lists several options for expanding the size of the informal helping network. Formal services are those provided by outside agencies.

Tables 11.3 and 11.4 focus on general institutional-level interventions.

Table 11.1. Level of Analysis—Personal

Intervention	Type of Disability			
	Sensory Loss	Physical Loss	Cognitive Loss	Social Loss
Prevention	Prevention or control of diseases which can cause sensory loss, e.g., diabetes, hypertension	Health education; Lifestyle change; Accident prevention; Oral hygiene; Flu vaccinations	Control of risk factors; Medical education; Mood control; Nutrition	Retirement preparation; Senior activities
Early Detection/Treatment	Glaucoma screening	Diabetes, hypertension screening; Cancer detection (mammography); Early signs of dehydration, incontinence	Identifying early signs of depression, cognitive loss, sensory loss	Targeting older groups; Post-retirement groups
Rehabilitation: Cognitive-Affective Approaches	Training in specific stress reduction and coping skills	Pain management training	Cognitive-behavioral treatment of depression in early Alzheimer's patients	Counseling; Psychoeducation
Somatic Treatment	Medication; Surgical procedures	Early and adequate treatment; Physical therapy; In-home treatment	Medical treatment of hypertention, diabetes	Use of caution in prescribing medications for this age group
Skills Training	Visual or auditory rehabilitation; Use of supplementary aids; Adherence	Occupational therapy; Medication adherence	Neurorehabilitation; Memory training	Adult education
Social Services	Talking books, sent by libraries, to the visually impaired	Specialized public transport for mobility impaired	Conservatorships	Community senior centers

Table 11.2. Interpersonal Level

Timing of Intervention		
Prevention & Early Detection	Rehabilitation	Social Services
• Family-oriented health education programs • Family & peer group-oriented health promotion strategies (e.g., smoking cessation, nutrition, physical activity)	• *Somatic Approaches:* - Family involvement & support in adherence to medication regimens, special diets, therapeutic exercise programs, etc. • *Behavioral Skills Training:* - Training of family caregivers in skills necessary to assist older adults - Peer-oriented skills training programs - Social skills training • *Cognitive–Affective Approaches:* - Psycho-educational stress management classes for disabled older adults and families - Family system interventions to relieve psychological distress - Support groups for disabled older adults and families	• *Informal Assistance:* - Cooperative sitting services among a group of caregivers - Arranging car pools for transportation - Spreading duties among other family members, e.g., assigning shopping, cleaning, and other chores • *Formal Assistance:* - Financial/legal services (e.g., estate planning, bill paying, tax services) - In-home medical services - Institutional care - Transportation services, e.g., discount fares on public transit, special vehicles, & services for the disabled - Shopping & delivery services, e.g., groceries, medications, mail order services, etc.

There are specific organizations that work with certain types of disabilities (e.g., the Lions Club has an interest in sight loss) but the tables have been constructed to emphasize the general features of all institutional interventions. Table 11.3 lists different types of institutions that can be the target of interventions. Service provider groups such as hospitals, physicians groups, retailers, and others may be offered training to improve their services to older adults. Business groups and service and fraternal organizations can be called upon for financing and other types of resources needed to develop and implement programs. Settings such as senior centers and retirement complexes may provide advertising, space, and endorsement of programs that they feel well benefit the older adults with whom they are in contact. There are also advocacy groups for individuals with specific diseases (e.g.,

Table 11.3. Institutional Level

	Target Organizations			
Advocacy/Umbrella Service Organizations	*Service & Fraternal Organizations*	*Service Provider Groups*	*Social/Recreation Programs*	*Residential Settings*
• Funding sources, e.g., United Way • Senior advocacy groups, e.g., AARP, Retired Federal Employees Association • Disease/disability specific groups, e.g., American Federation for the Blind; Parkinsons Foundation, Alzheimer's Disease & Related Disorders Association (ADRDA), Widow to Widow Organization	• Community groups, e.g., Lions Club, Soroptimists • Business groups, e.g., hospitals, local corporations and businesses	• Medical associations and training programs; health professional associations • Continuing education programs	• Senior centers • YMCAs, YWCAs • Church groups	• Retirement complexes • Mobile home parks

Alzheimer's Disease and Related Disorders Association) or who are simply part of the large group of older Americans (e.g., American Association of Retired Persons). These groups not only provide resources for specific programs but also act as political lobbyists and sources of information for their constituency.

Table 11.4 presents another target of institutional-level interventions: systems for coordinating institutional services delivered to individuals. A common complaint about the agencies and businesses serving the health care needs of older adults is the lack of inter-organizational cooperation and communication (Ruchlin & Braham, 1987). Table 11.4 presents several models of service coordination. There is a great need for empirical evaluations of these and other methods of coordinating services to older adults.

Table 11.5 presents two general areas of intervention at the societal level essential to maintaining the quality of life of older adults. The first area involves the establishment of public policies that promote a positive attitude toward later life and preserve meaningful roles for older adults in our society. The second area involves efforts to insure that an equitable proportion of the nation's resources are directed towards the needs of older adults. Specific targets in each of these areas are also presented in Table 11.5.

The federal government has established a structure of public agencies to provide for at least some of the needs of older adults. A summary of these national initiatives can provide a more comprehensive view of the societal-level interventions that have taken place in response to the growth of the older adult population in the U.S. The following information is adapted from Butler & Lewis (1982, pp. 415–419).

The Older Americans Act of 1965 created the Administration on Aging as a governmental body to address the needs of older Americans. The original act has been amended several times to create an interlocking system of local area agencies on aging, which provide or contract for a variety of services in

Table 11.4. Models for Coordination of Institutional Services

Retail Consumer Model	Private Case Management Model	Social Health Maintenance Model	Life Care Model
Individuals locate and contract for the services they need.	Individuals hire an individual or agency to locate and contract for needed services.	Based on the medical HMO model; Individuals purchase insurance from an organization that can provide a full range of personal care, medical care, and rehabilitative services.	Individuals buy into a residential community designed to provide a continuum of services as they are needed.

Table 11.5. Societal Level

GOAL: Increase public awareness of the potential and methods for maintaining quality of life as one ages.	GOAL: Generate government policies that will allocate a fair proportion of the nation's resources to provide for the needs of older adults.
Targets:	*Targets:*
• Media TV programming; Portrayal of late life in films; Positive portrayal of late life in advertising; Positive descriptions of late life in advertising	• General Income Social security benefits; Supplemental income (SSI) benefits; Personal retirement savings and income tax regulaitons
• Employment Retirement Policies Flexible retirement policies and programs; Part-time job opportunities	• Medical Care Medicare benefits; Medicaid benefits (long-term care); Catastrophic illness & long-term care expenses & income tax regulations
• Education Inclusion of information about aging in school curricula; Increased educational opportunities for older adults	• Direct Services Nutrition programs; Transportation services; Senior centers; Information & referral; Health and psychological care; Coordination of government services

their planning areas; state agencies on aging, which coordinate the efforts of their local area agencies and communicate with other state agencies; and the central Administration on Aging. This system has been mandated to provide: multipurpose senior centers and services in areas including nutrition, transportation, residential repair and renovation, and legal aid. The Administration on Aging also funds research in such areas as needs assessments, program evaluation, public policy, and demonstration programs. Other branches of the government distribute funds to cover necessities such as general income (Social Security, Supplemental Security Income) and health care (Medicare for acute care; Medicaid for acute and long-term care; Veterans Administration for military veterans). There are cooperating and independent agencies at both the state and local levels that also serve the needs of older adults. Clearly, developing methods of coordinating services among these systems, as well as those offered by the private sector and the older adult's informal support network, is a complicated and challenging task.

The tables presented above demonstrate the utility of the conceptual framework for both highlighting the diversity of strategies relevant to the health concerns of older adults and identifying common elements among those strategies. To be maximally useful, the framework must also offer a structure for developing integrated initiatives with which to address a specific health concern. The following section uses the framework to propose a coordinated series of strategies derived from both the psychological and public health literature for addressing the problems posed by Alzheimer's disease, one of the most devastating illnesses associated with aging.

ALZHEIMER'S DISEASE: A MULTILEVEL APPROACH

Alzheimer's disease (AD) is a brain disorder characterized by a progressive loss of memory and intellectual function (American Psychiatric Association, 1980). Its etiology is unknown and diagnosis is based on the elimination of other causes for the observed loss in intellectual function. The only definitive symptoms of the disease are specific neuropathological changes that can be observed on autopsy. AD develops slowly and its course varies from 3 to 20 or more years among afflicted individuals. The early stages are characterized primarily by memory loss and occasionally by subtle changes in personality. It is common for the disease to remain undiagnosed at this stage. The middle stages are accompanied by deficits in reasoning, judgment, and other forms of abstract thinking. Poor self-care and behavioral problems such as wandering become apparent. The late stage involves severe deficits in intellectual and physical functioning resulting in the need for total care. The prevalence of AD among people 65 years of age or older is approximately 6% but rises steadily with age to 20% for individuals 85 or older (Mortimer & Schuman, 1981). There are currently no treatments to prevent, cure, or arrest the progress of Alzheimer's disease. At first glance, this fact might suggest that AD is not yet a feasible target for public health initiatives. In spite of the absence of a medical treatment, however, the problem of AD is being attacked on many levels. We are proposing a three-phase initiative for the management of Alzheimer's disease in older adults. An overview of the initiative is provided below.

Overview of an Alzheimer's Disease Public Health Initiative

Alzheimer's disease is not currently preventable, nor can its debilitating effects be contained if it is diagnosed early in its course. Treatment of the disease is limited to the management of its symptoms and consequences. There appear to be three important stages in the management of AD in an older adult: diagnosis and early intervention, home care, and residential care.

Diagnosing AD is still quite difficult, especially in its early stages. The major goal of diagnosis is to eliminate the possibility that an individual's cognitive losses are the result of treatable disease (Gurland & Cross, 1987). Establishing that an individual is likely to have AD (a definitive diagnosis can not yet be made) also allows both the individual and his or her family to plan for future care needs. There are relatively few medical and behavioral specialists who are trained and experienced in the diagnosis of AD and this frequently makes it difficult for individuals to obtain timely and accurate information about the presence of the disease. In addition, there are secondary aspects of AD that may be treatable in its early stages. Depression and boredom are both possible targets for early intervention.

The second stage of management is home care. During the early and middle stages of the disease, it is often possible for the patient to remain at home if an appropriate system of home care services is available. The "system" often involves one primary caregiver, usually a spouse or adult child of the patient (Fitting et al., 1986). Home care provides the patient with the least restrictive and most familiar surroundings and, therefore, probably provides him or her with the best quality of life possible at that point in the disease process. We propose three methods for enhancing the experience of home care for both the patient and the primary caregiver: preliminary planning to insure that financial and legal resources are in place to facilitate long-term care; providing ongoing education, training, and support for the caregiver in methods of managing the physical and behavioral manifestations of AD; and development of both formal and informal service systems to ease the burden of responsibility on the caregiver. Each of these methods is described in greater detail below.

The final stage of care is often residential treatment. The late stages of Alzheimer's disease can prevent a multitude of care problems for some patients. Physical limitations or severe cognitive deficits may require that all personal care activities be done for him or her. Changes in personality sometimes lead to aggressive verbal or physical behavior or the tendency to wander away from home. The primary caregiver may not have the physical or emotional strength at this point to provide adequate care, at which point residential treatment becomes the only viable alternative. Residential care for AD patients can be both hard to locate and of poor quality because of the special management problems such individuals may exhibit in the later stages of the illness (Ruchlin & Braham, 1987).

Intervention strategies associated with each of the three phases of the proposed AD initiative are described in more detail in the following sections. The conceptual framework is used to organize the interventions into a coherent plan of action for addressing the needs of AD patients and their caregivers.

Diagnosis of Alzheimer's Disease and Preliminary Interventions

Currently, the diagnosis of AD frequently requires a combination of general medical, neurological, and neuropsychological assessments which are expensive and not readily available in many areas (Katzman, 1986).

Several institutional and societal level strategies must be employed to make diagnostic services for AD more available. Medical and psychological personnel involved in the care of older adults need more training in the diagnosis of AD, and centers that employ the necessary multidisciplinary staff to conduct AD assessments need to be established (Weiler, 1987).

Perhaps most importantly, basic research on the etiology and effects of AD needs to continue so that more efficient and accurate methods of diagnosing the disease can be developed. There have been increases in research support for Alzheimer's disease. Ten centers for research on Alzheimer's disease have been established nationwide and research monies for AD have increased from less than $4 million to about $65 million over the period from 1976 to 1986 (OTA, 1987). This increase is considered to be insufficient to many who point to the estimate from the National Institute on Aging that only $.01 of every $1.00 spent on AD goes to research (e.g., Weiler, 1987).

Although AD can not yet be effectively treated, some of its associated symptoms may be treatable. It is not surprising to discover that patients in the early stages of AD sometimes suffer from depression. Although incidence rates are hard to obtain, recent papers have reported that 25% to 30% of AD patients meet criteria for depression (Reifler et al., 1986). Although there have been no controlled studies of treatment for depression in AD patients, case reports suggest that effective treatment is possible. Reifler et al. (1986) reviewed medical records of patients with mixed AD and depression diagnoses and reported that approximately 85% of the cases responded positively to tricyclic antidepressants. Teri and Gallagher (in press) described the application of individual, cognitive–behavioral therapy to depressed individuals in the early stages of Alzheimer's disease.

More information is needed about the incidence of affective disorders in AD patients. Clinical depression and anxiety, especially in the early stages of the disease, may be treatable. These disorders could actually add to the individual's cognitive loss since they often affect cognitive functioning (Thompson, Wagner, Zeiss, & Gallagher, in press). Case reports suggest that depressed AD patients can benefit from medication (Reifler et al., 1986) and individual cognitive–behavioral therapy (Teri & Gallagher, in press); controlled studies are needed to verify these initial findings.

Although it is difficult to assess, AD patients may experience a great deal of boredom during certain stages of their illness. Moderate to severe memory loss interferes with many leisure activities such as reading, watching television, or pursuing hobbies. Caregivers complain that AD patients will follow them around the house or call them away from other activities, apparently because they want attention (Cantor, 1983; Robinson, 1983). Development of activities that are enjoyable and safe for AD patients at different stages of the illness might help to alleviate some of the patient's apparent boredom and attention-seeking behavior. Developing such activities for home use is a difficult undertaking, since it requires matching task demands with the individual's cognitive and physical abilities and activity preferences. It would provide a challenging and worthwhile project for an interdisciplinary team of psychologists, occupational therapists, and other health professionals who work with AD patients.

Home Care Strategies

Preliminary Planning for Long-term Care

Most people do not expect that they will be struck by a chronic, disabling illness such as AD. Consequently, it is not unusual for families caring for an AD patient to find that the financial and legal arrangements of the patient actually interfere with their ability to provide home care. Monies may be tied up in non-liquid assets and no one may have power of attorney status that allows them to manage the patient's legal affairs. To minimize these problems, an interpersonal-level strategy called Life Services Planning has emerged (Zuckerman, 1987). Life Service Planning (LSP) typically involves estate planning to insure that an individual's financial resources could be used effectively to obtain needed social services. LSP can also involve various legal actions to establish procedures to be followed in the event the individual is disabled and cannot perform certain activities (e.g., manage personal financial affairs, communicate a preference about the use of heroic medical procedures to sustain life).

A number of organizations are working on demonstration projects at the institutional level to develop and test procedures for making Life Services Planning available to the public. These organizations include the American Bar Association, the Older Americans Consumer Cooperative, and the Center for the Public Interest (Zuckerman, 1987). It is to be hoped that the results of these demonstration projects will encourage legal and financial management firms to offer similar services and that businesses will begin to include it as part of their retirement preparation programs.

Caregiver Education and Training

Studies have shown that most of the in-home care received by an AD patient is provided by a single individual, usually referred to as the primary caregiver (Fitting et al., 1986). It is important, therefore, to summarize what is currently known about this population of individuals.

Caregiver Profile. The following data on family caregivers was collected during the 1982 Long Term Care Survey and reported recently by Stone (1986). The majority of family caregivers were female (75%) and were usually the wives (23%) or daughters (29%) of the AD patients. The caregivers' average age was 57.3 years, although 35% of them were 65 years of age or older. The majority of respondents (64%) had been caring for their relative for a year or longer. Approximately 80% of the sample reported providing care seven days a week. The most frequently mentioned caregiving duties included: extra time spent transporting or shopping for the patient (86%), performing household chores such as preparing meals (80%), and assisting the patient with self-care activities such as bathing and dressing (66%).

Numerous studies have demonstrated that the role of caregiver is a stressful one (e.g., George & Gwyther, 1986). The emotional distress reported by caregivers has been referred to as caregiver burden (Zarit, Reeves, & Bach-Peterson, 1980) and caregiver strain (Cantor, 1983). Two studies have reported clinical levels of depression in 40% or more of their sample of caregivers (Coppel et al., 1985; Gallagher et al., in press). The factors that contribute to perceptions of distress and burden among caregivers have also been studied. Somewhat surprisingly, neither the number of symptoms exhibited by the patient, duration of the patient's illness, or the total number of caregiving activities performed for the patient were found to be major contributors to burden (George & Gwyther, 1986; Zarit, Reeves, & Bach-Peterson, 1980). Perceptions of burden have been found to be related to the caregiver's feelings of tolerance for the memory and behavior problems exhibited by their relative (Zarit, Reeves, & Bach-Peterson, 1980). Burden increases as the number of intolerable problems increase. Some studies (e.g., Cantor, 1983; George & Gwyther, 1986) have reported that spouses tend more than adult children to perceive caregiving as burdensome but the finding has not always been replicated (Robinson, 1983; Zarit, Reeves, & Bach-Peterson, 1980). Wives have been found to report higher levels of distress and burden than men when they assume the role of caregiver (Fitting et al., 1986; Zarit, Todd, & Zarit, 1986).

It is clear from this brief discussion that Alzheimer's disease has negative effects on the quality of life of the primary caregiver as well as the older adult afflicted with the disease. In addition, the level of burden perceived by the caregiver is positively associated with the decision to place the AD patient in a residential care facility (Zarit, Todd, & Zarit, 1986). For these reasons, many of the interventions proposed here to enhance home care focus directly or indirectly on decreasing the caregiver's feelings of burden and distress. Caregiver training strategies fall into two of the subtypes of rehabilitation strategies defined earlier in the chapter: skills training approaches and congitive–affective approaches.

Skills Training. Most individuals who find that they will be caring for an older adult with AD do not have much information about the disease, the types of disabilities it may cause, or how to manage them. They are also likely to feel significant emotional distress — the debilitating disease has been diagnosed in a person they love. At this point, caregivers could use both emotional support and information about the disease and its management. Support and education groups sponsored by the Alzheimer's Disease and Related Disorders Association (ADRDA) are available in many communities. Hospitals and medical centers may also conduct their own groups. Support groups often meet once or twice a month and the meetings are open to anyone who would like to attend. They provide basic information on a variety of topics and provide caregivers with an opportunity to share their experiences with one another.

The infrequent meetings and open enrollment of support and education groups make them a less desirable format for teaching caregivers specific skills they may wish to learn. A number of investigators (Haley, 1983; Pinkston & Linsk, 1984) have employed individual or classroom instruction to teach caregivers behavioral skills to assist them in controlling problematic patient behaviors such as wandering, constant repetition of the same question, and failure to perform self-care activities (Zarit, Reeves, & Bach-Peterson, 1980). Blake (1986) was able to teach caregivers how to design and use a variety of memory aids in the home to improve memory function of the AD patients for whom they were caring. These investigators found that caregivers were able to learn and apply these skills successfully. Training in the use of behavioral techniques did more than simply allow the caregivers to resolve a specific caregiver-related problem; it also provided them with a set of skills that could be used to address other problems and a means of communicating with their family member even if he or she was severely memory impaired or unable to comprehend verbal instructions. Training caregivers in the use of such behavioral techniques is a very promising technique and deserves further study.

D'Zurilla's (1986) review of the problem-solving literature indicates that people can learn problem-solving skills and use them effectively. Many interventions for caregivers include a problem-solving component (e.g., Gallagher, Lovett, & Zeiss, in press; Haley, Brown, & Levine, 1987) but do not specifically evaluate its effectiveness. Teaching problem-solving skills is a strategy also worthy of further study.

Environmental Design. A variety of environmental design techniques have been advocated to enhance AD patients' abilities to function in their living area (Calkins, 1987). Caregivers can be taught to make strategic use of simple signs, colors, patterns, and familiar furniture to help offset the problems created by memory loss. Potentially dangerous appliances in the home, such as the stove, can be fitted with safety devices to decrease the possibility of accidents due to inappropriate use. Adding a fence in the yard reduces the chances of a confused patient wandering away from home.

Family caregivers for AD patients may provide care for years and gradually encounter different demands as the disease progresses. It is not possible to determine when or if an individual caregiver will need specific training in behavior management skills, problem-solving skills, or home nursing skills. Ideally, community organizations such as hospitals, senior centers, and other agencies that serve older adults could continue to provide classes such as those described above on a regular basis.

Cognitive–Affective Approaches. Learning information and skills that help manage the effects of AD would be expected to decrease caregivers' feelings of burden. However, the demands of the role are great, even for individuals with good management skills. Other strategies to help reduce stress in the face of the difficulties encountered as a caregiver are also needed.

Such strategies might prove to be most effective if they are taught to caregivers who are experiencing early signs of distress. Unfortunately, it is extremely difficult to screen for early signs of caregiver distress. Alzheimer's disease develops insidiously, and many individuals are not aware that their spouse's or parent's unusual behavior is a symptom of AD (Chenoweth & Spenser, 1986). These individuals may be experiencing a great deal of distress but would be unlikely to seek services for caregivers since, without a diagnosis, they may not perceive themselves as being in a caregiver role.

There are also no measures of caregiver distress with sufficiently well-developed norms to establish cutoff scores to identify those individuals who are "too burdened." Finally, there are no prospective studies of the longitudinal experience of caregiving. Most efforts have been cross-sectional in design (e.g., George & Gwyther, 1986) or have obtained information about the very early stages of caregiving from retrospective reports (e.g., Chenoweth & Spenser, 1986). Procedures for identifying and reaching individuals who are serving as family caregivers, the development of a clinically useful measure of caregiver distress, prospective data about the "course" of caregiving, and interventions to help people manage stress during the early stages of caregiving are all areas in need of further research. The developmental/ecological approach described in chapter 6 suggests one method for developing potentially useful stress management interventions across the course of an individual's caregiving life.

A variety of programs designed to reduce caregiver distress have been described. Support and education groups, discussed above, are probably the most common (Gallagher, 1985). There is little empirical data concerning the effectiveness of these groups in reducing caregiver distress.

Another category of interventions are psychoeducational in nature. Psychoeducational interventions are designed to teach individuals specific skills to help them manage their own mood and behavior. Unlike support and education groups, the psychoeducational programs developed for caregivers have been professionally led, limited in duration, and closed to new membership once the program is begun. Haley, Brown, and Levine (1987) compared a wait-list control condition against a time-limited education and support group and a skills group which received the same material as the education group plus training in progressive muscle relaxation and other stress management techniques. They found that the caregivers enjoyed both groups but did not demonstrate significant changes in depression or life satisfaction compared to the wait-list controls.

A project currently underway at the Palo Alto Veterans Medical Center is comparing a wait-list control condition to an "Increasing Problem-Solving Skills" class and an "Increasing Life Satisfaction" class (Gallagher, Lovett, & Zeiss, in press). The "Increasing Life Satisfaction" class is based on Lewinsohn et al.'s (1986) work demonstrating that individuals can improve their mood by learning to identify pleasant events and incorporating these events into their daily activities. Preliminary results from the study indicate that caregivers attending either class demonstrate greater reductions in depression than those in the wait-list condition (Lovett & Gallagher, in press).

The available data on psychoeducational classes for caregivers is mixed. Differences in outcomes between studies may reflect differences in class content, instructional method, or the nature of the subject samples used. Further research is needed to identify the components of such interventions most helpful to caregivers.

Support groups and psychoeducational classes require caregivers to leave their homes in order to attend meetings. For many caregivers, this may require considerable planning and expense because of the need to locate a sitter for the patient, take time away from other important activities, and find transportation to the meeting place. A phone-based support system, such as that which has been used in other health-related areas (King, Taylor, Haskell, & DeBusk, 1988), might provide a more practical method for some caregivers to share their experiences and exchange information.

Developing Informal and Formal Support Systems

The primary caregiver of an AD patient often has need for help from other individuals. Caring for the patient, managing a household, and fulfilling responsibilities to other family members (and sometimes to a job) can require more hours than are available in the day. The specific types of activities with which the caregiver would like assistance can be quite varied. Some caregivers may need assistance with the personal care of the AD patient if heavy lifting is involved. Other individuals may prefer to receive assistance in home management tasks and perform the caregiving duties themselves. Data from the 1982 Long Term Care Survey (Stone, 1986) indicated that less than 10% of the caregivers sampled purchased such services.

The reasons for this were not clear but may include the lack of availability of services in some areas, lack of knowledge about the existence of services, and the expense of the services. There appears to be a need for the development of informal service delivery systems to supplement the efforts of the primary caregivers. Cooperative arrangements among a group of caregivers to provide sitting services, shopping services, and transportation pools might be feasible in some locations (Bradley, 1987). Little empirical work has been done to test the feasibility of establishing such informal service delivery systems.

Informal Systems

Both caregivers and AD patients complain that friends and acquaintances often avoid them once the symptoms of the disease become noticeable (George & Gwyther, 1986). This not only reduces recreational social contacts but limits the possibility of occasionally asking friends and neighbors for assistance. Increased public awareness of the nature of Alzheimer's disease might reduce this social avoidance by mitigating unrealistic fears individuals might have about the disorder. The popular media provides an excellent method of educating the public about issues such as Alzheimer's disease (see chapter 4). Feature stories in national news magazines and television documentaries about AD can help to raise public awareness and may eventually have very beneficial effects for the AD patient and his or her caregiver.

Formal and Professional Assistance

Many agencies and organizations provide services that can improve the quality of life of AD patients and their caregivers. Organizations serving the general population of older adults frequently offer services of interest: nutrition programs, transportation services, recreational activities, and others. Services that can enhance home care efforts fall into several broad categories: in-home services, community-based services, and advocacy services.

In-home Services. Many communities have private home health care agencies that can provide aides to supervise the patient while the caregiver is away from home or provide personal care services such as bathing and dressing. These agencies often have nurses who will provide home care to individuals suffering from substantial medical problems.

It is quite expensive to purchase home care services from for-profit agencies. Low-cost alternatives are required for individuals who need but cannot afford these services. Inexpensive or low-cost sitting services might be developed through volunteer organizations connected with churches, senior centers, or community service organizations. In-home care requiring medically trained personnel could be subsidized by public or private donations. Developing organizations to deliver low-cost in-home care for AD patients is likely to become a high priority goal in coming years as the number of AD patients continues to rise (OTA, 1987).

Community-based Services. The majority of community-based programs for AD patients and their caregivers are designed to offer respite services. Both the AD patient and his or her caregiver need time away from one another. Adult Day Care programs provide activities and socialization for AD patients and provide the caregiver with time needed to attend to other responsibilities. Adult Day Health programs are similar, also providing additional nursing and physical therapy services for individuals suffering from the effects of stroke, arthritis, and other physically debilitating diseases. Overnight respite programs are available through some nursing homes and other medical organizations such as certain Veterans Administration Medical Centers. They offer temporary, twenty-four-hour residential care for the AD patient for periods of several days to a week or more. This service is often needed when the caregiver becomes ill and requires time to recover. It also provides the caregiver with an opportunity to make needed trips out of town or simply catch up on lost sleep.

Other community-based interventions might be helpful to the AD patient and his or her caregiver. Some AD patients will wander away from their home and become lost. Police officers are usually responsible for searching for these people; however, there are a number of other workers who may be even more likely to observe a lost patient. Neighborhood firemen, meter readers for the power companies, and postal carriers may be in the area where an AD patient is presumed lost. A mechanism for alerting these individuals to the problem could greatly enhance the efficiency and effectiveness of a search. Before asking these workers to be involved in such a system, it would be useful to provide them with an educational program about Alzheimer's disease and how best to approach a patient who may be confused and afraid.

Advocacy Services. In addition to the agencies and organizations providing specific types of services, there is one organization that attempts to meet many of the needs of the AD patient. The ADRDA is a national group, with regional and local chapters, that organizes support groups, provides information and referral services, develops and distributes educational literature about AD, lobbies for legislative reforms to ease the financial burdens on AD patients and their caregivers, and funds research on AD. ADRDA has played a major role in making the country aware of the devastation caused by AD and generating both the services and research currently underway to combat the disease.

A continuing problem for caregivers attempting to use formal service systems is the lack of coordination between different public agencies and between public and private organizations. In 1980, the National Long Term Care Demonstration project, known as Channeling, was undertaken to evaluate the effectiveness of two different methods of coordinating services to older adults (Clark, 1987). The basic case management method utilized a case manager to arrange for needed services through existing public agencies. The financial control method also used case managers but expanded the types of services available and created a fund pool from which case managers could authorize the purchase of needed services up to a given maximum. Although there were no striking differences in the effects of the two systems on caregiver distress, there were some differences in the types of services used by the two groups. For example, caregivers under the financial control model use slightly more home management services. More such evaluations are needed to determine the most effective methods of assisting caregivers in providing home care.

The largest obstacle to the creation of support services for home care is monetary. It has been estimated that the indirect costs of community home care for AD patients in 1985 was $31.46 billion (Huang, Cartwright, & Hu, 1988). Home care services for Alzheimer's disease are rarely reimbursable through private insurance, Medicare, or Medicaid programs. Nursing home care, on the other hand, is reimbursable under Medicaid. The often prohibitive costs of home care can force an individual into a nursing home simply because that is the only form of care that receives a meaningful governmental subsidy.

There have been attempts to introduce legislation that would provide financial support for home care by allowing Medicare and Medicaid to cover outpatient services for AD, reduce the Medicare co-payment, and increase the reimbursement limit for mental health care. Tax credits and deductions for home care have also been proposed. Unfortunately, these bills would require additional federal expense now in the hope of minimizing long-term care costs in the future by reducing nursing home use. The current federal budget deficit lessens the probability of passing legislation that increases immediate costs.

Residential Care

The progressive nature of Alzheimer's disease results in increasing levels of disability and therefore places increasing demands on the caregiver. A point may be reached where the caregiver is unable to provide the level of care required by the patient. Unless the AD patient has enough money to pay for twenty-four-hour home care, a nursing home placement becomes necessary. Nursing homes are frequently seen as the option of last resort.

They are expensive and often place limits on the freedom of residents beyond that necessitated by their disability, and many have been cited for poor quality of care (Vladeck, 1980). Some AD patients pose special difficulties for nursing homes because of their tendency to wander or become confused and agitated (Gurland & Cross, 1987). It is unclear how many AD patients are placed in nursing homes at some point in the course of their disease; data suggest that almost fifty percent of the residents of nursing homes suffer from dementia (Gurland & Cross, 1987).

Theoretically, nursing homes could be operated in a manner that resulted in less restriction of personal freedom and provided better quality of care. The various programs for managing problematic behavior and the strategies for maximizing environmental design to assist AD patients could be applied in a residential care setting. The limiting factor appears to be money.

There are residential care facilities that operate differently than nursing homes. *Personal care homes* provide room, board, and some supervision and assistance with activities of daily living. They may be appropriate for some individuals in the early or middle stages of AD. *Life care communities* are a relatively new concept. Individuals purchase a residence in the community (usually an apartment) and pay an initiation fee (usually very large) to join. Members of the community are guaranteed lifetime care of whatever level may be needed. A particularly attractive feature of life care communities is the relatively wide variety of services available. House cleaning, meal preparation, and in-home personal care services are available if they are required to keep a resident in his or her apartment. The community also has its own nursing facility if an individual is unable to remain in his or her apartment. Life care communities are very expensive to enter and, like all businesses, are subject to the pitfalls of economic change and mismanagement. Their place in the long-term care system of the U.S. has not yet been firmly established.

Nursing home care is expensive. Estimates suggest that approximately $10.8 billion annually are spent on nursing home care for individuals with dementia (Freeland, Calat, & Schendler, 1980). Approximately one half of that amount was from private funds. Most of the remaining cost was covered by Medicaid. The majority of individuals who rely on Medicaid funds to cover nursing home fees were not initially poor. Their assets were "spent down" until they fell below the level set by the state for Medicaid eligibility (usually $2000–$4000; Estes, 1979).

There is a great need for long-range economic planning in the field of long-term care. Unless an effective treatment for Alzheimer's disease is discovered soon, the cost of care will escalate enormously. Clearly this is an area in which health care economists, along with other health professionals, can, and must, focus their attentions.

CONCLUSIONS

Older adults are clearly a population whose health needs and concerns are worthy of the attention of both psychologists and public health professionals. It is time that both groups embark upon programmatic and coordinated efforts to develop strategies to address these needs. In the current chapter, we have attempted to assist this process in several ways. It was suggested that the traditional focus of public health on the prevention of disease (Phillips & Gaylord, 1985) be modified for older adults to include the prevention or containment of disability.

A model for integrating work done in psychology and public health relevant to the goal of preventing disability was described.

The major goal of the model was to demonstrate that such seemingly disparate interventions as providing stress management training to caregivers and lobbying for reform in the Medicare laws have a common goal of reducing the level of dependence experienced by an older adult who has suffered a disability as a result of an illness or psychosocial loss.

The example of Alzheimer's disease was used to illustrate the manner in which a multilevel public health initiative for older adults could be developed. It also provided an opportunity to highlight some of the major issues in health care for older adults. These included the dearth of information available about preventing disabilities; the potential utility of training people in the use of cognitive and behavioral skills to help them manage the burdens of illness or disability; and the necessity of developing effective and cost-efficient methods of organizing service delivery systems that allow older adults to obtain only the services that they need and want.

We will end this chapter with an observation that calls into question the utility of designating older adults as a single target population for public health initiatives. Older adults constitute an *extremely* diverse group of individuals (Maddox & Douglas, 1974). It is therefore very difficult to make generalizations that are accurate for everyone over 65 years of age. A better approach, both for psychology and public health, would be a developmental model in which the effects of aging are studied in relation to various intervention strategies, disease entities, or types of disability. Through such approaches, older individuals can begin to be more systematically included in efforts to minimize the burden of illness — something they strongly deserve.

Synthesis & Epilogue

In this book we have attempted to integrate psychological and public health theory, principles, and methods in discussing intervention strategies for alleviating contemporary health problems. In addition to describing the use of techniques such as incentives, media, and community health promotion tactics, a synthesis of psychology and public health perspectives was explored as it applied to a number of different problem areas. In particular, the interventions discussed were typically multilevel and employed both psychological and public health components in the conceptualization, design, implementation, and evaluation processes presented.

We also tried to highlight some of the tensions that currently exist, and doubtless will continue to exist, between more individually focused perspectives and those perspectives with a more structural, societal orientation. It is quite clear that these contrasting perspectives have different value bases and lead to different theories, analyses, and courses of action. Some of the chapters examined the historical antecedents of different perspectives (e.g., labor and management's notion of such issues as occupational stress and safety; chapter 9). One of the chapters discussed how one manifestation of differing perspectives (rights of the individual versus societal protection) is a key issue in the AIDS epidemic (chapter 4). Two of the chapters (2 and 5) showed how these differing perspectives have enormous legal and economic consequences for the continuance of cigarette smoking (e.g., "freedom to choose"; banning cigarette advertising). In several of the chapters, therefore, we offered a number of possible ways to integrate perspectives and potentially resolve conflicts (e.g., exploit the market for healthier foods by having a properly informed public; chapter 8).

While the six problem areas chosen—community mental health, maternal and child/adolescent health, nutrition, worksite health and safety, environmental problems, and aging and health—are of major importance, they certainly do not cover all of the important health issues facing this nation. Not only were there areas that we did not cover directly (e.g., substance abuse; accident prevention outside of the workplace), but within each area we reviewed the content from a particular stance (e.g., the continual embrace of the waiting mode delivery system in mental health). Furthermore, in lieu of a more comprehensive approach we generally focused on a particular subarea (e.g., teenage pregnancy). Thus, it is quite true that this book has only just scratched the surface.

As we stressed in chapters 1 and 2, the approach presented is only a first step toward the synthesis and application of psychology and public health. The conceptual framework presented in chapter 2 is just one of many potential syntheses, frameworks, and areas of application that will undoubtedly be developed. Our firm expectation is that the wave of the future is various creative integrations of these two rich fields of study. At the present time, however, there remains little formal integration of the two.

In writing this book, we were made more aware of our own particular biases in relation to the issues discussed. Two of the authors (RW and AK) have degrees in clinical psychology, while the third (DA) has a degree in social ecology. While none of the authors has had extensive formal training in public health, each of us, in our own way, has become grounded in public health concerns and perspectives. As such, we have become increasingly involved in research and related activities that have led us to straddle both fields. One outcome of this is the fact that our perspectives on health-related issues have changed and in many respects broadened, as we suspect they have for others working in both areas.

We expect (and hope) that the few programs that have combined training in psychology and public health will continue to prosper. Another encouraging sign of increased connections between the two fields is that an increasing number of psychologists are being hired by schools of public health, and a growing number of public health professionals are becoming well versed in psychological theory and behavior change techniques (e.g., Stretcher et al., 1986). Thus, at least some individuals are having the fortunate opportunity to receive training in both disciplines. Although we believe that psychology and public health will continue to prosper and thrive as separate fields, the continued exploration of the interfaces between the two is deemed as timely and extremely important. The best methods for exploring these interfaces remain to be fully realized.

In addition to formal training opportunities at the graduate and postgraduate level, a number of large and visible projects which combine psychology and public health approaches have been mounted recently. Some of these projects have been described in this book. We anticipate that the success and visibility of many of these projects will serve to spark interest and awareness concerning what each field has to offer. In addition, it is our hope that fresh perspectives will emerge to help propel forward conceptual integrations of psychology and public health.

References

Abernathy, V. (1974). Illegitimate conception among teenagers. *American Journal of Public Health, 64*(7), 662–665.

Addiss, S. S. (1985). Setting goals and priorities: 1984 presidential address. *American Journal of Public Health, 75*, 1276–1280.

Adler, N. E., Cohen, F., & Stone, G. C. (1979). Themes and professional prospects in health psychology. In G. C. Stone, F. Cohen, & N. E. Adler (Eds.), *Health psychology* (pp. 573–590). San Francisco: Jossey-Bass.

Agras, W. S. (1982). Behavioral medicine in the 1980s: Nonrandom connections. *Journal of Consulting & Clinical Psychology, 50*, 797–803.

Aitken, P. P., Leathar, D. S., & Squair, S. I. (1986). Children's awareness of cigarette brand sponsorship of sports and games in the UK. *Health Education Research, 1*(3), 203–211.

Ajzen, I., & Fishbein, M. (1980). *Understanding attitudes and predicting social behavior.* Englewood Cliffs, NJ: Prentice-Hall.

Albee, G. W. (1986). Toward a just society: Lessons from observations on the primary prevention of psychopathology. *American Psychologist, 41*, 891–898.

Albright, C. L., Altman, D. G., Slater, M. D., & Maccoby, N. (1988). Cigarette advertisements in magazines: Evidence for a differential focus on women's and youth magazines. *Health Education Quarterly, 15*(2), 225–233.

Alcohol, Drug Abuse, and Mental Health Administration (1987). *ADAMHA update fact sheet.* Washington, DC: Public Health Service.

Aldous, J. (1982). *Two paychecks: Life in dual-earner families.* Beverly Hills, CA: Sage.

Allegrante, J. P., & Green, L. W. (1981). When health policy becomes victim blaming. *New England Journal of Medicine, 305*, 1528–1529.

Allegrante, J. P., & Sloan, R. P. (1986). Ethical dilemmas in workplace health promotion. *Preventive Medicine, 15*, 313–320.

Allen, J. R., & Curran, J. W. (1988). Prevention of AIDS and HIV infection: Needs and priorities for epidemiologic research. *American Journal of Public Health, 78*, 381–386.

Allgeier, E. R. (1981). Ideological barriers to contraception. In D. Byrne & W. A. Fisher (Eds.), *Adolescents, sex, and contraception.* New York: McGraw-Hill.

Altman, D. G. (1986a). A framework for evaluating community-based heart disease prevention programs. *Social Science and Medicine, 22*, 479–487.

Altman, D. G. (1986b, August). On the relationship between researchers and communities: A framework for the incorporation of research interventions in the community. Paper presented at the annual meeting of the American Psychological Association, Washington, DC.

Altman, D. G. (in press). The social context as a barrier to adopting healthy behaviors. In S. A. Shumaker, E. Schron, & J. K. Ockene (Eds.), *The adoption and maintenance of behaviors for optimal health.* New York: Springer.

Altman, D. G., & Cahn, J. (1987). Employment options for health psychologists. In

G. Stone, S. Weiss, J. Matarazzo, N. Miller, J. Rodin, C. Belar, M. Follick, & J. Singer (Eds.), *Health psychology: A discipline and a profession* (pp. 231–244). Chicago, IL: University of Chicago Press.

Altman, D. G., & Green, L. W. (1988). Interdisciplinary perspectives on behavioral medicine training. *Annals of Behavioral Medicine, 10*(1), 4–7.

Altman, D. G., & Jackson, C. (1984). Job stress and burnout: Research and intervention strategies. *Journal of Primary Prevention, 4*(4), 260–267.

Altman, D. G., & King, A. C. (1986). Approaches to compliance in primary prevention. *Journal of Compliance in Health Care, 1*(1), 55–73.

Altman, D. G., Flora, J. A., Fortmann, S. F., & Farquhar, J. W. (1987). The cost-effectiveness of smoking cessation programs. *American Journal of Public Health, 77*(2), 162–165.

Altman, D. G., Slater, M. D., Albright, C. L., & Maccoby, N. (1987). How an unhealthy product is sold: Cigarette advertising in magazines (1960–1985). *Journal of Communication, 37*(4), 95–106.

Altman, I. (1975). *The environment and social behavior.* Monterey, CA: Brooks-Cole.

Altman, I., & Rogoff, B. (1987). World views in psychology: Trait, interactional, organismic, and transactional perspectives. In D. Stokols & I. Altman (Eds.), *Handbook of environmental psychology* (pp. 7–40). New York: Wiley.

Altman, I., Vinsel, A., & Brown, B. B. (1981). Dialectic conceptions in social psychology: An application to social penetration and privacy regulation. In L. Berkowitz (Ed.), *Advances in experimental social psychology* (vol. 14, pp. 108–160). New York: Academic.

American Cancer Society (1987a). *Cancer facts and figures—1987.* New York: American Cancer Society.

American Cancer Society (1987b). *Smoke signals.* New York: American Cancer Society.

American Cancer Society (1987c). *Smoke fighting.* New York: American Cancer Society.

American Heart Association (1987). *Heart facts.* Dallas, TX: American Heart Association.

American Psychiatric Association (1980). *Diagnostic and statistical manual of mental disorders* (3rd ed.). Washington, DC: American Psychiatric Association.

American Public Health Association. (1980). Alternatives in maternity care. *American Journal of Public Health, 70*(3), 310.

American Public Health Association (1987). Taxation of tobacco products; advertising and promotion of tobacco products. *American Journal of Public Health, 77*(1), 102–103.

American Public Health Association (1988). Policy statements adopted by the governing council of the American Public Health Association—October 21, 1987. *American Journal of Public Health, 78*, 187–216.

Ames, B. N., Magaw, R., & Gold, L. S. (1987). Ranking possible carcinogenic hazards. *Science, 236*, 271–280.

Anastasiow, N. (1984). Preparing adolescents in child bearing: Before and after pregnancy. In M. Sugar (Ed.), *Adolescent parenthood.* New York: Spectrum.

Anderson, R. F. (1987). Solid waste and public health. In M. R. Greenberg (Ed.), *Public health and the environment: The United States experience* (pp. 173–204). New York: Guilford Press.

Anderson, R. G., & Meyerhoff, W. L. (1982). Otologic manifestations of aging. *Otolarynolology Clinica of North America, 15*, 353–370.

Antonovsky, A. (1979). *Health, stress and coping.* San Francisco: Jossey-Bass.

Antonovsky, A. (1987). *Unraveling the mystery of health: How people manage stress and stay well.* San Francisco: Jossey-Bass.

Ashford, N. A., & Caldart, C. C. (1985). The "right to know": Toxics information transfer in the workplace. *Annual Review of Public Health, 6,* 383–401.

Bachrach, K. M., & Zautra, A. (1986). Assessing the impact of hazardous waste facilities: Psychology, politics, and environmental impact statements. In A. H. Lebovits, A. Baum, & J. E. Singer (Eds.), *Advances in environmental psychology* (vol. 6, pp. 71–88). Hillsdale, NJ: Erlbaum.

Bagdikiam, B. H. (1985). The U.S. media: Supermarket or assembly line. *Journal of Communication, 35,* 97–109.

Bales, J. (1987). Drug tests: Little data, many doubts. *APA Monitor, 18*(8), 7.

Bales, R. F. (1970). *Personality and interpersonal behavior.* New York: Holt, Rinehart, & Winston.

Baltimore, D., & Wolff, S. M. (1986). *Confronting AIDS: Directions for public health, health care, and research.* Washington, DC: National Academy Press.

Bandura, A. (1973). *Aggression: A social learning analysis.* Englewood Cliffs, NJ: Prentice-Hall.

Bandura, A. (1977). *Social learning theory.* Englewood Cliffs, NJ: Prentice-Hall.

Bandura, A. (1982). Self-efficacy in human agency. *American Psychologist, 37,* 122–147.

Bandura, A. (1986). *Social foundations of thought and action: A social cognitive theory.* Englewood Cliffs, NJ: Prentice-Hall.

Barkan, J. D. (1985). Industry invites regulation: The passage of the Pure Food and Drug Act of 1906. *American Journal of Public Health, 75,* 18–26.

Barlow, D. H., & Hersen, M. (1984). *Single case experimental designs: 2nd edition.* New York: Pergamon Press.

Baum, A., Fleming, R., & Singer, J. E. (1982). Stress at Three Mile Island: Applying psychological impact analysis. In L. Bickman (Ed.), *Applied social psychology annual* (vol. 3, pp. 217–248). Beverly Hills, CA: Sage.

Baum, A., Singer, J. E., & Baum, C. S. (1981). Stress and the environment. *Journal of Social Issues, 37*(1), 4–35.

Bauman, K. E. (1987). *Development and evaluation of smoking prevention and cessation intervention using the mass media.* Ongoing project. School of Public Health, University of North Carolina.

Bayer, R. (1986). Notifying workers at risk: The politics of the right-to-know. *American Journal of Public Health, 76*(11), 1352–1356.

Beck, A., Rush, J., Shaw, B., & Emery, G. (1979). *Cognitive therapy of depression.* New York: Guilford.

Beck, R. N. (1987). Viewpoints: Health on the job. *HealthLink, 3*(1), 5.

Becker, M. H. (1986). The tyranny of health promotion. *Public Health Reviews, 14,* 15–25.

Becker, M. H., & Joseph, J. G. (1988). AIDS and behavioral change to reduce risk: A review. *American Journal of Public Health, 78,* 394–410.

Behrens, R. (1983). *Worksite health promotion: Some questions and answers to help you get started. A report of the Office of Health Promotion and Disease Prevention.* Washington, DC: U.S. Department of Health and Human Services.

Belar, C. (1987). The current status of predoctoral and postdoctoral training in health psychology. In G. Stone, S. Weiss, J. Matarazzo, N. Miller, J. Rodin, C. Belar, M. Follick, & J. Singer (Eds.), *Health psychology: A discipline and a profession* (pp. 326–334). Chicago, IL: University of Chicago Press.

Bell, C. S., & Levy, S. M. (1984). Public policy and smoking prevention: Implications for research. In J. D. Matarazzo, S. M. Weiss, J. A. Herd, N. E. Miller, & S. M. Weiss (Eds.), *Behavioral health: A handbook for health enhancement and disease prevention* (pp. 775–785). New York: Wiley.

Belloc, N., & Breslow, L. (1972). Relationship of physical health status and health practices. *Preventive Medicine, 1*, 409.

Benfari, R. C., Ockene, J. K., & McIntyre, K. M. (1982). Control of cigarette smoking from a psychological perspective. In L. Breslow, J. E. Fielding, & L. B. Lave (Eds.), *Annual review of public health* (vol. 3, pp. 101–128). Palo Alto, CA: Annual Reviews, Inc.

Bennetts, A. B., & Lubic, R. W. (1982). The free-standing birth center. *Lancet, 1* (February 13), 378.

Bergquist, C. L. (1986). Health promotion in the workplace. In *Michigan Department of Public Health, Worksite health promotion resource guide* (pp. 1–20). Ann Arbor, MI: Michigan Department of Public Health.

Bernstein, N. R. (1972). *APHA, the first one hundred years*. Washington, DC: American Public Health Association.

Berruta-Clement, J. R., Schweinhart, L. J., Barnett, M. W., Epstein, A. S., & Weikart, D. P. (1984). *Changed lives: The effects of the Perry Preschool Program on youths through age 19*. Ypsilanti, MI: High/Scope Educational Research Foundation.

Best, A., Thompson, S. J., Santi, S. M., Smith, E. A., & Brown, K. S. (1988). Preventing cigarette smoking in children. In L. Breslow, J. E. Fielding, & L. B. Lave (Eds.), *Annual review of public health* (pp. 161–202). Palo Alto, CA: Annual Reviews, Inc.

Bezold, C., Carlson, R. J., & Peck, J. C. (1986). *The future of work and health*. Diver, MA: Auburn House.

Birren, J. E., & Schaie, K. W. (Eds.). (1985). *Handbook of psychology and aging*. New York: Van Nostrand Reinhold.

Bittner, J. R. (1980). *Mass communication: An introduction* (2nd ed.). Englewood Cliffs, NJ: Prentice-Hall.

Black, J. S. (1987). The technological solution: Hard and soft paths, scientific uncertainty, and the control of technology. In M. R. Greenberg (Ed.), *Public health and the environment: The United States experience* (pp. 207–229). New York: Guilford Press.

Blackburn, H. (1972). Multifactor preventive trials (MPT) in coronary heart disease. In G. T. Stewart (Ed.), *Trends in epidemiology: Application to health services research and training* (pp. 212–230). Springfield, IL: Charles C. Thomas.

Blackburn, H., Luepker, R., Kline, F. G., Bracht, N., Carlaw, R., Jacobs, D., Mittelmark, M., Stauffer, L., & Taylor, H. L. (1984). The Minnesota Heart Health Program: A research and demonstration project in cardiovascular disease prevention. In J. D. Matarazzo, S. M. Weiss, J. A. Herd, N. E. Miller, & S. M. Weiss (Eds.), *Behavioral health: A handbook of health enhancement and disease prevention* (pp. 1171–1178). New York: Wiley.

Blake, W. (1986). *An evaluative investigation of the effects of establishing a personalized system of prosthetic aids to memory for demented persons in the home environment*. Unpublished doctoral dissertation. Blacksburg, VA: Virginia Polytechnic Institute and State University.

Blasi, V. (1986). The first amendment and cigarette advertising. *Journal of the American Medical Association, 256*, 502–509.

Blazer, D., & Williams, C. D. (1980). Epidemiology of dysphoria and depression in an elderly population. *American Journal of Psychiatry, 137*, 439–444.

Block, G., Dresser, C. M., Hartman, A. M., & Carroll, M. D. C. (1985). Nutrient sources in the American diet: Quantitative data from the NHANES II Survey. *American Journal of Epidemiology, 122*, 27–40.

Bloom, B. (1988). *Health psychology: A psychosocial perspective.* Englewood Cliffs, NJ: Prentice-Hall.

Bloom, B. L., Hodges, W. F., Kern, M. B., & McFaddin, S. C. (1985). A prevention program for the newly separated: Final evaluations. *American Journal of Orthopsychiatry, 55*, 9–26.

Blumenthal, D. S. (1985). A perspective on environmental health. In D. S. Blumenthal (Ed.), *Introduction to environmental health* (pp. 1–22). New York: Springer.

Bly, J. L., Jones, R. C., & Richardson, J. E. (1986). Impact of worksite health promotion on health care costs and utilization: Evaluation of Johnson & Johnson's Live for Life program. *Journal of the American Medical Association, 256*, 3235–3240.

Bohen, H., & Viveros-Long, A. (1981). *Balancing job and family life: Do flexible work schedules help?* Philadelphia: Temple University Press.

Bolton, F. G., Laner, R. H., & Kane, S. P. (1980). Child maltreatment risk among adolescent mothers: A study of reported cases. *American Journal of Orthopsychiatry, 50*, 489–504.

Bonam, A. F. (1963). Psychoanalytic implications in treating unmarried mothers with narcissistic character structures. *Social Casework, 44*, 323–329.

Boston Women's Health Book Collective. (1976). *Our bodies, ourselves: A book by and for women.* New York: Simon & Schuster.

Botvin, G. J. (1986). Substance abuse prevention research: Recent developments and future directions. *Journal of School Health, 56*(9), 369–374.

Botwinick, J. (1984). *Aging and behavior.* New York: Springer.

Bowers, T. G., Winett, R. A., & Frederiksen, L. W. (1987). Nicotine fading, behavioral contracting and extended treatment: Effects on smoking cessation. *Addictive Behaviors, 12*, 181–184.

Boyd, G. (1987). Use of smokeless tobacco among children and adolescents in the United States. *Preventive Medicine, 16*, 402–421.

Bradley, V. (1987). Alternate ways of accessing services/products. *Family caregiving project.* Rockville, MD: Project Share.

Brandt, A. M. (1987). *No magic bullet.* New York: Oxford University Press.

Brandt, A. M. (1988a). AIDS in historical perspective: Four lessons from the history of sexually transmitted diseases. *American Journal of Public Health, 78*, 367–371.

Brandt, A. M. (1988b). The syphilis epidemic and its relation to AIDS. *Science, 239*, 375–380.

Brenner, M. H. (1973). *Mental illness and the economy.* Cambridge, MA: Harvard University Press.

Breslow, L. (1982). Control of cigarette smoking from a public policy perspective. In L. Breslow, J. A. Fielding, & L. B. Lave (Eds.), *Annual review of public health* (vol. 3, pp. 129–151). Palo Alto, CA: Annual Reviews, Inc.

Brody, J. E. (1985). *Jane Brody's good food book: Living the high carbohydrate way.* New York: Norton.

Bronfenbrenner, U. (1977). Toward an experimental ecology of human development. *American Psychologist, 32*, 513–531.

Bronfenbrenner, U. (1979). *The ecology of human development: Experiences by nature and design.* Cambridge, MA: Harvard University Press.

Brooks-Gunn, J., & Furstenberg, F. F., Jr. (1985). Antecedents and consequences of parenting: The case of adolescent motherhood. In A. D. Fogel & G. F. Melson (Eds.), *The origins of nurturance.* Hillsdale, NJ: Lawrence Erlbaum.

Brown, S. L. (1985). Quantitative risk assessment of environmental hazards. *Annual Review of Public Health, 6,* 247–267.

Brownell, K. D. (1986). Public health approaches to obesity and its management. In L. Breslow, J. E. Fielding, & C. B. Lave (Eds.), *Annual review of public health* (vol. 7, pp. 521–533). Palo Alto, CA: Annual Reviews, Inc.

Brownell, K. D., & Felix, M. R. J. (1987). Competitions to facilitate health promotion: Review and conceptual analysis. *American Journal of Health Promotion, 2,* 28–36.

Brownell, K. D., Marlatt, A., Lichtenstein, E., & Wilson, G. T. (1986). Understanding and preventing relapse. *American Psychologist, 41,* 765–782.

Budd, J., & McCron, R. (1981). Health education and the mass media: Past, present, and potential. In D. S. Leather, G. B. Hastings, & J. K. Davies (Eds.), *Health education and the media* (pp. 33–43). Elmsford, NY: Pergamon Press.

Burden, D. S., & Klerman, L. V. (1984). Teenager parenthood: Factors that lessen economic dependence. *Social Work,* January/February, 11.

Bureau of National Affairs (1986). *Where there's smoke: Problems and policies concerning smoking in the workplace.* Washington, DC: Author.

Butler, R. N. (1980). Ageism: A foreword. *Journal of Social Issues, 36,* 8–11.

Butler, R. N., & Lewis, M. I. (1982). *Aging and mental health.* St. Louis, MO: C. V. Mosby.

Byers, S. K. (1987). Organizational stress: Implications for health promotion managers. *American Journal of Health Promotion,* Summer, 21–27.

Califano, J. A., Jr. (1986). *America's health care revolution: Who lives? Who dies? Who pays?* New York: Random House.

Calkins, M. P. (1987). Designing special care units: A systematic approach. *The American Journal of Alzheimer's Care and Research, 2,* 16–22.

Canada, M. J. (1986). Adolescent pregnancy: Networking and the interdisciplinary approach. *Journal of Community Health, 11*(1), Spring, 58–62.

Cantor, M. H. (1983). Strain among caregivers: A study of experience in the United States. *The Gerontologist, 21,* 471–480.

Cappel, D. B., Burton, C., Becker, J., & Fiore, V. (1985). Relationships of cognitions associated with coping reactions to depression in spousal caregivers of Alzheimer's disease patients. *Cognitive Therapy and Research, 9,* 253–256.

Carden, J. L., Jr. (1985). Hazardous waste management. In D. S. Blumenthal (Ed.), *Introduction to environmental health* (pp. 179–213). New York: Springer.

Cartwright, D., & Zander, A. (1968). *Group dynamics: Research and theory* (3rd ed.). New York: Harper & Row.

Cassell, J. (1976). The continuation of the social environment to host resistance. *American Journal of Epidemiology, 104,* 107–123.

Castleman, B. I., & Navarro, V. (1987). International mobility of hazardous products, industries, and wastes. *Annual Review of Public Health, 8,* 1–19.

Catalano, R. A. (1979). *Health, behavior, and community.* Elmsford, NY: Pergamon Press.

Catalano, R. A., & Dooley, D. (1983). The health effects of economic instability: A test of the economic stress hypothesis. *Journal of Health and Social Behavior, 23,* 133–147.

Cataldo, M. F., & Coates, T. J. (1986). *Health and industry: A behavioral medicine perspective.* New York: Wiley.

Cavins, H. M. (1943, April). The National Quarantine and Sanitary Conventions of

1857 to 1860 and the beginnings of the American Public Health Association. *Bulletin of the History of Medicine, 13*, 404.

Centers for Disease Control (1987a). Human immunodeficiency virus infection in the United States. *Morbidity and Mortality Weekly Report, 36*(49), 801–804.

Centers for Disease Control (1987b). Cigarette smoking in the United States, 1986. *Morbidity and Mortality Weekly Report, 36*(35), 581–585.

Chapman, F. S. (1987, February 16). Executive guilt: Who's taking care of the children? *Fortune*, pp. 30–37.

Chapman, S., & Fitzgerald, B. (1982). Brand preference and advertising recall in adolescent smokers: Some implications for health promotion. *American Journal of Public Health, 72*(5), 491–494.

Chave, S. P. W. (1984). The origins and development of public health. In W. W. Holland, R. Detels, & G. Knox (Eds.), *Oxford textbook of public health. Vol. 1: History, determinants, scope, and strategies* (pp. 3–19). Oxford: Oxford University Press.

Chavis, D. M., & Newbrough, J. R. (1986). The meaning of 'community' in community psychology. *Journal of Community Psychology, 14*(4), 335–340.

Chenoweth, B., & Spenser, B. (1986). Dementia: The experience of family caregivers. *The Gerontologist, 26*, 267–272.

Chesney, M. A., & Feurstein, M. (1979). Behavioral medicine in the occupational setting. In J. R. McNamara (Ed.), *Behavioral approaches to medicine: Application and analysis* (pp. 267–290). New York: Plenum Press.

Chilman, C. S. (1983). *Adolescent sexuality in a changing American society: Social and psychological perspectives for the human services professions* (2nd ed.). New York: Wiley.

Cirksena, K., Flora, J. A., Altman, D. G., Clark, M., Rogers, E., & Blaskovich, L. (1985, August). The "Healthy Living Project": Findings of a health diffusion project. Paper presented at the annual meeting of the American Psychological Association, Los Angeles.

Clark, R. (1987). Channeling effects on informal care. In *Family caregiving project conference on supporting family caregivers* (pp. 41–43). Rockville, MD: Project Share.

Coates, J. (1987). Major industrialists jumping on environmental bandwagon. *San Francisco Examiner*, June 14, p. A-9.

Coates, T. J., Barofsky, I., Saylor, K. E., Simons-Morton, K., Huster, W., Sereghy, E., Strough, S., Jacobs, H., & Kidd, L. (1985). Modifying the snack food consumption patterns of inner-city high school students: The great sensations study. *Preventive Medicine, 14*, 234–247.

Coates, T. J., Jeffrey, R. W., & Slinkard, L. A. (1981). Heart-healthy eating and exercise: Introducing and maintaining changes in health behaviors. *American Journal of Public Health, 71*, 15–23.

Cohen, A., Colligan, M. J., & Berger, P. (1985). Psychology in health risk messages for workers. *Journal of Occupational Medicine, 27*(8), 543–551.

Cohen, R. Y., Stunkard, A., & Felix, M. R. J. (1986). Measuring community change in disease prevention and health promotion. *Preventive Medicine, 15*, 411–421.

Cohen, S., & McKay, G. (1984). Interpersonal relationships as buffers of the impact of psychological stress on health. In A. Baum, J. E. Singer, & S. E. Taylor (Eds.), *Handbook of psychology and health: Vol. 4*. Hillsdale, NJ: Lawrence Erlbaum.

Cohen, W. S. (1985). Health promotion in the workplace: A prescription for good health. *American Psychologist*, February, 213–216.

Colletti, G., & Brownell, L. D. (1982). The physical and emotional benefits of social support: Application to obesity, smoking, and alcoholism. In M. Hersen, R. Eisler, & P. H. Miller (Eds.), *Progress in behavior modification* (pp. 109–178). New York: Academic Press.

Committee on Maternal Health Care and Family Planning (1978). *Ambulatory maternal health care and family planning services: Policies, principles, practices.* Washington, DC: American Public Health Association.

Cone, J. D., & Hayes, S. C. (1977). Applied behavior analysis and the solution of environmental problems. In I. Altman & J. F. Wohlwill (Eds.), *Human behavior and environment: Advances in theory and research* (vol. 2, pp. 129–179). New York: Plenum.

Conrad, P. (1987). Wellness in the work place: Potentials and pitfalls of worksite-site health promotion. *The Milibank Quarterly, 65*(2), 255–275.

Cooper, C. L., & Payne, R. (1980). *Current concerns in occupational stress.* New York: Wiley.

Cormier, A., Prefontaine, M., MacDonald, H., & Stuart, R. B. (1980). Lifestyle change on the campus: Pilot test of a program to improve student health practices. In P. O. Davidson & S. M. Davidson (Eds.), *Behavioral medicine: Changing health lifestyles* (pp. 222–255). New York: Brunner/Mazel.

Corso, J. F. (1977). Auditory perception and communication. In J. E. Birren & K. W. Schaie (Eds.), *Handbook of psychology and aging.* New York: Van Nostrand Reinhold.

Cowen, E. L. (1980). The wooing of primary prevention. *American Journal of Community Psychology, 8*, 258–284.

Cox, F. M. (1979). Alternative conceptions of community: Implications for community organization practice. In F. M. Cox, J. L. Erlich, J. Rothman, & J. E. Tropman (Eds.), *Strategies of community organization* (3rd ed., pp. 224–234). Itasca, IL: F. E. Peacock.

Crawford, R. (1978). Sickness as sin. *Health PAC Bulletin, 80*, 10–16.

Cruz, J., & Wallack, L. (1986). Trends in tobacco use on television. *American Journal of Public Health, 76*(6), 698–699.

Cummings, C. (1986). A review of the impact of nutrition on health and profits and a discussion of successful program elements. *American Journal of Health Promotion, 1*, 14–22.

Curran, J. W., Jaffe, H. W., Hardy, A. M., Morgan, W. M., Selik, R. M., & Dondero, T. J. (1988). Epidemiology of HIV infection and AIDS in the United States. *Science, 239*, 610–616.

Curtis, F. (1973). Observations of unwed pregnant adolescents. *American Journal of Nursing, 74*(1), 100–102.

Cushner, I. M. (1981). Maternal behavior and perinatal risks: Alcohol, smoking, and drugs. *Annual Review of Public Health, 2*, 201.

D'Augelli, J. F., & D'Augelli, A. R. (1977). Moral reasoning and premarital sexual behavior: Toward reasoning about relationships. *Journal of Social Issues, 33*(2), 126–135.

D'Zurilla, T. J. (1986). *Problem-solving therapy.* New York: Springer.

Damberg, C. (1984). *Worksite health promotion: Examples of programs that work. A report of the Office of Health Promotion and Disease Prevention.* Washington, DC: U.S. Government Printing Office.

Danish, S. J., Galambos, N. L., & Laquarta, I. (1983). Life development intervention: Skill training for personal competence. In R. D. Felner et al. (Eds.), *Preventive psychology: Theory, research, and practice.* Elmsford, NY: Pergamon Press.

Davidson, L. M., Baum, A., Fleming, I., & Gisriel, M. M. (1986). Toxic exposure and chronic stress at Three Mile Island. In A. H. Levovits, A. Baum, & J. E. Singer (Eds.), *Advances in environmental psychology* (vol. 6, pp. 35–46). Hillsdale, NJ: Lawrence Erlbaum.

Davis, H. (1987). Workplace homicides of Texas males. *American Journal of Public Health, 77*(10), 1290–1293.

Davis, J. K., Fink, R., Yesupria, A., Rajegowda, B., & Lala, R. (1986). Teenage pregnancy in an urban hospital setting. *Journal of Community Health, 11*(4), Summer, 259–267.

Davis, R. M. (1987). Current trends in cigarette advertising and marketing. *New England Journal of Medicine, 316*(12), 725–732.

Davis-Chervin, D., Rogers, T., & Clark, M. (1985). Influencing food selection with point-of-choice nutrition information. *Journal of Nutrition Education, 17*, 18–22.

Dawson, D. A. (1986). The effects of sex education on adolescent behavior. *Family Planning Perspectives, 15*(4), 162–170.

Dawson, D., Hendershot, G., & Fulton, J. (1987). Aging in the eighties: Functional limitations of individuals age 65 years and over. *Advance Data from Vital and Health Statistics, No. 133.* (DHHS Pub. No. (PHS) 87-1250). Hyattsville, MD: National Center for Health Statistics.

DeAmicis, L. A., Klorman, R., Hess, D. W., & McAnarney, E. R. (1981). A comparison of unwed pregnant teenagers and nulligravid sexually active adolescents seeking contraception. *Adolescence, 16*, 11–20.

DeLamater, J. (1981). Intrapersonal and interactional barriers to contraception. In D. Byrne & W. A. Fisher (Eds.), *Adolescents, sex, and contraception.* New York: McGraw-Hill.

Declining smoking rates reported, Roanoke Times and World News, September 15, 1987, p. 1.

DeLeon, P. H., & Vandenbos, G. R. (1987). Health psychology and health policy. In G. C. Stone, S. M. Weiss, J. D. Matarazzo, N. E. Miller, J. Rodin, C. D. Belar, M. J. Follick, & J. E. Singer (Eds.), *Health psychology: A discipline and a profession* (pp. 175–187). Chicago, IL: University of Chicago Press.

DeLeon, P. H., & Vandenbos, G. R. (1984). Public health policy and behavioral health. In J. D. Matarazzo, S. M. Weiss, J. A. Herd, N. E. Miller, & S. M. Weiss (Eds.), *Behavioral health: A handbook of health enhancement and disease prevention* (pp. 150–163). New York: Wiley.

Demkovich, L. E. (1986). Controlling health care costs at General Motors. *Health Affairs,* Fall, 58–67.

DeRose, A. M. (1982). Identifying needs, gaining support for, and establishing an innovative school-based program for pregnant adolescents. In I. R. Stuart & C. F. Wells (Eds.), *Pregnancy in adolescence: Needs, problems, and management.* New York: Van Nostrand Reinhold.

Detels, R., & Breslow, L. (1984). Current scope. In W. W. Holland, R. Detels, & G. Knox (Eds.), *Oxford textbook of public health, vol. 1: History, determinants, scope, and strategies.* Oxford: Oxford University Press.

Diamond, E., & Bellitto, C. M. (1986). The great verbal cover-up: Prudish editing blurs the facts on AIDS. *Washington Journalism Review, 8*, 38–42.

Dickey, G. (1987). Time for tennis to say no to cigaret ads. *San Francisco Chronicle.* February 17, p. 51.

DiFranza, J. R., Norwood, B. D., Garner, D. W., & Tye, J. B. (1987). Legislative efforts to protect children from tobacco. *Journal of the American Medical Association, 257*, 3387–3389.

Doll, R., & Peto, R. (1981). *The causes of cancer*. Oxford: Oxford University Press.

Dooley, D., & Catalano, R. (1980). Economic change as a cause of behavior disorder. *Psychological Bulletin, 87*, 450–468.

Drotman, D. P. (1987). Now is the time to prevent AIDS (editorial). *American Journal of Public Health, 77*, 143.

Dryfoos, J. G. (1983). Review of interventions in the field of prevention of adolescent pregnancy. Preliminary report to the Rockefeller Foundation, New York.

Dryfoos, J. G. (1984). A new strategy for preventing unintended teenage childbearing. *Family Planning Perspectives, 16*(4), 193–195.

Dryfoos, J. G. (1985). What the United States can learn about prevention of teenage pregnancy from other developed countries. Sex Information and Education Council of the U.S. (SIECUS) Report, Vol. XIV, no. 2, November.

Dryfoos, J. G., & Brindis, C. (1987, July). Planning and implementing a community wide program to reduce adolescent pregnancy. Paper presented at the Stanford Conference on Community Approaches to Health Promotion and Disease Prevention, Stanford University, Stanford, CA.

Edelstein, B. A., & Michelson, L. (Eds.). (1986). *Handbook of prevention*. New York: Plenum.

Edelstein, M. R., & Wandersman, A. (1987). Community dynamics in coping with toxic contaminants. In I. Altman and A. Wandersman (Eds.), *Neighborhood and community environments: Human behavior and environment* (vol. 9, pp. 69–112). New York: Plenum.

Edwards, L. E., Steinman, M. E., Arnold, K. A., & Hahanson, E. Y. (1981). Adolescent pregnancy prevention services in high school clinics. In F. F. Furstenberg, R. Lincoln, & J. Menken (Eds.), *Teenage sexuality, pregnancy, and childbearing*. Philadelphia: University of Pennsylvania Press.

Egger, G., Fitzgerald, W., Frape, G., Monaem, A., Rubinstein, P., Tyler, C., & McKay, B. (1983). Results of large scale media antismoking campaign in Australia: North Coast "Quit for Life" programme. *British Medical Journal, 287*, 1125–1128.

Eisen, M., Zellman, G. L., & McAlister, A. L. (1985). A health belief model approach to adolescents' fertility control: Some pilot program findings. *Health Education Quarterly, 12*(2), 185–210.

Eisenberg, L. (1977). The perils of prevention: A cautionary note. *New England Journal of Medicine, 297*(22), 1230–1232.

Elder, J. P., Howell, M. F., Lasater, T. M., Wells, B. L., & Carleton, R. A. (1985). Applications of behavior modification to community health education: The case of heart disease prevention. *Health Education Quarterly, 12*, 151–168.

Elias, M., Bruene, L., Clabby, J., Barbiere, M., & Heckelman, S. (1985). A multidisciplinary social problem-solving intervention for middle school students with behavior and learning disorders. *Advances in learning and behavioral disabilities, 4*, 49–75.

Elster, A. B., Lamb, M. E., Tavare, J., & Ralston, C. W. (1987). The medical and psychosocial impact of comprehensive care on adolescent pregnancy and parenthood. *Journal of the American Medical Association, 258*(9), 1187–1192.

Engel, G. L. (1977). The need for a new medical model: A challenge for biomedicine. *Science, 196*, 129–136.

Epstein, L. H., & Cluss, P. A. (1982). A behavioral medicine perspective on adherence to long-term medical regimens. *Journal of Consulting and Clinical Psychology, 50*, 950–971.

Epstein, L. H., & Masek, B. J. (1978). Behavioral control of medical compliance. *Journal of Applied Behavior Analysis, 11*, 1-9.

Eriksen, M. P., LeMaistre, C. A., & Newell, G. R. (1988). Health hazards of passive smoking. In L. Breslow, J. E. Fielding, & L. B. Lave (Eds.), *Annual review of public health* (pp. 47-70). Palo Alto, CA: Annual Reviews, Inc.

Erikson, E. (1968). *Identity: Youth and crisis*. New York: W. W. Norton & Co.

Erikson, M. P. (1986). Workplace smoking control: Rationale and approaches. *Advances in Health Education and Promotion, 1*(a), 65-103.

Ernster, V. L. (1985). Mixed messages for women: A social history of cigarette smoking and advertising. *New York State Journal of Medicine, 85*, 335-340.

Estes, C. L. (1979). *The aging enterprise*. San Francisco: Jossey-Bass.

Estes, C. L., & Lee, P. R. (1986). Health problems and policy issues of old age. In L. H. Aiken & D. Mechanic (Eds.), *Applications of social science to clinical medicine and health policy*. New Brunswick, NJ: Rutgers University Press.

Estes, E. H. (1977). Health experience in the elderly. In E. W. Busse & E. Pfeiffer (Eds.), *Behavior and adaptation in late life*. Boston: Little, Brown & Co.

Evans, G. W., & Cohen, S. (1987). Environmental stress. In D. Stokols & I. Altman (Eds.), *Handbook of environmental psychology* (pp. 571-610). New York: Wiley.

Evans, R. I. (1980). Behavioral medicine: A new applied challenge to social psychologists. In L. Bickman (Ed.), *Applied social psychology annual* (vol. 1, pp. 279-305). Beverly Hills, CA: Sage.

Evans, R. I. (1984). A social inoculation strategy to deter smoking in adolescents. In J. D. Matarazzo, S. M. Weiss, J. A. Herd, N. E. Miller, & S. M. Weiss (Eds.), *Behavioral health: A handbook for health enhancement and disease prevention*. New York: Wiley.

Faden, R. R., & Faden, A. I. (Eds.). (1978). Ethical issues in public health policy: Health education and life-style interventions. *Health Education Monograph, 6*, 177-257.

Faden, R. R. (1987). Health psychology and public health. In G. C. Stone, S. M. Weiss, J. D. Matarazzo, N. E. Miller, J. Rodin, C. D. Belar, M. J. Follick, & J. E. Singer (Eds.), *Health psychology: A discipline and a profession*. Chicago, IL: University of Chicago Press.

Farquhar, J. W. (1978). The community-based model of life-style intervention trials. *American Journal of Epidemiology, 108*(2), 103-111.

Farquhar, J. W., Fortman, S. P., Maccoby, N., Haskell, W. L., Williams, P. T., Flora, J. A., Taylor, C. B., Brown, B. W., Solomon, D. S., & Hulley, S. B. (1985). The Stanford Five City Project: Design and methods. *American Journal of Epidemiology, 63*, 171-182.

Farquhar, J. W., Fortmann, S. P., Wood, P. D., & Haskell, W. L. (1983). Community studies of cardiovascular disease prevention. In N. Kaplan & J. Stamler (Eds.), *Prevention of coronary heart disease* (pp. 170-181). Philadelphia: W. B. Saunders Company.

Farquhar, J. W., Maccoby, N., & Solomon, D. (1984). Community applications of behavioral medicine. In W. D. Gentry (Ed.), *Handbook of behavioral medicine* (pp. 437-478). New York: Guilford Press.

Farquhar, J. W., Maccoby, N., & Wood, P. D. (1977). Community education for cardiovascular health. *Lancet, 1*, 1192-1195.

Farquhar, J. W., Maccoby, N., & Wood, P. D. (1985). *Oxford textbook of public health*. Oxford: Oxford University Press.

Fawcett, S. B., Seekins, T., Whang, P. L., Muiu, S. (1984). Creating and using social technologies for community empowerment. In J. Rappaport, C. Swift, & R. Hess (Eds.), *Studies in empowerment: Steps toward understanding and action. Prevention in human services, 3*, 145–171.

Federal Trade Commission (1988). *Report to Congress: Pursuant to the Federal Cigarette Labeling and Advertising Act 1985*. Washington, DC: U.S. Government Printing Office.

Fein, G. G., Schwartz, P. M., Jacobson, S. W., & Jacobson, J. L. (1983). Environmental toxins and behavioral development: A new role for psychological research. *American Psychologist, 38*(11), 1188–1197.

Feis, C. L., & Simons, C. (1985). Training preschool children in interpersonal cognitive problem-solving skills: A replication. *Prevention in Human Services, 4*, 59–70.

Feldman, R. H. L. (1984). Evaluating health promotion in the workplace. In J. D. Matarazzo, S. M. Weiss, J. A. Herd, N. E. Miller, & S. M. Weiss (Eds.), *Behavioral health: A handbook for health enhancement and disease prevention* (pp. 1087–1093). New York: Wiley.

Felner, R. D., Farber, S. S., & Primavera, J. (1983). Transitions and stressful life events: A model for primary prevention. In R. D. Felner et al. (Eds.), *Preventive psychology: Theory, research, and practice*. Elmsford, NY: Pergamon Press.

Felner, R. D., Jason, L. A., Moritsugu, J. N., & Farber, S. S. (1983). *Preventive psychology: Theory, research, and practice*. Elmsford, NY: Pergamon Press.

Ferrara, A. J. (1984). My personal experience with AIDS. *American Psychologist, 39*(11), 1285–1287.

Fessenden-Raden, J., Fitchen, J. M., & Heath, J. S. (1987). Providing risk information in communities. Factors influencing what is heard and accepted. *Science, Technology, and Human Values, 12*, 94–101.

Fielding, J. A. (1984). Health promotion and disease prevention at the worksite. In L. Breslow, J. A. Fielding, & L. B. Lave (Eds.), *Annual review of public health* (vol. 5, pp. 237–265). Palo Alto, CA: Annual Reviews, Inc.

Fielding, J. E. (1979). Preventive medicine and the bottom line. *Journal of Occupational Medicine, 21*(2), 79–88.

Fielding, J. E. (1984). Health promotion and disease prevention at the worksite. *Annual Review of Public Health, 5*, 237–265.

Fielding, J. E. (1986). Banning worksite smoking. *American Journal of Public Health, 76*, 957–959.

Fine, S. J. (1981). *The marketing of ideas and social issues*. New York: Harcourt Brace Jovanovich.

Fineberg, H. V. (1988). Education to prevent AIDS: Prospects and obstacles. *Science, 239*, 592–596.

Finkel, M. L., & Finkel, D. J. (1981). Sexual and contraceptive knowledge, attitudes and behavior of male adolescents. In F. F. Furstenberg, Jr., R. Lincoln, & J. Menken (Eds.), *Teenage sexuality, pregnancy, and childbearing* (pp. 327–335). Philadelphia: University of Pennsylvania Press.

Fischhoff, B., Svenson, O., & Slovic, P. (1987). Active responses to environmental hazards: Perceptions and decision making. In D. Stokols & I. Altman (Eds.), *Handbook of environmental psychology* (pp. 1089–1133). New York: Wiley.

Fisher, J. D., Bell, P. A., & Baum, A. (1984). *Environmental psychology* (2nd ed.). New York: Holt, Rinehart, & Winston.

Fisher, S. M. (1984). The psychodynamics of teenage pregnancy and motherhood. In M. Sugar (Ed.), *Adolescent parenthood* (pp. 55–63). New York: Spectrum Publications.

Fiske, S. T. (1987). People's reactions to nuclear war: Implications for psychologists. *American Psychologist, 42*(3), 207–217.

Fitting, M., Rabins, P., Lucas, M. J., & Eastham, J. (1986). Caregivers for dementia patients: A comparison of husbands and wives. *The Gerontologist, 26*, 248–252.

Flavell, J. (1984, November). Cognitive development of adolescents. Paper presented at Conference on: *Unhealthful Risk-taking Behaviors in Adolescence*, Stanford University.

Flay, B. R. (1987). Mass media and smoking cessation: A critical review. *American Journal of Public Health, 77*(2), 153–160.

Flay, B. R., & Cook, T. D. (1981). Evaluation of mass media prevention campaigns. In R. E. Rice & W. J. Paisley (Eds.), *Public communication campaigns* (pp. 239–264). Beverly Hills, CA: Sage.

Fleming, I., & Baum, A. (1985). The role of prevention in technological catastrophe. In A. Wandersman & R. Hess (Eds.), *Beyond the individual: Environmental approaches and prevention* (pp. 139–152). New York: Haworth.

Flick, L. (1984). *Adolescent childbearing decisions: Implications for prevention*. St. Louis, MO: The Danforth Foundation.

Foege, W. H. (1987). Public health: Moving from debt to legacy — 1986 presidential address. *American Journal of Public Health, 77*, 1276–1278.

Foege, W., Amler, R., & White, C. (1985). Closing the gap. *Journal of the American Medical Association, 254*, 1355–1358.

Foster, S. E. (1986). *Preventing teenage pregnancy: A public policy guide*. Washington, DC: The Council of State Policy & Planning Agencies.

Fox, G. L. (1977). "Nice girl": Social control of women through a value construct. *Signs: Journal of Women and Culture in Society, 2*, 805–817.

Foxx, R. M., & Brown, R. A. (1979). Nicotine fading and self-monitoring for cigarette abstinence or controlled smoking. *Journal of Applied Behavior Analysis, 12*, 111–125.

Freedman, J. C. (1984). Effects of television violence on aggressiveness. *Psychological Bulletin, 96*, 227–246.

Freeman, E. W., Rickels, K., Huggins, G. R., Mudd, E. H., Garcia, C. R., & Dickens, H. O. (1980). Adolescent contraceptive use: Comparisons of male and female attitudes and information. *American Journal of Public Health, 70*, 790–797.

Freimuth, V. S., Hammond, S. L., & Stein, J. A. (1988). Health advertising: Prevention for profit. *American Journal of Public Health, 78*, 557–561.

Freudenberg, N. (1984). Citizen action for environmental health: Report on a survey of community organizations. *American Journal of Public Health, 74*(5), 444–448.

Friedman, L., & Haynes, S. G. (1985). An epidemiologic profile of the elderly. In H. T. Phillips & S. A. Gaylord (Eds.), *Aging and public health*. New York: Springer.

Friedman, M., & Friedman, R. (1979). *Free to choose: A personal statement*. New York: Harcourt Brace Jovanovich.

Friedman, S. M., Gorney, C. M., & Egolf, B. P. (1987). Reporting on radiation: A content analysis of Chernobyl coverage. *Journal of Communication, 37*(3), 58–67.

Fries, J. F., & Crapo, L. M. (1981). *Vitality and aging: Implications of the rectangular curve*. San Francisco, CA: W. H. Freeman.

Froines, J., & Baker, D. (1985). Workers. In W. W. Holland, R. Detels, & G. Knox (Eds.), *Oxford textbook of public health* (vol. 4, pp. 371–388). New York: Oxford University Press.

Fuchs, V. R. (1975). *Who shall live? Health, economics, and social choice.* New York: Basic Books.

Furstenberg, F. F., Jr., & Brooks-Gunn, J. (1986). Teenage childbearing: Causes, consequences, and remedies. In L. H. Aiken & D. Mechanic (Eds.), *Applications of social science to clinical medicine and health policy* (pp. 307-334). New Brunswick, NJ: Rutgers University Press.

Furstenberg, F. F., Jr., Herceg-Baron, R., Shea, J., & Webb, D. (1984). Family communication and teenagers' contraceptive use. *Family Planning Perspectives, 16*(4), 163-170.

Furstenberg, F. F., Jr., Masnick, G., & Ricketts, S. (1972). How can family planning programs delay repeat pregnancies? *Family Planning Perspectives, 4*(3), 54-60.

Furstenberg, F. F., Jr., Shea, J., Allison, P., Herceg-Baron, R., & Webb, D. (1983). Contraceptive continuation among adolescents attending family planning clinics. *Family Planning Perspectives, 15*, 211-217.

Furukawa, C. (1982). Adult health conference: Community-oriented health maintenance for the elderly. In T. Wells (Ed.), *Aging and health promotion.* Rockville, MD: Aspen Systems.

Gallagher, D. (1981). Behavioral group therapy with elderly depressives: An experimental study. In D. Upper & S. Ross (Eds.), *Behavioral group therapy.* Champaign, IL: Research Press.

Gallagher, D. E. (1985). Intervention strategies to assist caregivers of frail elders: Current research status and future directions. In M. P. Lawton & G. Maddox (Eds.), *Annual Review of Gerontology and Geriatrics, 5*, pp. 249-280.

Gallagher, D., Lovett, S., & Zeiss, A. (in press). Interventions with caregivers of frail elderly persons. In M. Ory & K. Bond (Eds.), *Aging and health care.* New York: Tavistock Publications.

Gallagher, D., Wrabetz, A., Lovett, S., Del Maestro, S., & Rose, J. (in press). Depression and other negative affects in family caregivers. In E. Light & B. Lebowitz (Eds.), *Alzheimer's disease treatment and family stress: Directions for research.* Washington, DC: U.S. Government Printing Office.

Garrison, E. G. (1987). Psychological maltreatment of children: An emerging focus for inquiry and concern. *American Psychologist, 42*, 157-159.

Garmezy, N. (1981). Children under stress: Perspectives on antecedents and correlates of vulnerability and resistance to psychopathology. In A. I. Rubin, J. Aronoff, A. M. Barclay, & R. A. Zucker (Eds.), *Further explorations in personality.* New York: Wiley.

Gatz, M., Popkin, S. J., Pino, C. D., & VandenBos, G. R. (1985). Psychological interventions with older adults. In J. E. Birren & K. W. Schaie (Eds.), *Handbook of the psychology of aging* (2nd ed.). New York: Van Nostrand Reinhold.

Gelfand, D. M., Ficula, T., & Zarbatany, L. (1986). Prevention of childhood behavior disorders. In B. A. Edelstein & L. Michelson (Eds.), *Handbook of prevention* (pp. 133-152). New York: Plenum.

Geller, E. S. (1986). Prevention of environmental problems. In B. A. Edelstein & L. Michelson (Eds.), *Handbook of prevention* (pp. 361-383). New York: Plenum.

Geller, E. S. (1987). Applied behavior analysis and environmental psychology: From strange bedfellows to a productive marriage. In D. Stokols & I. Altman (Eds.), *Handbook of environmental psychology* (pp. 361-388). New York: Wiley.

Geller, E. S., Winett, R. A., & Everett, P. B. (1982). *Preserving the environment: New strategies for behavior change.* Elmsford, NY: Pergamon Press.

George, L. K., & Gwyther, L. P. (1986). Caregiver well-being: A multidimensional examination of family caregivers of demented adults. *The Gerontologist, 26*, 253–259.

George, L. K., & Gwyther, L. P. (1985). Support groups for caregivers of memory-impaired elderly: Easing caregiver burden. Presented at Annual Vermont Conference on Primary Prevention, Burlington, Vermont.

George, M. D. (1925). *London life in the XVIIIth century*. New York: Alfred A. Knopf.

Gerrard, M., McCann, L., & Fortini, M. E. (1983). Prevention of unwanted pregnancy. *American Journal of Community Psychology, 11*, 153–167.

Gesten, E. L., & Jason, L. A. (1987). Social and community interventions. *Annual Review of Psychology, 38*, 427–460.

Gesten, E. L., Rains, M. H., Rapkin, B. D., Weissberg, R. P., Flores do Apodaca, R., Cowen, E. L., & Bowen, R. (1982). Training children in social problem-solving competencies: A first and second look. *American Journal of Community Psychology, 10*, 95–115.

Gibbs, J. O., Mulvaney, D., Henes, C., & Reed, R. W. (1985). Worksite health promotion: Five year trend in employee health care costs. *Journal of Occupational Medicine, 27*(11), 826–830.

Gibbs, M. S. (1986). Psychopathological consequences of exposure to toxins in the water supply. In A. H. Lebovits, A. Baum, & J. E. Singer (Eds.), *Advances in environmental psychology* (vol. 6, pp. 47–70). Hillsdale, NJ: Lawrence Erlbaum.

Gibbs, N. R. (1988). Grays on the go. *Time*, February 22, 1988, 66–75.

Giblin, P., Sprenkle, D. H., & Sheehan, R. (1985). Enrichment outcome research: A meta-analysis of premarital, marital, and family intervention. *Journal of Marital Family Therapy, 11*, 257–271.

Goldfried, M. R. (1980). Toward the delineation of therapeutic change principles. *American Psychologist, 35*, 991–996.

Goldston, S. E. (1986). Primary prevention: Historical perspectives and blueprint for action. *American Psychologist, 41*, 453–468.

Goodman, S. H. (1984). Children of disturbed parents: The interface between research and intervention. *American Journal of Community Psychology, 12*, 663–687.

Gordon, J. (1987). Workplace health promotion: The right idea in the wrong place. *Health Education Research, 2*(1), 69–71.

Gorn, G. T., & Goldberg, M. E. (1982). Behavioral evidence of the effects of televised food messages on children. *Journal of Consumer Research, 9*, 200–205.

Gostin, C., & Curran, W. J. (1987a). AIDS screening, confidentiality, and the duty to warn. *American Journal of Public Health, 77*, 361–367.

Gostin, C., & Curran, W. J. (1987b). Legal control measures for AIDS: Reporting requirements, surveillance, quarantine, and regulation of public meeting places. *American Journal of Public Health, 77*, 214–219.

Gottschalk, L. A., Titchener, J. L., Piker, H. N., & Stewart, S. S. (1964). Psychosocial factors associated with pregnancy in adolescent girls: A preliminary report. *Journal of Nervous and Mental Disorders, 138*, 524–534.

Government Accounting Office, Comptroller General's Report to the Congress of the United States (1979). *Conditions of older people: National information system needed*. (HRD 79-95, September). Washington, DC: U.S. Government Printing Office.

Gray, H. J. (1983). The role of business in health promotion: A brief overview. *Preventive Medicine, 12*, 654–657.

Green, L. W. (1979). Educational strategies to improve compliance with therapeutic and preventive regimens: The recent evidence. In R. B. Haynes, D. W. Taylor, & D. L. Sackett (Eds.), *Compliance in health care* (pp. 157-173). Baltimore, MD: Johns Hopkins University Press.

Green, L. W. (1984). Modifying and developing health behaviors. In L. Breslow, J. A. Fielding, & L. B. Lave (Eds.), *Annual review of public health* (vol. 5, pp. 215-236). Palo Alto, CA: Annual Reviews, Inc.

Green, L. W. (1986). Individuals vs. systems: An artificial classification that divides and distorts. *HealthLink*, September, 29-30.

Green, L. W. (1987). Letter to the editor. *Health Education Quarterly, 14*(3), 3-5.

Green, L. W., & Anderson, C. L. (1982). *Community health*. St. Louis, MO: Mosby.

Greenberg, M. R. (1987). *Public health and the environment: The United States experience*. New York: Guilford Press.

Greene, B. F., Rouse, M., Green, R. B., & Clay, C. (1984). Behavior analysis in consumer affairs: Retail and consumer response to publicizing comparative food price information. *Journal of Applied Behavior Analysis, 17*, 3-22.

Greene, B. F., Winett, R. A., Van Houten, R., Geller, E. S., & Iwata, B. A. (1987). *Behavior analysis in the community*. Lawrence, KS: *Society for the Experimental Analyses of Behavior*.

Greenwald, P., Lanza, E., & Eddy, G. A. (1987). Dietary fiber in the reduction of colon cancer risk. *Journal of the American Dietetic Association, 87*, 1178-1188.

Greenwald, P., Sondik, E., & Lynch, B. S. (1986). Diet and chemoprevention in NCI's research strategy to achieve national cancer control objectives. In L. Breslow, J. E. Fielding, & L. B. Lave (Eds.), *Annual review of public health* (vol. 7, pp. 267-292). Palo Alto: Annual Reviews, Inc.

Grobstein, C. (1983). Should imperfect data be used to guide public policy? *Science, 83*, 12, 18.

Grzelka, C. (1987). Employers ponder screening workers for drug use. *HealthLink, 3*(1), 13-14.

Guerney, B. G. (1986). Family relationship enhancement: A skills training approach. In L. Bond (Ed.), *Families in transition: Primary prevention programs that work*. Beverly Hills, CA: Sage.

Gurin, G., Veroff, J., & Field, S. (1960). *Americans view their mental health*. New York: Basic Books.

Gurland, B. J., & Cross, P. S. (1987). Public health perspectives on clinical memory testing of Alzheimer's disease and related disorders. In L. W. Poon (Ed.), *Clinical memory assessment of older adults*. Washington, DC: American Psychological Association.

Haglund, K. (1986). Hearings on passive smoking demonstrate the debate. *The Nation's Health*, April, 12.

Haley, W. D. (1983). A family–behavioral approach to the treatment of the cognitively impaired elderly. *The Gerontologist, 23*, 18-20.

Haley, W. D., Brown, S. L., & Levine, E. G. (1987). Experimental evaluation of the effectiveness of group intervention for dementia caregivers. *The Gerontologist, 27*, 376-382.

Hallett, R. (1986). Smoking intervention in the workplace: Review and recommendations. *Preventive Medicine, 15*, 213-231.

Hamburg, D. A., Elliot, G. R., & Parron, D. L. (1982). Health and behavior: Frontiers of research in the biobehavioral sciences. Washington, DC: National Academy Press.

Hamilton, J. R. (1972). The demand for cigarettes: Advertising, the health scare, and the cigarette advertising ban. *Review of Economics and Statistics, 54*, 401–411.

Hanlon, J. J., & Pickett, G. E. (1984). *Public health: Administration and practice* (8th ed.). St. Louis, MO: Mosby.

Hardy, J. B., King, T. M., & Repke, J. T. (1987). The Johns Hopkins adolescent pregnancy program: An evaluation. *Obstetrics & Gynecology, 69*, 300–306.

Harken, L. S. (1987). The prevention of adolescent smoking: A public health priority. *Evaluation and the Health Professions, 10*, 373–393.

Harper, A. E. (1984). A healthful diet and its implications for disease prevention. In J. Matarazzo, S. M. Weiss, J. A. Herd, N. E. Miller, & S. M. Weiss (Eds.), *Behavioral health: A handbook for health enhancement and disease prevention* (pp. 575–590). New York: Wiley.

Harris, R. H., English, C. W., & Highland, J. H. (1985). Hazardous waste disposal: Emerging technologies and public policies to reduce public health risks. *Annual Review of Public Health, 6*, 269–294.

Hart, S. N., & Brassard, M. R. (1987). A major threat to children's mental health: Psychological maltreatment. *American Psychologist, 42*, 160–165.

Hartsough, D. M., & Savitsky, J. C. (1984). Three Mile Island: Psychology and environmental policy at a crossroads. *American Psychologist, 39*(10), 1113–1122.

Harvey, M. R. (1985). *Exemplary rape crisis programs: A cross-site analysis and case studies*. (DHHS Publ. 85-1423). Washington, DC: U.S. Government Printing Office.

Hattie, J. A., Sharpley, C. F., & Rogers, H. J. (1984). Comparative effectiveness of professionals and paraprofessional helpers. *Psychological Bulletin, 95*, 534–541.

Health Insurance Association of America (1986). *Organizing a wellness council*. Washington, DC: Author.

Health Promotion Resource Center (1987). *A guide to comprehensive integrated community health promotion programs*. Stanford, CA: Author.

Heckler, M. M. (1985). The fight against Alzheimer's disease. *American Psychologist, 40*, 1240–1244.

Heimbach, J. T. (1981). Defining the problem: The scope of consumer concern with food labeling. In K. B. Monroe (Ed.), *Advances in consumer research* (vol. 8, pp. 515–521). Ann Arbor, MI: Association for Consumer Research.

Heller, K., & Monahan, J. (1977). *Psychology and community change*. Homewood, IL: Dorsey.

Heller, K., Price, R. H., Reinharz, S., Riger, S., & Wandersman, A. (1984). *Psychology and community change* (2nd ed.). Homewood, IL: Dorsey.

Heller, K., Swindle, R. W., & Dusenburg, L. (1986). Component social support processes: Comments and integration. *Journal of Consulting and Clinical Psychology, 54*, 466–470.

Henninger, D. G., & Nelson, G. (1984). Evaluation of a social support program for young unwed mothers. *Journal of Primary Prevention, 5*, 3–16.

Herold, E. S., Goodwin, M. S., & Lero, D. S. (1979). Self-esteem, locus of control, and adolescent contraception. *Journal of Psychology, 101*, 83–88.

Herzog, J. M. (1984). Boys who make babies. In M. Sugar (Ed.), *Adolescent parenthood* (pp. 65–73). New York: Spectrum Publications.

Hess, R. E., & Wandersman, A. (1985). What can we learn from Love Canal?: A conversation with Lois Gibbs and Richard Valinsky. In A. Wandersman & R. E. Hess (Eds.), *Beyond the individual: Environmental approaches and prevention* (pp. 111–123). New York: Haworth Press.

Hess, R. E. (1985). Beyond the individual: A practitioner's perspective. In A. Wandersman & R. E. Hess (Eds.), *Beyond the individual: Environmental approaches and prevention* (pp. 207–211). New York: Haworth Press.

Hill, R. D., Evankovich, K. D., Sheikh, J. I., & Yesavage, J. A. (1987). Imagery mnemonic training in a patient with primary degenerative dementia. *Psychology and Aging, 2*, 204–205.

Hinrichsen, G. A., Revenson, T. A., & Shinn, M. (1985). Does self-help help? An empirical investigation of scoliosis peer support groups. *Journal of Social Issues, 41*, 65–87.

Holahan, C. J., & Wandersman, A. (1987). The community psychology perspective in environmental psychology. In D. Stokols & I. Altman (Eds.), *Handbook of environmental psychology* (pp. 827–861). New York: Wiley.

Holden, C. (1987). Networks nix contraceptives ad. *Science, 238*, 887.

Hollander, R. B., & Hale, J. F. (1987). Worksite health promotion programs: Ethical issues. *American Journal of Health Promotion, 2*(2), 37–43.

Hollander, R. B., Lengermann, J. J., & DeMuth, N. M. (1985). Cost-effectiveness and cost–benefit analyses of occupational health promotion. In G. S. Everly & R. H. L. Feldman (Eds.), *Occupational health promotion: Health behavior in the workplace* (pp. 287–300). New York: Wiley.

Hopkins, J., & White, P. (1978). The dual-earner couple: Constraints and supports. *The Family Coordinator*, July, 253–259.

House, J. S., & Cottington, E. M. (1986). Health and the workplace. In L. H. Aiken & D. Mechanic (Eds.), *Applications of social science to clinical medicine and health policy* (pp. 392–416). New Brunswick, NJ: Rutgers University Press.

Hovland, C. I., Lumsdaine, A. A., & Sheffield, F. D. (1949). *Experiments on mass communication*. Princeton, NJ: Princeton University Press.

Huang, L., Cartwright, W. S., & Hu, T. (1988). The economic cost of senile dementia in the United States, 1985. *Public Health Reports, 103*, 3–7.

Huberman, A. M., & Miles, M. B. (1984). *Innovation up close: How school improvement works*. New York: Plenum.

Hubert, H. B. (1986). The importance of obesity in the development of coronary risk factors and disease: The epidemiologic evidence. In L. Breslow, J. E. Fielding, & L. B. Lave (Eds.), *Annual review of public health* (vol. 7). Palo Alto, CA: Annual Reviews, Inc.

Hutchings, R. (1982). A review of the nature and extent of cigarette advertising in the United States. In *Proceedings of the National Conference on Smoking and Health: Developing a blueprint for action* (pp. 249–262). New York: American Cancer Society.

Interdivisional Committee on Adolescent Abortion (1987). Adolescent abortion: Psychological and legal issues. *American Psychologist, 42*, 73–78.

Iscoe, I. (1982). Towards a viable community health psychology: Caveats from the experiences of the community mental health movement. *American Psychologist, 37*, 961–965.

Iverson, D. C. (1987). Smoking control programs: Premises and promises. *American Journal of Health Promotion, 1*(3), 16–30.

Jaccard, J. J., & Davidson, A. R. (1972). Toward an understanding of family planning behaviors: An initial investigation. *Journal of Applied Social Psychology, 2*, 228–235.

Jacobs, S., & Ostfeld, A. (1977). An epidemiological review of the mortality of bereavement. *Psychosomatic Medicine, 39*, 344–357.

Janis, I. L. (1983). The role of social support in adherence to stressful decisions. *American Psychologist, 38*, 143–160.

Janis, I. L., & Rodin, J. (1979). Attribution, control, and decision-making: Social psychology and health care. In G. C. Stone, F. Cohen, & N. E. Adler (Eds.), *Health psychology* (pp. 487–521). San Francisco: Jossey-Bass.

Janz, N. K., & Becker, M. H. (1984). The health belief model: A decade later. *Health Education Quarterly, 11*, 1–47.

Jason, L. A. (1987). Ongoing NIMH project on social transitions. Department of Psychology, DePaul University.

Jason, L. A., Felner, R. D., Hess, R., & Moritsugu, J. N. (1987). *Communities: Contributions from allied disciplines*. New York: Haworth Press.

Jason, L. A., Gruder, C. L., Martino, S., Flay, B. R., Warnecke, R., & Thomas, N. (1987a). Worksite group meetings and the effectiveness of a televised smoking cessation intervention. *American Journal of Community Psychology, 15*, 57–70.

Jaycox, S., Baronowski, T., Nader, P. R., Dworkin, R., & Vanderpool, N. A. (1983). Theory-based health education activities for third to sixth grade children. *Journal of School Health, 53*, 584–588.

Jeffrey, R. W., Forster, J. L., & Snell, M. K. (1985). Promoting weight control at the worksite: A pilot program of self-motivation using payroll-based incentives. *Preventive Medicine, 14*, 187–194.

Jessor, R. (1982). Critical issues in research on adolescent health promotion. In T. J. Coates, A. C. Petersen, & C. L. Perry (Eds.), *Promoting adolescent health: A dialog on research and practice*. New York: Academic Press.

Jessor, R. (1984). Adolescent development and behavioral health. In J. D. Matarazzo, S. M. Weiss, J. A. Herd, N. E. Miller, & S. M. Weiss (Eds.), *Behavioral health: A handbook for health enhancement and disease prevention* (pp. 69–90). New York: Wiley.

Jessor, R., & Jessor, S. L. (1977). *Problem behavior and psychosocial development: A longitudinal study of youth*. New York: Academic Press.

Johnson, C. A. (1983). *Prevention and control of drug abuse*. Los Angeles, CA: University of Southern California.

Johnson, D. L., & Breckenridge, J. N. (1982). The Houston Parent–Child Development Center and the primary prevention of behavior problems in young children. *American Journal of Community Psychology, 10*, 305–316.

Johnson, D. L., & Walker, T. (1985). The primary prevention of behavior problems in Mexican-American children. Paper presented at Social Research and Child Development Convention, Toronto.

Johnson, R. L. (1986). Preventing adolescent pregnancy: Meeting the comprehensive range of needs. *Journal of Community Health, 11*(1), 35–40.

Johnston, L. D. (1986, August). Testimony before the Subcommittee on Health and the Environment of the Committee on Energy and Commerce, United States House of Representatives, in Hearings on Cigarette Advertising and Promotion.

Joint Commission on Mental Illness (1961). *Action for mental health*. New York: Basic Books.

Jones, E. F., Forrest, J. D., Goldman, N., Henshaw, S. K., Lincoln, R., Rosoff, J. I., Westoff, C. F., & Wulf, D. (1985). Teenage pregnancy in developed countries: Determinants and policy implications. *Family Planning Perspectives, 17*(2), March/April, 53–63.

Jones, J. E., Namerow, P. B., & Philliber, S. G. (1986). Strategies for evaluating a contraceptive service for teenagers. *Health Care Management Review, 11*(1), 41–46.

Jones, R. C. (1987). Letter to the editor. *Journal of the American Medical Association, 257*(20), 2756–2757.

Jordon, T. J., Grallo, R., Deutsch, M., Deutsch, C. P. (1985). Long-term effects of early enrichment: A 20-year perspective on persistence and change. *American Journal of Community Psychology, 13,* 393–416.

Jorgensen, S. R. (1980). Contraceptive attitude–behavior consistency in adolescence. *Population and Environment, 3,* 174–194.

Judson, F. N., & Vernon, T. M. (1988). The impact of AIDS on state and local health departments: Issues and a few answers. *American Journal of Public Health, 78,* 387–393.

Kahn, R. L. (1981). *Work and health.* New York: Wiley.

Kahneman, D., & Tverskey, A. (1984). Choices, values, and frames. *American Psychologist, 39,* 341–350.

Kannel, W. B. (1983). An overview of the risk factors for cardiovascular disease. In N. M. Kaplan & J. Stamler (Eds.), *Prevention of coronary heart disease: Practical management of the risk factors.* Philadelphia, PA: W. B. Saunders.

Kanter, R. M. (1977). *Work and family in the United States: A critical review and agenda for research and policy.* New York: Russell Sage.

Kaplan, N. M. (1986). Dietary aspects of the treatment of hypertension. In L. Breslow, J. E. Fielding, & L. B. Lave (Eds.), *Annual review of public health* (vol. 7, pp. 503–519). Palo Alto, CA: Annual Reviews, Inc.

Kaplan, N. M., & Stamler, J. (Eds.). (1983). *Prevention of coronary heart disease.* Philadelphia, PA: W. B. Saunders.

Kaplan, R. (1984). The connection between clinical health promotion and health status. *American Psychologist, 39*(7), 755–765.

Kaplan, R. M. (1985). Quality-of-life measurement. In P. Karoly (Ed.), *Measurement strategies in health psychology* (pp. 115–146). New York: Wiley.

Katasky, M. (1974). The Health Belief Model as a conceptual framework for explaining contraceptive compliance. *Health Education Monograph, 5,* 232–243.

Katz, E., & Lazarsfeld, P. F. (1955). *Personal influence.* New York: Free Press.

Katzman, R. (1986). Dementia: Differential diagnosis of dementing illnesses. *Neurologia Clinica, 4,* 329–340.

Kazdin, A. E. (1984). *Behavior modification in applied settings* (3rd ed.). Homewood, IL: Dorsey.

Kegeles, S. M., Adler, N. E., & Irwin, C. E. (1988). Sexually active adolescents and condoms: Changes over one year in knowledge, attitudes, and use. *American Journal of Public Health, 78,* 460–461.

Khlentzos, M., & Pagliaro, M. (1965). Observations from psychotherapy with unwed mothers. *American Journal of Orthopsychiatry, 35,* 779–786.

Kiefhaber, A. K., & Goldbeck, W. B. (1984). Worksite wellness. In USDHHS, *Proceedings of prospects for a healthier America: Achieving the nation's health promotion objectives* (pp. 41–56). Washington, DC: U.S. Government Printing Office.

Kiesler, C. A. (1985). Prevention and public policy. In J. C. Posen & L. J. Soloman (Eds.), *Prevention in health psychology.* Hanover, NH: University Press of New England.

Killen, J. D., Maccoby, N., & Taylor, C. B. (1984). Nicotine gum and self-regulation in smoking relapse prevention. *Behavior Therapy, 15,* 234–248.

Kinch, R. A. H., Waring, M. P., Love, E. J., & McMahon, D. (1969). Some aspects of pediatric illegitimacy. *American Journal of Obstetric Gynecology, 105,* 20–31.

King, A. C., & Frederiksen, L. W. (1984). Low-cost strategies for increasing exercise behavior: Relapse preparation training and social support. *Behavior Modification, 8*(1), 3–21.

King, A. C., & Winett, R. A. (1986). Stress reduction for individuals at risk: Comparisons of women from dual-earner and dual-career families. *Family and Community Health, 9*, 42–50.

King, A. C., Carl, F. N., Birkel, L. P., & Haskell, W. L. (1988). Increasing exercise among blue-collar employees: The tailoring of worksite programs to meet specific needs. *Preventive Medicine, 17*, 357–365.

King, A. C., Dreon, D., Frey-Hewitt, B., Terry, R., & Wood, P. (1987, March). Low-cost strategies for maintenance of weight loss. *Proceedings of the Annual Conference of the Society of Behavioral Medicine*. Washington, DC: Author.

King, A. C., Flora, J. A., Fortmann, S. P., & Taylor, C. B. (1987). Smoker's challenge: Immediate and long-term findings of a community smoking cessation contest. *American Journal of Public Health, 77*, 1340–1341.

King, A. C., Haskell, H. L., Houston-Miller, N., & Blair, S. (1988). *Promotion of physical activity in communities: A manual for community health professionals*. Stanford, CA: Health Promotion Resource Center.

King, A. C., Saylor, K. E., Foster, S., Killen, J. D., Telch, M. J., Farquhar, J. W., & Flora, J. A. (1988). Promoting dietary change in adolescents: A school-based approach for modifying and maintaining healthful behavior. *American Journal of Preventive Medicine, 4*, 68–74.

King, A. C., Taylor, C. B., Haskell, W. L., & DeBusk, R. F. (1988). Strategies for increasing early adherence to and long-term maintenance of home-based exercise training in healthy middle-aged men and women. *The American Journal of Cardiology, 61*, 628–632.

King, A. C., Winett, R. A., & Lovett, S. B. (1986). Enhancing coping behaviors in at-risk populations: The effects of time management instruction and social support in women from dual-career families. *Behavior Therapy, 17*, 57–66.

Kinsey, A. C., Wardell, B. P., Martin, C. E., & Gebhard, P. H. (1953). *Sexual behavior in the human female*. Philadelphia, PA: W. B. Saunders.

Kirby, D. (1984). *Sexuality education: An evaluation of programs and their effects* (vol. 1). Santa Cruz, CA: Mathtec, Inc.–Network Publications.

Klepp, K. I., Halper, A., & Perry, C. L. (1986). The efficacy of peer leaders in drug abuse prevention. *Journal of School Health, 56*(9), 407–411.

Klesges, R. C., Vasey, M. M., & Glasgow, R. E. (1986). A worksite smoking modification competition: Potential for public health impact. *American Journal of Public Health, 76*, 198–200.

Knowles, J. H. (1977). The responsibility of the individual. In J. H. Knowles (Ed.), *Doing better and feeling worse: Health in the United States* (pp. 53–71). New York: Norton.

Kobasa, S. C. O. (1985). Longitudinal and prospective methods in health psychology. In P. Karoly (Ed.), *Measurement strategies in health psychology* (pp. 235–262). New York: Wiley.

Kotler, P. (1975). *Marketing for nonprofit organizations*. Englewood Cliffs, NJ: Prentice-Hall.

Kotler, P. (1982). *Marketing for nonprofit organizations* (2nd ed.). Englewood Cliffs, NJ: Prentice-Hall.

Kovar, M. G. (1986). Aging in the eighties: Preliminary data from the supplement on aging to the national health interview survey, United States, January–June 1984. *Advance Data from Vital and Health Statistics, No. 115*. (DHHS Pub. No. (PHS) 86-1250). Hyattsville, MD: National Center for Health Statistics.

Kozlowski, L. T. (1984). Pharmacological approaches to smoking modification. In J. D. Matarazzo, S. M. Weiss, J. A. Herd, N. E. Miller, & S. M. Weiss, *Behavioral health: A handbook for health enhancement and disease prevention* (pp. 713–728). New York: Wiley.

Kramer, K. D. (1987). *The effects of a participant modeling procedure on nutritious and lower cost food shopping.* Unpublished doctoral dissertation, Virginia Polytechnic Institute and State University, Blacksburg, VA.

Kramer, M. (1982). The continuing challenge: The rising prevalence of mental disorders, associated chronic diseases, and disabling conditions. In M. O. Wagenfield, P. V. Lemkau, & B. Justice (Eds.), *Public mental health*, Beverly Hills, CA: Sage.

Kraus, J. F. (1987). Homicide while at work: Persons, industries, and occupations at high risk. *American Journal of Public Health, 77*(10), 1285–1289.

Kristein, M. M. (1982). The economics of health promotion at the worksite. *Health Education Quarterly, 9*, 27–36.

Kristein, M. M. (1983). How much can business expect to profit from smoking cessation? *Preventive Medicine, 12*, 358–381.

Kuhn, A. (1975). *Unified Social Science: A System-Based Introduction.* Homewood, IL: Dorsey.

Kuhn, T. S. (1970). *The structure of scientific revolutions* (2nd ed.). Chicago, IL: University of Chicago Press.

Kuller, L. H. (1987). Letter to the editor. *Journal of the American Medical Association, 257*(20), 2757.

Kuller, L., Meilahn, E., Townsend, M., & Weinberg, G. (1982). Control of cigarette smoking from a medical perspective. In L. Breslow, J. A. Fielding, & L. B. Lave (Eds.), *Annual review of public health*, (vol. 3, pp. 153–178). Palo Alto, CA: Annual Reviews, Inc.

Lalonde, M. (1974). *A new perspective on the health of Canadians—A working document.* Ottawa: Information Canada.

La Rue, A., Dessonville, C., & Jarvik, L. F. (1985). Aging and mental disorders. In J. E. Birren & K. W. Schaie (Eds.), *Handbook of the psychology of aging* (3rd ed.). New York: Van Nostrand Reinhold.

Lamb, H. R., & Zusman, J. (1974). Primary prevention in perspective. *American Journal of Psychiatry, 136*, 12–17.

Lamb, M. E., & Sagi, A. (1983). *Fatherhood and family policy.* Hillsdale, NJ: Lawrence Erlbaum.

Landers, S. (1986). Latchkey kids. *The APA Monitor, 17*(2), 1.

Landers, S. (1987). Rising work stress claims hit employers in the pocket. *The APA Monitor, 18*(8), 6.

Lasater, T., Abrams, D., Artz, L., Beaudin, P., Cabrera, L., Elder, J., Ferreira, A., Knisely, P., Peterson, G., Rodriguez, A., Rosenberg, P., Snow, R., & Carleton, R. (1984). Lay volunteer delivery of a community-based cardiovascular risk factor change program: The Pawtucket experiment. In J. D. Matarazzo, S. M. Weiss, J. A. Herd, N. E. Miller, & S. M. Weiss (Eds.), *Behavioral health: A handbook of health enhancement and disease prevention* (pp. 1166–1170). New York: Wiley.

Laswell, H. D. (1948). The structure and function of communication in society. In A. Bryson (Ed.), *The communication of ideas* (pp. 57–79). New York: Harper & Row.

Lau, R., Kane, R., Berry, S., Ware, J., & Ray, D. (1980). Channeling health: A review of evaluations of televised health campaigns. *Health Education Quarterly, 7*, 56–89.

Lave, L. B. (1987). Health and safety risk analyses: Information for better decisions. *Science, 236*, 291–295.

Lazarsfeld, P. F., & Merton, R. E. (1971). Mass communication, popular taste, and organized action. In W. Schramm & D. F. Roberts (Eds.), *The process and effects of mass communication* (pp. 237–251). Urbana, IL: University of Illinois Press.

Lazarus, R. S. (1966). *Psychological stress and the coping process.* New York: Mc-Graw-Hill.

Lazarus, R. S., & Cohen, J. B. (1977). Environmental stress. In I. Altman & J. F. Wohlwill (Eds.), *Human behavior and environment: Advances in theory and research* (vol. 2, pp. 89–127). New York: Plenum.

Lazarus, R. S., & DeLongis, A. (1983). Psychological stress and coping in aging. *American Psychologist, 38,* 245–254.

Lazarus, R. S., & Launier, R. (1978). Stress-related transactions between person and environment. In L. Pervin & M. Lewis (Eds.), *Perspectives in international psychology.* New York: Plenum.

Le Duc, D. R. (1982). Deregulation and the dream of diversity. *Journal of Communication,* August, 164–178.

Ledwith, F. (1984). Does tobacco sports sponsorship on television act as advertising to children? *Health Education Journal, 43*(4), 85–88.

LeFebvre, R. C., Harden, E. A., Rakowski, W., Lasater, T. M., & Carleton, R. A. (1987). Characteristics of participants in community health promotion programs: Four-year results. *American Journal of Public Health, 77*(10), 1342–1344.

LeFebvre, R. C., Lasater, T. M., Carleton, R. A., & Peterson, G. (1987). Theory and delivery of health programming in the community: The Pawtucket Heart Health Program. *Preventive Medicine, 16,* 80–95.

LeFebvre, R. C., Peterson, G. S., McGraw, S. A., Lasater, T. M., Sennet, L., Kendall, L., & Carleton, R. A. (1986). Community intervention to lower blood cholesterol: The "know your cholesterol" campaign in Pawtucket, Rhode Island. *Health Education Quarterly, 13,* 117–130.

LeGrande, D. (1987). Viewpoints: Health on the job. *HealthLink, 3*(1), 7.

Leventhal, H., & Cleary, P. D. (1980). The smoking problem: A review of research and theory in behavioral risk modification. *Psychological Bulletin, 88,* 370–405.

Leventhal, H., Safer, M. A., & Panagis, D. M. (1983). The impact of communications on the self-regulation of health beliefs, decision, and behavior. *Health Education Quarterly, 10,* 3–29.

Levin, H. M. (1983). *Cost-effectiveness: A primer.* Beverly Hills, CA: Sage.

Levin, L. S. (1976). Self-care: An international perspective. *Social Policy, 7,* 70–75.

Levine, A. G., & Stone, R. A. (1986). Threats to people and what they value: Residents' perceptions of the hazards of Love Canal. In A. H. Lebovits, A. Baum, & J. E. Singer (Eds.), *Advances in environmental psychology* (vol. 6, pp. 109–130). Hillsdale, NJ: Lawrence Erlbaum.

Levine, J. A., Pleck, J. H., & Lamb, M. E. (1983). The fatherhood project. In M. E. Lam & A. Sagi (Eds.), *Fatherhood and family policy.* Hillsdale, NJ: Lawrence Erlbaum.

Levine, N. B., Dastoor, D. P., & Gendron, C. (1983). Coping with dementia: A pilot study. *Journal of the American Geriatrics Society, 31,* 12–18.

Levine, S., & Sorenson, J. R. (1984). Social and cultural factors in health promotion. In J. D. Matarazzo, S. M. Weiss, J. A. Herd, N. E. Miller, & S. M. Weiss (Eds.), *Behavioral health: A handbook of health enhancement and disease prevention* (pp. 222–229). New York: Wiley.

Levy, A. S., Mathews, O., Stephenson, M., Tenney, J. E., & Schucker, R. E. (1985). The impact of a nutrition information program on food purchases. *Journal of Public Policy and Marketing, 4,* 1–13.

Levy, S. (1985). *Behavior and cancer.* San Francisco: Jossey–Bass.

Levy, S. M., Hopkins, B., Chesney, M., Ringen, K., Nathan, P., & MacDougal, V. (1986). Cancer control at the community level: The modification of workers' behaviors associated with carcinogens. In M. F. Cataldo & T. J. Coates (Eds.), *Health and industry: A behavioral medicine perspective* (pp. 285–300). New York: Wiley.

Lewinsohn, P. M., & Libet, J. (1972). Pleasant events, activity schedules and depression. *Journal of Abnormal Psychology, 79,* 291–295.

Lewinsohn, P. M., Munoz, R. F., Youngren, M. A., & Zeiss, A. M. (1986). *Control your depression.* Englewood Cliffs, NJ: Prentice-Hall.

Lichtenstein, E. (1982). The smoking problem: A behavioral perspective. *Journal of Consulting and Clinical Psychology, 50,* 804–819.

Lieber, L. (1986). Coping with cocaine. *Atlantic Monthly,* January, 39–48.

Liebert, R. M., Sprafkin, I. N., & Davidson, E. S. (1982). *The early window: Effects of television on children and youth* (2nd ed.). Elmsford, NY: Pergamon Press.

Liem, R., & Ramsay, P. (1982). Health and social costs of unemployment: Research and policy considerations. *American Psychologist, 37,* 1116–1123.

Lindheim, R., & Syme, S. L. (1983). Environments, people, and health. *Annual Review of Public Health, 4,* 335–359.

Lippman, M. (1986). The moral imperative to correct deceptive cigarette billboard ads. *Tobacco and Youth Reporter, 1*(1), 10.

Lloyd, J. W., & Bettencourt, L. U. (1986). Prevention of achievement deficits. In B. A. Edelstein & L. Michelson (Eds.), *Handbook of prevention* (pp. 117–132). New York: Plenum.

Lochsen, P. M., Bjartveit, K., Hauknes, A., & Aaro, L. E. (1983, July). Trends in tobacco consumption and smoking habits in Norway. Report of the Norwegian Council on Smoking and Health. Presented at the fifth World Conference on Smoking and Health, Winnipeg, Canada.

Lorig, K., & Fries, J. F. (1986). *The arthritis helpbook.* Menlo Park, CA: Addison-Wesley.

Lorig, L., Kraines, R. G., Brown, B. W., & Richardson, N. (1985). A workplace health education program that reduces outpatient visits. *Medical Care, 23*(9), 1044–1054.

Lorion, R. P. (1983). Evaluating preventive interventions: Guidelines for the serious social change agent. In R. D. Felner, L. A. Jason, J. N. Moritsugu, & S. S. Farber (Eds.), *Preventive psychology: Theory, research, and practice.* New York: Pergamon Press.

Love, S. Q., & Ollendick, T. H. (1986). *Bulimic behaviors: A preliminary report on high risk situations for binge eating and purging.* Unpublished manuscript. Psychology Department, Virginia Polytechnic Institute and State University, Blacksburg, VA.

Lovelace, V. O., & Huston, A. C. (1982). Can television teach prosocial behavior? *Prevention in Human Services, 2,* 93–106.

Lovett, S., & Gallagher, D. (in press). Psychoeducational interventions for family caregivers: Preliminary efficacy data. *Behavior Therapy.*

Lundy, J. R. (1972). Some personality correlates of contraceptive use among unmarried female college students. *Journal of Psychology, 80,* 9–14.

Lyons-Ruth, K., Botein, S., & Grunebaum, H. U. (1984). Reaching the hard-to-reach: Serving isolated and depressed mothers with infants in the community. In B. Cohen & J. Musick (Eds.), *Parents and their young children.* San Francisco: Jossey-Bass.

Maccoby, E. E., & Jacklin, C. N. (1974). *The psychology of sex differences.* Stanford, CA: Stanford University Press.

Maccoby, N., & Alexander, J. (1980). Use of media in lifestyle programs. In P. O. Davidson & S. M. Davidson (Eds.), *Behavioral medicine: Changing health lifestyles* (pp. 351–370). New York: Brunner/Mazel.

Maccoby, N., & Altman, D. G. (in press). Disease prevention in communities: The Stanford Heart Disease Prevention Program. In R. Price, E. Cowen, R. Lorian, & J. Ramos-McKay (Eds.), *Casebook on model prevention programs*. Washington, DC: American Psychological Association.

MacDonald, A. P., Jr. (1970). Internal-external locus of control and the practice of birth control. *Psychological Reports, 27,* 206.

Maddox, G. L., & Douglas, E. (1974). Aging and individual differences: A longitudinal analysis of social, psychological and physiological indicators. *Journal of Gerontology, 29,* 555–563.

Mangald, W. D. (1981). Neonatal mortality by the day of the week in the 1974–75 Arkansas live birth cohort. *American Journal of Public Health, 71*(6), 601.

Mannarino, A. P., Christy, M., Durlak, J. A., & Magnussen, M. G. (1982). Evaluation of social competence training in the schools. *Journal of School Psychology, 20,* 11–19.

Manoff, R. K. (1985). *Social marketing: Imperative for public health.* New York: Praeger.

Marsiglio, W., & Mott, F. L. (1986). The impact of sex education on sexual activity, contraceptive use, and premarital pregnancy among American teenagers. *Family Planning Perspectives, 18*(4), 151–162.

Martin, J. E., & Dubbert, P. M. (1982). Exercise applications and promotion in behavioral medicine: Current status and future directions. *Journal of Consulting and Clinical Psychology, 50,* 1004–1017.

Martin, J. L., & Vance, C. S. (1984). Behavioral and psychosocial factors in AIDS: Methodological and substantive issues. *American Psychologist, 39*(11), 1303–1308.

Martin, M. J., & Silverman, M. F. (1986). The San Francisco experience with regulation of smoking in the workplace: The first twelve months. *American Journal of Public Health, 76*(5), 585–586.

Martin, M. J., Fehrenbach, A., & Rosner, R. (1986). Ban on smoking in industry. *The New England Journal of Medicine, 315*(10), 647–648.

Marx, J. L. (1980). Osteoporosis: New help for thinning bones. *Science, 207,* 628–630.

Maslach, C. (1982). *Burnout: The cost of caring.* Englewood Cliffs, NJ: Prentice-Hall.

Masters, W. H., Johnson, V. E., & Kolodny, R. C. (1988). *Crisis: Heterosexual behavior in the age of AIDS.* New York: Grove Press.

Mastria, M. A., & Drabman, R. S. (1979). The development of behavioral competence in medical settings. In J. R. McNamara (Ed.), *Behavioral approaches to medicine: Application and analysis* (pp. 33–63). New York: Plenum.

Matarazzo, J. D. (1980). Behavioral health and behavioral medicine: Frontiers for a new health psychology. *American Psychologist, 35,* 807–817.

Matarazzo, J. D. (1982). Behavioral health's challenge to academic, scientific, and professional psychology. *American Psychologist, 37,* 1–14.

Matarazzo, J. D. (1984). Behavioral health: A 1990 challenge for the health sciences profession. In J. D. Matarazzo, S. M. Weiss, J. A. Herd, N. E. Miller, & S. M. Weiss (Eds.), *Behavioral health: A handbook for health enhancement and disease prevention* (pp. 3–40). New York: Wiley.

Matthews, K. A., & Avis, N. E. (1982). Psychologists in school of public health:

Current status, future prospects, and implications for other health settings. *American Psychologist, 37*, 949–954.

Mattson, M. E., Pollack, E. S., & Cullen, J. W. (1987). What are the odds that smoking will kill you? *American Journal of Public Health, 77*(4), 425–431.

Mayer, J. A., Dubbert, P. M., & Elder, J. P. (1987). *Promoting nutrition at the point of purchase: A review*. Unpublished manuscript, Graduate School of Public Health, San Diego State University, San Diego, CA.

Mayer, J. A., Heinz, J. M., Vogel, J. M., Morrison, D. C., Lankester, L. V., & Jacobs, A. L. (1986). Promoting low-fat entree choices in public cafeterias. *Journal of Applied Behavior Analysis, 19*, 160–164.

McAlister, A., Puska, P., Koskela, K., Pallonen, U., & Maccoby, N. (1980). Psychology in action: Mass communication and community organization for public health education. *American Psychologist, 35*(4), 375–409.

McAlister, A., Puska, P., Salonen, J. T., Tuomilehto, J., & Koskela, K. (1982). Theory and action for health promotion: Illustrations from the North Karelia Project. *American Journal of Public Health, 72*, 43–50.

McCarty, D. (1981). Changing contraceptive usage intentions: A test of the Fishbein model of intention. *Journal of Applied Social Psychology, 11*, 192–211.

McGinnis, J. M. (1982). Targeting progress in health. *Public Health Reports, 97*, 295–307.

McGinnis, J. M., Shopland, D., & Brown, C. (1987). Tobacco and health: Trends in smoking and smokeless tobacco consumption in the United States. *Annual Review of Public Health, 8*, 441–467.

McGrath, J. E. (1970). *Social and psychological factors in stress*. New York: Holt, Rinehart, & Winston.

McGuire, W. J. (1980). The communication–persuasion model and health-risk labeling. In L. A. Morris, M. B. Mazis, & I. Barofsky (Eds.), *Banbury report: Product labeling and health risks* (vol. 6, pp. 99–122). Cold Spring Harbor, NY: Cold Spring Harbor Laboratory.

McGuire, W. J. (1981). Theoretical foundations of campaigns. In R. E. Rice & W. J. Paisley (Eds.), *Public communication campaigns* (pp. 67–83). Beverly Hills, CA: Sage.

McLeod, J. M., & Reeves, B. (1981). On the nature of mass media effects. In G. C. Wilhoit (Ed.), *Mass communication review yearbook* (vol. 2, pp. 245–282). Beverly Hills, CA: Sage.

McManus, J., Taylor, C. B., & Patrick, C. (1987). *Community approaches to the prevention and cessation of smoking*. Stanford, CA: Health Promotion Resource Center, Stanford University.

McMillan, D., & Chavis, D. (in press). A theory of sense of community. *Journal of Community Psychology*.

Mechanic, D. (1978). Considerations in the design of mental health benefits under national health insurance. *American Journal of Public Health, 68*, 482.

Melton, G. B., & Davidson, H. A. (1987). Child protection and society: When should the state intervene? *American Psychologist, 42*, 172–175.

Mendelsohn, H. (1973). Some reasons why information campaigns can succeed. *Public Opinion Quarterly, 37*, 50–60.

Mercer, R. T. (1979). *Perspectives on adolescent health care*. Philadelphia, PA: J. B. Lippincott Co.

Merwin, D. J., & Northrop, B. A. (1982). Health action in the workplace. Complex issues — no simple answers. *Health Education Quarterly, 9*, 73–82.

Messite, J., & Bond, M. B. (1980). Reproductive toxicology and occupational exposure. In C. Zenz (Ed.), *Developments in occupational medicine*. Chicago, IL: Year Book Medical Publishers, Inc.

Metropolitan Life Insurance Foundation (1982). *Statistical bulletin*, Jan.–Mar.

Meyer, A. J., Nash, J. D., McAlister, A. L., Maccoby, N., & Farquhar, J. W. (1980). Skills training in a cardiovascular health education campaign. *Journal of Consulting and Clinical Psychology, 48*(2), 129–142.

Michigan Department of Public Health (1986). *Worksite health promotion resource guide*. Ann Arbor, MI: Author.

Milby, J. B. (1982). Operant conditioning. In D. M. Doleys, R. L. Meredith, & A. R. Ciminero (Eds.), *Behavioral medicine: Assessment and treatment strategies*. New York: Plenum.

Milio, N. (1985). Health policy and the emerging tobacco reality. *Social Science in Medicine, 21*, 603–613.

Miller, A. B. (1986). Dietary fat and the epidemiology of breast cancer. In C. Ip, D. F. Birt, A. E. Rogers, & C. Mettlin (Eds.), *Dietary fat and cancer* (pp. 17–32). New York: Alan R. Liss.

Miller, C. (1987). *The effects of point-of-purchase information, prompts, and incentives in modifying nutritious entree selections in university student cafeterias*. Unpublished doctoral dissertation, Virginia Polytechnic Institute and State University, Blacksburg, VA.

Miller, C. A. (1975). Health care of children and youth in America. *American Journal of Public Health, 65*, 353.

Miller, G. A. (1969). Psychology as a means of promoting human welfare. *American Psychologist, 24*, 1063–1075.

Miller, W. B. (1981). Psychological vulnerability to unwanted pregnancy. In F. F. Furstenberg, R. Lincoln, & J. Menken (Eds.), *Teenage sexuality, pregnancy, and childbearing* (pp. 350–354). Philadelphia, PA: University of Pennsylvania Press.

Mitchell, F., & Brindis, C. (1987). Adolescent pregnancy: The responsibilities of policymakers. *Health Services Research, 22*,(3), 399–437.

Moore, G. T. (1987). Environment and behavior research in North America: History, developments, and unresolved issues. In D. Stokols & I. Altman (Eds.), *Handbook of environmental psychology* (pp. 1359–1410). New York: Wiley.

Moore, K. A., & Burt, M. R. (1982). *Private crisis, public cost: Policy perspectives on teenage childbearing*. Washington, DC: Urban Institute.

Moore, S. H., LoGerfo, J., & Inui, T. S. (1980). Effects of a self-care book on physician visits. *Journal of the American Medical Association, 243*(22), 2317–2320.

Moos, R. H. (1985). Evaluating social resources in community and health care contexts. In P. Karoly (Ed.), *Measurement strategies in health psychology* (pp. 433–459). New York: Wiley.

Morehouse, W., & Subramaniam, M. A. (1986). *The Bhopal tragedy: What really happened and what it means for American workers and communities at risk*. New York: Council on International and Public Affairs.

Morris, J. (1987). Medication side effects masquerade as Alzheimer's. *American Journal of Alzheimer's Care and Research, 2*, 8.

Morrison, D. M. (1985). Adolescent contraceptive behavior: A review. *Psychological Bulletin, 98*(3), 538–568.

Mortimer, J. A., & Schuman, L. M. (1981). *The epidemiology of dementia*. New York: Oxford University Press.

Moss, L. (1981). *Management stress*. Boston, MA: Addison-Wesley.

Munoz, R. F., Glish, M., Soo-Hoo, T., & Robertson, J. (1982). The San Francisco mood survey project: Preliminary work toward the prevention of depression. *American Journal of Community Psychology, 10*, 317–329.

Murphy, L. R., & Schoenborn, T. F. (1987). *Stress management in work settings.* Washington, DC: U.S. Department of Health and Human Services.

Murray, D. M. (1986). Dissemination of community health promotion programs: The Fargo–Moorhead heart health program. *Journal of School Health, 56*(9), 375–381.

Nader, P. R., Baranowski, T., Vanderpool, N. A., Dunn, K., Dworkin, R., & Ray, L. (1983). The family health project: Cardiovascular risk reduction education for children and parents. *Developmental and Behavioral Pediatrics, 4*, 3–10.

Naditch, M. P. (1984). The Staywell Program. In J. D. Matarazzo, S. M. Weiss, J. A. Herd, N. E. Miller, & S. M. Weiss (Eds.), *Behavioral health: A handbook of health enhancement and disease prevention* (pp. 1071–1078). New York: Wiley.

Nathan, P. E. (1984a). Johnson and Johnson's Live for Life: A comprehensive positive lifestyle change program. In J. D. Matarazzo, S. M. Weiss, J. A. Herd, N. E. Miller, & S. M. Weiss (Eds.), *Behavioral health: A handbook for health enhancement and disease prevention* (pp. 1064–1070). New York: Wiley.

Nathan, P. E. (1984b). The worksite as a setting for health promotion and positive lifestyle changes. In J. D. Matarazzo, S. M. Weiss, J. A. Herd, N. E. Miller, & S. M. Weiss (Eds.), *Behavioral health: A handbook for health enhancement and disease prevention* (pp. 1061–1063). New York: Wiley.

Nathanson, C., & Becker, M. (1983). Contraceptive behavior among unmarried young women: A theoretical framework for research. *Population & Environment, 6*, 39–59.

National Center for Health Statistics (1982). Contraceptive use patterns, prior sources, and pregnancy history of female family planning patients—United States, 1980 (*Advance data,* no. 82). Washington, DC: U.S. Government Printing Office.

National Center for Health Statistics (1984). Trends in teenage childbearing, United States, 1970–81 (*Vital and Health Statistics,* Series 21, No. 41, DHHS Publication No. (PHS) 84-1919, Public Health Service). Washington, DC: U.S. Government Printing Office.

National Center for Health Statistucs (1985). Advance report of final natality statistics, Trends in teenage childbearing, United States (1970–81). In S. Rosenbaum (Ed.), *A manual on providing effective prenatal care programs for teenagers.* Washington, DC: The Children's Defense Fund.

National Center for Health Statistics (1987). Advance report of final mortality statistics, 1985. *Monthly and Vital Statistics Report, 36*(5), suppl., August 28.

National Heart, Lung, and Blood Institute (1983). *Foods for health: Report of the pilot program.* Publication No. 83-2036. Washington, DC: National Institute of Health.

National Institute of Aging Task Force (1980). Senility reconsidered: Treatment possibilities for mental impairment of the elderly. *Journal of the American Medical Association, 244*, 259–263.

National Research Council (1987). *Risking the future: Adolescent sexuality, pregnancy, and childbearing* (vol. 1). Washington, DC: National Academy Press.

National Research Council (1986). *What is America eating?* Washington, DC: National Academy Press.

National Safety Council (1987). *Accident facts.* Chicago, IL: Author.

Navarro, V. (1976). *Medicine under capitalism.* New York: Prodist.

Nelson, K. A. (1987). Visual impairment among elderly Americans: Statistics in transition. *Journal of Visual Impairment and Blindness, 81*, 331–334.

Nesu, A. M. (1986). Efficacy of a social problem-solving therapy approach for unipolar depression. *Journal of Consulting and Clinical Psychology, 54*, 196–202.

Nietzel, M. T., & Himelein, M. J. (1986). Prevention of crime and delinquency. In B. A. Edelstein, & L. Michelson (Eds.), *Handbook of prevention* (pp. 195–222). New York: Plenum.

Nollen, S. D. (1982). *New work schedules in practice: Managing time in a changing society*. New York: Van Nostrand Reinhold.

Nyswander, D. B. (1942). *Solving school health problems*. New York: Oxford University Press.

O'Donnell, M. P., & Ainsworth, T. H. (1984). *Health promotion in the workplace*. New York: Wiley.

O'Donnell, M. P. (1986). Definition of health promotion: Part II: Levels of programs. *American Journal of Health Promotion, 1*(2), 6–9.

O'Donnell, M. P. (1986). Design of workplace health promotion programs. *American Journal of Health Promotion* (monograph).

O'Keefe, A. M. (1987). The case against drug testing. *Psychology Today*, June, 34–38.

O'Leary, K. D., & Wilson, G. T. (1987). *Principles of behavior therapy* (2nd ed.). New York: Holt, Rinehart, & Winston.

O'Malley, D. T., Heger, J. B., Trudgett, M., Mayo, S. T., & Gardner, L. B. (1987). Computerized nutrition education in the supermarket. *Journal of Nutrition Education, 19*, 159–162.

Office of Technology Assessment. (1987). *Losing a million minds: Confronting the tragedy of Alzheimer's disease and other dementias*. Washington, DC: U.S. Government Printing Office.

Olds, D. L. (1984). Final report. Prenatal/early infancy project — Maternal and child health research, NIMH. Washington, DC: National Institute of Mental Health.

Ollendick, T. H. (1987). *Ongoing projects on instruction in social skills as a preventive strategy with children*. Unpublished manuscript, Department of Psychology, Virginia Polytechnic University, Blacksburg, VA.

Ollendick, T. H., & Winett, R. A. Child behavior therapy as prevention: Conceptual and research issue. In P. H. Bornstein & A. E. Kazdin (Eds.), *Handbook of clinical child behavior therapy* (pp. 805–832). Homewood, IL: Dorsey Press.

Olsho, L. W., Harkins, S. W., & Lenhardt, M. L. (1985). Aging and the auditory system. In J. E. Birren & K. W. Schaie (Eds.), *Handbook of the psychology of aging* (3rd ed.). New York: Van Nostrand Reinhold.

Orleans, C. T. (1985). Understanding and promoting smoking cessation: Overview and guidelines for physician intervention. In W. P. Creger, C. H. Coggins, & E. W. Hancock (Eds.), *Annual review of medicine: Selected topics of clinical sciences* (vol. 36, pp. 51–61). Palo Alto, CA: Annual Reviews, Inc.

Ornitz, E. M. (1986). Prevention of developmental disorders. In B. A. Edelstein & L. Michelson (Eds.), *Handbook of prevention* (pp. 75–116). New York: Plenum.

Osborn, J. E. (1988). The AIDS epidemic: Six Years. In L. Breslow, J. E. Fielding, & L. B. Lave (Eds.), *Annual review of public health* (pp. 551–584). Palo Alto, CA: Annual Reviews, Inc.

Ouslander, J. G. (1982). Illness and psychopathology in the elderly. In L. F. Jarvik & G. W. Small (Eds.), *Psychiatric clinics of North America*. Philadelphia, PA: W. B. Saunders.

Paffenbarger, R. S., Hyde, R. T., Wing, A. L., & Hseich, C. (1986). Physical activity, all cause mortality, and longevity of college alumni. *New England Journal of Medicine, 314*, 605–613.

Palinkas, L. A., & Hoiberg, A. (1982). An epidemiology primer: Bridging the gap between epidemiology and psychology. *Health Psychology, 1*, 269–287.

Parkinson, R. S., & Associates (1982). *Managing health promotion in the workplace.* Palo Alto, CA: Mayfield Publishing Company.

Paul, E. W., & Schapp, P. (1982). Legal rights and responsibilities of pregnant teenagers and their children. In I. R. Stuart & C. F. Wells (Eds.), *Pregnancy in adolescence: Needs, problems, and management.* New York: Van Nostrand Reinhold.

Pechter, K. (1987). Corporate fitness and the collar barrier. *San Francisco Chronicle,* January 11, 13–15.

Pedro-Carroll, J. L., & Cowen, E. L. (1985). The children of divorce intervention program: An investigation of the efficacy of a school-based prevention program. *Journal of Consulting and Clinical Psychology, 53*, 603–611.

Pedro-Carroll, J. L., Cowen, E. L., Hightower, A. D., & Guare, J. C. (1986). Preventive intervention with latency-aged children of divorce: A replication study. *American Journal of Community Psychology, 14*, 177–187.

Pentz, M. A. (1986). Community organization and school liaisons: How to get programs started. *Journal of School Health, 56*(9), 382–388.

Perry, C. L., & Jessor, R. (1983). Doing the cube: Preventing drug abuse through adolescent health promotion. In T. J. Glynn, C. G. Leukefeld, & M. P. Ludford (Eds.), *Preventing adolescent drug abuse: Intervention strategies* (NIDA Research Monograph 47). Rockville, MD: National Institute on Drug Abuse.

Phillips, H. T., & Gaylord, S. A. (Eds.). (1985). *Aging and public health.* New York: Springer.

Piaget, J., & Inhelder, B. (1969). *The psychology of the child.* New York: Basic Books.

Pierson, D. E., Walker, D. K., & Tivnan, T. (1984). A school-based program from infancy to kindergarten for children and their parents. *Personal Guidance Journal, 62*, 448–454.

Pinkston, E. M., & Linsk, N. L. (1984). *Care of the elderly: A family approach.* Elmsford, NY: Pergamon Press.

Pitt, D. G., & Zube, E. H. (1987). Management of natural environments. In D. Stokols & I. Altman (Eds.), *Handbook of environmental psychology* (pp. 1009–1042). New York: Wiley.

Pitt, E. (1986). Targeting the adolescent male. *Journal of Community Health, 11*(1), Spring, 45–48.

Pleck, J. H., & Staines, G. L. (1982). Work schedules and work family conflict in two-earner couples. In J. Adlaus (Ed.), *Two paychecks.* Beverly Hills, CA: Sage.

Polich, J. M., Ellickson, P. L., Reuter, P., & Kahan, J. P. (1984). *Strategies for controlling adolescent drug use.* Santa Monica, CA: The Rand Corporation.

Polit, D. F., & Kahn, J. R. (1985). Project redirection: Evaluation of a comprehensive program for disadvantaged teenage mothers. *Family Planning Perspectives, 17*(4), 150–155.

Porter, P. J. (1981). Realistic outcomes of school health service programs. *Health Education Quarterly, 8*(1), 81.

Price, R. H. (1986). Stress management programming for worksite health promotion. In Michigan Department of Public Health, *Worksite health promotion resource guide* (pp. 1–29). Ann Arbor, MI: Michigan Department of Public Health.

Prochaska, J. O., & DiClemente, C. C. (1983). Stage process of self-change of smoking: Toward an integrative model of change. *Journal of Consulting and Clinical Psychology, 51*, 390–395.

Proctor, S. E. (1986). A developmental approach to pregnancy prevention with early adolescent females. *Journal of School Health, 56*(8), 313–316.

Prochansky, H. M. (1987). The field of environmental psychology: Securing its future. In D. Stokols & I. Altman (Eds.), *Handbook of environmental psychology* (pp. 1467–1488). New York: Wiley.

Purdom, P. W. (1980). *Environmental health* (2nd ed.). New York: Academic Press.

Pure Food and Drug Act of June 30, 1906, 34 Statute, 768 chapter, Public Law 384.

Puska, P. (1984). Community-based prevention of cardiovascular disease: The North Karelia Project. In J. D. Matarazzo, S. M. Weiss, J. A. Herd, N. E. Miller, & S. M. Weiss (Eds.), *Behavioral health: A handbook for health enhancement and disease prevention* (pp. 1140–1147). New York: Wiley.

Puska, P., Iacono, J., Nissinen, A., Vartiainen, E., Dougherty, R., Pietinen, P., Leino, U., Uusitalo, U., Kuusi, T., Kostiainen, E., Nikkari, T., Seppala, E., Vapaatalo, H., & Huttunen, J. E. (1985). Dietary fat and blood pressure: An intervention study on the effects of a low-fat diet on two levels of polyunsaturated fat. *Preventive Medicine, 14*, 573–584.

Puska, P., Nissinen, A., Tuomilehto, J., Sulonen, J. T., Kaskela, K., McAlister, A., Kottke, T. E., Maccoby, N., & Farquhar, J. W. (1985). The community-based strategy to prevent coronary heart disease: Conclusions from the ten years of the North Karelia Project. In L. Breslow, I. B. Lave, & J. E. Fielding (Eds.), *Annual review of public health* (vol. 6, pp. 147–193). Palo Alto, CA: Annual Reviews, Inc.

Puska, P., Salonen, J., Nissinen, A., Tuomilehto, J., Vartiainen, E., Korhonen, H., Tanskanen, A., Rommquist, P., Koskela, K., & Huttunen, J. (1983). Change in risk factors for coronary heart disease during 10 years of a community intervention programme (North Karelia Project). *British Medical Journal, 287*, 1840–1844.

Puska, P., Salonen, J. T., Tuomilehto, J., Nissinen, A., & Kottke, T. E. (1983). Evaluating community-based preventive cardiovascular programs: Problems and experiences from the North Karelia Project. *Journal of Community Health, 9*(1), 49–64.

Puska, P., Tuomilehto, J., Salonen, J. T., Nissinen, A., Virtamo, J., Björkvist, S., Koskela, K., Neittaanmäki, Takalo, T., Kottke, T. E., Mäki, J., Sipilä, P., & Varuikko, P. (1981). *Community control of cardiovascular diseases: The North Karelia Project.* Copenhagen: World Health Organization.

Rachlin, H. S., & Braham, R. L. (1987). Long-term care: A review for the general internist. *Journal of General Internal Medicine, 2*, 428–435.

Ralph, N., & Edgington, A. (1983). An evaluation of an adolescent family planning program. *Journal of Adolescent Health Care, 4*(3), 158–162.

Randolph, L. A., & Gesche, M. (1986). Black adolescent pregnancy: Prevention and management. *Journal of Community Health, 11*(1), Spring, 10–18.

Rappaport, J. (1977). *Community psychology: Values, research, action.* New York: Holt, Rinehart, & Winston.

Rappaport, J. (1981). In praise of paradox: A social policy of empowerment over prevention. *American Journal of Community Psychology, 9*, 1–25.

Rappaport, J. (1987). Terms of empowerment/exemplars of prevention: Toward a theory for community psychology. *American Journal of Community Psychology, 15*(2), 121–148.

Reeves, R. S., Foreyt, J. P., Scott, L. W., Mitchell, R. E., Wohlleb, J., & Gotto, A. M. (1983). Effects of a low-cholesterol eating plan on plasma lipids: Results of a three-year community study. *American Journal of Public Health, 23*, 873–877.

Reifler, B. V., Larson, E., Teri, L., & Poulsen, M. (1986). Dementia of the Alzheimer's type and depression. *Journal of the American Geriatric Society, 34*, 854–859.

Reppucci, N. D. (1987). Prevention and ecology: Teen-age pregnancy, child sexual abuse, and organized youth sports. *American Journal of Community Psychology, 15*, 1–22.

Rice, R. E., & Paisley, W. J. (Eds.). (1981). *Public communication campaigns.* Beverly Hills, CA: Sage.

Richardson, B. W. (1887). *The health of nations, a review of the works of Edwin Chadwick* (vol. 2). London: Longman, Green & Co.

Rickards, L. D., Zuckerman, D. M., & West, P. R. (1985). Alzheimer's disease: Current congressional response. *American Psychologist, 40*, 1256–1261.

Riessman, F. (1985). New dimensions in self help. *Social Policy, 15*, 2–5.

Roberts, B. B., & Thorsheim, H. I. (1986). A partnership approach to consultation: The process and results of a major primary prevention field experiment. In J. Kelly (Ed.), *Ecological theory: Guidelines for doing consultation as a preventive service (Prevention in Human Services*, Vol. X). New York: Howarth Press.

Robertson, L. S., Kelley, A. B., O'Neill, B., Wixom, C. W., Eiswirth, R. S., & Haddon, W., Jr. (1974). A controlled study of the effect of television messages on safety belt usage. *American Journal of Public Health, 64*, 1071–1080.

Robinson, B. C. (1983). Validation of a caregiver strain index. *Journal of Gerontology, 38*, 344–348.

Robinson, J. C. (1987). Worker response to workplace hazards. *Journal of Health Politics, Policy, and Law, 12*, 665–682.

Robinson, J. P. (1977). *How Americans use time.* New York: Praeger.

Roccella, E. J. (1982). Selected roles of the federal government and health promotion/disease prevention focus on the worksetting. *Health Education Quarterly, 9*, 83–91.

Rodin, J. (1984). Overview: Healthful diet. In J. D. Matarazzo, S. M. Weiss, J. A. Herd, N. E. Miller, & S. M. Weiss (Eds.), *Behavioral health: A handbook for health enhancement and disease prevention* (pp. 549–551). New York: Wiley.

Rodin, J., & Stone, G. C. (1987). Historical highlights in the emergence of the field. In G. C. Stone, S. M. Weiss, J. D. Matarazzo, N. E. Miller, J. Rodin, C. D. Belar, M. J. Follick, & J. E. Singer (Eds.), *Health psychology: A discipline and a profession* (pp. 15–26). Chicago, IL: University of Chicago Press.

Rodin, J., & Wack, J. T. (1984). The relationship between cigarette smoking and body weight: A health promotion dilemma. In J. D. Mutarazzo, S. M. Weiss, J. A. Herd, N. E. Miller, & S. M. Weiss (Eds.), *Behavioral health: A handbook for health enhancement and disease prevention* (pp. 671–690). New York: Wiley.

Rogers, E. M. (1983). *Diffusion of innovation* (3rd ed.). New York: Free Press.

Rogers, E. M., & Kincaid, D. C. (1981). *Communication networks: Toward a new paradigm for research.* New York: Free Press.

Rogers, E. M., & Shoemaker, F. (1971). *Communication of innovations.* New York: Free Press.

Rosen, G. (1958). *A history of public health.* New York: M. D. Publications.

Rosenbaum, S. (1985). *A manual on providing effective prenatal care programs for teenagers.* Washington, DC: The Children's Defense Fund.

Rosenberg, M. J., & Weiner, J. M. (1988). Prostitutes and AIDS: A health department priority. *American Journal of Public Health, 78*, 418–423.

Rosenberg, M. S. (1987). New directions for research in the psychological maltreatment of children. *American Psychologist, 42*, 166–171.

Rosenstock, I. M., Stergachis, A., & Heaney, C. (1986). Evaluation of smoking prohibition policy in a health maintenance organization. *American Journal of Public Health, 76*(8), 1014–1015.

Roskin, M. (1982). Coping with life changes: A preventive social work approach. *American Journal of Community Psychology, 10*, 331–340.

Ross, H. L. (1982). *Deterring the drinking driver: Legal policy and social control.* Lexington, MA: D. C. Heath & Co.

Rotter, J. B. (1966). Generalized expectancies for internal versus external control of reinforcement. *Psychological Monographs, 80* (1, Whole No. 609).

Rowe, J. W., & Kahn, R. L. (1987). Human aging: Usual and successful. *Science, 237*, 143–145.

Rowe, M. J., & Ryan, C. C. (1988). Comparing state-only expenditures for AIDS. *American Journal of Public Health, 78*, 424–429.

Rozin, P. (1984). The acquisition of food habits and preferences. In J. D. Matarazzo, S. M. Weiss, J. A. Herd, N. E. Miller, & S. M. Weiss (Eds.), *Behavioral health: A handbook for health enhancement and disease prevention* (pp. 590–607). New York: Wiley.

Rubenstein, L. Z., Josephson, K. R., Nichol-Seamons, M., & Robbins, A. S. (1986). Comprehensive health screening of well elderly adults: An analysis of a community program. *Journal of Gerontology, 41*, 342–352.

Rubin, D. M. (1987). How the news media reported on Three Mile Island and Chernobyl. *Journal of Communications, 37*(3), 42–57.

Rubin, K. (1987, March). Whose job is child care? *Ms.*, pp. 32–44.

Ruchlin, H. S., & Braham, R. L. (1987). Long-term care: A review for the general internist. *Journal of General Internal Medicine, 2*, 428–435.

Ruckelshaus, W. D. (1983). Science, risk, and public policy. *Science, 221*, 1026–1028.

Rudd, J. R., & Geller, E. S. (1985). A university-based incentive program to increase safety belt use: Toward cost-effective institutionalization. *Journal of Applied Behavior Analysis, 18*, 215–226.

Rundle, R. L. (1987). New efforts to fight heart disease are aimed at blue-collar workers. *Wall Street Journal*, March 25.

Runyan, C. W., DeVellis, R. F., DeVellis, B. M., & Hochbaum, G. M. (1982). Health psychology and the public health perspective: In search of the pump handle. *Health Psychology, 1*(2), 169–180.

Russell, L. B. (1985). *Is prevention better than cure?* Washington, DC: The Brookings Institute.

Russell, M., & Guber, M. (1987). Risk assessment in environmental policy-making. *Science, 236*, 286–290.

Russell, M. A. H. (1976). Tobacco smoking and nicotine dependence. In R. J. Gibbons, Y. Israel, H. Kalant, R. Popham, W. Schmidt, & R. Smart (Eds.), *Research advances in alcohol and drug problems* (vol. 3). New York: Wiley.

Ruttenberg, R., & Powers, M. (1986). Economics of notification and medical screening for high-risk workers. *Journal of Occupational Medicine, 28*(8), 757–764.

Rutter, M., Maughan, B., Mortimore, P., & Outston, J. (1979). *Fifteen thousand hours: Secondary schools and their effects on children.* Cambridge, MA: Harvard University Press.

Rychtarik, R. G., Fairbank, J. A., Allen, C. M., Roy, D. W., & Drabman, R. S. (1983). Alcohol use in television programming: Effects on children's behavior. *Addictive Behaviors, 8,* 19–22.

Saegert, S. (1987). Environmental psychology and social change. In D. Stokols & I. Altman (Eds.), *Handbook of environmental psychology* (pp. 99–128). New York: Wiley.

Salguero, C., Schlesinger, N., & Yearwood, E. (1984). A mental health program for adolescent parents. In M. Sugar (Ed.), *Adolescent parenthood* (pp. 181–194). New York: Spectrum Publications.

Salguero, C. (1984). The role of ethnic factors in adolescent pregnancy and mother-hood. In M. Sugar (Ed.), *Adolescent parenthood* (pp. 75–98). New York: Spectrum Publications.

Sallis, J., Hill, R., Killen, J., Telch, M., Flora, J. A., Girard, J., & Taylor, C. B. (1986). Efficacy of self-help behavior modification materials in smoking cessation. *American Journal of Preventive Medicine, 2,* 342–344.

Sanders, I. T., & Brownlee, A. (1979). Health in the community. In H. E. Freeman, S. Levine, & L. G. Reeder (Eds.), *Handbook of medical sociology* (pp. 412–433). Englewood Cliffs, NJ: Prentice-Hall.

Sandman, P. M., Weinstein, N. D., & Klotz, M. L. (1987). Public response to the risk from geological radiation. *Journal of Communication, 37*(3), 93–108.

San Francisco Chronicle (1985). More TV than ever. April 27, p. A1.

Sarason, S. B. (1974). *The psychological sense of community: Prospects for the community psychology.* San Francisco: Jossey-Bass.

Sarason, S. B. (1981). *Psychology misdirected.* New York: Free Press.

Scales, P., & Beckstein, D. (1982). From macho to mutuality: Helping young men make effective decisions about sex, contraception, and pregnancy. In I. R. Stuart & C. F. Wells (Eds.), *Pregnancy in adolescence: Needs, problems, and management* (pp. 264–289). New York: Van Nostrand Reinhold.

Scales, P. (1981). Sex education in the '70s and '80s: Accomplishments, obstacles and emerging issues. *Family Relations, 30,* 557.

Scales, P. (1986). The changing context of sexuality education: Paradigms and challenges for alternative futures. *Family Relations, 35,* 265.

Schacter, S. (1982). Recidivism and self-cure of smoking and obesity. *American Psychologist, 37,* 436–444.

Schaffer, C., & Pine, F. (1972). Pregnancy, abortion, and the developmental tasks of adolescence. *Journal of the American Academy of Child Psychiatry, 11,* 511–536.

Scharf, K. R. (1984). Funding for pregnant adolescents: A legislative history. In M. Sugar (Ed.), *Adolescent parenthood* (pp. 197–215). New York: Spectrum Publications.

Schinke, S. P., Gilchrist, L. D., & Small, R. W. (1979). Preventing unwanted adolescent pregnancy: A cognitive–behavioral approach. *American Journal of Orthopsychiatry, 49*(1), 81–88.

Schofield, W. (1969). The role of psychology in the delivery of health services. *American Psychologist, 24,* 565–584.

Schucker, R. L. (1983). *Implementation of a revised food labeling policy: Evaluation and tracking.* Washington, DC: Food and Drug Administration.

Schultz, H. W. (1981). *Food law handbook.* Westport, CT: NVI Publishing Co.

Schwartz, J. L. (1987). *Review and evaluation of smoking cessation methods: The United States and Canada, 1978-1985.* Washington, DC: USDHHS.

Schwartz, J. L., & Weiss, S. (1978). Behavioral medicine revisited: An amended definition. *Journal of Behavioral Medicine, 1*, 249-251.

Schwertfeger, R., Elder, J. P., Cooper, R., Lasater, T. M., & Carleton, R. (1986). The use of telemarketing in the community-wide prevention of heart disease: The Pawtucket Heart Health Program. *Journal of Community Health, 11*(3), 172-180.

Scott, R. R., Denier, C. A., Prue, D. M., & King, A. C. (1986). Worksite smoking interventions with nursing professionals: Long-term outcome and relapse assessment. *Journal of Consulting and Clinical Psychology, 54*, 809-813.

Seekins, T., Fawcett, S. B., Elder, J. P., Jason, L. A., Schnelle, J., & Winett, R. A. (1988). Multistate evaluation of child-restraint laws. *Journal of Applied Behavior Analysis, 21*, 251-259.

Seligman, M. E. P. (1975). *Helplessness: On depression, development, and death.* San Francisco, CA: W. H. Freeman.

Senate Special Committee on Aging (1983). *Developments in aging 1982: Vol. 1.* Washington, D.C.: U.S. Government Printing Office.

Seneca, J. J. (1987). Economic issues in protecting public health and the environment. In M. R. Greenberg (Ed.), *Public health and the environment: The United States experience* (pp. 351-377). New York: Guilford Press.

Sensenig, P. E., & Cialdini, R. B. (1984). Social-psychological influences on the compliance process: Implications for behavioral health. In J. D. Matarazzo, S. M. Weiss, J. A. Herd, N. E. Miller, & S. M. Weiss (Eds.), *Behavioral health: A handbook of health enhancement and disease prevention* (pp. 384-392). New York: Wiley.

Sewell, W. R. D. (1980). Environmental decision-making: The unevenness of commitment. In N. M. Trieff (Ed.), *Environment and health* (pp. 605-624). Ann Arbor, MI: Ann Arbor Science Publisher, Inc.

Shapiro, L. Health or hype? *Newsweek*, February 22, 1988, 67-68.

Shattuck, L. (1850). *Report of the Sanitary Commission of Massachusetts: 1850.* Cambridge: Harvard University Press, 1948.

Sherry, S. (1985). *High tech and toxics: A guide for local communities.* Sacramento, CA: Golden Empire Health Planning Center.

Shopper, M. (1984). From (re) discovery to ownership of the vagina—a contribution to the explanation of nonuse of contraceptives in the female adolescent. In M. Sugar (Ed.), *Adolescent parenthood* (pp. 35-54). New York: Spectrum Publications.

Shure, M. B., & Spivack, G. (1982). Interpersonal problem-solving in young children: A cognitive approach to prevention. *American Journal of Community Psychology, 10*, 341-356.

Sidel, V. W. (1987). Medical haves and have-nots. *San Francisco Chronicle*, September 16, 6.

Simon, H. (1979). Rational decision making in business organizations. *The American Economic Review, 69*, 493-513.

Simopoulos, A. P. (1986). Introduction. In L. Breslow, J. E. Fielding, & L. B. Lave (Eds.), *Annual review of public health* (vol. 7, pp. 475-480). Palo Alto, CA: Annual Reviews, Inc.

Singer, E., & Endreny, P. (1987). Reporting hazards: Their benefits and costs. *Journal of Communication, 37*(3), 10-26.

Singer, J. A., Neale, M. S., & Schwartz, G. E. (1987). The nuts and bolts of assessing occupational stress: A collaborative effort with labor. In L. R. Murphy & T. F. Schoenborn, *Stress management in work settings* (pp. 3–29). Washington, DC: USDHHS.

Singer, J. E., & Krantz, D. S. (1982). Perspectives on the interface between psychology and public health. *American Psychologist, 37*, 955–960.

Singer, J. L., & Singer, D. G. (1983). Psychologists look at television. Cognitive, developmental, and social policy implications. *American Psychologist, 38*, 826–834.

Slaughter, D. T. (1983). Early intervention and its effect on maternal and child development. *Monograph of Social Research and Child Development, 48* (4, No. 202), 99.

Sloan, R. P. (1987). Workplace health promotion: A commentary on the evolution of a paradigm. *Health Education Quarterly, 14*(2), 181–194.

Slovic, P. (1987). Perception of risk. *Science, 236*, 280–285.

Slovic, P., Fischhoff, B., & Lichtenstein, S. (1980). Informing people about risk. In L. A. Morris, M. B. Mazis, & I. Barofsky (Eds.), *Banbury report: Product labeling and health risks* (vol. 6, pp. 165–181). Cold Spring Harbor, NY: Cold Spring Harbor Laboratory.

Solomon, D. S., & Maccoby, N. (1984). Communication as a model for health enhancement. In J. D. Matarazzo, S. M. Weiss, J. A. Herd, N. E. Miller, & S. M. Weiss (Eds.), *Behavioral health: A handbook for health enhancement and disease prevention* (pp. 209–221). New York: Wiley.

Sommer, R. (1987). Dreams, reality, and the future of environmental psychology. In D. Stokols & I. Altman (Eds.), *Handbook of environmental psychology* (pp. 1489–1511). New York: Wiley.

Sonenstein, F. L., & Pittman, K. J. (1984). The availability of sex education in large city school districts. *Family Planning Perspectives, 16*, 19.

Spivak, H., & Weitzman, M. (1987). Social barriers faced by adolescent parents and their children. *Journal of the American Medical Association, 258*(10), 1500–1504.

Stern, M. P., Farquhar, J. W., Maccoby, N., & Russell, S. H. (1976). Results of a two-year health education campaign on dietary behavior: The Stanford Three Community Study. *Circulation, 54*(5), 826–833.

Stern, P. C., & Oskamp, S. (1987). Managing scarce environmental resources. In D. Stokols & I. Altman (Eds.), *Handbook of environmental psychology* (pp. 1043–1088). New York: Wiley.

Stokols, D. (1980). The use of intrapersonal and contextual theories in social psychology. In R. F. Kidd & M. J. Saks (Eds.), *Advances in applied social psychology* (vol. 1, pp. 198–211). Hillsdale, NJ: Lawrence Erlbaum.

Stokols, D. (1987). Conceptual strategies of environmental psychology. In D. Stokols & I. Altman (Eds.), *Handbook of environmental psychology* (pp. 41–70). New York: Wiley.

Stokols, D., & Altman, I. (1987a). *Handbook of environmental psychology*. New York: Wiley.

Stokols, D., & Altman, I. (1987b). Introduction. In D. Stokols & I. Altman (Eds.), *Handbook of environmental psychology* (pp. 1–4). New York: Wiley.

Stone, G. C. (1979). Psychology and the health system. In G. C. Stone, F. Cohen, & N. E. Adler (Eds.), *Health psychology* (pp. 47–75). San Francisco, CA: Jossey-Bass.

Stone, G. C. (1983). Proceedings of the National Working Conference on Education and Training in Health Psychology. *Health Psychology, 2* (suppl.).

Stone, G. C. (1987). The scope of health psychology. In G. C. Stone, S. M. Weiss, J. D. Matarazzo, N. E. Miller, J. Rodin, C. D. Belar, M. J. Follick, & J. E. Singer (Eds.), *Health psychology: A discipline and a profession* (pp. 27–40). Chicago, IL: University of Chicago Press.

Stone, G. C., Cohen, F., Adler, N. E. (1979). *Health psychology.* San Francisco, CA: Jossey-Bass.

Stone, G. C., Weiss, S. M., Matarazzo, J. D., Miller, N. E., Rodin, J., Belar, C. D., Follick, M. J., & Singer, J. E. (1987a). *Health psychology: A discipline and a profession.* Chicago, IL: University of Chicago Press.

Stone, G. C., Weiss, S. M., Matarazzo, J. D., Miller, N. E., Rodin, J., Belar, C. D., Follick, M. J., & Singer, J. E. (1987b). Health psychology in the twenty-first century. In G. C. Stone, S. M. Weiss, J. D. Matarazzo, N. E. Miller, J. Rodin, C. D. Belar, M. J. Follick, & J. E. Singer (Eds.), *Health psychology: A discipline and a profession* (pp. 513–524). Chicago, IL: University of Chicago Press.

Stone, J. T. (1987). Interventions for psychosocial problems associated with sensory disabilities in old age. In B. Heller, L. Flohr, & L. S. Zegans (Eds.), *Psychosocial interventions with sensorially disabled persons.* San Francisco, CA: Grune and Stratton.

Stone, R. (1986). Caregivers of the frail elderly: A national profile. *Family Caregiving Project.* Rockville, MD: Project Share.

Stone, R. A., & Levine, A. G. (1985). Reactions to collective stress: Correlates of active citizen participation at Love Canal. In A. Wandersman & R. Hess (Eds.), *Beyond the individual: Environmental approaches and prevention* (pp. 153–177). New York: Haworth.

Stop smoking or be fired, employees told. *San Francisco Chronicle.* January 20, 1987, p. 3.

Straus, D. B. (1987). Collaborating to win. In M. R. Greenberg (Ed.), *Public health and the environment. The United States experience* (pp. 271–292). New York: Guilford Press.

Stretcher, V. J., Devellis, B. M., Becker, M. H., & Rosenstock, I. M. (1986). The role of self-efficacy in achieving health behavior change. *Health Education Quarterly, 13,* 73–91.

Stuart, I. R., & Wells, C. F. (Eds.). (1982). *Pregnancy in adolescence: Needs, problems, and management.* New York: Van Nostrand Reinhold.

Stunkard, A. J., Felix, M. R. J., & Cohen, R. Y. (1985). Mobilizing a community to promote health: The Pennsylvania County health improvement program (CHIP). In J. C. Rosen & L. F. Solomon (Eds.), *Prevention in health psychology* (pp. 143–190). Hanover, NH: University Press of New England.

Sugar, M. (1984a). Adolescent decision-making toward motherhood. In M. Sugar (Ed.), *Adolescent parenthood* (pp. 21–33). New York: Spectrum Publications.

Sugar, M. (1984b). *Adolescent parenthood.* New York: Spectrum Publications.

Surgeon General (1979). *Healthy people.* Washington, DC: USDHHS.

Surgeon General (1985). *The health consequences of smoking: Cancer and chronic lung disease in the workplace.* Washington, DC: U.S. Government Printing Office.

Surgeon General (1988). Report on nutrition and health. Washington, DC: US Government Printing Office.

Sutherland, J. W. (1973). *A general systems philosophy for the social and behavioral sciences.* New York: George Braziller.

Sweetgall, R. (1985). *Fitness walking.* New York: Perigee.

Syme, S. L., & Alcalay, R. (1982). Control of cigarette smoking from a social perspective. In L. Breslow, J. A. Fielding, & L. B. Lave (Eds.), *Annual review of public health* (vol. 3, pp. 179–199). Palo Alto, CA: Annual Reviews, Inc.

Tartinger, D. A., Greene, B. R., & Lutzker, J. R. (1984). Home safety: Development and validation of one component of an eco-behavioral treatment for abused and neglected children. *Journal of Applied Behavior Analysis, 7,* 159–174.

Taylor, R. L., Lam, D. J., Roppel, C. E., & Barter, J. J. (1984). Friends can be good medicine: An excursion into mental health promotion. *Community Mental Health Journal, 20,* 294–303.

Taylor, S. E. (1987). The progress and prospects of health psychology: Tasks of a maturing discipline. *Health Psychology, 6*(1), 73–87.

Taylor, S. E., & Clark, L. F. (1986). Does information improve adjustment to noxious medical procedures? In M. J. Saks & L. Saxe (Eds.), *Advances in applied social psychology* (vol. 3, pp. 1–28). Hillsdale, NJ: Lawrence Erlbaum.

Teel, S. J., Teel, J. E., & Bearden, W. O. (1979). Lessons learned from the broadcast cigarette advertising ban. *Journal of Marketing, 43,* 45–50.

Telch, M. J., Killen, J. D., McAllister, A. L., Perry, C. L., & Maccoby, N. (1982). Long-term follow-up of a pilot project on smoking prevention with adolescents. *Journal of Behavioral Medicine, 5*(1), 1–8.

Teri, L., & Gallagher, D. (in press). Cognitive behavioral interventions for depressed patients with dementia of the Alzheimer's type. In T. Sunderland (Ed.), *Depression in Alzheimer's disease: Component of consequence?* New York: Grune and Stratton.

Terris, M. (1981). The primacy of prevention. *Preventive Medicine, 10,* 689–699.

The Alan Guttmacher Institute (1981). *Teenage pregnancy: The problem that hasn't gone away.* New York: Author.

The Alan Guttmacher Institute. (1986). *Teenage pregnancy in developed countries.* New Haven, CT: Yale University Press.

Thompson, L. W., Gallagher, D., & Breckenridge, J. S. (1987). Comparative effectiveness of psychotherapies for depressed elders. *Journal of Consulting and Clinical Psychology, 55,* 385–390.

Thompson, L. W., Wagner, B., Zeiss, A., & Gallagher, D. (in press). Cognitive/behavioral therapy with early stage Alzheimer's patients: An exploratory view of the utility of this approach. In E. Light & B. Lebowitz (Eds.), *Alzheimer's disease treatment and family stress: Directions for research.* Washington, DC: U.S. Government Printing Office.

Thornberry, O. T., Wilson, R. W., & Golden, P. (1986). Health promotion and disease prevention provisional data from the National Health Interview Survey: United States, January–June 1985. *NCHS Advance Data, 119,* May 14.

Thornburg, H. P. (1972). A comparative study of sex information sources. *Journal of School Health, 48,* 88.

Tietze, C. (1981). Teen pregnancies: Looking ahead to 1984. In F. F. Furstenberg, R. Lincoln, & J. Menken (Eds.), *Teenage sexuality, pregnancy, and child-bearing* (pp. 150–154). Philadelphia, PA: University of Pennsylvania Press.

Timberlake, B., Fox, R. A., Baisch, M. J., & Goldberg, B. D. (1987). Prenatal education for pregnant adolescents. *Journal of School Health, 57*(3), 105–108.

Tobacco and Youth Reporter. (1986). R. J. Reynolds reaches kids with "Moviegoer." *1*(1), 13–14.

Todd, J., & Todd, T. (1985). *Lift your way to youthful fitness.* Boston: Little, Brown and Company.

Tones, B. K. (1981). The use and abuse of mass media in health promotion. In D. S.

Leather, G. B. Hastings, & J. K. Davies (Eds.), *Health education and the media* (pp. 97–114). Elmsford, NY: Pergamon Press.

Trickett, E. J. (1987). Community interventions and health psychology: An ecologically oriented perspective. In G. Stone, S. Weiss, J. Matarazzo, N. Miller, J. Rodin, C. Belar, M. Follick, & J. Singer (Eds.), *Health psychology: A discipline and a profession* (pp. 151–163). Chicago, IL: University of Chicago Press.

Trieff, N. M. (1980). *Environment and health.* Ann Arbor, MI: Ann Arbor Science Publisher.

Tuomilehto, J., Pietinen, P., Salonen, J. J., Puska, P., Nissinen, A., & Wolf, E. (1985). Nutrition-related determinants of blood pressure. *Preventive Medicine, 14*, 413–427.

Turiel, I. (1985). *Indoor air quality and human health.* Stanford, CA: Stanford University Press.

Twardosz, S. (1987). The importance of day care ecology. *The Community Psychologist, 20*, 18.

Twardosz, S., Cataldo, M. F., & Risley, T. R. (1974). Open environment for infant toddler day care. *Journal of Applied Behavior Analysis, 7*, 529–546.

Tye, J. B. (1985). *A note on public policy issues in the cigarette industry.* Unpublished manuscript, Stanford Graduate School of Business, Stanford, CA.

Tye, J. B., Warner, K. E., & Glantz, S. A. (1987). Tobacco advertising and consumption: Evidence for a causal relationship. *Journal of Public Health Policy, 8*(4), 492–508.

U.S. Bureau of the Census (1984). *Statistical abstract of the United States.* Washington, DC: U.S. Government Printing Office.

U.S. Department of Health and Human Services (1980). *Promoting health/preventing disease: Objectives for the nation.* Washington, DC: U.S. Government Printing Office.

U.S. Department of Health and Human Services (1982). *Health, United States, 1980.* DHHS Publication No. (PHS) 82-1406. Hyattsville, MD: Author.

U.S. Department of Health and Human Services (1986). *Health United States, 1986.* Hyattsville, MD: Author.

U.S. Department of Health and Human Services (1987a). *Smoking and health: A national status report.* #87-8396. Washington, DC: USDHHS.

U.S. Department of Health and Human Services (November, 1984). *Proceedings from Prospects for a Healthier America: Achieving the nation's health promotion objectives.* Washington, DC: U.S. Government Printing Office.

U.S. Department of Health and Human Services (1987b). *National survey of worksite health promotion activities: A summary.* #PB88-129390. Washington, DC: USDHHS.

U.S. Department of Health, Education, and Welfare, Federal Council on Aging (1979). *Mental health and the elderly: Recommendations for action.* (DHEW Pub. No. 80-209607). Washington, DC.

U.S. Department of Health, Education, and Welfare/Public Health Service (1984). *Healthy people: The surgeon general's report on health promotion and disease prevention.* Washington, DC: U.S. Government Printing Office.

U.S. Government Accounting Office, Comptroller General Report to the Congress of the United States (1979). *Conditions of older people: National information systems needed.* HRD 79-95, Sept.

U.S. Public Health Service (1983). *Pregnancy and infant health. Public Health Reports*, Sept.-Oct., 24–40.

U.S. Public Health Service (1983). *Sexually transmitted disease control. Public Health Reports*, Sept.–Oct., 49–55.

Udry, J. R., Billy, J. O. G., Morris, N. M., Groff, T. R., & Raj, M. H. (1985). Serum androgenic hormones motivate sexual behavior in adolescent boys. *Fertility and Sterility, 43* (January), 90–94.

Ulene, A. (1980). The media, insurance industry and health. In *Health, education, and promotion: Agenda for the eighties* (pp. 52–54). *Proceedings of a conference sponsored by the Health Insurance Association of America*, American Council of Life Insurance, Atlanta, Georgia.

Unger, D. G., & Wandersman, A. (1985). The importance of neighbors: The social, cognitive, and affective components of neighboring. *American Journal of Community Psychology, 13*, 139–169.

Van Houten, R., Rolder, A., Nau, P. A., Friedman, R., et al. (1985). Large-scale reductions in speeding and accidents in Canada and Israel: A behavioral ecological perspective. *Journal of Applied Behavior Analysis, 18*, 87–93.

Veninga, R. L., & Spradley, J. P. (1981). *The work stress connection: How to cope with job burnout*. Boston: Little, Brown and Company.

Vickery, D. M., & Fries, J. F. (1981). *Take care of yourself: A consumer's guide to medical care*. Reading, MA: Addison-Wesley.

Vickery, D. M., Kalmer, H., Lowry, D., Constantine, M., Wright, E., & Loren, W. (1983). Effect of a self-care education program on medical visits. *Journal of the American Medical Association, 250*(21), 2952–2956.

Videka-Sherman, L. (1982). Effects of participation in a self-help group for bereaved parents: Compassionate Friends. *Prevention in Human Services, 1*, 69–78.

Vincent, M. L., Clearie, A. F., & Schluchter, M. D. (1987). Reducing adolescent pregnancy through school and community-based education. *Journal of the American Medical Association, 257*, 3382–3386.

San Francisco Chronicle (1987). Vital statistics. October 10.

Vladeck, B. C. (1980). *Unloving care: The nursing home tragedy*. New York: Basic Books.

Wadden, T. A., & Brownell, K. D. (1984). The development and modification of dietary practices in individuals, groups, and large populations. In J. D. Matarazzo, S. M. Weiss, J. A. Herd, N. E. Miller, & S. M. Weiss (Eds.), *Behavioral health: A handbook for health enhancement and disease prevention* (pp. 608–631). New York: Wiley.

Wagner, B. (1985). *Systematic process and outcome evaluation in mental health clinics*. Unpublished master's thesis, Department of Psychology, Virginia Tech, Blacksburg, VA.

Wagner, J. A., & Winett, R. A. (1988). Promoting one low-fat, high-fiber menu item in a fast-food restaurant. *Journal of Applied Behavior Analysis, 21*, 123–127.

Wahler, R. G., & Graves, M. G. (1983). Setting events in social networks: Ally or enemy in child behavior therapy? *Behavior Therapy, 14*, 19–36.

Wahler, R. G. (1980). The insular mother. Her problems in parent–child treatment. *Journal of Applied Behavior Analysis, 13*, 207–220.

Walker, W. B. (1987). *An interactive computer network system for assessment and treatment of stress*. Unpublished dissertation, Virginia Polytechnic Institute and State University, Blacksburg, VA.

Wallack, L., & Winkleby, M. (1987). Primary prevention: A new look at basic concepts. *Social Science & Medicine, 25*, 923–930.

Wallack, L. (1987). Letter to the editor. *Health Education Quarterly, 14*(4), 383–385.

Wallack, L. M. (1981). Mass-media campaigns: The odds against finding behavior change. *Health Education Quarterly, 8*, 209–260.

Waller, P. F. (1985). Preventing injury to the elderly. In H. T. Phillips & S. A. Gaylord (Eds.), *Aging and public health*, New York: Springer.

Wallston, K. A., Wallston, B. S., Smith, S., & Dobbins, C. J. (1987). Perceived control and health. *Current Psychological Research and Reviews, 6*(1), 5–25.

Wallis, C. (1987, June 27). Who's bringing up baby? *Time*, pp. 54–60.

Walter, H. J., Hofman, A., Connelly, P. A., Barrett, L. T., & Kost, K. L. (1985). Primary prevention of chronic disease in childhood: Changes in risk factors after one year of intervention. *American Journal of Epidemiology, 122*, 772–781.

Wandersman, A. (1981). A framework of participation in community organizations. *Journal of Applied Behavioral Science, 17*, 27–58.

Wapner, S. (1987). A holistic, developmental, systems-oriented environmental psychology: Some beginnings. In D. Stokols & I. Altman (Eds.), *Handbook of environmental psychology* (pp. 1433–1465). New York: Wiley.

Ware, J. E., Manning, W. G., Duan, N., Wells, K. B., & Newhouse, J. P. (1984). Health status and the use of outpatient mental health services. *American Psychologist, 39*, 1090–1100.

Warheit, G. J., Bell, R. A., & Schwab, J. J. (1977). *Needs assessment approaches: Concepts and methods.* Rockville, MD: U.S. Department of Health, Education, and Welfare.

Warner, K. E. (1977). The effects of the anti-smoking campaign on cigarette consumption. *American Journal of Public Health, 67*(7), 645–650.

Warner, K. E. (1981). Cigarette smoking in the 1970's: The impact of the antismoking campaign on consumption. *Science, 211*, 729–731.

Warner, K. E. (1985). Cigarette advertising and media coverage of smoking and health. *New England Journal of Medicine, 312*(6), 384–388.

Warner, K. E. (1986a). *Selling smoking: Cigarette advertising and public health.* Washington, DC: American Public Health Association.

Warner, K. E. (1986b). Selling health: A media campaign against tobacco. *Journal of Public Health Policy, 7*(4), 434–439.

Warner, K. E. (1986c). Smoking and health implications of a change in the federal cigarette excise tax. *Journal of the American Medical Association, 255*(8), 1028–1032.

Warner, K. E. (1987a). Selling health promotion to corporate America: Uses and abuses of the economic argument. *Health Education Quarterly, 14*(1), 39–55.

Warner, K. E. (1987b). Television and health promotion: Stay tuned. *American Journal of Public Health, 77*, 140–142.

Warner, K. E., & Murt, H. A. (1984). Economic incentives for health. In L. Breslow, L. B. Lave, & J. E. Fielding (Eds.), *Annual review of public health* (vol. 5, pp. 107–133). Palo Alto, CA: Annual Reviews, Inc.

Warren, N. J., Grew, R. S., & Ilgen, E. R. (1984). Parenting after divorce: Preventive measures for divorcing families. Research prepared for NIMH conference on Children and Divorce, Washington, DC.

Webb, G., Briggs, C., & Brown, R. (1972). A comprehensive adolescent maternity program in a community hospital. *American Journal of Obstetrics & Gynecology, 113*, 511–523.

Wehlage, G. G. (1982). *The marginal high school student: Defining the problem and searching for policy.* Madison, WI: Wisconsin Center for Education Research.

Weick, K. (1984). Small wins: Redefining the scale of social problems. *American Psychologist, 39*, 40–49.

Weiler, P. G. (1987). The public health impact of Alzheimer's disease. *American Journal of Public Health, 77,* 1157–1158.

Weinstein, N. D., Sandman, N. D., & Klotz, M. L. (1987, August). Underestimating and overestimating in radon risk perception. Paper presented at the annual meeting of the American Psychological Association, New York.

Weiss, B. (1983). Behavioral toxicology and environmental health science. *American Psychologist, 38*(11), 1174–1187.

Weiss, S. M. (1982). Health psychology: The time is now. *Health Psychology, 1*(1), 81–91.

Weiss, S. M. (1984). Community health promotion demonstration programs: Introduction. In J. D. Matarazzo, S. M. Weiss, J. A. Herd, N. E. Miller, & S. M. Weiss (Eds.), *Behavioral health: A handbook of health enhancement and disease prevention* (pp. 1137–1139). New York: Wiley.

Weiss, S. M. (1987). Health psychology and other health professions. In G. C. Stone, S. M. Weiss, J. D. Matarazzo, N. E. Miller, J. Rodin, C. D. Belar, M. J. Follick, & J. E. Singer (Eds.), *Health psychology: A discipline and a profession* (pp. 61–74). Chicago, IL: University of Chicago Press.

Werner, C. M., Altman, I., & Oxley, D. (1985). Temporal aspects of homes: A transactional perspective. In I. Altman & C. M. Werner (Eds.), *Home environments* (vol. 8, pp. 1–32). New York: Plenum Press.

Whelan, E. M., Sheridan, M. J., Meister, K. A., & Mosher, B. A. (1981). Analysis of coverage of tobacco hazards in women's magazines. *Journal of Public Health Policy, 2,* 28–35.

Wicker, A. W. (1979). *An introduction to ecological psychology.* Monterey, CA: Brooks-Cole.

Wilbur, C. S., & Garner, D. (1984). Marketing health to employees: The Johnson & Johnson Live for Life program. In L. W. Frederiksen, L. J. Solomon, & K. A. Brehony (Eds.), *Marketing health behavior: Principles, techniques, and applications* (pp. 137–163). New York: Plenum Press.

Wilkens, L., & Patterson, P. (1987). Risk analysis and the construction of news. *Journal of Communication, 37*(3), 80–92.

Wilkie, F. L. (1980). Blood pressure and cognitive functioning. In S. G. Haynes & M. Feinlab (Eds.), *Second conference on the epidemiology of aging.* Washington, DC: U.S. Government Printing Office.

Wilkie, W. L., McNeill, D. L., & Mazis, M. B. (1984). Marketing's "scarlet letter:" The theory and practice of corrective advertising. *Journal of Marketing, 48,* 11–31.

Williams, A. F. (1982). Passive and active measures for controlling disease and injury: The role of health psychologists. *Health Psychology, 1*(4), 399–409.

Wilson, G. T. (1984). Weight control treatments. In J. D. Matarazzo, S. M. Weiss, J. A. Herd, N. E. Miller, & S. M. Weiss (Eds.), *Behavioral health: A handbook for health enhancement and disease prevention* (pp. 657–670). New York: Wiley.

Winett, R. A. (1983). Comment on Matarazzo's "Behavioral health's challenge . . . ". *American Psychologist, 38,* 120–121.

Winett, R. A. (1985). Ecobehavioral assessment in health lifestyles: Concepts and methods. In P. Karoly (Ed.), *Measurement strategies in health psychology* (pp. 147–182). New York: Wiley.

Winett, R. A. (1986). *Information and behavior: Systems of influence.* Hillsdale, NJ: Lawrence Erlbaum.

Winett, R. A. (1987). Prosocial television for community problems: Framework, effective methods, and regulatory barriers. In L. A. Jason, R. D. Felner, R. Hess,

& J. N. Moritsugu (Eds.), *Communities: Contributions from allied disciplines.* (pp. 117–160). New York: Haworth Press.

Winett, R. A. (1988). *Ageless athletes.* Chicago, IL: Contemporary.

Winett, R. A. (1988). Video-feedback systems to promote nutritious purchases. Ongoing project, Department of Psychology, Virginia Polytechnic Institute and State University, supported by The National Cancer Institute.

Winett, R. A., & Kramer, K. D. (1988). A behavioral systems framework for information design and behavior change. In J. Salvaggio & J. Bryant (Eds.), *Media use in the information age.* Hillsdale, NJ: Lawrence Erlbaum.

Winett, R. A., & Neale, M. S. (1981). Flexitime and family time allocation: Use of a self-report log to assess the effects of a system change on individual behavior. *Journal of Applied Behavior Analysis, 14,* 39–46.

Winett, R. A., Hatcher, J. W., Fort, T. R., Leckliter, I. N., Love, S. Q., Riley, A. W., & Fishback, J. F. (1982). The effects of videotape modeling and daily feedback on residential electricity conservation, home temperature and humidity, perceived comfort, and clothing worn: Winter and summer. *Journal of Applied Behavior Analysis, 15*(3), 381–402.

Winett, R. A., Kramer, K. D., Walker, W. B., Malone, S. W., & Lane, M. K. (1987). Effective consumer information interventions: Concepts, design, and impacts using field experiments. In A. deFontenay, D. Sibley, & M. Shugard (Eds.), *Telecommunications and demand modeling: An integrative review.* Amsterdam: North Holland.

Winett, R. A., Kramer, K. D., Walker, W. B., Malone, S. W., & Lane, M. K. (1988). The effects of modeling, feedback, and goal setting on nutritious and economical food purchases. *Journal of Applied Behavior Analysis, 21,* 93–101.

Winett, R. A., Leckliter, I. N., Chinn, D. E., Stahl, B., & Love, S. Q. (1985). Effects of television modeling on residential energy conservation. *Journal of Applied Behavior Analysis, 18*(1), 33–44.

Winett, R. A., Neale, M. S., & Williams, K. R. (1982). The effects of flexible work schedules on urban families with young children: Quasi-experimental, ecological studies. *American Journal of Community Psychology, 10,* 49–54.

Winkler, R. C., & Winett, R. A. (1982). Behavioral interventions in resource conservation: A systems approach based on behavioral economics. *American Psychologist, 37*(4), 421–435.

Winslow, C. E. A. (1920). The untilled field of public health. *Modern Medicine, 2,* 183.

Winslow, C. E. A. (1923). *The evolution and significance of the modern public health campaign.* New Haven, CT: Yale University Press.

Withington, A. M., Gimes, D. A., & Hatcher, R. A. (1983). *Teenage sexual health.* New York: Irvington Publishers.

Wright, J. C., & Huston, A. C. (1983). A matter of form: Potentials of television for young viewers. *American Psychologist, 38,* 835–844.

Wright, S., & Cowen, E. L. (1987). The effects of peer teaching on students' perceptions of class environment, adjustment, and academic performance. *American Journal of Community Psychology, 13,* 417–431.

Yalom, I. D. (1985). *The theory and practice of group psychotherapy* (3rd ed.). New York: Basic Books.

Yokley, J. M., & Glenwick, D. S. (1984). Increasing the immunization of preschool children: An evaluation of applied community interventions. *Journal of Applied Behavior Analysis, 17,* 313–325.

Zabin, L. S., & Clark, S. D. (1983). Institutional factors affecting teenagers' choice and reasons for delay in attending a family planning clinic. *Family Planning Perspectives, 15*(1), January/February, 29–39.

Zabin, L. S., Kantner, J. F., & Zelnik, M. (1979). Risk of adolescent pregnancy in the first months of intercourse. *Family Planning Perspectives, 11*, 215–226.

Zarit, S. H., & Zarit, J. M. (1982). Families under stress: Interventions for caregivers of senile dementia patients. *Psychotherapy: Theory, Research and Practice, 19*, 461–471.

Zarit, S. H., Reeves, K. E., & Bach-Peterson, J. (1980). Relatives of the impaired elderly: Correlates of feelings of burden. *The Gerontologist, 20*, 649–655.

Zarit, S. H., Todd, P. A., & Zarit, J. M. (1986). Subjective burden of husbands and wives as caregivers: A longitudinal study. *The Gerontologist, 26*, 260–266.

Zelnik, M., & Kim, Y. J. (1982). Sex education and its association with teenage sexual activity, pregnancy and contraceptive use. *Family Planning Perspectives, 14*, 117.

Zelnik, M., & Shah, F. K. (1983). First intercourse among young Americans. *Family Planning Perspectives, 15*(2), 64–70.

Zifferblatt, S. M., Wilbur, C. S., & Pinsky, E. (1980). Changing cafeteria eating habits. *Journal of the American Dietetic Association, 76*, 15–20.

Zilbergeld, B. (1978). *Male sexuality*. Boston: Little, Brown and Company.

Zuckerman, D. (1987). Consumer directed preventive services: Life service planning. *Family caregiving project conference on supporting family caregivers* (pp. 41–43). Rockville, MD: Project Share.

Author Index

Subject Index

About the Authors

Richard A. Winett (Ph.D., State University of New York at Stony Brook) is professor of psychology and director of graduate studies at Virginia Polytechnic Institute and State University. His major interest is the use of various media-based strategies in large-scale disease prevention and health promotion efforts. During Dr. Winett's career he has published about 100 articles and received seven major federal grants.

Abby C. King (Ph.D., Virginia Polytechnic Institute and State University) is presently research associate at the Stanford Center for Research in Disease Prevention, Stanford University School of Medicine. Dr. King has published journal articles in areas related to primary prevention of chronic disease. Among her research interests are prevention and amelioration of diseases and health enhancement in older adults.

David G. Altman (Ph.D., University of California, Irvine) is the associate director of the Health Promotion Resource Center at Stanford University. Dr. Altman's primary research interests include community health promotion, tobacco advertising, public health policy, and program evaluation, with recent publications in all four of these areas.

*Out of print in original format. Available in custom reprint edition.